AGRIPPINA

AGRIPPINA

Mother *of* Nero

Anthony A. Barrett

B T Batsford Ltd, London

© Anthony A. Barrett 1996
First published 1996

Printed in Great Britain by Butler & Tanner, Frome,
Somerset

Published by B.T. Batsford Ltd
4 Fitzhardinge Street, London W1H 0AH

A CIP catalogue record for this book is available
from the British Library

ISBN 0 7134 6854 8

The jacket illustration shows a sculptured head of
Agrippina (Ny Carlsberg Glyptotek, Copenhagen).

Contents

Illustrations

Photographs
(Between pages 138 and 139)

Stemmata

Figures

Stemma I

The Julio-Claudians

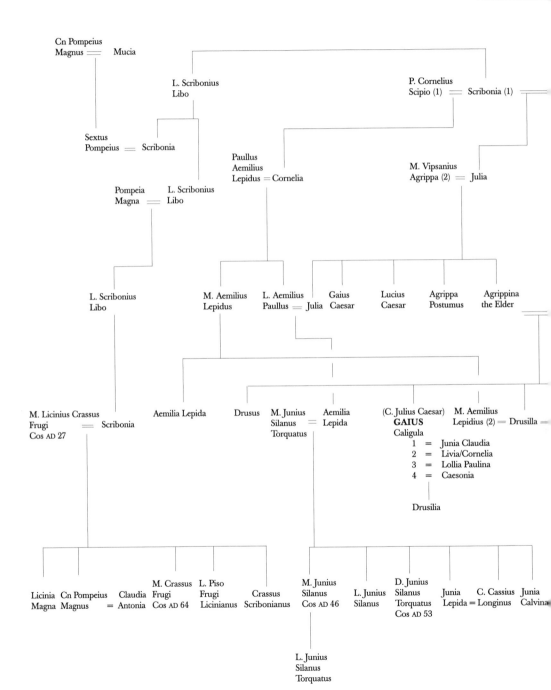

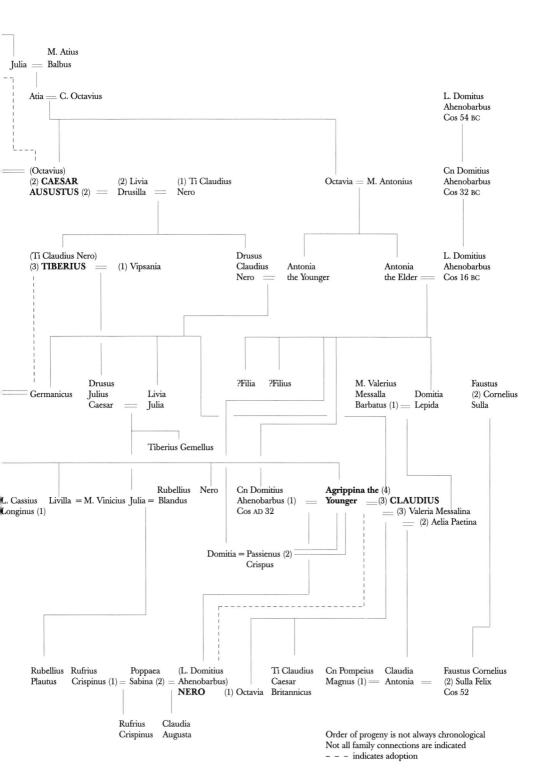

Rubellius
Plautus

Rufrius
Crispinus

Claudia
Augusta

Order of progeny is not always chronological
Not all family connections are indicated
- - - indicates adoption

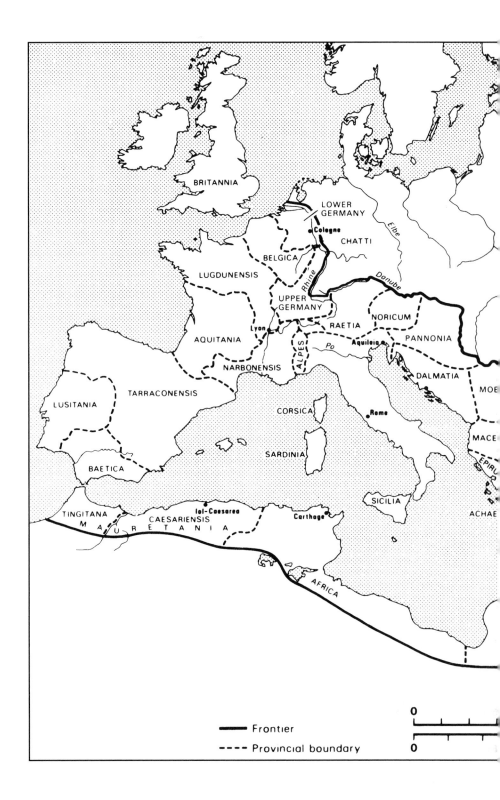

BRITANNIA

LOWER GERMANY

Cologne

CHATTI

BELGICA

LUGDUNENSIS

Rhine

UPPER GERMANY

Danube

NORICUM

Lyon

RAETIA

PANNONIA

AQUITANIA

ALPES

Po

Aquileia

NARBONENSIS

DALMATIA

MOE

TARRACONENSIS

CORSICA

Rome

LUSITANIA

MACE

SARDINIA

EPIRU

BAETICA

SICILIA

ACHAE

TINGITANA

Iol-Caesarea

CAESARIENSIS

M A U R E T A N I A

Carthage

AFRICA

Elbe

Frontier

Provincial boundary

0

0

The Roman world in AD 41

Danube
MOESIA
THRACIA

Phasis
HIBERI
Artaxata
ARMENIA

PONTUS et
BITHYNIA

GALATIA

ASIA
CAPPADOCIA

Ephesus
LYCIA
CILICIA
P A R T H I A
Tigris
Euphrates
Athens
Antioch
SYRIA
Seleucia
Ctesiphon

CYPRUS

JUDAEA

Alexandria
ARABIA

RENE

AEGYPTUS

Nile

500 Miles

800 Km

Foreword

Through some perverse and mysterious quirk of nature, the villains of history, rather than the saints, are what excite the popular imagination. Characters like Rasputin, Dr Crippen, Vlad the Impaler are undoubtedly evil, but they are also so colourful and so alluringly sinister, that they fascinate at the same time as they repel. At first glance Agrippina the Younger clearly deserves membership in this select company. She plotted against her brother Caligula (as well as sharing his bed), she murdered her husband Claudius with a deadly mushroom, and she tried (unsuccessfully) to cope with a rebellious teenage son, Nero, by sharing his bed too. She was finally eliminated by that same Nero through a scheme as ingenious and outlandish as any in the history of crime – an irresistible combination of treachery, incest and murder. Or so tradition has it. Whether these things actually happened is another matter altogether. At one level it makes hardly any difference, since historical reputations are a product of perception, not of reality. But at another level the issue is an important one. The complete truth about Agrippina may be unobtainable by now, but the serious reader is entitled to hope for a version that comes as close to that truth as the evidence allows, rather than a string of entertaining but dubious anecdotes. That kind of sober reappraisal of the evidence is the objective of this biography.

Time has certainly not been kind to Agrippina's memory. She suffers one accidental disadvantage, essentially trivial but often a curse on posthumous reputations. She had a parent of the same name, not as famous (infamous in her case) but prominent enough for the activities of mother and daughter to be occasionally confused. Far more serious, Agrippina's sordid popular image has eclipsed her more significant accomplishments. Along with Livia, the wife of the first Roman emperor, she represents a political paradox of the early Roman empire, the woman who managed to exercise great power and influence in a society that offered no constitutional role to powerful and influential women. It is this achievement, to be empress in an empire that allowed only emperors, that makes her accomplishments interesting and worthy of serious study. But not to the Romans – they saw the elevation of women like Agrippina as an inversion of the natural order, and the preoccupation of the ancient writers with the evils of female ambition all but blinded them to any admirable qualities they might have possessed.

Modern scholars, of all national backgrounds, have with very few exceptions treated Agrippina no less harshly than did their ancient counterparts. In the first monograph devoted to her, *Agrippina die Mutter Neros*, written in German over a century ago, the distinguished writer Adolf Stahr accepted the hostile ancient testimonia uncritically. More recent treatments have maintained this tradition. Syme calls her 'violent', 'truculent and merciless', 'corrupt but vigorous' and speaks of her 'robust criminality'. To Dudley she is a 'Clytaemnestra' of a woman. Mellor considers her 'loathsome' and 'treacherous', and complains of her 'murderous immorality'. Fabia calls her '*dure, vindictive, impitoyable*'. Lackeit, in the entry on Agrippina in the influential Paulys *Real-Encyclopedie der classischen Altertumswissenschaft*, portrays her as a depraved and power-hungry monster, who exercised a demonic influence over her husband and son. The excellent brief study by Werner Eck, *Agrippina, die Stadgründerin Kölns*, is on the whole more balanced, but he still portrays her as an essentially ruthless woman. Modern scholars generally share the revulsion felt by the ancients towards a woman who presumed to be ambitious and was therefore 'greedy for power' (Dudley), driven by '*orgueil ambitieux*' (Fabia) or '*ehrgeizigen Streben*' (Domaszewski).

The actual record, however, suggests very strongly that both ancient and modern writers offer a lop-sided portrait, at best. Agrippina's presence seems to have transformed the regime of her husband, the emperor Claudius. Only a secure ruler can be an enlightened ruler. She appreciated that such security depended on the loyalty of the troops, especially the praetorian guard garrisoned in Rome. This much, admittedly, involved no great insight, but her cleverness lay in recognizing that it was not enough to control their commander, who might be removed peremptorily; she also hand-picked the middle officers, and through them kept a secure grip on the rank and file. In addition, she understood that, while senators in Rome might not command armies, they did, more than any other group, represent the pride and traditions of the old republican Rome. Coercion and force could make them servile, but also sullen and dangerous, while diplomacy and tact would mould them into helpful collaborators. Similarly, the one colony founded under her sponsorship, Cologne, stands out as a remarkable instance of co-operation between the Romans and the local population. The evidence suggests that after her marriage to Claudius, Agrippina inverted the normal progression of a monarchical regime, changing it from a repressive dictatorship marked by continuous judicial executions to a relatively benign partnership between the ruler and the ruled. Also, the ascendancy she enjoyed after her son Nero's accession coincided with the finest period of his administration, and her final departure from the scene seems to have removed the restraining check to his descent into erratic tyranny.

Thus Agrippina's contribution to her time seems on the whole to have been a positive one. This does not mean, of course, that she was a paragon of virtue and a woman of sterling character, worthy of the devout and unstinting admiration bestowed on her by her one major apologist, Guglielmo Ferrero. Writing at the beginning of this century, Ferrero portrayed her as a splendid heroine of duty. In fact, the evidence, honestly and fairly evaluated, seems to suggest that she was a distinctly unattractive individual. But in her defence it might be pointed out that politically ambitious people tend not to be appealing at the very best of times. And politically ambitious people who have to make their way in a monarchical system can generally succeed only through behaviour that is by most norms repellent. If we add to this formula a politically ambitious woman in a monarchical structure that had no formal provision for the involvement of women, the odds are almost insurmountable in favour of her being, by necessity, rather awful. It is when Agrippina is judged by her achievements, rather than by her personality or character, that she demands admiration.

Clearly the Roman imperial system was unfair to a woman like Agrippina, whose talents and energies were such that she would have achieved high office, quite likely the principate itself, had she been a man. Moreover, this unfairness might provide legitimate ammunition for the social activist. But students of history, having once observed the inequality, are likely to gain little historical insight by dwelling on it. It must be left to others to draw any social and political lessons that are to be learned from the historian's discoveries. Also, this book is organized in what might well seem at first sight an old-fashioned and even patronizing scheme, since it approaches Agrippina as the daughter of an acclaimed and much-loved prince, the sister of an emperor, the wife of another emperor, and the mother of yet another – in each case, it might be objected, as the appendage of a significant man. But in the setting of ancient Rome these subordinate roles are what, in fact, defined her sphere of operations, as she was fully aware. The brilliant exploitation of that position, so as to exercise enormous *de facto* power and influence, was her own great achievement. The inability to reconcile maternal and political instincts was her one crucial failing.

Underlying any study of ancient history is the problem of the source material available to us. Three names will constantly reappear throughout this work: Tacitus, our most important historical writer, the biographer Suetonius and Dio, the Greek historian of the early third century. A separate chapter will consider the value of these and others for the topic in hand, but it should be noted at the outset that the standards of care and accuracy we associate with modern historical scholarship must not be sought in even the best ancient literary sources. Moreover, in any period of historical writing there can be no such thing as an untainted judgement since, despite any genuine desire to be honest and precise, the historian will inevitably be corrupted by an inherited way of viewing the world. The theoretical deconstructionist would deny that meaningful history can be written. This book takes a more pragmatic approach and assumes that even behind reports that are contradictory or, when consistent, patently absurd, there lurks a reality capable of being at least partially unearthed. Now the distortion of the record to add colour or to serve personal or political ends is a hindrance to the historian, but is not an insurmountable obstacle. Far more problematic is the common tendency of the ancient sources, especially when they are dealing with certain groups (like ambitious women), to think in stereotypes and to tailor the evidence to fit some imaginary preconceived type-model. Agrippina is more than once linked with a contemporary rival as being her equal in 'beauty and corruption', the implication being that women could achieve mastery only through sexual allure, and through being immoral enough to exploit that allure. Stereotypical thought is particularly dangerous because it can produce a series of events that is consistent and plausible, but no less distorted and inaccurate than the product of prejudice or an overheated imagination.

Sometimes the fictions that the ancient sources pass on can be almost as useful to us as the truth, since they have considerable value in conveying what was believed at the time. There was, for instance, a tradition that Agrippina was a cruel and dangerous woman. Whether or not she really was, that very reputation must have affected the behaviour of potential enemies. This point is particularly important in one specific area. The charge of poisoning is frequently levelled during the Julio-Claudian period, especially against women. Now whenever murder by that method is alleged in antiquity, modern scholars tend dutifully to collect the ancient testimonia to reach a scholarly conclusion about the true cause of death. Such detailed work is probably wasted effort.

Even in our own day, with the help of science, the opportunity for exhumation, police investigation and a systematic court procedure, it is notoriously difficult to determine the truth in poisoning cases. That said, when the ancient sources allege poisoning, the charge can give us an insight into how contemporaries looked upon the individual under suspicion. Thus, whether or not Agrippina was a poisoner is probably less important politically than the mere reputation of poisoner, since even if it was totally undeserved the public perception would have been a potent deterrent to opposition.

The study of the ancient past presents its own special problems for the historian. So negligible is the information on figures like Agrippina that many aspects of her life and career remain a mystery, and it must be acknowledged that the result of any research can be only an approximation of the full picture. The biographer also faces another, more serious, obstacle, the contentious issue of the historical value of studying the lives of 'important' people. Personal lives, admittedly, offer a limited picture of an era and a society. But of course similar reservations can be raised about any other single historical approach. Biography is only one tool alongside others, with its own peculiar set of limitations and strengths. What cannot be contested is that intelligent readers, who have no axe to grind and no turf to protect, continue to use biography as a valid means of enhancing their understanding of the past.

To understand Agrippina, we must understand the system that shaped and defined her. Thus an attempt is made to explain how the Augustan system was established and evolved down to her time, stressing those incidents that involved female members of the imperial house, figures like Livia, Messalina and also republican women like Fulvia, who in a sense laid the groundwork for Agrippina. In the tradition of biographical writing, a chapter is dedicated to Agrippina's parents, where the information is by necessity cursory since they could arguably merit separate monographs in their own right. Considerable space is devoted to the individuals and institutions which make up the contemporary background to Agrippina's career. Much of this material will be familiar to the specialist, whose indulgence is accordingly sought.

Some familiar and elementary concepts are explained for the benefit of the non-specialist. Since family connections are a constant frustration when dealing with the Julio-Claudians, individual relationships are often repeated for the sake of clarity. Names, both of people and of places, appear in their most familiar forms, even at the risk of some inconsistency. In particular, Agrippina is identified as the 'Elder' or 'Younger', or by means of a family relationship (as in the title of the book), only when the context seems to demand it. To avoid confusion, Nero, the future emperor, is referred to as such throughout, even before he formally acquired the name through adoption by the emperor Claudius. The flamboyant Jewish ruler 'Herod' Agrippa is given that familiar though technically incorrect form of his name. Roman praenomina (given names) are written out in full (except in the notes), not in the conventional abbreviated form. Discussions that are unduly complex or threaten to obstruct the flow of the narrative are assigned to appendices.

Monetary amounts are expressed in the standard Roman fashion, in sestertii (abbreviated 'HS'). It is always a risky process to speculate about monetary equivalence, but as a very rough guide it might be noted that the annual pay for an ordinary legionary soldier in the relevant period was 225 denarii, before deductions, or 900HS expressed in sestertii.

Agrippina and some of her contemporaries are illustrated through sculpted heads and decorated gems. In each case, the attribution is based on scholarly opinion and a secure identification cannot be guaranteed.

The task of writing an academic book can be much lightened by the support of individuals and institutions, and such has been my own experience. I have benefited from the thoughtfulness of the staff of various libraries: the Bodleian and Ashmolean in Oxford, the Cambridge University Library, and especially the circulation division of the Library of the University of British Columbia. Several bodies have allowed me to illustrate items from their collections; individual acknowledgements are attached to the plates. A grant from the Social Sciences and Humanities Research Council provided a welcome term's leave from my regular teaching and administrative duties to concentrate on writing the text. As on a previous occasion, I have been permitted to use, with minor adaptations, Tony Birley's map of the Roman world and Miriam Griffin's family tree of the Julio-Claudians. Rochelle Ramay prepared the map of the Baiae area for me. My colleague James Russell allowed me to draw on his deep knowledge of Roman archaeology. Dr D. G. Roberts provided useful information on dental matters. Brian Rose granted me a preview of his manuscript on Roman sculptural groups. My family has supported and encouraged me throughout, reading the early versions and subjecting the preliminary draft to detailed scrutiny and forthright comment. The manuscript was read by Tony Birley and Barabara Levick, both of whom saved me from a number of errors and offered useful leads, and for their generous help I owe to them a major debt of gratitude (as I do to the anonymous reader for Yale University Press). The completed version was read by my friend Karl Sandor, who offered a number of insightful suggestions. The final copy was corrected by Alexis Davis, and Peter Kemmis Betty and Charlotte Vickerstaff have helped the book into Press with their usual perfect blend of patience and persistence. I wish finally to record my gratitude to Graham Webster, who initially stimulated my interest in ancient biography and many years ago taught a traditional Classicist the importance of evaluating ancient literary sources in the context of the material remains.

Significant Events
and Figures

14
19 August   Death of Augustus

15?
6 November   Birth of Agrippina

16   Recall of Germanicus from Germany

17
26 May   Germanicus' triumph
autumn   Departure of Germanicus for the east

19
10 October   Death of Germanicus

26   Clash between Agrippina the Elder and Tiberius
                         Departure of Tiberius from Rome

28   Marriage of Agrippina the Younger and Domitius

29
early   Death of Livia
                         Exile of Agrippina the Elder and her son Nero

31
18 October   Death of Sejanus

32   Consulship of Domitius

33
18 October   Death of Agrippina the Elder

37   Albucilla affair
16 March   Death of Tiberius
                         Accession of Caligula
15 December   Birth of Nero (?)

39
late   Exile of Agrippina and Livilla

40
late?   Death of Domitius

41
late January   Assassination of Caligula
                         Accession of Claudius
after January   Recall of Agrippina and Livilla
                         Exile and death of Livilla

	Exile of Seneca
	Marriage of Agrippina and Passienus (?)
47	Presence of Agrippina and Nero in Rome
48	Death of Messalina
49	
1 January	Marriage of Claudius and Agrippina
later	Recall of Seneca
	Death of Lollia
50	Bestowal of title of Augusta on Agrippina
	Adoption of Nero by Claudius
	Foundation of Cologne
51	
by March	Manhood ceremony of Nero
later	Appointment of Burrus as praetorian prefect
	Death of Vitellius
	Surrender of Caratacus
52	Inquiry into affairs in Judaea
	Draining of the Fucine Lake
53	Grant of judicial powers to procurators
	Presentation by Nero of cases in court
	Nero's appointment as prefect of the city
	Downfall of Titus Statilius Corvinus
	Death of Lepida
	Marriage of Nero and Octavia
54	
13 October	Death of Claudius
later	Accession of Nero
	Consecration of Claudius
	Death of Marcus Junius Silanus
	Death of Narcissus
	Crisis in Armenia
	Reception of Armenian ambassadors
55	Clash between Nero and Agrippina over Acte
	Removal of Pallas
	Death of Britannicus
	Departure of Agrippina from the palace
	Charge of conspiracy against Agrippina
	Revival of Agrippina's influence
56/57	Agrippina honoured on Alexandrian coins
57	
6 November	Celebration of Agrippina's birthday by the Arval Brethren
	Allusion to affair between Agrippina and Seneca
57/58	Agrippina honoured on Alexandrian coins
58	
6 November	Celebration of Agrippina's birthday by the Arval Brethren

59

19–23 March	Murder of Agrippina
June	Return of Nero to Rome
	Death of Domitia

62   Death of Burrus

65   Pisonian conspiracy
                       Death of Faenius Rufus
                       Death of Seneca

68

9 June   Death of Nero

Whereabouts of Agrippina

On 6 November (15?) Agrippina was born in Ara Ubiorum (Cologne). In 16 she was in Ambitarvium just above Coblenz, where her sister Drusilla was born.

In 17 Agrippina accompanied her parents to Rome. They would have lived in the residence of her father, Germanicus. That house is described by Josephus as being adjacent to the house of Caligula, which probably refers to the large Claudian block in which Caligula seems to have taken up residence (Jos. *Ant.* 19.117). Kokkinos (1992), 67, 152 has observed that there are close connections between the household staffs of Germanicus and Antonia the Younger and believes that their house was one and the same, to be identified with the house of Livia.

On the arrest of her mother, Agrippina the Younger went to live with Livia in her house on the Palatine, until 28.

In 28 Agrippina was outside Rome for her wedding, possibly in Campania (the ceremony was attended by Tiberius).

After her marriage in 28 Agrippina probably joined her husband in his house on the Via Sacra (possibly located to the north of the site of the Arch of Titus)

Agrippina was in the imperial villa at Antium when Nero was born, probably in 37.

In 39 Agrippina may well have been staying on her estate at Mevania when she was arrested on the orders of Caligula.

Late in 39 Agrippina was exiled to the island of Pontia.

On Claudius' accession in late January 41, Agrippina returned to Rome. Her movements are uncertain for the next few years.
In 47 Agrippina was in Rome, after an apparent absence. She may have lived in the house of Domitius on the Via Sacra.

After her marriage to Claudius in 49, Agrippina would have moved to his residence on the Palatine, probably in the large Claudian insula. Possibly on her initiative the palatial Domus Tiberiana was constructed, as a symbol of her status. She continued to live there to 55.

In 55 (Tac. *Ann.* 13.18.5) Nero deprived her of her guard and moved her to the house of Antonia. Dio 53.27.5 alludes to a house of Marc Antony on the Palatine, which Antony might have inherited from Fulvia. It seems to have been given to Marcus Agrippa and later burnt down.

Agrippina spent much of her last months in her villas, at Tusculum and Antium (Tac. *Ann.* 14.3.1).

In 59 she spent time at Antium, almost certainly in the great imperial villa there, before making her fateful journey south to meet Nero. There she probably stayed at the villa once owned by Antonia the Younger at Bauli.

After her death she was buried by the road between Misenum and Baiae.

Agrippina's Husbands

1 Gnaeus Domitius Ahenobarbus
2 Gaius Sallustius Crispus Passienus
3 Tiberius Claudius Caesar (Claudius)

Agrippina's Alleged Lovers

Her brother Caligula: Dio 59.22.6; 26.5; Eutropius 7.12.3; Jerome *ab Abr.* 178 (Helm); Schol. Juv. *Sat.* 4.81; Orosius 7.5.9; Aur.Vict. *Caes.* 3.10; Anon. *Epit. de Caes.* 3.4

Aemilius Lepidus, husband of her late sister: Tac. *Ann.* 14.2.4: Suet. *Cal.* 24.3; Dio 59.22.6,8

Tigellinus, later prefect of the guard: Dio 59.23.9; Schol. Juv. *Sat.* 1.155

Seneca: Dio 61.10.1 (cf Tac. *Ann.* 13.42.5)

Her uncle Claudius (before their marriage): Tac. *Ann.* 12.5.1; Suet. *Claud.* 26.3; Dio 60.31.6; 61.11.3–4
Faenius Rufus, later prefect of the guard: Tac. *Ann.* 15.50.4

The freedman Pallas: Tac. *Ann.* 12.25.1, 65.4, 14.2.4; Dio 61.3.2; Probus, in Schol. Juv. *Sat.* 1.109

Aulus Plautius, young nobleman: Suet. *Nero* 35.4

Rubellius Plautus, son of Julia, granddaughter of Tiberius: Tac. *Ann.* 13.19.3

Her son Nero: Tac. *Ann.* 14.2; Suet. *Nero* 28.2; Dio 61.11.3-4

Agrippina's Alleged Victims

(mode of death as supplied by the source, without implication of validity)

Passienus, her second husband, poisoned: [Suet.] *Vita Passieni* (probably between 44 and 47)

Calpurnia, distinguished woman admired by Claudius. Banished, according to Tacitus; executed, according to Dio: Tac. *Ann.* 12.22.3, 14.12.6; Dio 60.33.2b (49)

Lollia Paulina, ex-wife of Caligula, candidate for marriage to Claudius, executed: Tac. *Ann.* 12.22.1-4; Dio 60.32.3 (49)

Titus Statilius Taurus, consul AD 44, forced into suicide: Tac. *Ann.* 12.59.1 (53)

Domitia Lepida, mother of Messalina and sister-in-law of Agrippina, executed: Tac. *Ann.* 12.64.4-6, 65.1-2 (54)

Claudius, her husband, poisoned: *Apoc.* 1-6; Jos. *Ant.* 20.148, 151; *Octavia* 31, 44, 64, 102, 164–5; Pliny *NH* 22.92; Juv. *Sat.* 5.146-8, 6.620-3 (along with scholiast); Tac. *Ann.* 12.66-67; Martial 1.20; Suet. *Claud.* 44.2-46; *Nero* 33.1, 39.3; Dio 60.34.2-6, 35; Philost. *Apoll.* 5.32 (hos phasi); Aur. Vict. 4.13; Anon. *Epit. de Caes.* 4.10; Oros. 7.6.18; Zosim. I.6.3 (54)

Marcus Junius Silanus, potential rival to Nero, poisoned: Pliny *NH* 7.58; Tac. *Ann.* 13.1.1-2; Dio 61.6.4 (54)

Britannicus, stepson, poisoned: Schol. Juv. *Sat.* 6.124; 628 (55)

Junia Silana, enemy of Agrippina, exiled: Tac. *Ann.* 13.22.3 (55)

Calvisius and Iturius, clients of Junia Silana, exiled: Tac. *Ann.* 13.22.3 (55)

Atimetus, freedman of Domitia Lepida, executed: Tac. *Ann.* 13.22.3 (55)

1
Background

The republic that was established in Rome after the expulsion of its kings, an event traditionally dated to 510 BC, served its purpose well for some four centuries. But its final century was one of increasing chaos and disorder. The growth of an overseas empire, in particular, created opportunities and temptations too attractive for most to resist, and the political scene was dominated by a succession of military commanders with their own excessive personal ambitions. The most famous of these commanders was without doubt Julius Caesar, whose assassination in 44 BC heralded the republic's end.

Caesar belonged to a distinguished family, the Julians, whose name would be invoked repeatedly by generations of his successors. In the funeral oration that he gave for his aunt Julia in 68 BC he reminded his audience of the tradition that the Julian *gens* had existed since the foundation of Rome and was descended from the goddess Venus, through her son Aeneas and her grandson Julus, a happy fiction that was later to be given a veneer of respectability by the poet Vergil in his great national epic, the *Aeneid*. The Julii attained prominence in the fifth and fourth centuries, but then, despite their splendid divine ancestry, sank into obscurity for 200 years. By the time of Caesar they had once again come to prominence.[1]

Caesar's ultimate political ambitions are something of a mystery, and whether or not he aimed at the restoration of a monarchical system is far from clear. But it was nature that denied him the ultimate satisfaction of a monarch, that of being succeeded by his own son. He married several times and had a reputation among his soldiers for sexual prowess but despite all these assets he produced only one legitimate child, a much-loved daughter, who on her death left no surviving offspring. Caesar's sister Julia did better, with two granddaughters and a grandson, Octavius. This sickly and unprepossessing youth was Caesar's closest male descendant. He was destined to change the course of history.

The custom of great Roman families who faced extinction through a lack of male heirs was the very practical one of simply acquiring a son from another prominent family. Hence Caesar adopted his great-nephew Octavius, who in the Roman manner assumed his adoptive father's name, technically followed by a modified form of his own, Octavianus (although he in fact avoided use of this final part of his name, which would have drawn attention to his adopted status). Few men can be said to have used their inheritance more effectively than did Octavian. Styling himself the son of the deified Caesar, he made claim at the age of 18 not only to his adoptive father's estate but also to his political legacy.

The fact that the republic was now little more than a fiction was demonstrated just over a year after Caesar's death by the legal establishment of a triumvirate, or committee of three men, who divided the Roman world between them with virtually absolute powers. The rivalry between the most powerful two, Octavian and Marc Antony, persisted for over a decade. The battle of Actium in 31 BC, however, saw the defeat of the combined forces of Antony and his mistress Cleopatra, and left Octavian the undisputed master of the Roman world, a position that he was to maintain until his death in AD 14. The durability of his power was due in no small part to the remarkable constitutional changes he initiated.

After Actium, Octavian began the process by which the institutions of the republic could theoretically be confirmed, while he, for all practical purposes, remained in control. He accordingly handed back the extraordinary powers that he had accumulated. In return he received other powers nominally bestowed by the senate and the Roman people, as well as a new title, Augustus. It was the constant preoccupation of Augustus to present himself as princeps, the 'first citizen', a magistrate whose office might involve major responsibilities but who remained in the end essentially no different from other magistrates. By holding significant offices concurrently, with special privileges attached to them, he succeeded in controlling political and military affairs throughout the Roman empire for the rest of his life. This change was regretted by some leading families, who resented the surrender of their political power, but most Romans no doubt welcomed the peace and stability that the principate brought with it.

Under the Augustan settlement, the main deliberative and legislative body remained the senate, which by now consisted essentially of about 600 former magistrates of the rank of quaestor or above. The quaestorship, like the other magistracies, was open only to men, in this case men who had reached at least the age of 25, and the position generally involved financial duties. Twenty were elected annually. It might be followed by one of two offices, either that of aedile, concerned mainly with municipal administration, or of tribune, appointed originally to protect the interest of the plebeians. By this period the old political distinctions between the plebeians and high-born patricians had disappeared for practical purposes, and the tribune was concerned chiefly with minor judicial matters. The quaestor could, if he chose, pass directly to the next office in the hierarchy, the praetorship (twelve elected annually) and be generally responsible for the administration of justice. Finally, he could be elected to one of two consulships, the most prestigious office in the state and one that was eagerly sought after. Formally this could happen only after the age of 42, but an ex-consul in his family line enabled a man to aspire to the office at a much earlier age, possibly by 32, and members of the imperial family sooner still.[2] The holding of a senior magistracy, possibly the consulship itself, elevated the holder's family, whether patrician or plebeian, to the rank of the *nobilitas*. Once he had held the appropriate office, a man could usually expect to serve as senator for life. But there were exceptions. In the early republic the position of censor was established, to maintain the official list of citizens. He could expel from the senate those members whose conduct was deemed wanting on legal or moral grounds. The office had begun to lose much of its prestige by the late republic and its powers were assumed by the emperors.

On the expiry of their term, consuls and praetors would often be granted a province, which by this period generally indicated a territory organized as an administrative unit. In their provinces the ex-magistrates would continue to exercise their authority in the capacity of their previous offices, that is as *propraetor* or *proconsul*. In 27 BC Augustus placed his own territories at the disposal of the senate. They for their part granted him control over a single huge 'province', involving at its core Gaul, Syria and most of Spain, for a period of ten years, with the possibility of renewal. It was in these 'imperial' provinces that the Roman legions, with some minor exceptions, were stationed. Augustus received the power to appoint their governors (*legati Augusti*) and the individual legionary commanders (*legati legionis*), and was thus effectively commander-in-chief of the Roman army, a position fortified by the establishment of a central state fund to provide pensions for retired soldiers. The élite of the army were the praetorians, essentially the emperor's personal guard, stationed in Rome and other parts of Italy, and enjoying special pay and privileges. The acme of the soldier's career, the 'triumph' that followed a major military victory and involved a splendid military parade through Rome, became the prerogative of the imperial family. The victorious commander, who had achieved his success as viceroy of the emperor, had to be satisfied, unless he was a member of the imperial family, with the lesser honour of triumphal *insignia*. Governors of the remaining 'public' provinces (*proconsules*) were normally chosen by lot. Egypt was in a special position, legally assigned to Augustus but in effect looked upon almost as a quasi-private domain where he ruled as successor to the Ptolemies.

The smooth operation of the Augustan system required a steady supply of administrators, which would in turn depend ultimately on a healthy birth rate. To encourage stable marriages and the procreation of legitimate children among upper-class families, Augustus enacted a body of social legislation. This provided incentives in the form of improved career prospects and other advantages for both men and women willing to assume their responsibilities, and corresponding penalties against those who were not.

From 31 BC to 23 BC Augustus held a continuous consulship. After the latter date he held the office on only two occasions. This change reflects a growing confidence in his position, but also a desire not to block the ambitions of others or to limit the potential pool of administrators of consular rank. Also, to this end, from 5 BC it became usual for consuls to resign office in the course of the year, to allow replacements ('suffects'). In return for giving up his consulship in 23 BC, Augustus was granted 'greater authority' (*imperium maius*); since it was 'greater' than that of other magistrates, this authority prevailed in the public as well as imperial provinces, and did not lapse when he passed within the boundaries of the city of Rome. It was probably in 23 BC also (there is some disagreement on the matter) that he assumed the traditional authority of the plebeian tribunes, the *tribunicia potestas*. This conferred certain privileges, such as the right to convene the senate and popular assemblies, and to initiate or veto legislation. It would also make more logical the grant of *sacrosanctitas*, a privilege associated with the tribunes, which had been conferred on him earlier and which had made an attack on his person an act of sacrilege. The symbolic importance of the tribuncian *potestas* is illustrated by the practice adopted by emperors of dating their reigns from the time of its assumption.

Below the senators, rated on the basis of their financial worth, stood the equestrians, roughly the entrepreneurial middle class, who had before this period generally found themselves excluded from service to the state. The Augustan settlement opened up major opportunities for the equestrians, including the government of certain smaller provinces, with the rank of prefect or procurator (the latter became the usual title during the Claudian period). At the pinnacle of the equestrian career were the four great prefectures of Egypt, the praetorian guard, the *annona* (corn supply) or the Vigiles (city police).

Nothing better exposes the fiction that the emperors were essentially regular magistrates than the law that dealt with treason (*maiestas*). The precise nature of this crime, which predates the imperial period, is unclear. In about 100 BC a *Lex Appuleia de Maiestate* was enacted, apparently to punish the incompetence of those who had mishandled the campaign against the hostile Germanic tribes, the Teutones and Cimbri. The charge seems to have involved negligence rather than criminality. Somewhat later, under the dictator Sulla, a *Lex Cornelia de Maiestate* was aimed at preventing army commanders from taking their armies out of their provinces. Under Caesar this law was replaced by a *Lex Julia de Maiestate*. The actual misdemeanours covered by Caesar's legislation are not clear, nor is the penalty – it may technically have been death, but in practice resulted in a form of exile. Caesar's law was replaced by a later *Lex Julia* under Augustus, one that resulted in significant changes. The Augustan law was interpreted to include verbal abuse and slander in its definition of *maiestas laesa*. It protected the state against ambitious army commanders, and from threats against the security of the state, much as it had done during the republic. But there was now a new element. It protected the emperor against personal attacks, both physical and, more significantly, verbal; lèse majesté as we know the expression. Gradually the penalties became more and more severe, leading to death. The imprecision of the crime and the inducement offered to the original complainant, in the form of a portion of the fine imposed in the case of conviction, inevitably encouraged the proliferation of the semi-professional accuser (*delator*). *Maiestas* trials were the most hated feature of the principate, and on accession each Julio-Claudian emperor after Tiberius foreswore at least those cases that involved slander (an undertaking that inevitably proved impossible to sustain). Given the imprecise nature of the crime, it was open to serious abuse, especially since the princeps had the power to conduct proceedings *in camera*. There was a common belief that influential figures in court, especially the imperial wives, were heavily involved in many of the trials.[3]

The formal involvement of women in public life was limited essentially to certain priestly offices and, in particular, to membership in the Vestal Virgins. Vesta was the goddess of the hearth, and her state cult was established in the round temple near the Regia in the forum. It housed a sacred fire and the community of Vestals (who numbered six in the Augustan period) were charged with tending it. A Vestal was expected to remain chaste for the duration of her service (normally thirty years), after which she was free to marry (but rarely did). She was removed from the control of her paterfamilias (see below) but came under the authority of the pontifex, who could punish her by scourging for letting out the sacred fire or by death for violation of her chastity. She enjoyed several privileges, such as special seats at the games and sacrosanctity; these special privileges would gradually be acquired also by prominent women of the imperial family.

The only other quasi-political role for an upper-class Roman woman was to strengthen family alliances through marriage. Daughters, even wives, would find themselves used as political tools. As Pomeroy has observed, even the nation's founding hero Aeneas of Troy, according to tradition, broke off an affair with Queen Dido of Carthage, whom he loved, and planned a dynastic marriage with the daughter (whom he had never met) of the Italian King Latinus. This practice became very common in the late republic. Thus Caesar sought to cultivate Pompey's adherence by offering him marriage with his daughter Julia. Octavian broke off an earlier engagement to become betrothed to Marc Antony's daughter, but in turn broke this pact to marry Scribonia, who was connected to Pompey's renegade son, Sextus Pompeius. He also arranged the marriage of his sister, Octavia, to Marc Antony.

At first sight the Augustan reforms might seem to have no political significance for a woman like Agrippina. As a result of the changes he initiated, a man as humble as a freedman (a liberated slave) could aspire to the governorship of a province, as happened to Felix, the procurator of Judaea, before whom Saint Paul was granted his famous hearing. But such opportunities remained barred to women, no matter how high born or accomplished. All the same, in its own curious way the imperial system did allow a limited group of women certain political advantages. From 27 BC men who held office did so as servants of the emperor. Power, in the sense of the ability to influence 'policy', resided in the first instance with the emperor. Beyond this, as in any quasi-monarchical system, it was exercised by those lucky enough to win his ear. Such individuals might be holders of high office, like powerful army commanders, governors of important provinces, prefects of the imperial guard or even able freedmen performing key tasks within the emperor's chancery. But they might also be personal friends, either foreign or Roman, and they might also be wives. The involvement of the imperial wives in this process caused deep bitterness among contemporary Romans, and this resentment had a serious impact on the way such powerful women are presented by the literary sources. The ill-feeling had its roots in long-held views about the role that women should properly expect to play within the framework of the Roman state.[4]

By the Augustan age some Roman women had managed to acquire personal wealth and independence undreamt of in Classical Athens and still regularly denied them even in many otherwise progressive states before the twentieth century. The ancient form of Roman marriage, whereby a bride was passed over to the total authority (*in manus*) of her husband was by this time little more than a historic relic, and from a relatively early period women had acquired the power to inherit, own and bequeath property. Nominally this power was administered under the direction of a man. A daughter remained under the authority of her paterfamilias (usually her father, but possibly her paternal grandfather or even great-grandfather if he was alive). On the death of the paterfamilias, custody over her passed technically to a guardian, normally the closest male relative. The wealth and prominence of a number of women in the late republic show that this apparently draconian control was less irksome in practice than in theory, and could be avoided by a range of devices, such as an appeal to a magistrate. Even the formal and legal restrictions were removed under Augustus from those women who had borne three or four children.

In one particular respect the Romans were relatively enlightened – in their attitude towards the education of young girls. Unlike boys, girls generally did not study outside the home with philosophers or rhetoricians, largely for the simple practical reason that they tended to be married by the time such arrangements would normally come into force (p. 40). But they did share domestic tutors with their brothers before marriage, and the evidence indicates that in Agrippina's day husbands encouraged their wives after marriage to continue their intellectual and artistic pursuits. Pliny the Younger, for instance, was pleased to find his young wife reading and memorizing his writing, and setting his verses to music. Cornelia, the wife of Pompey, was well versed in literature, music and geometry, and in the habit of listening to philosophical debates. Caerellia, a friend of Cicero, was interested in philosophy and was so anxious to get a preview of his *De Finibus* that she used the copyists hired by Cicero's friend Atticus to get unauthorized access to it.[5] One of the most celebrated speakers of the late republic was Hortensia. She belonged to a large group of wealthy women whose male relatives had in 42 BC been proscribed, and who were taxed to provide revenues for the triumvirs. The women congregated in the forum to protest, and Hortensia gave a celebrated speech on their behalf. Almost a century and a half later Quintilian testifies to the eloquence of her oratory and says that her works were still read on their own merits and not just because of the novelty that they were written by a woman.[6] The phenomenon of the educated woman is confirmed by the remarks of the misanthropic Juvenal, who declares his horror at females who pontificate on literature, discourse on ethics, quote lines of verse that no-one has heard of and correct your mistakes of grammar.[7] Thus when we hear of the younger Agrippina writing her memoirs, and of the emperor Tiberius responding to her mother's taunts in Greek, presumably expecting to be understood, it should come as no surprise that both mother and daughter had developed sophisticated literary skills.

This enlightened attitude did, to some degree, have an ulterior motive. Quintilian advocates that mothers should be educated so that they might educate their sons in turn.[8] In the *Dialogus* attributed to Tacitus, Vipstanus Messala fondly recalls worthy women of the old republic. For such women the highest praise was that they devoted themselves to their children.[9] First in the list of those Tacitus admired (it includes also the mothers of Caesar and of Augustus) comes Cornelia, daughter of Scipio Africanus, who bore twelve children, including the two famous Gracchi brothers. She was widely acclaimed as the prototype of the sophisticated mother, dedicated to her sons' education and constantly in the company of Greeks and scholars. Cicero, who had read her letters, comments that her sons were nurtured by her speech as much as by her breast.[10] This tradition continued into the imperial period. Tacitus speaks with admiration of Julia Procilla, the mother of his father-in-law Agricola, a contemporary of Agrippina who, like her, kept a close supervision over her son even to the extent of discouraging, as did Agrippina, his enthusiasm for philosophy (an excessive interest in that subject was not considered proper in a Roman senator).[11] No one would have been surprised by Agrippina's tight control over the upbringing and education of her son Nero, or over the potentially more sinister control that she exercised over the tutors of her stepson Britannicus.

While mothers were expected to communicate their learning to their children, it was from their fathers that they supposedly acquired their inborn talents and they were not reluctant to proclaim their paternal inheritance. Thus Cornelia, despite her own contribution to the education of her sons, the two Gracchi, drew constant attention to her father Scipio Africanus and followed tradition by recording her paternity ('Cornelia, daughter of Africanus') on the base of her well-known portrait statue (otherwise considered *avant garde* by Pliny because the figure wore no straps on the shoes). It was claimed that she goaded her sons to be ambitious by reminding them that she was famous as the daughter of Scipio Africanus rather than as the mother of the Gracchi brothers.[12] Agrippina was the daughter of probably the most admired Roman of his age, Germanicus, and she similarly had no scruples about constantly exploiting the connection, even though her father died before he could have had any practical influence over her.

Co-existent with the relatively advanced position of Roman women and the history of their gradual, albeit partial, emancipation was another attitude that has more to do with myth than truth, and which went beyond the simple idea that a woman should commit herself to the welfare of her children. Romans nostalgically recreated the figure of the Roman woman of olden times, devoted to her husband whom she of course obeyed unquestioningly, and to the frugal and industrious running of her household in an age when women were virtuous, marriages were stable, and husbands and wives went through life in unruffled bliss. *Domum servavit. Lanam fecit* ('She kept house. She made wool') is how the familiar tomb inscription of the end of the second century BC summed up the virtues of a worthy wife. The women of Augustus' family, despite their education and hard-won legal rights, were expected to perpetuate this myth, and he spread the story that his simple clothes were all woven by his sister, wife or daughter.[13]

The motif of the woman who duly excluded herself from involvement in political matters became hallowed in tradition. From time to time females were conceded an important part in critical moments in the history of the state. But, while their behaviour could be heroic, it was essentially passive or supportive in its nature, as when the women of Rome reputedly donated their hair for bowstrings during the siege of the Capitol by the Gauls in 390 BC.[14] Otherwise they might act collectively to entreat male Romans to pursue a particular course of action, like the abducted Sabine women who interceded between their new Roman husbands and their former families, and forged an alliance between the two groups, or like the deputation of women, led by his wife and mother, who in 491 BC supposedly dissuaded Coriolanus from making war on Rome.[15]

Perhaps the most heroic legendary woman was Lucretia. According to tradition, the sons of the last Roman king, Tarquin, wagered with a cousin, Collatinus, on the relative behaviour of their wives in the absence of their husbands (they were on campaign). They returned to Rome, where it was found that the wives at the royal palace had given themselves over to dissipation, but at Collatinus' house his wife Lucretia was found industriously spinning with the female slaves. Tragedy ensued. One of the sons, Sextus Tarquinius, was so smitten by Lucretia that he returned a few days later and forced her to submit to his lust, threatening that if she refused he would kill her and a male slave and leave both bodies in her room, pretending that they had been caught *in flagrantibus* and executed. Next day Lucretia summoned her family and revealed the story to them, before stabbing herself to death. The event supposedly so inflamed the populace that according to tradition it led to the end of the monarchy and the establishment of the republic. Lucretia was thus the victim of unintentional sexual allure and her decency would not let her come to terms with it. Agrippina's sexual sins would by contrast seem all the greater in that she actually exploited her sexual charms to advance her own political ambitions.

Balancing these idealized portraits from early Rome were others that showed the baneful effect that ambition could have on women. Tullia, daughter of King Servius Tullus, is a perfect example. She brought about the death of her husband and sister in order to marry her sister's husband, Tarquinius Superbus, whom she persuaded to seize the throne from her father. As she drove back to the senate after the putsch her carriage was blocked by the body of her dead father. She coolly took the reins from the distraught driver and drove over the corpse. She was thus the prototype of the ruthlessly ambitious woman, assumed to be willing to stoop to anything, including murder of her kin, to achieve her goal. The reality that such tales belong to the realm of legend rather than history does not affect their potency. The Romans instructed through *exempla*, and such stories of idealized womanhood or the calamity of perverted womanhood would have been absorbed at an early age and have encouraged them to think of women in simplistic stereotypes.[16]

By the second century BC the record of historical events becomes more secure and the element of fantasy recedes. A theme that prevails from now on is that of the corroding effect of female emancipation. Throughout the republic men seem to have had an irrational fear of the danger that the growing independence of women posed. The most celebrated statesman to give voice to such views was the austere Cato the Elder, who was obsessed by the notion of moral decay. He made the observation that Rome might rule the world but Romans were ruled by their wives. Cato got his main chance in 195 BC. In this year the Oppian Law, which during the war against Hannibal had imposed restrictions on the personal extravagance of women, was to be repealed. The women demonstrated in the streets, and Cato, consul at the time, took the opportunity to deliver a speech (in vain) in which he warned of their growing power. The speech as preserved in Livy's text may not be genuine, but the sentiments expressed certainly fit what we know of Cato. Men have lost control over their wives, he insists, and this laxity lies at the root of the contemporary problem. Excessive female independence has overwhelmed freedom in the home and now threatens to trample it underfoot in the Forum. If women are allowed to gather together and confer in secret, men will be in danger of destruction.[17] This attitude did not die with Cato. In his *De Republica*, written in the first century BC, Cicero, a man generally associated with relatively liberal views, allows Scipio to deliver a long paraphrase of Plato to the effect that unless slaves obey their masters and wives their husbands anarchy will prevail. 'What an unhappy state it would be where women seize the prerogatives of men, the senate, the army and the magistracies!'[18] Such an attitude certainly carried over into Agrippina's own day. In AD 21, during a debate in the senate on the proconsulships of Asia and Africa, Caecina Severus moved that provincial governors should be prohibited from allowing their wives to accompany them to their provinces. There is great danger, he claimed, in the practice. Whenever governors are tried after their term for corruption, the majority of the indictments are against the wives. Given the chance, women become ruthless intriguers, ambitious for power. They parade among the soldiers, keep the centurions at their elbows.[19]

Women ambitious for themselves or for their sons were thought to be impervious to the kinds of restraint that kept men within the bounds of decency. Even the much-admired Cornelia was suspected of murdering her son-in-law, the great Scipio Aemilianus, with the help of her daughter, Sempronia, to prevent him from annulling the legislation of her sons. A particularly sinister aspect of ambitious women was that their weapon of choice was supposed to be poison. The earliest recorded example is a striking one, the great series of poison trials of 331 BC when the deaths of several prominent citizens were attributed to what Livy calls a *muliebris fraus* ('female treachery'). The phrase is identical to that used by Tacitus to explain the death in AD 19 of Germanicus, supposedly poisoned through the indirect agency of Augustus' wife, Livia.[20] In 180 BC there occurred an incident that sounds like a rehearsal for the charge that would later be made against Agrippina as a woman willing to stop at nothing to promote the interests of her son. In that year the consul died and it was determined that he had been poisoned by his wife Hostilia, who wanted to create a vacancy for her son.[21] There can be little doubt that such stories, handed down as popular lore from generation to generation, would have influenced attitudes about the deaths of Augustus and Claudius who, it was assumed, had similarly to make way for Livia's son Tiberius and Agrippina's son Nero.

While it is clear that throughout Roman history a number of women had in one particular or another anticipated Agrippina, it was not until the final century of the republic that a real prototype for the powerful political woman emerged. The change in status is symbolized by the recognition given to Roman women in an important public ceremony, the funeral oration. Long observed in the case of male ancestors, the first speech in commemoration of a woman was that given in 102 BC by the consul Quintus Lutatius Catulus on behalf of his mother Popilia. At the time of her death Popilia was elderly, and it was thirty years before the honour was granted to a young woman, when Julius Caesar delivered the oration at the funeral of his wife Cornelia. The custom became well established. Caesar made a similar and more famous speech on behalf of his aunt Julia, and Caesar's late sister Julia was honoured in 51 BC by her grandson, the 12-year-old Octavius.[22]

From this time we see an assault on the established tradition that had generally excluded females from the political arena. Women with formidable political influence now become almost an institution.[23] This change no doubt reflects the great wealth of many women of the period, exemplified by Terentia, the wife of Cicero, who had a personal fortune greater than her husband's and who combined these resources with political ambition, being more inclined, as Plutarch observed, to involve herself in Cicero's political activities than in his domestic life.[24] Again, there is need for caution. The notion that women of high birth played a key role in late republican politics became almost formulaic among historical writers. It is consequently difficult in individual cases to determine to what extent their influence is real and to what extent it arises from rhetorical exaggeration, feeding long-held imaginary fears by drawing upon familiar stereotypes.

Certainly there was never a question of women holding political office in their own right – the exercise of power would always be from the *domus* ('home') through their husbands. In the late republic the use of marriage as a political tool was given a new twist and women began to pursue marriage connections on their own initiative, to further *their own* ambitions. Their tactics were invariably trivialized and condemned as improper. Agrippina was criticised for supposedly using her feminine charms to ensnare a defenceless Claudius, and views of her conduct would have been shaped by stories of similar women in the late republic. The aristocratic and ambitious Valeria, for instance, deliberately flirted with the dictator Sulla at the games. So charmed was he by her good looks and saucy manner that they ended up married. Similarly, the noted beauty Praecia, a woman of great charm and wit, brought the powerful Cornelius Cethegus under her spell and he, like Claudius generations later, supposedly did nothing without her approval – power, it was claimed, passed entirely into her hands. Lucullus, the consul of 74 BC, used bribery and flattery to persuade Praecia to work on his behalf, and she eventually secured a command in Cilicia for him.[25] An even more striking parallel is provided by Chelidon, the mistress of Verres, the corrupt governor of Sicily from 73 to 70 BC. She supposedly used her hold over Verres to prop up her power and build up her fortune. As long as her lover was governor, Cicero maintains, Chelidon controlled contracts and settled civil cases for a price; men had to go through her to have their disputes settled. When Verres decided a case she need only whisper in his ear for him to call the parties back and change his judgement.[26]

Perhaps Sallust provides the best illustration of how the assessment of a women's power could be hopelessly distorted. In his account of the conspiracy of Catiline (63 BC), the historian claims that Catiline attracted around him a number of women who had fallen into debt through their extravagance. These he hoped to recruit for a variety of purposes, supposedly to start fires in Rome, to win over their husbands to the cause or, if that failed, to murder them. Chief among such corrupt females was the aristocratic matron Sempronia. She was beautiful and came of good family. She was also well read, a witty talker with a good brain, but she turned her assets to bad purpose and cheated to escape debts, and was even involved in murder. She was a woman lacking in self-restraint and decency, who committed crimes *virilis audaciae* ('of male boldness'), a phrase reminiscent of Tacitus' description of Agrippina's regime as a *quasi virile servitium* ('a kind of male tyranny'). This is a damning character sketch, yet when we examine Sallust's narrative for details of the actual events we find that he fails in fact to assign Sempronia any role in the actual conspiracy, nor is mention made of her in any of the other accounts of the conspiracy that have survived. Again, the broad description of her character, totally unsupported by concrete examples, seems to cater to the obsessive and exaggerated fear of the damage that would inevitably result from women's involvement in public affairs.[27]

Of all the notable late republican women none more closely parallels Agrippina than Fulvia. Like her, she clearly possessed qualities of determination, courage and political skill, and also like Agrippina she is savaged by an almost uniformly hostile tradition, one so hostile that the truth at times seem hopelessly buried in exaggeration and misinterpretation. In her person she represented all the characteristics that the Romans feared as the outcome of female emancipation and the perversion of the idealized notion of a Roman matron. Plutarch observed that she did not think it worthwhile to dominate a man not in public life – she wanted to rule a ruler and command a commander.[28] The daughter of the Sempronia associated by Sallust with the Catilinarian conspiracy, Fulvia was descended on her father's side from a plebeian family that could lay claim to ancient distinction but had of late been politically inactive. Her father Marcus Fulvius Bambalio is dismissed by Cicero as a nonentity (*homo nullo numero*) who acquired his curious cognomen from a stammer, while her grandfather made his mark by dressing up in theatrical costumes and throwing money from the rostra to the poor.[29] But she married three prominent political figures, all tribunes of the plebs and committed supporters of Caesar: Publius Clodius, Gaius Scribonius Curio and Marc Antony. In the last four years of her life (she died in 40 BC) she was active in support of her third husband Antony and thus fell foul of Cicero and, more significantly, Octavian, so she has inevitably faced considerable hostility in the historical tradition. This tradition presents her as a ruthless virago who made a career of battling for power on her husbands' behalf.[30]

Fulvia made her first appearance in the public arena after the death of her first husband, the infamous demagogue Publius Clodius, killed in a fracas with his enemy Milo in 52. She displayed his body to the crowds who congregated outside their house on the Palatine, and gave evidence against Milo in the subsequent trial.[31] In his unsuccessful defence of Milo, the text of which was revised for publication, Cicero raised the traditional bogey-man of the emasculated husband (he reappears later in the person of the emperor Claudius) with his assertions that Fulvia never let Clodius out of her sight, except apparently on the key occasion of the fracas. Her behaviour could, of course, be evidence of nothing more sinister than close affection.[32]

Fulvia probably married Antony before 45 BC, and Cicero appears to hint (without supporting evidence) that she had already begun an affair with him while was she married to Clodius.[33] As Antony's wife, she would suffer from the invectives of his two most vitriolic and influential opponents, Cicero and Octavian. In 44 Cicero associates her with an act of brutal savagery – she was present and her face was spattered with blood when Antony executed a number of centurions, on the refusal of the legions to obey his commands at Brundisium. Antony had, in fact, treacherously invited the centurions to his house and Fulvia's presence there should not be considered at all remarkable.[34] Tradition gives her the last laugh in her quarrel with Cicero. When the orator was put to death and his head delivered to Antony she allegedly spat on it, pulled out the tongue and stuck hairpins in it, amidst much ribaldry. The story, as will be seen, is curiously reminiscent of the reported treatment of Julia Livilla and Lollia Paulina, by Messalina and Agrippina respectively.[35]

The spirit of unrestrained hostility towards Fulvia manifested by Cicero was maintained after his death by Octavian. By an agreement among the triumvirs there were widespread proscriptions and seizure of land in 43, and Octavian would have found it expedient to shift the resulting odium onto his partners in the triumvirate, especially onto the shoulders of a supposedly scheming and ambitious woman.[36] A deliberate campaign of denigration would account for a story about her abuse of the political process to acquire property, a story reminiscent of those later told about Agrippina and other women of the imperial family. Fulvia coveted the fine house of a certain Caesetius Rufus. He at first refused to sell, but when the proscriptions began he offered it as a gift. It did him no good; he was proscribed in any case and his head supposedly passed on to Fulvia to be impaled by her on a pole.[37]

After the victory at Philippi in 42 BC, Antony departed for the east and Octavian in 41 undertook the task of confiscating land from a number of Italian cities in order to found colonies for military veterans. In doing so he was met by the resistance of Lucius, brother of Antony and guardian of his interests. Lucius recruited the aid of Fulvia, and at his instigation she appeared with Antony's children before his old soldiers and urged them to remember their loyalty to their commander.[38] Lucius meanwhile took up the cause of dispossessed Italians. In the autumn of 41 he gathered his troops at Praeneste to launch an attack on Rome. Fulvia joined him there, and, according to the tradition, girded a sword, issued the watchword, harangued the troops and held councils of war with senators and knights. This is the kind of behaviour that evoked special dread in republican writers, and in critics of Agrippina and of her mother – the presumption of a woman who would seek to command the loyalty of the troops. The writer Florus describes her as *gladio cincta virilis militiae* ('girt with the sword of a man's [or, her husband's] campaign'). Dio, who may well have been using Octavian's memoirs, says that the future emperor took particular offence at her military posturing (which might well have stood in stark contrast to his own reputation as something of a poltroon). The poet Martial later excuses the raunchy character of his own verses with an epigram supposedly by Octavian. The poem suggests that Fulvia is battling out of sexual frustration, and she challenges him with the taunt '*aut futue aut pugnemus*' ('either screw me or let's fight'). Octavian, who presumably thought it less daunting to tussle with Fulvia on the battlefield than in the bed, decided to fight.[39]

Octavian met the military threat and forced the surrender of Lucius' forces at Perusia. After the fall of the town, Fulvia fled with her children to join Antony and his mother in Athens. But she had not earned his gratitude. He blamed her for the failures in Italy and she fell ill at Sicyon on the gulf of Corinth, where she died in mid 40 BC, heartbroken over her husband's ingratitude and infidelities. Antony in the meantime had departed for Italy without visiting her sickbed.[40] The final irony in the story is that later in the year Antony would marry Octavia, the sister of the very man who had directed his energies so vigorously against Fulvia precisely because she was defending Antony's interests.

Fulvia's story contains many of the ingredients that will be found in Agrippina's career – venality, cruelty, sexual infidelity, suborning of troops, and the ultimate ingratitude of the men for whom they made such sacrifices. Prototypes can easily become stereotypes. The similarities should alert us to the likelihood that accounts of Agrippina's life and career have been moulded by a standardized preconception of the politically ambitious woman.

2
Family

Agrippina, great-granddaughter of the revered Augustus, would make much of her Julian descent, a descent that came through the bloodline and was not conferred merely through adoption. This dynastic connection was in itself powerful enough, but she could boast another family distinction since she belonged to the second great house to give its name to the first generation of Roman emperors, the proud and haughty Claudians. This particular link would come through her great-grandmother Livia, a woman who in many respects provided a model for the central role that Agrippina was herself to occupy in the Roman state.

Livia's name resulted from her father's adoption into the family of the Livii Drusi, but she was by descent a Claudian, belonging to a family that had already gained prominence in the time of the Roman kings and which produced a series of eminent office-holders during the subsequent republic. In fact, the Claudian republican record was more distinguished than that of the Julians, by whom in the play of imperial politics it was to be eclipsed. At the same time, the Claudians gained a reputation for disdainful arrogance, a reputation not enjoyed exclusively by the men. One early Claudia, for instance, was the daughter of the famous Appius Claudius Caecus, censor in 312 BC, and sister of a naval commander who managed to lose an entire fleet in action. She caused an outrage on one occasion when her carriage was blocked by a throng of people and she wished out loud that the crowd could be forced into the fleet, and her brother brought back to command it. Again, when Appius Claudius Pulcher, consul of 143, was refused permission by the senate to celebrate a triumph after a military campaign of dubious value, he decided (being a Claudian) to ignore the ban and celebrate one in any case. To add insult to injury, his daughter, another Claudia and a Vestal Virgin, joined him in his chariot, since her sacrosanctity would protect him from prosecution.[1]

When Livia's path crossed that of Augustus (or Octavian, as he then was) she was married to Tiberius Claudius Nero, member of a minor branch of the Claudians. In November 42 she bore him a son, Tiberius, destined to succeed Augustus as the least charismatic of the Julio-Claudian emperors. Velleius Paterculus calls Livia's first husband *clarissimus* ('most distinguished') and a man of great spirit and learning, but he seems in reality to have been a professional failure.[2] A supporter of Antony, he was forced to flee from Italy and to suffer a number of humiliations in exile, almost losing Livia in Sparta when the family was caught in a forest fire. Livia's dress and hair were scorched in the mad rush to safety.[3] As would Agrippina later, Livia clearly found her first husband a disappointment; both women made up for this disappointment with their subsequent matches.

As a consequence of the short-lived peace settlement agreed between Antony and

Octavian at Brundisium in 40, Tiberius Nero was able to make use of the general amnesty to return with his wife and child to Italy.[4] The return was to prove a fateful one for the history of the Roman world. Octavian became infatuated with Livia. Unfortunately we have no direct information on their courtship. Tacitus says that Octavian was driven by *cupidine formae* (essentially 'lust') and suggests that Livia might not have discouraged his attentions, *incertum an invitam*. She was a woman of considerable ambition, and probably concluded that her first husband's track record hinted at less than outstanding prospects. The new match would have brought some benefits to Octavian. The name of Livia's grandfather, Livius Drusus, was revered by Italians as the champion of their demands for Roman citizenship, but the advantages would hardly have been overwhelming, and Octavian seems to have been motivated primarily by pure erotic attachment. Passion is the only explanation for their unseemly hurry to be married. Octavian divorced his pregnant wife Scribonia, claiming that she was impossible to live with – Seneca describes her as an 'overbearing woman'. But her true qualities would come to the fore almost forty years later, when her daughter Julia was sent into a bleak exile and Scribonia volunteered to accompany her. In any case no-one can have been deceived since Octavian proceeded immediately to arrange his marriage to the similarly pregnant, and similarly divorced, Livia. It took place on 17 January 38 and three months later Livia's second son, Nero Claudius Drusus, grandfather of Agrippina, was born.[5]

In 36 BC Octavian was granted the sacrosanctity enjoyed by the tribunes, and in the following year the same privilege was legally granted to his wife Livia and his sister Octavia. This was an important innovation, since it conferred on a non-Vestal woman the attribute of an office, indeed an office that would become central to the notion of the principate. The idea does not seem to have been received well, and most Romans probably thought that Octavian had gone too far. In any case the experiment was not repeated for other women of the imperial house. They would instead receive the sacrosanctity of the Vestals who, unlike the tribunes, did not play a political role in the state. The bestowal of the Vestal privileges was thus a much lesser violation of propriety and tradition in the eyes of the traditionalists. All the same, in 36 BC the first step had been taken in a process that would culminate in the person of Agrippina and see the emperor's consort elevated to a symbolic status of near-parity with her husband.[6]

Like some of the republican women before her, Livia became extremely rich, with financial interests in Italy, estates in Asia minor and Egypt, and mines in Gaul. Burrus, the famous prefect of the praetorian guard during Agrippina's ascendancy, was procurator of one of Livia's estates. Rank certainly had its privileges and she would have had complete freedom in the administration of her wealth, since she received the exemption from guardianship granted under her husband's moral legislation to those worthy ladies who had, unlike Livia, actually borne three children. She was also exempt from the provisions of the *Lex Voconia*, which limited the amount a woman could inherit. The size of her fortune is indicated by the fact that on her death she bequeathed to Galba 50 million HS.[7]

If the position of Augustus within the Roman state was made deliberately ambiguous, then that of his wife was even more so. She could not base her status on tenure of office or by virtue of great achievements in war. She enjoyed her privileged position only by virtue of being the wife of the princeps. Perhaps her great achievement was the way in which she managed to turn this ambiguity to her advantage. It enabled her to cast her own definition of her political role, which gave her an influence over affairs of state to a degree unprecedented for a woman. Generally, she appears to have conducted herself with great skill, as a discreet background adviser, with a good sense of how to tread the careful mid-course between docile passivity and unwelcome intrusion into spheres where women by law, custom or social climate would not be welcomed.

Livia, like Agrippina, is treated harshly by the literary sources, especially Tacitus. A number of striking parallels emerge in the careers of both. Each was a clever and ambitious woman who won the affections of a princeps and used her position to promote the prospects of her son by the weapons of intrigue and scheming, and even of murder – both are accused of eliminating rivals and husbands. It has often been observed that there was a fundamental difference between them, in that Livia did not earn a reputation for exploiting sex as a political weapon. Tacitus, for instance, concedes that she possessed an 'old-fashioned' virtue. But sex was clearly an important factor in clinching her marriage to Octavian. Their hasty wedding, for which a special dispensation from the Pontifical College was needed, raised disapproving eyebrows, and there was persistent gossip that the child born three months later (Drusus) was Octavian's.[8] From this point on, comparison between the supposed sexual standards of Livia and Agrippina is hardly relevant; Livia had nothing political to gain from sexual intrigue, since her husband the emperor survived long enough for her to ensure the succession for her son. She was still the target of inevitable abuse for immoral behaviour, but since any infidelity on her part could not be dredged up (there was simply no evidence of any), she was blamed instead for Augustus' moral lapses, real or imagined, and charged with turning a blind eye to his peccadilloes and even with procuring young women for him.[9]

During the lifetime of Augustus the preoccupation of Tacitus and the other sources is with Livia as the obsessive mother of a potential successor, rather than with her role as consort of Augustus. It is clear, however, that she was in many respects Augustus' mental equal, if not his superior, and it is hardly surprising that he sought her advice and counsel in affairs of state, and even prepared written memoranda of topics to discuss with her in private.[10] Her stature was close to that of an *amica principis*, a kind of privy councillor. This is illustrated by the affair of Cornelius Cinna, charged some time before AD 5 with plotting against Augustus, and pardoned by him on the advice of Livia just before a planned meeting of the *consilium* to decide his case (the meeting was cancelled). Livia had astutely advocated a selective exercise of clemency to deal with those suspected of disloyalty.[11] It is probably not far off the mark to see their relationship paralleled in that of Agrippina and Claudius, even though the literary sources have depicted the latter situation as the manipulation and domination of an incompetent and ineffective ruler. Instances of overt and public involvement by Livia in her husband's business are difficult to document, but they must have occurred. Her presence during a fire after Tiberius' accession, bringing relief and encouraging the soldiers and citizens alike (foreshadowing yet again similar activity of Agrippina), reminded people, according to Suetonius, of what she used to do while Augustus was alive.[12]

As noted, it was the issue of the succession that was to preoccupy Livia, as it would Agrippina. Augustus' position in the state, although given legitimacy by the traditional republican institutions he had manipulated, had no real precedent. The novelty of his situation made itself apparent when he came to consider what would happen after his death. Now Mommsen claimed that the principate was incompatible with heredity and that there was an inherent contradiction between the two. He argued that the powers were bestowed on the princeps through a legal process, and were comparable to those held by magistrates. To Mommsen, then, the principate was personal, not institutional, and it was the prestige of the princeps that justified the authority conferred on him.[13] But this may be to take too formal a view of the situation. Despite a traditional antipathy towards the notion of kingship, Romans did make considerable allowance for the principle of heredity in public life. Throughout their history certain family names had constantly reappeared in the record, the Claudii, the Aemilii, the Cornelii and others, families that had almost reserved for themselves the consulate, whose sons, for all intents and purposes, would eventually succeed their fathers in office. Powerful families that did not have male issue would have recourse to adoption to create an artificial male line. Nor is this all; under the republic a powerful family would have a number of 'clients' who could be expected to supply broad political support and loyalty, and the sons would inherit these clients.[14] It might be going too far to say that Augustus laid down a legal principle of hereditary succession, but when the Julio-Claudian dynasty ended in AD 68 the short-lived emperor Galba could claim that Rome had in a sense become the 'inherited property of a single family'. Galba broke the sequence when he succeeded Nero, but Vespasian, who established a new dynasty in 69, felt no reticence in informing the senate that 'either his sons would succeed him, or no-one would'.[15] In fact it was mainly the awareness of her descent from Augustus that would fuel the political ambitions of Agrippina. The prospect of her becoming, by virtue of this descent, ruler in her own right was never a serious one. This was not possible for a woman. Caligula supposedly did intend to designate his favourite sister Drusilla as his successor, but his decision is associated with activities that illustrate his mental instability.[16] The Julian link did, however, give Agrippina a near-mystical status and would provide a powerful basis for the claims that were made on behalf of her son.

To avoid the conflict that would be inevitable if powerful noble families competed for power, Augustus may have thought it desirable for the succession to fall to someone from his own kin. But conveniently for him this noble motive would have coincided with a natural impulse to be succeeded by someone of his own blood line. The fact that he designated as successors a series of adopted, rather than natural, sons might have made his conduct a little easier for traditional Romans to stomach. But it should not be mistaken for deliberate policy. Livia supposedly conceived a child by him, but it was born prematurely and did not survive.[17] No other children followed, and in fact no Julio-Claudian emperor at the time of his death left a son (or grandson) old enough to succeed him. Since Augustus had no surviving male issue, he was obliged to make adoptions within the family. It is noteworthy that those who were seen as potential successors, Marcellus, Gaius and Lucius Caesar, all came through the *female* line. This tradition was repeated with the accession of Caligula and, although broken by Claudius, was revived by the last Julio-Claudian emperor, Nero.[18]

The appointment of a successor contained its own perils. In restoring the monarchical principle, Augustus must have been fully aware of the general offence that he would cause. He was also shrewd enough to appreciate that since the only *undisputed* successor could be a natural son, those members of his own entourage excluded by the process would be bound to feel aggrieved. Thus he proceeded cautiously. His first inclination seems to have been to choose Marcus Claudius Marcellus, son of his sister Octavia. Marcellus was admitted to the senate and married to Augustus' daughter, Julia. Unfortunately for the dynastic plans Marcellus fell seriously ill in 23 BC, and, despite the best efforts of the celebrated physician Antonius Musa, did not recover – the first major setback to Augustus' scheme. Dio reports with scepticism the rumour that Livia was responsible for the death.[19]

Augustus now tried a different course. He turned to his old friend and ally, Agrippa, the architect of the victory over Antony at Actium. Agrippa divorced his wife Marcella (Octavia's daughter and Augustus' niece) in 21 to marry the widowed Julia, and in 18 received tribunician powers for five years, a clear sign that he was to preside should Augustus not survive. The plan seemed to work well. In 20 a son, Gaius Caesar, was born to Julia and, to confirm the line, a second, Lucius Caesar, arrived in 17. Augustus was delighted, and soon after Lucius' birth signalled his intentions by adopting both boys. Two daughters, Julia and Agrippina, mother of her more famous namesake, completed the family circle. In 12 BC Agrippa, having served his purpose with eminent distinction, died.[20]

After her husband's death Julia bore a third son, the appropriately named Agrippa Postumus. Although later adopted by Augustus, he would play no part in public life and would be dropped from any schemes for the succession. Shortly after receiving the toga of manhood (*toga virilis*) in AD 5 he fell into unspecified disgrace. The official reason was gross immorality and bestial behaviour (*ferocia*) and it is not impossible that he suffered from some sort of mental deficiency. However it is difficult to avoid the suspicion that he had become involved in some kind of unsavoury political activity, and that the claims of defective character were meant simply as a cover to remove him from the scene. At any rate his family broke its ties with him and he was eventually sent into permanent exile on the island of Planasia, near Corsica.[21]

The loss of his old friend Agrippa created special problems for Augustus. In his grandsons he had heirs of his own line, but there was no-one to safeguard their interests after his death. Julia would clearly have to remarry, and the obvious candidate for the vacant position of husband was Livia's older son Tiberius. He had remained essentially outside the line of succession up to this point, and had pursued his own outstanding diplomatic and military career. Apart from his public achievements, his domestic situation was particularly successful; he was happily married to Vipsania, Agrippa's daughter, who bore him a son, Drusus, probably in 14 BC.[22] Tiberius thus offers a perfect object lesson in the folly of the pursuit of power. Had he remained satisfied with this secondary role he could have enjoyed a successful and fulfilled life, but his entry onto the centre stage of political life would bring him nothing but bitterness and frustration. Clearly lacking the foresight to realize this, he divorced Vipsania, pregnant at the time (she lost the child), and married the emperor's daughter.

Tiberius' military career continued to prosper, as did that of Drusus, his younger brother. Drusus had also made a successful first marriage, to the worthy Antonia the Younger, daughter of Marc Antony and Augustus' sister Octavia. They produced three children: Germanicus, father of Agrippina, destined to be the most admired man in the Roman world, Claudius, destined to astonish the world and become emperor, and Livilla, destined to become notorious as mistress of the wicked Sejanus. While Tiberius was engaged in subduing Pannonia, Drusus conducted a celebrated campaign in Germany. By 9 BC he had advanced as far as the Elbe, when disaster struck. During a riding accident his horse fell on him and broke his thigh. He died just before his brother, who had travelled day and night, was able to reach him. Tiberius, displaying an impressive dignity and deportment, accompanied the body on foot the whole way to Rome. As they passed through the towns people greeted the procession with the enthusiasm normally reserved for triumphs. In Rome fulsome eulogies were presented by Augustus and Tiberius, and the title of Germanicus was posthumously conferred on Drusus and his descendants. Drusus is highly relevant to the story of his granddaughter Agrippina. He was the first to establish a powerful and enduring link between her family and the northern legions. More importantly, through his personal charm and popularity, he laid the foundations for the legendary reputation of his son, Germanicus, Agrippina's father. It was popularly believed that Drusus was committed to some sort of restoration of the republic. As the memory of the chaos of that era's final decades receded, latent dissatisfaction over the imperial system made such a sentiment appealing. Whether or not Drusus actually held such ideas (and it seems unlikely that he would have advocated the total restoration of the pre-Augustan system) is not important. The *perception* that he did was enough to win him widespread affection, and was the basis for the belief that Augustus was involved in his death, a piece of gossip related with warranted scepticism by Suetonius. When Drusus was cut down in his prime, the goodwill that he had enjoyed was inherited by his son Germanicus, whose temperament and political views were similar to his father's. This goodwill would in turn be exploited by Germanicus' daughter Agrippina, although nothing would have been further from *her* mind than the restoration of the republic.[23]

Tiberius now replaced Drusus in command of the armies of the Rhine and was rewarded with a triumph on his return, and a second consulship. But, despite the public acclaim and professional success, the uncertainty over his political future made his position basically untenable. The question of the succession played constantly on his mind, and he resented being in the shadow of his stepsons Gaius and Lucius, Augustus' obvious favourites. Eventually his feelings of resentment and a growing antipathy between himself and his wife, Julia, drove him to insist on being allowed to retire to the island of Rhodes.[24]

That there were private difficulties between Julia and Tiberius cannot be doubted, and it is hardly surprising. Julia was a highly intelligent woman, well read and knowledgeable, with a penchant for lively and witty company. She was also quite 'bohemian' and considered any behaviour socially acceptable if her own personal inclinations recommended it. She shocked her father by her roué young friends and her provocative style of dress. Augustus, who had pretensions to old-fashioned morality and austerity, was not well suited to be the father of an independent and highly spirited daughter. He nagged her about her friends, her bold language, her clothes, even about her habit of removing prematurely grey hairs. He also tried to keep her under rigid supervision, informing even the most respectable young men who called on her that they were not welcome in the emperor's home. Augustus' attempts to safeguard his daughter's virtue met with inevitable failure. Julia took lovers from at least the time of her marriage to Agrippa, and supposedly recommended the safe period afforded by pregnancies, commenting that she only 'took on passengers when carrying freight'.[25]

Julia reportedly had long nursed a passion for the taciturn Tiberius and their marriage at first was fairly harmonious. But their personalities were so at odds they were almost bound to drift apart. The death of their only child broke the last bond, and the affection gradually turned to contempt. Nor did Julia's sexual habits change, and Tiberius, like Agrippa before him, had little choice but to endure her infidelities.[26] However irksome she found her father, Julia could never forget that she was his daughter. Hence she grew to despise Tiberius as her inferior – the first woman to claim superiority through possession of the divine blood of Augustus. It was a claim that would be repeated by her daughter, Agrippina the Elder, and in turn by her daughter Agrippina. She was encouraged in her contempt for Tiberius by her current lover, Sempronius Gracchus, a kinsman of the famed Gracchi brothers and the first member of the family to be mentioned in the record since the days of his famous predecessors. He induced her to write a letter to Augustus some time after Tiberius' departure for Rhodes, denouncing her husband in violent terms.

With Tiberius out of the picture, it might have been hoped that Julia could fade into the background but her behaviour, in fact, became even more spirited and provocative, and it was probably inevitable that it would lead to scandal. The climax came in 2 BC, when the 60-year-old Augustus was shattered by a personal disaster. Seneca provides the fullest account, claiming, no doubt with exaggeration, that Julia, who would now have been 38, had scores of lovers and roamed about the city looking for thrills, even prostituting herself with strangers in the forum at the statue of Marsyas. When Augustus learned of this his first thought apparently was to put her to death, and he responded to the news that one of Julia's friends, a freedwoman called Phoebe, had hanged herself with the comment that he wished he was Phoebe's father. In the event, he limited himself to denouncing his daughter in a letter to the senate and requesting strict exile. Despite the generous attempt of Tiberius to bring about a reconciliation between father and daughter, she was sent to the island of Pandateria, off the coast of Campania. This small island, under 3.2km (2 miles) long, boasted an imperial villa and even a small grape cultivation, which was plagued by field mice. Julia, however, was reputedly denied every luxury, even wine, and no-one was allowed to land at the island without exhaustive enquiries. She was even prohibited in her father's will from being allowed into his Mausoleum after her death. Her only comfort was her mother Scribonia, still unmarried since her divorce from Augustus, who offered voluntarily to accompany her daughter. Following vociferous and repeated popular demands for her return, Augustus lightened the punishment somewhat five years later, allowing her to move to Rhegium on the mainland, but the sentence of exile remained in force. Her situation grew worse with Tiberius' accession. The modest allowance made by her father was stopped and she was reduced to destitution. She went into a decline and died in the early months of Tiberius' reign.[27]

Julia's disgrace brought down others also. Velleius provides the names of five male accomplices. At the top of the list stands Jullus Antonius, the son of Augustus' arch-rival Marc Antony and the famous Fulvia. He had received generous treatment from the emperor, and had married Octavia's daughter Marcella after her divorce from Agrippa. Jullus was the only man recorded as dying as an *immediate* result of the scandal, either by suicide or execution (the distinction is not significant).[28] The other men implicated in the case seem to have suffered relegation, a mild form of exile. Dio mentions that a number of women were charged at the same time (the above-mentioned Phoebe might well have been one of them), but that they were treated leniently.[29]

The 'Julia affair' is highly relevant to any account of Agrippina's career, since she would similarly be exiled in 39 under circumstances that recall those of her grandmother's. The details of both cases are murky. The sources place great emphasis on the moral aspect of Julia's conduct and Tacitus comments on the excessive punishment meted out to her, observing that Augustus overstepped the mild penalties of earlier times and even the penalties prescribed by his own laws in classing sexual misconduct as sacrilege and treason. Thus he almost warns us against inferring from the excessive penalties that the charges concealed political misconduct. The general testimony of the ancients is clearly that Julia and her associates committed moral transgressions, and fell foul of the moral legislation that Augustus himself had enacted.[30] But many scholars insist that the claims of sexual misconduct by members of the Julio-Claudian family were largely specious devices to conceal serious political threats, and that charges of adultery or moral depravity could be used to eliminate dangerous claimants or their supporters. The prominence of the men involved in Julia's case obliges us to consider the possibility of a political dimension very carefully. In fact the borderline between immorality and conspiracy is a fine one, when the imperial family is involved. An amorous entanglement with a ruler's daughter must always involve a mixture of both erotic attraction and political ambition. Under English law, for instance, it is still a treasonable offence, punishable by death, to be involved in a sexual liaison with the spouse of the heir to the throne.[31] If the paramour is someone with an impressive personal pedigree the situation becomes especially dangerous, even if there is no overt conspiracy. Augustus may have been willing to turn a reluctant blind eye to Julia's previous indiscretions, but an affair with a man of Jullus' stature, especially when Tiberius was absent, must have seemed fraught with peril. Julia's letter to her father, which was eventually to cost its co-author Sempronius his life, may have well been the last straw; the attack it contained on Tiberius, while intended to be personal, had inevitable political implications.

While the full meaning of the Julia episode eludes us, it does contain elements that are recognizable. It illustrates the veil of secrecy and obscurity that falls over events when a female member of the imperial house is involved in any scandal. This was in the nature of things; since women could not seek power directly for themselves, any attempt to further their ambitions would need to involve intrigue and third parties. Augustus' response shows also that in the ruling imperial family the pursuit of power, and the suppression of threats to that power, counted in the end for more than affection.

Further misfortunes were to befall Augustus. Lucius Caesar, on his way to Spain in AD 2 fell ill at Marseilles and died. Later, Augustus' last remaining hope, Gaius Caesar, died of wounds on his way back from the east in AD 4. Inevitably, Livia is blamed in the literary sources for both deaths. Augustus was devastated by the turn of events and was now reduced to one viable candidate, Livia's son, Tiberius (Agrippa Postumus was never seriously considered). He had been allowed to return from Rhodes in AD 2 through his mother's aggressive lobbying efforts.[32] He was now finally adopted (along with Agrippa Postumus) but under circumstances that left no doubt about his true position in the scheme of things. Just prior to his own adoption he was obliged to adopt his nephew Germanicus, son of his late brother Drusus and Antonia.

The dynastic significance of Augustus' new arrangements soon became clear when, probably in the following year, Germanicus married Augustus' granddaughter, Agrippina the Elder, daughter of Agrippa and the disgraced Julia. This was to prove an extremely fruitful union. Agrippina the Elder bore Germanicus nine children, six of whom would survive infancy. The first three were all sons: Nero, her eldest (not to be confused with her grandson Nero, the future emperor), Drusus (a confusingly popular name of imperial princes) and Gaius (more familiar as the emperor Caligula). Three daughters, the younger Agrippina, Drusilla and Livilla, followed.

In the Augustan scheme Agrippina the Elder would provide the required Julian blood link for his ultimate successor. Indeed, she would prove to be the only Augustan descendant of her generation to sustain his hopes. Her brothers Gaius and Lucius were dead, and her third brother Agrippa Postumus in disgrace and exile. She did have a sister. Unfortunately, Julia the Younger chose to follow in their mother Julia's footsteps, which not unexpectedly also led to her mother's fate. As confusing as the scandal of Julia the Elder might seem, the events surrounding her daughter's disgrace are even more obscure (and not helped by the loss of much of Dio's narrative for AD 8, the year in question).[33] Julia the Younger was married to Lucius Aemilius Paullus, consul in AD 1 and they produced a daughter Aemilia Lepida but beyond this we know very little of her earlier life, apart from Pliny's remark that Julia owned the largest house in Rome and the smallest dwarf. Tacitus informs us that she was convicted of adultery (in AD 8) and exiled to Trimerus off the Apulian coast, where she was sustained by allowances from Livia until her death twenty years later. Augustus' resentment was evident – he pulled down her splendid house (the fate of the dwarf is unrecorded) and decreed that her ashes were to be refused admission to his Mausoleum. He would not allow a child born to Julia after the scandal had broken to live or even to be acknowledged.[34]

This affair raises the usual questions about the severity of this Julia's punishment for apparently moral lapses. An entry in the notoriously unreliable scholiast on the poet Juvenal connects her relegation with the execution of her husband for *maiestas*.[35] The scholiast who, among other blunders, conflates Julia with her mother, must be treated with considerable caution. There is some evidence that Paullus had indeed been involved in a conspiracy, but it occurred some two years earlier and this lapse of time surely dissociates his fall from Julia's. It has been suggested that if Paullus was in fact off the scene by AD 6 the child borne by Julia two years later, clearly illegitimate, might well have been the reason for her own disgrace (it is otherwise difficult to explain why Augustus should have cast out his own great-grandchild).[36]

This was the second scandal to overwhelm the house of Augustus in a single decade. The precise details are not really crucial to the issue at hand; the consequences of the affair are far more significant. From now on, all the hopes of Augustus resided in the family of Julia's sister Agrippina and the exemplary Germanicus.

3
Daughter

Of all the people who would play a part in Agrippina's life none had a greater influence on her than her parents. She would barely have known her father – she was not yet five when she last saw him – but she was always conscious of his almost mystical reputation, and of the compelling magic of his name. She could hardly have felt otherwise, since she spent her formative years with a mother who was obsessed by the notion that her family was born to rule and that her husband, endowed by nature to be an outstanding princeps, had been cheated of his proper birthright.

Although the evidence indicates that Agrippina the Elder and Germanicus were a devoted couple, they could not have been more different in temperament and personality. Agrippina was proud, quick-tempered, intolerant, liable to fly off the handle, a woman of *tumultuaria incapacità* as Paratore describes her.[1] She presents a serious problem to the ancient sources, since she was essentially an unattractive individual but was at the same time on the right side, an opponent of Tiberius and his odious servant Sejanus, prefect of the praetorian guard. Tacitus goes to great pains to avoid overtly condemning behaviour that he would castigate in her daughter. Thus when he describes the elder Agrippina as *aequi impatiens, dominandi avida*, a woman lusting after power with no sense of what was right or fair, one whose female limitations had been replaced by ambitions better suited to a man (the archetypal object of dread, as has been seen, for Roman men), the charges are not denied; but they are placed in the mouth of Tiberius, as if to suggest that, while not necessarily untrue, they are discredited by association.[2]

Agrippina the Younger did share with her mother an obsessive conviction of her right, as a descendant of Augustus, to continue the line of the Julian succession. But she would learn from her mother's fate that a direct, head-on attack was not the right weapon for a woman in the political arena, and would use that knowledge to succeed where her mother had failed.

Germanicus was what would be called today a 'charismatic' leader, especially if we take the cynical attitude that charisma means that image takes precedence over substance. He inherited the popularity of his father Drusus, whose military achievements in Germany had been outstanding and who was thought to have favoured the restoration of republican government. Also, he was able to contribute a genuinely affable and charming personality. 'The radiant figure compounded of all virtues and excellence to set against the dark soul of Tiberius,' Syme calls him.[3] The general adulation is a key element in the popular favour initially shown towards his children, especially Caligula and, of course, Agrippina. Suetonius provides a mini-biography, appended as an introduction to his *Life of Caligula*. He describes Germanicus as the supreme individual of his age, handsome, courageous, the best in both physical and mental qualities, moreover a distinguished man of letters, the author of a version of Aratus' *Phaenomena* and of

Greek comedies. These exemplary qualities did not, however, turn his head, and he was noted for his concern for others and his ability to inspire affection. So loved was he that when he went out in public his life was often at risk from the throngs of enthusiastic admirers. Suetonius can find only one fault, his skinny legs, and even this is turned to his advantage since he could show strength of character in building them up with rigorous horseback rides after meals. Tacitus saw him as the epitome of moral rectitude and admired his *civile ingenium, mira comitas* ('courteous nature and exceptional affability'), in contrast to the aloofness and arrogance of Tiberius. He reports that in his funeral eulogies he was likened to Alexander the Great, only better, and would have eclipsed his celebrated predecessor both in military fame and personal qualities if only he had lived longer.[4]

Such a paragon of virtue was not, in fact, unique. For parallels we need look no further than the fawning adulation that welcomed the accessions both of Caligula and Nero, models of charm, promise and civility until grim reality intervened. Germanicus preserved his reputation by dying early, before he could become emperor and be obliged to face major responsibilities and problems. Even during his lifetime there were occasions when his motives and intentions might have been beyond reproach, yet he still managed to bungle things. Tacitus is obliged by the extant record of events to criticize him on specific points of detail, whether a blunder in military strategy in Germany or an absence of judgement in pandering to the demands of the Rhine mutineers following the death of Augustus. But these details are not allowed to detract seriously from the overall glowing picture.[5]

In the minds of the general public Germanicus could do no wrong (even when he clearly did) and this spiritual quality was supposedly passed on to his family, to his son Caligula, who was thought to have inherited his father's sterling character, to his brother Claudius, said to have been the choice of the praetorians as emperor precisely because of his kinship with Germanicus, and to his daughter Agrippina, who was able to combine this kinship with her blood link, through her mother, to Augustus. Agrippina the Younger does seem to have inherited some of Germanicus' tact and diplomatic skills, although of course the hostile sources portray these same qualities as the sinister mastery of intrigue and manipulation.

Only one shadow, according to Tacitus, darkened Germanicus' otherwise brilliant horizon – he was hated by Livia and Tiberius because of the republican sympathies he supposedly inherited from his father. There is no serious evidence in their actual behaviour of any antipathy. For his part, Germanicus, in all his public actions, demonstrated consistent loyalty towards Tiberius, who in turn treated his stepson courteously and fairly. Also, Tacitus claims that there was what he called typically feminine friction, *muliebres offensiones*, between Livia and Agrippina the Elder, for which he places the blame squarely on Livia. He does concede that Agrippina had a fiery spirit, but not to worry, her moral integrity and wifely sense of duty, he claims, directed this passion to worthy ends.[6] Two Tacitean themes can be observed here, the notion of irrational hatred between women and the deft conversion of failings into qualities when it suited the historian's purpose.

Apart from the birth of their first two sons, Nero (not the emperor) and Drusus, little is known of the early activities of Agrippina the Elder and Germanicus. His first recorded activities (in AD 7) are in Pannonia, where he eventually gained a reputation for military prowess and personal bravery by helping Tiberius to suppress a revolt. In AD 12 he campaigned in Germany, again with Tiberius. Agrippina spent the summer of that year in Antium, where Augustus owned a favourite villa, and on 31 August bore her third son Gaius, known more familiarly as Caligula, who would reign briefly but notoriously as emperor.[7] That same year Germanicus held the consulship, marked in the record by little other than the slaughter of 200 lions during the festival to honour Mars (Ludi Martiales).[8]

Early in AD 13 Germanicus returned to the north, accompanied, probably from the outset, by his wife Agrippina and his two eldest sons, Nero and Drusus. He was to be governor of the Three Gauls, a position that gave him authority over the eight legions on the Rhine (at this period the districts of Upper and Lower Germany were military zones rather than regular provinces). By May of the year 14 Agrippina was pregnant again (she apparently lost the child). Germanicus at this time was in Gaul carrying out a census, and Agrippina, presumably because of her pregnancy, decided not to accompany him. This we can judge from a letter written by Augustus on 18 May, preserved in Suetonius, in which the emperor writes of sending the infant Caligula to join his mother and expresses the hope that she will be in good health when she rejoins her husband.[9] We cannot be sure where she was at this time, but Ara Ubiorum (the future Cologne), where she would enjoy the protection of the nearby Legions I and XX, is a strong candidate. When little Caligula joined his mother he became the favourite of the soldiers, dressing up in a diminutive soldier's uniform and wearing small *caligae*, the hobnailed boots worn by Roman soldiers, which gave him his familiar nickname. Tacitus' handling of this episode is interesting. Caligula's imposture of a miniature soldier was almost certainly his mother's idea, or at the very least condoned by her, and was an undisguised attempt to court the popularity of the legions, behaviour which, had it been exhibited by her daughter, would have been condemned outright as a shameless scheme to extend her influence. Tacitus must report the story, but again he deflects potential criticism. He emphasizes the jealousy and ill-will that Tiberius harboured towards the idea that she 'paraded' (*circumferebat*) her son in military garb and Tiberius, not Tacitus, draws the inference that she was behaving *ambitiose*. The impression is completed by the observation that the incident was exploited by Sejanus, with the aim of denigrating Germanicus and his wife. The further detail that Agrippina the Elder required her son to be addressed as 'Caesar Caligula' is again noted as behaviour that angered Tiberius rather than as something that Tacitus himself condemned.[10] The likelihood that the reports were true is skilfully buried beneath the indignation over the insinuations of the sinister praetorian prefect and his suggestible master.

On 19 August AD 14 a chapter of Roman history ended when the 76-year-old Augustus died at Nola in Campania. There were rumours that Livia was responsible for his death, even a suggestion that she smeared poison on the pears that her husband collected fresh from the trees. Supposedly she was alarmed by a rumour that Augustus had sailed secretly to visit Agrippa Postumus and was planning to restore him to favour. A striking echo of this rumour can be heard in the later claim that Agrippina the Younger plotted the murder of her husband Claudius because he had been reconciled with his son Britannicus. As Augustus lay dying, Livia acted promptly. A letter was despatched to Illyricum to recall her son Tiberius. She arranged for the house and street to be guarded by pickets, and hopeful bulletins were released at intervals to give her time to ensure her son's smooth succession. Her first priority would have been to eliminate Agrippa Postumus, although it is far from clear who gave the actual orders for his execution. Again, reports of Livia's conduct parallel what is told about Agrippina following the death of Claudius.[11]

After a show of reluctance, Tiberius, at the age of 55, took Augustus' place. In Rome the first dramatic change to catch attention was in the status of his mother. In his will Augustus accepted Livia into the Julian family. Also, he bestowed on her the name of Augusta. The use of this term, with its semi-religious connotations, had enormous symbolic importance for the Romans since its masculine counterpart embodied the moral and political authority of the princeps. It alone of the titles appended to the name of the princeps distinguished him from the magistrates of the republic. Livia's elevation to Augusta would in turn tend to elevate her beyond the rank of the emperor's widow (or mother). In a sense it represents the culmination of a lengthy process, whose early stages may be detected in the anonymous *Consolatio ad Liviam*, written in 9 BC on the occasion of the funeral of her son Drusus, where Livia is called, in the feminine form, a *Romana princeps*. Tiberius in fact felt that the title of Augustus was excessive even for the princeps and declared his intentions of not using it except when dealing with foreign rulers, a hope impossible to maintain in practice, as even his very early coins indicate. Its bestowal on Livia no doubt caused her son some unease, and probably marked the first stage in his efforts to distance himself from her. He refused, for instance, to be designated as *Iuliae filius* ('son of Julia') and prevented the senate from granting his mother the further titles of *parens patriae* or *mater patriae*. This should not be regarded as spite – there is no reason why Tiberius should have felt any animosity towards Livia at this time; rather he had a feeling for strict constitutional procedure, and Dio has Tiberius reminding his mother at the time of the accession of the need to maintain proper behaviour.[12]

The situation was bound to create friction between mother and son and, although there are few serious problems recorded in the early years, relations probably soon deteriorated. Livia lost no opportunity to remind Tiberius that he owed the accession to her (as Agrippina the Younger was to remind her son Nero, equally ineffectively and with similar consequences). Dio claims that she attempted to manage everything as if *autarchousa* ('sole ruler'), and behaved quite unlike the oldfashioned traditional woman, receiving senators and others at her house and entering the visits into the public records. Her name was constantly advertised in public documents since the letters of Tiberius for a time went out in her name as well as the emperor's, and communications were addressed to both alike. Gradually Tiberius found this too much to stomach and Suetonius claims that he went out of his way to avoid meeting her or having to talk to her. Again, all of this will be replayed in the difficulties that arise between Agrippina and her son Nero within a few months of his taking power.[13]

Outside Rome the death of Augustus had a disturbing effect on the northern legions, where harsh conditions of service were a cause of deep resentment. Drusus, Tiberius' son by his first wife, Vipsania, was sent to the Danubian province of Pannonia, where riots broke out, and succeeded in preventing a serious mutiny through firmness and discipline (and a lucky eclipse of the moon). The disturbances on the Rhine had their main focus in Lower Germany, where the dissatisfaction is given a political flavour in the literary sources, who all insist that the soldiers wanted Germanicus to seize power. This idea is unconvincing, given his later trouble in persuading the soldiers to obey him.[14] Germanicus was in Gaul when news of the emperor's death reached him, and quickly departed for Germany, his concern about the legions probably aggravated by anxiety over his pregnant wife, who was presumably now in Ara Ubiorum with her children. He dealt first with Lower Germany, where discipline had collapsed and several centurions had been murdered. On arrival he demonstrated what can only be described as vacillation, incompetence and weakness. When appeals to the soldiers' loyalty failed to work, he melodramatically threatened to commit suicide and was jokingly told to go ahead. His impotence is illustrated by his final act of desperation, when he produced a forged letter from Tiberius purporting to meet some of the concessions demanded, and backed this up by bribes taken from the official funds. He bought a respite, but it was to be very brief. A deputation from the senate arrived and the soldiers got it into their heads that its members were there to cancel the agreements. Germanicus and the senators were subjected to insult and humiliation, and even his own officers were critical of his lack of resolution.

The crisis was solved in the end by a brilliant stroke. Soldiers throughout the ages, for all their occasional brutality, tend to maintain certain codes, one of which is a patronizing protectiveness towards women and children of their own side. Agrippina realized this, and had exploited the sentimentality by dressing up the infant Caligula as a boy-soldier. It was almost certainly she who now thought up the scheme to end the mutiny – at any rate Tiberius gave her the credit for it. The whole incident displays her sense of theatre, as well as a cool courage that may have been beyond Germanicus. Threats and bribes were abandoned. Instead, Germanicus announced to the soldiers that he could no longer trust them with his wife's safety and that she would be sent into the territory of the Treveri. Clasping her son Caligula, and followed by the tearful wives of the Roman officials, Agrippina made her way out of the camp, pretending to be reluctant and insisting that as granddaughter of Divus Augustus she was willing to stay and face the danger. The soldiers had enormous respect for her, as a daughter of Rome's most illustrious family, and a woman *insigni fecunditate* and *praeclara pudicitia* ('outstandingly prolific and of impeccable moral character'). Embarrassed and ashamed, they surrendered their weapons. So says Tacitus. In reality the surrender might not have proceeded quite so smoothly; another tradition, found in Suetonius and in Dio, suggests that some of the soldiers confirmed Germanicus' lack of faith in their reliability and seized Agrippina and Caligula. They let her go when they saw that she was pregnant, and it was only when they finally realized that they could achieve little by continuing to hold Caligula hostage that they let him go too.[15] What may well have been a series of sordid events was perhaps sanitized by the sources to enhance Agrippina's dignity and presence of mind. But in any case the crisis was over, and Germanicus was saved by his wife and child. It remained to punish the ringleaders – typically he left it to the soldiers to deal with them, and they did so with gusto. The concessions that he had granted the men were all to be annulled by Tiberius.[16]

Agrippina the Elder had been an invaluable asset to Germanicus in handling the mutinies, and she was to perform further distinguished service in the following year. We have scant information about the precise movements of the armies during the campaigns on the northern frontier during AD 15 and instead are offered a series of scenic incidents, 'enhanced by eloquence and invention', as Syme observes.[17] Germanicus felt a natural ambition to emulate his father Drusus by attempting to push the Roman frontier as far as the Elbe. His operations began well, and he advanced as far as the Teutoburg Forest. A funeral mound was raised there to the legionaries who had died in the disastrous expedition of Varus in AD 9. He now made the mistake of overreaching himself. He set off in pursuit of Arminius, the German chief who had inflicted the earlier defeat on the Romans, and almost repeated Varus' error of falling into a fatal trap. He only just escaped and in full retreat the Romans made a dash for the Rhine. At this point Agrippina once again came to the rescue of her husband, even more dramatically. Tacitus describes how the 'great-spirited woman' (*femina ingens animi*) assumed the duties of a commander (*munia ducis*), helping the soldiers who had lost their equipment by handing out clothing and supplying dressings for the wounded. But this was the least of her contributions. Word reached the military zone that the Roman troops had been trapped and that the Germans were pouring west, even threatening Gaul. Panic spread, and there were hysterical demands that the bridge over the Rhine at Vetera (Xanten) be destroyed to stem the barbarian hordes. It was Agrippina who stepped in to block its demolition. She thus saved her husband's army from being trapped on the other side of the river, and saved her husband's reputation from a blow that even he could not have withstood. Tacitus cites Pliny the Elder (probably in his work on the German Wars) for the splendid figure of Agrippina standing at the bridge as the soldiers returned, praising them and expressing the gratitude of the Romans for their sacrifice.[18] Behaviour that in other women would certainly have earned Tacitus' contempt is described with implicit admiration. Tiberius was not so impressed. He voiced the historic fear that women now had more influence over the soldiers than legionary commanders or provincial legates (*duces* and *legatos*), and that the generals were out of a job since their women did the rounds of the troops, parading before the standards and distributing bonuses.

Some of the responsibility for the near-débacle should probably be borne by Aulus Caecina, with whom Germanicus had divided tactical command of the Roman forces in Germany. Caecina may well have felt particularly humiliated that his units owed their survival to a woman. He was the senator who, in AD 21, proposed the motion that no provincial governor should be allowed to take his wife with him to his province, since their presence had a harmful effect on military activities (p. 8). Among other things, Caecina asserted, women would parade among the troops. He cited the example of a woman, unnamed, who had presided over the manoeuvres. The allusion would have been intended for the notorious case of Plancina, wife of Piso, the legate of Syria (see below), but it can hardly have escaped the senators that the cap also fitted Agrippina.[19]

Agrippina's courage in defending the bridge at Xanten in 15 is all the more remarkable in that she was pregnant at the time. On 6 November she gave birth at the Rhine settlement of Ara Ubiorum to her first daughter, her namesake Agrippina (see Appendix I). The birthplace was historically significant. The people of the area, the Ubii, had been friendly to Rome since the time of Julius Caesar. In 38 BC, to avert the threat of hostile pressure from the Suebi, Agrippina's grandfather Agrippa transferred them from the right to the left bank of the Rhine. Later, about 9 BC, an *Ara Romae et Augusti* ('Altar of Rome and Augustus') was built there for the future province of Germany. Legions I and XX were housed nearby. Agrippina's daughter would nurse an affection for her place of birth, which was reciprocated; its later name of Cologne derives from the *colonia* that was established there under her sponsorship. Agrippina the Younger's birth occurred when her mother was at the apogee of her power and reputation. Her early years would be shaped and guided by someone who could feel that her horizons were unlimited.[20]

Germanicus carried out further campaigns in 16, transporting his legions down the Weser. A disastrous storm dispersed the ships, some of which beached up as far away as Britain. Fresh incursions into Germany followed. The infant Agrippina seems to have been living at this time in Ambitarvium, probably located on the lower Mosel just above Coblenz, and in the latter part of the year her sister Drusilla was born there (the actual month is unknown, but a sufficiently long interval must be allowed after the birth of Agrippina). Pliny the Elder mentions that among the local attractions of Ambitarvium were altars inscribed OB AGRIPPINAE PUERPERIUM ('in honour of Agrippina's delivery').[21]

Tacitus would have us believe that the year 16 ended with the Romans full of confidence and Germanicus convinced that with one more push he could extend Roman sway as far as the Elbe. The decision of Tiberius to recall him at this point might well have been seen by the young commander and his wife as a deliberate insult, inspired by malice and jealousy.[22] This would have been an unfair assumption. Tiberius was cautious and careful by nature, and he probably foresaw that the ultimate conquest of Germany required a process of gradual pacification, backed up by well-developed communications. He wrote diplomatically at the end of the year, suggesting that the Romans should stay their hands until the Germans started to fall out amongst themselves as, given time, they almost certainly would. In addition, Tiberius might well have had some misgivings about a popular commander who had control of eight legions, and he was also properly concerned that if there was any glory to be distributed it should go equally to Germanicus and to Tiberius' own son Drusus, also at this time pursuing a military career. The two young men were, in Tacitus' words, *egregie concordes* ('outstandingly harmonious'), a bond that would have been cemented by Drusus' marriage to Germanicus' sister Livilla.[23]

The return of her father from Germany would have brought Agrippina the Younger for the first time to Rome, where she would have taken up residence with her parents in the district where the most dramatic episodes of her eventful life would be played out. The Palatine Hill rises to the south of the Forum Romanum and is today dominated by the remains of the huge palace complex, the Domus Augustiana, begun by Domitian after AD 80. The palace remains conceal the fact that there are in reality two summits, the Germalus, and to its south-east the main summit, the Palatine. This latter name tends to be used loosely for the hill as a whole.[24] The Palatine (in this broad sense) was the original site of the ancient walled city of Rome, and is thus closely associated with the city's earliest history. During the republic it became one of the most fashionable residential districts for well-to-do citizens. Clodius, his rival Milo, Cicero, Marc Antony – all seem to have owned houses there.[25] The most extensive residence was that of the

Claudii, which seems to have occupied a whole block (*insula*) and was the birthplace of Tiberius. Augustus also was born on the Palatine, and moved to its ancient south-west corner after his marriage to Livia. Germanicus similarly had a home here, as we know from a chance remark of Josephus, who reports that after the murder of Caligula in his palace on the Palatine the assassins sought their escape and went through the adjoining house of Germanicus.[26] Its precise location is unknown.

Germanicus might have felt a private snub over his recall from Germany, but he kept it to himself, and Tiberius for his part was determined that there would be no public hint of official displeasure. On his return to Rome he received official sanction of his German campaigns, and on 26 May 17 celebrated a lavish triumph for his supposed victories over the tribes west of the Elbe. His achievements in Germany, if more apparent than real, and distinguished by more than a fair share of serious errors of judgement, did in the end produce a strong bond between him and the German legions and confirmed his heroic image in Rome. The triumph of Germanicus would be the last vivid memory Romans would have of him, and it was a memory that his daughter would exploit to the full.[27] The procession wended its way to the Capitol, accompanied by massive spoils and numerous captives, along with the traditional tableaux depicting mountains and rivers of Germany and the victorious battles of the Romans. Germanicus rode in a chariot, and with him were his five children, including the little Agrippina. Whatever Germanicus' private ambitions, or lack of ambitions, his wife and the older children can hardly have resisted feeling that the world lay open to them, not that little Agrippina, only a year and half at the time, would have had any proper appreciation of the magnitude of the occasion.

The splendid triumph granted Germanicus and the promise of a consulship for the following year would not in themselves have made up for the loss of his German command. In the event, Tiberius was able to offer more substantial compensation, an important mission to negotiate with Parthia over the disputed status of Armenia. Rome was determined to keep the mountainous country in friendly hands as a buffer state, and to resist Parthia's long-standing claims on the territory.[28] The task seemed perfectly suited to Germanicus' diplomatic skills. In the autumn of 17 he set out, accompanied by a large retinue, as well as his yet-again pregnant wife, and his son Caligula. The other children, including Agrippina, were left in Rome, possibly under the care of Germanicus' brother Claudius, since Tiberius' son Drusus was on campaign at the time.[29] Their progress to the east had the air not of a Roman official going to his *provincia* but rather of a great triumphal procession, as cities tried to outdo one another in the lavishness of their hospitality. After visiting his stepbrother Drusus in Dalmatia, Germanicus proceeded to Nicopolis, the city founded by Augustus near Actium to commemorate his great and decisive naval victory over Antony and Cleopatra. He remained there until 18, when he entered into his second consulship. In Athens he tactfully heaped compliments on the city and praised it for its great heritage. From there the entourage travelled to Euboea, then Lesbos, where Agrippina gave birth to the last of her children, a daughter Julia Livilla (see Appendix 1). The island of Lesbos was ultra-loyal to the Julio-Claudians, as its numerous coins and inscriptions show. Agrippina and her new daughter probably stayed there while Germanicus took Caligula on a grand tour of north-west Asia Minor. Eventually the family was reunited to continue the journey east.

In Rhodes Germanicus encountered Gnaeus Calpurnius Piso, the newly appointed legate of Syria. The role that Piso and his wife Plancina were to play in subsequent events is a murky and contentious one. Piso was a stubborn, even arrogant, man, reluctant to give in even to Tiberius. Tacitus implies that he understood his appointment as intended to scuttle Germanicus' mission or even to bring about something far more sinister. Tacitus adds that Livia, out of typically female spite, gave Plancina instructions to keep Agrippina in check, perhaps being anxious to prevent in Syria another public performance like the incident at the Rhine bridge.[30] Of course, Tiberius may well have recognized that, for all his other qualities, there was a certain unstable streak in Germanicus which had led to major setbacks in Germany; Piso's assignment might well have been the relatively innocent one of exercising a steadying influence over his young colleague.

Once Piso had reached Syria, he seems to have ingratiated himself with the legionaries by bribes and relaxed discipline. He also replaced the long-standing officers with men of his own choosing. His wife Plancina supposedly missed no opportunity to denigrate Agrippina, but at the same time took a leaf out of her book, taking part in the cavalry exercises and the infantry manoeuvres. She was thus unable to limit herself to *decora feminis* ('what was fitting for a woman'), as Tacitus observes, tactfully ignoring the obvious precedent set by Agrippina herself.[31]

Whether or not hostile forces were conspiring against him, Germanicus performed his duties effectively. He went first to Armenia where he established Zeno/Artaxias as a pro-Roman ruler – he would last sixteen years in power – and incorporated a number of old kingdoms into the empire.[32] With these tricky diplomatic problems settled, he went to Syria. His relations with Piso were decidedly cool, perhaps because of a genuine uncertainty over their respective spheres of authority. After a series of clashes Piso decided that the best course of action was to leave. He had scarcely begun his return journey, however, when news arrived that Germanicus had fallen seriously ill. The revelation that spells and curses were found in his house, along with other evidence of witchcraft, simply hardened Germanicus' suspicions that Piso and his wife had conspired to murder him. His condition grew steadily worse and on 10 October AD 19, he died, at the age of 33. Convinced that he had been poisoned, just before his death he asked his entourage to bring Piso and Plancina to justice, and to exploit the affection that Romans felt for Agrippina ('granddaughter of the deified Augustus') in their efforts. To Agrippina he left telling instructions that she was to put aside her harsh manner (*exueret ferociam*) and to learn to compromise, while not provoking those more powerful than her in her own bid for power (*aemulatione potentiae*). Ironically, such implied criticism from Germanicus does not seriously damage Agrippina's image, since he would clearly have set demanding standards for tact and diplomacy. Following his death the body was laid out in public, to show proof of the poisoning, and after a splendid funeral in Antioch was cremated and the ashes collected for return to Rome.[33]

Reports of Germanicus' death produced a great outpouring of grief, and a spate of extravagant honours.[34] But nothing could match the theatrical return of the grieving widow. By October the safe sailing season had already passed. Only in dire emergencies would a Roman venture on a sea voyage that late in the year. But Agrippina understood the importance of timing and the need to arrive in Rome while memories were still fresh. Late in 19 she set sail, grief-stricken and physically ill, accompanied by Caligula and the infant Livilla and, of course, Germanicus' ashes. She reached Corcyra, just opposite the Italian coast, and there she delayed for a few days to compose herself and deal with her grief, according to Tacitus, but probably to ensure that news of her imminent arrival would reach Italy. Finally, as her ship approached the harbour of Brundisium, the crowds thronged into the area. People of all sorts and conditions turned up, residents of the local towns along with large numbers of old soldiers who had seen service with Germanicus. By the time Agrippina's ship sailed into view every vantage point had been taken up by onlookers – the harbour itself, the city walls, even private houses. The vessel came to dock, the oarsmen rowing at a special funereal pace. The crowd fell silent, and when Agrippina, clasping the urn to her and keeping her eyes steadily downcast, appeared with her children Caligula and Livilla as if on cue the spectators uttered a loud groan.

Tiberius sent two cohorts of praetorians to escort Germanicus' widow, and they accompanied her through the towns of southern Italy, carrying bare standards and reversed *fasces* (the *fascis* was the traditional symbol of office). As they passed through the towns officials poured out to pay their final respects, and in *coloniae* (p. 114) the people put on black clothing and the equestrians donned their formal purple-striped robes of state, burning incense and garments as they did at funerals. At Tarracina, the coastal town on the Appian way, some 95km (60 miles) south-east of Rome, Tiberius' son Drusus, together with Germanicus' brother Claudius and Agrippina's other children, met the procession. The young Agrippina would have been just over four at this time, and the dramatic reunion with her mother on this momentous occasion is likely to have been among her earliest distinct childhood memories. It would have been a potent one.

As the family proceeded along the Appian way it was met by the consuls, Marcus Valerius and Marcus Aurelius, as well as other senators, and people continued to stream out to witness the great historical event. The ashes were placed in the mausoleum of Augustus with great pomp and ceremony, and that night the Campus Martius blazed with torches. There was a great upsurge of sympathy for Germanicus' widow, who was praised as an ornament to her country (*decus patriae*) and an unparalleled example of old-fashioned virtues (*unicum antiquitatis specimen*). More ominously, people also proclaimed her as the last representative of the line of Augustus.

Noticeably absent from the activities were Tiberius and Livia. The emperor issued a public statement that the imperial family should bear its losses with private dignity. The officers of the state were mortal, he observed ponderously; only the state itself was immortal. These thoughts are entirely in character for Tiberius, who would have found the circus-like atmosphere of Germanicus' last rites extremely distasteful. But they would have done nothing to endear him to the general public, or to diminish the popularity of Agrippina.

Tiberius might have hoped that the feverish obsession with Germanicus would soon diminish, but it was not to be. Bowing to popular demand, he brought Piso and his wife to trial – Piso for poisoning Germanicus, for arrogant behaviour towards his superior and for sedition, Plancina for engaging with him in blasphemous rites and sacrifices. Whatever the merits of the case, public feeling was running so high that Piso bowed to the inevitable and committed suicide. Tiberius then intervened on behalf of Plancina at the instigation of his mother, as is confirmed in a recently discovered contemporary account of the trial issued on the instruction of the senate. Livia's interference merely hardened suspicions of official involvement in Germanicus' murder and heightened fears for the safety of Agrippina and her family.[35] Ironically, as events would prove, it was Livia who, despite her personal animosity, protected Agrippina, just as she had protected Plancina. Her own later death would leave both exposed (Plancina eventually took her own life).[36]

On their return to Rome Agrippina's two eldest sons seem to have been placed in the care of Tiberius' son Drusus, who had considerable affection for them and treated them kindly (Caligula and the daughters seem to have been left with their mother.) The gesture may be taken to mean that Tiberius intended to give the two boys their due place in the line of the succession. He was probably also determined to take them from the control of a headstrong and ambitious woman who would poison their minds against the emperor. The brothers would not have had far to move. Drusus almost certainly occupied part of the large Claudian residence on the Palatine, which would now become the new home of Germanicus' two sons. Until her marriage the younger Agrippina probably continued to live with her mother, sister and Caligula in their nearby family residence.[37]

In the year that Germanicus died, Tiberius' son Drusus had cause to celebrate when he became the father of twins, one of whom, Tiberius Gemellus, survived infancy.[38] Tiberius' line now seemed secure but he dutifully continued to advance the careers of Agrippina's sons. In 20 the eldest, Nero, was presented to the senate on reaching the age of majority (14). He was granted a priesthood and the promise of an acceleraed quaestorship. As a final gesture of goodwill he was betrothed to Drusus' daughter, Julia.[39]

During this period there is no hint of any personal animosity between Agrippina and Drusus, and in any case they would soon have found common cause in combating a formidable enemy, the ruthless and ambitious prefect of the praetorian guard, Lucius Aelius Sejanus. Already in favour by the time of Tiberius' accession, Sejanus was first appointed joint prefect with his father, and two years later sole prefect. He succeeded in making himself indispensable to the emperor, and must have been a charming and persuasive man. He built up a power base both in the army and the senate, and by 20 was already highly enough regarded by Tiberius to be described as the 'partner of his labours' (*socius laborum*). Sejanus' prospects were confirmed when permission was granted for his daughter Junilla to be betrothed to Claudius Drusus, the son of Germanicus' brother Claudius (the future emperor). Unlike his father, the young Claudius Drusus was physically adept. To prove the point, a few days after the betrothal he nonchalantly threw a pear into the air and caught it in his mouth, proceeding then to choke to death.[40]

Sejanus' precise intentions are unclear and it is not certain whether he saw his future as princeps or in the more limited role of regent. But of his ambition for power there can be no doubt, and two people in particular stood in his way, Agrippina the Elder and Tiberius' son Drusus. His primary hostility would of course have been directed at Drusus, since the two men were in competition for Tiberius' affection and confidence. Sejanus sensed that Drusus was most vulnerable in his domestic life, and directed his attention towards his wife Livilla. The two became lovers, and it was later claimed that they plotted against Drusus' life.[41]

The year 23 saw two important developments. Sejanus concentrated the nine cohorts of the praetorian guard into a single set of permanent barracks just outside the city, at the Porta Viminalis.[42] Also, in September, Tiberius' son, Drusus, died. It was claimed some years later that he was poisoned. The eldest sons of Germanicus and Agrippina, Nero and Drusus, aged 17 and 16, were now the obvious candidates for the succession, since all other potential aspirants were too young for consideration. Tiberius treated them generously. Had Agrippina shown an equal goodwill, with even a fraction of the diplomatic skill that her late husband could muster or that her daughter would later demonstrate, she might well have built up a base of support in the imperial home that would have withstood the assault that Sejanus was planning. Her behaviour was in fact the very opposite to what was called for in the circumstances. Ever since Germanicus' illness she had convinced herself that Tiberius was determined on the destruction of her family. She also, as the granddaughter of Augustus, could not stop thinking of Tiberius just as her mother Julia had thought of him, as an unworthy supplanter. She was determined to push the interests of her sons by whatever means. Her utter conviction of the rightness of her cause, and her total lack of tact or subtlety in promoting it, would lead to disaster.

Agrippina's single-minded obsession with the rights of her sons would inevitably have aroused the concerns and suspicions of Tiberius' mother Livia, and his widowed daughter-in-law Livilla, since both women would naturally have entertained hopes for Livilla's son Gemellus. Sejanus was aware of this tension, and with considerable political astuteness made his initial attack on Agrippina an indirect one, exploiting the latent ill-will of potential opponents. Agrippina's arrogant pride over her Augustan heritage and the general popularity she enjoyed outside through the memory of Germanicus made it easy to convince rivals in the imperial household that she was nursing ambitions for power.[43]

Tiberius found the palace intrigue unsettling, and his sensitivity over the issue is well illustrated by his reaction to an incident that may have been no more than a simple blunder on the part of officialdom. Early in 24, as the priests were taking the customary vows for the emperor's well-being, they incorporated Agrippina's eldest sons Nero and Drusus into their prayers (see p. 52). Tacitus admits that their inclusion involved nothing more sinister than standard sycophancy, intended to please Tiberius. In the event, he was furious that the youths should be elevated to his level and suspected that Agrippina had allies in the priestly college, where they were manoeuvring for her benefit. The anecdote, trivial enough in itself, is of considerable interest in showing that already by 24 Tiberius was feeling uneasy about Agrippina's ambitions. Naturally Sejanus (and probably Livia and Livilla) made every effort to encourage these suspicions, feeding the emperor the idea that there was a serious division in the body politic and that a definable faction supporting Agrippina had emerged, the *partes Agrippinae*.[44] Bauman has argued that this supposed group represents the 'first specific political movement to be headed by a woman'. But the truth of Sejanus' charge is very difficult to assess and it is not clear just how organized the supporters of Agrippina were. She clearly had considerable backing in the senate, and seems to have enjoyed the sympathies and affection of a wide section of the Roman population. There is, however, little evidence of a coherent and orchestrated effort by her adherents to support her claims and it is unlikely that their action was broadly enough based to justify description as a 'movement'.[45]

From this point on, the battle moves into a new phase, in the courts.[46] Immediately after his reference to the supposed emergence of an Agrippinian faction, Tacitus recounts the first of a plethora of overtly 'political' trials, the case launched by Sejanus against Gaius Silius and his wife Sosia Galla. Silius had been legate of Upper Germany in 14, and had put down a serious rebellion that broke out in Gaul in 21 under the Gallic notables Julius Sacrovir and Julius Florus. For this he won the *ornamenta triumphalia*. Sosia was a close friend of Agrippina, and it was into Silius' protection that Germanicus had threatened to send his wife during the Rhine mutinies (the Treveri came under his jurisdiction). It was now, in 24, charged that Silius had in fact been in league with Sacrovir and had succeeded in making himself rich from the revolt; his wife was supposedly his accomplice. Tacitus is highly sceptical about the charge of *maiestas*, but concedes that there were reasonable grounds for suspecting extortion. Silius committed suicide and Sosia was exiled.

What threat did this couple pose? Was their prosecution simply a device to intimidate Agrippina's supporters? The ancestors of the Aeduan Sacrovir and the Treveran Florus had been enfranchised by Julius Caesar and his patronage would have passed to his descendants. Bauman proposes tentatively that, as such a descendant, Agrippina might have had a call on their loyalty. Also, there could have been mixed feelings in Rome about the Gallic crisis of 21. So deep was the resentment felt towards the imperial regime that some might even have welcomed a disaster. Tiberius' suspicions of treason could therefore have been more reasonable than Tacitus is willing to concede.[47]

The elimination of a number of Agrippina's friends gave Sejanus a false sense of confidence. By 25 he felt that his influence was powerful enough for him to seek permission to marry Drusus' widow Livilla. He tried to win over Tiberius by the argument that the union would strengthen the emperor's house, and in particular the children, against Agrippina's scheming. Sejanus had taken a gamble and he found that he had miscalculated. Tiberius was no fool. No matter how intensely offended he might be by Agrippina, he recognized her as a fact of life. To antagonize her even further would merely aggravate the danger of divisions and factions. Sejanus' request was rejected, with the vague promise that the faithful prefect would receive his due reward at some point in the future.[48]

To Sejanus this refusal represented only a temporary setback. His campaign against Agrippina's friends continued unabated. In 26 a charge of *maiestas*, by means of spells and poison, coupled with an accusation of adultery, was brought against Claudia Pulchra, Agrippina's second cousin and close friend. Agrippina felt that this attack hit too close to home, and indignantly interceded with Tiberius. To judge from the accounts of Tacitus and Suetonius, she behaved with the kind of headstrong arrogance that her dying husband had warned her against. Always fierce (*atrox*), says Tacitus, she was now 'inflamed' (*accensa*). She burst in on the emperor while he was making a sacrifice to Augustus and launched into a scathing assault, scorning him for his hypocrisy in honouring his predecessor Augustus, but at the same time persecuting Augustus' descendants. She then uttered her most hurtful barb, one that betrayed her constant preoccupation. She pointed out that the prosecution of Claudia Pulchra was nothing more than a smokescreen. The real target was the genuine descendant of Augustus (*caelesti sanguine ortam*) – herself. It is difficult to imagine anything more calculated to arouse the resentment of Tiberius, a man who had spent so many years waiting in the wings while Augustus tried desperately to secure the succession for one of his own. Tiberius was more given to abstruse scholarship than to personal violence and it was therefore not out of character for him to respond with a taunting line of Greek verse, that Agrippina should not think of herself as wronged just because she was not queen. Whether the incident occurred precisely as described is not especially important. There can be little doubt that a deep gulf had arisen between the emperor and Augustus' granddaughter. Nor did the clash do Claudia Pulchra any good. Together with her lover she was convicted, although nothing is known of the penalty.[49]

Immediately after this incident Tacitus reports a second meeting between Tiberius and Agrippina. She was now physically ill and worn out by the stress of the Claudia Pulchra trial. She might well have been feeling particularly vulnerable. She asked permission to marry, arguing that she was lonely and still young enough. Having produced nine children, she would, under Augustus' moral legislation, already have been free from the tutelage of a guardian. Her request must have been to Tiberius as princeps, rather than as the adoptive father of her husband. For his part, he must have felt a dilemma and have seen the political implications both of acceding and of refusing. He adopted the politic course of postponing a decision. There may also have been a purely personal reason for his unwillingness to grant permission. The intended husband is not named, but Agrippina's known association with Asinius Gallus makes him the most likely candidate. Tiberius could hardly have failed to resent Gallus, who had married Vipsania after her divorce from Tiberius, and who, until her death in 20, seems to have enjoyed with her the happy married life that Tiberius had once known. The latent ill-will was aggravated by an incident at the very outset of the reign. In the debate in the senate over the succession Tiberius made the suggestion that he should receive not the entire principate but whatever portion the senate might allot him. Gallus broke in with a pointed question, 'Which portion?' He tried to gloss over the interjection, but Tiberius could not be mollified and continued to bear a grudge.[50]

It is far from certain when Agrippina's request was made, but it would have been out of place immediately after the confrontation over Claudia Pulchra. Agrippina reminded Tiberius that she was still young, but she would already have been about 40 years old if the request was made in AD 26. Moreover, Suetonius claims that after the clash over Claudia Pulchra, Tiberius held no further proper conversation with Agrippina. Tacitus' information came from the famous memoirs of Agrippina the Younger (p. 198). The incident might have appeared there without any indication of chronology, and simply have been added by the historian at what he considered a dramatic point.[51]

Sejanus meanwhile continued his assault. Some of Agrippina's friends were now on his payroll, and they planted in her mind the notion that poisons had been prepared for her. So highly strung was she that she might well have been prepared to believe the story, which would have seemed more convincing if she was indeed ill at the time. At the next dinner with Tiberius she sat in tense silence and declined the food offered her. Tiberius could hardly fail to notice (he may well have been tipped off) and was offended. To test her, he took some fruit and passed it to her, making some casual comment about its quality. She declined to taste it and passed it on to her slave. Tiberius pointedly said nothing to her but observed to his mother Livia that he could hardly be blamed if he decided on stern treatment for someone who would accuse him of poisoning her. To many the rebuke seemed to contain an ominous threat.[52]

Tiberius had by now endured enough of the strife and intrigue of palace life in Rome and decided that it was time to take his leave. At some point in 26 he left the city for Campania, and went from there to Capri. He was not destined to return to Rome, except for his own funeral. Whether or not, as Tacitus claims, it was through the urging of Sejanus that he left cannot be determined. The sources also suggest that he might have been determined to get away from his interfering mother. The tension between Tiberius and Livia had grown, and he had already removed her entirely from involvement in public affairs.[53] After 26 he was to see her only once, and that briefly, and refused to visit her when she was ill.[54] His departure certainly served Sejanus' purpose, since it removed one of the few checks on the prefect's campaign against Agrippina. As in the past, he planned his attack indirectly and chose as his target Nero, her eldest son. Nero tended to express his views forcefully and bluntly, habits he may well have picked up from his mother. Sejanus bribed his freedmen and clients to egg him on. He made a number of foolish remarks which were duly noted down and passed on to Tiberius. Sejanus had also discovered that Nero's brother Drusus resented him as their mother's favourite, and exploited his jealousy. This is the only hint that Tacitus gives of ill-feelings *within* Agrippina's family, yet another example of the historian's reticence over matters that made him uncomfortable.[55] Caligula was only 14 by mid-26, probably too young yet to be the target of Sejanus' plots.

Attacks on Agrippina's supporters continued unabated into 27. Quinctilius Varus was the son of Claudia Pulchra, and betrothed to Agrippina's daughter Livilla although they did not marry. He was charged (we do not know the details, but probably for *maiestas*). Luckily the absence of Tiberius from Rome, at this stage assumed to be temporary, provided Agrippina's supporters with a breathing space. They succeeded in postponing the trial until Tiberius' anticipated return to the city. Nothing is known of the ultimate verdict, or even if the case was proceeded with.[56]

In the same year Sejanus finally made his move against his main target – Agrippina herself. The events that led up to her downfall, which happened alongside that of her son Nero, are extremely difficult to disentangle, and contradictory versions have come down in the sources. Tacitus asserts that the final attack did not take place until after Livia's death, in 29. Suetonius, on the other hand, says that *after* Agrippina had been banished her son Caligula was placed in the care of a very much alive Livia. In addition, Pliny also says that the trial of Titus Sabinus, a supporter of Agrippina, which took place in 28, arose *ex causa Neronis* ('as a consequence of Nero's case'), clearly implying that Nero was charged by 28 at the very latest and thus before Livia's death. Although not quite so explicit, Velleius certainly implies that Livia died after the fall of Agrippina and Nero.[57] These contradictions have been much discussed by modern scholars and, while certainty is impossible, the sequence followed here is based on the suggestion of Eckhard Meise, that Sejanus' attack was launched in two stages, the first some time before 29 and the second, and more serious one, after Livia's death.[58]

According to Tacitus, from 27 on Sejanus dropped all pretence and made no secret of his campaign against Agrippina and Nero. He instructed the praetorians to keep watch over them and to submit detailed reports on their daily activities. This suggests that mother and son were being kept under house arrest, and Seneca mentions (without any indication of date) that Agrippina had a splendid villa at Herculaneum where she was held under guard (the villa was destroyed later by Caligula).[59] Nero's whereabouts are unknown, but he may well have been under similar restraint. In that case Caligula, almost certainly along with the young Agrippina and their two sisters, could have been sent to stay with their great-grandmother Livia while their mother's movements were restricted. This arrangement would at any rate reconcile the accounts of the ancient sources. Suetonius does admittedly refer to the actual *banishment* of Agrippina (*ea relegata*) as occurring before 29, but in a context where his narrative is very condensed, and the expression might be used loosely to describe not banishment proper but her forced detention in Herculaneum.

Livia at this period seems to have occupied private quarters on the Palatine, the so-called 'Casa di Livia', identified by an inscription IULIA AUGUSTA found there on a lead pipe. This building had originally been the home of Augustus and Livia, and the emperor seems to have allowed it to remain as a private residence of his wife when he built a new residential complex to the south of it. It is a relatively modest house of tufa and concrete with a brick facing in *opus reticulatum*, its inner walls decorated with wall paintings. Its modest scale would, of course, have suited the underplayed image that Augustus sought to convey.[60] This was the 11-year-old Agrippina's second place of residence in Rome, where she would have lived with Caligula and her sisters for a year or so, in a house filled with tension and foreboding.

Sejanus' soldiers seem to have done their work efficiently, and Agrippina's eldest son, the headstrong and outspoken Nero, was probably foolish enough to play into their hands. Enough damaging material was collected to justify some sort of proceeding and, as a result of what was disclosed there (we have no details), Sejanus launched an investigation of Sabinus, probably late in 27. This man had been a close friend of Germanicus and after the latter's death had often been seen in public in the company of Agrippina and her children, and had been a frequent visitor to their home. Sejanus had long been planning a case against Sabinus but had bided his time, perhaps in the hope of netting both him and Agrippina together. He was now ready to strike. Latinius Latiaris, a casual acquaintance of Sabinus, was used as the agent. He invited him to his home, making a pretence of sympathy for Agrippina, and managed to elicit some ill-considered remarks about Tiberius. What Sabinus did not realize was that Latiaris had henchmen hiding in the attic, taking down his every word. He was arrested on the spot. A report was hastily despatched to Tiberius, who wrote to the senate on 1 January 28, denouncing him. He was tried and executed, his body thrown down the Gemonian stairs. In the letter that Tiberius sent to the senate afterwards, thanking them for the punishment of a man he described as an enemy of the state, he noted that his life was under constant threat from his enemies. No names were mentioned, but according to Tacitus the senators had no doubt that he meant Agrippina and Nero.[61]

The attack on Agrippina seems to have been held momentarily in check and at some point in 28, during a time of danger and disaster for her family, her daughter, Agrippina the Younger, was married to Gnaeus Domitius Ahenobarbus (the event will be considered in detail in the next chapter.) The marriage seems to have had no effect on the status of her mother, whose continued security appears to have depended on Livia's protection, an ironical situation given that the two women supposedly despised one another. But the prospect of Sejanus taking control would hardly have been any more attractive to Livia than it was to Agrippina, and while Livia was alive he would have hesitated to reveal his ultimate ambitions. This situation changed early in 29, with the death of Livia. She claimed that she kept herself alive by regularly drinking the wine of her home area Pucinum. The recipe was effective, but it could not be permanent and finally, at the age of 86, even she had to yield to the course of nature. Tiberius was at long last free of his interfering mother but could not get over his feelings of bitterness. He did not attend her simple funeral (the eulogy was given by Caligula, who had been living with her) and refused to allow her to be deified, or her will to be executed.[62]

The precise details of what followed are unclear, but it seems that Sejanus conveyed a detailed and devastating attack on Agrippina and Nero to Tiberius. The strategy clearly worked, and Tiberius in turn sent a letter to the senate denouncing both (there was a popular belief that the letter had been sent earlier and suppressed by Livia). He did not go so far as to charge them with *maiestas*, but instead accused Nero of sexual depravity and took Agrippina to task for her arrogant language and haughty attitude (*adrogantiam oris* and *contumacem animum*). The senate was placed in a difficult position by the ambiguity of Tiberius' accusation. 'Hard-liners' demanded that charges be levied. Agrippina's supporters would clearly have resisted this. In the middle was the majority of senators, who were afraid to act either way in the absence of clear directions from Tiberius. In fact, he probably had no stomach for a direct charge of treason against popular members of the imperial family. Junius Rusticus, who had been appointed by Tiberius as the official recorder of the senate's proceeding and presumably someone who had some sense of the emperor's wishes, advised the consuls not to put forward a motion for a trial.[63]

Agrippina had always believed in the power of public opinion. We see evidence of this on numerous occasions, such as her attempts to win over the ordinary soldiers in Germany and Syria, and the grand spectacle she engineered when she returned to Italy with the ashes of Germanicus. Yet in the end her popularity was to prove her downfall. When Germanicus' remains were brought to Rome there had been a great upsurge of popular sympathy for his widow and her children. There was a similar groundswell of support in 29. A mob surrounded the senate-house waving effigies of Agrippina and Nero, and noisily proclaiming that the letter from Tiberius was actually a forgery. Pamphlets were also distributed anonymously, supposedly listing charges made by senior senators against Sejanus.[64] None of these demonstrations was aimed directly at Tiberius, on the contrary the demonstrators seem to have gone out of their way to confirm their loyalty to the emperor, suggesting instead that he had been duped by his prefect. All the same, any leader conscious of his own unpopularity will always find it difficult to stomach the popularity of others in his court circle. The demonstrations, described by Sejanus in exaggerated terms, elicited yet another angry letter from Tiberius to the senate. He repeated his earlier charges against Agrippina and Nero, and insisted that he would determine their fate in a closed hearing. At this crucial point in the crisis there is a gap in the text of Tacitus, and the narrative does not resume until the year 31. There are also major gaps in Dio's account. Hence any reconstruction must at best be tentative. To judge from Tiberius' final instructions, Agrippina and Nero were tried *in camera*, and we learn in a different context that one of the main accusers was Avillius Flaccus, the Prefect of Egypt.[65] There is no other information on the trial, nor on the role that Flaccus might have played in it. Despite any pretence adopted for public consumption, it may well be that they were accused of inciting rebellion. There was evidence that some supporters had urged them to seek refuge with the Rhine armies, or to take a stand in the forum by the statue of Divus Augustus and call upon senators and ordinary people to join their cause.[66] Tacitus claims that these suggestions were made by *agents provocateurs*, who were rebuffed, but it cannot be established conclusively that Tiberius' suspicions were groundless.[67] In any case, both Agrippina and Nero were declared public enemies (*hostis*), clearly implying a charge of some sort of political misdemeanour, and both were banished, Nero to Pontia and Agrippina to Pandateria. She was not an easy prisoner and could be controlled only through coercion – she lost an eye in a struggle with a centurion. She also went on a hunger strike and had to be force-fed.[68] But in the end her courage and determination would not be enough to save her.

4
Sister

By 28 the bitter clash between Tiberius and Agrippina the Elder was moving towards its grim climax. The arrest of Agrippina's closest ally Sabinus would have left no-one in doubt that a campaign was now being waged against her in deadly earnest. Not only in Rome was there a sense of doom – Agrippina's sister, the younger Julia, finally died in wretched and lonely exile. Farther afield, the Romans suffered a major reverse in the Lower Rhine region of Germany. Some 900 Roman prisoners were put to death after a hopeless battle against the Frisians, and another 400 committed suicide to avoid a similar fate. Tiberius despaired of any effective response, and adopted the time-honoured political device of simply keeping the public in the dark about the true extent of the disaster.

The younger Agrippina could hardly have been unaware of such happenings – they must have been topics of conversation and gossip in the home of her great-grandmother Livia, who was looking after her at the time. How well she comprehended the issues is a different matter, since by the end of the year she was still only 13. But she was not too young to marry. The normal age of marriage for women in the Roman world seems generally to have been in the late teens (ten years later for men), but among the upper-class women marriage at 15 was regular and even earlier unions were common in aristocratic circles, especially if there were political advantages to the match. In Agrippina's case, the chosen husband (chosen by Tiberius, that is) was a member of a distinguished family, Gnaeus Domitius Ahenobarbus.[1]

Tacitus records the event at the end of his narrative of AD 28, in fact as the very last item although he could have merely added the information as an appendage to the year's events, without intending an exact date.[2] Whenever precisely the marriage took place, it would have meant an important change in Agrippina the Younger's life. She would have moved from Livia's house on the Palatine to the residence of her new husband. Domitius owned a family home on the Via Sacra, the important thoroughfare that passes through the Forum and then rises to the east up the spur of the Velia between the Palatine and the Oppian Hills. The house was located on this rise and would have commanded a fine view of the Forum. It would also have been comfortable; at any rate, Domitius four years later added a conspicuous baths wing, a display of irresponsible self-indulgence that caused his mother much anxiety (see p. 43). The house, which has been indentified by the archaeologist A. Carandini with the residence located beneath Hadrian's Temple of Rome and Venus, was still standing some thirty years later when their only son Nero was emperor, and it even became a place of veneration, with sacrifices carried out by the Arval Brethren on Domitius' birthday (11 December).[3]

Since the marriage marked an important stage in Agrippina's life, and by a certain standard she might now *technically* be considered an adult, this might be a useful point to attempt a general portrait. It is not an easy task. None of the ancient sources attempts a balanced assessment of her character and abilities. Most of the characterizations seem little more than clichés. No truly distinctive or idiosyncratic personality can be said to emerge. When she is mentioned it is invariably as someone reacting to circumstances, and the descriptions tend to be shaped by those circumstances.

Agrippina's native ability can be inferred from her later career and from her literary activities as the writer of memoirs. We can assume that as one of the children of Germanicus she would have been well educated. We can also assume that even in her early youth she would have learned from her mother a powerful sense of her important place in the scheme of things, a place intended for her as a daughter of the acclaimed Germanicus and of Agrippina the Elder, the last surviving grandchild of Augustus. The unfortunate fates of her mother and brothers would also have taught her the need for caution and diplomacy in political matters, a principle she maintained in her later life and which she would neglect only once, with disastrous results, when she had to deal with her own son.

On her physical appearance we are slightly better informed. She was in good general condition, still able, even when she had reached the age of 43, to swim to safety after a shipwreck in the cold March seas, despite a wound and despite having earlier attended a lavish banquet. Only one specific physical feature is recorded by Pliny the Elder: on the right side of her upper jaw she had a double set of canine teeth, a relatively uncommon dental abnormality that in antiquity was supposed to portend Fortune's favour (double canines on the left were unlucky), but probably had the effect of making her face slightly lop-sided. It is just possible that the effects of this are reflected in her sculpture (see below).[4] Tacitus speaks in general terms of her physical allure; when comparing her on separate occasions to two contemporary women (Junia Silana and Domitia Lepida), he claims in each instance that the women were well matched in their moral depravity and were equals in their *forma,* where the context requires that this word be understood in a positive sense of 'beauty'. Dio calls her *kale* ('beautiful'). We might also add the macabre anecdote that after her death Nero supposedly remarked on seeing her naked body that he had never realized she was so lovely.[5] These stories have a distinct rhetorical ring, and perhaps reflect an ancient stereotype that linked physical charms to moral degradation. Agrippina was clearly not sexually repellent, as the tradition of a host of lovers makes clear, but there is probably little more that we can safely infer about her appearance from the sources.

Roman coins can tell us much about the appearance of the individuals depicted, since the imperial coinage and, to some extent, local issues (on the distinction, see p. 225) aspire to a degree of realism. The most useful for this purpose are, of course, the large bronzes, especially the sestertii. Unfortunately, in the case of the younger Agrippina only one certain sestertius is known, that minted under Caligula showing all three sisters on the reverse, on a scale that allows no scope for facial features or individualism (Pl. 10). One other Agrippina sestertius has been tentatively identified. Its obverse depicts a draped female bust, facing right, with the hair in a long plait, and identified as 'Agrippina Augusta, daughter of Germanicus and wife of Claudius', hence dated 49–54 (Pl. 7). The face is rather severe, with a prominent nose, but otherwise unremarkable. The resemblance of this piece to the memorial sestertius of Agrippina's mother, issued

under Caligula (both have the covered carriage, the *carpentum*, on the reverse) is probably more striking than could be explained by a mother-daughter relationship, and the
earlier issue might have served as a model (Pl. 8, p. 226). A dupondius of the same date
depicts a similar head (facing left) and identical legend; only two examples are known
(one now missing), neither sufficiently well preserved to provide useful details. The precious metal issues, gold aurei and silver denarii, have relatively small flans on which
detailed characterization is more difficult. The Claudian coins honouring Agrippina
reveal a face with heavy rounded features, while issues dated to early in Nero's reign
depict his mother with the same heavy features, rather jowly, with a prominent nose.[6]

Sculpture must be used with some caution, since Roman sculpted heads are very
rarely found with inscriptions and are identified largely on the basis of resemblance to
coin types. The process is far from scientific, as the widely differing attributions of the
same piece frequently attest. There is, in the case of Agrippina, a general scholarly consensus that at least one portrait-type can be identified with near-certainty, represented
by a fine piece in Copenhagen (Pl. 3). The hair is parted in the middle, lies flat for a
short distance at each side of the straight parting, then rises in tiers of curls over the
temples. The centres of the curls are drilled. At the back the hair is tied in a plait and
long corkscrew strands (usually two) fall from behind the ear. The forehead is low, with
level eyebrows, and the face tends to be broad and short. The cheekbones are fairly
prominent, the chin broad. Most of the portraits have an appearance of superiority, with
a slightly masculine cast to the face. The nose is often prominent, with a rounded tip.
The lips tend to be tightly set, with the upper one protruding above the lower. This last
feature may be an idealized depiction of the distortion of the upper lip usually associated with a double canine, but a similar, though not so pronounced, feature is noticeable
on Caligulan sculpture and it may be a family trait. The face is far from beautiful, and
one must also make allowance for a degree of idealization. The sculpted reliefs from the
sebasteion at Aphrodisias add the further detail that Agrippina was probably quite tall,
taller than her husband Claudius (who is himself described as tall by Suetonius) and of
about the same stature as her 17-year-old son Nero (Pls 18–19).[7]

The material evidence, then, suggests that Agrippina was probably not especially
beautiful in the normally accepted sense of the word. This is not a trivial issue. The literary sources portray her as an alluring woman who succeeded by using her sexual
charms to ensnare defenceless victims like Claudius, a woman for whom sex was a means
not so much to pleasure as to power. The limited evidence on her physical appearance
tends to indicate that the sources thought in stereotypes, as they often do. Agrippina's
achievements can probably be more fairly attributed to ability and perseverance than to
standard 'feminine charms'.

Agrippina may not have been the clichéd beauty that the sources allege, but she was
intelligent, and of impeccable lineage. She should have had good marriage prospects –
were they realized in Domitius? The question is an important one. The main key to
Agrippina's later motivation is family pride, an emotion that would have been implanted and nurtured by her mother. But a 13-year-old is still at an impressionable age. It is
reasonable to ask if her embryonic sense of being born to play a part in the greater destiny of Rome, albeit through a husband or son, was reinforced by the choice of her first
marriage partner. Seneca the Elder calls Domitius *nobilissimus,* Velleius *clarissimus,*

Josephus *episemos* ('prominent') and Juvenal says that it was his *son* (Nero) who dishonoured the name of the Domitii. Suetonius does describe Domitius as a man *omni parte vitae detestabilis* ('despicable in every aspect'), but his interest was not so much in Domitius as an individual in his own right but rather as the father of the evil and depraved Nero, and he admits his intention of showing that Nero acquired the vices of his ancestors as a kind of natural inheritance. The only failing on which we do have reliable evidence is a tendency to indolence, which, as mentioned, caused his mother some distress. Seneca the Elder relates the anecdote that Antonia was troubled by her son's lack of ambition, since he first built a baths annexe to his house and then started to seek out the rhetoricians and spent his time declaiming. The professional wit Asilius Sabinus tried to put her mind at rest, and make himself seem rather clever in the process, by alluding to a Greek proverb that described incompetents as people who can neither 'swim nor spell'. Domitius, he reassured her in elegant iambics, had at least got the order right, 'diving first, then writing'. It seems that Domitius did not live up to the distinguished record of his ancestors or to the promise that his mother saw in him, but this did not mean that the marriage was anything but honourable. Tacitus certainly felt that it was, and it prompted him to observe that Domitius was linked by blood to the imperial family through Augustus' sister Octavia (Domitius' mother was Antonia the Elder, daughter of Octavia and Marc Antony). Tiberius clearly felt that the ceremony occasioned no shame, since he attended it himself (*coram*), presumably while visiting Campania. It has also been noted that, amidst the uncertainty facing the family of Germanicus, the marriage would have provided a degree of protection to the young Agrippina.[8]

Domitius could certainly boast an outstanding ancestry, with an unbroken line of consuls stretching back over several generations. Originally a plebeian family, the Domitii had, with others, been elevated by Octavian to the rank of patricians, probably in 30 BC.[9] According to tradition, they received their cognomen *Ahenobarbus* ('bronze-bearded') during the conflict between the Romans and the Latins. In one version of the story, at the battle at Lake Regillus in about 496 BC the Romans were aided by the timely intervention of the sons of Jupiter, Castor and Pollux, who, to prove their divinity to an understandably sceptical Lucius Domitius, touched his dark beard (*barba*), whereupon it turned bronze-red (*ahenea*). The red beard, as well as numerous public distinctions and honours, became the distinguishing mark of the family.

Suetonius enumerates the immediate ancestors of Agrippina's husband. He first records Gnaeus, the consul of 122 BC, who had a flair for showmanship that would manifest itself in his distant imperial descendant, the emperor Nero. To celebrate a victory, Gnaeus rode through Gaul on an elephant, followed by his troops. In his list Suetonius conflates Gnaeus with his son of the same name, consul of 96, of whom it was said that his bronze beard should cause no surprise since he had a face of iron and a heart of lead.[10] In the next generation, Lucius, consul of 54 BC, was a man of violent temper but also strangely indecisive. He supposedly attempted suicide by poison, changed his mind and vomited it up; he then bestowed freedom on his doctor, who had known his master well enough to ensure that the normally fatal draught actually contained less than a fatal dose. But Lucius was also a man of considerable courage and a key figure in the move to deprive Julius Caesar of his command in Gaul. Most important for our purposes is the evidence of his prodigious family wealth. It became a byword in Agrippina's day and may well have served her in building up her large body of supporters. During the civil war Lucius was able to raise troops for Pompey's side by promising land from his own estates. He died at the battle of Pharsalus, where Caesar defeated the forces of Pompey in 48 BC.[11]

Lucius' son Gnaeus, consul of 32 BC, was implicated in the murder of Julius Caesar but was eventually reconciled to Antony and offered a major naval command, which he declined on the eve of Actium, before defecting to Octavian (to join his mistress, according to Antony). He was of little assistance in the battle and died a few days later. His son, Lucius Domitius, consul of 16 BC, father-in-law of Agrippina and grandfather of Nero, was a man described by Suetonius as arrogant, extravagant and cruel, whose gladiatorial shows were so brutal that they offended even Roman taste. But this portrayal is not reflected by other sources. Velleius rejects the charge of extravagance with the observation that Gnaeus was paradoxically a man of distinguished simplicity (*eminentissimae ac nobilissimae simplicitatis*). Tacitus calls him a *vir nobilis* and records his achievement of taking Roman arms further across the Elbe than anyone before, for which he won the *ornamenta triumphalia*. Also, the fact that he was named executor of Augustus' will suggests an individual with outstanding personal qualities. More significantly, his adherence to Octavian's cause was considered so crucial that he was given the hand of Octavia's daughter, Antonia the Elder (Antonia the Younger married Livia's son Drusus).[12]

Agrippina's husband thus came from a prestigious family. He cannot be seen as a husband likely to bring Agrippina down to earth after the heady atmosphere that her mother had engendered. Antonia, his mother, might have harboured fears about his fecklessness, but Tiberius was willing to give him his chance. He was granted the consulship in AD 32 and permitted the unusual privilege of being allowed to stay in the office for the whole year. Although his only recorded accomplishment in office was the building of his bath-house, further responsibilities followed. In 36 a massive fire in Rome destroyed much of the Aventine and part of the Circus Maximus. Tiberius generously paid full compensation for the properties, at a cost of 100 million HS, and to deal with the claimants set up a commission, consisting of Domitius and the other husbands of the four imperial princesses.[13]

As Agrippina's husband, Domitius could have hoped for a consulship at the very least by the normal age for men of less well-connected noble families. Since his tenure of the office fell in 32, his birth may be placed in about 2/1 BC, and he was probably about 30 at the time of his marriage to Agrippina. This seems to rule out one of the anecdotes related by Suetonius, who claims, as an example of Domitius' brutality, that when he went to the east in Gaius Caesar's entourage (in 1 BC) he slew one of his own freedmen for refusing to drink as much as he ordered and was then dismissed by Gaius. Domitius would have been far too young, and Suetonius may have conflated the mission of Gaius Caesar with that of Germanicus in AD 17, or he may have confused Domitius with someone else; Syme has argued that there could have been an older, unrecorded brother who behaved outrageously on Gaius' expedition.[14]

Few other achievements are recorded for Domitius. Suetonius claims that while racing his chariot on the Appian Way (an echo of his son's later obsession with chariots) Domitius knocked down and killed a young boy, and it was believed that he did it deliberately. In Rome he got into an altercation with a Roman knight and intentionally, it was claimed gouged out one of his eyes. He was supposedly dishonest in his business practices, cheating bankers in at least one transaction and, during his praetorship, skimming off the prize monies awarded to winners in the chariot races. These last two stories of Suetonius do tally with the other evidence that Domitius was to some degree preoccupied with money (see below), but such anecdotes should generally be treated with caution. In any case Domitius' unattractive personal traits would have been less important than the family distinction and considerable wealth that he brought to the marriage.

Domitius also brought Agrippina new living relatives. Two of these, his sisters, both play prominent roles in Agrippina's later life, by seeking to block her ambitions. Before her marriage to Domitius, Agrippina had belonged to a family beset by outside foes. She now had the opportunity to observe a family troubled by internal tensions, and in particular to observe the destructive effect that love of money had on the life of the Roman aristocracy. This experience might have strengthened her resolve to view wealth as something not worth pursuing for its own sake but rather as a means to an end, usually a political end.

There are several ancient references to a sister of Domitius, referred to as Lepida, or Domitia Lepida, or Domitia. Nowhere is there an explicit statement that there was more than one sister; Suetonius comes closest when in the same passage he speaks first of Domitius' 'sister', and then of his 'sister Lepida'.[15] The accumulation of references from all sources, however, leaves no doubt that there were two, usefully referred to as Lepida and Domitia. Since both sisters became embroiled in serious conflict with Agrippina and since both competed with her for Nero's affections, there is an enormous risk that they could have been confused by the sources with one another. Basic typologies emerge – anecdotes about sexual impropriety are *generally* assigned to Lepida, those about meanness generally to Domitia.

Their roles in the story of Agrippina will emerge in due course, but some preliminary observations will be useful. First, Domitia.[16] In AD 55 Agrippina refers to her as an *anus* ('old woman'). While allowance must be given for rhetorical embellishment, the claim is supported by Dio who observes that when poisoned (by her nephew the emperor Nero) in 59 Domitia was close to dying of old age anyhow.[17] This would make her older than Domitius, who was probably born, as noted above, in about 2 BC. Her only recorded husband is Gaius Sallustius Crispus Passienus, who later divorced her and married Agrippina (p. 84), an obvious source of ill-feeling between the two women. No other husband is attested, though Syme believes that there might have been two earlier marriages (see Appendix II).

Domitia was notorious for her meanness. She once charged a certain Junius Bassus with claiming that she sold old shoes. He responded indignantly: 'I deny it emphatically – I said that you *bought* them.' This mean streak did not, however, prevent her from taking her brother to task for the same fault and she ridiculed him for cheating the winners in the chariot races. Inevitably, she and her brother ended up in a legal dispute about the family wealth. She probably saved money by having her husband Passienus plead her case; at all events he is on record as referring to the wealth *qua uterque abundabat* ('which both [Domitius and Domitia] had in abundance'), and as making the trenchant observation that there was nothing the two of them were less short of than what they were fighting over.[18]

Domitia had estates in Ravenna, where she built splendid gymnasia that were still in use in Dio's time in the early third century. She also had a villa at Baiae, where she constructed elaborate fishponds which Agrippina, in a later dispute, cited as examples of frivolity. In Rome, in the region across the Tiber, she owned gardens that would later house Hadrian's tomb and later still become one of the favourite retreats of the emperor Aurelian.[19]

The other sister, Lepida, was probably the youngest of the Domitii siblings, since she is said by Tacitus, with some laxity, to be close in age to Agrippina.[20] She was married first to Messala Barbatus, to whom she bore Messalina (to become the infamous wife of Claudius). She entered her second marriage, almost certainly in the early 20s (probably as widow rather than divorcée), to Faustus Cornelius Sulla, who held the consulship in 31 then disappears from the record. Their son, of the same name, was engaged to Antonia, the emperor Claudius' daughter. He would later be put to death on the orders of Nero.

Lepida was described by Tacitus as no less immoral than Agrippina; just before the death of Tiberius, she and her brother Domitius were charged with incest, but escaped prosecution owing to the change in rulers, suggesting that the indictment was probably malicious and unsubstantiated (see below).[21] Like her sister she was wealthy. She had holdings in Calabria, and there is also evidence of an estate at Fundi and of granaries at Puteoli, used to store grain in transit from Egypt.[22]

Agrippina's marriage in AD 28 had no effect on the major political battle being waged in Rome. Her mother continued to suffer, although very little is known about her from now until her death. With Agrippina the Elder, as well as Tiberius, away from Rome, Sejanus was able to consolidate his position. His influence now extended even to Germany, with results that would later prove highly significant for Agrippina. Lower Germany was governed by Lucius Apronius, the father of one of Sejanus' close friends. Upper Germany in 29 went to Gnaeus Cornelius Lentulus Gaetulicus. He was married to a daughter of Apronius and his daughter was betrothed to Sejanus' son.[23] In Rome Sejanus completed the elimination of Agrippina the Elder's remaining supporters, the most prominent being Asinius Gallus (almost certainly the man she had earlier hoped to marry). He was denounced in 30 by Tiberius, probably on a charge of illicit relations with Agrippina the Elder, and held without trial in solitary confinement. He was dead by 33 (through forced or voluntary starvation), his case still unheard.[24]

In the same year, AD 30, Sejanus felt able to move against Agrippina's second son, Drusus. The rift between Drusus on the one side and his mother and his brother Nero on the other was clearly a serious one, even though the sources are reticent on the matter. He had allowed himself to be used by Sejanus in his political battles against his family and was foolish enough to believe that the ambitious prefect looked upon him as a friend. Drusus' wife, Aemilia Lepida, was persuaded by Sejanus to bring a number of charges against him (their exact form is unknown) and in 30 Drusus was sent to Rome from Capri and formally accused. No further details of the indictment have survived, but he was convicted and declared a public enemy (*hostis*), and imprisoned in a cell beneath the imperial residence on the Palatine.[25]

Finally Sejanus was betrothed to Livilla and chosen by Tiberius to be his partner in the consulship in 31 but, with ultimate success almost in his grasp, he was abruptly toppled from power. The circumstances are not clear, nor are the emperor's motives in wanting to rid himself of his prefect, although Tiberius claimed afterwards that it was because he had plotted against the offspring of Germanicus. Indeed, shortly before Sejanus' fall Nero had died in mysterious circumstances. Officially he was said to have committed suicide, although Suetonius suggested that he did so when falsely informed that he had been sentenced to death.[26] Tiberius' version of Sejanus' crimes may be intended to mask the truth about his own behaviour, but it could be that Sejanus' action against the young prince finally opened the emperor's eyes. In any case, Sejanus was lured to a meeting of the senate on the Palatine in October 31 and in a carefully orchestrated operation was arrested and strangled in prison. The command of the praetorians passed to Quintus Naevius Cordus Sutorius Macro, the organizer of the putsch. Sejanus' destruction dragged down a number of other victims in its wake, including his former wife Apicata. Before her suicide she dropped another bombshell. In a letter to Tiberius she revealed that eight years previously her husband and Livilla had poisoned Drusus. The charge may or may not have been true, but Tiberius believed it. Livilla was executed, starved to death by her mother, according to one tradition.[27]

Caligula had already been summoned to join his grandfather Tiberius in Capri sometime in 31 and was clearly a serious candidate to succeed to the principate. Tiberius treated him fairly, even generously, and he was made joint heir with the emperor's natural grandson Tiberius Gemellus. Sejanus' successor, Macro, recognized a rising star in the young Caligula and a role as kingmaker for himself. He wasted no opportunity to strengthen Caligula's position and, most importantly, to convey to others that, when the dramatic moment arrived, Germanicus' youngest son would have the crucial support of the praetorian guard. Caligula received further encouragement from a newfound friend, Herod Agrippa, a colourful member of the ruling family of Judaea, whose friendship with the Caesars would prove very lucrative and bring him his own kingdom. Caligula also played his proper part and any resentment he may have felt over the treatment of his mother and brothers was carefully masked.[28]

If Tiberius did not show any vindictiveness towards Caligula, nor did he show any inclination to forgive either Agrippina the Elder or her son Drusus. The fall of Sejanus, and the exposure of his long record of political machinations, did not persuade the emperor that somehow Germanicus' family had been wronged. Drusus was the first to go. In AD 31 an imposter, claiming to be Drusus, had emerged in Asia and Achaea and had collected a considerable following before eventually being tracked down and exposed as a phoney.[29] The real Drusus was still in the far less exotic confines of the Palatine prison. Rumours of a different kind circulated in 33, that there had been a *rapprochement* with Tiberius. They proved to be as false as the imposter, and any hopes that might have been raised were dashed when it was disclosed that Drusus had in fact been starved to death in his prison. His end was a protracted one and in the last agonizing stages he even ate the stuffing from his mattress. As a final grim touch, a detailed record was kept of his last days, together with his final crazed denunciation of Tiberius, all of which was read to the senate, where he was vigorously denounced as a public enemy (*infestum reipublicae*) and *exitialis in suos*.[30] This last charge, that he was 'destructive of his own kin', is an interesting one, as it suggests that his association with Sejanus and his role in the death of his brother Nero was probably more sinister than the sources care to acknowledge. Moreover, while Tiberius was admittedly an aloof and unsympathetic individual, there is little concrete evidence that he was gratuitously cruel. The horrendous punishment meted out to Drusus clearly had to be motivated by something much stronger than personal dislike.

The horror of Drusus' death had scarcely subsided when it was revealed that his mother, Agrippina the Elder, had also died. Apparently she starved herself to death, despite efforts to force-feed her. Tiberius reported the death to the senate, claiming that her suicide was prompted by the news that her lover Asinius Gallus had died. The sources reluctantly concede that the emperor was not, in fact, directly responsible for her end.[31] By a bizarre coincidence she died on 18 October 33, exactly two years to the day after Sejanus' death. Tiberius in his report could not avoid drawing attention to this ominous coincidence, and 18 October was marked as a black day in the calendar. Tiberius also observed that he had not had her strangled and dragged over the Gemonian stairs (the fate of common criminals), and the senate passed a decree thanking him for his *clementia*. Tacitus narrates these proceedings in the senate without comment; Suetonius sees them as a piece of grim irony. But again, it is difficult to avoid the conclusion that Agrippina's transgressions were far more serious than mere displays of arrogance and rudeness, the only shortcomings admitted by the sources.

In many ways Agrippina the Elder was probably not a pleasant individual. She was clearly self-centred and arrogant, faults that the favourable sources and even her husband concede. Yet she was a woman of immense courage, unwilling to compromise her convictions, and the manner of her death was one that required enormous willpower. She had devoted her life to ensuring that a son of Germanicus, of the direct line of Augustus, would one day enter the inheritance stolen from her husband. Ironically, she was to achieve her aim in the end. Her favourite Nero was dead, as was her second son Drusus, but she was survived by a third, virtually unknown outside his immediate family circle, and, in her last lonely days on Pandateria, little could she have dreamt that less than four years later Caligula would be acclaimed as princeps by a jubilant empire.

In the year of her death Agrippina's two unmarried daughters received husbands. The delay in their marriages (their sister had been married five years earlier) can be explained by the recent turmoil, caused initially by Sejanus and latterly by Agrippina the Elder. By 33 things seemed to have settled down. But Tiberius remained cautious. The matches seem to reflect a deliberate intention on his part to select unpromising partners, so as to ensure that the succession would not be complicated by unwelcome rivals. Drusilla was married to Lucius Cassius Longinus, who like Domitius came from a noble family but similarly lacked personal ambition or drive. Livilla was given to Marcus Vinicius, whose grandfather had been a close friend of Augustus. Marcus was a retiring man of no great promise, with an interest in literature inherited from his father. He held the consulship in 30 and it was probably expected that this would be his last public role. He was destined, however, to rise briefly to prominence after the murder of Caligula. Julia, daughter of Tiberius' late son Drusus, was also married at this time to Rubellius Blandus, a union so mediocre that her whole household was plunged into gloom.[32] In the same year Agrippina's only surviving brother Caligula also received a bride, Junia Claudia, daughter of the prominent consular Marcus Junius Silanus.[33]

Unfortunately we have virtually no information about Agrippina's life with Domitius during the final years of Tiberius' reign. In a typically confused and garbled entry, the scholiast on the *Satires* of the poet Juvenal seems to suggest some sort of *ménage à trois*, or perhaps more accurately *à cinq*, involving the hated Ofonius Tigellinus, later the brutal prefect of the guard under Nero, together with Agrippina and her husband (mistakenly called Lucius by the scholiast), as well as her sister (called Fulvia!) and husband. The scholia on the poems of Juvenal seem to derive from a commentary composed about AD 400 and are riddled with errors and misunderstanding. This particular entry is almost certainly of little or no value as evidence of the sexual diversions of Germanicus' daughter. But there may be a kernel of truth in it. Tigellinus could at one time have been a close acquaintance of this branch of the imperial family. If so, he might have been fostered as the kind of individual whose social assets were minimal but who had given signs of being useful as a political ally. The association seems to have led later to his banishment (see below).[34]

It is in this context that we should view a curious incident in AD 37, the year of Tiberius' death and of Caligula's succession. A lady named Albucilla, who had acquired fame as a connoisseur and collector of lovers, was indicted for acts of *impietas* against the emperor. Accused with her, as partners in both her crime and her bed (*conscii et adulterii*), were three prominent Romans: Vibius Marsus, Lucius Arruntius and Agrippina's husband Gnaeus Domitius. The political credentials of the first two are impressive. Lucius Arruntius was a very distinguished figure, much admired by Augustus, who, according to Tacitus, once remarked that Lucius had both the ability and the inclination to become his successor. Either from fear, or as a special favour, when he was appointed legate of Hispania Citerior by Tiberius he did not assume his command but governed *in absentia*. In 31 he succeeded in warding off a politically motivated charge of *maiestas*. In addition, he was the adoptive father of Arruntius Furius Camillus Scribonianus, who was to earn his place in history in 42 as governor of Dalmatia and the first imperial legate to lead his troops in rebellion against his emperor, Claudius. The son was consul in AD 32 as colleague of Domitius, and married to a Vibia, whose name suggests a link with Vibius Marsus. This last individual would certainly have added popular prestige to any political action. Suffect consul in 17, he seems to have been in Syria during Germanicus' commission, perhaps as a legionary legate, and was a serious candidate to replace Piso as governor of Syria (he would eventually serve in that capacity under Claudius). He accompanied the elder Agrippina on her return to Rome, and would thus have enjoyed the image of a Germanicus loyalist.

The case, with its charges of sexual misconduct, bears all the hallmarks of a political trial. Unfortunately neither Tacitus nor Suetonius provides any direct information on the political dimensions of the case, and the relationship between Albucilla and the three men accused with her is not defined beyond adultery. Tacitus does, however, give a prominent role to Macro, adding the detail that the prefect took charge of the preliminary interrogation of witnesses and the torture of slaves. Dio provides a summary of the events, and adds the tantalizing detail that the real object of Macro's attack was in fact Domitius. Macro at this time was preoccupied with Caligula's (and hence his own) prospects. His personal role in the campaign against the Albucilla group leads inevitably to the suspicion that they were either seen as threatening the orderly succession of Caligula, or as threatening Macro's pre-eminent position of influence over him. If Dio is correct that Macro was especially hostile to Domitius, it would be because, as husband of Germanicus' daughter Agrippina, he might have seemed the key player. If this was indeed Macro's thinking, he would not have needed to pursue his vendetta after the accession of Caligula, as the group would no longer represent a danger. Perhaps a similar intent underlaid the abortive prosecution of Domitius and his sister, already noted, on a charge of incest.[35] Arruntius killed himself before the trial, proclaiming that life had been bad enough under Tiberius and Sejanus but would be sheer hell under Caligula and Macro. Domitius and Marsus simply played for time, and they survived Tiberius' death unscathed. Only Albucilla faced actual proceedings; she was found guilty, and after a botched suicide attempt thrown into prison. She would not emerge alive.

This affair might well represent the first recorded attempt to elevate Agrippina the Younger to the position of the emperor's consort. Domitius' failure to live up to the expectations both of his mother, and, more important, of Agrippina, now 21 years old, might have prompted the latter to goad him into some sort of political action. He could well have resented her interference; certainly there are hints of marital discord later in the year, and any tensions would inevitably be aggravated by the charge of incest launched against Domitius and his sister Lepida, even if it was groundless. But Agrippina's initial generous treatment by Caligula shows that she was certainly not suspected of any kind of disloyalty. Whatever her role in what turned out to be a débâcle, she was old enough to draw the conclusion, at the very least as a spectator, that any such political initiative required two essential ingredients to ensure success. The support of a substantial group of powerful and influential members of the senatorial class was invaluable, but, even more important, such an endeavour could not succeed without military support, ideally that of the praetorian guard. Agrippina would take these lessons to heart.

Early in March 37 Tiberius fell ill in Campania. As he grew weaker he developed a chill and was obliged to retire to his villa at Misenum, where he still managed to continue his lively dinner parties and to entertain his old friends. He continued to get worse, however, and eventually had to take to his bed. Finally his doctor Charicles reported to Macro that the emperor had only two days to live, and the prefect set in motion his carefully arranged plans. He spoke to the key people in the immediate court circle, probably using a mixture of encouragement and threats, and sent messengers to bear instructions to the army commanders and provincial governors. On the emperor's death on 16 March, Macro hastened to Rome, where he persuaded the senate (he would have prepared his allies beforehand) to nullify Tiberius' will, which named Caligula and Tiberius Gemellus as his heirs, and to acclaim the young Caligula as successor.[36]

The news of Tiberius' death was greeted in the city with disbelief at first, followed by jubilation. The senate, in particular, seems to have been genuinely enthusiastic about the change of rulers. Caligula accompanied Tiberius' body when it set out from Misenum for its final journey to Rome, but the journey was more like a triumph than a funeral procession, as the people thronged to catch a glimpse of the new emperor. It was noted that Italy had last seen crowds of this size when they came out to greet Germanicus on his travels. Caligula was a total unknown, apart from two details. The first was the self-evident fact that he was not Tiberius – many people would probably have been well disposed to almost any successor, but he was also the son of Germanicus. This converted a favourable reception to a rapturous welcome on the apparently naive assumption that he would have inherited all the qualities his much-loved father was popularly supposed to have possessed (and they had in fact never actually been tested in the father). Nor was this reaction confined to Italy. Philo reports (allowance must, of course, be made for exaggeration) that throughout the whole of the empire there was a holiday atmosphere, with celebrations and revelry exhibited by every class of society.[37] The episode is highly relevant to the future career of Agrippina, demonstrating as it does the powerful emotional attachment to Germanicus' name, an attachment she would often exploit. Her son Nero, grandson of Germanicus, would receive the same rapturous reception by senate and people alike.

Caligula entered the city on March 28 and went before the senators. The meeting was a significant one for Roman history since in a single session they confirmed absolute power on him, the first time that this had happened in Rome. Any reservations that might have been expected would have been largely alleviated by the demeanour of the young princeps, who made a great show of deference to the senate. In particular, he went to some length to demonstrate his *pietas*, that distinctively Roman virtue which combines veneration for the gods with that of the family. The display of regard for his great-grandfather Augustus was to be expected as a matter of political expediency, and reached its climax in the dedication of the Temple of the Divus Augustus (p. 55). In respecting his grandfather Tiberius, he had to tread more warily – an excess of affection for a hated ruler would clearly cause more offence than would studied indifference. The proper balance seems to have been struck. There was a fine funeral where Caligula delivered a eulogy before the remains were interred, probably in the mausoleum of Augustus.[38] Divine honours were requested, but when the senate delayed getting around to the vote, the matter was allowed to drop.

When it came to his immediate family Caligula showed no restraint. Honours were bestowed on his parents. The Arvals carried out sacrifices on their birthdays, and the stain of the *dies nefastus* was lifted from Agrippina the Elder's.[39] The month of September was renamed 'Germanicus'.[40] Two issues of gold and silver coins were minted, depicting either the head of Germanicus or of Agrippina the Elder on the reverse with appropriate identifying legends.[41]

There is no evidence that Caligula had made any effort to secure the release of his mother or brothers while he was with Tiberius on Capri, or that he showed any particular concern for them. He now made up for this neglect. In a highly public spectacle he sailed to Pontia and Pandateria in person to recover the remains of Agrippina and Nero. It would not have been an easy task. To start with, the weather was bad, which made the crossing difficult (although it made his devotion seem all the more impressive). Also Nero's remains had been scattered to prevent any attempt at burial. But he persisted and the ashes were brought in urns, first to the port of Ostia and from there on up the river Tiber to Rome where they were carried by the equestrians in solemn procession (nicely timed for midday), and placed in the mausoleum of Augustus. Thus in the end Agrippina the Elder occupied the place that was rightfully hers, in the resting place of her deified grandfather. The inscription beneath her urn has survived, a simple but explicit message, identifying the bones of 'Agrippina, daughter of Marcus Agrippa, granddaughter of Divus Augustus, wife of Germanicus Caesar and mother of Gaius Caesar (Caligula)'. Games were instituted in her honour, and a carriage (*carpentum*) assigned to carry her image in the circus procession. The *carpentum* is commemorated on the reverse of a sestertius of Caligula, while the obverse depicts Agrippina's head. The coin is noteworthy as the first minted in Rome to commemorate a deceased member of the Julio-Claudian family on both sides, and seems to have been used later as a model for a similar type honouring Agrippina the Younger (p. 225). The villa at Herculaneum, the scene of his mother's earlier imprisonment, was destroyed. Further honours were also decreed for Caligula's dead brothers. Cenotaphs were built to commemorate Drusus, whose remains were not found. Statues of both youths were ordered and a special coin was issued, a dupondius depicting Nero and Drusus on horseback, their cloaks flying behind them.[42]

Caligula did not limit himself to honouring the dead. His grandmother Antonia the Younger (sister of Gnaeus Domitius' mother) received the rights once bestowed on Livia, which included the privileges of the Vestal Virgins. She was also appointed priestess of Augustus, and perhaps most significantly received the title of Augusta. Antonia, a level-headed woman of integrity, may well have felt uncomfortable with this evocative title and have declined to use it in Rome during her lifetime. Its first datable epigraphic appearance in Italy occurs after her death, in the Arval record of 38.[43] Even Caligula's uncle Claudius, the lame and much-ridiculed brother of Germanicus, was not excluded, and could be said for the first time to have been shown the deference owed a member of the imperial family. On 1 July he entered the consulship, along with Caligula, holding the office for two months, and was given the task of arranging the contracts for the statues of Nero and Drusus.[44] (He made a mess of the job.)

Yet, amidst all the displays of family affection and *pietas*, nothing could match the honours that Caligula heaped on Agrippina the Younger and her two sisters. All three received striking privileges, some of them unprecedented. They were awarded the rights of the Vestal Virgins, which would have given them such important legal advantages as exemption from the authority of a male guardian. It would also have brought a number of practical 'perks', such as the freedom to view public games from the front seats (Augustus had banished women generally to the upper seats). The sisters were also included in the annual vows taken for the emperor's well-being. They were not the first to be singled out for such an honour; Livia's name had been included in the same vows, and later Sejanus was added. But inclusion was still a great, albeit not unprecedented, distinction, and its status can be gauged by the angry reaction of Tiberius when Germanicus' sons Nero and Drusus were included without his authority (p. 33). Much more unusual in terms of constitutional practice, the sisters were included in the formula that the consuls used when proposing motions to the senate. This declaration traditionally involved the hope that such a proposal would be beneficial to the state; under Augustus it was expressed in the form of good fortune for Augustus and his house. Caligula ordained that the sisters be specifically mentioned: *quod bonum felixque sit C. Caesari sororibusque eius* ('may this be good and fortunate for Gaius Caesar and his sisters').[45]

Perhaps most extraordinary of all the privileges granted the sisters was the instruction that they were to be included in the vow of allegiance taken to the emperor: *neque me liberosque meos cariores habebo quam Gaium habeo et sorores eius* ('nor shall I consider myself or my children more precious than I do Gaius and his sisters'). This is a remarkable development. The oath of loyalty was a highly important and significant institution under the principate, and one that the emperors took very seriously. It is recorded that after Augustus' death Tiberius made sure that it was taken by the consuls, then by the praetorian prefects and prefects of the *annona* (corn supply), followed by the senators, soldiers and people. We hear that when the rebellion broke out on the Rhine Germanicus immediately took the oath of loyalty himself, then saw that it was taken by his officials and the Belgic communities. This procedure was probably re-enacted by all the other provincial governors. On Caligula's accession Vitellius, governor of Syria, was in Jerusalem when news reached him of Tiberius' death, and he proceeded immediately to administer the oath of loyalty to the new emperor. It is not certain when in the imperial period the oath became an annual event. At the time of Tiberius' accession one senator, Valerius Messala, suggested that allegiance be sworn annually but his idea was not adopted at the time. After the fall of Sejanus in 32 Tiberius might have felt that it would be useful to have an annual reminder of the loyalty due the emperor, to accompany the oath introduced in that year to uphold Tiberius' *acta* and those of Augustus. There is no precedent for Caligula's inclusion of his sisters. In fact, after the fall of Sejanus, the senate explicitly prohibited the taking of oaths in the name of anyone other than the emperor. Caligula's actions represent a key stage in the elevation of the women of the imperial house, not to the status of joint ruler, of course, but to a more symbolic recognition that they shared in the mystique and majesty of the principate.[46]

In the course of his first year, Caligula issued his most remarkable coin, a type previously unknown in Roman numismatics. A sestertius, with the traditional head and legend of the emperor on the obverse, depicts Caligula's three sisters on the reverse (Pl. 10). They stand side by side, their bodies facing forward, each identified by name. On the left Agrippina represents *Securitas,* with her head turned to the right and a cornucopia in her right hand. Her right arm rests on a column and her left hand on Drusilla's shoulder. Drusilla as *Concordia* stands in the centre, her head turned left. She holds a flat dish, or *patera,* in her right hand and a cornucopia in her left. Finally Julia Livilla stands at the right, representing *Fortuna,* her head turned to the left, a rudder in her right hand and a cornucopia in the left. This remarkable coin prompted imitations both within and outside the empire. The city of Apamea in Bithynia minted a version of the type, as did Herod Agrippa for his own kingdom, and Cappadocia minted didrachms in honour of Claudius' wife Messalina, whose reverses, depicting the emperor's three children, were clearly based on the Caligulan prototype.[47]

It is difficult to be sure about Caligula's motives in bestowing these honours. On the one hand they served a purely political purpose. He seems to have based his right to rule essentially on his descent from Augustus, which gave his claim a quasi-constitutional authority, and the fact that he was Germanicus' son, which made him the unanimous choice of all sectors of Roman society. On both counts the promotion of members of his own family would, in a sense, enhance also the legality of his own claim. At the same time, we should not exclude an element of genuine and naive affection. Caligula had lived the last six years of his life under the constant supervision of his grandfather

Tiberius, an upright individual perhaps, but not someone given to displays of warmth and affection. The young man had to suppress any feelings for his mother and brothers, simply to survive. When the repressive cloud was lifted, it would be quite natural for him to want to give way to normal family sentiments but of course there was also a danger, once the euphoria of the early months had dissipated, that this excessive affection might turn into bitter recrimination.

The close bond between Caligula and his sisters inevitably gave rise to coarse rumours. Suetonius claims that when Caligula stayed at the house of Antonia, on the death of Livia in 29, his grandmother caught him committing incest with Drusilla. He adds for good measure that this was not the only time or the only sister – he had got up to the same with Agrippina and Livilla also. Other literary sources make similar claims.[48] Charges of this nature are notoriously difficult to prove or disprove, even in contemporary contexts; when made about unpopular figures of distant antiquity the truth is particularly elusive. As a general principle, one should be highly sceptical. Accusations of incest were traditionally levelled against the prominent and powerful (Agrippina's husband, it will be remembered, supposedly committed incest with his sister) and were a handy smear, essentially impossible to disprove. In Caligula's case we should be particularly suspicious. Suetonius tells us that the thing Caligula admired most about himself was his *adiatrepsia*, a word that seems to mean something like 'shamelessness'.[49] In essence he loved to shock people. An anecdote that has been preserved about Passienus Crispus illustrates this. Passienus, a man celebrated for his wit, was reputedly asked by Caligula, when the two of them were on some sort of journey, whether Passienus had, like the emperor, enjoyed his (own) sister. Caligula probably hoped to shock and embarrass him, but his attempt was cleverly parried by his companion's response of *nondum* ('not yet!'). The account of this exchange would inevitably have added fuel to the rumours. Of course it may never have taken place, especially since there were no witnesses (*nullo audiente*). The only source could have been Crispus himself, who might have gilded the lily to make himself look clever. If it did in fact happen, it might betray nothing more than two individuals trying to be outrageous and witty, rather than formally baring their souls with confessions of past (or future) sexual misbehaviour.[50] Another serious problem is that no charge of incest is made against Caligula by either Seneca or Philo, both of whom are viciously hostile towards him and especially offended by his immorality, and had the advantage of being contemporaries in contact with close court circles. By inference, it can also be safely assumed that this particular charge was not mentioned in the lost chapters of Tacitus' *Annals*.[51] In dealing with the later issue of the incestuous advances that Agrippina supposedly made on her son Nero (see p. 182), Tacitus makes no reference to any similar conduct between Agrippina and her brother. This is an argument *ex silentio*, of course, although in this instance a powerful one. The historian does claim that her incestuous behaviour in AD 59 could be blamed on a similar 'lifestyle' in her earlier years, but attributes the corruption to her affairs with her brother-in-law Lepidus and freedman Pallas. In fact, as her ultimate act of moral degradation, he cites her marriage to a paternal uncle (Claudius). Thus this first juicy anecdote about Agrippina's sexual proclivities must be deemed unproven and improbable.

The honours heaped on Agrippina and her sisters seem to stand in contrast to the treatment of their husbands, whose careers were not promoted to the extent that might have been expected. Domitius fades from the picture after 37 until his death in 40. Although he survived the Albucilla affair and was not considered dangerous, he was probably regarded with a degree of suspicion. Nor is there any hint that Agrippina made any further effort to promote her husband's prospects. Livilla's husband, Marcus Vinicius, is not heard from until the end of Caligula's reign, when his interest in the succession suggests that Caligula might have been prudent not to have advanced him earlier. Drusilla was married to the insipid Lucius Cassius Longinus, until she was relieved of him to marry her brother's favourite, Marcus Lepidus.

Two events are recorded for Agrippina during the remainder of AD 37. The Temple of Divus Augustus, decreed shortly after that emperor's death and constructed between the Capitoline and Palatine during the reign of Tiberius, was completed by Caligula and consecrated during the last two days of August, the whole occasion marked by a splendid ceremony and the issue of a commemorative coin.[52] Extravagant games were staged, which included a two-day horse-race and the slaughter of 400 bears. In the front seats Caligula was accompanied by Agrippina and her two sisters, an appropriate privilege for the recipients of the rights of the Vestal Virgins. A trivial honour, it might seem, but in the eyes of the Romans it would have conferred enormous status.[53]

The second, more significant, event occurred at the end of 37. By this time dramatic developments had occurred in Rome, though their precise details are very obscure. At some point after the end of the summer, probably in September, Caligula fell seriously ill and there were fears that he might not recover.[54] When he did, probably in October, a great change in the political atmosphere followed. Some have speculated that the illness brought on some sort of mental derangement. Another possibility is that the illness was so protracted that his entourage had to make arrangements for the smooth running of the state, and perhaps even for the grooming of a successor. Such actions might afterwards have been misunderstood or, at the very least, viewed with suspicion by Caligula. At any rate, the festive aura of the accession had clearly evaporated.

The first important result of the change seems to have been the death of Tiberius Gemellus, adopted as Caligula's son on his accession. Late in 37 the charge was made that Gemellus had planned for Caligula's death and had tried to benefit from his illness. Soldiers were sent to force him to take his own life. Philo, a source sympathetic to Gemellus, makes the chilling observation that many approved the forced suicide as an act of political expediency, since the stability of the state would suffer if there were two perceived rivals for power (a similar argument will be used to defend Nero's supposed murder of his stepbrother Britannicus). Gemellus' death seems to have been followed closely by that of Caligula's father-in-law Marcus Junius Silanus (his daughter, Caligula's first wife, had died some three years previously). Silanus was apparently tried before the senate (the charges are not clear), and cut his own throat with his razor.[55] It may have been a heightened concern about his security that prompted Caligula to give serious thought to the issue of his own succession. At any rate, some time before the end of the year he was married again, this time to Livia Orestilla (there is some confusion over her name). The marriage did not last long; she may have been put aside for failing to become pregnant.[56]

In this heavy atmosphere of political trials and imperial marriages Agrippina, on 15 December, gave birth to a son, Lucius Domitius Ahenobarbus, known more familiarly by his later name, Nero (on the date, see Appendix III). The birth occurred nine years after the marriage, a considerable delay, given the traditional attitude of the Roman aristocracy towards the merits of producing offspring quickly. The pregnancy clearly began soon after the death of Tiberius, and might have been planned – the Domitii had a tradition of only sons, which enabled a concentration of property (the Romans did not follow the principle of primogeniture in inheritances).[57] At the time of delivery Agrippina was in the imperial villa at Antium (Anzio), the fashionable coastal resort to the south of Rome. Augustus was very fond of the place, and it was to Antium that in about 3 BC a deputation from the senate travelled to offer him the title of *pater patriae* ('father of the nation'). On the coast beyond the west pier the remains of an imperial villa, known as the 'Villa Neroniana', are still visible, with structures dating from the second century BC to the third century AD. The villa faced the sea and had terraces, covered galleries, and an open-air bay with seating (*exedra*), surrounded by a colonnade. There was also a theatre, built on an artificial terrace. Erosion from the sea has destroyed much of the later structure, and the famous World War II campaign added to the damage; consequently our knowledge of this part of the villa is to some extent based on seventeenth-century illustrations. Also, to the east of the pier well-preserved floors have survived, similarly belonging to the structure's earliest phases. Coarelli speculates that Augustus had inherited the villa from his great-grandfather and had initiated considerable rebuilding. Later phases can be attributed to Nero, Domitian, Hadrian and Septimius Severus.[58] Agrippina had clearly decided to stay in this splendid setting during her confinement. Ironically, it was almost certainly from this same villa that she set out on her final journey, to die in 59 on the orders of the son she was carrying in 37.

Nero's birth was attended by a favourable omen. Just before dawn, and before he came into contact with the earth (he would have been placed at his father's feet for formal acknowledgement), he was touched by the rays of the sun. This happy sign was countered by the date, time and manner of his birth, however, since a number of people determined that his horoscope was very unfavourable. One of the astrologers, possibly the son of the famous Thrasyllus who had such influence on Tiberius, supposedly forecast that he would rule but would murder his mother, eliciting from Agrippina the celebrated response: 'Let him kill me, only let him rule!' (*occidat dum imperet*). The incident may not be true, but is a vivid illustration of the courage that the tradition attributed to her.[59] The birth was very difficult. It involved a breech delivery, a very dangerous and painful procedure in antiquity. Apart from the pain, a breech birth was, unlike the rays of the sun, distinctly ill-omened, and Pliny the Elder remarks that Agrippina's grandfather Agrippa was the only known case of someone born feet first who turned out later to be a success in life. Agrippina found the experience so traumatic that she saw fit to record it in her memoirs.[60] Although she had two husbands after Domitius, she produced no more children, possibly unwilling to repeat the agony that she suffered with Nero.

Eight days after the birth a *lustratio* was carried out in the presence of close relatives, a traditional ceremony where sacrifices were performed and infants given names. The occasion provides us with the only clue about the state of Agrippina's married life. When being congratulated by his friends, Domitius, who was supposedly able to predict his son's depravity from his own and Agrippina's character, is quoted as insisting that whatever was born of him and Agrippina would be bound to be loathsome and a public disaster (*detestabile et publico malo*).[61] The story cannot be dismissed, but it is distinctly implausible - whatever his attitude towards Agrippina, Domitius would have been unlikely to make such a denigrating remark about his first-born son (if intended seriously). A second incident is reported from the same ceremony. Agrippina asked her brother to suggest a name for the child. Caligula offered 'Claudius', supposedly looking at his uncle at the time and intending his remark as a joke. We are told that Agrippina was offended by the suggestion, given that their uncle was considered a laughing-stock. It is difficult to know what to make of this anecdote, which may have been invented at a later period when Caligula had fallen out with Agrippina. Claudius' praenomen was 'Tiberius' and 'Claudius', the nomen of the Claudian tribe, if adopted as a praenomen would have been a distinguished one and not inappropriate for a boy whose lineage was partly Claudian. In any case, Caligula treated his uncle with respect in the first year of his reign and his relations with his sister seem to have been totally harmonious at this period. If Caligula did indeed suggest 'Claudius' it might have been intended as a sincere offer, perhaps declined by Agrippina because the name might somehow overshadow Nero's Julian bloodline. It would certainly be unwarranted to use it as a proof of a rift in the family harmony, or as the first stage of the dynastic strife that would divide Caligula from his sisters.[62]

The historical record is totally silent on the activities of Agrippina for AD 38, although events were set in motion that were to affect her greatly. The year had a colourful start, when on 1 January a deranged slave called Machaon climbed onto the couch in the Temple of Jupiter Capitolinus, made some fiery predictions, then killed a puppy and himself. The first major political event to be recorded was the fall of Macro, Sejanus' replacement as prefect of the praetorian guard. The sources provide little information on how he was brought down (as the man who engineered Sejanus' fall, he would presumably have taken every possible precaution) or why Caligula should have decided to rid himself of someone who had played a key role in his accession. It may well be that Macro had been somehow involved in the negotiations with Gemellus and Silanus, and that his removal was delayed because it would require long and careful planning.[63] The other noteworthy death of the year had no overt political implication. On 10 June Agrippina's sister Drusilla died. Their brother Caligula was overwhelmed by the loss and heaped special honours upon her, one of which broke new ground. On 23 September (significantly the birthday of Augustus) Drusilla was consecrated as a goddess. A gold effigy was designed for the senate-house, as well as one to stand alongside Venus in that goddess' temple in the Forum. Her worship was to be overseen by a college of twenty priests, both male and female.[64] These honours were certainly generous, and unprecedented for a woman, but they are not the great violation of Roman tradition that is sometimes claimed. The worship of the imperial family, even during their lifetimes, was widespread outside Italy, and perhaps within Italy. In Rome Tiberius blocked the deification of Livia after her death, but the very fact of the prohibition suggests that the issue must have been taken seriously. In the end Livia was deified, by Claudius in 42, and Nero went on to bestow the same honours on Claudia and Poppaea, his daughter and second wife.[65] The combination of both men and women in the priesthood also had its precedents – Livia had been a priestess of Augustus under Tiberius, as had

Antonia under Caligula. Nevertheless the official worship of Drusilla *in Rome* did mark another stage in the gradual elevation of the imperial women to a status ever closer to that of the male members of the ruling family.

Drusilla had been married in 33 to the nonentity Lucius Cassius Longinus. The marriage did not last. They were divorced, and she next married Marcus Aemilius Lepidus (Stemma II). This man was to play an important role in the story of Agrippina and precise information on him would be most welcome. Unfortunately, his background is unclear, except that he was a member of the Aemilii Lepidi, one of a group of powerful noble families whose ambitions were generally kept in check by marriages with members of the imperial family (see family tree, Appendix IV). An Aemilius Paullus, for instance, had married Julia the Younger. Marcus Lepidus thus would already have had connections with the palace before his marriage to Drusilla, and would clearly have seemed marked for a promising future. Caligula did nothing to dispel this impression. Lepidus was given the right to stand for office five years before the legal age, and Dio even claims that he was publicly identified by Caligula as his successor. It is not clear what is meant by Dio's assertion, which might have been based on the acceleration of Lepidus' career, and the issue is confused by Suetonius' testimony that during his illness Caligula designated *Drusilla* as heir both to his worldly goods and to his domain (*bonorum atque imperii*). Unless Caligula was delirious at the time, the second claim is implausible. There is the technical problem that the succession could not properly be bequeathed in a will, but there is a second, more serious, difficulty. Romans had grown accustomed to the notion of powerful women in the imperial court, but they were not yet ready for a female princeps, and if Caligula's intention had been to weaken Gemellus' prospects he would presumably have nominated a male heir. Dio's claim that Lepidus was intended as Caligula's successor is more feasible. In any case there can be no doubt of Lepidus' privileged position. He was on intimate personal terms with the emperor, so intimate that the inevitable lewd stories were told about them.[66] A statue of Lepidus was even located in the imperial *sebasteion* at Aphrodisias (see p. 215), part of a group that included statues for Germanicus and Agrippina the Elder. He is, in fact, the only husband of an imperial princess to attract any attention, however garbled, from the sources during Caligula's lifetime and the only one even mentioned in Suetonius' *Life of Caligula.*[67]

The death of Drusilla does not seem to have placed any strain on the close relations between Caligula and Lepidus, who remained in the city after his wife's death and delivered the funeral eulogy. He still carried weight with the emperor several months after the death and in October 38 was influential enough to intervene in the case of Avillius Flaccus, the incompetent governor of Egypt, during whose term Alexandria had been rocked by bloody clashes between its Greek and Jewish population. Flaccus was condemned to death, but the penalty was overturned, and he was instead sent into a comfortable exile. If Lepidus continued to entertain hopes for the succession, his prospects would clearly have diminished later in the year, when Caligula decided to remarry. The new imperial wife, Lollia Paulina, who would eventually fall victim to Agrippina, was a noted beauty and a woman of considerable wealth. The elder Pliny reports seeing her at a dinner party bedecked with emeralds and pearls, some 40 million HS worth. In case anyone had the poor taste to be unconvinced of their value, she

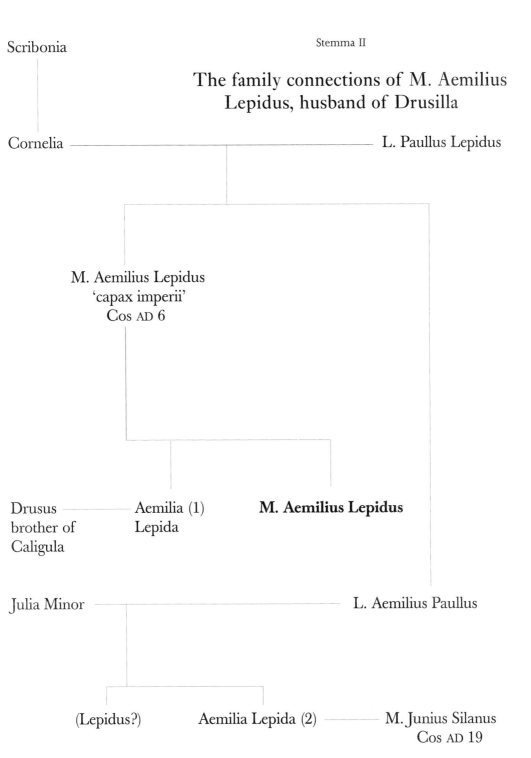

Scribonia

The family connections of M. Aemilius
Lepidus, husband of Drusilla

Cornelia ———————————————————————— L. Paullus Lepidus

M. Aemilius Lepidus
'capax imperii'
Cos AD 6

Drusus ————— Aemilia (1)   **M. Aemilius Lepidus**
brother of   Lepida
Caligula

Julia Minor ————————————————————— L. Aemilius Paullus

(Lepidus?) ———— Aemilia Lepida (2) ——— M. Junius Silanus
                                        Cos AD 19

carried the bills of sale on her person and readily produced them. This new setback to Lepidus' hopes was short-lived, the marriage barely lasted longer than Caligula's previous effort.[68]

The year 39 is an important one in the story of Agrippina since it is the first where her active participation in Roman political life can be clearly identified. Unfortunately, it is also one of the most confused periods of the Julio-Claudian era. What is beyond doubt is that in 39 the tension between the emperor and senate developed into a sort of open warfare. *Maiestas* trials, abolished during the early period of goodwill, were reintroduced. The situation was clearly much more serious than it had been in 37, when central figures like Gemellus or Macro were eliminated. In 39 the unrest seems to have spread more widely. Caligula's tactic was to inspire a collective fear in the senate, in the reasonable hope that from an instinct for self-preservation the members would denounce their fellows. Dio follows the confrontation with the famous incident at the Bay of Naples, where Caligula built a massive bridge of boats and rode a chariot from one side to the other. The purpose of this bizarre incident may have been in part to put on a massive and extravagant show of force, simply to rub the noses of his enemies in his awesome power.

Another important event of the same year, probably belonging to the spring, was a personal one. Caligula married, for the fourth and final time. He rid himself of Lollia, possibly on the grounds that she was barren.[69] His next wife, Milonia Caesonia, was neither beautiful nor young, and had a reputation for high living and low morals. She seems to have been born about AD 5 and was thus about seven years older than her husband. She had already borne three daughters before the marriage (a good sign of fertility) and was far pregnant with her fourth, Julia Drusilla, when she married the emperor. Caligula was devoted to the child, and even quipped that the precocious savagery she displayed in attacking her little friends was absolute proof of his paternity.[70]

At the political level, life was not so harmonious. In September Caligula removed the two consuls from office (one of them committed suicide), and followed this with a wave of arrests.[71] His major anxiety would, of course, have been over the loyalty of the powerful provincial legates, who had legions under their command. It was probably in 39 that Lucius Vitellius, the highly successful governor of Syria, a man in command of four legions, was replaced. Vitellius (later a very close ally of Agrippina) was not in disgrace, perhaps not even under suspicion, but Caligula may have wanted to prevent him from becoming too popular. Calvisius Sabinus, governor of Pannonia, was not thought so innocent. Although he commanded only two legions in Pannonia, their proximity to Italy made him potentially dangerous. Accused of *maiestas* after the fall of Sejanus in 31, he had emerged unscathed. This time he was not so lucky. On his return to Rome in 39 he was charged, along with his wife Cornelia. The precise details are lost, but Cornelia was accused of having 'gone the rounds' of the sentries dressed as a soldier and of having 'watched the soldiers on manoeuvres' – the kind of behaviour, as has been seen so often, that caused the Romans deep unease. In the great tradition of high-profile Roman political trials, treason and sex always seemed to go together. Cornelia supposedly favoured the guards while on her rounds, and was caught in the heat of passion in the headquarters building. Cornelia and Sabinus recognized the inevitable and committed suicide.[72]

Potentially the most serious threat to any emperor came from the Roman presence in Germany, home to no fewer than eight legions. This threat would in 39 involve Caligula in the most serious crisis of his reign (excluding his assassination, of course!), a crisis that would bring Agrippina onto the centre stage of political life. Command of the two military zones of Germany was in theory separate, but in actual fact was close to united in 39. The legate of Upper Germany was the same Gaetulicus who had survived the downfall of Sejanus. He had acquired his post in 29, succeeding his brother and thus acquiring troops who already felt bound to his family. Moreover, Gaetulicus' father-in-law, Lucius Apronius, was legate of Lower Germany (he had been there since AD 24) and Tacitus implies that *his* four legions were somehow under the control of his son-in-law. Gaetulicus certainly seems to have been an ambitious man, and did not scruple to play the politician. This brought its own dangers. His daughter had been betrothed to Sejanus' son, a useful connection as long as Sejanus was alive but potentially a lethal one after his fall. Gaetulicus clearly felt himself at risk. He saved himself by a deftly written letter to Tiberius, in which he declared his loyalty to the emperor, suggesting that just as Tiberius ought to retain his principate so Gaetulicus should retain his province. The thinly veiled threat had its effect, and he was allowed to remain in place.[73]

Gaetulicus unfortunately incurred the serious displeasure of Caligula, who proved more resolute than Tiberius. His fall had serious and widespread repercussions, and among those who were brought down at the same time we can include Marcus Lepidus and Agrippina. The precise connection between the various parties involved is murky indeed, and one of the great mysteries of Caligula's reign. It is established that some time in 39, after the beginning of September, Caligula left Rome hurriedly for the north, where he planned to carry out a campaign against Germany and Britain. By 27 October the dramatic news of a thwarted military coup had reached Rome, and the Arvals on that day recorded sacrifices *ob detecta nefaria con[silia/in C. Germani]cum Cn. Lentuli Gaet[ulici* ('to mark the exposure of the evil plots of Gnaeus Lentulus Gaetulicus against Gaius Germanicus').[74] We know little about the context or the details of Gaetulicus' downfall. Dio reports that Caligula did little of military significance against the enemy while he was in the north, but inflicted much harm on citizens and allies, and put many individuals to death on the pretence of rebellions and plots but in reality because they were rich. Dio declares that he will thoughtfully spare the reader the tedium of reading the victims' names (!) and will restrict himself to noting prominent individuals. At the top of his list is Gaetulicus. Suetonius in the *Life of Caligula* says nothing about Gaetulicus other than that he wrote some flattering verses about the emperor. In the *Life of Galba* he merely notes that Gaetulicus was Galba's predecessor in the German command, and had been casual in imposing discipline.[75]

It may be that Gaetulicus' removal was essentially a non-political event, decided on the simple grounds of incompetence. He does seem to have been a lax commander, and his unwillingness to impose strict discipline was notorious.[76] The need for a firm commander, of the stature of Galba, was clearly imperative, especially in view of the planned invasion of Britain, not a feasible project until the Rhine frontier was secure, yet Gaetulicus would not have been an easy man to dislodge. He had cultivated the popularity of the troops in his four legions, and his influence extended over the four legions of the lower Rhine as well, in addition to the two new legions currently being raised in

Germany for the British expedition. Moreover, he had shown after the fall of Sejanus that he was not the kind of individual who would willingly give up his authority. The most expeditious course for the emperor might have been to fabricate a claim of rebellion and to use that to engineer his forced removal.[77]

While mere incompetence could have been a contributory factor in Gaetulicus' fall, it can hardly be the full explanation. Some have seen Gaetulicus as a participant in a general conspiracy, as a member of the old Sejanus party or as one of the pro-Gemellus group.[78] But there is no hint of an involvement in any broad political movement in Rome, or even that such a movement in fact existed. Another possibility is that he had forged ties with specific individuals – Sabinus, governor of Pannonia, is one possibility, and it has been argued that Sabinus' wife Cornelia may have been Cornelia Gaetulica, sister of Gaetulicus.[79] This is a rather tenuous link on which to base the idea of a conspiracy, but we cannot rule out the possibility that the trial of Sabinus might have alerted opponents of Caligula to the need to take quick and decisive action. At the very least, Sabinus' fall would have served to put the politically astute Gaetulicus on his guard. Two names are specifically linked to Gaetulicus' downfall. One is Lucilius Junior, the friend of the writer Seneca. He was a self-made man, born in humble circumstances, who rose to equestrian rank and became an elegant writer. Seneca dedicated his *Quaestiones Naturales* to him and praised Lucilius' courage in adversity, implying that he was at the very least threatened with torture, if not actually tortured, but that throughout the ordeal he stood true to his friendship with Gaetulicus and could not be persuaded by Caligula to betray his loyalty. Unfortunately we have no further information on Lucilius' part in the affair. He did at one time govern (as procurator) a section of the mountainous area between Gaul and Italy, and in any kind of military action directed from the north would have played a key role in guarding the Little and Great Bernard Passes. If he had been a personal friend of Gaetulicus he might have been an object of suspicion by Caligula and have been pressured into denouncing him which, as a man of principle, he apparently refused to do. The very fact that there seems to have been some sort of enquiry implies very strongly that something more serious than Gaetulicus' incompetence was involved.[80]

The second name is even more intriguing. If Gaetulicus had planned to move his army against Caligula it would clearly have been prudent for him to link up with an ally in Rome, one who had some family and social standing. There are grounds for thinking that he might have made just such a contact since the second individual associated with Gaetulicus was no less than Caligula's brother-in-law, Marcus Lepidus. As examples of the prominent individuals put to death, Dio lists Lepidus second, immediately after Gaetulicus. He admittedly does not specifically claim that the two men were involved *together*. The connection between the two is made explicit only by Suetonius in the *Life of Claudius* (but not in the *Life of Caligula*), where he records that Claudius was sent to Germany to congratulate Caligula on the exposure of the *Lepidi et Gaetulici coniuratio* ('the conspiracy of Lepidus and Gaetulicus').[81]

The general uncertainty about the exact nature of the plots against Caligula in late 39 makes the reconstruction of the events of that year especially difficult. Caligula left Rome in September, accompanied by a unit of praetorians and a motley collection of actors, gladiators and women. He stopped first at Mevania, a beauty spot favoured by prosperous villa-owners on the river Clitumnus, about 150km (100 miles) from Rome, probably in the villa that Agrippina possessed there (Phlegon confirms the existence of an estate of Agrippina at Mevania, and the presence of a hermaphrodite there in 53!).[82] There he joined Lepidus, Agrippina and Livilla, unless they had already set out with him from Rome. It is likely that he stayed for a time, protected by the praetorians from potential enemies both in Rome and in the Rhine armies, while he put his counterplans into operation. Agents, probably including Galba, the next commander of the Rhine armies, were despatched to Germany to remove Gaetulicus and to prepare the way for the arrival of the emperor. Caligula's investigations might well have revealed some disturbing information since he apparently began to fear for his personal security, to judge from the prophecy delivered by the famous oracle at Mevania, which supposedly advised him to increase his German bodyguard.

The plot now grows thicker. Lepidus, it emerged, had been playing a dangerous sexual game, carrying on an affair with *both* of his late wife's sisters, Agrippina and Livilla. Lepidus thus joins the list of Agrippina's many recorded lovers. The revelation seems to have come at Mevania and from there a bill of accusation was rushed to the senate in Rome, where an enquiry into their conduct was held. Caligula provided a lengthy indictment of immoral behaviour on the part of Lepidus and his two mistresses and made public a collection of letters, obtained surreptitiously, purporting to prove the adultery. There was a further bombshell. The emperor then explicitly charged all three with conspiracy, through being party to the plots hatched against him. Political scandals involving the imperial family were often concealed, as has already been noted, under the pretence of sexual adventures. The aim is clear – to conceal what might have been serious political activities with charges that trivialize the political motives of the conspirators and make them seem simply depraved, degenerate and perhaps slightly ridiculous. In this case, the claim of sexual misconduct, based on the evidence of letters between Lepidus and the sisters, might at first sight provoke scepticism. In the absence of the actual documents, we do not know if the proof of misbehaviour was explicit or inferred and it seems unlikely that these highly sophisticated individuals would have been so foolish as to leave such damning evidence lying about. But the charge of moral misdemeanours is supported by the other literary sources. Tacitus, it has been noted, saw the affair between Agrippina and Lepidus as the beginning of her moral corruption and the tradition is still found in the early fifth century, when the poet Namatianus tells how Lepidus' ambition drove him into adultery.[83]

It should also be noted that on this occasion the claim of sexual misdeeds was not intended as a diversion, to cloak more sinister activities. Unusually for a case that went right to the heart of the imperial family, Caligula made no secret of the political crimes of the accused. Lepidus' game is not easy to define. Links between him and an embryonic opposition to Caligula have been suggested, a group that might have included the dismissed consuls of 39.[84] But there is scant evidence that Lepidus had broad political ties. He had evidently been willing to intercede on behalf of Flaccus, the former prefect of Egypt, and have his sentence reduced, but the nature of their friendship is unknown to us. The only other hint of political alliance comes to light at the end of Caligula's reign. Lucius Annius Vinicianus, a relative, possibly a nephew, of Livilla's husband Vinicius, was one of the more prominent conspirators involved in the final move against

Caligula. According to Josephus, he bore a grudge against Caligula in part because of his old friendship with Lepidus and a desire to avenge the latter's death. He also supposedly recognized that the friendship could make him a potential target. But we must be cautious about such claims. Several highly favoured Romans tried, after Caligula's death, to excuse their collaboration with the regime by pretending that they had, in fact, been in imminent danger of execution. Vinicianus was among those who did well under Caligula. He had been co-opted into the Arval Brotherhood and received a consulship. He might therefore have later exaggerated his closeness to Lepidus, one of Caligula's most prominent victims, to preserve his own reputation in the early years of Claudius' reign.

Lepidus had clearly been Caligula's favourite. He was an unlikely individual to turn against the emperor on grounds of principle, and adherents of any planned rebellion could hardly have been expected to place much confidence in the depth of his commitment. It is far more likely that any part he played in the opposition resulted from personal and private ambitions. Caligula's marriage to Caesonia could have been the trigger.[85] Lepidus might still have entertained hopes for himself even after Drusilla's death, and his influence in the issue of Flaccus' sentence suggests that he still commanded considerable affection from the emperor. Caligula's serious illness might have led to expectations that the emperor, although still young, had not long for this world, and he still had not produced a surviving legitimate child. Lepidus' prospects would clearly be much strengthened by a renewed tie to the imperial family, and he might well have set his sights on one of Caligula's surviving sisters. Of the two, Agrippina, who had borne a son, would have seemed to offer the better prospect.

Thus Lepidus had motives for a liaison beyond simple sexual pleasure – he needed a princess of the Julian house if he was to have a serious claim on the throne. What of Agrippina? Her husband Domitius suffered from dropsy and in 39 may well have been very ill (he died in 40). It might have seemed politically prudent for Agrippina to seek a liaison with a man of Lepidus' eminence, perhaps with the ultimate intention of marriage. As Griffin puts it, 'Even if we assume her too hard-headed for emotional indulgence, practical considerations might tempt her to a liaison with the heir apparent; there was the future of her son to be secured.'[86] Agrippina's son Nero was born in AD 37. In the absence of any son of Caligula, Nero's prospects were excellent, given his mother's family prominence and imperial connections. The death of Drusilla without issue would clearly strengthen his claim. It might at first sight seem that Nero's prospects were neither particularly strengthened nor weakened by his mother's association with Lepidus, who would be thought a useful ally only while Caligula was alive and he was the emperor's favourite. That he might have been hand-picked by the emperor as his successor would hardly have been a recommendation if a new regime was to be installed after that same emperor had been deposed. But our reservations about Lepidus surely reflect the loss of the source material for the period. If Agrippina had sought a lover for political ends, it must have seemed that Lepidus was the best candidate. He presumably had qualities that we can not appreciate. Tacitus would almost certainly have had something to say about them in the missing books of the *Annals*. Certainly, in the later extant narrative he implies that Lepidus brought advantages to Agrippina in AD 39, and asserts that she became sexually involved with him *spe dominationis* ('through her ambition for power'). In this matter, her conduct would be consistent with her later image, since she acquired the reputation of using sex, like money, as a tool for political ends.[87]

Caligula's marriage to Caesonia would have represented a serious setback to the ambitions both of Lepidus and Agrippina. Caesonia came from a highly fertile family. Her mother, the frequently married Vistilia, had borne at least seven children, a fact recorded by Pliny the Elder in his *Natural History*, because of her unusual gestation periods.[88] Caesonia had herself borne three children before her marriage to Caligula and was already pregnant before their wedding. In addition, Lepidus might have seen signs that his influence had begun to wane in the ultimate fate of Flaccus. Philo claims that Caligula came to regret his decision to remit Flaccus' death sentence and despatched assassins to his exile home of Andros. A grim manhunt followed. They tracked down their quarry to the interior of the island, then stabbed and clubbed him to death. His body was thrown into a shallow pit. His ties to Lepidus clearly did him little good in the end.[89]

The motives and activities of Lepidus and Agrippina are problematic enough when considered in isolation. They become more complex when others enter the equation. First, Gaetulicus. Agrippina later in her career demonstrates a keen appreciation of the value of military support in any political initiative. She might, on this occasion, have seen in Gaetulicus the best hope for a military power-base; her own links with Germany both through her father and through the circumstances of her own birth would have helped.[90] Then there are the supporters of Agrippina (and Livilla) in the senate. We have no specific names, but it is recorded that in the latter part of 39 many Romans were tried because of their sympathy for the two sisters, even men at the rank of aedile and praetor.[91] This development implies considerable sympathy for Agrippina among the senators, whose motive might have been simple self-preservation. Caligula had earlier given clear evidence of his vindictiveness and many may have felt that they had nothing to lose by switching allegiance. The existence of such supporters, again, is not surprising when seen in the context of the tactics that Agrippina demonstrated later in her career, when any political action she undertook was preceded by a careful preparation of allies in the senatorial ranks.

Probably the most curious aspect of this whole confused affair is the charge that Lepidus was supposedly plotting with, and having affairs with, *both sisters at the same time*. Lepidus, it might be argued, was hedging his bets – and was not very discreet about it if he was writing to, as well as sleeping with, both women. But the thinking of the sisters is more baffling. Both had a great deal to lose, and they must have had powerful motives for undertaking a highly risky course of action that might and, as events show, in fact did lead to death and exile. One of them could possibly have hoped to occupy a position of quasi-imperatrix in any political realignment; they can hardly both have hoped to do so. If Lepidus did manage to succeed and marry Agrippina, Livilla would be left out and her privileges and status would hardly have been improved (and the converse would have been true had he married Livilla). In fact all three had benefited enormously from Caligula's accession. With the death of Drusilla they were to all appearances the most favoured and privileged individuals in Rome. The notion of the double sexual liaison seems to be the kind of recurrent theme the historical tradition loves (both Tigellinus and Seneca were similarly accused of having affairs with *both* sisters) but at the very least the close relationship probably reflects collaborative political activity and we must ask if there could have been circumstances under which the death of Caligula could have suited the purpose of all three individuals – Lepidus, and Agrippina, and Livilla.

The answer may be found in the general events of AD 39. The sources for that year are highly confused but it is clear that by now the tensions between Caligula and the senators and, more important, the army commanders had reached a crisis. No ruler could alienate both groups, as he would eventually discover to his cost. It might be an overstatement to claim that in 39 Caligula was conducting a purge of military commanders, but to any observer it must have been apparent that his cavalier attitude towards the powerful and prestigious had set him on a course of ruin. When he was assassinated in 41 it was seriously hoped that his regime would be followed not by another Julian emperor but by the restoration of the old republic – only the timely intervention of the praetorian guard and the disorganization of the senators prevented that from happening. But there would have been some who in 39 might have felt that the end of the imperial system would not be in their interest, and would have been chagrined to realize that such an end could be the inevitable and speedy result of Caligula's behaviour. His two sisters, and probably Lepidus, might have been of that number and this consideration seems the only one that could have made the removal of Caligula in favour of another claimant from, or linked to, the line of Augustus and Germanicus, in the interest of both sisters. Such considerations might have led to precautionary exchanges about the future in the event that Caligula should leave the scene. The crackdown reported among high officials sympathetic to Agrippina in Rome after the disclosure of the plot suggests that she, or more strictly her son Nero, could count on considerable support to fill the gap. Livilla's interest, then, might not necessarily have been the anticipation of power but rather the desire to avoid the destruction of the principate with the subsequent loss of her own privileges and favours, or perhaps an even worse fate should Caligula continue to reign and alienate supporters not only of himself but even of the institution itself. The Roman constitution did not possess a simple and painless mechanism for dislodging a princeps, and forcible removal of the incumbent was the only real option open to those seeking change.

Whatever the motives of the conspirators, the outcome of their trial could hardly have been in doubt. When the senate had reached its predictable verdict Lepidus was condemned to death, and his throat was cut by a praetorian tribune.[92] Agrippina's punishment was less final, but no less dramatic. In a cruel parody of the return of her mother from Syria with Germanicus' remains, she was forced to carry the urn containing the bones of Lepidus back from Mevania to Rome. It is in this bizarre and humiliating posture that she makes her first vivid entry onto the stage of Roman history. She was in all likelihood accompanied by three daggers, which Caligula sent to the city for deposit in the Temple of Mars Ultor, to symbolize the three daggers designed to take his life. The deposit of these weapons suggests that the emperor felt that the threat on his life had been a serious one. It finds a later echo when Nero, after the conspiracy of 65, dedicated the dagger of the would-be assassin Scaevinus in the Temple of Jupiter on the Capitol. The senate seems to have been willing to play along with this charade.

On Agrippina's arrival no less an individual than the future emperor, Vespasian, later to emerge as a man of solid good sense but at that time a praetor with his future to make, proposed a motion that the bones of the conspirators be cast out unburied. He further ingratiated himself by asking the senate, probably on a later occasion, for special games for Caligula's victories in Germany, topping it all off with special thanks to the emperor for a personal invitation to dinner. Vespasian would live to regret his behaviour. It is probably from this date that Agrippina began to nurse a hatred towards him, which may have contributed to his semi-retirement during the period of her ascendancy.[93]

Caligula's northern journey took him to Gaul, where he auctioned off the possessions of his two sisters, including their slaves and freedmen. A consummate salesman, he exploited the social pretensions of the locals and the cachet of any item connected to the imperial house. He arranged for goods to be transported north from the old Palatine residence. It was no minor production. Suetonius says that Caligula commandeered so many wagons for the task that the bread supply was interrupted through the strain on transportation. The usual allowance for exaggeration must be made but a sale of mammoth proportions seems to lie behind the story.[94]

It is interesting that two other men who fell under suspicion in 39 were both linked sexually with Agrippina. One has already been recorded – Ofonius Tigellinus, a man later to surpass Sejanus' reputation for evil, as Nero's praetorian prefect. Supposedly, like Lepidus, he was banished on a charge of adultery with both sisters (p. 49). It is very difficult to evaluate the significance of Tigellinus' role and any connection with a putative conspiracy. The picture is further confused by the claim in the scholiast that he also had affairs with Vinicius and Domitius, husbands of Livilla and Agrippina. This persistent theme of the double adulterous affair casts some doubt on the supposedly similar conduct of Lepidus.[95]

The second individual is already familiar as an important literary source for the period, and from now on will become one of the key participants in the story of Agrippina: the philosopher, statesman and writer, Lucius Annaeus Seneca. Like Lepidus and Tigellinus, he will come to be accused of improper sexual relations with *both* sisters. Seneca's sex life is a matter for speculation, but there can be little doubt that his and Agrippina's career were closely interconnected.

Although a prolific author, Seneca provides relatively little autobiographical information in his works and, despite his later fame, there is considerable uncertainty about his early life. His father (Seneca the Elder) was a celebrated teacher of rhetoric in their home town of Cordoba in southern Spain, and also won considerable fame in Rome for history and oratory. Seneca the Younger's birth-date is unknown, but from scattered comments in his works it should probably be placed in the final years of the first century BC. As a young man, he would inevitably have received a traditional training in rhetoric but an early inclination towards philosophy was discouraged by his father, possibly because he thought that it would be a hindrance to his son's political career. He spent some time in Egypt, where his uncle was prefect, then after 31 accompanied his widowed aunt to Rome, where he obtained the quaestorship.[96] At this time he might have made the acquaintance of the wealthy and influential Passienus Crispus (husband of Domitia and later to be husband of Agrippina, see p. 84), with whom his father had close personal connections.[97] He still had not obtained a praetorship by 39 but, while his political career might have been less than distinguished, his literary reputation grew and by Caligula's day he had become the most fashionable writer in Rome. He was married by 41 (he lost a son in that year), but his marital status in 39 cannot be determined.[98]

Under the year 39 Dio cites two examples of orators whose eloquence aroused the envy of Caligula and who were lucky to escape with their lives. The first was the brilliant and versatile Domitius Afer, who reputedly saved his skin by declaring himself overcome by Caligula's brilliance and by diplomatically announcing that he feared him more as speaker than as emperor. Far from being punished, Afer was appointed consul later the same year. The second orator was Seneca, who made the mistake of pleading a case well in the senate while the emperor was present. Supposedly in a fit of jealousy, Caligula ordered him put to death but rescinded the instruction when what Dio calls a 'female acquaintance' of Seneca intervened with a logical argument for clemency. She pointed out that he was seriously consumptive and would probably die soon in any event, and thus save the emperor the unpleasantness of having to arrange his elimination.

Why should Caligula have been hostile towards Seneca? There is some evidence that Caligula, a would-be scholar himself, was irritated by the other's current popularity. He disparagingly categorized him as 'sand without lime' and dismissed his works as mere *commissiones* (something like 'light entertainment'). But these attacks may not be too significant; Caligula is also recorded as making abusive comments about Homer, as well as claiming that the poet Vergil had no talent and that Livy was a shoddy historian. He clearly aspired to be something of an *enfant terrible* in matters of literary taste. In any case, a dislike of Seneca's literary style can hardly be considered seriously as the grounds for a sentence of death, even under Caligula.[99] Inevitably we look for a political dimension to Seneca's career, hinted at by the possible involvement of his close friend Lucilius with Gaetulicus. To throw further light on this issue we must jump ahead a little. In 41, after the murder of Caligula and the accession of Claudius, Seneca was exiled on the grounds of sexual misconduct with Agrippina's sister, Livilla. He was recalled in 49 through the intercession of Agrippina, who considered him bound to her as an ally *memoria beneficii* ('through the memory of her act of kindness'). Later (in 58) he would be accused of having been Agrippina's lover.

There has long been a suspicion that Seneca's punishment under Claudius in 41 should be linked to events of 39, and that he was involved on that earlier occasion in some sort of political intrigue with the two sisters. Certainly it seems clear by the blunt way Tacitus introduces him in 49 (when relating his recall from exile) that the historian had already dealt with Seneca in some detail in the books of the *Annals* now missing, and had presumably given the grounds for the presumption of Agrippina in 49 that she could have complete faith in his loyalty. Dio's account of Seneca's near-escape in 39 is not placed within the events of the conspiracy of that year, but Dio's narrative sequence of this period is hopelessly confused and he probably wished to associate Seneca's fate with that of Afer, the other disgraced orator, by describing the two in the same context. It has even been argued that the mysterious female friend of 39 might have been none other than Agrippina, and that the favour later binding Seneca to her dates from this earlier intervention. But why Dio would have chosen not to name her is unclear. His source might have been someone favourable to Seneca, such as the historian Fabius Rusticus (p. 201), who might have wanted to avoid mentioning items that lent weight to the stories of Seneca's supposed sexual liaison with her. Why in that case refer to the mystery woman at all? Of course, it must also be considered possible that the incident of Seneca's narrow escape from Caligula never actually took place and was his own later confection to enhance his image.[100]

The link between Seneca and the conspirators remains elusive. His role would have had to be fairly minimal, given that he survived the aftermath. His *modus operandi* later in his political career seems to suggest that his style was one of compromise, diplomacy and intrigue rather than direct confrontation, and it is difficult to imagine him actively and aggressively involved in a dangerous political movement. As a friend of Livilla and Agrippina, he might have been drawn into their deliberations and even have discussed in an abstract and academic way the future nature of Rome's government (Agrippina later refers scornfully to him as a man of inaction, with a *professoria lingua*.) Thus, while he might have fallen under a vague suspicion, in the end it was perhaps concluded that he was not particularly dangerous.[101]

Agrippina and Livilla were both exiled to the Pontian isles; the sentence involved the loss of their property which, as indicated, was auctioned off in Gaul in the winter of 39–40.[102] The small volcanic island of Pontia lies off Cape Circe, some 110km (70 miles) west of Naples, the largest of a cluster to which it gives its name and which also includes Pandateria. The islands were rich in Homeric tradition and associated variously with the home of Circe or of the Sirens, both of whom had the reputation for luring men who should have known better to their destruction – ominous destinations for imperial women charged with sexual impropriety. Agrippina and Livilla would almost certainly have been bound for Pontia and Pandateria, the final home of their brother Nero and their mother respectively; the islands had been imperial property probably from the time of Augustus. Nero's wife Octavia eventually went to Pandateria and, in listing the victims who had preceded her, Tacitus includes Agrippina the Elder and her daughter Livilla. He does not mention Agrippina the Younger, a woman far more famous than her sister, which makes it more than likely that she did not serve her time there but went instead to the main island of Pontia.[103] During the republic there was a settlement on Pontia, of which no trace has survived, and it would almost certainly have passed from the scene by Agrippina's time. All the same, Strabo, writing in the Augustan period, describes the island as well peopled. There were at least two villas, both dating from the early Julio-Claudian period. One of them, some 40,000sq m (9.9 acres) in extent, with a fine solarium attached, was located on the promontory that faces north-east in the southern section of the island, near the natural harbour, and probably dates from the Tiberian era. Along the heights of the promontory several structures have been detected, including one described as an odeon or small theatre. At the base of the headland, facing the bay at water level, there is a system of rock-cut chambers and basins (the Grotto of Pilate), possibly rock-cut fishpools. Agrippina would have been relatively comfortable, and she would have enjoyed a large staff, as is indicated by the references to freedmen in inscriptions well into the second century.[104] Her main problem, shared by all imperial exiles, would have been boredom. The only distinctive feature of the region is described with some relish by Pliny the Elder – an exotic kind of shellfish that flourished in the Pontic waters. It stood up like a pig's leg and had a gaping toothed orifice at least 30cm (1ft) wide, hardly a substitute for the sophisticated company Agrippina would have enjoyed at the centre of things in Roman society. Perhaps most unnerving of all would have been the memory of her mother's exile, from which she had not returned, and the fear that she was destined to follow the same fate.[105]

Agrippina's husband Domitius now departs permanently from the scene. He was still in Rome in late October 39, as proved by his presence in an Arval ceremony held shortly before 27 October. We do not know if he also attended the meeting of the 27th, as the list for that day is missing. The names of the participants would in fact be of considerable interest, since that was the day when the exposure of Gaetulicus' treachery was celebrated. The Arval record of June 40 has survived and Domitius is missing from it. He might well have left Rome at the end of 39 when his wife's disgrace became public.[106] Near the end of 40 he died of dropsy in the Etruscan city of Pyrgi, and thus occupies a special place in history as the only one of Agrippina's husbands she was *not* accused of murdering (a difficult crime to commit from a distant island!).[107] The infant Nero was placed in the care of his aunt Domitia who, despite her formidable reputation, looked after him with much affection. For this Agrippina never forgave her.

Caligula remained bitter towards the two people he felt had, more than any others, betrayed his deepest trust. While he was still in the north, at Lyons, a deputation of senators led by his uncle Claudius arrived to offer him congratulations on having escaped death. They were treated with great discourtesy (there is a tradition that Claudius was pitched into the Rhône), and informed that henceforth Caligula's family (presumably his two sisters) were to receive no further honours. He constantly sent them both terrifying messages, including the witticism that he had swords as well as islands.[108]

If Caligula believed that the execution of Gaetulicus and Lepidus, and the banishment of Agrippina and Livilla, would liberate him from the danger of conspiracies, he was soon to be proved mistaken. When he returned to Rome in mid-40 his antagonism towards certain of the senators had reached new heights. There is evidence of a series of plots, culminating in the final successful one. The conspiracy that rid the world of Caligula contained all the necessary ingredients – high-minded soldiers, ambitious soldiers, high-minded senators, ambitious senators and in the shadowy background Caligula's uncle Claudius, both high-minded and ambitious, conveying an air of confusion and bemused indecision but surely more aware of what was happening than he chose to allow the historical tradition to record. In January 41, during theatrical performances on the Palatine, Caligula was trapped in an underground passage of the imperial complex and despatched by disaffected tribunes of the praetorian guard. As Dio observed, on that day Caligula finally learned that he was not a god.

5
Niece

The assassination of Caligula was the prelude to a blissful, if short-lived, period of illusion. The senators, convinced that the republic had been restored, were assembled by the consuls on the Capitol (the senate building was shunned because its name, the Curia Julia, evoked the memory of the Julian house). Here they charged Caligula with unspecified crimes, and some even demanded that they delete the legislation of the imperial period from the record and destroy the temples dedicated to the Caesars. They were brimming with confidence. They were also totally out of touch with reality. In particular, they had little sense of the mood of the people, who were less than enthusiastic about the prospect of a return to the republican system, with its privileges for the old nobility.

In essence, neither the senators nor the people would be key players in the events that rapidly unfolded. While others debated, the praetorians carried Claudius to their camp at the Viminal gate, where they acclaimed him as emperor. The senators seemed at first undaunted by the news. They were reluctantly prepared to face the inevitability that the principate would survive, but they proceeded to bicker impotently about who among them would be the best candidate to head it. One name put forward was Marcus Vinicius, husband of Livilla. Although there is no evidence of his involvement in the actual conspiracy, his emergence at this stage perhaps hints at his complicity. Another candidate was the wealthy Gaul, Valerius Asiaticus, who at a mass rally after the assassination had in effect offered his own name. He responded to popular demands for the identity of the assassin with the ambiguous assertion that he wished it were himself.[1] By next morning, however, the heady atmosphere was much evaporated and the senators' confidence had begun to ebb away. A mere 100 turned up for that day's meeting. In a sense the events of that day vindicated the Augustan system, since the hostility towards the imperial house was dwarfed by the inability of individual senators to stomach the prospects of a colleague taking over. Claudius meanwhile took the precaution of administering an oath of loyalty to the praetorians, and sweetened it with a generous donative. A senatorial deputation reached him and forthwith went over to his side. Resistance quickly collapsed. The restored republic had lasted less than twenty-four hours.

Claudius was in his 50th year when he succeeded his nephew as princeps. He was lacking in administrative training (although hardly more so than his predecessor) and until his consulship in 37 had held mainly ceremonial posts. To the literary sources his lack of experience was a minor matter. Much more serious was what was viewed as general mental incompetence. He is portrayed as an absurd figure, physically awkward, absent-minded, impractical, the constant butt of jokes, his numerous illnesses aggravated by a life of self-indulgence. Worst of all, he was someone who could be easily manipulated and deceived by cunning and deceitful freedmen and a series of wives with stronger wills than his own. 'Wholly under the control of the freedmen and wives he behaved not as a prince but as a servant,' Suetonius observed.[2]

Claudius did indeed suffer from physical infirmities. These seem to have dated back to the time of his birth, to judge from his mother Antonia's uncharitable remark that he was a monster, a *portentum hominis*, that nature had only begun but not finished off. His precise disability is uncertain but we do have details of its symptoms. He dragged his right leg, his head and hands shook slightly, and he had difficulty with speaking. But he had a good mind, as his extensive historical and literary pursuits prove. Antonia might have referred to him as a fool and Augustus seems to have felt that he might be mentally backward, but these attitudes essentially reflect an age that saw a close link between intellectual and physical abilities. His exclusion from a political career clearly had nothing to do with lack of competence and much to do with the fear that his presence on the political stage would excite ridicule.[3]

Claudius married four times, Agrippina being his last wife. Did her willingness to marry him suggest an excessive political ambition that drove her to accept a physically repulsive husband? There are no good grounds for believing this. Claudius' earlier marriages to women of distinguished families suggest that his physical shortcomings were probably much exaggerated by the sources, notwithstanding the obvious attractions of his high birth. Also, if he had been an object of such deep contempt it would have been unthinkable for the praetorians to have acclaimed him as princeps at such a critical point, without any apparent reservations.[4] Nor was he incapable of thinking for himself, as will become apparent. He rejected the suggestion of the senate that one of his wives, Messalina, receive the title of Augusta; also, despite her best efforts, his next wife Agrippina was not able to save her agent Tarquitius Priscus from condemnation.[5]

The murder of Caligula and the way Claudius attained the accession are familiar to us for their anecdotal qualities. Perhaps because we are inured to the usurpations of the later Roman empire the contemporary impact of Claudius' putsch has generally been unappreciated. It was undoubtedly less accidental than the sources tend to indicate, and he was surely to some degree at least personally responsible for the turn of events, even though there was an attempt to keep his role secret.[6] Claudius had in fact seized power by military force and throughout his reign was conscious of the danger that he could be removed in the same manner. The praetorian tribune, Chaerea, the supposed ringleader of the plot against Caligula, was put to death. At least one of the praetorian prefects had been involved (the other, totally unknown, may also have had a role). They were too dangerous to be left in office, and were dismissed, to be replaced by new men. The replacements, Rufrius Pollio and Catonius Justus, were probably not personal friends of the new emperor (Claudius' contact with the military had been minimal) and they were not destined to last beyond AD 43.[7] An aggressive military campaign in Britain was designed at least in part to establish Claudius' credentials as commander of the Roman troops.

Claudius' task in confirming his position with the military, while immediate and urgent, would prove less complex than his relationship with the senate, a problem that would not be solved until his marriage to Agrippina. The principate from the outset meant a loss of privilege and power for the senatorial order. But it was a loss in which they generally acquiesced. In the case of the accession of Tiberius and Caligula, and of

Nero later, the process by which this power was conferred by the senate on a single individual was specious if not fraudulent. In Claudius' case the offence to the body politic was much greater, since even the formality of acquiescence was absent from what was blatantly a coup d'état, carried out in an atmosphere of hostility and betrayal. Far from acclaiming the new princeps, the senators began by declaring him a *hostis*. After his accession he did not enter the senate chamber for thirty days, and when he did he was accompanied by a bodyguard.

Josephus describes Herod Agrippa as urging Claudius at the outset of his reign to be conciliatory towards the senate. The advice was sound, but not pursued systematically until Claudius' marriage to Agrippina. Until then, he had other powerful weapons to deal with a hostile and resentful body. One was to attempt to change the character of the body. Thus in 47/8 he revived the censorship after a lapse of 68 years, and held the office personally along with Lucius Vitellius. This has been seen by some as a display of antiquarianism. Far from it – the censor could control the make-up of the senate. Old senators could be removed from their places and new ones 'adlected' (added without the preliminary qualifications), while loyal senators could be appropriately rewarded (the triple consulship of Vitellius shows how).[8] Claudius also had at his disposal a much more sinister tool. Suetonius and the *Apocolocyntosis* agree in their assertion that thirty-five senators were put to death by him; they differ in the number of equestrians (Suetonius over 300, *Apocolocyntosis* 221). The names of eighteen of the senators are known, as well as the wives of two of the eighteen and five other women. Also to be taken into account are the accomplices of the rebellious provincial legate Scribonianus (see below), whose names might have been known had Tacitus' account for the year of the rebellion (AD 42) survived. It has been noted that when Claudius went to Britain to share in its conquest all those senators who accompanied him received triumphal *ornamenta*, but of the nine who are known by name no fewer than five were subsequently put to death. By contrast, in the first seventeen years of Tiberius' reign (four more than the total for Claudius) not one senator has been identified as being executed. Friction between Claudius and the equites is more difficult to explain, and might have resulted from their perception of a diminished status, as functionaries who were now obliged to take orders from freedmen.[9] In this tense and dangerous situation, we read of Claudius' wives eliminating individuals depicted by the ancient sources as their own rivals. But the emperor's wives should be seen more properly as his accomplices and allies rather than as hostile agents undermining a benign and generous regime, and Claudius should be seen as happy to use them to help secure his own ends (although in Agrippina's case, as will be shown, the claim of political murders was much exaggerated). Bauman's comment that Messalina was 'in a certain sense Claudius' Sejanus, hunting out his enemies and destroying them' is doubtless justified, and Agrippina filled a parallel, though different, role.[10]

Another difficulty that Claudius faced, one that would in time prove to be to Agrippina's advantage, was that he did not belong to the line of Augustus and could not make an exclusive claim to the principate on the basis of descent. This absence of a Julian link made him particularly sensitive to the threat posed by certain families who resented their loss of power and privilege with particular acuteness, and consequently had to be bought off through marriage to the imperial house. The Aemilii Lepidi have already been noted – but the most striking example is that of the Junii Silani, who figure largely in the story of Agrippina. Described by Syme as 'abnormally prolific and prominent' under the Julio-Claudians, this family was also excessively proud and its own distinctions, as well as its connections by marriage with the ruling family, gave its members a presumption that they had inherited a central role in Rome's governance. Tacitus refers to their *claritudo* ('splendid fame'), and observes that they had become so arrogant by 65 that a proposal was made that year in the senate that the month of June (*Junius*) be renamed because of the unfortunate associations of its current name.[11] Two branches are generally recognized: from the one, Decimus Junius Silanus was involved in the scandal of the younger Julia and barred from holding office as a result. His brother Marcus was the father-in-law of Caligula and was driven to suicide on suspicion of conspiracy. A third brother, Gaius, was relegated to an island (in 22) on charges of extortion and *maiestas* after his governorship of Asia, while Gaius' son, Gaius Appius Silanus, was put to death under Claudius, almost certainly for complicity in some form of treasonable opposition (see below). Of the other branch Marcus Junius Silanus was consul in 19 and governor of Africa, and enhanced the nobility of the family by marrying Aemilia Lepida, daughter of Julia the Younger. Together they produced three sons, Marcus, consul 46, Decimus, consul 53, and Lucius, and two daughters, Junia Lepida and Junia Calvina. All three sons would be linked with opposition to the principate and committed suicide or were executed. Lucius killed himself at the time Claudius married Agrippina, Marcus was eliminated on Nero's accession in 54 and Decimus survived long enough to be forced into suicide in 65. Marcus' son, Lucius Silanus Torquatus (like his uncle he adopted the proud ancestral cognomen of Torquatus), was similarly executed as a conspirator in 65. One of the daughters, Junia Lepida, married the famous jurist Gaius Cassius Longinus, and her husband would also be involved in the conspiracy against Nero in 65. The other, Junia Calvina, was accused of incest with her brother and banished through Agrippina. The Junii Silani provide one example of the still-powerful sense of resentment. But there were other ambitious and dangerous descendants of important republican families, such as the two men who could trace their lineage from Pompey-Scribonianus, leader of a major rebellion in 42 (see below), and Pompeius Magnus, Claudius' son-in-law, who similarly came to a sad end.[12]

In dealing with these threats, both the real and the imaginary, Claudius would have sought support not only from his wives but also from two other important groups – freedmen and friendly senators. Agrippina (and Messalina) sought similarly to build up their own support from the same quarter, forming complex networks of alliances which cannot be properly examined in isolation. As a class, the senators harboured resentment towards Claudius but there would have been some who realized that their future lay with the principate. The most prominent of such men was Lucius Vitellius, the father of the future short-lived emperor of AD 69. He would prove a consistently loyal servant both of Claudius and of Agrippina. Vitellius was a man of undoubted abilities. He was an outstanding legate of Syria and an individual of great charm and tact, who reputedly escaped Caligula's wrath for his failure to see the moon in attendance of the emperor by his protestations that 'only you gods are permitted to see other gods', and who carried Messalina's right shoe on his person, frequently stopping to kiss it. His services were rewarded with an extraordinary series of three consulships. Vitellius will play an important part in Agrippina's schemes, and he used his abilities as a mediator and negotiator with consummate skill. [13]

While not a man noted for moral courage or independence of spirit, Vitellius was considered free from profound flaws of character. The same cannot be said for Claudius' other senatorial lieutenant, Publius Suillius Rufus. Suillius was the son of the famous six-times-married Vistilia and half-brother of Caesonia, the last wife of Caligula. As quaestor of Germanicus, he was a natural target of Sejanus. He was convicted of judicial corruption but almost escaped banishment until Tiberius intervened and argued vehemently that a sentence of exile was required in the national interest. Tacitus says that Tiberius' interjection was much criticized at the time; later his insight was praised. The career of Suillius illustrates how volatile alliances would be, and how dangerous it can be to construct political pacts on the basis of family connections. Although he served under Germanicus, by 41 Suillius had shifted allegiance completely to become an ally of Messalina. If Vitellius was a go-between and diplomat, Suillius was a weapon of vengeance. His most famous victims would be Julia, the granddaughter of Tiberius, and the distinguished Gallic senator, Valerius Asiaticus. His connections (through Caesonia) with Caligula do not seem to have damaged him, and early in Claudius' reign he received the consulship. He also seems to have been unharmed by the later involvement of his son, Suillius Caesoninus, in the scandal of Claudius' wife Messalina (the son was banished). Suillius was probably too valuable to the princeps as a vigorous and ruthless accuser, and by serving his master in this role he became one of the most hated men in Rome, with a list of prestigious victims, although it can perhaps be argued in his defence there is no evidence that he deliberately contrived the condemnation of the innocent. By the late 50s, when hostility towards Agrippina was no longer dangerous, he launched an attack on her, charging her in the senate with immoral behaviour.[14]

Although he might have been able to count on the support of a small number of individual senators, Claudius' estrangement from the body as a whole would almost inevitably have made him dependent on his own household, specifically his wives and his freedmen. Freedmen from the east (particularly from Greece) who had special skills and professions had long enjoyed an important place in Roman homes. Under Augustus the distinction between the functions of the household and of the state, especially in financial matters, became blurred, and freedmen began to play a role in the process of government. Inevitably some became extremely influential, and as a consequence much resented. Augustus generally kept them at a distance, although there were exceptions and some of his freedmen became proverbial for their wealth. Under Tiberius, Nomius acquired furnishings extravagant enough to be recorded by Pliny, while Hiberus was for a time governor of Egypt. By the end of the reign an unnamed Samaritan freedman was wealthy enough to lend Herod Agrippa the enormous sum of 1 million drachmae, used to pay off his debts to Antonia and curry favour with Tiberius' successor.[15]

It was during Caligula's rule that the freedmen as a *group* rose to prominence and became a highly visible phenomenon in the system of imperial government. Several names have passed down to us, the most famous of whom was Callistus. He is seen offering advice on several important decisions, such as the acquittal (and subsequent elevation) of the orator Afer in 39. His status is shown by the significant role he seems to have played in Caligula's assassination and Claudius' accession.[16]

The growing importance of the imperial freedmen can be seen, in part, as a natural development. As the palace bureaucracy grew and the complexity of administration grew with it, there would have been an increasing tendency for the emperor to rely more and more on his own personal advisers. Given that the nature of the relationship was as much personal as official there would also have been another inevitable tendency. While the power of the freedmen did initially rise from their official positions and at the outset would have depended on the competent discharge of those duties, as they grew closer to the centre of power their careers would have depended increasingly on the degree of personal influence they would exercise over the princeps. In the atmosphere of palace intrigue, they could hardly have kept themselves aloof from the manipulation and scheming that lay at the heart of political life through the Julio-Claudian period. Such intrigue would encourage the growth of factions, all at one level working loyally in the interests of their master but at another working for their own survival. It is not surprising that a senate that felt itself increasingly excluded from the real exercise of power should have resented the imperial freedmen as a class.

This general tendency would have been aggravated by Claudius' peculiar situation. The gulf between him and the senate, the hostility felt towards him as the usurper of their privileges, would have led him, whatever his better instincts, to seek advice and guidance generally from outside this class. The dissatisfaction of the senate is hardly surprising, and one of the promises made by Nero when trying to win senatorial backing on his accession was that he would keep the principate free of improper influence, and the palace out of the affairs of state. Modern scholars generally acknowledge that Claudius dominated the situation rather than was dominated by it, and it is probably fair to see his relationship with his freedmen, as with his wives, as one of converging interests.[17] The scheming to eliminate dangerous rivals was intended essentially to strengthen his insecure position. If at times he seemed to distance himself from what was happening by a show of bemused confusion and ignorance, we should not be deceived. The manner of his accession offers a good clue to the remainder of his regime.

The place of Agrippina in the Claudian system is so tightly bound up with those of his two most prominent freedmen, Narcissus and Pallas, that an outline of their earlier careers and lives is appropriate. Of all the Julio-Claudian freedmen, it is probably fair to say that none has established his place in the tradition so strongly as has Narcissus. As his name indicates, he was, like most of the powerful freedmen, Greek by origin. His family background and date of birth are unknown, but by the time of his death in 54 he seems to have been well past his prime – Tacitus notes his ill-health and Seneca his gout.[18] Nor is his earlier career documented; in particular the tradition that he was a eunuch is based on dubious sources. He had probably already been granted his freedom under Caligula, to judge from his rapid rise to power during Claudius' reign.[19] Under Claudius his function was *ab epistulis*, which gave him control over the correspondence both received by and transmitted from the princeps, and afforded an excellent control over politics in general.[20] He built up a network of power within the palace, and used it well to bring down Messalina: the freedman Euodos whose task it was to ensure that at the critical moment Messalina would be put to death was clearly his underling, as were the two courtesans who initially betrayed her to Claudius. He also had his allies at the upper end of the social scale: Messalina for a time found him a useful agent, Vitellius sought his help, and Vespasian owed his initial advancement to him.[21] He played a central role in some of the key developments of Claudius' reign: the death of Appius Junius Silanus, the suppression of the mutiny on the eve of the invasion of Britain and, most significantly of all, the downfall of Messalina. In the course of the last he briefly found himself in the extraordinary position of controlling the praetorian guard, and afterwards was given the *ornamenta quaestoria* ('quaestorian trappings'). During the course of this remarkable career Narcissus acquired not only power but also a considerable fortune. Dio speaks of cities and kings paying court to him, and of his amassing more than 400 million HS, while Suetonius records the quip that Claudius once complained about the low state of his funds and commented that he would have enough to spare if he went into partnership with Narcissus and Pallas.[22]

Narcissus does seem to have been genuinely loyal to Claudius' interests and until the marriage to Agrippina was the most influential of the freedmen. He was the arch-enemy of Agrippina (see p. 128). She for her part had an ally in the other powerful freedman of the period, Marcus Antonius Pallas. Although Pallas came into his own with Agrippina's ascendancy, Tacitus points out that he was highly prominent even before her predecessor Messalina's fall. His origins also are obscure. He was still a slave (of Antonia) in the year of Sejanus' fall (31), and was almost certainly freed some time before her death in 37, since he took his nomen from her. This suggests a birth about the turn of the century (Roman law discouraged emancipation of slaves before they reached 30). His name Pallas indicates that he too was Greek, and this is borne out by the fanciful tradition reported by Tacitus that he was descended from the kings of Arcadia.[23]

Pallas first appears during the fall of Sejanus. He was clearly held in very high regard by his mistress, Antonia, since he was entrusted by her with the crucial letter to Tiberius that exposed the ambitious prefect. This service would have been an appropriate occasion for his emancipation.[24] Claudius would have assumed his mother Antonia's rights and responsibilities as patron, and Pallas would accordingly in turn have entered his service. We hear nothing further about him until Tacitus alludes to his cautious behaviour during the Messalina affair. Dio makes no reference to him until 48, with Claudius' marriage to Agrippina. Under Claudius he became a *rationibus,* in charge of accounts, the official who would, in a sense, regulate the financial activities of all the procurators of the imperial provinces. He occupied a special place within the imperial household and his ties with Agrippina were so close that it was inevitably claimed that they were lovers (p. 128). Also, like Narcissus, Pallas amassed an enormous fortune, put at 3 million HS by Tacitus and at 4 million by Dio.[25] Like Narcissus, he would be granted the insignia of a magistrate (the more elevated one of praetor, in his case). His service was to suggest the format of a *senatus consultum* (the first stage in the enactment of a law) on the union of free women with slaves (p. 128).[26]

In addition to his undue dependence on his freedmen, Claudius was supposedly a dupe also of his wives, of whom Agrippina was the fourth. He was betrothed first to Aemilia Lepida but the engagement was broken off when her mother, Julia the Younger, fell in disgrace in AD 8. There followed a second betrothal, to Livia Medullina, whose family was linked with the legendary Camillus. This second attempt was no more successful, as she died on her wedding day. Finally a marriage did take place, to Plautia Urgulanilla, daughter of Marcus Plautius Silvanus, consul of 2 BC, distinguished for his military achievements in the Balkans. She bore Claudius two children. First came Drusus, who suffered the untimely and bizarre death at the time of his betrothal to Sejanus' daughter (p. 32). Sometime in the mid-20s Claudius divorced Plautia but a few months after the divorce she gave birth to a daughter, Claudia. Claudius initially planned to raise the child, then apparently began to entertain doubts about her paternity – Suetonius cites the freedman Boter – and repudiated her, placing her back in the care of her mother. Claudia may have been dead by the time of her father's accession; certainly she plays no role in his plans for the succession. According to Suetonius, the grounds for the divorce were gross lewdness (infidelity) and the suspicion of murder. It is not made clear whose murder was involved and the reference to 'suspicion' suggests that she was not charged. There was a celebrated scandal in AD 24 when Plautia's brother Plautius Silvanus threw his wife Apronia out of a window to her death. Silvanus claimed that he had been asleep at the time but an investigation headed by Tiberius in person revealed that there had been a struggle. Silvanus committed suicide and the full circumstances of the case never came out; his first wife Numantina was formally accused of sending him insane by drugs and witchcraft, but was acquitted. The presence of the emperor Tiberius suggests that the case assumed a very high profile, and Plautia's association with it could have been reason enough for Claudius to divorce her.[27]

Some time before 28 Claudius took his second wife, Aelia Paetina, of the Aelii Tuberones, a kinswoman of Sejanus but perhaps remotely so, and it would be risky to read too much into the political connection. She was in fact a woman of some importance, and wealthy enough to own a pottery factory. She bore him a daughter, Antonia, no later than 29. The marriage with Aelia ended probably by AD 38. There was no scandal – Suetonius reports that Claudius divorced her *ex levibus offensis* ('for trivial offences') and the fact that she would later be a candidate for remarriage to Claudius suggests that the divorce was purely political, perhaps reflecting her husband's elevated status on the accession of Caligula.[28]

If Claudius' first two wives failed to make their mark on history, his third, the notorious Messalina, more than made up for them. This next marriage, which occurred sometime during Caligula's reign, would have seemed an advantageous one from Claudius' point of view.[29] Both Messalina's father, Messalla Barbatus, and her mother, Domitia Lepida (Agrippina the Younger's sister-in-law), were grandchildren of Augustus' sister Octavia, which gave her a blood link to Augustus, although admittedly not one as direct or potent as Agrippina's. Moreover, she had family connections that would have been an asset in the post-Tiberian period. Her aunt Claudia Pulchra had suffered under Sejanus, as had Pulchra's son (Messalina's cousin), Quinctilius Varus. Given Messalina's excellent connections, the marriage might reflect Claudius' rise in favour as a result of the accession of Caligula.

In certain respects Messalina resembles Agrippina and assessments of her reflect the irresistible comparison. Syme describes her as an 'avid, envious and vindictive' woman who exploited her domination through 'intrigue and crime' and whose concentrated ambition would 'stop at nothing', expressions very similar to those he uses about Agrippina.[30] The major difference, at least in their image, came in their private lives. As will be seen, Agrippina supposedly used sex as a means to political ends. For Messalina sex in generous amounts, from as many sources as possible, was an end in itself or so we are asked to believe. The sources are replete with accounts of her infidelities. Among the more colourful anecdotes, Juvenal depicts her attending brothels under an assumed name, Pliny has her accommodating twenty-five men in a single twenty-four-hour session, and Dio claims that she organized orgies with upper-class women, their husbands invited as spectators. Messalina may well have enjoyed a varied and active sex life, but the powerful Narcissus was to find it politically expedient to blacken her name with charges of gross immorality, to which she was not given the chance of responding, and the more lurid episodes may originate from his indictment.[31]

A daughter, Octavia, was born in 39 (or early 40) and a son, Tiberius Claudius Caesar Germanicus (Britannicus), shortly after Claudius' accession, in February 41. The birth of Britannicus was a joyous occasion for Claudius. On public occasions he would hold him up for the applauding masses or show him off to the praetorians.[32] Claudius had thwarted an attempt to restore the republic and the birth of a successor and the establishment of a new dynasty would have seemed a propitious event. When Claudius was offered the title of Britannicus, to mark his triumph in 44, he refused it for himself, but did accept it on behalf of his son.[33]

In honouring women of the imperial family, Claudius showed the same sensitivity to Roman feelings as Tiberius. He was prepared to heap lavish distinctions on the dead women of his family. Thus games were established to mark the birthday of his mother Antonia. Livia in 42 finally received the deification withheld from her by her son Tiberius, and was given a statue in Augustus' temple. Such behaviour should be seen not only as a manifestation of *pietas*, but also as an attempt to confer a dynastic respectability on Claudius' own reign.[34] Messalina received the honours due to the wife of the emperor. Her birthday, for instance, was officially celebrated and statues erected in public places. After the British campaign she was accorded the privilege of occupying the front seats at the theatre, one that Livia and Caligula's sister had received, and also of using the *carpentum,* or covered carriage, on sacred occasions, a privilege previously limited to such prominent individuals as Vestals and priests. But this was as far as Claudius was prepared to go. Even these special distinctions might have been restricted to the occasion of the British celebrations in 44, as Suetonius seems to imply, and have been intended to enhance the splendour of that particular occasion. Most significantly, he refused to allow Messalina the title of Augusta, offered presumably by the senate when she produced a male heir. Claudius no doubt felt that such an award would have gone beyond honouring her as an appendage to his own regime, and would have elevated her to a quasi-constitutional position that was out of character with Roman tradition. Significantly, the same privilege was not withheld later from Agrippina.[35]

In the eyes of many, the accession of Claudius marked a dark day in Rome's history. But for Agrippina and her sister Livilla it would have been a cause of celebration. Their isolation from Roman life and society was to end. They were among those considered unjustly banished by Caligula and accordingly recalled from their island exiles by Claudius, with their property restored to them. Agrippina was now 25 years old and clearly determined to revive her fortunes. Unfortunately the loss of Tacitus' *Annals* for this period (the narrative does not resume until AD 47) creates considerable uncertainty about her activities.

Agrippina's first recorded action is a striking one – arranging a proper funeral for her dead brother Caligula. On the evening of the assassination his lifeless body had been removed to the gardens of the Lamii, an imperial estate on the Esquiline Hill just beyond the city limits. No Roman seems to have had the courage to take over the arrangements for the final disposal of the remains, and the task fell to his old friend Herod Agrippa. Since he was busily occupied with co-ordinating Claudius' take-over, Agrippa had time to arrange only for a preliminary dressing of the body. It was then given a hasty cremation and placed under a light covering of turf on the Esquiline. On their return from exile, Agrippina and Livilla wasted no time in exhuming Caligula and giving him a proper cremation and burial. The final resting place is unknown, but it may have been in the Mausoleum of Augustus.

One possible explanation for the prompt action of the sisters might have been superstition, since it was believed that the ghost of Caligula haunted the Lamian gardens and had been seen there by the caretakers. Presumably his spirit was demanding a proper burial, since the apparitions ceased after the sisters had done their duty. Not one to do things by halves, Caligula reputedly also haunted the part of the palace where he had been murdered, and similarly desisted when his body had been properly disposed of.

Superstition, however, probably played a very small part in their considerations; a political motive is more likely. They would have known that little opprobrium would attach itself to sisters performing an act of *pietas* for a dead brother, no matter how appalling his behaviour had been in life. Had he been officially declared a public enemy, *hostis*, as many thought he should have been, the situation might have been different. But in the event their action becomes a standard *topos* in the literary sources for funerals of despotic emperors. Thus Nero's remains were supposedly given a similar treatment by his nurses, Egloge and Alexandria, helped by his mistress Acte, an old enemy of Agrippina. Domitian was similarly cremated by his nurse Phyllis.[36] Given the treatment that Caligula had meted out to his sisters two years earlier, family devotion probably played no greater a part in their actions than did superstition, but there were considerable political advantages to be derived. While Caligula had offended large elements of the senatorial order and alienated certain members of the praetorian guard, his death was not welcomed in all quarters, a fact that seems to have caused the sources some embarrassment. In the temporary theatre on the Palatine, which he had left minutes before his murder, the news of Caligula's assassination was received with grief and shock, explained away by Josephus with the observation that many in the audience were slaves, children and silly women, people who knew no better. While the death of Tiberius had been greeted throughout Rome with jubilation, Caligula's murder, by contrast, inspired no celebration, for which Suetonius gives the lame excuse that the populace believed he was still alive and the report of his death a trick dreamt up by Caligula himself to test them. A popular meeting in the Forum, during which demands were made that the assassins be brought to account, is presented to us in disparaging terms which convey the idea of an unruly rabble.[37]

Agrippina would have realized that an immediate attempt to tap the support of this not inconsiderable element which still felt affection for Caligula would have been foolish. But with the passage of time the nostalgia for the bloodline of Germanicus and of Augustus would inevitably return, and the brief aberration in the promise that this line held for Rome would fade from popular memory. Agrippina's appeal for support would not rest on a logical argument that her family had brought good government, but on the irrational and almost mystical power transmitted to her from her forbears. For all his sins, Caligula had shared in this power and to have refused him his final symbolic ritual would have left the mysticism tarnished.

It has been claimed that from the outset Agrippina set her sights on Claudius and began a campaign to supplant Messalina. This is nothing more than speculation. Given that her sister Livilla was apparently barren (at any rate she bore no children), Agrippina would have been conscious of representing the last hope for the continuity of Germanicus' line. But if she did entertain hopes of attaining the supreme position as early as 41 it is unlikely that she would have risked anything as foolish as overt action. She was a shrewd judge of character (except her own son's) and would have had sufficient insight to appreciate that Messalina lacked the proper temperament to build up her position gradually and systematically, and that patience would be the best weapon.[38] The fate of Livilla would have prompted her to be cautious.

That Messalina felt she had something to fear from the sisters is certainly suggested by what happened to Livilla, and to her associate Seneca. She had returned to Rome with Agrippina on Claudius' accession. Although she had no children, she might have been seen as a potential threat because of her marriage to Marcus Vinicius, who had apparently not displayed any particular ambition before Caligula's death but afterwards became prominent as a candidate for the principate. Technically the marriage with Vinicius should have been terminated on her conviction for adultery, but, like Agrippina, Livilla must have had her conviction annulled or have received a special dispensation by Claudius (she is certainly described by Dio as Vinicius' wife at the time of her death).[39]

Under the year 41 Dio reports that Messalina was offended by Livilla because she did not show her proper respect, and was jealous because Livilla was very beautiful and spent a lot of time alone with Claudius. Messalina therefore engineered her second exile and subsequent death, by trumping up a number of charges, including that of adultery with Seneca. Dio also implies that the punishment met with general disapproval.[40] The charge of lack of respect in itself is not a serious one but it might conceal the idea that Messalina felt that her position and status as empress were somehow threatened. Similarly, the notion of pure sexual jealousy can surely be ruled out since Claudius' sexual appetite was widely recognized, and widely gratified, and if Messalina feared Livilla on the score of an amorous relationship with Claudius it would be because of the political implications of such an affair. But caution is necessary. The charge that Livilla was often alone with Claudius looks very much like yet another stock situation. An almost identical claim will be made later about *Agrippina* and Claudius. Moreover Dio's assertion that Messalina fabricated the charges of adultery against Livilla seems to be cast into doubt by his own later testimony. Under the year 58 he reports an attack on Seneca by the evil informer Publius Suillius, whose charges included the claim that Seneca committed adultery with Agrippina (p. 180). Seneca was not satisfied, reports Dio, probably paraphrasing the arguments of Suillius, with his earlier affair with Livilla, the one that led to his banishment. This evidence at the very least implies that there was a general belief in a liaison.[41]

It is likely that Livilla fell victim to the general tension and paranoia that surrounded the court in the period following the accession. Messalina may have been given a predominant role in her downfall simply to reinforce the tradition that Claudius was the inept fool who followed the dictates of his wife. Suetonius claims that it was Claudius who put Livilla to death *incerto crimine* ('on an unspecified charge'), with no defence allowed, a fairly common procedure in Claudian *maiestas* cases. (Suetonius makes no mention of Seneca in this context, and confuses the issue by recording it in a passage that deals with the involvement of wives and freedmen in all of Claudius' important decisions.)[42] Also, the *Apocolocyntosis* claims that Claudius was responsible for Livilla's death.[43] His wife may well have fed his suspicions, but they would probably have been suspicions already implanted by the behaviour of Marcus Vinicius. That Livilla, as daughter of Germanicus and granddaughter of Augustus, posed a serious threat to Claudius is indicated by her ultimate fate. She was banished, probably to Pandateria, and Dio reports that 'not much later' Messalina arranged her death, apparently by starvation. Her remains were eventually brought back to Rome, probably when Agrippina became influential, and laid to rest in the mausoleum of Augustus.[44] Curiously, Livilla's husband, Marcus Vinicius, survived her. He died in 46 and was given a state funeral, although there were rumours that he was poisoned by Messalina because he refused to sleep with her, and, ironically, suspected her of killing his wife.[45]

The fate of Livilla's collaborator, Seneca, seems to confirm that there was a political dimension to her fall. The late-first-century scholar Valerius Probus is cited by the scholiast on Juvenal for the information that Seneca was relegated to Corsica *quasi conscius adulteriorum Juliae* ('on the grounds of being guilty of [or 'privy to'] adulteries with Julia Livilla'). Whether or not they were in fact lovers is largely irrelevant, since the punishment meted out to both cannot have been simply for an affair, which could at best have been only the pretext. As a close confidant and supporter of Livilla, Seneca may have been seen by Messallina and Claudius as a champion of the old Julian faction. He was tried before the senate, which voted for conviction and the death penalty.[46] In the event, he was exiled to Corsica. This seems to suggest that he was potentially dangerous enough to be removed, but not dangerous enough to be put to death. The choice of the death penalty in an adultery case is surprising, and the only clear precedent would seem to be Jullus Antonius' fate after the famous Julia affair, where Tacitus sees fit to comment on the excessive nature of the punishment. The charge against Seneca may have arisen from paranoia pure and simple.

Tacitus later reports, in the context of Seneca's recall by Agrippina in 49, that the philosopher was at that time *infensus Claudio dolore iniuriae* ('hostile towards Claudius through resentment over the wrong done to him)', where *iniuria* could reflect either the public view of his conviction or simply Seneca's own opinion. Certainly in the *Helvia*, which he wrote to his mother from exile, Seneca takes the stance of someone wronged, which suggests that the notion of his innocence would at the least not have appeared ridiculous to the reader. Moreover, he expressed to the freedman Polybius the hope that if Claudius were to review his case, the emperor's sense of justice (*iustitia*) would persuade him of the wrongful conviction.[47]

That Messalina probably played a predominant role in bringing down Seneca is indicated by the simple fact that he was not recalled until after her death. Also, Seneca himself implicates her in his account of the conduct of his friend Lucilius. It will be remembered (p. 62) that he praised Lucilius for staying loyal to Gaetulicus (in 39). Seneca then goes on to congratulate him also for standing up against the combined forces of Messalina and Narcissus in his devotion to his friends. The allusion must surely be to the events of 41.[48]

Unlike Livilla, Seneca was allowed to live, and it has been suggested that the reduced sentence came about through the intercession of Agrippina, who would recall her *beneficium* when she later engineered his recall.[49] Such an intervention is unlikely. Agrippina was probably keeping the lowest of profiles at this time, and would probably have felt that her circumstances required not intervention but protection, both her own and her son Nero's (she had recovered him from her sister-in-law Domitia). She might also have felt the need for financial help. When her first husband died, Caligula seized his property.[50] This was restored by Claudius, but Caligula's extravagant lifestyle may well have left it much depleted. Both her political and financial fortunes would be revived by a successful marriage.

Agrippina's first choice for a new husband is said to have fallen on the aristocratic Servius Sulpicius Galba, the future emperor. Galba would have been a good catch and his qualifications say much about Agrippina's judgement. His family was an ancient patrician one and to convince doubters he reputedly carried about a copy of his family tree, with its ancestry traced back to Jupiter. Within the recorded historical period his line could boast a succession of consuls from the earliest days of the republic. On his mother's side Galba could point to his descent from Lucius Memmius, the conqueror of Corinth, and Quintus Lutatius Catulus, the distinguished scholar and soldier who came to great prominence at the beginning of the first century BC.[51] He was also very wealthy, in part because of the favour of older women. He was adopted by the wealthy Livia Ocellina (his father's second wife) and, even more significantly, enjoyed the favour of the other, more famous, Livia (Augustus' wife), who fostered his career and left him 50 million HS in her will. Suetonius claims that because the amount was designated in figures and not written out, Tiberius, her heir, reduced the bequest to 500,000. Suetonius adds that Galba never received even that, but it is more than likely that he would have done so when Caligula on his accession in 37 honoured Livia's bequests (none of them had apparently been paid by Tiberius).[52]

Galba was married, probably in AD 20, to Aemilia Lepida, daughter of Manius Aemilius Lepidus.[53] According to Suetonius, the presence of the wife posed no real obstacle and Agrippina made a pitch for Galba while Aemilia Lepida was still alive. This caused such a scandal that Aemilia Lepida's mother came up to Agrippina in the company of a group of Roman ladies and gave her a tongue-lashing, which ended with a slap on the face. Unfortunately this incident is dated by Suetonius immediately after the death of Agrippina's husband Domitius, by which time she was almost certainly enjoying the peace and quiet of exile in Pontia and Galba was serving in Germany, having replaced Gaetulicus as commander. Also such a blatant and clumsy attempt to acquire Galba would have been quite untypical of Agrippina. The incident, if it occurred, probably did so after Aemilia Lepida's death, by which time Galba was in any case a much better catch. As commander in Germany he had performed brilliantly, so well that the timetable for the invasion of Britain in 43 was changed when he fell ill. Perhaps more significantly, his was one of the names touted as a suitable successor after Caligula's assassination. But, for all his ambitions, Galba might have felt that a link with Agrippina would bring more dangers than advantages and he passed up on the opportunity.[54]

Agrippina's second choice was an older man, probably more prominent than the scant notices in the historical records imply. Because of the loss of the relevant section of Tacitus' *Annals*, Gaius Sallustius Passienus Crispus is known only from occasional references in inscriptions and stray allusions in the literary sources. In the absence of Tacitus, the longest entry is the brief biography recorded in the scholiast on Juvenal, a source of information usually to be mistrusted but sometimes, as on this occasion, containing highly useful material.[55] Even the scholiast's evidence has come down to us by a happy accident. He had not realized that a reference in Juvenal to the 'old age of Crispus' in fact referred to a totally different man, Quintus Vibius Crispus, a dangerous smooth-tongued *delator* ('informer') of the Domitianic period. Wrongly assuming the Crispus to be Passienus Crispus, Agrippina's second husband, the scholiast appended a brief biography. Passienus, a native of the town of Visellium, was a man of letters, a wit with a sometimes cruel but always clever tongue, a favourite of both Caligula and Claudius. Agrippina's family background would have made her feel at home in a setting of literate sophistication, although Passienus' great wealth would also have been a considerable inducement. It resulted from his adoption by Gaius Sallustius Crispus, the great- nephew of the famous historian, and the close adviser of Augustus and Tiberius (he played a prominent role in the elimination of Agrippa Postumus in AD 14). He had no natural sons, and when he died in AD 20 he left Passienus with a considerable fortune and useful political contacts. It was almost certainly from his adoptive father that Passienus acquired his estate across the Tiber.[56]

The young Passienus first made his mark in public in the Centumviral Court, a special tribunal which dealt with important civil actions, and in consequence earned a statue in the Basilica Julia in the Forum. He was awarded his first consulship in 27 and by 44 he had held the office a second time. From summer 42 to summer 43 he was proconsul of Asia, and was a generous benefactor according to an inscription from Ephesus, the administrative centre of the province.[57] His progress seems to have been based on his rhetorical abilities: a speech of his on behalf of Volusenus Catulus was still well enough known to be cited by Quintilian some fifty years later. Passienus would have wanted to reinforce this natural talent with an advantageous wife and married Domitia, the sister of Domitius Ahenobarbus, thus becoming Agrippina's brother-in-law. Tacitus describes Domitia as immoral and violent, and her meanness, as has been indicated, was legendary. The political advantages of the marriage might then have been bought at a price, but in any case Passienus seems to have earned the imperial favour by his own merits rather than powerful connections, and to have been sought out for his sharp wit and what seems to have been an outrageous sense of fun. His *bon mot* about his first wife and her brother has already been noted, when in a bitter lawsuit he noted that each already had in abundance the very thing they were striving to get. This wit was combined with a lively sense of humour that could sometimes be outlandishly eccentric. Pliny records his curious behaviour on his estate at Corne near Tusculum. The property contained an outstanding beech tree which

Passienus pretended to have fallen in love with – he would embrace it and kiss it, and lie underneath it pouring wine over its trunk. The most famous incident associated with him has already been mentioned, when he cleverly parried Caligula's question about whether he had slept with his sister by responding, 'Not yet.' Much of his humour was dangerously directed against his imperial masters. He was the author of the famous comment on the relationship between Tiberius and Caligula, that the world had never known a better slave or a worse master. Unlike Seneca, however, who seemed to reserve his barbs only for dead emperors, Passienus was not afraid to take on the living in his comment that he would prefer the esteem to the generosity of some men, such as Augustus, while from others, such as Claudius, he would rather have the generosity.[58]

Seneca pays Passienus an extraordinary compliment, claiming that he was the most 'subtle' thing he had come across: *quo ego nil subtilius novi*.[59] Further evidence of friendship with Seneca is found in two poems addressed to a Crispus from the motley collection grouped under the conventional title of *Anthologia Latina* (some of which are attributed to Seneca). One of the Crispus poems, written in elegiac couplets by a man supposedly in exile, reflects a usual flattering style typical of Seneca and describes Crispus as the sole comfort in his affliction. Another, in hendecasyllables, is a lament on the death of Crispus, the writer's *praesidium* and *voluptas* ('his defence and pleasure').[60] It is thus possible that Senceca might have worked to cultivate a liaison between his two friends, but in fact not a single detail of Passienus' courtship of Agrippina has come down to us.

It is interesting to note that, in describing Passienus' marriage to Agrippina, Pliny observes that he became *clarior* ('more distinguished') as a result of it, an unmistakable reference to the potency of the Augustan/Germanican connection, since at this time Agrippina would have had few other material assets to offer. We cannot be sure that he obtained his divorce in order to marry Agrippina, but in any event it is likely that the new marriage took place relatively soon after her return from exile in 41. In that case Agrippina could well have spent 42–3 with him in Asia, when a statue was apparently erected to her as Passienus' wife in the Asclepieion at Cos.[61] His second consulship in 44 might have been in recognition of his new family connection. It also has to be assumed that somehow Agrippina's conviction as an *adultera* had been revoked, since marriage to a woman so stigmatized would have been an offence. A pardon would in fact have been appropriate, in light of Dio's comment that Agrippina was among those *unjustly* condemned.[62] Passienus' desire to conclude a political marriage for his own career advancement, possibly putting his current wife aside in the process, would not, of course, have endeared Agrippina to her former sister-in-law, and it is hardly surprising that evidence of antagonism emerges later.

We have no information whatsoever on how well or badly the marriage fared. Opportunely for Agrippina, Passienus died in the 40s, leaving her a wealthy woman. The precise date of the death is uncertain, although Syme observes that it must surely have occurred before 47, when Tacitus' narrative resumes, or we would have expected an obituary notice. He received a public funeral and was buried in a tomb on the Appian way. The poet Martial referred to the monument at the end of the century, by which time it had started to fall into disrepair. After his death, the inevitable rumours circulated about the causes. The scholiast on Juvenal reports that Agrippina murdered her husband after being made his heir, adding that it was *per fraudem* ('treacherous-ly'), artfully implying poison, the murder weapon impossible to disprove and traditionally associated with ambitious women. The death, from a purely political standpoint, can be seen as convenient, since it provided Agrippina with the financial means to build a *clientela*, and it freed her for the time when Claudius himself became available as husband. But that is far from proof that Passienus' end was anything other than natural.[63]

If Agrippina had at the time of her return begun to formulate schemes to manoeu-vre herself into the centre of power, she managed to conceal these ambitions and she in fact drops from the historical narrative until the eve of Messalina's fall. She would have been wise to exercise extreme prudence since the fate of her family members and friends, such as Livilla and Seneca, showed how dangerous and vulnerable her posi-tion was. The only identifiable event that might belong to the immediate aftermath of Passienus' death is the appointment of Asconius Labeo as Nero's *tutor* ('guardian'). Little is known of Asconius. His family came from Padua, which prided itself as the birthplace of the great scholar Asconius Pedianus, and another Asconius Labeo is testified there as a local priest. Agrippina may have spent the first years after Passienus' death in that region. A tutor would, of course, have been assigned by the urban praetor to Nero on the death of his natural father, Domitius, and it is possible that Asconius was appointed on that earlier occasion. At any rate, Nero remembered his old guardian with fondness, and when emperor granted him the *orna-menta consularia*.[64]

A hint that Messalina might have felt threatened by Agrippina may be seen in another entry of the scholiast on Juvenal, this time on the fate of Tigellinus. This man, it is claimed, had been banished in 39 on the charge of improper relations with the sisters of the emperor, Agrippina and Fulvia (sic), and had gone to Greece to make a living as a fisherman (p. 67). He seems to have benefited from the general amnesty at the beginning of Claudius' reign and to have returned to Italy. Significantly, how-ever, he was not allowed to return to Rome and he instead used an inheritance to buy land in Apulia and Calabria (where Domitia Lepida also had estates) to start a busi-ness breeding horses. The embargo might well have been due to Messalina, who could have feared a potentially dangerous combination of old intriguers from AD 39. We do not hear of him again until 62, when he is appointed prefect of the guard, but, given the importance of the post, he must already have been at the court for a number of years.[65]

Claudius clearly shared Messalina's fear of conspiracy, and what the sources char-acterize as paranoia might have been a response to genuine threats. His reign claimed a large number of prominent victims. The first to be recorded was Gaius Appius Silanus.[66] Dio reports that he had been recalled from Spain on some pretext, then married to Messalina's mother (divorced, perhaps recently, by Passienus). Appius had many of the characteristics that would have marked him out as dangerous – high birth, influential family and a history of opposition to the principate. His execution in 42 might have resulted from his involvement in some sort of conspiracy, perhaps the major one which broke out later in the year, rather than a refusal to sleep with

Messalina (the claim made by the sources).[67] It is to be remembered that Appius was one of the five nobles accused of *maiestas* under Tiberius in AD 32, and one of the only two survivors of the affair. Also, he was linked to the Junii Silani, a family with a history of resentment towards the imperial family.[68]

At any rate, the death of Appius is followed by the most dramatic event of the reign, one that would affect Claudius greatly and in its own way pave the route for Agrippina's arrival. Dio observes that Appius' fate opened the eyes of Romans to the reality of the new regime. One man who felt particular resentment was Annius Vinicianus, the second survivor of the conspiracy trial of 32. He has been identified as one of the key figures in the assassination of Caligula, and doubtless nursed his own ambitions for the principate. Vinicianus found common cause for resentment with Quintus Pomponius, consul at the time of Caligula's assassination.[69] A successful conspiracy requires troops, and Vinicianus turned for support to Lucius Arruntius Camillus Scribonianus, consul of 32, and in 42 legate of Dalmatia, in command of two legions. Scribonianus was the adopted son of Lucius Arruntius, the man charged along with Agrippina's husband Domitius in the Albucilla affair of 37. Scribonianus rebelled against the emperor, the only provincial legate to do so before the fall of Nero, and reportedly was supported by a large number of senators and equestrians. Claudius was thrown into the depths of despair; needlessly so. Within five days the rebellion had fizzled out and Scribonianus fled to the island of Issa, where he was murdered.[70]

The failure of the Dalmatian rebellion also led to the suicide of Vinicianus, and to the deaths of many others besides. Dio says that Messalina and Narcissus used the occasion as an excuse for a general purge of their enemies, both men and women.[71] It is remarkable that Agrippina emerged from this assault unscathed, since the threat seems to have rekindled the fear of dynastic rivals. Julia, the daughter of Tiberius' son Drusus and his unfortunate wife Livilla, had been in 33 married to the innocuous Rubellius Blandus, to whom she bore a son, Rubellius Plautus. She plays no significant part in events before her death.[72] It is difficult to see why she should have been a target of Messalina or of Claudius, unless it was through fear that her son Rubellius might become a rival to Britannicus. Julia's death bears certain similarities to Livilla's and they are grouped together in the sources. Dio places it in 43, claiming that it was engineered by Messalina in the same fit of jealousy that had compelled her to destroy Livilla. Tacitus also attributes her downfall to Messalina, with the evil Suillius as agent. Suetonius, implying that the wives and freedmen were responsible, relates that she was put to death *incerto crimine*, with no defence allowed, while the *Apocolocyntosis* blames Claudius for the death. The affair illustrates how difficult it is to determine the truth about policies decided within the secrecy of palace walls.[73] Julia anticipated execution by taking her own life.[74]

On the eve of the invasion of Britain in 43 the commander of the praetorians, Catonius Justus, was executed. Dio places responsibility for this on Messalina and claims that it was to prevent the prefect from reporting her dissolute life. Catonius had been an adherent of Julia's father Drusus and was a member of the delegation that Drusus sent to Tiberius during the Pannonian mutiny. He might therefore have been sympathetic to Julia. Catonius' colleague, Rufrius Pollio, seems to have accompanied

Claudius to Britain and to have been honoured by the emperor on his return. But he too, almost certainly, was executed and the removal of the pair afforded Messalina the opportunity to appoint in their places men whose loyalty could be depended on, Lusius Geta and Rufrius Crispinus. Both were later characterized as *Messalinae memores et liberis eius devincti* ('faithful to Messalina's memory and bound to her children').[75] In the end, Messalina's attempt to control the praetorians did not protect her, as similar measures would later protect Agrippina so effectively. One reason was the emotional and almost mystical attachment that the praetorians felt to the memory of Germanicus, an accident of birth over which Messalina had no control. Quite apart from this, however, Agrippina realized that prefects could be removed swiftly. She would make sure that she infiltrated the praetorians thoroughly, not only at the top.

The absence of Agrippina from the recorded events of the reign between Claudius' accession and the eve of Messalina's fall speaks volumes for her good sense. She should have been the main target of Messalina's vengeance. Her son made her far more dangerous than her sister Livilla, and her blood-link to Augustus and Germanicus made her a much more formidable rival than Julia. Tacitus, in describing the events of 47, says that Messalina had always been *infesta* ('hostile') towards Agrippina.[76] But when Agrippina and her son appear once again in his narrative the context suggests that there was something novel in their appearance in Rome. The *Annals* are missing up to AD 47 but, all the same, we would have expected some hint of any clashes in the other sources. This creates the suspicion that Agrippina might have spent much of the time since her return from exile away from Rome, possibly in Asia, possibly at Passienus' Tusculan estate, possibly in Padua, the home of Asconius Labeo, Nero's tutor, patiently waiting until word came down that Messalina had overplayed her hand and was at last vulnerable. What is quite clear is that in the intervening years Claudius and Messalina continued to be obsessed by the memory of the rebellion of Scribonianus and lived in constant fear of further sedition.

In 43, when Claudius went to Britain to play a personal role in the surrender of the British tribes, he took with him anyone who could be considered a threat. Other plots followed later, that of Asinius Gallus in 46, and of Taurus Statilius Corvinus in the same or following year.[77] At some point, perhaps early in 47, his son-in-law Pompeius Magnus, husband of his daughter Antonia, was put to death, reputedly because he had been caught in the act with a male lover. The political dimension of the affair is established, however, by the fact that both Pompeius' mother Scribonia and his father Crassus Frugi were also executed, although it is curious that neither Suetonius nor Dio connect the cases (Tacitus' narrative does not resume until mid-47). We do not know what the real case against Pompeius might have been. He was a vain and arrogant young man, and his manner might have persuaded Messalina that he was becoming a rival to Britannicus.[78] Antonia was now quietly married to Cornelius Faustus Sulla, Messalina's brother, a safe nonentity.[79]

The most distinguished of those Romans who died just prior to Messalina's fall was undoubtedly Valerius Asiaticus, the ex-consul from Narbonese Gaul, the last surviving figure suspected of personal ambitions in the death of Caligula. His trial coincides with the resumption of Tacitus' narrative, missing since the death of Tiberius. The motives given for his downfall are frivolous in the extreme. He had acquired the gardens of Lucullus, which Messalina desired, and was supposedly upset because he was the lover of Poppaea Sabina, her rival for the actor Mnester (Poppaea's daughter would become the emperor Nero's second wife). Asiaticus was tried by Claudius in the palace. Suillius handled the case against him but did not do it effectively, and Claudius was apparently willing to acquit. Vitellius went through the motions of speaking for the defence, and, egged on by Messalina who was present, turned the case on its head by concluding with a plea for mercy on the basis of Asiaticus' services to the state, in that he should be allowed to choose his own manner of dying. This supposedly confused Claudius into thinking that guilt had already been established, and he supported Vitellius' plea. Asiaticus committed suicide, as did Poppaea Sabina later, driven to it by Messalina because of rivalry for the favours of Mnester. The motives have been so trivialized that it is difficult to know what sort of threat Asiaticus posed. The claim that Messalina coveted his gardens is weakened by the fact that an identical motive is claimed for Agrippina's later attack on a Statilius Taurus (p. 135).[80]

Asiaticus' death may well have alarmed many senators, and Messalina compounded the damage by alienating support in another quarter. She brought about the execution of the powerful freedman Polybius, again one of her supposed lovers. Polybius was at this time a *libellis*, handling petitions on behalf of the emperor. He exercised considerable influence, and for that reason Seneca addressed a *Consolatio* to him, in the clear hope that he might bring about the philosopher's recall. He may well have taken up Seneca's appeal, which would have earned him Messalina's enmity and his own subsequent death. Messalina's reasons are probably less significant than the consequences. Polybius was the first of the very powerful freedmen to lose his life through palace intrigue, and his fate was a warning to the others not to 'put their trust in princes', or at least not all of it and not in this particular princess.[81]

Asiaticus died in 47, a year that represents a turning point in the fortunes of Messalina, since it is at this time that Agrippina comes back on the scene. No reason is given for her return to Rome, if she had in fact been away. One may speculate that friendly elements within the palace had kept a watching brief for her, and the top candidate for such a role is the freedman Pallas. There may be a hint of such activity in Tacitus. In his account of the events of this period he describes Pallas as *flagrantissima gratia* ('at the red-hot peak of favour'). This statement is surprising.[82] Narcissus, as Tacitus clearly indicates, was then the dominant freedman, although Pallas' power and influence would grow enormously after Agrippina's marriage to Claudius. Tacitus' comment then might be a cryptic allusion not to the general favour that Pallas enjoyed in the court at that period, but to the particular favour of Agrippina specifically.

At any rate, AD 47 saw the first recorded clash between Agrippina and Messalina, under circumstances that suggest a considerable amount of orchestration. In this year the Secular Games were held. This important festival had been ordained by the sacred collection of oracles in the Sibylline books and had been celebrated at least as early as 249 BC. Theoretically it marked the passing of 100 years, the beginning of the new era, but opportunistic political leaders allowed themselves considerable flexibility with the calendar. Thus Augustus had staged a splendid celebration only sixty-four years earlier, in 17 BC, marked by a famous hymn composed for the occasion by the poet

Horace. There were three successive days and nights of sacrifices and games, and another seven of varied entertainments in the theatre and circus. The Romans had a strong sense of symbolic occasion and if the line of Germanicus was to reassert itself this would afford the ideal setting.

During the games in the circus the young men performed the *Lusus Troiae*, the ancient equestrian parade traditionally staged by boys from the upper crust of Roman families. Among those taking part in 47 were Britannicus and Nero, respectively 6 and 9 years old. Nero was greeted by wild applause, which could hardly have been spontaneous, and received a noticeably more enthusiastic reception than did Britannicus. The power of popular approval tends to be ignored as an element in Roman history, but popular opinion could have a considerable effect on the morale and self-confidence of the ruler. It is in this context that Tacitus relates a common tale told about the young Nero, that serpents had watched over him in his infancy. Nero made the story more credible by self-deprecatingly insisting that there had, in fact, been only one. The emergence of this anecdote precisely when Nero came to public attention suggests that it was deliberately spread at this point by Agrippina or her agents. An anecdote recounted by Suetonius shows how imaginatively the tale could be embellished. The dead skin of a snake was found in Nero's bed, and the rumour was spread that Messalina, fearing him as a rival for Britannicus, had sent assassins to murder him as he took his noon nap. The assassins were not especially tough and were frightened away by a snake that darted out from under his pillow. To keep the story alive, Agrippina had the snake's skin put in a golden bracelet, which Nero wore on his right arm.[83]

Agrippina showed great skill in her bid for popular support by shifting the focus away from herself. She could not play a formal role in the governance of the state and could not hope to win sympathy for being cheated of such a hope. Instead, she cleverly ensured that attention would fall on her son, exploiting the memory of Germanicus and the sympathy that Nero enjoyed as the last male survivor of the line. This line had, of course, passed on through the female side, and such support for Nero would not only satisfy Agrippina's natural maternal urges but also vindicate her in her belief that she had a special role to play in Rome's destiny.

Any sympathy that Agrippina garnered would have come not so much through her own efforts but rather through the passive part that she would play as the object of Messalina's persecution. None of the sources other than Tacitus mentions an early clash between the two determined and ambitious women, and he limits himself to observing Messalina's long-standing hostility to Agrippina, which presumably means that she had always recognized the danger represented by her rival and her son; at this particular point (the display of popular approval for Nero), Tacitus says that Messalina became more agitated (*commotior*), and would have launched into a full-scale attack on Agrippina with an army of accusers had she not suddenly become preoccupied by a new *grande passion*.[84] In the dramatic events that surround her notorious affair no role is recorded for Agrippina, but that she had at least a background part to play can hardly be doubted.

To Tacitus Messalina and Agrippina were equally evil, but he recognized that they were quite different women. Messalina was essentially amateurish, and motivated *per lasciviam* ('by lust'). Agrippina he saw as almost sexless, for whom passion was simply a means to a political end.[85] Yet up to this point Messalina's behaviour seems, to the extent that the limited sources allow us to tell, not to have differed greatly from Agrippina's. Now a contrast seems to emerge. Agrippina, so tradition has it, was to perish because of an insatiable lust for power, Messalina, we are to believe, because of the insatiable lust for a man.[86] This picture is almost certainly misleading, and Messalina's motives may well in reality have been no less political than were Agrippina's. As Tacitus explains the affair, she had by 47 developed a passion for an extremely handsome young man, Gaius Silius, whose father (of the same name) and mother had been convicted during the ascendancy of Sejanus for supposed complicity in the rebellion of Sacrovir (p. 34). At the time of his involvement with Messalina, Silius was consul-designate and probably in his early 30s. He was married to Junia Silana, of the family of the powerful Junii Silani (she is generally identified as the daughter of Marcus Silanus, the consul of 15, and thus sister-in-law of Caligula).[87] Messalina contrived to have Junia Silana turfed out of the marital home and divorced so that she might monopolize her husband. Silana would thus have been a natural ally of Agrippina, and may well have rendered her service during the scandal.

The adulterous couple apparently made no attempt at concealment. They moved about with a retinue of followers, and Messalina showered wealth and honours on her paramour. Some of Claudius' household staff of slaves and freedmen were even transferred to his house, as were some of the palace furnishings! Tacitus' account of the affair is interrupted by events in Rome and abroad, and resumes under the year 48. By then the idea of simple adultery had lost its novelty for Messalina and she was eager for something more ambitious. Silius for his part was unwilling to wait for Claudius to die of old age. He declared himself single, childless and ready to marry Messalina and to adopt Britannicus.

The two lovers seized the opportunity when Claudius left Rome for Ostia. Free from his supervision, they went through the complete ritual of a marriage ceremony. In order to avert the scepticism that might greet such a story, Tacitus admits that it might seem incredible, but that he is not making things up for sensational purposes – everything he reported he had heard from his elders or seen written. Suetonius expresses similar concerns that his reader will find the story unbelievable, and adds the even more incredible detail that Claudius signed the contract with his own hand. The explanation offered by Suetonius is that the marriage was a feigned one, intended to avert from Claudius a calamity that had been predicted to fall upon Messalina's husband. There may be some truth to Suetonius' version – it is perhaps the least unsatisfactory explanation of the bizarre episode. The congruence of the sources, and their concern that the story would sound unbelievable, combine to make it plausible. It is worth noting in particular that the *Octavia*, written probably not long after the event, and generally somewhat sympathetic to Messalina as the victim of ungovernable passion, accepts the marriage as a fact.[88]

If Silius and Messalina did go through a ritual marriage *pro forma* with Claudius' consent they might have hoped later to turn the arrangement to their political advantage in a move to supplant Claudius. At any rate, by now the powerful freedmen had begun to feel consternation and to appreciate the damage that a powerful but reckless

Messalina could wreak on their own positions. They also appreciated that Silius was not simply an adulterous lover, and that a consul designate with patent ambitions represented a threat they had never had to fear when stories circulated that harmless characters like the actor Mnester were sharing her bed. They differed in their reactions to the crisis. Narcissus was clearly the activist of the three. Callistus, Tacitus observes, had learnt under Caligula that masterly inactivity was usually the best guarantee of security. For Pallas' inactivity he can offer no explanation other than cowardice. But Pallas might well have been Agrippina's agent and have received instructions to distance himself from any direct involvement. He adopted the more prudent policy of provoking Narcissus into assuming the high-risk key role in exposing Messalina. Narcissus had been her ardent supporter, but would have recognized that her growing unpopularity following the death of Valerius Asiaticus threatened to bring him down at the same time.

Narcissus now set to work. Two concubines, Cleopatra and Calpurnia, were instructed by the freedman to convey the warning to Claudius (Narcissus clearly knew his master's recreational activities) and he was persuaded by them to call in Narcissus for advice. The freedman performed brilliantly. It was not Messalina's adulteries, he claimed, that caused him concern, disingenuously asking forgiveness for his silence over her previous indiscretions. The crisis in this case was that a marriage had taken place and that Claudius was, in effect, divorced. The contract, he added ominously, had been made public and been seen by the senate, the people and *the soldiers* (meaning the praetorian guard). His recommendation was that Claudius should go straight from Ostia to Rome and to the praetorian camp.

While this was going on, Messalina and Silius and their friends were enjoying a Bacchic revel, dressed up to look the part, with the wine flowing freely. This story, if true, suggests a disturbing incompetence on their part in wasting the crucial time that should have been spent in winning the support of the praetorians. During the frivolity a celebrated doctor, Vettius Valens, climbed a tall tree and, when asked what he could see, replied 'a terrible storm over Ostia'. They were soon to discover that the storm had shifted its path. Messengers arrived with the devastating news that Claudius had uncovered their scheme and was on his way to take revenge. Panic took over. Silius rushed off to the Forum, and the other revellers dispersed, to be hunted down and arrested by the centurions. Messalina escaped through the city on foot then took a lift on a refuse cart heading in the direction of Ostia, hoping to meet her husband on his way to the city. The threat to Claudius had dissipated, but en route to Rome from Ostia he had no way of knowing that the danger had passed. His uncertainty is revealed in an extraordinary decision to relieve Geta temporarily of his command for one day and to place Narcissus in charge of the praetorians. Narcissus knew Claudius' propensity for panic (he had displayed it during the rebellion of Scribonianus) and made sure that he travelled with him in the carriage back to Rome. It was just as well, since Claudius' other companions Lucius Vitellius and Caecina Largus (the emperor's colleague in the consulship six years earlier) were still uncertain about how things would turn out and would not commit themselves unequivocally against Messalina, fencing the emperor's questions with ambiguous replies.

Messalina finally reached Claudius, but her appeal for a hearing was blocked by

Narcissus, as was her attempt to bring the children into the emperor's presence. Narcissus took him to Silius' home, where he showed him the Claudian heirlooms that had been stripped from the palace. Claudius was driven to fury. He went to the praetorian camp and instituted makeshift trials. Silius was put to death, followed by a number of equestrians, including the prefect of the Vigiles and Vettius Valens, the tree-climbing doctor. Senators were also executed; others were banished, including Suillius Caesoninus, the son of Claudius' famous prosecutor. To show fair treatment without class distinction, the wretched Mnester was also put to death. As was appropriate for a foreigner of his lowly station, he grovellingly begged for mercy.

By early evening, according to Tacitus, Claudius had vented his rage and was beginning to feel more benign, a happy condition helped by wine. Narcissus, we are told, saw the need for decisive action and ordered the praetorians, under the supervision of a freedman, Euodus, to finish off Messalina, and represented the orders as the emperor's. They found her in the Gardens of Lucullus preparing her petition to Claudius, along with her mother Lepida – mother and daughter had become reconciled in her final hours. When she saw the praetorians approach, Messalina accepted the inevitable and ended her own life, helped by a tribune. The report of her death was taken to Claudius, who acted with apparent indifference, and Suetonius even suggests that on taking his place at dinner he asked why Messalina had not come. His bewildered air was probably a ruse intended to distance himself from what had happened. [89] At any rate he did not oppose the senatorial decree that Messalina's name be removed from inscriptions and her statues destroyed.[90] He also saw to it that in recognition for his service in the affair Narcissus was given the *ornamenta praetoria*.

The narrative details of the Messalina affair are not particularly important for the story of Agrippina. Of more interest are her motives. It is unfortunate that the one well-documented *cause célèbre* involving an imperial woman is in its basic motivation no less obscure than those scandals sparsely covered by the sources. But clearly more than sexual passion was involved – the constant concern about the loyalty of the praetorians and the severe punishment meted out to her followers confirm this. It is worth noting that Pliny identified Vettius Valens, the tree-climbing doctor, as a man who built up followers and power (*adsectatores et potentiam*) and there can surely be little doubt of a conspiracy, albeit an incompetent one. The main difficulty is to determine what the two main participants hoped to achieve. Silius' incentive, and his willingness to use Messalina as a route to power, are comprehensible. Also, if there was a fear that Claudius might die soon, it might well have been in Messalina's interest to seize the initiative and take pre-emptive action, since Britannicus was too young to assume power automatically. But there is no evidence that Claudius' death was imminent and, although in delicate health, he lived for a number of years more. Moreover, his departure for Ostia suggests that he was not in immediate danger of expiring.

In fact, Messalina had a tremendous amount to lose. She enjoyed power and prestige, her son was destined to succeed Claudius and to judge from the sources, allowing of course for exaggeration, she was able to enjoy her sexual adventures without interference from a *mari complaisant*. It would have taken a dramatic development, and perhaps unscrupulous advisers, to persuade her to jeopardize all of these advantages, and to see a situation where the future of Britannicus would be more secure with

Silius as stepfather than with Claudius as father, especially since she supposedly feared that her lover might not follow through with the arrangement.[91] The most convincing context is provided by the arrival of Agrippina and her son on the scene. The reaction of Messalina to the displays of popular sympathy for the young Nero and his mother might have been only the tip of the iceberg. This scenario, of course, would require that Agrippina had built up considerable support among those close to the emperor. Senators like Vitellius, and freedmen like Pallas, motivated by their own sense of self-advancement and self- preservation, would have been natural targets of her interest. If Messalina had a sense that a pro-Agrippina block was emerging and might, in the absence of prompt counter-measures, be unstoppable, she could have been driven to desperate action. Under such circumstances, she might have sought the insurance of a 'marriage' to Silius.[92] In any case, Messalina's demise left the field open to Agrippina. She was now poised to move finally into the position of power that her birth and lineage had foreordained.

6

Wife

The Messalina affair exposed the vulnerability of Claudius' regime. He did his best to put on a bold face and even tried to find humour in his predicament, supposedly announcing to his praetorians that he had taken a pledge to remain a widower, and that if he showed any inclination to go back on his word they had his permission to put him out of the way.[1] If Agrippina had somehow engineered Messalina's fall by provoking her to desperate action she might be expected to find such comments discouraging, but she would surely have had the political commonsense to appreciate that they were not meant seriously. Claudius clearly would not stay unmarried. Tacitus claims that he could not take celibacy and needed to be under a wife's thumb (*coniugum imperii obnoxio*).[2] Neither comment should be taken too seriously. The absence of a wife did not mean celibacy for someone of Claudius' wealth and status, and the second charge is the standard sneer directed against him. Claudius would need a wife, not for sex or companionship, nor out of any masochistic desire to be dominated, but because he needed a political ally to help him keep at bay the forces still threatening to topple his principate. And he needed an ally he could rely upon. He had tried to seek links with the noble houses and they had failed. He must have realized, as Agrippina shrewdly gambled he would, that the only effective security would come from a union *within* the imperial house.

According to Tacitus, there was great competition among potential candidates for the position of Claudius' fourth wife, each parading her physical charms, her family connections and fortune, and each of the three front runners actively promoted by a powerful freedman. They were Claudius' former wife Aelia Paetina, favoured by Narcissus, Lollia Paulina, Caligula's ex-wife, favoured by Callistus, and Agrippina, who enjoyed the support of Pallas. Claudius reputedly wavered between one and another, depending on the argument he had last heard, until he finally called a meeting and asked each of the freedmen to present his case.

The meeting held to reach the final decision on Claudius' fourth wife is presented in almost ironical terms by Tacitus, as a sort of parody of a formal *concilium* of the emperor's close friends and advisers. While his account probably owes much to his imagination, there is no reason to doubt that a considerable amount of lobbying did actually take place.[3] Narcissus would have realized that he had been completely outmanoeuvred by Pallas. By putting himself on the line in the Messalina crisis he made it almost inevitable that Britannicus, Claudius' likely successor, would bear a grudge against him. Having incurred this potential odium, he would have been dismayed to discover that the leading candidate to replace Messalina was the patron of one of his rival freedmen. His only hope was to promote a candidate of his own. His choice fell on Claudius' ex-wife Aelia Paetina, surely a long shot at best and one difficult to explain. Narcissus' prominence at the beginning of Claudius' reign suggests that he had been in the emperor's household long before he came to power, and he may well have known Aelia when she was Claudius' wife.[4] She had the presumable advantage that Claudius already knew her and her arrival on the scene would ensure a minimum of domestic disruption. Moreover she was the mother of Antonia and Claudius would have the option of designating Antonia's husband Felix Sulla as his heir, not so much in his own right but rather, in view of his apparent lack of ambition, to hold the fort for Britannicus until the lad came of age.[5]

Tacitus tells us that Callistus led the argument against Aelia, claiming that her long-standing divorce disqualified her and that if brought back to the palace she would be all the more arrogant. For his part, he urged the case of Caligula's former wife, Lollia Paulina. Callistus had, of course, been a highly influential freedman under Caligula and would have known Lollia then. She was a woman of striking appearance, from a family whose beauty supposedly went back at least three generations. They were also enormously wealthy and Lollia may have benefited from the financial acumen of her grandfather Marcus Lollius, consul in 21 BC, a man described by Velleius as rapacious and devious, who left a fortune on his death in disgrace in AD 2, probably by suicide. Lollia's wealth was legendary, and her habit of carrying bills of sale to prove the unbelievable cost of her best jewellery has already been noted. The wealth would have been an attraction but it is difficult to see what other positive advantage she could be thought to bring. Callistus argued that because she was barren and not subject to parental rivalry she would make a suitable parent for the stepchildren, a plea that seems almost desperate.[6]

Whether or not there was ever a *formal* discussion, the debate would in any case have been moot, since the third candidate, Agrippina, had overwhelming advantages over the other two. She had the strong support of Pallas and we must assume that there had been close contact between them before the issue of the marriage arose.[7] Even if Pallas did have a vested interest in his candidate's case, nevertheless the arguments placed in his mouth were compelling. The marriage would avoid the danger of outsiders trying to arrogate the power and prestige of the imperial house to themselves. Moreover, Agrippina belonged by blood to both branches of the imperial family. She was a Julian, through her mother Agrippina, and a Claudian, through her father Germanicus. She could thus play an important role in bridging the divide that had bedevilled politics almost since the beginning of the principate, a rift whose origins lay in the simple fact that Augustus and Livia had not produced surviving children. The strife between the rival factions of the imperial family had poisoned the atmosphere of Tiberius' reign and led to the destruction of Agrippina's mother and two of her brothers. A marriage between Claudius and a member of both sides of the family would heal many old wounds and would considerably reduce the threat of a coup. Agrippina would also bring with her a grandson of Germanicus, an unimpeachable candidate for the succession. The last consideration is of considerable significance. An attractive and popular successor-in-waiting would reduce the incentive to replace an unpopular regime. Claudius clearly felt so beleaguered that his primary concern was not the usual one of the succession by his natural son but the guarantee that his regime would survive, even if it meant that an outsider would follow him as emperor.

Claudius was not a Julian, not even by adoption, since his father Drusus, unlike Tiberius, had never been adopted by Augustus. He could claim a Julian *connection*, of course, through his mother, Antonia the Younger, and her mother Octavia, sister of Augustus and wife of Marc Antony. But this association did not have the force of descent from the emperor himself, as was revealed in Augustus' own words in two letters he wrote to Livia, where in each case he referred to Claudius as *her* grandson.[8] In fact Claudius was more directly descended from Antony, Augustus' opponent. The Antonian descent was further emphasized in his son Britannicus, as Messalina was granddaughter of Antonia the Elder.

Nero was also related to Antony – his grandmother on his father's side was the same Antonia the Elder. But, more important, on his mother's side Nero could boast descent from Augustus. The importance of this asset cannot be overstated. The Augustan link is a theme that is constantly reiterated by Tacitus. It will be recalled how at the funeral of Germanicus onlookers observed that Agrippina (the Elder) alone represented the true blood of Augustus, not to suggest that her children were somehow disenfranchised but rather to contrast her with Tiberius, who was Augustus' son by adoption, not through the bloodline. The theme will come to the fore again on the accession of Nero, when rivals were removed because of their link, however remote, with the line of the first princeps.[9] Suetonius quotes the first line of a popular epigram that associates Nero with the legendary founder of the Julian line, the Trojan hero Aeneas: 'Does anyone deny that Nero is from the great line of Aeneas?' and Dio recalls a supposed prophecy by the Sibyl that refers to Nero as *eschatos Aineadôn* ('last of the sons of Aeneas'). Dio also recounts a popular tradition that the end of the line of Aeneas and Augustus was marked by the death of Nero, because (rather illogically) a famous laurel tree planted by Livia in 37 BC and the breed of white chickens established at the same time both died when Nero did. Dio on two occasions refers emphatically to Nero's descent from Augustus, once when he contrasts Nero's journey to the east (to perform in the arena and on the stage) with that of Augustus, and once when he laments the spectacle of a descendant of Augustus giving performances on the lyre. Claudius, on the other hand, he calls merely 'son of Drusus, the son of Livia', just as Tacitus calls Britannicus the 'last of the Claudii'.[10]

Claudius' own detachment from the Julian line clearly lies behind his decision to adopt the 'title' Caesar. This was strictly a name (*cognomen*), acquired by Octavian when he was adopted by Julius Caesar, and transmitted from him through Tiberius and Germanicus to Caligula. Its close association with the Julian family, including those members who were Julian only by adoption, gave it a powerful place in the imperial idea. It is with the accession of the non-Julian Claudius that it might be said to begin its life as a title. It is a useful illustration of the powerful appeal of the Augustan connection, one that Agrippina would later seek to exploit. Not everyone was impressed. In the *Apocolocyntosis* Augustus complains of Claudius *sub meo nomine latens* ('masquerading under my name'). In the same work the patently crooked Diespater makes the argument that Claudius should become a god on the basis of his being bound to Augustus by blood, an argument whose validity can be measured by his next claim, that he surpassed all men in wisdom.[11]

Apart from his Augustan link Nero offered another, perhaps even greater, advantage in that he was the grandson of Germanicus (*Germanici nepos*). On his first appearance on the public stage the crowd had sympathized with him as the last *suboles virilis* ('male offshoot') of the family. It was from his *mother's* side that he could trace this descent, but this was not a problem.[12] Similar claims through the female side will be made for Rubellius Plautus, son of Julia, granddaughter of Tiberius *cui nobilitas per matrem ex Julia familia* ('who acquired nobility from the Julian family [sc. by adoption] through his mother'). Marcus Junius Silanus is thought of as a potential claimant to the throne in 54, even though his descent from Augustus is through three women – Julia the Elder, her daughter Julia the Younger, and her granddaughter (Silanus' mother), Aemilia Lepida.

The common interests of Claudius and Agrippina would result in a perfect partnership, since she shared his view of the union of the dynastic traditions of the two families as the source of strength and stability. She was to remain loyal to this ideal even after Claudius' death, and the later conflict with her son would to no small extent derive from this loyalty.[13] Pallas' arguments prevailed, helped, the sources tell us, by the 32-year-old Agrippina's seductive guiles. She spent many hours in Claudius' company, using her position as niece as an *entrée*, and winning over her impressionable uncle with little endearments and kisses, even, according to Tacitus, engaging in an *amor inlicitus*. Not too much weight should be given to these claims. They bear a striking resemblance to her sister Livilla's reported efforts to entrap Claudius with similar seductive enticements. It would be going too far to claim that there was no exchange of affection between the two, but if there were lengthy close discussions they would probably have involved backroom political strategy rather than sexual encounters.[14]

Agrippina was thus poised on the point of marriage, and she found herself so placed because of her enormous reserves of patience and her skill in carefully preparing her ground. These characteristics she was to retain. Even before the marriage took place she got down to the task of strengthening the position of her son Nero. He was three years older than Britannicus and in Claudius' eyes would provide assurance of an untroubled succession. There were historical precedents for an arrangement whereby two potential successors were groomed, not necessarily with the intention of joint-rule but rather to provide a fail-safe in the event of the death of either one. Thus Augustus had adopted his grandsons Gaius and Lucius, and Tiberius had been instructed to adopt Germanicus to form a pair with his own son, Drusus, and on his death left behind two candidates, Caligula and Tiberius Gemellus. Agrippina would have appreciated that for all the attractions of such an arrangement it did involve potential dangers, especially if, as in the present case, the two potential successors belonged to different families. She could not afford to wait on events and found herself in a situation similar to Livia's, manoeuvring to protect her son's prospects. In this she had an advantage that Livia did not enjoy. Whatever his true character, the young Nero presented to the outside world the image of a personable and attractive youth, almost a second Germanicus, the ideal candidate for those who entertained the hopes of an enlightened and liberal principate.

Agrippina would have seen her first priority as the confirmation, through Nero, of the newly forged link between the Julian and Claudian branches of the imperial family. The obvious way to cement this relationship would be through a further marriage. Claudius' daughter by Messalina, Octavia, perhaps 8 or 9 years old, and thus some four years from marriageable age, was the ideal partner and both Tacitus and Dio insist that Agrippina had already begun to hatch her scheme in late 48, even before she was married to Claudius.[15] She did face one serious obstacle, that Octavia was already betrothed, to Lucius Junius Silanus. Claudius would have the option of simply breaking off the engagement. The fact that he decided not to do so reflects the power and status of the Junii Silani.

Lucius Junius Silanus was born about AD 26/7. As the son of Marcus Junius Silanus, consul of 19, and Aemilia Lepida, daughter of Julia the Younger, he had the right family connections, especially on the Julian side, to ensure a favoured career. He was apparently inducted into the Salii (priests of Mars) in 37/8 and went on to serve on the Vigintivirate (board of magistrates). He was for a brief period prefect of the city, in 41, soon after Claudius' accession. Engaged to the emperor's daughter Octavia, his future must have seemed assured. In 43 he accompanied Claudius on the British expedition, and after the surrender of the British tribes was sent ahead to Rome to announce the victory. He was granted triumphal insignia, despite his youth, almost certainly in connection with the triumph of 44. During that triumph Silanus climbed the steps of the Capitol at Claudius' side (the second son-in-law, Pompeius, was on the other side). Claudius also worked to ensure the popularity of both. In a distribution of some 300 HS each to the people, Lucius Silanus and Pompeius were allowed to distribute the money on Claudius' behalf. Silanus was co-opted into the Arval Brotherhood and is recorded as a member there between 43 and 48. As a further mark of high imperial favour he was allowed an accelerated quaestorship and by 48, the year before his death, had held a praetorship, again by very accelerated promotion. As praetor, he received financial backing from Claudius to stage a particularly lavish gladiatorial show.[16]

Lucius Silanus had managed to survive the purge that swept away Claudius' other son-in-law Pompeius (p. 88). Agrippina would clearly find him a tough opponent. To dislodge him from an almost unassailable position to make way for Nero, she had in effect to destroy him. Her response to the challenge illustrates the exacting thoroughness of which she was capable. The attack on Lucius was made in the one quarter where he seemed vulnerable. That Agrippina was the brains behind the campaign that followed seems beyond doubt, and Tacitus described Lucius' fall as her *scelus* ('wicked crime'), the first to be recorded after she had become Claudius' intended wife. To some degree this reference foreshadows the death of Lucius' brother Marcus Silanus, which will similarly be mentioned as her first crime, this time after her son Nero had become emperor in 54. She appears to have had the backing of a number of freedmen, who supposedly feared retribution from Britannicus for their role in bringing down Messalina. Dio's simplistic suggestion that the freedmen feared Lucius because he was a 'good man' (*aner agathos*) is not persuasive.

The actual mechanics of the attack on Lucius Silanus were handled by Vitellius, Claudius' closest ally in the senate and a man who would henceforth see himself as an equally devoted servant of Agrippina, *ingruentium dominationum provisor* ('with a sharp eye for rising power'). The notion that the scheme might have been engineered by Vitellius without any prompting from Agrippina can surely be ruled out. He was a minister, not an initiator, and a high-risk independent assault by him on the son-in-law of the emperor can be ruled out of serious consideration.[17] Vitellius was censor in 48, and one of his duties was to scrutinize the senatorial ranks for those guilty of moral turpitude. Lucius Silanus, it emerged, had a skeleton lurking in his closet. He had a sister, Junia Calvina; she is described as *decora* ('comely') and *procax* (difficult to translate, but something like 'rather wild'), and Lucius, as Tacitus concedes, was unduly demonstrative in his affection for her. By coincidence, she had until very recently been Vitellius' daughter-in-law but family connection carried little weight with Vitellius and he placed the worst possible complexion on this affection between brother and sister, charging Lucius with incest and castigating a relationship which Tacitus describes as 'unguarded rather than incestuous'. Whatever the precise truth of the matter, Vitellius' insinuation was not his own invention. It is echoed in the *Apocolocyntosis*, where Junia, described as *festivissima* ('very lively and charming'), is called *Venus* by everyone but her brother Silanus, who preferred to call her *Juno*. The author suggests that those who do not understand the allusion should look for a precedent in Alexandria. The point of the witticism is that Juno was *soror et coniunx* ('sister and wife') of Jupiter, just as in Egypt the brother and sister of the ruling dynasty married one another. Moreover, the fact that neither Suetonius nor Dio avoids raising the issue of incest suggests that the charges of Vitellius were broadly accepted.[18]

As Claudius' son-in-law Silanus would have had little general incentive to plot against the emperor, but if he got wind of a plan to discredit him he might have tried to take some countermeasures, which could be construed or misrepresented as active opposition. Such behaviour might underlie the garbled report of Dio that the freedmen persuaded Claudius to put Silanus to death, on the grounds that he was conspiring against him. Silanus was in fact not executed. A direct accusation for *maiestas* could probably have succeeded (evidence could always be trumped up), that perhaps is how Messalina would have proceeded. But direct action was not necessary; Agrippina's method was much cleverer. Just as she had waited to allow Messalina to destroy herself, so she now put Silanus in a position where he might do the same, shamed by a charge that, if not true in all particulars, had enough substance to ensure that he would be affected by the scandal. Agrippina put her plan into operation quietly and discreetly, the hallmark of her method. Lucius probably had no idea that a plot was being hatched against him. Indeed, the lustrum of the senatorial order was already complete when an edict was carried by the senate expelling him from its order. As a final humiliation, he was obliged to resign his praetorship on the very last day of his term and, in accordance with Roman custom, the vacancy was filled, if only for a day, in this instance by Eprius Marcellus, later to become notorious as an unscrupulous prosecutor.[19]

It is likely that Claudius and Agrippina kept their intentions to marry secret until after Lucius' expulsion, to allay suspicions that they had had a hand in his exposure. Once he had been disgraced there was no need for further secrecy and they could now proceed with their double plan, the marriage between Claudius and Agrippina and the betrothal of Nero and Octavia. The lengths that Claudius was willing to go to secure both shows how thoroughly he was convinced of the benefits both measures would bring.

His own marriage was the first step.[20] It might seem at first sight that there could not be any serious obstacle to such a match. Each was free to marry after the deaths of Passienus and Messalina. But both Roman law and tradition stood solidly in the way. Agrippina was the daughter of Claudius' late brother, and a marriage between uncle and niece was strictly disallowed. This was no piece of arcane and recondite legal pedantry but a time-honoured and familiar prohibition, and even without his scholarly background Claudius could not have been unaware of it. Nor was it something that Romans would easily turn a blind eye to. Tacitus insists, in his brief survey of Agrippina's sexual improprieties, that the marriage to her uncle represented the depths of her moral degradation. Also, in the *Octavia* the nurse character declares that Claudius' marriage to the daughter of his brother involved 'a wicked marriage bed and a torch for mourning', and was the cause of all the calamities that followed.[21]

The legal obstacle to the marriage was in fact serious enough to cause an initial postponement of their plans, through fear of violent public reaction. The ever-loyal Vitellius once again came to the rescue, and a scenario was devised in which Claudius could be seen not to be pushing his own agenda but rather yielding to the insistent demands of the senate and ordinary people. The indirect manipulation of the business of the senate by imperial interests was not without precedent. One is reminded of how Caligula arranged through the prefect Macro for Tiberius' will to be annulled in the senate. Also, after her marriage Agrippina would persuade the consul designate to frame a *sententia* in which the senate would urge Claudius to betroth Octavia to Nero. Having learned the technique from his mother, Nero reputedly planned to use the same tactics after his accession to further his plans to marry his freedwoman. This procedure should not be seen as excessive interference in the working of a legislative body, but rather as care and forethought in the managing of state affairs.[22]

Early in 49 Vitellius entered the senate and delivered an effective speech, aimed at winning senatorial approval for the union (the summary provided by Tacitus is probably based on senate reports). His opening points were general and unobjectionable, emphasizing the need for Claudius to have a wife to provide relief from the burdens of public office. The wife should be a woman of noble birth, with experience of motherhood, since she would share the upbringing of Britannicus and Octavia. The final qualification was purity of character. Vitellius' arguments would not necessarily have been persuasive, but he would hardly have made claims that risked exciting ridicule. The fact that he used moral rectitude as the culminating argument of a case that was intended to lead inexorably to Agrippina is a clear indication that the charges of sexual misconduct which had been brought against her by Caligula in 39 were not taken too seriously, and that she had at any rate succeeded in cultivating a reputation for propriety and respectability since her return to Rome. Vitellius then ingeniously suggested that the process could enhance that body's powers, since by giving their assent they would establish a precedent by which the *senate* would determine the nature of an emperor's marriage. He drew the contrast between the current situation and that of Claudius' predecessors, who had taken their wives 'from the wedding-beds of others' – clearly he had in mind Augustus, who had taken Livia from her husband Tiberius Claudius Nero, and Caligula, whose second wife was already betrothed and the third already married when he chose them as brides. Vitellius had prepared his ground well. He now reached the tricky part. Marriage with a brother's child, he claimed, was not incestuous or impious but novel, customary in other countries and not prohibited by any law. In Rome marriage between cousins had at one time been prohibited but had become common with the passage of time. Using an argument that has a clear resonance in modern judicial discussions, he concluded that the definitions of moral standards change as society changes.[23]

The speech had the desired effect. Given their lead, no doubt, by well-primed friends and allies of Agrippina sitting in the chamber, the senators poured out of the house in a body, declaring that if Claudius refused to listen to their appeal they would force him. They were joined by insistent crowds.[24] The demonstrations of excessive enthusiasm for an emperor who was not especially popular suggests that, beyond the opportunity to ingratiate themselves, senators and people alike positively approved of marriage with the daughter of Germanicus, and did indeed see such a union as a means of averting future conflict over the succession. The original plan had been for the throng to make its way up the Palatine to the palace but Claudius, possibly on the advice of Agrippina, exploited this opportunity for a public relations coup and came down to meet them in the Forum and to listen to their shouts of encouragement. A further meeting of the senators was hastily arranged, where Claudius took the floor and formally asked for a decree that would make legitimate the marriage between a man and his brother's daughter, not only in his case but as a general principle.

The freedom to marry a brother's daughter remained in force until 342. The fact that such a lengthy period elapsed before the legislation was repealed (in the Christian period) has been taken to suggest that Claudius' plans to marry Agrippina were not as shocking to the general conscience of the day as Tacitus' narrative, and the Octavia, seem to imply. On the other hand, there was no stampede to follow Claudius' example. The literary sources mention only two cases, an unnamed freedman and the equestrian Alledius Severus, a *primipilaris* (centurion of the first rank), whose motive was to curry favour with Agrippina and whose marriage was attended by Claudius and Agrippina personally.[25] Claudius still left prohibited a union between a man and a uterine niece (that is, the daughter of his sister, rather than of his brother), a ban that was not lifted during the Roman period. He presumably sensed the lingering prejudices over this matter and saw no need to push the principle further than required by immediate expediency.[26]

Once the decree had been passed, Claudius and Agrippina hesitated no longer and in 49 the marriage was speedily concluded. From now on, Dio asserts, Agrippina had Claudius under her complete control. Tacitus' assessment is more sophisticated. To him the marriage represents a transformation in the development of the Roman state. Affairs were now under the control of a woman but not a woman like Messalina, who had used the power of the state simply as a means to indulge in excesses. Agrippina's lust was not for passion, but for power. She introduced a 'tightly drawn servitude, one that might have been imposed by a man' (*adductum et quasi virile servitium*). She could not in fact have been more different from Messalina. In her private life Tacitus sees her as an austere person, totally free of promiscuous conduct, unless it was intended to contribute to her power. Even her greed for money he saw as a device for reinforcing her power.[27] Tacitus is surely right about Agrippina's aversion to private excess. She had not been present in Rome during the last year of her brother Caligula's reign, but on her return from exile she could not have failed to realize that his extravagant public projects and his personal self-indulgence had created a serious financial crisis, leading to a groundswell of opposition and even to riots. She was a calculating individual and would have had the wisdom to avoid Caligula's mistakes. But where Tacitus and Dio are mistaken, or deliberately misrepresent her, is where they present the Roman state as being in the thrall of a woman. This, of course, is consistent with their depiction of Claudius as a dupe, who was completely under the influence of wives and freedmen. Rather he was in the enviable position of having a wife who shared his view of the world, and who would be an aggressive supporter of his political agenda.

It has been suggested that a visible commemoration of the marriage has survived in the form of a remarkable cameo now in Vienna, the Gemma Claudia (Pl. 6). Four heads are depicted. On the right Germanicus and Agrippina the Elder emerge from cornucopiae and face on the left the heads of Claudius and the younger Agrippina in a matching configuration. The ensemble rests on pieces of armour, presumably representing the victories of the two brothers in Germany and Britain. Agrippina the Elder wears a helmet, her daughter a crown in the form of a turreted wall, whose precise significance in this context is uncertain.[28]

The joy that marked the marriage was overshadowed by a particularly embarrassing development. In his capacity as Pontifex Maximus, Claudius prescribed expiatory sacrifices to be carried out by the priests in the grove of Diana, to purge the supposed incest of Lucius Silanus and his sister. Some might, as Tacitus claims, have considered his attitude hypocritical. The ill-feeling would have been aggravated by a dramatic turn of events. Ashamed and humiliated, Lucius Silanus decided to put an end to it all and took his own life. The circumstances are unclear, but he seems to have timed his suicide to coincide with their wedding day, to ensure that it would achieve the maximum possible effect. [29] There was no way of escaping the odium that the young man's tragic end was bound to create. Claudius' one hope was that people would draw a contrast between Silanus, on the one hand, who along with his sister had gone ahead and committed a universally abhorred sin, and the emperor on the other, who had sought the guidance of the people and the senate to help him in his moral dilemma.[30]

Dio claims that after the marriage Agrippina moved to the palace and began to take complete control of her husband, through a mixture of intimidation and bribery. Her usual tactic was to arrange for the freedmen to persuade Claudius of the wisdom of her advice, and she also arranged approval beforehand from all sources – the ordinary people, the praetorian guard, the senators.[31] Dio's emphasis on the passivity of Claudius can be largely discounted but he is surely right in conveying the sense that from this time on policy was pursued in a much more highly organized and systematic fashion, and that Agrippina brought to the marriage a keen political sense that controversial policies should be preceded by careful groundwork and the building up of approval and consensus.

The day-to-day activities of Agrippina after her new marriage are beyond the range of our knowledge, and were probably little understood even by her contemporaries. But the impact of her arrival in the palace is probably best judged by results. Claudius' reign falls into two almost equal parts, from his accession in AD 41 to the death of Messalina in 48, followed by the ascendancy of Agrippina down to his death in 54. The success of any regime might well be gauged by the intensity and consistency of the opposition. The absence of proper statistics makes this a difficult thing to calculate with precision. The literary sources have a tendency when dealing with the Julio-Claudian emperors to speak about widespread opposition and bloodbaths. When such claims are made in very general terms it is impossible to distinguish reality from rhetorical exaggeration. But there is one possible measure. The deaths of prominent individuals tend to be recorded by name and, while the accumulation of such names hardly constitutes sufficient statistical data to determine social trends, it should provide a rough-and-ready guide to the mood of the times.

The sources agree that the number of senators put to death by Claudius was thirty-five; the figure for equestrians who suffered the same fate is given variously as 221 or over 300. The more prominent of these can be identified. In the period under review, the *Annals* of Tacitus are missing for all but the final phase of Messalina's tenure as imperial wife, but are extant for the whole of Claudius' Agrippina period, and consequently a higher proportion of named victims should be expected. But when we compare the figures of both periods as evidence of political opposition, the result is surprising and surely significant.

The list of known senatorial, senior equestrian and even prominent freedmen victims in the 'Messalina period' is extensive (no distinction is made here between execution and suicide in anticipation of execution). Livilla, Agrippina's sister and Claudius' niece, went down early in the reign, exiled in 41 and afterwards put to death. Her associate Seneca was actually sentenced to death, although he managed to escape with exile. Gaius Appius Silanus, husband of Messalina's mother, was executed in 42. His death was the spark that inspired Scribonianus, the legate of Dalmatia, to lead an unsuccessful rebellion against the emperor, which resulted in failure and Scribonianus' suicide. A number of other prominent Romans died in connection with the rebellion. These included Annius Vinicianus, related to Livilla's husband and possibly at one time a contender for the principate, and Caecina Paetus, who committed suicide along with his famous wife Arria because of his complicity in the revolt. Another possible collaborator was Pomponius Secundus, consul of 41, put to death for unspecified action against the emperor. In 43 Julia, the granddaughter of Tiberius, was forced into suicide, and the same period saw the deaths of Catonius Justus and probably Rufrius Pollio, prefects of the guard. Some three years later Asinius Gallus, son of Tiberius' first wife, and Statilius Corvinus rebelled with the help of a few slaves. Asinius was only exiled, but Statilius may have been put to death. Probably early in the following year Gnaeus Pompeius Magnus, the son-in-law of Claudius, was executed, as were his father Marcus Crassus Frugi and his mother Scribonia. The same year also saw the death of Valerius Asiaticus, the wealthy and prominent senator from Narbonese Gaul, who had held two consulships. It was followed by the forced suicide of his supposed mistress Poppaea Sabina. To this list we might add the prominent freedman Polybius. The Messalina scandal brought down in its wake Gaius Silius and the senator Juncus Vergilianus, as well as a number of prominent equestrians, Titus Proculus, *custos* ('guardian') of Messalina, the doctor Vettius Valens, their henchmen Pompeius Urbicus and Saufeius Trogus, Decrius Calpurnianus, prefect of the Vigiles and Sulpicius Rufus, procurator of the gladiatorial school. In the period that followed Claudius' marriage to Agrippina, Dio claims that she used murder for profit. But, despite the more detailed documentation now possible because of the resumption of Tacitus' *Annals*, there is a curious dearth of solidly identifiable victims. Lollia, the former wife of Caligula, was put to death, and the consular Statilius Taurus, whose gardens Agrippina coveted, committed suicide in 53 in anticipation of a condemnation to death. Sosibius, the tutor of Britannicus, was eliminated and Lepida, Agrippina's former sister-in-law, was executed shortly before Claudius' death. All of these seem to have been condemned in open trials rather than through *in camera* proceedings. No other victims are named. Lucius Silanus did commit suicide but it was to avoid shame and humiliation rather than to escape judicial execution.

It is apparent that the mood and atmosphere of Claudius' reign improved measurably during its latter half and there are several recorded instances where issues were handled with the maximum co-operation between palace and senate, instead of the confrontation that had earlier been so common. Moreover, the attitude of the senators seems to have changed from sullen hostility to supportive collaboration. There is nothing to indicate that the original intense hostility gradually lost its force by the late 40s, which would have been one explanation for the change in the temper of the regime. The pattern of executions in the first half of Claudius' reign is erratic and spasmodic, as severe towards the end of this initial phase as it had been at the beginning. A distinct change did occur towards the end of the decade, and it is difficult to avoid the conclusion that much of the impetus for this change for the better should be attributed to the influence and efforts of Agrippina.

The influence of Agrippina on the senate would have been considerable. Pliny the Elder notes an occasion when they passed a decree supposedly on her orders (*iubente Agrippina*), bestowing the praetorian insignia on Pallas (see below). Pliny is clearly determined to give his own twist to the situation, simplistically presenting as a command what would have been an efficient and vigorous campaign to win over senatorial support.[32] Nor is there evidence of consistent vindictiveness against senators who did not share her views. In this context it will be useful to consider the issue of the future emperor Vespasian, who is often cited as an example of Agrippina's enmity. Prior to AD 52 he enjoyed a promising career. He received his first important command in Germany when he became legate of Legio II shortly before the invasion of Britain in 43, an appointment he owed to Narcissus. The assignment of that legion to the invasion offered an opportunity for military glory and Vespasian's successes were rewarded by the *ornamenta triumphalia*. He was granted a suffect consulship in 51, which he held for the last two months of the year. From that point on, however, his career stalled and there is no record of further office until his governorship of Africa, in the early 60s. Suetonius claims that his forced retirement was due to the ill-will Agrippina bore towards him over his friendship with Narcissus. Certainly Agrippina must have had little love for Vespasian, given his behaviour towards her and her allies after the failed conspiracy of 39 (p. 67). But it is difficult to accept Suetonius' claim that she blocked his career. Clearly she was unable to prevent his consulship in 51, when she was at the height of her power and influence with Claudius. His son Titus remained a favourite at court, enjoying the friendship of Britannicus and dining in the palace (he was allegedly present at Britannicus' last meal). Moreover, Agrippina's eclipse after late 55 (the last time she seems to have been able to influence appointments) did not lead to a resumption of Vespasian's career. The main reasons for the hiatus in his progress must lie elsewhere.[33]

Once the marriage between Claudius and Agrippina had taken place, the groundwork for the next stage in their plan ('their' rather than 'her' is used advisedly) could be laid. The consul-designate Mammius Pollio, supposedly corrupted by a bribe, introduced a motion in the senate that called upon Claudius to betroth Octavia to Nero, another example of a friendly senator used as agent of the emperor's policy. Tacitus says that the proposal was made in the same terms Vitellius had used in canvassing support for the earlier marriage, which implies that once again the argument focused on the political advantages to be gained from a reconciliation between the two factions of the imperial family.[34]

Before the betrothal was concluded, however, Agrippina brought about a further change that was to have far-reaching consequences both for Roman political history and for her own future – the recall of Seneca, eventually to assume the duties of tutor to her son Nero. Seneca, as noted earlier (p. 81), had been banished on the grounds of involvement in an adulterous affair with Agrippina's sister Livilla. His offence had clearly been a serious one in Claudius' eyes, and, until the marriage to Agrippina, the emperor held firm in his resolve not to allow his return. According to one tradition, Seneca was on the point of setting out for Athens when he was summoned to Rome.[35] A reason for the recall is offered by Tacitus – he says that Agrippina wanted to avoid having her reputation based solely on 'crime' and saw the chance for popularity through association, by championing the return of a man of considerable literary distinction. By this time he had written three *Consolations*, most of his essay on anger, the *De Ira*, and at least one of his scientific publications, a lost treatise on earthquakes. Claudius must have been persuaded that Seneca could perform such a valuable service by using his literary skills to promote the emperor's political programme that his previous crimes should be overlooked. If, as Tacitus claims, Seneca still nursed a hatred towards Claudius for what he considered the unfairness of his treatment, he had the good sense to keep his resentment well concealed. He would have had a good incentive to do so. His return was approved in 49 and it was topped off the next year by his appointment as tutor to Nero and election to a praetorship (see Appendix VI).

Why would Agrippina have wanted Seneca to be Nero's tutor? Admittedly, when Nero stayed with his aunt Domitia during his mother's exile his education had been sadly deficient; it was even claimed, no doubt with exaggeration, that he had been taught by two instructors, a dancer and a barber. Agrippina would naturally not have allowed this neglect to continue once she returned to Rome and resumed supervision of her son. Her first appointments are indicated in an entry in the famous Byzantine encyclopedia, the 'Suda', which identifies two distinguished philosophers as Nero's instructors. One of them, the peripatetic Alexander Aegeus, wrote a commentary on Aristotle and was cited by Alexander of Aphrodisias. He was assisted as tutor by another philosopher, Chaeremon of Alexandria, a member of the embassy sent from Alexandria to Rome in 41 to present the case of the Greeks in an enquiry on the Greco-Jewish clashes in that city and a writer on Egyptian culture and history.[36] As Nero came to manhood, Agrippina would have been less committed to Nero's *philosophical* education. In the tradition of Cornelia, mother of the Gracchi, and of Seneca the elder, she discouraged her son from philosophical studies as an impediment to a ruler. She probably shared the prejudice that philosophy, and stoicism in particular, was irreconcilable with an active political life. Her motive in appointing Seneca as tutor would have been largely political. She was aware of the role of teachers in shaping an individual's political attitudes, and seems to have blamed Britannicus' tutors for antipathy between him and Nero. She would have wanted Nero to be taught by a brilliant mind whose political views on the best way to rule the Roman state coincided with her own. She and Seneca had been kindred spirits in 39. He had been in Rome to witness the outcome of one emperor's rule and had somehow incurred the wrath of the emperor who succeeded him. Both Agrippina and Seneca, consequently, would have seen the value of a 'constitutional' form of principate that operated through consensus and the liberalism of the ruler rather than through the simple exercise of power, and the advantages of imparting this principle to Nero.[37]

This political alliance between Agrippina and Seneca also provides incidental evidence of Agrippina's powerful influence, since it was almost certainly with her support that Seneca's relatives began to prosper. His father-in-law Pompeius Paulinus was placed in charge of the corn supply (*praefectus annonae*) not long after 49, and his brother Junius Gallio was appointed governor of Achaea for 51/2. His brother-in-law, the younger Aulus Paulinus, served as legate in Lower Germany in 55 and must accordingly have held a (suffect) consulship before that.[38]

Did the relations between Agrippina and Seneca have a closely personal, as well as a political, basis? There are hints that this might have been the case. For the evidence we must move forward in time to 58, when the notorious *delator* (informer) Publius Suillius accused Seneca of having had an affair with Agrippina (p. 81).[39] The accounts of his charge clearly show that there was a widely held belief that Agrippina and Seneca were at some point lovers. They give no clear indication of when. An illicit affair while Claudius was alive would have been extremely dangerous (given the fate of Messalina and her lover), yet would have been politically appropriate since Agrippina and Seneca were working together for the same goals. The sense of shared challenge (and danger) would have disappeared after the death of Claudius and the accession of Nero, at which point Seneca and Agrippina become increasingly estranged at both the personal and the political level. The collapse of a love affair might go a long way to explain the ill-will that later arose between them. It may be, of course, that the story of the affair is a complete fabrication, the sort of charge that could easily be (and frequently was), levelled against the prominent, and one which was unprovable but also difficult to refute.

Agrippina had clearly acted quickly in securing the recall of Seneca. She also moved hastily in dealing with what she perceived to be a potential threat to her position – the continuing challenge apparently posed by Lollia Paulina, who had been her rival for the hand of Claudius after the fall of Messalina.[40] It is not clear why Lollia should still have been considered dangerous, and Tacitus explains the intensity of Agrippina's hostility with the stereotypical observation that she was *atrox odii* ('unrelenting in her hatred'). This explanation is not satisfactory and apparently no hostility was manifested against her other rival Aelia Paetina. Moreover, an unnecessary direct head-on attack against her opponents was not typical of Agrippina. It is possible that Lollia was not herself an active opponent of Agrippina, but was considered by the anti-Agrippina forces as a likely candidate to replace her should she be brought down (Lollia certainly had sufficient wealth to support any such campaign). What is clear is that the attack came from both Agrippina and Claudius. Agrippina initiated the charge, that Lollia had consulted astrologers and had sought information from the oracle of Apollo at Colophon about the recent marriage (behaviour considered typical of would-be traitors). But it was Claudius who took up the case in the senate, where he refused Lollia a hearing. He made a long speech about her family distinction (omitting, however, any mention of her marriage to

Caligula), her link with the Volusii on her mother's side, her uncle Cotta Messalinus and her previous marriage to Memmius Regulus. This sounds as though Claudius was putting forward arguments that would bolster her suitability as an imperial wife, but he presumably intended to emphasize the depths to which she had sunk. Her behaviour was harmful (*perniciosa*) to the state, he claimed (it is not revealed how) and she should be deprived of her wealth, to prevent her from using it for criminal activity.

Lollia was thus obliged to forfeit her property, with the exception of 5 million HS, a pitiful amount from such a vast fortune, and she was relegated from Italy. The fine would go into imperial coffers (see p. 132). The relatively mild treatment was deceptive and probably intended to put her supporters off their guard. At some point later a praetorian tribune was despatched to track her down and put her to death. Dio adds the grisly detail that Agrippina, to make sure that she was dead, arranged for her head to be cut off and transported to Rome. She did not at first recognize her, but confirmed the identity by checking the teeth, which had certain peculiarities. The story is reminiscent of Fulvia's supposed treatment of Cicero's head but is neverthless plausible; Agrippina's double canine might have encouraged her to take a special interest in the teeth of others. Lollia's ashes were returned to Rome after Agrippina's death.

Tacitus and Dio also mention the fate of an otherwise unknown woman of rank, Calpurnia (both describe her as 'distinguished', presumably to avoid confusion with the concubine of that name involved in the downfall of Messalina). She was praised casually by Claudius and subsequently banished although, in contrast to Lollia, she was not put to death because the comment had been a casual one.[41] The allusion is cryptic, but she must have been considered more dangerous than is implied by the sources since her exile was to last for ten years. She enjoyed the general amnesty that followed Agrippina's death and was allowed to return to Rome in AD 59.

Agrippina could have felt well satisfied with her achievements in 49. She had married the emperor, betrothed her son to his daughter, arranged the recall of an influential ally and the expulsion of more than one potential rival. But she was not one to rest on her laurels, and the following year saw her achieve new heights. Her success was symbolized by a highly significant event, the conferment on her in AD 50 of the title of Augusta.[42] From now on her official name in coins and inscriptions is Iulia Augusta Agrippina, a change of great symbolic importance. She was in fact the first wife of a *living* emperor to share in the distinction of this title. Livia received it as a widow, when it could not threaten to eclipse the status of her husband. Antonia seems also to have been granted the rank by her grandson Caligula in 37, but she similarly did not pose a threat to the emperor and was by then a very elderly woman (she would die within months). Poppaea, the wife of Nero, would become Augusta when her daughter Claudia was born at Antium in January 63 and it became the regular title for the wife of the princeps from the accession of Domitian in 81.[43] The significance of Agrippina's elevation cannot be exaggerated. Perhaps more than anything else, it conveyed the notion of empress, not, of course, in the technical sense of a person having the formal authority to make legally binding decisions, but as someone who could lay equal claim to the majesty that the office of emperor conveyed. She now received another important distinction, that of participating in the daily *salutatio*. When courtiers and clients paid homage to the emperor, as they did each morning, they would henceforth do the same to her.[44]

The title of Augusta would enhance Agrippina's status in the eyes of the public and this elevated status is reflected in the coins produced by the imperial mint in subsequent years. Precious metal coins issued officially in Rome had prior to the marriage emphasized on their reverses the domestic and foreign achievements of Claudius. This now changes. For the very first time the emperor and his consort appear on the same issue. Claudius is depicted on the obverse, with a draped bust of Agrippina, identified as Agrippina Augusta, on the reverse (Pl. 16). She wears ears of corn, a recurring feature also of other imperial women and seemingly suggesting an association with Demeter and fertility. An official silver coin of Ephesus, dated 50/51, similarly carries an obverse head of Claudius and a reverse of Agrippina Augusta. Another Ephesian issue depicts jugate heads of Claudius and Agrippina Augusta (that is, facing in the same direction with one superimposed over the other, Pl. 12). The head of the emperor and of his wife appearing *together* on the same face of a coin is a remarkable first for Roman official (as opposed to local) coinage. The jugate heads, first developed by Ptolemy II to celebrate his marriage to his sister Arsinoe, signal very strikingly the official sanction of the role of Agrippina as Claudius' partner. Such types were already familiar in local coinage but here it is the pervasiveness of Agrippina's image that is striking. She appears on Claudian coins from at least twenty-one cities, as opposed to Messalina's nine. Agrippina also appears facing the emperor on local coins of Assus and jugate with him at Mostene, Smyrna and Nysa (probably), while Messalina shares with Claudius the same face of only one known coin, a local issue of Tralles.[45]

Another striking feature of Agrippina's iconography is that sculpted heads attributed to her from the Claudian period are sometimes adorned with a diadem. This was an exceptional honour. The diadem was properly the attribute of a goddess, and allowed to mortals only after death. It is likely that Agrippina was the first to receive this distinction during her lifetime – another striking demonstration of her elevated position.[46]

Agrippina would also have made sure that her portrait would appear on statues all through the empire. She has been identified in nine known extant monuments featuring statuary groups. In the basilica of the Italian town of Velleia she appears with Claudius and a very youthful Nero, thus early in the marriage before Nero's assumption of the *toga virilis*.[47] The most striking group appears on a relief from the *sebasteion* of Aphrodisias (p. 18). There are three figures. Agrippina stands at the left, her right hand clasping the right hand of Claudius, who stands in the centre. On Claudius' left a figure in a toga, presumably a personification, crowns him with an oak wreath.[48] In her left hand Agrippina holds a bunch of corn ears, associated, as on the imperial coins, with Demeter.[49] This piece combines two themes Agrippina would have wanted to emphasize. The oak crown was a powerful symbol in Julio-Claudian iconography. Originally it was given to acknowledge the saving of another man's life; when associated with the emperors, it represented their role in the saving of the state. In 27 BC, when Augustus made the gesture of restoring the republic, the senate voted him an oak crown. A similar crown appeared on the pediment of the Palatine residence early in Claudius' reign.[50] Its image appears on coins of Augustus, Tiberius and Caligula, as well as on those of Claudius, where it is usually accompanied by a legend inherited from Augustus, *ob cives servatos* ('for saving his fellow-citizens'), and it will reappear on Nero's issue. The figure in the toga almost certainly represents the senate, which had the authority to grant the award, and its bestowal marks the constitutional accord between emperors and senate. This is combined with the powerful image of marital harmony – the clasped hands represent in most likelihood *concordia* between man and wife, while at the same time they suggest a kind of equality of the two parties. Agrippina is cleverly placed alongside Claudius and the personified senate as the third element in the working of the Roman state.

Although proof is impossible, there is good reason to believe that Agrippina might well have sought at this point to establish a more visible reminder of her status in Rome. The part of the Palatine Hill that dominated the north slope above the Forum Romanum was occupied in the latter part of the Julio-Claudian period by a massive palace complex, the Domus Tiberiana, constructed on a platform 15,000sq m (18,000sq yds) in area. Built over by the Farnesi Gardens in the fifteenth century, it has not been systematically excavated. The northern range is best known; tiles indicate that Domitian rebuilt the complex after 80 and that Hadrian made further alterations in the early second century. It was long believed that the first Domus Tiberiana was built piecemeal, but a recent archaeological survey by the Swiss Institute in Rome has decided emphatically against this theory, and has concluded that the geometric structure of the palace argues strongly for its being the uniform concept of a single individual. The expression 'Domus Tiberiana' might seem logically to suggest that the original structure should be dated to the reign of Tiberius, but in fact the name is used for the first time in extant sources in a context that postdates Tiberius' death by more than thirty years, the conspiracy of the short-lived emperor Galba in 69. It may have been coined to define the original structure, to draw a distinction with the later period when the general term *palatium* became associated specifically with the huge palace complex built over the area by Domitian. In fact, it would have been totally out of character for Tiberius, who had a distinct and notorious aversion to grandiose architectural ventures, to have undertaken a luxurious project on the scale of the Domus Tiberiana. He would almost certainly have contented himself with the already grand family complex that the Domus replaced. It would not have been out of character for Caligula, of course, but there is no reference to his building a palace on the Palatine; in fact, Suetonius locates his planned new residence not on the Palatine but on the Capitoline hill. Also Josephus' description of the aftermath of Caligula's assassination indicates that in 41 the imperial residence on the Palatine was still made up of individual houses, such as that of Germanicus: 'since the palace, although one complex, had been increased a part at a time and as a result the additions were named for the members of the imperial family who completed or began some part of the whole' (loosely paraphrased and the text is very uncertain).[51]

The Domus had almost certainly been built by the time Claudius died in 54. At any rate, Suetonius states that on the morning following his death the doors of the palace were dramatically opened and the young Nero emerged to be proclaimed by the praetorians *pro gradibus palatii* ('before the steps of the palace'), a clear allusion to the stairs that would have been necessitated by the huge podium. The historical evidence, then, suggests that the Domus Tiberiana is almost certainly Claudian and the building technique, a mixture of tile and travertine blocks, suits a late Claudian date. One further detail helps to date the complex after his marriage to Agrippina. The structure of the podium has its closest parallel in Rome in the massive platform of the Temple of Divus

Claudius, begun by Agrippina on her husband's death at the north-west corner of the Caelian Hill. The temple, although authorized by the senate, was very much Agrippina's personal project and her later eclipse meant that it had to wait until the reign of Vespasian for its completion. The author of the Domus Tiberiana and of the Temple of Claudius is probably one and the same, and both express Agrippina's grandiose concept of the role of herself and of Claudius in the overall scheme of things.[52]

The bestowal of the title of Augusta on Agrippina is placed by Tacitus among the events of AD 50. The very first event of that year to be mentioned is Agrippina's thrust to hurry forward the adoption of Nero by Claudius. She made use of Pallas as an intermediary to argue her case with her husband, but we can be sure that Claudius would hardly have allowed his mind to be made up for him on an issue that lay at the very heart of his principate.[53] The adoption of Nero, who was older than Britannicus and would thus become the prime candidate for the succession, must have been seen by Claudius as in his own best interest. The desire to be succeeded from within one's own line is a natural impulse, but had no constitutional validation in Rome. During the first two centuries of the empire only two emperors, Marcus Aurelius and Vespasian, were succeeded by their natural sons, through the accident that they were the only ones who had surviving sons to succeed them. The argument was supposedly presented to Claudius that the adoption of Nero would somehow protect Britannicus, but this was surely specious. Claudius' desire to be succeeded by his own son was secondary to his desire to survive, by signalling to any would-be rivals that on his own removal they would have to deal with the problem of two potential successors.

Technically it could be argued that Tacitus was wrong in claiming that Claudius gave Nero precedence in the succession over Britannicus, as there was no constitutional arrangement by which the successor could be formally designated. Britannicus was not actively excluded. It could have been claimed that he was simply too young for the offices and responsibilities that befell Nero when he reached manhood. But Claudius had considerable political sense and could not have failed to appreciate how his actions would be interpreted. The promotion of Nero at a time when Britannicus was legally unable to be advanced clearly meant that on the death of the emperor Nero's superior experience and his longer exposure to public and political life would make his position virtually unassailable. Events confirm that this was in fact the case.[54]

There was another issue, on which the sources are somewhat reticent. Tacitus says that Britannicus was passed over even though some insisted that he was a bright boy. Tacitus admits, however, to some scepticism about this claim of superior intelligence, which was never put to the test, and he suggests that it might have been the result of a kind of compensatory sympathy. Tacitus does reveal later (after Britannicus' death, in fact) that the young man had suffered from epilepsy since childhood. Caligula was also an epilepsy sufferer in his infancy and this did not seem to pose a serious obstacle to his claim to succeed. If, however, Britannicus suffered from a serious form of the disease (which may in fact have killed him), it could well have jeopardized his prospects. The only hint that something of this nature might have proved an obstacle is an anecdote preserved in Suetonius. Narcissus brought in a physiognomist to examine Britannicus and was told that he would never rule (although his friend Titus, the son of Vespasian, one day would). Whatever the merits of the argument that concern over Britannicus' health was a factor in Claudius' decision to favour Nero, there is certainly little merit in the speculation that the emperor had doubts about Britannicus' paternity. It is true that Nero supposedly charged that Claudius was not Britannicus' father and the idea receives indirect support from the *Octavia*, where it is claimed that Messalina's conduct put Octavia's paternity in doubt. But caution needs to be exercised over such claims – they look very much like a standard *topos*. Tiberius Gemellus was also reputedly denied his fair claim to the succession because his grandfather Tiberius suspected that he might not be legitimate. While Claudius allowed Britannicus to occupy second place in the succession league, there is no hint that he ever personally turned against his son.[55]

The case for Nero's adoption was presented by Claudius in the senate (we need not take too strongly Tacitus' claim that he simply regurgitated Pallas' arguments). He used the precedents of earlier emperors, Augustus, who had advanced his stepsons Tiberius and Drusus even though he had grandsons in the wings, and Tiberius, who had adopted Germanicus even though he had a son (Drusus) of his own. The appeal was made that Claudius should similarly have someone to share the burden of office. It was noted at the time, either by *periti*, 'expert observers' (according to Tacitus) or by Claudius himself (according to Suetonius, probably correctly), that there was no recorded case of an adoption in the patrician branch of the Claudian family. The recent precedent of Tiberius seems to have been conveniently ignored. He had adopted Germanicus before his own adoption by Augustus into Julian line, when he was still a Claudian.[56]

The procedure was not a simple one. On the death of his paterfamilias Domitius, Nero was technically *sui iuris* ('under his own authority'), in the sense that he did not fall under the authority of a paterfamilias, even though a guardian would be technically responsible for his affairs until he came of age. The only way in which he could be adopted, and could then pass under the authority of a new paterfamilias, was by a complex process of adoption known as *adrogatio*, which involved legislation (a *lex curiata*) from the people's assembly, the *comitia centuriata*, on the motion of the Pontifex Maximus or his deputy (the latter must presumably have been involved in those procedures that involved the emperor, who routinely held the chief pontificate himself). This procedure would be preceded by a formal investigation by the pontiffs to ensure that the adoption was valid. They would need to determine a number of things: whether the adoptive parent was beyond the age when he could expect to bear natural children, established traditionally at 60, and also whether he had a child from a previous union. Suetonius indicates that this was the form used by Augustus when he adopted Agrippa Postumus and Tiberius, and it is safe to assume that it would have been used by Tiberius in the adoption of Germanicus (cited by Claudius), and Caligula in the adoption of Tiberius Gemellus (not cited, but probably from tact rather than unsuitability as a legal precedent).[57] Certainly Claudius met the first requirement. But the existence of a natural son Britannicus caused problems and criticism, just as similar concerns seem to have been raised by Tiberius' adoption of Germanicus. These obstacles were not strictly legal. The pontiffs could, and frequently did, relax the rules if there was a reasonable cause, a *iusta causa adrogandi*, and Claudius, as Pontifex Maximus, could have ensured approval. Similar problems were overcome by Tiberius, who faced the double obstacle of having a son (Drusus) and being only 46 years old at the time. The difficulty was political. There would be a temptation for observers to recall the irregularity of

Claudius' marriage to Agrippina.[58]

None of the sources is explicit about how the issue was resolved but a hint is provided later by Tacitus. When the issue of Nero's status was supposedly raised by Britannicus (see below), Agrippina protested to her husband that questions were being raised, even though the adoption had been carried through on the instructions of the people (the *lex curiata*) and a resolution of the senate (*censuerint Patres*).[59] The passing of a *lex* was routinely preceded by a senatorial decree, but Agrippina's emphasis on the senate's role suggests that in this instance it was more than routine. In the case of her marriage to Claudius, Agrippina had manoeuvred things so that the senators prevailed on the emperor to go through with it. It seems likely that the same happened on this occasion. The comment that the Claudii had never before adopted could well be an assertion by Claudius himself as he allowed himself to be prevailed upon by an insistent senate. The handling of the whole issue bears all the hallmarks of Agrippina.[60]

The senate approved the adoption, which was enacted on 25 February 50, as indicated in the Arval record. It is from this point that Agrippina's son officially acquired his familiar name, Nero, when, instead of Lucius Domitius Ahenobarbus, he became, through adoption, Nero Claudius Drusus Germanicus Caesar.[61] Although he had been adopted by no less a figure than the emperor, Nero's inscriptions at this time continue to stress his descent on the Julian side and from Germanicus. When the Arvals made vows at some time between 50 and 54 for his recovery from an illness Nero appears to be described (the record is fragmentary) as the *suboles* ('offspring') of Agrippina before he is mentioned as the son of Claudius. This theme is reflected in three places which had strong links with the Julio-Claudian dynasty. An inscription from Pergamum, the centre of the imperial cult in Asia, identifies Nero as the son of Claudius the emperor and as grandson of Germanicus. In other words, it traces his descent first through his (adoptive) father but then through his *mother's* line. Ilium (Troy) had strong links with the Julian house which, by tradition, was founded by the Trojan Aeneas, son of Venus, though his son Iullus. An interesting statue group is known from that city, a group set up by the inhabitants to honour Claudius' children Britannicus, Antonia, Octavia and Nero. The letter-forms in the dedication to Nero are smaller, creating the impression that his inscription was squeezed in afterwards, either after his adoption or to mark the service he performed a year or two later on behalf of the city. In the inscription Nero is called 'Caesar', while Britannicus is not. Even more noteworthy is the detail that Nero is the only one of the children to be called *syngenes tes poleos*, 'kinsman of the city'. Both details emphasize his Julian descent. One inscription from Aezani in the province of Asia goes so far as to make no mention of Claudius, and refers to Nero as the son of *Theas Agrippeines* ('Divine Agrippina'), adding that he is her *natural* son (*phusei*).[62]

Although she had worked to establish Nero's precedence over Britannicus, Agrippina would have appreciated that she would gain nothing by antagonizing her stepson needlessly. She would also have accepted that if Nero did not survive Claudius, the succession should pass to his stepbrother. She made an effort to show kindness to Britannicus, which Tacitus describes as hypocritical and which was supposedly seen as such by Britannicus. Certainly the evidence indicates that relations between Agrippina and Claudius' daughter Octavia were always close and cordial. Her gestures may have been genuinely meant, but kind gestures could not alter the reality that Nero's arrival on the scene had displaced Claudius' son.[63]

Agrippina would have had to ensure that Nero would be fit and ready to assume office when the time came, and some time after the adoption in February she arranged the appointment of Seneca as his tutor. Suetonius reports that on the night following the appointment Seneca had a dream that he was teaching Caligula – a dream that would prove prophetic when Nero began to display cruelty on a level that would rival his predecessor's. The story, at least in the damning form it takes, is to be treated with the greatest caution – it would have required a bravado that Seneca did not possess for him to have made such a vision public, and in any case he states in his own writings that he did not believe in premonitions derived from dreams.[64] It could not have escaped Seneca that any contribution he might make to Nero's prospects could come about only at a cost to Britannicus. He later revealed to Nero that he realized that his role was to further his pupil's expectations (*spei tuae admotus*). It has even been suggested that his grudge against Claudius could have inspired him to damage Britannicus' chances deliberately . Of course, Nero was clearly destined to be the successor and Seneca might have argued that he could at least play his part in ensuring that the new ruler should be as enlightened as possible, in which he seems to have been to some degree successful. Such an educational programme can hardly have offended Agrippina – the desire for a better entente between the senatorial oligarchy and the imperial power was probably one both she and Seneca shared. What she did not anticipate was that the bond that developed between teacher and willing pupil would, when it came to a clash, prove stronger than that between son and mother.

In AD 50 Agrippina's powers and influence, already persuasive in Rome, were given distinct recognition outside Rome also, when a *colonia* was founded in her birthplace, Ara Ubiorum. The *colonia* was an ancient and well-established Roman institution. Its origins go back at least to the fourth century BC, when families were sent to defend the coastline of Italy and settled in outposts at Ostia, Antium and Tarracina, where they received generous allowances of land. By the late second century colonies had been established beyond Italy, the first overseas venture being the Gracchan settlement at Carthage. By this time they had a political, as well as a strategic, function, as a device to encourage emigration of the urban masses and to provide land for veterans. Eventually the tradition grew of granting the title of *colonia* to *municipia* as means of elevating their status and conferring full Roman citizenship.

The establishment of colonies was clearly an important element of Claudian policy. It was a means of creating clients throughout the empire, but it also fostered his enlightened aim of spreading Roman citizenship beyond Italy, paralleled by the policy of encouraging the admission of wealthy and deserving individuals from Gaul into the Senate. Claudius thus established settlements in the east, at Ptolemais (Acre) in Syria and Archelais in Cappadocia, as well as in the Balkans, at Siculi (Biac) and possibly Aequum in Dalmatia and Savaria in Pannonia. At Camulodunum (Colchester) in Britain he established *Colonia Victricensis* for veterans of Legio XX, when that legion moved from Colchester to Gloucester in AD 49.[65]

The new *colonia* at Ara Ubiorum extended Agrippina's influence beyond Rome into an area where she always felt that she had a special role to play. More than eighty years previously (38 BC) her maternal grandfather Marcus Agrippa had moved the friendly

Ubii from their location on the far side of the Rhine to the left bank (p. 27). Her father Germanicus and paternal grandfather Drusus were both associated with conquests in the region, and it was during her father's campaigns that she was born there. Some time after her birth the settlement was rebuilt on the Roman pattern. By AD 50 the two legions originally stationed there had long been transferred to Neuss and Bonn and in that year, Tacitus informs us, 'to advertise her strength in the provinces', Agrippina arranged for the establishment of a *colonia* of veterans in the place of her birth. The community received its title from her and Claudius' names, *Colonia Claudia Ara Augusta Agrippinensium*, establishing once again a parity between Agrippina and her husband in an important political act. While Tacitus gives Agrippina a key role in the matter, the founding of what later became Cologne was completely in harmony with Claudian policy elsewhere in the empire and is, in fact, another good example of Agrippina and the emperor working in partnership. There is, however, an interesting difference between the provisions made there and the normal arrangement at other foundations. The settlement at Cologne seems to have involved the traditional allotment of land to veterans along with the simultaneous elevation of the status of the existing town of Ara Ubiorum to a *colonia*, a privilege in which the original inhabitants could share. It would thus confer at least Latin rights, and possibly full citizenship, on the *whole* community. As a consequence, Cologne avoided the traumatic experience of Colchester, where the brutal confiscation of land without any compensating benefit for the local community was to be the flash- point leading up to the Boudican rebellion. The Ubii were pleased to be able to call themselves *Agrippinenses* from now on. It is impossible to attribute this policy directly to Agrippina but it bears all the signs of her strategy of anticipating difficulties and clearing away the obstacles beforehand, and the use of her name by the inhabitants suggests a special feeling of gratitude.[66] By the late 60s there had been so much intermarriage between new settlers and the original inhabitants that it was difficult to distinguish between Romans and Ubii among their offspring, and Cologne had so prospered that it was envied and resented by other German communities. The Agrippinenses would only reluctantly become involved in the rebellion of Julius Civilis which broke out in the Rhine area in AD 69, and quickly went back to their old allegiance afterwards.[67]

The founding of the new *colonia* may well have given Agrippina more than symbolic honours, since the people of Cologne might have assumed the status of her clients and she of their patron, a powerful one at that, who could represent their interests in time of trouble. This collaboration was an extension of an old established tradition of the patron/client relationship, whereby powerful families originally offered assistance to their poor counterparts in return for broad political services. By the third century BC Roman military commanders began to assume a new form of general patronage over people conquered by them, and this seems to be the origin of a third and related kind of patronage, whereby towns appointed powerful individuals to speak for them in Rome or to act as arbitrators in disputes.[68]

The patronage of the imperial family would bring considerable prestige as well as practical benefits, and it was sought by a number of communities in the Alpine regions, in Spain and in Asia.[69] Many of the clients would have come originally to Augustus by virtue of conquest, but others could have developed through family association. Ilium (Troy) had close connections with the Julian family. Julius Caesar confirmed privileges the town had enjoyed in the form of immunities and extended territory; there was a claim that he planned to move the seat of government from Rome to Ilium. The recognition of Augustus as their patron is associated with the simultaneous establishment of the imperial cult.[70] Before his accession Tiberius was patron of Epidaurus, a city that had a long and traditional association with the imperial family.[71] In Cologne's case, the association was obvious. Agrippina had been born in the town, and her grandfather Agrippa had played a part in its early history. From Tiberius on it was the regular practice for emperors to decline patronage of communities. Whether Agrippina would have felt herself bound by similar ethical restraints we cannot tell. Also, if she did become patron she may not have been the only one. The town of Canusium, for instance, could in AD 223 boast a list of thirty-one senators and eight knights as their patrons, who shared the role. Unfortunately no similar document for Cologne has survived. But, whether as patron or as friend, Agrippina would certainly have maintained a close interest in the colony and have fostered its loyalty and allegiance.[72]

In 51 Claudius entered his fifth consulship, the first since the fall of Messalina, probably to mark the tenth anniversary of his accession.[73] The timing was fortunate, since he would be able to honour as consul the first event recorded by Tacitus for the year, the elevation of his stepson Nero to the status of manhood. If the gods are to be believed (and they sent no shortage of omens to make their point clear), this laid the foundations for calamities that would plague Rome for years to come. Owls infested the Capitol, buildings were destroyed by earthquakes and as people tried in panic to escape they were trampled to death. There was a corn shortage and a subsequent famine, all sure signs of divine disfavour. But for Agrippina, at least, the year would be cause for jubilation. As the elder of the two sons, Nero would naturally take precedence over Britannicus, and when he reached official manhood, by assuming the *toga virilis*, he would in a quasi-legal sense be deemed competent to assume the principate. At the beginning of the year he was in his 14th year. The normal occasion for the rites of manhood was 17 March, the festival of Liberalia, but there is evidence that Nero's ceremony was brought forward. He was already consul-designate by at least 4 March 51, since he begins to be identified as such on inscriptions from 51 on, and the month and day are confirmed by anniversary celebrations in later Arval records. An authority on Roman constitutional history like Claudius would hardly have allowed election to such a high office had Nero been technically under age, just as Augustus was greatly offended by the unauthorized selection of Gaius Caesar as consul in 6 BC before he was of age.[74]

At the same time as his election as consul-designate (the office to be assumed in his 20th year), Nero also received the title of *princeps iuventutis* ('the leader of the youth'), a position analogous to that of *princeps senatus* (the 'president of the senate') and usually intended to mark its holder as a potential successor (it had earlier been conferred for that purpose on Gaius and Lucius Caesar by Augustus).[75] There was now a striking difference in the relative standing of Nero and Britannicus, and this difference was publicly reflected in the official coin issues assigned to the remaining years of Claudius' reign. Among gold and silver issues (aurei and denarii) struck at Rome between 51 and 54 were coins with obverse portraits either of Agrippina, wearing the crown of corn ears, or of Claudius, and on the reverse of both the head of Nero, identified as *princeps iuventutis*. The appearance of the designated successor on the reverse of a coin depicting the emperor's spouse is yet another numismatic innovation. Another two issues bear the bust of Nero on the *obverse*, identified as *cos design* ('consul-designate'), while the reverses celebrate either his nomination as *princeps iuventutis* or his co-option into the four major priestly colleges. These issues are also unprecedented in imperial coinage; other than on posthumous commemorative pieces, the obverse had always shown the emperor. Britannicus' only appearance in official issues is on an earlier coin issued in Caesarea in Cappadocia in 46, where he appears, along with his sister Octavia and half-sister Antonia, on an imitation of the Caligula 'three sisters' sestertius. Outside Rome, Nero and Britannicus receive fairly balanced treatment on coins, since explicit instructions to elevate Nero at the expense of his stepbrother would have been difficult to convey discreetly to distant communities.[76]

The manhood ceremony was followed by the usual manifestations of public generosity, handouts for the troops and for the general public, as well as a parade drill of the praetorians, headed by Nero in his capacity of *princeps iuventutis*. Tacitus says that all this happened because Claudius gave in to the 'sycophantic urgings' of the senate. What this probably means, of course, is that careful groundwork had been carried out in the senate before the event, and in this we can surely detect once again the hand of Agrippina.

The public could not have failed to see the parallels between Claudius and Augustus, who held consulships in 5 and 2 BC when he introduced Gaius Caesar and Lucius Caesar respectively to public life. The remission of statutory years for Nero's consulship also had precedents – Marcellus, Augustus' nephew, was the first member of the family known to receive this favour.[77] The remarkable feature of Nero's advancement, however, is that as consul-designate he was to be allowed proconsular authority outside the city limits. This measure gave him a power that was independent of his status as Claudius' son, and which he would therefore continue to exercise after Claudius' death. It must have been deemed essential for him to have this safeguard, and Agrippina no doubt felt it no less essential to remind the public that he enjoyed it. Thus in the circus games following the ceremony Britannicus wore the white and purple toga of youth, while Nero wore the magisterial robes which marked the tenure of *imperium*. None of the spectators could have been left in any doubt about who was intended for the succession.[78]

The Roman public would be reminded of the new situation in the palace in a much more concrete fashion. In 43, as a consequence of Claudius' victories in Britain, the senate had voted him arches in both Boulogne, his embarkation point, and Rome. The Rome monument was constructed as part of the Aqua Virgo and takes the form of an engaged triumphal arch at the point where the aqueduct passes over the Via Lata, completed in 51. Its inscriptions, duplicated on the north and the south face, included a set of eight of members of his family, probably in association with relief sculpture (the sculpture is now lost). One group consisted of the names and titles of Antonia, Agrippina, Nero and, almost certainly, Germanicus. The other set included Britannicus, Octavia and two further unidentified individuals. Agrippina is identified in large letters as IULIA AUGUSTA at the head of the inscription, stressing her Julian descent and her status as Augusta, and she is further described as daughter of Germanicus. Nero's inscription stands next to his mother's and is of great interest since it traces his descent on his mother's side, through her father Germanicus and her grandmother Antonia. His status as consul-designate and *princeps iuventutis* is recorded, as well as the induction into the four major Roman priesthoods celebrated on contemporary coin issues (see above). Another inscription of the period records his additional induction in 51 into the order of the Sodales Augustales, the body charged with the cult of Divus Augustus and Divus Julius.[79]

Thus far it might be said that the distinctions bestowed on Nero inevitably enhanced his position relative to that of Britannicus, but up to now they should not be seen as part of any campaign specifically to discredit his stepbrother. In 51 the situation changed and the catalyst seems to have been a casual incident. At a chance meeting, Nero greeted his brother as 'Britannicus' and the latter reputedly answered with 'Domitius', the name he held before his adoption by Claudius.[80] Suetonius portrays the mistake as innocent, as the result of habit (*ex consuetudine*), an unlikely explanation given that the change of name had taken place about a year earlier. Nero reputedly took offence, and in revenge tried to persuade Claudius that Britannicus was illegitimate. In later years Nero clearly held the name of the Domitii in great honour, and supposedly declared his intention in the last year of his life of abandoning his adoptive name and reverting to his original nomen of Domitius.[81] But Britannicus can hardly have intended the gesture as a compliment. Agrippina exploited the insult, representing it to Claudius as the first symptom of internal strife which could turn into a catastrophe unless Britannicus was protected from corrupting influences. She convinced Claudius of the risk of factions within the palace, the very danger that their marriage had been intended to eliminate. Claudius was paranoid about the threat to his security and authorized an immediate purge of Britannicus' advisers. This represents a further stage in a process which Agrippina seems to have initiated the previous year, when she tried to check the malign influence of some members of Britannicus' entourage. At that time she began slowly and gradually (*paulatim*) to deprive Britannicus of his old tutors. Now the loyal freedmen were removed, as well as the few old tutors who still remained. The most important of these, Sosibius, was put to death, on the grounds of plotting against Nero. Britannicus' old retainers would have been loyal to the memory of Messalina, and Agrippina and Claudius were probably prudent in their decision to have them removed.[82]

More significantly, Tacitus claims that Agrippina began to remove any officers of the praetorian guard at the rank of centurion or tribune who had shown Britannicus sympathy, and to replace them with her own men. She was able to do this, Tacitus notes, by manipulating bogus promotions. That the wish of the imperial house should have influenced the disposition of the officer ranks of the praetorians is not at all surprising, and conforms to Roman practice and tradition. The innovation in this case was that the influence was exercised ultimately not by the emperor, but by his wife. So thorough was her intervention that the effect of her handiwork would be felt for years afterwards, and would have a dramatic impact on political events.[83]

By what process were these officers appointed? A centurion in both the praetorian and the legionary service would command eighty men, a praetorian tribune a whole cohort (the size of the praetorian cohort at this time, whether 500 or 1000 soldiers, is uncertain). There is ample evidence to show that legionary centurions often owed their appointments to decisions made on the spot by the governors of the provinces where they would serve. Tacitus reports that in AD 18 Piso, on his arrival in Syria, sought to win over the legions by using bribes to ingratiate himself with the soldiers and by dismissing the long-service centurions and the stricter tribunes, replacing them with his hangers-on. That such appointments could be made by an 'old boy' network without reference to the emperor is illustrated by the activities of the younger Pliny, who was able to secure from Neratius Marcellus, appointed governor of Britain in about AD 101, a commission as military tribune for his younger contemporary, none other than the future biographer Suetonius. Pliny's letter seems to indicate that this kind of patronage was not out of the ordinary, and what is particularly striking is that Neratius seems to have sent Pliny a blank commission document, with the name to be filled in. When Suetonius, in the end, decided to pass over the chance to go to Britain, Pliny was able to transfer the position to someone whom Suetonius, in his turn, wanted to advance.[84] But while appointments at this level could be decided locally, there were occasions when the emperor took a personal hand. The poet Statius describes the work of an imperial freedman, an *ab epistulis* to Domitian, whose duties included giving guidance to the emperor on who would 'command a century or a cohort'. Juvenal saw the centurionate as something that could be lobbied for, presumably in Rome, and in the Hadrianic period Florus could speak of the great honour felt in the receipt of a centurionate from the emperor. The direct involvement of the emperor in such appointments could have a major impact on subsequent events. During the struggle for imperial power in AD 69 there was sympathy in Britain among the troops of Vespasian's old Legio II for the claim of their old commander, but they faced resistance from other legions, where Vitellius had taken a direct hand in the appointment of centurions.[85]

Tacitus claims that Agrippina got rid of the sympathizers of Britannicus by bogus promotions. In fact the study of epigraphical material has shown that it was a *regular* feature in the Roman army for service as a centurion or tribune in the praetorian guard to be followed by promotion to the higher centurionates of the legion.[86] The career of Marcus Vettius Valens, who belongs to this general period, provides an excellent illustration of the phenomenon:

M. Vettio M(arci) f(ilio) Ani(ensi tribu) Valenti
mil(iti) coh(ortis) VIII pr(aetoriae)
benef(icario) praef(ecti) pr(aetorio)
donis donato bello Britan(nico)
torquibus armillis phaleris
evoc(ato) Aug(usti)
corona aurea donat(o)
(centurioni) coh(ortis) XVI vig(ilum)
(centurioni) stat(orum)
(centurioni) coh(ortis) XVI urb(anae)
(centurioni) coh(ortis) II pr(aetoriae)
exercitatori equit(um) speculatorum
princip(i) praetori leg(ionis) XIII Ge(minae) ex
trec(enario)
[p(rimo) p(ilo)] leg(ionis) VI Victr(icis)
donis donato ob res prosper(e) gest(as)
contra Astures torq(uibus) phaler(is) arm(illis)

trib(uno) coh(ortis) V vig(ilum)
trib(uno) coh(ortis) XII urb(anae)
trib(uno) coh(ortis) III pr(aetoriae)
[...] leg(ionis) XIIII Gem(inae) Mart(iae) Victr(icis)
proc(uratori) imp(eratoris) Neronis Caes(aris) Aug(usti)
prov(inciae) Lusitani(ae)
patron(o) coloniae '

To Marcus Vettius Valens, son of Marcus, of the tribe
Aniensis
soldier of praetorian cohort VIII
beneficarius of the praetorian prefect
granted awards in the British war of
torcs, armbands, disks
evocatus Augusti
awarded a gold crown
centurion of cohort VI of the *Vigiles*
centurion of the *statores*
centurion of urban cohort XVI
centurion of praetorian cohort II
trainer of the mounted scouts
staff adjutant of Legio XIII Gemina, formerly *centurion*
trecenarius
[chief centurion] of Legio VI Victrix
granted awards for successful campaigns
against the Asturians of torcs, disks, armbands
tribune of cohort V of the Vigiles
tribune of urban cohort XII
tribune of praetorian cohort III
[chief centurion?] of Legio XIV Gemina Martia Victrix
procurator of Imperator Nero Caesar Augustus in the province
of Lusitania
patron of the *colonia* [87]

Valens began his career as a ranker in the praetorians and after his initial term of
service reached the level of *evocatus* (a status that tended to precede the centurionate),
from which he progressed through the centurionates of the Rome units, the *vigiles*,
the *cohortes urbanae*, and the praetorian prefects. After service in Legio VI as chief
centurion (if the inscription has been correctly restored), he returned for tribunacies
in the Rome cohorts, followed probably by a chief centuriate in Legio XIV. His career
was concluded by a civilian post. His progression indicates that there was nothing at
all sinister or unusual about praetorians being moved out of Rome to hold senior positions in the legions. To remove unwelcome praetorian officers from the scene,
Agrippina chose a particularly astute stratagem; she adopted a procedure that was
standard military practice and by, in effect, *rewarding* men she could not fully trust she

much reduced the danger of resentment and resistance.

The changes made in the command of the guard would have profound consequences. Clearly the support of a loyal *prefect* of the praetorians was an invaluable political tool (and one that Agrippina would arrange in due course). But the change of officers at a lower level would have an effect on the rank and file which the more remote prefect could not possibly match. Agrippina shrewdly moved to make these lower-level appointments before the selection of a new prefect, who might take umbrage at a large-scale re-posting of his officers.

The penetration of the guard would not be total – there is a hint that after Claudius' death there were still some elements sympathetic to the cause of Britannicus. But it was certainly thorough, with long-lasting effects. Some of those advanced at this time are recognizable later. Their number probably included Julius Pollio, praetorian tribune in 55, with a reputation as a staunch supporter of Nero, and supposedly his agent in arranging the poisoning of Britannicus (see p. 170).[88] Others would feel complex pulls of loyalty when Nero later became estranged from his mother. When he came to plan her murder, one of the great obstacles that he faced was the divided commitment of the guard. Six years after her death, two of the leading participants in the great conspiracy against Nero in 65 were Faenius Rufus, prefect of the praetorians, and the tribune Subrius Falvus. The plot was betrayed and both were put to death. For Faenius' motives we have the evidence of the odious Tigellinus, who claimed that the former prefect was still mourning Agrippina (and had been her lover) and was determined to avenge her. For Subrius we have his own testimony. After being charged, he proudly confessed his involvement, claiming that he had been the most loyal supporter of Nero in the early days, for as long as he deserved that loyalty, but he began to despise him when he turned into a wastrel after the murder of his mother Agrippina and wife Octavia.[89]

The most dangerous part of Agrippina's plan to ensure the loyalty of the praetorians would be the dismissal and replacement of the old prefects. The circumstances in which this was engineered are not clear, but it may be that she exploited the unrest caused by the shortage of grain in 51. Public expressions of distress over such shortages were certainly not unknown in Rome. What distinguishes the disturbances of 51 is that Claudius became drawn into them. While sitting in judgement in the Forum he was surrounded by a noisy mob, who pelted him with pieces of bread and shouted abuse. The praetorians forced a passage for him, and he managed to escape into the palace by a back door.[90] Dio even claims that Agrippina instigated the riots herself but he is undercut by Tacitus and Suetonius, who concede that there was deeply rooted dissatisfaction over the famine. No doubt she exploited the fracas to persuade Claudius, prone as he was to paranoia about his safety, that the praetorians had allowed his security to be compromised.

There was probably a lurking suspicion that the current prefects Lusius Geta and Rufrius Crispinus still harboured a sense of loyalty towards Messalina, and were sympathetic towards her children.[91] They had been appointed in about AD 47, to replace those prefects who had taken over in the early days of the accession. Geta has left the more vivid impression of the two, because of his role in the events surrounding Messalina's fall. When the scandal broke, he left it to Narcissus to inform the emperor, and when later asked to conduct an investigation he took no initiative but merely conceded that Narcissus had told the truth, suggesting that Claudius go to the camp in person to test the guards' loyalty. Clearly he was not a commander to inspire confidence, which is why Claudius temporarily entrusted his personal security to Narcissus. Less is known about Crispinus. He seems to have played an active role as Messalina's hireling, and in 47 was given the task of arresting Valerius Asiaticus. He was absent from the events of 48 and it might have been suspected that he deliberately made himself scarce.

Like prefects before him, Geta was dislodged by the traditional bribe, the prefecture of Egypt. There he might well have been kept under the watchful eye of Tiberius Claudius Balbillus, an active supporter of Agrippina, rewarded by her in 55 by being himself appointed prefect of Egypt. In 51 he was probably already in the country, in charge of the museum, shrines and library at Alexandria and other cities (see p. 177). It is important to note that Geta did not suffer the common fate of ex-praetorian commanders, including at least one of his immediate predecessors, that of being executed. This can perhaps be seen as yet another indication of Agrippina's non-confrontational style of operation. On the fate of Crispinus we have no information, but the silence of the sources tends to suggest that he did not meet with a violent end either.

Agrippina succeeded in persuading her husband that the efficiency and discipline of the guard were jeopardized by its division between two commanders, who were often in rivalry with one another. Their replacement, as single prefect without colleague, was a man destined to play a prominent role in the next decade, Sextus Afranius Burrus. He is described by Tacitus as someone who enjoyed a lofty military reputation but remained conscious of who had given him his position. Most of what is known about Burrus' earlier career is based on an inscription from a statue erected at Vasio (Vaison), a prosperous and well- appointed town in Gallia Narbonensis, to honour him as the town's patron. He was almost certainly a native of the town and probably had an estate in the area, since another inscription found there mentions one of his freedmen. His nomen *Afranius* indicates that his family might have received its citizenship during the final chaotic days of the republic, when the Pompeian supporter Lucius Afranius was active in the area. His age is not given (a birth between 10 BC and the turn of the century fits well with later events), nor does the summary of his earlier career provide evidence for the military distinction that impressed Tacitus or the details of how he came to the attention of Agrippina. He first held the rank of military tribune and followed this with service as procurator of Livia, presumably as agent on one of her estates. He is next mentioned as procurator of Tiberius and Claudius, which could have meant the governorship of a procuratorial province (see below for the different types of procuratorships), where he could have had some military experience. But it is difficult to see how he could have won militarily distinctions as provincial procurator, since his duties would have been essentially civil. During military crises procuratorial provinces generally came into the orbit of the governor of the nearest imperial province. His military 'reputation' might simply reflect the high regard in which he was held by the praetorians, and may have had more to do with honesty and fairness than prowess in battle. The final honours to be mentioned on the Vaison inscription are the insignia of a consul, *ornamenta consularia*, distinctions that Claudius bestowed frequently, but which in Burrus' case probably postdate the accession of Nero (and may have been for services during the accession). No earlier connection with Agrippina is attested. She may have seen him, along with Seneca, as a beneficial and stabilizing influence in preparing her son for his succession and have supported his appointment for that reason rather than because of close political connections.[92]

The appointment of Burrus can have left Romans in little doubt about the strength of Agrippina's position. Not all would have been happy. There would still have been some who supported the claims of Britannicus, and there would have been conservative senators who disapproved of such power in any woman, whatever her political position. A last-ditch effort was made to thwart her through an indirect attack on one of her key supporters, when a senator Junius Lupus brought a charge of *maiestas* against Vitellius.[93] Tacitus claims that Claudius was prepared to take the charges seriously but was prevented by his wife, who dissuaded him with threats, an implausible scenario and simply an attempt to reinforce the view that Claudius was under the thumb of his wife (and freedmen). But it is astonishing that the charge should have been brought at all. Vitellius had enjoyed a distinguished military career outside Rome, and at court he had put aside higher personal ambition in favour of serving the reigning princeps. His repeated consulships (he held three) show the high regard in which he was held by Claudius. By 51 he was elderly and his departure from the narrative suggests that his death, from a stroke, occurred not long after. It would surely have been out of the question for him to consider some personal putsch against Claudius or against Agrippina, who still continued to champion him.

The attempt to bring down Vitellius also suggests great courage on the part of Junius Lupus, in daring to bring an action against the most favoured of the emperor's friends. It has even been suggested that Lupus was, in reality, acting on the instructions of Claudius. The emperor might have been concerned about the growing ambitions of his wife and have wanted to give a warning both to her and to Vitellius, whose loyalties might seem to be shifting focus. This too is hardly likely. The evidence indicates that Claudius and Agrippina were acting in total concert at this time, and for at least the next two years. In any event, the incident left Agrippina in an even stronger position, since the failure of the case would frighten off potential opponents. Lupus is more likely to have been the dupe of a group within the senate, perhaps traditionalists who opposed Agrippina's powerful position or a remnant of the supporters of Messalina (who would be looking for the accession of Britannicus). The mission of Lupus (who is unknown before this incident) seems an almost suicidal one but is perhaps understandable if, as has been suggested, he was a relative of Lucius Junius Silanus, the disgraced suicide, and his affectionate sister Junia Calvina, and thus motivated by a passionate individual hatred rather than rational political judgement. His punishment was less severe than might have been expected. Tacitus suggests that Vitellius could, if he had wished, have asked for a capital charge to be laid but was satisfied with a sentence of exile (the details of the indictment are not made clear). After his brief appearance at the centre of events, Lupus passes back into historical oblivion.

Roman military success gave Agrippina another opportunity for a public demonstration of her elevated status as Augusta. The British leader Caratacus, son of Cunobelinus, had continued to mount a strenuous opposition to the Romans from the time of the invasion of the island in AD 43. In 51 he was eventually captured and brought to Rome, where in a grand ceremony he and the other British prisoners paid homage to Claudius, attended by members of his praetorian guard. Not only to

Claudius; Agrippina sat on a neighbouring tribunal close by and the Britons honoured her in exactly the same manner. Dio says that it was one of the most remarkable sights of the time, and Tacitus notes that it was without precedent for a woman to sit in state before Roman standards and acutely observes that in doing so she claimed a partnership in the empire her ancestors had created. He presumably means by this that by her near-equal status to Claudius in the ceremony she was claiming a sort of authority over the praetorians – the familiar bugbear of a woman commanding troops. It is unlikely that she intended any such arrogation of authority. It would have seemed entirely appropriate to her that the daughter of Germanicus and granddaughter of Drusus, great conquerors in the north-west, should join in presiding over the formal and final (as it would have seemed) surrender of the British. It was probably in connection with the celebration of this second great military achievement that she was first granted the use of the covered carriage, the *carpentum,* reserved previously for priests. Messalina had been allowed to use it, but probably only during the specific occasion of the British triumph in AD 44. Agrippina appears to have been granted the privilege of its general use during religious festivals.[94]

The strength of Agrippina's influence can be gauged by the fact that she was able to affect events in the provinces as well as in Rome. We have evidence of her sponsoring games in the province of Asia, at Adalia and Mytilene.[95] Such public generosity was expected of members of the imperial family. Her real power-plays would have been enacted behind the scenes and we are fortunate enough to have evidence of a specific intervention, in the affairs of Judaea. The region had enjoyed a period of autonomy under the rule of the pro-Roman ruler, Herod Agrippa, close friend both of Claudius and of Caligula. On his death in 44 the kingdom reverted to the status of a Roman province, governed by a procurator. The reimposition of Roman rule initiated a period of increasing disorder, one that was to result eventually in open revolt. Nationalist feeling was offended by the loss of self-government, and almost from the outset the Roman authorities were confronted by violent challenges to their authority. The situation was complicated by the disruptive presence of a series of powerful local leaders, presenting themselves as messiahs, men like Theudas, who planned to re-enact Moses' crossing of the Red Sea. They were viewed by the Romans as dangerous political agitators and dealt with ruthlessly.[96]

For the first few years following Herod Agrippa's death disturbances were limited and order of a kind was maintained. The appointment of Ventidius Cumanus in about 48 brought this relative calm to an end and marked a turning point in the history of the province, after which violent hostility to Rome became so deeply rooted that effective central control became almost impossible. The deterioration was heralded by two serious incidents, the second of which involved the direct intervention of Agrippina. In the first, a soldier from the Roman garrison guarding the temple enclosure in Jerusalem during Passover bared his bottom and broke wind. The crowd was incensed, and hurled stones at the soldiers and insults at Cumanus. He called in reinforcements and in the panic that followed large numbers of Jews were crushed to death. The casualty figures were exaggerated and some reports put them as high as 30,000.[97] Little direct blame can be laid at Cumanus' door over this specific incident and Josephus places the responsibility squarely on the shoulders of the individual soldier. But the conflict does illustrate the tense atmosphere in Jerusalem and the degree of mistrust that had developed between Cumanus and the Jews.

The second incident had more serious consequences. In 51 a gang of Samaritans attacked a number of Galilean pilgrims on their way to Jerusalem. At least one of the pilgrims, and possibly more, was killed, and the Galileans asked Cumanus to launch an investigation and to punish the wrong-doers. Cumanus brushed aside the complaint on the grounds of being preoccupied by more serious matters, and this led to the inevitable, though probably baseless, charge that he had been bribed.[98] When word of the attack reached Jerusalem, the Judaeans were roused to passion; groups of them volunteered to go north to aid the Galilean cause and a number of Samaritan settlements were destroyed. Cumanus finally realized that he faced a serious situation. He took five cohorts into the field, reinforced a number of Samaritan irregulars and clashed with the joint units of Judaeans and Galileans, taking several prisoners in the process. Most of the remainder dispersed, but one of their leaders managed to evade arrest and a number of the rebels rallied to him. From various strongpoints, they launched raids throughout Judaea.[99]

At this stage the Samaritans appealed to Ummidius Quadratus, who as governor of Syria had overall authority for the military administration of Judaea. The request suggests that Josephus' account, which places the blame on the Samaritans, might not be balanced. Quadratus was subsequently approached also by the Jews, who expressed the fear that Cumanus had been bribed and that their conduct would be misrepresented. In response, he announced that he would delay judgement and go to the province of Judaea to hold a proper enquiry. At this stage a new character appears on the scene, Felix, the brother of Pallas, Agrippina's freedman-ally. Confusingly, Tacitus asserts that Felix was procurator of Samaria during the time Cumanus was procurator of Galilee, and suggests that the two men *shared* the jurisdiction of the province of Judaea from the outset, and that both were profiting from the spoils of the brigands. This is a remarkable piece of information and difficult to reconcile with Josephus' account unless Josephus is anxious to play down Felix's role, with its implication that the Jews had powerful friends on the spot. Certainly Josephus portrays Cumanus as able to operate freely within Samaria, Felix's supposed territory. The issue is complex and controversial, and it is tentatively assumed here that Samaria was detached from the remainder of Judaea in 51, at the time of Quadratus' enquiry, and that Felix's appointment there dates from then. Whenever he received the office, there can be little doubt that his elevation would have been due to Agrippina, the patron of his brother. Moreover, since Agrippina's sympathies, as will emerge, were pro-Jewish, it is to be expected that Felix would have reflected her sentiments.[100] Quadratus appointed a tribunal and allowed Felix to sit as a judge, perhaps a careful move to avoid offending someone who had powerful friends in Rome. At any rate, Quadratus concluded that the Samaritans were basically culpable, although he maintained a balance by executing both the Jewish and the Samaritan rebels captured by Cumanus. But he was still not satisfied that he had heard the whole truth. He went on to Lydda in Judaea proper where he instituted a second enquiry. At this hearing the weight of the evidence presented seems to have been heavily against the Jews and eighteen were beheaded. Quadratus may well have concluded that events had by now overtaken him, and have sensed that he might be called upon to take measures that would not be pleasing in high circles in Rome. He decided to hand over the matter to the emperor. Deputations from both the Jewish and Samaritan sides were dispatched to Italy to present their cases before Claudius. Another traveller was Cumanus, sent by Quadratus to face a charge of maladministration. The former High Priests Jonathan and Ananias (whose son Eleazar would be a leading figure in the revolt of 66 and whose own loyalty was not above suspicion) and Ananus, the superintendent of the temple, were also sent, in chains, to face the inquiry.[101] Felix may have returned to Rome at the same time, probably early in 52.

Our only source for what happened at the hearing in Rome is Josephus.[102] He suggests that Claudius' freedmen and *philoi* (presumably his council of advisers) took the side of the Samaritans, which might suggest that the evidence in their favour was overwhelming. But the Jews had powerful supporters. Agrippa II, son of Herod Agrippa, had been appointed King of Chalcis (in the Lebanon valley) in 49.[103] He was in Rome at the time of the enquiry, either by chance or with the specific intention of attending. Agrippa had a friend at court in the person of Agrippina. In the *Antiquities* Josephus says that Agrippina threw her weight behind the Jewish cause; interestingly, in his *Bellum*, published under Vespasian, no mention is made of her, possibly to avoid suggesting that the Jews were supported by one of Vespasian's old opponents. According to Josephus, Agrippina persuaded the emperor to give the case what the historian describes as a proper hearing in conformity with proper legal procedure. Suetonius does hint that Claudius had a general habit of giving judgement after hearing only one party to a suit, and the *Apocolocyntosis* claims that he did so on occasion without hearing *either* party.[104] But, in view of the elaborate preparations, summary judgement in the current crisis can probably be ruled out and Josephus' carefully chosen language more likely conceals an active intervention by Agrippina for the Jewish cause.

It is not clear why Agrippina should have been pro-Jewish but her sympathies may well have arisen from personal connections rather than any developed political policy. Herod Agrippa had been very active in establishing close rapport with members of the imperial family, and had exploited the ties that already existed with the Jewish ruling dynasty. These existed between the women, as well as the men. Antonia, the grandmother of Agrippina, was a friend of Herod Agrippa's mother, Berenice (niece of Herod the Great), and Berenice's mother, the famous Salome, was a personal friend of Augustus' wife Livia. Herod Agrippa's son, Agrippa II, would have fallen heir to the nexus of personal alliances forged by his father and such connections were a powerful driving force in Roman political life.[105]

Given his lead by Agrippina, Agrippa II spoke earnestly on the Jewish side at the hearing and Claudius' final decision suggests that the behind-the-scenes manoeuvring paid off. The Samaritans were found ultimately responsible for the incident and Cumanus was deemed to have behaved negligently. Three of the Samaritans were executed and Cumanus was exiled. The Jews seem to have escaped further punishment. A tribune named Celer was ordered to be dragged around Jerusalem in a public spectacle then beheaded, a remarkable punishment for a Roman, and it may be that he was the soldier who had originally exposed himself in public.

Another apparent outcome of the hearing and of Agrippina's intervention was that Felix was now sent by Claudius as procurator of Judaea. Felix was a freedman (*libertus*), and the appointment of someone of that rank as a procurator or prefect is almost without parallel.[106] His selection was thus a remarkable one and further evidence of Agrippina's power and influence. Felix certainly felt indebted to her and Judaean coins that appear in 54, the first procuratorial coins to be minted in Judaea since Pontius Pilate's time, some twenty years earlier, honour Agrippina, depicting her name within a wreath on the reverse.[107] It is difficult to assess how wise the appointment of Felix was, and what light it throws on Agrippina's judgement. One might argue that, given the sensitivity of the situation, the absence of any major disaster during his term is, in a sense, a point in Felix's favour. Tacitus has little time for him and accuses him of using his brother's influence to get away with things in the province and of behaving brutally and licentiously. But we would not expect Tacitus to have much sympathy for a powerful freedman, and a brother of Pallas into the bargain.

Felix's humble status certainly does not seem to have held him back. He achieved two distinguished marriages, first to Drusilla, granddaughter of Antony and Cleopatra, and later to a second Drusilla, the daughter of Herod Agrippa and thus sister of Agrippa II, after she had left her husband Azizus, King of Emesa.[108] As governor he dealt with a number of cases of unrest involving brigands and nationalist prophets who were stirring up resentment against the Romans. He also faced the complex problem of the relations of the Jews with their neighbours. During his term a particularly serious incident occurred in Caesarea, where the demands of the Jews of Caesarea for equal status with the Greeks of the city led to street fighting.[109] Although in general probably pro-Jewish, Felix tried in this case to maintain an even-handed approach and sent a delegation from both sides to Rome. Josephus records charges that Felix allowed his troops to be brutal towards the Jews and to loot their houses, but he also concedes the possibility that the troops had acted on their own initiative and that Felix stopped them as soon as he was alerted. In any case, on his recall (the precise date is uncertain) a delegation of Jewish leaders from Caesarea (probably the one sent by Felix) charged him with unspecified misdeeds. Josephus claims that he was saved only though Pallas' intercession, although by that time Pallas had certainly been dismissed from office (see p. 169). In the event Nero would decide in favour of the Greeks.[110]

Josephus' interest in Judaea provides evidence that Agrippina intervened successfully in events of that province. It is fair to speculate that she was similarly involved in quiet, behind-the-scenes intervention in other provinces which had no Josephus to record their history.

Agrippina owed her success, whether in Rome or abroad, primarily to two strategies. She prepared her groundwork carefully and patiently, and she ensured that she had useful friends in useful places. Vitellius had of course been her chief ally in the senate. His death would leave a serious gap but there were at least two other senators she could count on, Barea Soranus and Marcus Tarquitius Priscus, as will emerge in the subsequent narrative. Another important group to attract much interest were the freedmen, whose role in her schemes was emphasized in the sources because of the prejudice that it would create against her. Through them Agrippina built up a network of alliances within the palace. A few individual names are known, such as Xenophon, the palace doctor, but her chief supporter was Pallas. His services were outstanding. He championed her suitability as wife for Claudius and Nero's suitability as a adopted son, but he also had a crucial administrative function. As *a rationibus* he played a key part in the management of the imperial finances, and it was through him that Agrippina could exercise an influence in this sphere (see below). Their collaboration was so close that it inevitably gave rise to a story reported in Tacitus and hinted at in Dio that they were involved in a sexual liaison. Probus records that someone even scribbled a graffito about the scandal on the statue of Minerva (the Roman equivalent of Pallas Athene) on the Palatine: *Pallas s'aitiontai* (Greek: 'Pallas, they charge you').[111] Whether or not they had an adulterous affair is impossible to determine, but the charge would almost inevitably be made about two people who both incited envy and antipathy. On the surface it seems implausible that Agrippina, with her heightened sense of importance as the descendant of Augustus and daughter of Germanicus, would have condescended to a liaison with an ex-slave. For his part, Pallas would not have needed sexual favours to work for a powerful patron like Agrippina. In any case, it would be a mistake to think of him as merely Agrippina's creature. Clearly he enjoyed the confidence of Claudius too. It appears that the emperor in AD 52 consulted Pallas about the appropriate treatment of free women who married slaves.[112] Pallas' suggestion was that they should be reduced to the rank of slave if they married without the consent of the new husband's master, but to that of freedwoman if they had his permission. Claudius adopted his recommendation and the senate decreed accordingly. The originator of the idea was revealed and the consul-elect, Barea Soranus, moved that he be awarded the praetorian insignia and a grant of 15 million HS. The senator Cornelius Scipio added that, although descended from the Kings of Arcadia (presumably through Pallas, the son of the Arcadian King Evander), Pallas had unselfishly devoted himself to the public good as a servant of the emperor. Pallas declined the cash, saying that he was content with the honour. A further decree was passed praising Pallas' old-fashioned frugality, a decree summarized in an inscription on his tomb and described by Pliny the Younger as sickeningly fulsome. The award of the *praetorian* insignia, when compared to Narcissus' receipt of *quaestorian* insignia for his contribution to the downfall of Messalina, was no doubt intended deliberately to acknowledge that Narcissus had been eclipsed. Pliny the Elder attributes the special treatment of Pallas to the machinations of Agrippina, and was almost certainly right. At the very least Pallas' success, and the appointment about the same time of his brother Felix as procurator of Judaea, would serve to advertise the power of her patronage.[113]

In Tacitus' narrative the arch-opponent of Agrippina within the palace was Narcissus (Dio records that Callistus was dead by 51). Of all the freedmen he had initially been closest to Claudius, to the degree that his assistance was called upon even to deal with a potential mutiny of the troops before their departure for Britain in 43 (he resolved the issue successfully), and he was given temporary authority over the praetorians during the Messalina débâcle in 48. His services during the latter crisis should have brought him to the pinnacle of power, but ironically they may have had the opposite effect. His key role in the events, including his brief command of the praetorians, caused jealousy within the palace and deep offence to traditionalists, and aggravated the hostility that his support of Claudius had already engendered among some of the senators.

Narcissus would have resented the increasing power and influence of Agrippina, and he would certainly have resented his own subsequent eclipse by Pallas. But there is no inherent reason why he could not have supported her, even though he had championed a different candidate as Claudius' fourth wife. In fact, it would have been very much to his advantage to court her favour. He had stuck his neck out during the fall of Messalina, which left him exposed.[114] Agrippina's closeness to Pallas would, of course, have been an obstacle to any rapprochement and she might have mistrusted someone prepared so aggressively to bring about the ruin of an emperor's wife, even if that wife had been determined to thwart her plans. But the main impediment was that Narcissus' sense of danger seems to have been secondary to his own personal pride and abiding sense of grievance. The sources consistently show Agrippina and Narcissus at odds. There is one exception: Dio, in an epitome provided by Zonaras, says that in 51 Agrippina exercised total authority, since she dominated Claudius and had won over Pallas *and Narcissus*.[115] This is a remarkable passage. It is, of course, possible that there was a convoluted and short-lived realignment of loyalties within the palace, but the chances are remote – it would have been astonishing for such a dramatic shift to have escaped notice by Tacitus or any other source. There is a more plausible explanation. Dio later reports that in 68, after the fall of Nero, his successor Galba arrested the scum that had risen to the surface during the previous reign, and ordered them to be led in chains through the city and put to death. They included Helius, Patrobius, Narcissus and the poisoner Locusta. Now the Narcissus mentioned here had enjoyed the favour of Nero and was clearly alive at the time, in 68, but Narcissus, the loyal freedman of Claudius, died shortly after his master in 54. There is thus good reason to believe that there were at least two freedmen called Narcissus prominent in the palace in the Claudian/Neronian period, one of whom was an active supporter of Nero, and that Dio (or Zonaras) has confused the two.[116]

The private tensions between Agrippina and the first Narcissus became common knowledge when they publicly feuded over one of the great public work projects initiated by Claudius – the draining of the Fucine Lake in central Italy. The enterprise was intended to prevent constant flooding in the area and to create new farmland by putting the reclaimed territory to profitable use. It involved the digging of a tunnel some 5km (3 miles) beneath the limestone of Mount Salvio, to provide a channel into the river Liris. Private companies were brought in to share the work, in return for the freehold of the reclaimed land; 30,000 men were engaged on the project for eleven years, some tunnelling in the darkness below, others lifting the spoil to the surface in hoists. Pliny concluded that it was one of Claudius' most astonishing achievements and it is testimony to the continuing regard felt for Narcissus by the emperor that he was placed in overall charge of the project, as a special assignment, since such a responsibility could hardly have fallen within the sphere of his regular duties. [117]

The opening of the tunnel in 52 was planned as a great public spectacle. A mock naval battle was arranged on the Fucine Lake with ships and 19,000 combatants, divided into the opposing sides of 'Rhodians' and 'Sicilians'. A visible memento of the event has survived on a temple wall at nearby Alba Fucens in the form of a graffito depicting a quadrireme (a ship with four banks of oars). The lake was enclosed by a wooden wall, with stands, to accommodate an enormous crowd, and the surrounding hills were thronged with thousands of people who had come in from the neighbouring towns or even from Rome itself. Among the spectators were Claudius and Nero, dressed in military garb (no mention is made of Britannicus), and Agrippina, who wore a beautiful cloak woven with threads of gold. Pliny the Elder was present for the celebrations and provides an eye-witness account of Agrippina's presence. The golden cloak was not only an object of beauty but also highly symbolic, as apparel associated with royalty. A small gilt bronze head, almost certainly of Agrippina, has been found at the nearby town of Alba Fucens and it is suggested that she and Claudius might have stayed in the town and presented the magistrates with the portrait (along, perhaps, with one of Claudius, p. 217). The naval battle ran its course and the spectacle finally reached its climax, the opening of the sluices. The anticipated torrent of water did not materialize. The tunnel had not been sunk at even the mean depth of the lake. A meagre and humiliatingly dismal trickle was all that emerged.[118]

An appropriate interval was allowed for the channel to be dug deeper. To ensure a good turn-out for the second opening, a gladiatorial show was staged on pontoons laid on the lake and at the outlet of the discharge a banquet was arranged, attended by Claudius and, almost certainly (although she is not mentioned), by Agrippina herself. On this second occasion the opening of the channel produced the very opposite result. The outrush of water tore away part of the structure, and Claudius and his party were nearly drowned.

Agrippina's presence at the opening of the Fucine Lake was to be expected. She had a keen interest in public works, no doubt as a way of keeping herself prominently in the public eye and associated with popular activities. During a great fire, for instance, which damaged much of Rome at this time, she made a point of accompanying Claudius as he lent his assistance. It is hardly surprising, then, that she should have been furious with Narcissus for the embarrassment she must have felt over the Fucine project. He was blamed for the disaster and it was even hinted that he had misappropriated some of the funds, then deliberately arranged the collapse to conceal his misdeeds. The incident caused a public row, and a charge of embezzlement was engineered by Agrippina. Narcissus hit back, but seems to have had no *specific* charge to lay at Agrippina's door. Instead he accused her of *inpotentiam muliebrem* ('female imperiousness') and *nimias spes* ('excessive ambition'), standard charges made against women who aspired to play a political role, and thus designed to appeal to deep-seated prejudices. The lines were clearly drawn now between Agrippina and the freedman, and we might date from this incident the beginning of the end for Narcissus. [119]

Closely allied to Agrippina's involvement in public works was her interest in financial matters. The eclipse of Narcissus and the inevitable improvement in the standing of Pallas would have offered additional scope to show her skills in this area. While there is little direct evidence for Agrippina's influence on financial policy, it can certainly be inferred. By comparison with his predecessor, Claudius was careful and responsible but he still had massive financial outlays. Various taxes thought up by Caligula towards the end of his reign had proved highly unpopular and his successor had no choice but to eliminate them. The cost of maintaining the extra legions for the British campaign would have been an additional drain on resources. In his personal habits Claudius was given to sex, gluttony and gambling, relatively inexpensive pursuits compared to some of Caligula's grandiose extravagances, but when political necessity demanded it he would not stint. Caligula had doubled Tiberius' bequest of 1000 HS to each praetorian; Claudius increased this amount to 15,000 HS to each man. Then there was the massive cost of worthy public enterprises, the refurbishing of the aqueduct system, the rebuilding of the port of Ostia and the draining of the Fucine Lake.[120] The economic and financial difficulties, and the subsequent potential for dissatisfaction, would have increased as the reign progressed. The very fact that there was no financial crisis nor, apparently, serious hardships, suggests that the administration of Claudius' finances was competent and well managed.

Agrippina's close interest in financial matters cannot be doubted. She would have seen how Caligula's difficulties came about largely because of his financial mismanagement. Her own strictly disciplined view of financial affairs is illustrated in the anecdote told about her final hours. She realized that her son had made an attempt on her life by wrecking the ship on which she was travelling, and that a second attempt was bound to follow. But her thoughts did not dwell on matters of heaven and the afterlife. Almost her last recorded action was to arrange the will of her friend Acerronia, who had died in the shipwreck. She gave instructions that it be sought out and the deceased's effects be placed under seal, presumably on the assumption that she had been designated as heir.[121]

Wealth for its own sake was generally not of great interest to the early emperors. Stories are told of Caligula rolling on gold coins, drinking pearls dissolved in vinegar and of his extravagantly equipped barges and sumptuous villas. But he is the exception. Augustus, Tiberius and Claudius lived relatively simple lives and saw their enormous wealth as a means of maintaining or increasing their power. Agrippina adhered to this tradition, something that the Romans found surprising in a woman. In commenting on the changes that she brought about on her marriage to Claudius, Tacitus, as noted earlier, describes the kind of strict, almost masculine, domination that she exercised over the state and observes that she had an insatiable desire for wealth, but with the intention of using it to win supporters for autocratic rule. A similar situation is described by Dio, who claims (under AD 49) that she set about accumulating great wealth, exploiting every possible source and overlooking no-one, no matter how modest their resources, but that she did so for Nero.[122]

Agrippina's influence on financial policy would have been exercised through Pallas, and made possible by the peculiarity of the financial system of the early Roman empire. Under the republic the main state treasury, the *aerarium,* was located in the temple of Saturn under the Capitol, and contained supplies of coins and precious metals, as well as important state documents. In the provinces public revenues were collected and dispensed through the *fiscus* or special fund of the provincial governor, with funds presumably moving between the governor's *fiscus* and the central treasury in Rome.[123] With the emergence of the imperial system the organizing of state finances becomes very unclear, largely because of the ambiguity of the sources, which, in turn, probably reflect the ambiguity of the situation. In particular, the distinction between the emperor's private wealth (his *fiscus* in the strict sense) and the public funds that he held in charge is not clear, nor the relationship between the 'public' *aerarium* and the 'imperial' *fiscus.*[124] For practical purposes, the revenues that actually went into the emperor's *fiscus* were mostly 'public' and by a process that is not well documented he was able to treat them in a sense as his own.[125]

The movement of funds was not exclusively one way. The emperor, from Augustus on, would on occasion place what he defined as his private wealth at the disposal of the state. Thus Augustus subsidized the public revenues with as much as 2,400,000,000

HS.[126] This massive expenditure from supposed 'private' funds must surely mean that, as the chief executive of the state, the princeps was able to exercise some general control over the state's finances and thus have access to them. It was this control that enabled Augustus to deliver his *rationes imperii* ('imperial accounts'), including the reserves in the public treasury and in the provincial coffers and what was due in taxes. Eventually, formal accounts ceased to be given (they were revived briefly by Caligula), and inevitably the distinction between public and private resources became blurred. Thus Tacitus is able to report that in 32, with the fall of Sejanus, the late prefect's property was withdrawn from the treasury and transferred to the imperial *fiscus*, 'as if the distinction mattered', and Dio claimed that the emperor was equally the controller of his own and the public monies.[127] So it was that the imperial property, from Tiberius on, passed from emperor to emperor and the inheritance of the emperor's private resources seems to have been exempt from the usual provisions of private law. Vespasian apparently left a will (Domitian suspected that his brother Titus tampered with it), but otherwise there is no good evidence of an emperor making a will after Claudius.[128] Otho acquired Nero's slaves, Vitellius took over the imperial residences in Rome and squandered their contents, and Vespasian sold off most of the imperial palaces in Alexandria.[129]

The imperial *fiscus* seems to have been derived in part from funds which could legitimately be regarded as private, but also from sources that were essentially public. It was able to make its claim on certain taxes. Hence Suetonius records that when at one point Livia tried to pressure Augustus into granting citizenship to a Gaul, he refused but offered the man in question relief from tribute, declaring that he would rather suffer a loss to his *fiscus* than see the Roman citizenship debased.[130] Where no heir had been stipulated in an estate, and no-one with a fair claim came forward, the *bona vacantia* fell to the state and initially enriched the public *aerarium*.[131] But perhaps as early as Tiberius such intestate estates passed into the imperial *fiscus*. Tacitus reports that in AD 17 a prosperous lady, Aemilia Musa, died intestate and that the *fiscus* had a claim on her property, which Tiberius waived when he discovered a member of the same family.[132] A similar rule applied to the property of those who had been condemned. This had also fallen to the public treasury under the republic, but in 26 BC the senate decreed that the property of Cornelius Gallus, the disgraced governor of Egypt, should after his conviction fall to Augustus. This must be what Dio means when he claims, in a confused statement, that Agrippina murdered people as a means of making money. As an example of those she 'murdered' he cites Lollia, adding that her murder was occasioned also by jealousy. But the only way that Agrippina could profit from enemies like Lollia would not be through murder in the sense in which the word is normally used, but through their condemnation by a legal process. The imperial *fiscus* would have benefited from Lollia's initial conviction (followed by banishment), but her later execution would have no financial implications. Murder pure and simple would bring no obvious financial returns, unless the victim had no known heirs.[133]

It is likely that the emperor used the same staff to administer both his private properties and revenues and those of the public monies over which he had jurisdiction.[134] This is, in a sense, the origin of the position held by Pallas, the *a rationibus*.[135] Somewhat later the poet Statius enumerates the duties of the *a rationibus* under Domitian. He had to keep a check on the expenditure of the imperial palace and on the revenues of the emperor's estates, but he also had public functions, such as disbursements in areas like the armies, roads and grain distribution.[136] When Pallas retired, he insisted that his accounts with the *aerarium* be considered balanced. He clearly feared an audit which might reveal improper conversion of public monies.

Pallas was *a rationibus* and head of the *fiscus* by at least 48, when he supposedly played a role in persuading Claudius to choose Agrippina as his next wife. Tacitus comments that his position gave him virtual control over the state, and this suggests that under him the finances of the imperial *fiscus* were brought under centralized control. This is not to say that the funds themselves were centralized in Rome. Vast sums must have flowed in and out of the provincial *fisci*, and between them and the central *fiscus* in Rome. This operation would have been co-ordinated and supervised by Pallas. He would thus have been in charge of a bureau of accounts (*rationes*), supervising the emperor's income from the whole empire, with particular care for the needs of the army and the coinage.[137] One piece of financial mischief has been attributed to him. Plated denarii (coins with a base core plated with silver) had been around for a long time before Claudius, but under Claudius the proportion of plated denarii increased considerably. It is scarcely possible to attribute them to deliberate government policy – sub-standard denarii would have impaired imperial credit. It may be that Pallas profited directly by diverting silver stocks.[138] Pallas' position would have given Agrippina unique access to the financial operations of the state. That they worked together closely in this sphere is suggested by what happened to Pallas later. Tacitus' account of the freedman's fall is highly significant, since he presents the removal of Pallas from control of the finances in Nero's reign as a device to reduce *Agrippina's* power. The sequence of events is particularly telling. Under the year 55 Tacitus describes how Agrippina bitterly opposed her son over an affair with a freedwoman, Acte (p. 167). After failing to move him by threats she tried indulgence, even, Tacitus says, offering to transfer to her son her 'private' resources, which were no less great than his own. This cannot surely refer to her *private* resources in the sense of her own *patrimonium*. It would have been out of the question for Agrippina to cede this to Nero and leave herself totally bereft. Nor could her own resources have matched those of the princeps. It seems more likely that the allusion is a confused reference to her control over the *fiscus*, exercised through Pallas. It can clearly be no accident that the removal of Pallas follows *immediately* in the next section of Tacitus' narrative.[139] The dismissal is preceded by an apparently trivial incident which may well be related to this situation. Tacitus reports that during that period Nero selected a dress and jewels from the collection that had once adorned the wives and matrons of the imperial family and sent it to his mother as a gift. Tacitus observes that this was an act of considerable generosity since he happened to have chosen some of the choicest items. Agrippina, however, seems to have been unimpressed and to have complained that he was dividing up resources that he had received entirely from her (*cuncta ex ea haberet*). The expression is a curious one. There is no possibility that these garments were Agrippina's private inheritance. As part of the imperial property they would have been in the grey area of property that was both public and private (they were certainly not bequeathed to Nero by Claudius, whose will was never published).[140]

One of the measures to which we might attribute the influence of Agrippina –

working in concert with Pallas, of course – was the decision made by Claudius in 53 to confer judicial powers on procurators so that their decisions would have the same authority as his own. The emperor brought this issue up several times in the senate, smoothing the way for its enactment by a senatorial decree. The office of procurator involved one of three basic functions in the Claudian period. It could refer to the governorship of a small province. Clearly these procurator- governors would have exercised a criminal and civil jurisdiction in their own areas from the outset, as is well illustrated by events in Judaea where Coponius, the very first equestrian governor, had the right to impose the death sentence. There were also procurators assigned to the imperial provinces governed by legati; these men, of equestrian rank, were the equivalent of the quaestors in senatorial provinces, responsible for the collection of tribute, payment of troops and the like. Finally there were those procurators in charge of the emperor's private property throughout the empire, in both the imperial and senatorial provinces. In AD 23 a case had been brought against Lucilius Longus, the procurator of the imperial estates in the senatorial province of Asia, for making unauthorized use of troops. Tiberius insisted that his jurisdiction extended only over the slaves and revenues of his property, and that if Lucilius had usurped some of the authority of a governor he had overstepped the mark (he was banished). In treating the Lucilius case, Dio comments that during his period procurators were allowed to do nothing beyond collecting the traditional revenues, and that in the case of disputes had to go to court on an equal footing with ordinary citizens. At the end of the relevant section dealing with Claudius' new legislation, Tacitus mentions that the emperor by his new measure elevated *freedmen* to be his equal, which suggests strongly that it was the patrimonial (estate) procurators (sometimes equestrians, but often freedmen) whose powers were now elevated, although whether the change would apply to both imperial and public provinces is still not made clear. This new legislation represented, if not a major shift in policy, formal and legal recognition of a de facto situation that had evolved over the past twenty years or so. It was a financially shrewd move that could only benefit the imperial *fiscus*, since the procurators would now have formal juridical powers in cases to which they were a party. Tacitus notes that the issue was raised several times in the senate before actually being implemented. The tactic of preparing the senate by frequently broaching the subject is the hallmark of Agrippina's strategy and this, along with her collaboration with Pallas, leaves little doubt about her influence in bringing about this measure.[141]

For all her interest in the details of administration, Agrippina would not have forgotten that her key short-term task was to groom Nero to take over when Claudius died. It was particularly important that people grow familiar with the idea of him as the appropriate successor. By AD 53 he was in his sixteenth year and ready to be introduced to his public. He would make his entrée as an advocate for a number of cities presenting their cases in Rome. This would give him a chance to show off the skills that his tutor Seneca had supposedly imparted to him. The cities were no doubt carefully selected. Ilium (Troy), for instance, was exempted from tribute after a speech in which Nero expatiated at length on the city's associations with Aeneas, the founder of the Julian line, a speech which would, of course, have drawn attention to Nero's own Julian descent. His eloquence also won financial reparations for Bononia (Bologna) which had suffered a devastating fire, and a remission of tribute for Apamea in Asia Minor after it was partly destroyed by an earthquake. Both causes would have seemed to portend a liberal and generous princeps-to-be. In addition, his successful speech in favour of the restoration of the liberties of the Rhodians would have won him favour in the Greek world.[142]

Nero had further opportunities to display his talents. It was the tradition for the emperor to depart from Rome each year for the three days of the Latin Festival, when he joined representatives of the old Latin league and presided over the archaic rituals of Jupiter Latiaris on the Alban Mount. Affairs in Rome were left in the hands of a prefect of the city. In 53, when Claudius made the traditional journey, he entrusted the task to Nero.[143] One of Nero's duties would have been to hear cases, and probably from concern over his deputy's relative youth the emperor had instructed that significant proceedings be held over. This did not happen. So great was the desire to plead before Nero that some of the most celebrated *patroni* vied to present their important cases before him.[144]

Some time after this (the date is not clear) Claudius fell ill, and Dio notes that Agrippina lost no opportunity to exploit even this misfortune to boost her son's popularity. She had him conduct games (Dio says horse races, Suetonius bear-baiting) for Claudius' recovery. But she was not content merely with a public display of filial *pietas*. Claudius' illness brought home to her that Nero's position, although strong, was still not unassailable and with the careful organization that typified her political career she initiated two measures. It was almost certainly as a result of the illness that she persuaded Claudius to inform the senate that, should he die, Nero was already capable of taking over the administration of the state. The letter he sent to the senate to convey this information is in many ways an extraordinary document, the most explicit public statement by a living princeps that he was designating his successor.[145]

Agrippina's other move was to bring about Nero's marriage to Octavia.[146] In promoting this union, she was faced by a familiar obstacle, the renewed suspicion of incest – Nero and Octavia were by law brother and sister. Other societies, such as the Greeks, would not have regarded an adoptive relationship of this type as an impediment to marriage but it was prohibited in Roman law and, if such marriages did take place, they have not left much trace in the sources.[147] Because of the scandal raised by the earlier suicide of Silanus (p. 103) and the reservations felt over Claudius' own marriage to Agrippina, the emperor would have been anxious to avoid even the hint of technical incest. He therefore arranged to have Octavia first adopted by another family, which would annul her legal status of Nero's sister.

The year was to claim one more victim, through action forced upon Claudius, as Tacitus sees it, by Agrippina's scheming (*artes*).[148] Her target was Titus Statilius Taurus, the grandson of one of Augustus' great generals, and himself consul in AD 44 with Passienus Crispus (her previous husband) and afterwards proconsul of Africa. A charge was brought by Tarquitius Priscus, one of his officials in Africa, of corruption and addiction to magical superstitions (the previous year had seen a fruitless senatorial decree banishing astrologers from Italy). Titus committed suicide before a verdict was reached.

Titus was almost certainly the brother of Taurus Statilius Corvinus, consul of 45, who in 46 became involved with the ugly and diminutive Asinius Gallus in a conspiracy against Claudius, and there may have been good reason to be suspicious of him.[149]

Tacitus' explanation was that Agrippina fabricated the charges against Titus because she was anxious to acquire his gardens. This sounds suspiciously like a standard *topos*, since the same claim was made against Messalina in connection with the gardens of Valerius Asiaticus. But it could well be a garbled version of something close to the truth. The gardens of Statilius, to judge from the location of an inscription recording their owner's name, seem to have been located just outside the Porta Maggiore, at the confluence of several aqueducts completed in 52/53, and thus at the heart of the city's water supply system. As we know from Frontinus, the Roman government had the right to expropriate in the area adjacent to an aqueduct at a fair evaluation, and there is evidence that Claudius may have used this method of expropriation by quasi-eminent domain in such enterprises as the enlargement of Ostia. We may have an illustration here of Agrippina's disciplined approach to financial problems – the exploitation of a charge of impiety, which may have been well grounded, as a device to help finance a key imperial project without resorting to costly expropriation.[150]

The accuser Tarquitius was himself punished, by expulsion from the senate. Tacitus claims that the penalty was imposed because of his attack on Titus and against the wishes of Agrippina. If he is right, it suggests that a body of opposition to Agrippina had now built up in the senate and contradicts the notion that she was in complete control over the affairs of state. In fact, Tarquitius' expulsion might have been far less sinister. He may have brought the charges against Titus in the hope of financial rewards in order to redeem his own poverty (as accuser he would receive a share of any penalty after conviction). The suicide of the accused would have frustrated this effort and Tarquitius might then have fallen victim to a law enacted in the previous year, requiring poverty-stricken senators to renounce their senatorial rank. He was eventually recalled, and was himself later charged with extortion during his subsequent governorship of Bithynia.[151]

There is some evidence that Tarquitius might have served Agrippina on another occasion. Among the more intriguing pieces of evidence for the period is a collection of documents known as the *Acts of the Pagan Martyrs*, which survive in fragments of Greek papyri and constitute the record of trials of prominent Alexandrian (Greek) nationalists held before Roman emperors. The language of these tracts is highly charged against what the writer saw as oppressive Roman masters, who conspired with Jewish extremists to abolish the privileges of the city. They are, of course, thoroughly biased, so great care must be exercised in their use but they can be of some value, if only for evidence that certain *in camera* proceedings did take place. One sub-group of four papyri, the so-called *Acts of Isidore*, offers a verbatim account of a hearing by Claudius and his council, on 30 April and 1 May of an unspecified year, to receive the complaints of an Alexandrian embassy led by Isidore the gymnasiarch (an Alexandrian official) and his colleague Lampon against Agrippa (either Herod Agrippa or his son Agrippa II, depending on the date). We do know that Agrippa II was certainly in Rome for Claudius' inquiry into the disturbances in Judaea, and a date of 30 April 53 for the appearance of the embassy is very possible. The proceedings took place before thirty-six senators in one of the imperial gardens, and several *women* (*ton matronon*) were present (including Agrippina, according to one tentative emendation of the very fragmentary text). One passage records a debate concerned with the advisability of giving Isidore a hearing at all. The text is highly corrupt, but it is clear that a certain 'Tarkyios' rose and insisted that if Rome took any notice of the Alexandrian claims the whole (of Egypt?) would be upset; he was answered by 'Aouiolaos' who persuades Claudius to grant Isidore a hearing. In the proceedings on the following day there was a bitter exchange and Isidore and Lampon were condemned to death. The evidence is very tenuous, but 'Tarkyios' may well be Tarquitius. The use of an agent to promote her position would be typical of Agrippina, and her indirect involvement in this matter would be consistent with the pro-Jewish sentiments she revealed during the Cumanus inquiry.[152]

The year 53 had been a remarkable one for Agrippina, for a variety of reasons. On her estate at Mevania, for instance, a young Syrian woman in her service turned spontaneously into a man on the eve of her wedding.[153] Agrippina's reaction to this novel occurrence is not recorded. Nor is her reaction to recent political developments, but she must surely have ended the year feeling highly satisfied. She was now married to the emperor and her son, already adopted, was now married to the emperor's daughter, marked as his successor, and successfully introduced to public life. Nero was, in fact, ready to take his place as emperor. The only obstacle was that the office was already occupied, but not for much longer.

Claudius had vacated the throne, along with his earthly existence, before the end of 54. The last recorded victim of Agrippina before this happened was the mother of Messalina, Agrippina's sister-in-law Lepida, who re-enters the narrative for the first time since her daughter's suicide. Agrippina had not hesitated earlier to rid herself of potential rivals, such as Lollia Paulina. But the action against Lepida represents a new type of attack, one against a member of the imperial family. Tacitus trivializes the clash between the two women, saying that it arose from 'female reasons' (*muliebribus causis*) between women who were alike in looks, age and wealth, but also equally unchaste and in constant rivalry in their vices.[154] This sounds inherently implausible and is likely to be a combination of stereotyping and personal antipathy towards both women. The second stated reason for their mutual hostility was jealousy over Nero. Tacitus describes Agrippina as *trux* and *minax* ('grim and threatening') in her dealings with her son, suggesting that she was trying through Seneca to teach him discipline and self-restraint, while Lepida was easy-going and generous with the lad. It is very possible that Tacitus has confused Lepida with Nero's other aunt, Lepida's sister Domitia. It was Domitia who took responsibility for the infant Nero after Agrippina's banishment in 39, and indulged him to the extent of allowing him a dancer and a barber as tutors. He continued to be the favourite of Domitia right up to her death and she, as will be seen, continued to excite Agrippina's jealousy. At any rate, during the hearing Nero showed Lepida no sympathy and publicly gave evidence against her at his mother's bidding.

What Tacitus does not emphasize in this context is that Lepida was Messalina's mother, and hence grandmother of Britannicus. Even though there had been an apparent rift between herself and her daughter, she would have had an interest in her grandson's succession. Through her descent from Octavia, Augustus' sister, she could boast a powerful lineage that would remind people that Britannicus also had Julian links, even if they were not as strong as Nero's.[155] She was accused of magical acts against Agrippina (a form of *maiestas* against the emperor's wife) and also with failing to keep the slaves in her Calabrian estates in order, thereby threatening the security of Italy, a charge which would have evoked memories of the great slave rebellions of the late republic. This latter claim seems to suggest a fear that she was training armed bands for use in some sort of putsch. The evidence seems to have been powerfully persuasive, since she was convicted and put to death despite the strenuous resistance of Narcissus.

Throughout her political life Agrippina's name would often be linked with murder, the common experience of women like herself, or Livia, or Messalina, who had reached positions of great power and influence. The popular image of Agrippina the homicide is based almost entirely on her supposed role in one famous incident, the death, by poisoned mushroom, of her husband Claudius.[156] The actual evidence for murder, by her or anyone else, is slender indeed.

The year 54 began with enough heavenly signs to warn those sensitive to such things of the imminence of the emperor's end. A comet appeared, the traditional harbinger of the death of a sovereign, enriched on this occasion by a shower of blood, and a thunderbolt fell from the sky and played around the tents and standards of the praetorians. The tomb of Claudius' father, Drusus, was also struck by lightning. In Rome a swarm of bees came to rest on the pediment of the Capitol, and the door of the Temple of Jupiter Victor, the place where the senate had met immediately after Caligula's assassination, opened of its own accord. There were rumours of the births of hermaphrodites and a pig was born with the claws of a hawk. One officer from each of the chief magistracies of that year died within a few months of taking office. Even Claudius supposedly had a premonition and appointed no magistrates beyond the month when he died (October), and on his last sitting in the senate declared several times that he had reached the end of his mortal career.

Inevitably, after the fact, the sources would look retrospectively for more down-to-earth signs of the disaster to come and, perhaps equally inevitably, would read deep meaning into casual events and comments. Suetonius records a jocular remark of Claudius, made after he condemned a woman for adultery. It was his fate to suffer the wickedness of his wives, he claimed, and then to punish them, a comment reported by Suetonius in the form of a witty wordplay – *omnia impudica, sed non impunita matrimonia* ('all his marriages were unchaste but not unchastened'). Tacitus elevates this witticism into a bald statement of fact, conveying an unmistakable and sinister threat, delivered by Claudius when his guard is down because of alcohol (*tremulentulus*): *fatale sibi ut coniugum flagitia ferret, dein puniret* ('it was fated for him that he was to endure the sins of his wives, then inflict punishment'). Tacitus' intentions are patent – he wants to build up a presumptive case against Agrippina by suggesting she was terrified by the comment and panicked into a swift reaction.[157]

Dio claims that by 54 the emperor had become aware of Agrippina's 'actions' and was angered by them; the actions are not specified, nor the process by which they were supposedly revealed. Suetonius says less specifically that near the end of his life Claudius began to repent his marriage and the adoption of Nero. Tacitus places the initiative for smoking out Agrippina with Narcissus, claiming that he had grown increasingly suspicious of her (although his suspicions should surely have been alerted from the fall of Lucius Silanus even before the marriage). Tacitus' summary of Narcissus' position seems uncharacteristically naive. The freedman took the position that he was doomed, no matter whether Britannicus or Nero succeeded, but he was devoted to Claudius' interests and those interests, he felt, would best be served by Britannicus' succession.

1 Agrippina (*Museo Archeologico, Milan*)

2 Agrippina
(*Schloß Fasanerie, Fulda*)

3 Agrippina (*Ny Carlsberg Glyptotek, Copenhagen*)

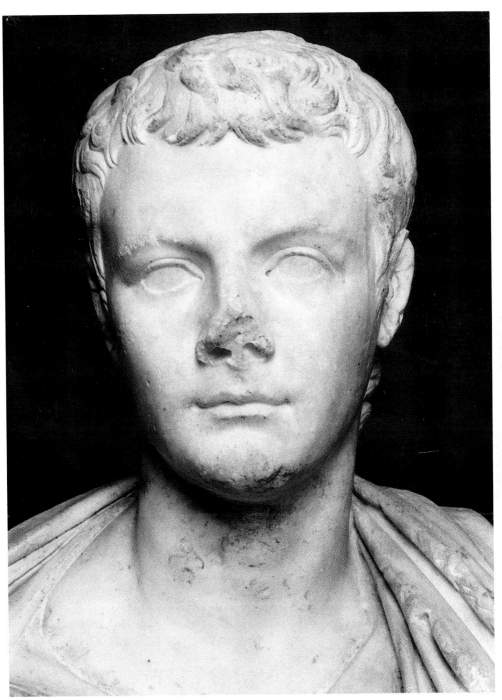

4　Caligula (*Virginia Museum of Fine Arts*)

5   Agrippina the Elder (*German Archaeological Institute, Rome*)

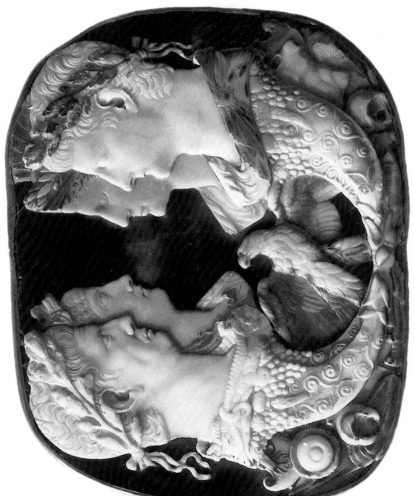

6 Cameo depicting Claudius and Agrippina (*left*) and Germanicus and Agrippina the Elder (*right*) (*Kunsthistorisches Museum, Vienna*)

7 Sestertius: Agrippina
(*Staatliche Museen, Berlin*)

8 Sestertius: Agrippina the Elder
(*British Museum, London*)

9 Dupondius: Germanicus
(*British Museum, London*)

10 Sestertius: Agrippina and
her sisters
(*British Museum, London*)

11 Coin of Apamea: Agrippina
and her sisters
(*British Museum, London*)

12 Tetradrachm of Ephesus:
Agrippina and Claudius
(*Ashmolean Museum,
Oxford*)

13 Aureus: Nero and Agrippina
(*Ashmolean Museum, Oxford*)

14 Aureus: Nero and Agrippina
(*Ashmolean Museum, Oxford*)

15 Tetradrachm of
Alexandria: Agrippina
(*Ashmolean Museum,
Oxford*)

16 Denarius: Agrippina
(*Ashmolean Museum, Oxford*)

17 Drachm of Caesarea in
Cappadocia: Agrippina
(*Ashmolean Museum, Oxford*)

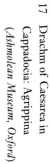

7   Sestertius: Agrippina
    (Staatliche Museen, Berlin)

8   Sestertius: Agrippina the Elder
    (British Museum, London)

9   Dupondius: Germanicus
    (British Museum, London)

10   Sestertius: Agrippina and
      her sisters
      (British Museum, London)

11   Coin of Apamea: Agrippina
      and her sisters
      (British Museum, London)

12   Tetradrachm of Ephesus:
      Agrippina and Claudius
      *(Ashmolean Museum,
      Oxford)*

13   Aureus: Nero and Agrippina
      (Ashmolean Museum, Oxford)

14   Aureus: Nero and Agrippina
      (Ashmolean Museum, Oxford)

15   Tetradrachm of
      Alexandra: Agrippina
      *(Ashmolean Museum,
      Oxford)*

16   Denarius: Agrippina
      (Ashmolean Museum, Oxford)

17   Drachm of Caesarea in
      Cappadocia: Agrippina
      (Ashmolean Museum, Oxford)

6 Cameo depicting Claudius and Agrippina (*left*)
   and Germanicus and Agrippina the Elder (*right*)
   (*Kunsthistorisches Museum, Vienna*)

18   *Sebasteion* relief from Aphrodisias depicting Agrippina
and Claudius (*Institute of Fine Arts, New York*)

19 *Sebasteion* relief from Aphrodisias depicting Agrippina
and Nero (*Institute of Fine Arts, New York*)

Narcissus considered himself an expert in bringing down imperial wives who enjoyed the favours of paramours. He had ruined Messalina and Silius, and believed that he had sufficient material to do the same to Pallas and Agrippina (the manuscripts are corrupt at this point). He was supposedly indiscreet enough to pass these views on to his friends, thus conveniently offering Agrippina an opportunity to find them out, and he also passed them on to Britannicus on a number of occasions, each time embracing the lad and looking forward to the day when he would officially reach manhood (probably 15 March 55, if the ceremony was not advanced). Then, Narcissus declared, he could rout the enemies of his father and even punish the slayers of his mother (a suicidal proclamation, if ever there was one!). Claudius is given no part in this version of the rapprochement with Britannicus and Tacitus implies a continuing coolness between father and son when he later says that Agrippina, having resolved on murder, decided against a slow poison lest it alert her husband and at that point bring about a renewed affection for his son.

The whole episode as conveyed by Tacitus, in particular Narcissus' final noble gesture in offering to lay down his own life, is totally implausible and is usefully compared with what is evidently the account of the same event in Suetonius and Dio. In their versions it is not Narcissus but *Claudius* who hugs Britannicus and makes amends, and they both have *Claudius* not only looking forward to the day when his son will reach manhood but even prepared to declare him immediately as his successor, 'so that the Roman people would at last have a genuine Caesar'.[158] It is likely that Suetonius and Dio reflect the version that was originally (though probably inaccurately) transmitted, and that Tacitus has given Narcissus an exaggerated role in his account in order to have a freedman, rather than Claudius himself, take the initiative and thereby to reduce Claudius to an essentially passive figure. But, of course, if Claudius at this point had really become so weak-minded one might wonder why Agrippina and Pallas were unable to have Narcissus removed. The emperor was surely very much still in control at the time.

Whether or not this essentially private encounter actually took place between Claudius and his son, and whether Claudius entertained the intentions ascribed to him, is another matter altogether. He would surely have realized that a volte-face over the succession would have caused massive disruption in the state, and have introduced into his reign the very instability he seemed to be at such great pains to avoid. This seems to be another instance where the record has been tailored to support a particular interpretation of later events. The encounter between Britannicus and Claudius/Narcissus is intended to provide a plausible motive for Agrippina's decision to murder Claudius when she did, and is very reminiscent of the rumour of Augustus' final rapprochement with Agrippa Postumus, a development that supposedly persuaded Livia to murder her husband. If, as is most likely, the story about Claudius and Britannicus was fabricated it was very probably the invention of those people hostile to Nero's accession, although Agrippina herself has also been blamed for spreading the tale during the later period of her estrangement from Nero.[159] Only one practical development is recorded as a result of Claudius' supposed change of heart. Suetonius reports that shortly afterwards he made his will (the contents are not revealed) and marked it with the seal of all the magistrates.[160]

An opportunity for murder finally presented itself in October when Narcissus, his health broken by his anxiety about the succession, went off to Campania to take the cure. The freedman suffered from gout and, according to Dio, was persuaded by Agrippina to go to Sinuessa. Its baths were famous and even reputed to cure insanity.[161] His absence on general grounds of health is easily explicable, but he was a shrewd strategist and his departure at this time on Agrippina's suggestion is very difficult to reconcile with Tacitus' picture of a man who felt that the struggle over the succession was about to reach a stormy climax. Dio's comment that Narcissus guarded his master so carefully that had he been present in Rome the murder would not have taken place also suggests that prior to October there had been no dramatic turn that would have alerted him to danger. Moreover if Claudius had changed his mind over the succession issue, as he was reputed to have done, Narcissus would surely have learned of it and his absence under such circumstances would have been extraordinary.

The ancient sources are in general agreement that Agrippina was guilty of murder, with few exceptions. Josephus expresses reservations on two occasions, with the comments *logos ên para tinôn* ('it was reported by some') and *kathaper ên logos* ('according to report'). Philostratus, in his life of Apollonius of Tyana, displays the same caution, *hôs phasin* ('so they say'). But these two are in a distinct minority, Nero is generally not implicated. Tacitus' account is the most detailed. He states that Agrippina had been resolved on murder for some time and had sought advice on different types of poison. She needed some drug that would offer a good balance between slow- acting properties (which would tip off Claudius) and rapid effects (which would arouse the suspicion of others). She therefore sought something powerful which would befuddle his mind and provide for a prompt, but not too speedy, death. The problem was especially complicated since not only did Claudius, like all emperors, take the standard antidotes as a matter of routine, but his excessive consumption of alcohol had built up a sort of immunity.[162] She finally procured the right product from Locusta, known to her from a recent poisoning charge. Locusta was to be a loyal servant to the family, reputedly supplying poison later to eliminate Britannicus also and providing Nero with a suicide draught in his last hours (it was stolen, along with his bedclothes, by his slaves). She was executed, with Narcissus II and others, by Galba. Once the drug was made available, the task of administering it was given to Halotus, Claudius' food-taster. This stain on his reputation did no harm to Halotus since, despite being generally unpopular he was rewarded with a procuratorship by Galba in AD 68.[163]

The tradition that Claudius was despatched by a mushroom goes back at least to the elder Pliny, who is presumably among the contemporary historians (*temporum illorum scriptores*) cited by Tacitus for the manner of the death, as well as its setting, a palace banquet, on the night of 12 October. Suetonius found a similar version in his sources (*alii tradunt*), but was aware of a variant in more than one authority (*quidam tradunt*) that the poison was administered by Halotus on the Capitol when Claudius was dining there with the priests. This basic uncertainty over the circumstances clearly casts doubts about the validity of the general charge. Tacitus adds the detail that the poison was sprinkled on a particularly appetizing specimen (Dio adds the further detail that Agrippina artfully ate the rest herself).

One might wonder why a skilled poisoner would not simply have provided a poisonous species of mushroom rather than an edible one that had been tampered with. The poisonous capabilities of mushrooms were well known in the ancient world – Domitian, for instance, refused to eat them. A careless choice of species at a banquet would later remove in one fell swoop the prefect of the watch, Seneca's friend Annaeus Serenus, along with several of his officers. Pliny implies that Agrippina did in fact carry out the deed with a poisonous rather than a poisoned item and this version probably circulated during the next reign, when a witticism was attributed to Nero that mushrooms were the 'food of the gods', in the words of a common Greek saying, since Claudius became a god by eating one.[164]

Inevitably the precise details of what ensued vary. In Suetonius' version, many (*multi*) say that as soon as Claudius swallowed the poison he lost the power of speech and was afflicted with a terrible pain, which lasted all night until he died, just before dawn. This tallies generally with Dio's report that Claudius seemed to be overcome by drink, a not uncommon habit and one not likely therefore to arouse suspicion, and was carried out of the banquet and died without regaining speech. But Suetonius reports that several authorities (*nonnulli*) distinguished between two phases in his final night. In the first he passed out, then emptied the contents of his stomach by vomiting, after which, it is implied, he seemed to recover. Tacitus reflects the latter tradition in his much more dogmatic version, which has Claudius survive the first dose, either because of his generally sluggish condition or because of his alcohol-induced immunity, and has him pass the poison by a bowel movement. Tacitus and Suetonius (in an alternative version of events) report that Claudius was then given a second dose. It is worth noting that none of the accounts tallies with the notion that Agrippina had acquired a 'medium-action' poison from a highly skilled poisoner, and one suspects that the tradition arose because Claudius apparently survived his initial bout of illness.

Both agree that Agrippina had the help of the doctor Gaius Stertinius Xenophon who, Tacitus claims, was happy to commit crimes for profit. Xenophon had been highly regarded by Claudius and had sufficient influence to persuade the emperor to grant immunity from taxation to his home district, on the island of Cos. He managed to amass a fortune in the course of his professional life and among his various ventures was a health resort in Naples. It may well have been he who persuaded Narcissus to go to Sinuessa.[165] Tacitus says that it is believed (*creditur*) that Xenophon placed a feather dipped with a speedy poison into Claudius' throat on the pretence of inducing vomiting. In Suetonius' account the colourful suggestion is made that Xenophon might have used a poisoned enema, introduced through a syringe (medically all but impossible), although he prosaically allows that it might have been put in a bowl of soup. The issue of Agrippina's guilt is impossible to determine at this remove. In terms of motive, the advantages and disadvantages are more or less evenly balanced. Nero was still relatively young, but the longer the succession was delayed the older Britannicus would be, and the more realistic his claim. The mere fact that a charge is made is not in itself significant, since such accusations followed the deaths of most of the prominent members of the Julio-Claudian family. It is hardly astonishing that Claudius should have died when he did; he had suffered from ill-health since childhood. A surprisingly large number of magistrates died in the months before Claudius' passing (and were considered portents of his death), so it may have been one of the more unhealthy summers which, according to the *Apocolocyntosis*, Claudius was in the habit of spending by holding court in Rome instead of going to a country retreat. Since in this same work it is Febris (Fever) who carries off Claudius, this might suggest a tradition that he died of malaria. In fact, several natural causes for his death have been proposed, including gastro-enteritis and heart failure.[166] The report of Claudius' passing, whether natural or induced, was supposedly kept secret for a while. The senate was convened and the priests made their vows for his recovery, at the very moment when his lifeless body was being covered with warm blankets to hinder rigor mortis and prevent the time of death being known. Even comic actors were summoned, on the pretence that he had asked for entertainment. Agrippina refused admission to the palace (echoing Livia's conduct on the death of Augustus) and issued regular bulletins, holding out hope for recovery. She prevented Britannicus from leaving his room but kept him in her sight and hugged him, offering comfort and sympathy. Claudius' daughters Antonia and Octavia were also detained. The reason for the delay is offered by Tacitus and Suetonius – to keep the main body of the praetorians in the dark until the preparations for Nero's succession were completed. This is plausible, but accords ill with the notion that Claudius was the victim of premeditated murder, in which case the perpetrators would have had ample opportunity to complete such preparations ahead of time. In any case, Tacitus seems to imply that the unit of the guard that first greeted Nero as he emerged from the palace had not in fact been primed beforehand. Both sources add a second reason, which may not be unrelated to the first, that the delay was intended to make the death fit an auspicious moment as predicted by the astrologers. This idea receives some support in the *Apocolocyntosis*, where 13 October, the official day of Claudius' death, is described as the *initium saeculi felicissimi* ('the first of a highly auspicious age'), and where Mercury asks the Fates to release Claudius and to let the astrologers be right for once.[167]

Finally all was ready, and the truth could be made public. Shortly after midday on 13 October 54 the word was given that the emperor was dead and, to judge from the *Apocolocyntosis*, the official report stated that he died happy, watching the performance of the comic actors brought in to entertain him when he was indisposed. Before the news had time to sink in, the succession of Nero was a *fait accompli*.[168]

7
Mother

The morning of 13 October 54 found the palace seized by feverish activity, totally concealed from the unsuspecting public outside its walls. By noon everything was in place.[1] The hours since Claudius' death would have given Burrus sufficient time to ensure a loyal cohort of guards on duty (although, in the event, they seem to have been taken somewhat by surprise). Seneca used the time to prepare the statements that the young Nero would make to the senate and the praetorians, and to invest them with sufficient elegance and earnestness to guarantee a good first impression. Also, while praetorian support was crucial in the first few days, the adherence of the legions stationed on the frontiers was needed to ensure the continuing viability of the new regime. After Tiberius' death, the praetorian prefect Macro had made sure that formal notice of Caligula's take-over was despatched immediately to provincial legati. On Claudius' death, Agrippina in a sense assumed Macro's old role and she would similarly have recognized the need for haste, to forestall the risk of any move by Britannicus' supporters. In the early days of the new reign Agrippina had a reputation for writing regularly to foreign nations, to client kings and to provincial governors. There can be little doubt that it would have been she who carried out this task on the first crucial morning of her son's accession.[2]

Finally the palace doors burst open to reveal Nero, not the gross specimen that self-indulgence would create within a few short years, but a handsome and attractive young man. Burrus came out with him and it must be assumed that, if the prefect had spent the early hours with the members of the guard, he had returned to the palace in the meantime. The soldiers stationed at the foot of the steps did not in fact greet Nero spontaneously, a curious omission if they had been properly prepared for the occasion. Burrus gave them their cue, and then they cheered and acclaimed their new emperor. They should by now have been good at this – some of them might already have given an identical performance twice before, first for Caligula, then four years later for Claudius. The anticipation of the traditional show of generosity before the day was over would have given the occasion an extra lift.

The first necessity was to move Nero without delay to the praetorian camp at the Viminal Gate. As the guards accompanied his litter from the Palatine, one or two of them looked around and asked about Britannicus. This might suggest a lingering sense of duty towards Claudius' natural son, but it could also have been nothing more than curiosity. At any rate, if the Britannicus loyalists were testing the waters, they found them distinctly cool. Any support for the younger prince was clearly scattered and unorganized. No interest was shown in the enquiry by the rest of the guards and the matter was simply dropped. The incident is a further hint that the guard had not been thoroughly primed. Britannicus was in the meantime still in the palace, where Agrippina was consoling him and, of course, keeping him out of the way until her son's elevation was firmly in place.[3]

When Nero reached the praetorian barracks the not-quite-17-year-old delivered a superb speech, not a difficult task since, like shrewd politicians of a later era, his mother had engaged a speechwriter, in this case Seneca, the most celebrated literary figure of his age. The speech was brief and to the point, to suit its audience, but it had the right effect and the troops proclaimed Nero as imperator, perhaps not surprisingly since, as anticipated, he was extremely generous. He emulated the grand gesture of Claudius thirteen years earlier, reputedly handing out in the neighbourhood of 15,000 or 20,000 HS to each member of the guard.[4]

After her marriage to Claudius, Agrippina had encouraged the notion of senatorial co-operation, to allay resentment over the undeniable fact that her husband had attained the purple by a military coup, pure and simple. She was deeply conscious of the value of ensuring that once the real power had been secured the notional source of that authority should be assuaged and flattered. The same principle was applied to the new regime. Nero was taken immediately (*raptim*) from the praetorian camp to the senate house. There his reception was no less rapturous. Tacitus records a number of decrees (*senatus consulta*), and Suetonius implies that Nero received his powers *en bloc* (*honores immensi*), just as Caligula had.[5] We have some idea of the nature of these powers from the text of a later law which granted imperial powers to Vespasian on his accession in AD 69, the *Lex de Imperio Vespasiani*, a copy of which was recorded on a bronze tablet and has luckily been preserved. Among its provisions is a key clause which gives the princeps the right and power to do whatever he thinks is in the interest of the state. This clause almost certainly goes back to Caligula's accession, when massive powers were bestowed on that emperor by a naive senate, and it can be assumed to be among the privileges granted Nero. The senate could not technically confer these powers itself. It could acclaim the new ruler as imperator but beyond this it had powers only to pass a senatorial decree (*senatus consultum*), the first stage of the formal process by which the princeps' (tribunician) authority would some time later be technically conferred by the popular assembly (*comitia*) through a law (*lex*). At this last point, Nero would become princeps in the full sense of the concept (in his case the formal process would not be completed until 4 December).[6] It would not look good to be too greedy, of course, and in a civilized display of moderation Nero, like Caligula and emperors before him, postponed acceptance of the title of 'father of the nation' (*pater patriae*).[7] Finally by late evening, after a brilliantly successful beginning, he could at last return to the palace.

For Nero it had been a long and exhausting, and exhilarating, first day, but there had been good reason to have him pack everything in before it ended. He dated his acclamation as emperor (*dies imperii*) from 13 October, marked on its anniversary by Arval sacrifices to celebrate his assumption of imperium (*ob imperium Neronis*). There was a diplomatic ambiguity about the day that bears all the hallmarks of Agrippina's subtle manoeuvring. Depending on one's point of view, he might be said to begin his reign from the first military acclamation by the praetorians, or it could be claimed that the senate had played the key constitutional role, since they would almost certainly at their first meeting have proclaimed Nero as imperator, just as they did Caligula in 37. In the foolish euphoria that invariably seemed to attend the accession of future tyrants, both sides could congratulate themselves and Agrippina could in turn congratulate *herself* on this shrewd diplomatic move, so typical of her political style.[8]

As late evening closed in on the first meeting in the senate, members with a sense of precedent and tradition would have wondered when they would finally reach the spicy part of the agenda, the reading of Claudius' will. Their expectations were reasonable. Augustus' will seems to have been read at the very first meeting of the senate convened to meet Tiberius; when Tiberius in turn died, Macro, the praetorian prefect, lost no time in rushing to Rome to announce the emperor's death and to publish his will (if only to have it annulled).[9] The anticipation at this first meeting must have been intense. Dio might echo the feelings of some in his assertion that after Claudius' death the principate belonged by strict *justice* (*kata to dikaiotaton*) to Britannicus, Claudius' natural son, even though by law (*ek nomou*) it fell to Nero, through adoption. But these sentiments have no basis in Roman constitutional theory and in any case, to judge from all the evidence available to us, Claudius seemed to put more emphasis on 'law' than 'justice', whatever Dio meant by the term. He certainly made sure that Nero received all the perks that would have marked him out as successor. One hope, surely a forlorn one, remained for the Britannicus loyalists – that the late emperor had perversely expressed intentions in his will which were completely at variance with his actions for the previous four years. But if there was any sense of mounting excitement as the time for the reading grew closer, the meeting must have ended on a flat note. There was no reading of the will; by now, indeed, there may have been no will. Dio charges that Nero destroyed Claudius' last testament and seized all the power (*ten archen pasan*). His clear implication is that Britannicus had been favoured in the document, which fits Suetonius' claim that Claudius had changed the key clauses to reflect the last-minute rapprochement with his son. Tacitus explains its suppression, as he has a habit of doing, in ambiguous terms, 'in case the preference of the stepson over the son (*antepositus filio privignus*) might create a sense of injustice and upset the ordinary people (*vulgus*)'.[10] This makes little sense if Tacitus means to suggest that it was *Claudius* who had given Nero priority, and that people would be offended by his choice – the suppression would simply serve to transfer the odium from Claudius to Agrippina and her allies. Tacitus' words are sensibly taken to mean that there was a fear that offence might be taken at the preference shown the stepson not by *Claudius* but by the *senate* (with the implication that Claudius had, in fact, placed Britannicus' name first and his wishes had been ignored). Certainly people were amused when Nero later took credit for prosecuting people who had tampered with wills and punished others for the very crimes he was suspected of, and the sense of irony felt on this later occasion might have been prompted by the rumours surrounding the fate of Claudius' will.[11] The failure of the sources to mention a single specific detail of the contents suggests strongly that we are dealing with pure guesswork. Evidently the contents, whatever they might have been, were not publicly known, a situation that inevitably encouraged speculation. Two observations might be made. Claudius was in many ways a traditionalist, with a close interest in Roman constitutional history. Augustus had shown the way by introducing his successor to public life by sharing office with him. If Claudius did decide to name his natural son as his successor, he was clearly prepared to deliver him as a hostage to fortune, declining right to the end to give him any of the credentials that would have validated his prospects. This could not be reversed by a simple clause in a will, and Claudius would have been aware of the precedent created by the treatment of Tiberius' final instructions. Tiberius' will had simply been declared null and void by the senate through the machinations of an energetic praetorian prefect.

Claudius' final instructions may well have been suppressed by Agrippina, but the reasons need not have been narrowly constitutional. His will, like Tiberius' before him, might have had political *implications* but in law, like the will of any citizen, it would have involved essentially a disposition of his estate. Suetonius records that Claudius on his last visit to the senate commended *both* of his sons to the care of the members, and for all that he seems to have groomed Nero as his successor, for reasons already given, there is no hint of any kind of personal breach with Britannicus. Claudius might thus have intended his estate to be shared equally between the two young men, and to have indicated this intention in his will.[12] Agrippina was keenly interested in monetary affairs and had the benefit of advice from Pallas, a shrewd financial manipulator. The ultimate disposition of Tiberius' estate would have provided her with a guiding precedent. Tiberius appears to have instructed that his possessions be shared equally between his two grandsons. The will was annulled, but afterwards the estate was not divided between those who should have had a claim in a normal non-testamentary situation, his five surviving grandchildren. It passed entirely to Caligula, with the implication that the principle had been accepted that a new princeps was vested, on his succession, not only with his predecessor's imperial powers but also, by virtue of the office, with his predecessor's estate. In fact, after Claudius, emperors seem almost without exception to have given up making wills, and after Nero's death in the turbulent 68–9 period the imperial properties passed successively and automatically into the hands of each new, short-lived princeps. The decision not to make public Claudius' will would almost certainly have been Agrippina's and would have been a calculated gamble. There were certain disadvantages. Inevitably, the fact that the document did not see the light of day would be bound to lead to conjecture about its contents, which the pro-Britannicus elements would have exploited. The stories of Claudius' change of heart in the last few months would have been fuelled by such speculation. Balancing these considerations, Nero, as princeps, would have had an undisputed claim on the whole estate in the absence of a will, and Agrippina would not be associated with the public process of dismantling the last measure of her husband. The precedent offered by Macro's annulment of Caligula's will was not one to be emulated by her, except as a very last resort.[13]

So Claudius' will was never read at the first meeting, but he was not neglected and Nero ensured that his stepfather would leave the world in fine style (and at public expense). Suetonius describes the funeral approved by the senate as 'splendid' (*apparatissimo funere*) and Tacitus says that the send-off followed exactly the pattern voted earlier for Augustus. Its scale is attributed to Agrippina, who, he says, was determined to match Livia's lavish extravagance (*magnificentia*).[14] Nor should this surprise us. Agrippina had seen herself not as a female interloper but as a partner of Claudius, and her son not as a usurper but as Claudius' considered choice as successor. The treatment of Claudius after his death might be seen as a crude political device to impress senate and public with a display of piety, but it would also have been a genuine reflection of what Agrippina believed her partner and her son's predecessor deserved.

The protocol for Claudius' funeral had been established by the ritual followed for Augustus and Tiberius. There would be a lying-in-state for five days (until 18 October), followed by cremation. Six days later the bones would be placed in the mausoleum. The surviving description of Augustus' funeral allows us to reconstruct the arrangements made by Agrippina for Claudius. The corpse was carried in a coffin, inside a couch-shaped catafalque of gold and ivory. A wax image of the emperor in triumphal garb was carried by the magistrates-elect; a similar image of gold was carried by senators and a third was placed on a triumphal chariot. Behind this followed the traditional procession of actors wearing the death masks of Claudius' ancestors. After the traditional eulogy the procession made its way to the Campus Martius, where priests, knights and praetorians made circuits of the pyre, the last group placing on it any triumphal decorations they had received from the emperor. The pyre was finally lit by centurions of the guard. After the funeral proper a *iustitium*, or period of public mourning, followed. We do not know how long it was but it is unlikely that Agrippina would have followed the Augustan model for this part of the ritual, since Augustus' death was followed by a few days of mourning for the men but a whole year for the women. She would have been too shrewd to risk trying public patience with a period of similar length for the far less popular Claudius.[15]

Funeral eulogies were traditionally given by young men from the deceased's family. For Claudius the duty was performed, appropriately, by Nero. The speech was a highly polished piece of writing provided, of course, by Seneca. It did contain one surprise. The standard references to the antiquity of Claudius' family and the attainments of his ancestors were received respectfully by the audience, as was the praise of his literary achievements and his successes abroad. But Nero went on to praise Claudius' foresight and wisdom (*providentia* and *sapientia*). This was too much even for a reserved and proper Roman audience, and people could not help chuckling. The incident might have involved nothing more than an unfortunate over-use of clichés, leading in this case to a degree of social embarrassment. But we cannot completely rule out a more sinister scenario, and a preview of things to come. Seneca had a clever sense of parody, and he might well have deliberately exaggerated Claudius' political and intellectual skills beyond the conventional level as a safe means (he was not one to court danger) of ridiculing his former employer. As will emerge later, Seneca seems to have encouraged his pupil in an 'anti-Claudian' direction, and it is not impossible that he cleverly used this panegyric as the first salvo of this campaign.[16]

On 19 October, the day after the funeral, Nero entered the senate, where he would make an important speech, outlining his programme and principles of government. He also came with a request, readily approved, that his late stepfather be made a god.[17] The deification of Claudius would have been deemed essential by Agrippina as a formal sanctioning of the regime of which she had been an inseparable part, but the privilege was not automatic. Divine honours had been requested for Tiberius but were not granted because of a distinct lack of enthusiasm in the senate (the issue was never raised for Caligula). Claudius had much more powerful forces at work for him. Tacitus was generally impressed by the thorough and disciplined way Agrippina managed business while Claudius was alive. We can be sure that, for at least the initial period of the new reign, she continued to demonstrate the same prudence and shrewdness. She would have ensured through allies in the senate that the deification would pass off smoothly, which it did. Once he had officially become a god, Claudius' cult would have to be arranged. The Sodales Augustales, the body responsible for the worship of the first emperor, and which now included Nero, were also given responsibility for the most recently deified Caesar. Priests (*flamines*) were appointed, and Agrippina was appointed *flamenica* (female priest). Livia had been granted a similar honour in the case of Augustus.[18]

The consecration of Claudius would have been an important personal triumph for Agrippina, and would also have encouraged her to hope that in due time the same boon would befall her. At a more practical level, she would have appreciated that it gave Nero an important propaganda tool, since he could from now on style himself as Divi Filius, the son of a deified father. Nor did he hesitate to use the title. On the earliest gold and silver issues, Divus Claudius is mentioned both on the obverse (as Agrippina's husband) and the reverse (as Nero's father). On the slightly later series minted in AD 55 the same double allusion is found, and the reverse also depicts four elephants drawing a chariot, on which are seated two radiate figures (the radiate crown is the symbol of divinity), Claudius and a companion, perhaps Augustus or a personified spirit.[19] On Neronian local coinage the association between Divus Claudius and Nero is pervasive.[20]

One final honour awaited Claudius now that he had been promoted to divine rank. Any self-respecting god required a place of worship. After their apotheoses, both Julius Caesar and Augustus were voted their own temples. The completion of the latter's was much delayed by the cautious and penny-pinching Tiberius, but its eventual dedication provided one of the most splendid spectacles of Caligula's reign. The energy and initiative for the Temple to the Divine Claudius, according to Suetonius, came from one source, Agrippina. Taking her cue from the massive grandeur of the imperial palace (the Domus Tiberiana) on the Palatine, for which, it has been suggested, she might have been largely responsible, she undertook construction of the new temple on the Caelian Hill. It was not finished at the time of her death in 59 and what had been erected was partly dismantled in the later rebuilding of the area after the great fire of 64 to make way for the extravagant complex of Nero's Golden House. It was eventually rebuilt by Vespasian. Consequently, much of Agrippina's project is lost to us, but we do know that it was planned on a grand scale, as can be judged from the remains of the massive platform, measuring 200m x 160m (650ft x 525ft) and dwarfing any other sacred precinct in Rome.[21] Part of the retaining wall which supported the great platform of Claudius' temple has survived in the form of a double order of arcades in elaborate rusticated masonry (Fig. 2). In the lower section the arches are rectangular, with a cornice supported by short Doric pilasters; the upper ones are rounded, between pilasters. The keystones of the upper arches project considerably and much of the facing is left rough. Within the arches are walls; on the ground they are in brick-faced concrete, cut by a doorway; on the upper level they are in rusticated travertine, with windows to provide light for a range of rooms behind. The rusticated masonry is very reminiscent of Claudian structures, such as the Porta Maggiore and the Aqua Virgo, and this wall is most likely part of the original structure as built by Agrippina. But since the façade is built against the core of an earlier platform, we cannot rule out Vespasianic reconstruction; if Vespasianic, the style of the wall very probably follows that of the original it replaced. Hence it is also very possible that the overall design of the temple adopted by

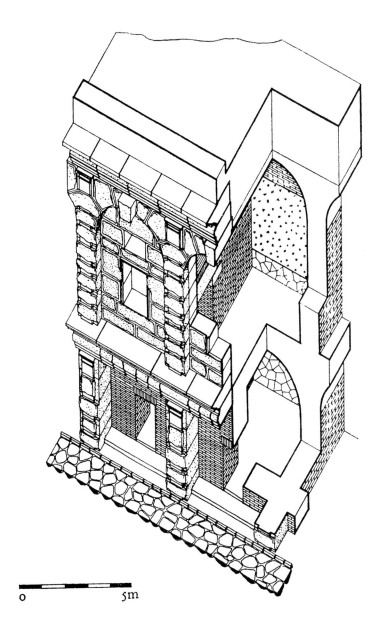

0   5m

Fig. 2 The Temple of Divus Claudius: podium façade

Vespasian similarly followed the plan and style of the earlier structure. The Vespasianic design appeared on the famous marble plan of Rome executed at the end of the second century. With the subsequent loss of the crucial parts of the marble plan, the design is now known to us by drawings made before the loss (Fig. 3). The temple shown in the drawing has a frontal row of five columns, generally considered by scholars to be an incorrect representation of the more usual hexastyle (six-column) arrangement. It stood slightly to the east of the centre of the platform, facing west across the shorter axis. The open area around it was planted with trees. In addition it seems that a portico honouring Claudius was built in association with the temple, a clever way of combining the elegant and symbolic with the essentially functional, a tradition Claudius had himself maintained, and also an effective way to ensure that the public would be constantly reminded of the two individuals, Claudius and Agrippina, to whom they owed the amenity. Martial seems to suggest that since the portico stood just outside the range of Nero's Golden House, it was not dismantled and was still in public use in his own time.[22]

The early days of Nero's reign represented the acme of Agrippina's achievement. She was now arguably the most powerful person in Rome. Both Suetonius and Dio claim that at first Nero left all public and private business in the hands of his mother. This claim is difficult to document and is probably something of an exaggeration. Tacitus in fact records few specific details of direct political power exercised by Agrippina at the outset, beyond the elimination of potential rivals. All the same it would have been natural for Nero to have been heavily dependent on her until he could find his own feet. Certainly, there were many outward signs of deference. The very first watchword that he gave to the praetorian guard was *Optima Mater* ('Best Mother'), and he would ride with her through the streets in a litter or make a special show of devotion by walking beside her as she was carried.[23]

Two of Agrippina's privileges had clear political connotations. Tacitus reports that meetings of the senate were convened on the Palatine, to enable her to follow the proceedings, and he uses the imperfect tense (*vocabantur*, '*used to be* convened') to imply strongly that she was allowed this privilege repeatedly. Agrippina was able to enter discreetly by a newly installed rear door and would stay concealed behind a thick curtain. This was a signal honour. Dio observes that, even though Livia for practical purpose ran the empire, she never committed the impropriety of entering the senate chamber. Nor, of course, did Agrippina actually enter the chamber. Nero would later maintain before the senate that one of Agrippina's sins had been that she could barely be restrained from breaking into the senate, a charge framed in such a way that it effectively admits that she never in reality did so. Only one single source, one of Dio's epitomators, John of Antioch, claims that she did in fact enter.[24] Agrippina's behaviour was not nearly as remarkable as Tacitus wants to imply. Meetings on the Palatine were not uncommon under the Julio-Claudians, and under Augustus they were regularly held, for his convenience, in the library and portico of the temple of Apollo. Tiberius also arranged meetings there, both early and late in his reign, and it was on the Palatine that the senate held its famous session to denounce Sejanus, and where Claudius summoned the members after he seized power in 41. The choice of the Capitol for the senate meeting which immediately followed Caligula's assassination can be explained by the dangerous situation on the Palatine, where the murder had taken place. There are several recorded

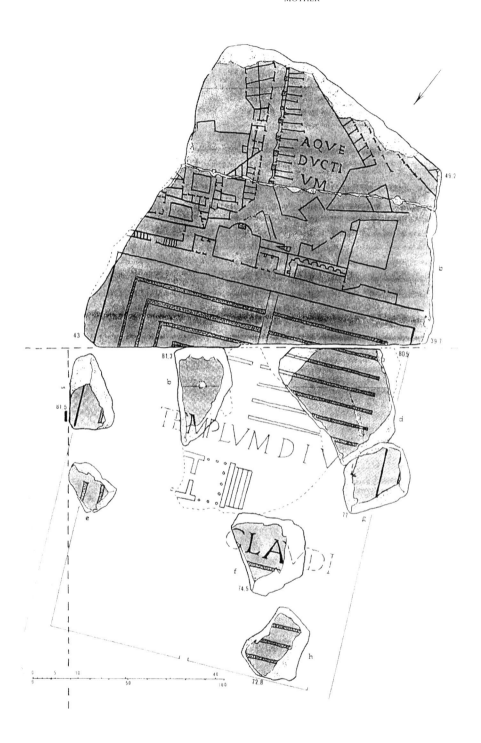

Fig. 3 The Temple of Divus Claudius on the marble plan of Rome.

instances when interested parties were allowed to watch the proceedings in the house, but obliged to do so standing at the bar. The four sons of the wretched Marcus Hortalus, for instance, watched the senatorial debate, similarly on the Palatine, while their father pleaded for financial relief and was subjected to a stern and humiliating lecture by Tiberius.[25] Agrippina's privilege was a mark of her prestige and power – but she was careful not to offend tradition.

Another highly political gesture was the granting to Agrippina of two lictors. Lictors were the attendants of magistrates and other people of high rank and station, such as the chief Vestal Virgin (who was allowed only one). Their function was to precede the officials, carrying the emblem of *fasces* or bundled rods, and to move bystanders out of their path. Livia had been allowed a lictor, but only when she carried out her sacred duties as priestess of Augustus – Tiberius made a special point of banning her from using him otherwise. In Agrippina's case, Tacitus seems to imply that the lictors were granted as a general privilege. Like the use of the covered carriage, the *carpentum,* this prerogative was of more symbolic importance than practical use, but the symbol would have been a powerful one. Lictors suggested the power and authority of the magistrates. Agrippina's privilege would have served to elevate her in the public mind to the status of a woman who had a quasi-official share in the administration of the principate.

Agrippina's elevated status is also reflected in the imperial coinage. It is impossible to exaggerate the impact that the numismatic innovations of Nero's reign would have had on his contemporaries. Agrippina became the very first woman during her lifetime to share with a reigning princeps the face of an official coin minted in Rome (she had similarly appeared on Claudian coins minted in Ephesus). Gold and silver coins issued during Nero's first year, beginning in late 54, depict busts of Nero and his mother facing one another (Pl. 13). The legend identifies Agrippina as Agrippina Augusta, the wife of the Deified Claudius, the mother of Caesar, and thus brings together on a single coin the three roles that brought her the greatest pride. Nero's own legend is reserved for the back of the coin, together with the familiar motif of the oak wreath (the *corona civica*) with the legend *ex sc* ('with senatorial authority'). This arrangement involves a remarkable association of the emperor with his mother and is the most powerful hint that Agrippina saw herself as a kind of regent, or co-ruler, with her son, a position that had no precedent in Roman law or tradition. Outside Rome a parallel series may have been minted in the imperial mint at Caesaria in Cappadocia. Here drachms and didrachms and 12 and 24 *as* pieces, undated but clearly belonging to early in the reign, to judge from the youthful Nero depicted on the obverse, identify him as the son of the deified Claudius, while his mother appears on the reverse, veiled or bare-headed, identified as Agrippina Augusta, Mother of the Augustus.[26] The relationship between the young emperor and his mother is reflected in the inscriptions of the period. Nero is called the son of Divus Claudius, but his descent from Germanicus, Tiberius (through adoption) and Augustus (again through adoption) are invariably included; these ancestors are all on his mother's side. He is in fact the first princeps who does not limit himself in his inscriptions to his paternal descent.[27]

Nothing better symbolizes Agrippina's special position than a striking relief from the Sebasteion at Aphrodisias, depicting Nero and his mother (Pl. 19). The portrait type is that of the early Nero, one that might well have been created on his accession, and reflects the image that appears on contemporary coins – the good restrained princeps in the mould of Germanicus, as opposed to the later depictions which portray him as the more flamboyant established emperor. Agrippina carries a cornucopia (reflecting her traditional association with Demeter, see p. 223), and crowns her son with a laurel wreath. Nero is in military garb and carries a spear, and the relief seems to portray his promotion to emperor as the crowning of a military victor. Rose suggests that the pose might have been inspired by a similar arrangement of the cult statue of Augustus being crowned by Roma in the temple they shared at Pergamum.[28] He is dressed as a soldier, appropriately, since his acclamation by the senate would not have been as 'princeps' but as the more distinctly military 'imperator'. But on his feet he does not wear soldiers' boots, rather civilian sandals with toe caps and straps which cross over the feet and then are wrapped around the ankle and tied at the front. We might have expected Nero to receive the crown from an abstract figure, on the lines of the personification of the senate which bestows the oak crown on Claudius on another relief from the same site. In this case, it is the mother who performs this crucial role of initiation. The impression that all of this made on the popular mind is reflected in the slightly later *Octavia,* where the character of Agrippina speaks of 'the whole world which my love gave to the youth to rule' (*totum ... orbem quem dedit ... puero regendum noster ... amor*).[29] Further evidence of Agrippina's special position comes to us from an interesting inscription found at Corinth, in the form of a dedication to Gaius Iulius Spartiaticus, who had been elevated to equestrian status by Claudius, clearly dead at the time of the inscription, since he is identified as *Divus Claudius.* Spartiaticus is attested as the procurator *Caesaris et Augustae Agrippinae* ('procurator of Caesar and Agrippina Augusta'); the 'Caesar' can hardly be other than Nero, and Agrippina thus owned property jointly with the emperor. The procurator was of course the servant of the private estate of the emperor. But the division between the public and private income of the emperor, if distinct in law, was blurred in common perception and this inscription is in effect a striking piece of documentary evidence which brings her very close to the status of co-regent. It is also possible that a Eutychus, identified in another inscription as *procurator Augustorum* ('procurator of the Augustus and Augusta'), may similarly have administered the joint property of Nero and his mother.[30]

The practical application of Agrippina's enhanced power immediately after the accession is more difficult to determine. There was certainly a belief early in the reign that she took a direct part in the handling of 'foreign policy' when Parthia invaded Armenia and provoked yet another Armenian crisis. Many in Rome were concerned that the response to the threat would be under the control of a woman.[31] But Tacitus is ambivalent about her role in this campaign and observes that many Romans were confident that Seneca and Burrus would have the final word.

Agrippina would have seen her main and immediate task as that of eliminating any threat of potential rivals to Nero. Tacitus dramatically introduces Book XIII of the *Annals,* which begins with Nero's accession, with the statement that the first victim in the new regime was Marcus Junius Silanus, governor of Asia. The narrative device is reminiscent of the way he introduces Tiberius' reign with the murder of Agrippa Postumus, in each case setting a chilling tone for what was to follow. Admittedly, in Marcus Silanus' case Tacitus ascribes the crime explicitly to Agrippina, saying that

Nero was ignorant of any plot; Pliny is in fact the only source to place the blame on Nero rather than on Agrippina. He makes the crime seem especially heinous by stressing that it was inconceivable that Marcus' behaviour could have provoked his murder, since he was an apathetic creature, so despised by earlier emperors as to earn from Caligula the tag of 'golden sheep'. Perhaps, but it is worth noting that his consulship in 46 lasted for the whole year (a relatively uncommon honour) and that he was competent and energetic enough to govern the important province of Asia without apparent mishap.

Tacitus provides two reasons for Agrippina's action. She had driven Marcus' brother Lucius Junius Silanus to suicide in 49 to clear the path for Nero to be betrothed to Octavia just before her own wedding. He suggests that consequently she feared Marcus' vengeance. This is hardly convincing, as he would surely have been no less a threat in any of the previous five years. The second motive offered is more plausible, that many people thought that Nero was too young and that the principate should go to man of mature years (Marcus was 40), of good character (as he supposedly was) and of noble family. Marcus was the son of Aemilia Lepida, great-granddaughter of Augustus. He was thus what Rudich calls a 'dynastic dissident', someone automatically at risk simply because of his kinship with the imperial family. And he was a Junius Silanus on his father's side, a member of a family which entertained constant ambitions for power and perhaps felt that the succession of a new and very young emperor was an ideal time to mount a personal challenge.[32]

Marcus, we are asked to believe, was one of a rare breed, a man without a past. It might have proved difficult to make a trumped-up charge of treason stick. Instead Agrippina reputedly decided on the traditional woman's weapon, poison, even using the same brand that had worked so well on Claudius. Her agents in crime were two employees of the palace stationed in Asia, the equestrian procurator Publius Celer and the freedman Helius, in charge of the imperial revenues in the province. Marcus was eliminated over dinner, with no attempt made to conceal the crime, according to Tacitus, to some degree contradicting the notion that they used the 'Claudius' poison the speciality of which was supposedly concealment. Whether or not Helius and Celer were guilty, they suffered no immediate repercussions and Nero later held them both in very high regard. Helius had been Claudius' freedman but, unlike Pallas, continued to be favoured by the new emperor. Nero later left him in charge when he went to Greece in 67, handing over Italy for him to plunder, as Dio puts it. After Nero's fall Helius would be dragged through the Forum to his death by Galba, to the applause of bystanders. Celer similarly enjoyed Nero's favour and when he was charged with extortion in the same province, Asia, in 57, the emperor managed to draw out the case until the accused died of old age.[33]

Whether or not Agrippina was responsible for the murder of Marcus Junius Silanus (if he was in fact murdered at all) will never be known. Certainly, it could not have happened immediately. There is the very practical consideration that some time would have had to elapse simply for her to communicate her instructions to Asia, and the death could not have occurred immediately at the outset of the reign. The parallel drawn with the elimination of Agrippa Postumus, who would have been put to death on the spot in Rome, is clearly intended for literary effect. But the truth is largely irrelevant. A *reputation* for eliminating opponents promptly and efficiently was enough to provide a powerful deterrent to any would-be claimants. It is conceivable that, even if his death had been natural, Agrippina would not have been unhappy for others to think otherwise. There were potential rivals (with claims at least as good as Marcus') in the wings. If they did nurture secret ambitions for the purple they seem to have been scared off, but only for the time being. All seem to have been considered dangerous when Agrippina was no longer on the scene, and all came to sorry ends. The brother of Marcus, for instance, Decimus Silanus Torquatus, had credentials as impressive as his brother's and might have posed a potential threat. At any rate he would be forced to commit suicide in 64, reputedly because of his Augustan lineage and his supposed imperial aspirations. Marcus' son, Lucius Junius Silanus Torquatus, might have seemed a lesser threat since he was one generation further from Augustus and if he were older than Nero it could hardly have been by much (his father was born in 14). All the same, he was later seen as a rival and Nero had him put to death in 65. Rubellius Plautus was the son of Rubellius Blandus and Julia, Tiberius' granddaughter. He was banished in 60 amidst widespread speculation that he was the natural candidate to replace Nero, and was put to death two years later. Yet another, if more remote, rival might be found in Faustus Cornelius Sulla, the half-brother of Messalina and husband of Antonia, Claudius' daughter. At any rate he was banished to Massilia in 58 on the bizarre charge of being the leader of a gang of thugs who attacked a party of revellers returning from the Mulvian bridge, a group that was thought to include Nero. Faustus was also eliminated later, at the same time as Rubellius Plautus. The fact that several years could elapse before Nero felt obliged to take any action against unwelcome rivals suggests that Agrippina (or her reputation) had been totally effective in 54.[34]

One further irritant remained to be dealt with. The freedman Narcissus, in a milieu whose motives seem always to be self-serving, appears to have remained stubbornly loyal to Claudius. He was in Sinuessa when his master died, taking the cure for gout, and perhaps rather foolishly returned to Rome on receiving the news. He had been an extremely powerful and extremely wealthy individual, but his position was highly vulnerable. It had depended on the continued patronage of a single individual, Claudius. When that individual passed from the scene, Narcissus found himself with no natural allies. Quite apart from the enmity of Agrippina, he had hardly endeared himself to the senate. The *Apocolocyntosis* charges that a whole procession of senators and knights had been marked for death by him, and his prominent role in the downfall of Gaius Silius in particular would have cost him support among those senators who might have been Agrippina's natural opponents. After his return to Rome he was placed under a rigorous guard and before the end of the year he was dead, murdered or forced to commit suicide. By an odd irony his death occurred at the tomb of Messalina. Just before he died Narcissus behaved oddly, carrying out what Dio describes as a 'splendid deed' (*lampron ergon*). His privileged position in the palace as *ab epistulis* would have given him access to sensitive correspondence, and he had held onto a number of letters with incriminating material about Agrippina and others. His final gesture before departing this life was to burn them all. It is difficult to understand why Narcissus should have felt the need to protect Agrippina's reputation, and why Dio would have thought it reason for congratulation that evidence of her crimes had gone up in smoke. Two rational explanations suggest themselves. One is that Narcissus' gesture might have been a last desperate attempt to survive the new regime by ingratiating himself with Agrippina. Possibly, but he would have been politically astute enough to realize that in destroying the letters he was discarding his last bargaining chip. It is more likely that the tradition has distorted the event and that he nobly destroyed documents that might harm worthy individuals, even though this might mean the incidental destruction of material that could blacken the name of his arch-enemy Agrippina. The decision to give loyalty priority over revenge would have been passed down in the tradition as a noble act.

Only one individual is recorded as feeling any regret over the demise of Narcissus, and that surprisingly is Nero (*invito principe*). Tacitus claims that his hidden vices nicely matched Narcissus' greed. Hardly an adequate explanation. If Nero did oppose Narcissus' death, it is more likely because he saw him as a foil to use against his mother's interference (depending on when precisely the death occurred). It is also possible that Tacitus in describing Narcissus' standing with Nero has confused him with the less familiar Narcissus II, a close associate of the emperor (p. 129).[35]

No matter how valuable Agrippina might be to Nero, it was almost inevitable that she would find it difficult to maintain her predominant position of influence and power. The root causes of the strain that developed between her and her son are not particularly difficult to understand. Nero was a very young man, with an inflated opinion of his own talents and abilities, and it would have been natural for him to want to show that he was capable of establishing his own, independent, role. The enormous debt that he owed his mother for helping to assure the accession would initially have been a reason for gratitude, and in an older man might have remained so. In a self-centred 17-year-old it was bound to become a cause of resentment. Nor did Agrippina's attitude help. A daughter of the imperial family, someone who had been able to exercise great tact and diplomatic skill when dealing with senators and army officers, she was surprisingly inept at handling her teenage son. She assumed that he would have the same appreciation of her skill and talents that had been shown by her late husband Claudius, a man of considerable political sophistication. She tried to dictate his choice of friends, and Tacitus describes her as *trux* and *minax* in her dealings with him ('grim and menacing'), *quae filio dare imperium, tolerare imperitantem nequibat* ('[someone] who knew how to hand over the rulership to her son, but was unable to endure his ruling'). Suetonius reports that Nero for his part was offended by her excessive surveillance and her constant criticism of his behaviour, to the extent that he threatened to run away and leave Rome. Nero was a vain individual; what he wanted to hear was flattery. There were some, including Seneca, who knew that this was the key to a ruler's heart, or at least a ruler like Nero. In the *Apocolocyntosis* Apollo declares that Nero is 'similar to me in his countenance and similar to me in beauty, and not inferior to me in voice and song' (*mihi similis vultu similisque decore/ nec cantu nec voce minoris*), and that 'his gleaming countenance shines forth with gentle gleam and his neck is handsome as the hair falls over it' (*flagrat nitidus fulgore remisso/ vultus, et adfuso cervix formosa capillo*). Agrippina was too close to Nero to indulge in this kind of nauseating adulation, but a mother who constantly reminded him that he was an immature youth who needed to adhere to her advice and guidance would soon wear out her welcome.[36]

An inevitable cause of dissension would have been Nero's spending habits. Agrippina had handled money with respect, seeing it as a political tool, to be carefully husbanded.

She would perhaps not have disapproved of her son's abolition or moderation of some of the more oppressive taxes, or his occasional distribution of money to the populace, or the annual grants to impoverished senators. Such acts of generosity were expected of an emperor and could have distinct political benefits. But Nero was also a notorious spendthrift, in the grand style of Caligula, with no real concept of frugality. An anecdote reported by Dio illustrates the problem. Nero reputedly ordered that 10 million HS be given to Doryphorus, his freedman *a libellis*. To bring home the enormity of his extravagance, Agrippina piled the money up before him, hoping that the sight of it would persuade him to change his mind. When he learned the true amount, he admitted his mistake – he had not realized it was so little. He made amends by doubling the total![37] The anecdote may in its details owe more to imagination than truth but it surely reflects in broad terms the impression made by Nero on his contemporaries, an impression of youthful extravagance and arrogance.

This generally difficult situation would have been aggravated by the novel circumstances of Nero's accession. Not only did Nero owe his rule to someone else, someone who was still on the scene and wanted a share in his government, but he owed it to a *woman;* indeed, he owed it to his mother. Expressions of concern about his youth might have given him a certain perverse pride. But he would have been irked by mutterings heard at the end of AD 54, when the new crisis emerged in Armenia and people were worried that it would be beyond the competence of a youth *under the sway of a woman*.[38]

Those anxious about the handling of the Armenian crisis were consoled by the discovery that Nero in fact sought the guidance not of his mother but of Seneca and Burrus, two men whose understanding of worldly matters was widely acknowledged. Tacitus, who is borne out by Dio, says that Seneca and Burrus offered a rare example of men who exercised power *in partnership* (*in societate potentiae*), sharing an influence that was equal but came from different sources. Burrus was a military man who provided a model of duty. His role may have been to set the proper tone of old-fashioned Roman *gravitas*, to take a stand as someone not prepared to compromise his principles for expediency. Seneca brought wise political counsel, presented with eloquence and charm. They thus balanced one another and tried to ensure that, if Nero was not committed to the path of virtue, his misbehaviour might at least be kept within reasonable bounds. It is very difficult to understand how in practice such a partnership could have operated and it is generally assumed that Burrus must have been subordinate to Seneca, in the sense that the philosopher and teacher is likely to have played the more active political role in advising and guiding.[39]

In fact, it is probably misleading to consider Seneca and Burrus as *partners*. Each had a distinct function. At a key moment, such as the accession, it is Burrus who has the crucial task, as prefect of the guard, and it may have been for his service in this matter that he was granted the *ornamenta consularia*, celebrated on the monument erected to him in his home town of Vasio.[40] In such matters as the preparation of speeches for the senate it is Seneca who comes to the fore. Apart from their guidance over the Armenian crisis (described in very broad terms, and seen essentially as a general counterpoint to the influence of Agrippina), there is no actual recorded instance of their acting in concert. They do appear together at times of crisis, as during the final hours leading up to Agrippina's murder, and it is claimed that they attended Nero's early theatrical performances, prompting him and giving the audience the lead on how to react.[41] But on none of these occasions do they seem to have a properly thought-out and agreed agenda that would characterize a working partnership.

Suetonius depicts Nero as very much his own man. On the other hand, Tacitus and Dio suggest that Seneca and Burrus managed him, although they differ in their understanding of how this was done. Dio has the young emperor hand over complete control of the state to them. Tacitus portrays them as giving in to Nero's personal inclinations to some extent, not, however, as a device to exclude him from a serious role in governing, but rather to ensure that Agrippina's influence would be kept in check. Hence, he does have Nero act independently, but only at times. This inconsistency in the literary sources seriously compromises our understanding of how Nero worked within the Augustan system at the beginning of his reign and, in turn, our proper understanding of his mother's role during the same period.

Dio insists that Seneca and Burrus took the government entirely into their own hands, and that their control of affairs met with general approval. He goes on to say that the two advisers made many changes in existing *kathestekota* ('institutions' or 'regulations') and abolished some altogether, enacting many new laws and leaving Nero to indulge himself. Dio's suggestion has an appealing simplicity but is impossible to substantiate. Nowhere in his narrative is there any single example of such innovation or legislation, nor is there any reference to Seneca and Burrus working to implement an imperial edict or senatorial measure. The original text of Dio's history is missing for this period, of course, and has to be reconstructed from his later epitomators, but it is difficult to believe that they somehow omitted every single reference to any kind of legislative programme.[42] Tacitus does provide some details of reforms, but he thought them far less impressive than they appeared and clearly did not see them as the distinguishing features of the new regime. Suetonius cites Nero's reforms simply as an illustration of the attractive aspects of his personality rather than as part of a formal programme emanating from Seneca (or Burrus), nor does he give Seneca any role in their implementation. Seneca held a suffect consulship at some point in the mid-50s (the exact year is uncertain), yet a decree passed during his term of office comes down to us not in his name but in that of his colleague Trebellius Maximus (the *senatus consultum Trebellianum*).[43] There is no mention even of Seneca's presence in the senate, let alone a speech. This seems an astonishing omission in a man of such celebrated oratorical gifts, particularly since Tacitus is far more interested in him as a politician than as a philosopher.[44] It is likely that he was less active as a legislator than as a background figure, a role rightly stressed by Griffin. Certainly the terms used to describe him, *amicus* (friend) or *magister* (teacher), suggest a general influence on behaviour rather than an active role as initiator of a legislative programme.[45] Seneca seems to have seen his task as conveying to the young emperor the notion that the principate was invested with enormous powers, but that the wise ruler could achieve more success by exercising these powers in a spirit of mercy and leniency, motivated by a sense of *clementia*. It is no accident that his *De Clementia* was written about this time, containing a judicious blend of flattery and advice, and similar sentiments are voiced by the contemporary poet Calpurnius Siculus, a shadowy figure but almost certainly a contemporary of Nero, who speaks of 'clemency smashing the mad blades' (*insanos contudit enses*).[46] A nice illustration of Seneca at work will occur at the beginning of 55. Plautius Lateranus had been ejected from the senate for enjoying the pleasures of Messalina. He was restored to his rank by Nero, in the context of a pledge of clemency made by Nero acting as Seneca's mouthpiece. Given his vanity, Nero would probably have been easily persuaded by the argument that generosity was a sure-fire way of gaining admiration.[47]

The nature of Seneca and Burrus' influence over Nero and of their contribution to the waning role of Agrippina represents the most difficult historical problem of Nero's early reign. Since the rivalry for the ear of a sovereign by necessity takes place behind the scenes, it is not surprising that our understanding of events is hopelessly obscure. This is a perfect example of the problem raised by Dio when he concedes that everything Nero and his mother said or did to each other was reported in such a garbled form that in the absence of hard and reliable information people had recourse to guesswork, and passed on their guesses as facts. An illustration of the confusing picture that emerges is the report in Dio that Seneca had an affair with Agrippina (and had to fight off formal charges of adultery), at the very time he was supposedly involved in a bitter struggle with her. The difficulty is compounded by Tacitus' technique. As Syme has observed, the concentration on a small number of personalities in Tacitus' Neronian books creates serious disadvantages, since events remain unexplained and there is no coherent presentation of 'policy'.[48]

Whatever the precise part that Seneca and Burrus played there is no doubt that Agrippina very soon found that her place at the right hand of her son had to be shared with others. Tacitus' claim, however, that *from the outset* Seneca and Burrus had to combine to resist Agrippina's savagery (*ferocia*) is surely an exaggeration. Nor should we accept without scrutiny Tacitus' assertion that the distinctions heaped on her at the beginning were purely for public consumption (*propalam*). Popular opinion distinguished the two groups, according to Dio, and saw Nero's mother as the 'stronger' and Seneca and Burrus as the 'wiser', presumably a distinction between the control of the sources of power, such as the army and senate, as exercised by Agrippina, and the ability to change policy by personal influence, as exercised by Seneca and Burrus. The picture may not be far from the truth. While Agrippina clearly began to lose some of the affection of her son, she remained to the end a powerful woman, one to be respected and feared, if not loved.[49]

The situation was highly ironic. It was Agrippina who had won Seneca's reprieve from exile and had given him the role of Nero's tutor, and it was almost certainly she who had engineered Burrus' appointment as commander of the guard. Both men would surely have been basically sympathetic to her views, and it is difficult to believe that any profound ideological differences could have separated them. Seneca, sensing the mood of the times, emphasized *clementia* as the key to a successful reign; Agrippina emphasized diplomacy and the building up of a powerful clientele. The two approaches are hardly irreconcilable. Moreover Seneca was a highly political man, at the centre of court life since his return, and he must have been aware of the sometimes sordid machinations conducted on behalf of his pupil. Burrus had participated in them in directly. When it served their career, the two men did not find themselves out of sympathy with either Agrippina's political ends or her methods. The parting of the ways for Agrippina and her two old allies may well have been brought about by nothing more complicated than a natural instinct for self-preservation. For as long as Claudius was alive, Agrippina's influence over him, even if in fact largely benign in its results, would inevitably have caused offence. But the aggressive wife who influenced affairs indirectly through a compliant husband was a familiar phenomenon, one that Romans had learned reluctantly to live with. Certainly Seneca and Burrus did not feel that the patronage of such a woman was to their disadvantage. But with the accession of Nero, Romans were faced with a true novelty and a deeply disturbing one, a woman who seemingly sought power in her own right. The *Octavia* probably reflects contemporary feelings on the issue. In the play the character of the nurse describes Agrippina as *regnum petens* ('pursuing rule', line 159), and claims that *ausa imminere est orbis imperio sacri* ('she dared to strive after imperium over a sacrosanct world', line 156), a line whose full connotations are difficult to convey, since *sacer* is often used with specific reference to the sacrosanctity of the princeps.[50] Clearly to many Romans Agrippina would have seemed in 54 not merely offensive, but a dangerous threat to the whole Roman order. Certainly Nero would later play on such fears in his efforts to justify himself after her death, by claiming that she had aspired to a *consortium imperii*, and tried to suborn the praetorians. A clever operator like Seneca, who always had his finger to the political wind, would certainly have realized soon after the accession that Agrippina was heading for a major fall and that she would bring down her cronies with her. The instinct for survival, always strong in Seneca, would have told him that the time was opportune for a switch in allegiance. Burrus was an old-fashioned soldier with a strong sense of loyalty and his attitude towards Agrippina seems to have been ambivalent. To the end he was unwilling to betray her, yet even he recognized that she represented a danger from which he should maintain a prudent distance. The situation may well parallel the earlier predicament of Agrippina and her sister Livilla in 39, when the disastrous conduct of their brother Caligula forced them into opposition to him (see p. 66). The 'rift' between Agrippina and her two former creatures thus probably had more to do with simple expediency than with dogma.

There was, however, one important area where divergent viewpoints were likely to cause tension. Agrippina would have looked back on Claudius' reign, or at least its last five years, as one of triumph, when she took her place at the side of the princeps, and came close to the rank of co-ruler, sharing in the decisions and enjoying many of the trappings of authority. She would thus have regarded the Claudian 'legacy' as her own and any attempt to dismantle his achievements as a personal affront. Seneca, on the other hand, bore a personal grudge towards the former emperor as the man who had humiliated and exiled him, and had ignored his sycophantic appeals for clemency. He no doubt concealed his animosity while his patron was alive; after his death the temptation to seek some sort of posthumous revenge must have been irresistible. There was a clear opportunity to do so. Nero would have felt a natural and understandable desire to make his own mark, and to move out of his adoptive father's shadow. Also, any credit given to Claudius was likely to enhance Nero's position less than it would improve Britannicus' prospects. At the outset Nero had to show the expected piety towards his predecessor. Once his position was secure, however, he could start to distance himself from Claudius, then even begin to denigrate him. The downgrading of Claudius would have been taken by Agrippina as a personal affront.

In a battle where one side's challenge is to encourage the personal inclinations of a vain young man with absolute power and the other's is to try to discourage those inclinations, the outcome will hardly be in doubt. Would this have resulted in *bitter* enmity between Agrippina and Seneca (and Burrus)? Probably not, and it is possible that the sources have misrepresented a careful distancing as deep animosity. Certainly, Nero believed right up to the moment of his mother's death that Burrus' loyalty was split between her and himself, and in 58 Romans could be reminded, without any hint of irony, that Seneca at one time had been Agrippina's lover. This charge reflects current gossip and its truth or untruth is perhaps not as significant as the fact that, even if not true, it must not have seemed inherently implausible at the time.

The first signs of the strain that would cause the rift between mother and son can be detected at a very early stage, and it will be appropriate at this point to return to the narrative of events. As noted earlier (p. 147), after Claudius' funeral Nero spoke in the senate, requesting apotheosis for his predecessor and setting forth the principles on which his rule would be based. Such an occasion would be expected to call forth conventional and all-too-familiar platitudes. In fact, Nero's speech was specific and pointed. While Tacitus does not explicitly attribute the text to Seneca, it does follow his praise of the latter's literary talents and the reported comment that old-timers were quick to note how Nero was the first princeps to rely on borrowed eloquence. The authorship can hardly be doubted.[51]

Nero began by acknowledging that he ruled with the authority of the senate and the consensus of the army – a good way to flatter the body he was addressing, and to remind them at the same time who was really in charge. He then cited the models he would follow for excellence in government (Augustus in particular) and went on to observe that his youth had not been disturbed by civil conflict or by domestic strife (*domesticis discordiis*). This very last point, in a speech totally devoid of irony and acclaimed by the senate, is another sign that the claims of strife between Agrippina and Claudius towards the end of the latter's reign must have been exaggerated. Nero was thus starting out with a clean slate, with no hatred and no desire for vengeance. The spirit of the address is reflected in the poet Calpurnius Siculus, who speaks of a new golden age (*aurea ... renascitur aetas*) heralding the end of civil strife.[52]

Thus far the speech seems to have followed the standard banalities. What would have suddenly caught attention and have roused the somnolent was that Nero abruptly went on to distance himself from what he saw as the abuses of the previous reign. He would not set himself up as a judge in every legal proceeding, or allow himself to be subjected to influence from private individuals. He would put an end to venality and intrigue in his household. The affairs of the palace and the affairs of government would be kept separate. The senate would return to its old prerogatives. Italy and the public provinces would fall under the legal jurisdiction of the consuls. The emperor's jurisdiction would be over the armies committed to his charge.

Agrippina might have felt that to deliver a speech lauding Claudius, followed shortly afterwards by a second one criticizing his deficiencies, was not in the best of taste, but she was a realist and played the political game. Like the senators, she appreciated that a maiden speech in the Curia would inevitably include a solemn declaration to follow the model of Augustus. Even the implied criticism of Claudius might merely reflect the need felt by every new emperor to place his own stamp on the principate. Hence it is unlikely that at this early stage the speech would have caused Agrippina any particular unease, or the more astute of the senators any particular comfort. Nor would any special significance be seen by her in the fact that the speech was inscribed on a silver plaque to be read out every time the new consuls took office. The senate had similarly been charmed by Germanicus' son Caligula when he delivered his first formal and flattering address to them after Tiberius' death. Even the silver plaque is reminiscent of the golden shield the senate decreed in Caligula's honour, which was carried to the Capitol each year with much ceremony.[53]

What would come as a surprise was that Nero, under the guidance of Seneca, actually made a serious effort to live up to his promises. 'He kept his word,' comments Tacitus. Senators would have been pleased by the deference that he showed them, a deference that seems to be marked even in coinage, since in contrast to earlier practice the legend SC (*senatus consulto*, 'by a decree of the senate') appeared regularly on his initial gold and silver issues (see Appendix IX).[54] But they would have been even more impressed by his genuine determination to eliminate the more blatant abuses of Claudius' reign. In particular, the concentration of judicial functions in the emperor's hands had increased the scope for corruption, and this corruption was associated especially with the issues raised by the Lex Cincia. This law, originally enacted in 204 BC, had required advocates to perform without a fee. It had clearly lapsed by 17 BC when Augustus made an effort to revive it. It continued to be evaded afterwards and under Claudius there was a public scandal when Samius, a Roman knight of some stature, was tricked into paying the evil Suillius Rufus 400,000 HS (the details are obscure). Facing apparent ruin, Samius had committed suicide. The consul-designate Gaius Silius (soon to become notorious through the Messalina affair) courted popularity among senators and the public in 47 with his demand that sanctions be enacted under the existing law. Claudius sought a compromise and, instead of another futile attempt at an outright ban on fees, imposed a limit of 10,000 HS as the maximum advocates could receive. In practice, this limitation seems to have had little effect and unscrupulous individuals like Suillius continued to prosper. Under Nero's legislative programme a total ban on lawyers' fees was imposed. The abolition caused Agrippina offence; her concern was not so much with the intrinsic issue (hardly likely to be of major concern to her) but rather, as Tacitus observes, with what she saw as the subversion of the policies of Claudius. Such a subversion, in turn, reflected on her role as Claudius' consort and partner, and represented a serious symbolic assault on her own standing.[55]

In camera trials were another obvious cause of distress. They had been known from the time of Augustus, the conviction of the poet Ovid being the most famous. The best-known Claudian example was the case of Valerius Asiaticus, where Claudius was supposedly tricked by Messalina. The presence of wives in such proceedings caused special disquiet. There was no way to control their interference since, unlike trials held before the praetors and in the senate, *in camera* proceedings followed no fixed rules and were handled by the arbitrary dispensation of the princeps. There is no real evidence that such trials were particularly oppressive under Claudius and the situation if anything seems to have improved after his marriage to Agrippina, but there was room for reform and Nero, guided by Seneca, sought to reduce personal intrusion in the administration of justice. Calpurnius Siculus speaks of laws being restored and cases returning to the Forum, consuls presiding over busy tribunals. Suetonius records procedural improvements, unfortunately undated. Nero's method of consultation was to make each member of his *consilium* (advisory board) give an opinion individually in written form, which the emperor read in private. This level of confidentiality would have prevented powerful individuals, like Agrippina, from manipulating the outcome of the *consilium's* deliberations. These good intentions could not be sustained. In the trial of Anicetus in 62 Tacitus observes that friends of the emperor were brought in to take part in what was a mockery of a regular *consilium;* after the exposure of the conspiracy of Piso in 65, the *consilium* assembled to try the accused was made up only of the evil Tigellinus and Nero's wife Poppaea.[56]

Nero's next allusion to Claudian abuse might well have seemed a pointed reference to Agrippina, when he acknowledged that Claudius had allowed affairs of state (*respublica*) to be compounded with those of the household (*domus*), with inevitable widespread intrigue and bribery. The general belief that Claudius was the dupe of his wives and freedmen is a familiar theme of his reign. This clearly was not a situation created by Agrippina, since Narcissus, Callistus and Messalina had all been powerful operators before she came on the scene. But she had certainly used favourites and clients for political ends; both she and they had prospered as a result, and her continuously *successful* use of behind-the-scenes manoeuvring must have been especially galling. The resentment over the role of Claudius' wives continued to fester long after his death. When Suillius was charged in 58 with having brought malicious charges against a number of prominent individuals during Claudius' reign, he claimed at first that he had been acting under orders. But Nero's examination of his predecessor's records unearthed no such orders, and Suillius consequently changed tactics, claiming that the instructions had come not from the emperor but from Messalina. The assertion was not challenged but neither was it accepted as a reasonable defence, on the grounds that Suillius had evidently been willing to act as the agent for the *saeviens impudica* ('the wild whore').

At the outset, Nero did change conditions within the palace. The dismissal of Pallas (see below) and the requirement that he render an account to the treasury would have been applauded as an enlightened and reassuring way of handling over-powerful freedmen. Nero's wife Octavia played no part in affairs of state, whether by policy or inclination. The danger of female influence on Nero would come from his mother, not his wife. Agrippina might have bristled at the suggestion that she was an intriguer – she had surely seen herself rather as Claudius' trusted and welcomed adviser, but her self-assessment was not shared by the outside world, which would have considered her influence over Nero equally malign. The grumbling about her during the Armenian crisis is a good illustration of public disquiet. If Seneca advised Nero to curb her influence, or at the very least the public perception of it, that suggestion would have been sound and not inherently hostile to Agrippina, however difficult she might have found it to accept the wisdom of his advice.[57]

In fact, Nero would find the promises to distinguish *domus* and *respublica*, and to eliminate the appearance of improper political influence, with its attendant bribery and favouritism, very difficult to sustain. Already in 55, Paris, the actor and freedman of Nero's aunt Domitia, is seen playing a serious role in political intrigue and orchestrating an attack on Agrippina. Doryphorus, who succeeded Callistus as a *libellis,* received lavish gifts, as noted above (p. 157); there was a belief that Pallas was able use his influence to secure the acquittal of his brother Felix from a charge of extortion brought by Jewish subjects; the Syrian Beryllus, who looked after the emperor's Greek correspondence, was able to obtain concessions for his fellow-countrymen. That said, it is fair to conclude that there was nothing in the early years of the reign to match Narcissus negotiating with mutinous troops, or Pallas advising Claudius on matters of state and being in turn rewarded lavishly by the senate. The first recorded example of a freedman causing serious public offence was Polyclitus, who was sent on a special commission to Britain in 61 and whose retinue was on a truly regal scale, a burden to the communities of Italy and Gaul.[58] The promise made in Nero's speech that the senate would have jurisdiction over Italy and the public provinces is difficult to evaluate; Nero actually passed edicts which affected all the provinces, not just the imperial ones. If his undertaking to separate his private home from the state had any meaning, it should have signalled an end to the juridical powers of the procurators of the emperor's private estates in the provinces. The powers of jurisdiction that Claudius granted, almost certainly with the active collaboration of Agrippina, may well have been rescinded. The nature of the evidence prevents any conclusive verdict on this question. Procurators are seen exercising independent authority in the imperial provinces, as in the famous case of Catus Decianus, whose arrogant conduct in Britain was a contributory factor to the rebellion of Boudicca. But the known cases of procuratorial high-handedness seem to involve *public* officials. It is, however likely that any noble intentions of Nero would have degenerated in the course of his reign. The private procurators may well have had their powers curbed in 54 but by at least Domitian's time they seem once again to have possessed juridical authority, perhaps even within Italy itself.[59]

Whether or not the procurators lost their special powers, to the inevitable dismay of Agrippina, must remain an open question. But one other issue *did* cause her bitterness – the change in the system of financial obligations. Almost all senatorial offices involved a contribution towards public games or some other communal good. Traditionally the quaestors were obliged to provide for the paving of roads. In 47 the sycophantic Publius Dolabella moved that quaestors-designate should pay for an annual gladiatorial show from their own pockets (which Tacitus considered tantamount to putting up the quaestorship for auction). This requirement was among those repealed by Nero. Such was the force of habit that, after the formal obligation was lifted, quaestors seem to have felt social pressure to continue making a contribution and under Domitian the legal requirement was reintroduced. Nero's change, like the revised Lex Cincia, was opposed, unsuccessfully, by Agrippina. Again Tacitus does not say that she resisted the change *per se* (she could hardly have considered it significant). Rather she resented the sabotaging of the acts of Claudius. This particular measure had been instituted in 47, and could not even have been one of her own projects. Her attempt to uphold it illustrates vividly the commitment that she felt to the Claudian legacy.[60]

The incident that tradition sees as bringing matters to a head was a purely symbolic one. Both Tacitus and Dio emphasize the significance of an awkward misunderstanding that occurred at the end of 54. As a consequence of the Armenian crisis, an embassy representing that country's pro-Roman faction had arrived in Rome. No arrangement was made for Agrippina's formal participation in the ceremonies marking the visit, perhaps wisely in view of the earlier public disquiet about her influence over policy in the region. Her exclusion, whether deliberate or unintended, almost led to a horrendously embarrassing incident. As Nero sat on the tribunal to hear the representatives, he was astonished, as was his entourage, to see Agrippina approach, with the clear intention of coming up to join him. During the previous reign, Agrippina had grown accustomed to receiving foreign deputations at the same time as her husband (most notoriously during the formal surrender of Caratacus, when she sat up on a neighbouring tribunal to receive him as he was received by Claudius). The Armenian incident represents an escalation in her ambitions, since she had every intention of joining the princeps on the same tribunal. The tense situation was defused by the adroit intervention of Seneca (Dio credits Burrus also). On his advice, Nero descended and greeted his mother, as if paying her special respect. Nero's gesture was ambiguous and may not have been intended deliberately to belittle her. Indeed, it may in effect have had the opposite intention, to save her from public humiliation and to avoid inflaming feelings, but it did convey to her that her authority and status were subject to limitations. This event is represented as a turning-point in Agrippina's standing. Dio sees it as the moment when Seneca and Burrus were able to wrest control of the state entirely from the hands of Agrippina and take matters into their own charge. This is clearly an overstatement, but does contain a germ of truth.[61]

There was a further blow. We are told by Dio that after the deification of Claudius Seneca wrote a parody, the *Apocolocyntosis* ('Pumpkinification'), widely assumed to be the familiar extant parody that is generally known by that name (although it is given a different name in the manuscripts). Seneca's work, whether or not it is the extant piece, was apparently composed not long after Claudius' consecration as a god (it was perhaps performed during the Saturnalia of 54) and attracted much attention. The surviving parody clearly belongs to that period and both ridicules and condemns Claudius as a fool and a murderer. Nero's reign evokes optimistic expectations and Agrippina personally emerges unscathed. She is not in fact mentioned, hardly surprisingly, since she would clearly still have been in a position to punish overt critics, but the institutions to which she had dedicated herself were made to seem ridiculous. The blow to Agrippina's pride, perhaps delivered under the guise of licensed hilarity, must have been immense.[62]

As Nero sought to distance himself from Claudius, he went out of his way to emphasize his filial piety towards Domitius Ahenobarbus, his natural father and Agrippina's first husband. Suetonius notes the special honours paid to Domitius, almost certainly at the very outset of the reign, and Tacitus records under 54 that Nero asked the senate to decree a statue to his father. The Arval Brethren commemorate Domitius' birthday on 11 December, starting in 55 at the latest (the relevant section of the record is missing for 54). The birthday ritual took place every year after that up to and including 59 on the Via Sacra, in front of the home where, it will be recalled, Domitius had during his consulship self-indulgently added a bath-house. The record for subsequent years is also missing. It would be unfair to deny Nero some vestigial affection for his natural father (whom he can hardly have remembered), but there is surely a political dimension to these measures in that they further de-emphasized the link with his predecessor Claudius. Such gestures would have caused Agrippina considerable dismay.[63]

While Claudius might have been downgraded, or even on the appropriate occasion, mocked, it is unlikely that Nero would have overtly repudiated him, certainly during Agrippina's lifetime. Even Seneca would probably have felt that an open breach would have been counter-productive. Pliny the Younger does claim that Nero deified Claudius only to ridicule him, but he was probably applying too literal an interpretation to the *Apocolocyntosis* and may have read too much into Nero's quips in dubious taste about mushrooms being the food of the gods (p. 141). Suetonius goes so far as to assert that Nero rescinded Claudius' consecration (restored later by Vespasian) and destroyed the temple on the Caelian.[64] This last claim is simply unconvincing. It is true that after its appearance on the initial issues of the Roman mint in 54, any reference to Divus Claudius is restricted in 55 to gold quinarii and after that disappears from coins minted in Rome. But at the imperial mint at Caesarea in Cappadocia coins depicting Divus Claudius, and identifying him as Nero's father, continue to be minted throughout the reign. They are technically undated, but a general idea of the phases of minting can be gauged by the maturing bust of Nero on the obverse. Moreover, the filiation 'Son of the Deified Claudius' continues to appear in inscriptions until the 60s, not surprisingly, given the advantage for Nero in continuing to style himself as the son of a god.[65] In fact, even in the chaotic period immediately following Nero's death in 68 Claudius continues to be found as *ho theos Klaudios* ('the god Claudius') in an Alexandrian inscription, and 'Divus Claudius' in the Arval Acts for January and March 69. There is one important omission, in the law passed by the senate confirming Vespasian's imperium in 69, where he appears simply as Tiberius Claudius Caesar Augustus Germanicus without the honorific *Divus*. This might represent a deliberate earlier downgrading of Claudius by the senate, but it is more likely that the cult of Divus Claudius simply fell into disuse. This neglect might have misled Suetonius about Nero's behaviour. At any rate during Vespasian's reign, Divus Claudius appears in such official documents as the records of restored aqueducts and the oaths taken by candidates for office, and we find games still being given on his birthday as late as 124.[66] Moreover, while Nero clearly made no effort to complete the temple, left unfinished at Agrippina's death, any destruction would not have been vindictive but rather part of the programme of clearing up the Caelian Hill and other areas in preparation for the building of his Golden House.

That a complete break from the Claudian past can be ruled out is suggested by Suetonius' report that Nero toyed with the idea of withdrawing from Britain but decided not to do so out of respect for Claudius. When this happened is not made clear, but the most plausible context for the episode is the early part of the reign. When Nero came to power in 54 the governor of Britain was Aulus Didius Gallus, a man who despite an impressive military record earned the contempt of Tacitus, who considered him apathetic and prone to leave the serious work to his subordinates. Didius certainly faced serious problems. No sooner had he dealt with the raids of the Silures of Wales (who defeated one of his legions) than serious divisions within the Brigantes, a pro-Roman tribe in the north, required Roman intervention. If Tacitus' strictures of Didius reflect official thinking, it might have seemed that progress in Britain had become bogged down and a new emperor who had set up the rule of Augustus as his ideal could have decided to limit Rome's military commitments. The decision to continue honouring Claudius' policy in Britain might be seen as an early instance of a clash between

Agrippina and Seneca/Burrus, with Agrippina prevailing. But there could have been other reasons. Dio reveals that Seneca had investments of 40 million HS in Britain, and it would have required considerable altruism on his part to have advocated a Roman withdrawal. The decision by Nero to stay represents the triumph of policy over personal inclination. Claudius had garnered enormous prestige from the British campaign. An early withdrawal would have meant abandoning his major political achievement, and it would also have resulted in a major loss of face for the Romans and for their new emperor, one that could have led to a considerable decline in respect for Rome in other troublespots, like Armenia.[67]

Tacitus reports that AD 55 saw the beginning of the gradual decline of the *potentia matris*, the powerful personal influence that Agrippina had exercised over Nero as his mother. It has also been claimed that this change can be detected in imperial coin issues. The first gold and silver coins of the reign had depicted facing heads of Nero and Agrippina. A second series, issued in the the first year of the reign but after the assumption of Nero's first consulship in January 55, continue to show Nero and Agrippina on the obverse, but the heads on these slightly later coins are now jugate (ie. both facing right), with Nero's superimposed over his mother's (Pl. 14). Moreover, Nero's legend appears on the obverse while Agrippina's is restricted to the reverse, which depicts the divine Claudius on a chariot pulled by elephants. Some see this series, coming after the initial one with the *facing* heads, as a subtle and gradual degradation of Agrippina's prestige, but one should be cautious. Examples of the 'initial' series, although technically limited to only the first two-and-a-half months, are far commoner than the 'second', which were minted during the remaining nine-and-a-half months of the year. This suggests, as one might have expected, that after the dies were cut in late 54 for the first series the coins produced would have continued to be issued well into the new year, so that, for practical purposes, the two series were essentially contemporaneous. It would also be perverse to demote an individual by according her what were still exceptional public honours, with a barely discernible diminution from a slightly earlier honour. Certainly, when the jugate type was introduced by Ptolemy II in the third century BC to celebrate his marriage to his sister, Arsinoe II, the emission was intended as a mark of honour. The local coins of Claudius, in which there could have been no intention to demote Agrippina, depict the emperor and his wife both jugate and facing, without any apparent discrimination. Ephesus issued both types. Also, local coins depicting Nero and Agrippina do not seem to discriminate between the two versions.[68]

Agrippina's attempt to establish a place for herself in her son's regime created serious and perplexing constitutional problems. However, the reason for the initial deterioration in their relationship, if Tacitus is right, was on the surface a purely personal one. Nero had earlier fallen for a freedwoman from Asia Minor, Acte, and had begun an affair with her. Most people in court circles would have considered such a liaison to be almost inevitable and not particularly harmful. Nero's arranged marriage to Octavia seems not to have been happy and there was probably general relief that the young emperor had found an outlet in someone of Acte's rank, thus sparing the reputation of a respectable woman of social standing. Seneca actively encouraged him, even recruiting the help of a close friend and kinsman, Annaeus Serenus, the prefect of the Vigiles (he would later die, along with a company of centurions and tribunes, from eating poisonous mushrooms). Serenus played the part of Nero's stalking-horse, creating the public impression that it was he who was Acte's lover, and even passed on gifts to her from Nero at their bogus trysts. Other accomplices in the affair were Marcus Otho, the future emperor, and Claudius Senecio, a close friend of Nero in 55, but by 65 a participant in the Pisonian conspiracy against him (he would lose his life as a result).[69]

Agrippina, according to Tacitus, behaved 'as women do' and, instead of waiting for the affair to run its course, lashed out against Acte, using abusive expressions like 'her freedwoman rival' (*liberta aemula*) or 'her daughter-in-law the maid' (*nurus ancilla*). She also expressed loud disapproval of Nero's choice of friends and, according to Dio, had some of them eliminated. Predictably, her vigorous opposition served to drive Nero into downright disobedience and, according to Dio, into the control of Seneca.

Agrippina's handling of the affair seems mystifying. Some scholars accept the stereotype of the possessive mother and are persuaded by Dio's suggestion that Nero's passion for Acte was incompatible with his mother's notion of total control. But this scenario requires an almost unbelievable obtuseness on Agrippina's part, and an uncharacteristic over-reaction to a situation that was hardly uncommon among the men of Rome's ruling class. Her anxiety may, in fact, have been well founded. Although Acte was not of free birth, she became a woman of some substance, and inscriptions indicate that she owned a considerable household. Her relationship with Nero was not a casual affair that could be expected simply to fade away. She seems to have remained genuinely attached to him right to the end, and even arranged his funeral in the family tomb on the Pincian Hill. Under the Lex Julia enacted by Augustus in 18 BC, marriage between a freedman or freedwoman and a member of the senatorial order was prohibited and there are few, if any, exceptions recorded in the Julio-Claudian period. But a situation very close to marriage could exist; Vespasian, for instance, later lived with Caenis, the former freedwoman of Antonia, who was his wife in all but name (*paene iustae uxoris loco*) until she died. Agrippina was committed to the Nero–Octavia marriage for more than sentimental reasons. It represented the culmination of her political goals and the final union of the Julian and Claudian families which she symbolized in her own person. Agrippina recognized that Acte was more than just a passing fancy and she may well have entertained a genuine, and perhaps well-grounded, fear that her young and irresponsible son would seek to exercise his authority as princeps and marry her, as Agrippina seemed to hint with her slur of 'daughter-in-law the maid'. Indeed, Suetonius says that Nero came very close to a regular marriage with Acte (*iusto matrimonio*) and that to this end a number of men of consular rank were bribed to swear that she was actually of royal birth, possibly descended from the Attalids, the powerful dynasty of Asia. This scheme may lie behind Dio's claim that she was adopted into the family of Attalus.[70] Although Agrippina may have had good cause for concern, her heavy-handed behaviour as the disapproving mother alienated her son even further. She seems to have realized this, and decided to change her tack and make up for her harsh reaction. Perhaps taking a leaf from Seneca's book, she now assumed the role of sweet indulgent mother, even allowing him to use her chambers for his trysts.[71] This type of behaviour was alien to Agrippina and it is not surprising that it was not kept up. She was, by nature, discreetly assertive and accustomed to dealing with people through the medium of power and authority. In any case, Nero's friends tipped him off him about what she was up to and warned him to be on guard against her insincerities. Agrippina had not succeeded as a domineering mother and her experiment in leniency seems to have been short-lived. She now decided to play the card of indispensable political ally. Nero did, indeed, owe his position to her, and she was determined not to let him forget it. Dio quotes the terse claim 'I made you emperor', perhaps intended as a hint that he would find it difficult to maintain his position without her help.

Seen in this light, the Acte episode probably was, as Tacitus claimed, another turning-point in this early phase of Nero's reign. By the end of the crisis, Agrippina was no longer the close confidante of her son, but she was still a powerful figure, too powerful for Nero to provoke directly. Instead he attempted an indirect challenge, probably under the guidance of Seneca. If Agrippina could not be removed from her position of dominance, he could at least get rid of those on whom her 'female arrogance' (*muliebris superbia*) depended. The main target of the attack was Pallas. He represented more than any other the old Claudian regime and his control of finance gave him, along with Agrippina, virtual control over government. Besides which, Nero seems to have disliked him personally. The precise mechanism used to fire him is unknown, but there may have been some charge of financial improprieties. Evidently a plea bargain was arranged. If Pallas would agree to resign and go peacefully there would be no retrospective enquiry into his accounts, which would be taken as balanced. He gave up office in style, accompanied by a great army of attendants, and as he left Nero is said to have remarked wryly that he was on his way to swear himself out of office (high magistrates at the end of their terms took an oath that they had acted in accordance with the laws).[72]

The removal of Pallas marked a significant stage in Nero's determination to distance himself from his predecessor. It also represented a serious blow to Agrippina. Tacitus claims that the freedman's fall pushed her into a new and highly dangerous stage in her relationship with her son, a phase of 'terror and threats' (*terror et minae*). While she had been active in promoting Nero's candidacy for the succession, she had almost certainly been as much motivated by her concept of the central role due to her as a descendant of Germanicus and Augustus as she had been driven by biological instinct. If Nero as princeps could help her to play that role, so much the better; if he would not, Tacitus claims, she would turn elsewhere. The decision of Claudius to champion Nero over Britannicus could be cited as a precedent for the triumph of *realpolitik* over ties of blood. She now, it is claimed, reversed the process. Tacitus has her make thinly veiled threats and dwell on the suitability of Britannicus as a candidate, suggesting that she would bring everything down by exposing all the dark secrets of Nero's accession, the true circumstances of her marriage to Claudius and, her own poisonings. This reported exchange can surely be no more than a dramatic device, to convey in vivid images Tacitus' own assessment of the shift in power in the palace; as reported, it is distinctly implausible. However much Agrippina wanted to clip Nero's wings, she would hardly have been prepared to do so by revealing her own dark side and by destroying her own credibility and influence completely, thus exposing herself to enormous personal risks.

While Tacitus may have offered little more than speculation about the confrontation between Agrippina and her son, he does show a good understanding of the nature of her power. As long as she had been the victim of the hated Messalina, Agrippina had enjoyed widespread popular support. Once she herself became the powerful and influential woman, this popularity would have quickly dissipated. There was little prospect of her winning broad backing in the senate, nor was there any doubt about where her real strength did lie, as Tacitus appreciated. She was, he claims, prepared to go to the praetorian camp and raise her standard there, and to offer the guard the choice between herself on the one side and, as she put it, the crippled Burrus (he apparently had a maimed hand, although this is the only mention of it) and the pedantic Seneca on the other. Agrippina may well have thrown out unmistakable hints about her influence with the guard. But the notion of her threatening to rally them to her standard must be treated with considerable scepticism. The image seems to reflect the traditional fear that Romans had of powerful women seizing command of troops and is reminiscent of the similar charge made against her mother, that she was prepared to go to Germany and lead the northern legions against Tiberius. The primary function of Tacitus' claim of Agrippina's conversion to the cause of Britannicus is surely to lay a foundation for the theme of his next section, Nero's decision to murder his stepbrother. Nero was driven to it, he claims, because Agrippina repeated her threats with increasing urgency (*urgentibusque ... minis*). This supposed challenge, incidentally, is the only recorded instance of Agrippina making a personal attack on Seneca and Burrus, despite the bitter hostility that is generally assumed between them.

The dramatic confrontation between Agrippina and Nero is followed in Tacitus' account by the no less dramatic death of Britannicus. Earlier in 55 he had clearly not been seen as a threat, and an attempt by some to revive the *maiestas* law by charging an equestrian Julius Densus with sympathy towards Britannicus was a failure. Agrippina's outburst supposedly changed things. The ancient sources are in agreement that his death was murder. Tacitus adds a bizarre detail found in several contemporary authors, and represented also in one of Dio's epitomators, that Nero had buggered him a few days earlier, and his passing was to be seen as a blessed deliverance! A trivial incident, perhaps based on a misunderstanding, had alerted Nero at the end of 54. During the Saturnalia in late December, the young men threw dice for who would be 'king' of the festivities. Nero won and imposed various forfeits, including one on Britannicus to start a song (Suetonius for good measure adds that Nero was jealous of his stepbrother's singing voice). Britannicus' choice of party piece seems to have been an injudicious one, since it contained ambiguous subject matter and seemed to suggest that he had been cheated of his inheritance. Nero's suspicions were raised, and they hardened as the strain between himself and his mother grew.

The literary tradition provides us now with a vivid scenario. Nero was offered a wonderful opportunity. The poisoner Locusta, who had reputedly performed sterling service in the matter of Claudius' passing, happened at that time to be under detention with the praetorian guard. Through Julius Pollio, the tribune responsible for guarding her, Nero made arrangements for her to supply him with poison. Ironically, Britannicus' tutors and attendants had been dismissed by Agrippina some time earlier and replaced by men who would not encourage any aspirations he entertained for power. Tradition has it that these new tutors, appointed on her instructions, administered the first dose of poison. Locusta had deliberately diluted it to avoid giving the game away, but it was so weak that it had no effect and Britannicus passed it in a bowel movement. Nero was furious – he threatened Pollio with imprisonment and Locusta with death (to encourage her he had her flogged). Locusta responded well to the incentive and got seriously down to work, experimenting on various animals. When she had achieved the instantaneous death of an unsuspecting pig (earlier experiments on a young goat had proved abortive), they decided that they were at last ready. To assume maximum effect, the occasion chosen for the crime was a dinner attended by nobles and members of the imperial family, including Agrippina. Since Britannicus used a food-taster, a scheme had to be devised to get the poison to him. It was not particularly sophisticated. He was offered a very hot drink (the Romans added hot water to their wine) and, when he asked for it to be cooled, cold water containing the poison was added. Its effect was immediate (as the hapless pig could have attested). He lost his speech and began to gasp for breath. Nero's response was distinctly casual. He merely remarked that Britannicus was suffering one of his regular epileptic attacks, and that he would recover. Agrippina showed no reaction but Tacitus, who apparently can read her mind on this occasion, asserts that she was overcome by terror and panic, and realized that the path was now open for her own murder. Nor did Nero's wife Octavia give any sign of special concern and Tacitus, who apparently read her mind also, claims that she managed to conceal her emotions. Britannicus was carried away on a stretcher and with admirable aplomb the diners continued with their meal.

Britannicus did not survive. His body soon turned dark and, perhaps because of the disfiguration, the funeral was hastily arranged, either that night, according to Tacitus (who adds unconvincingly that the pyre had been arranged in advance), or next day, according to Suetonius. Both agree that the final rites were carried out in a heavy rainstorm, which the bystanders took as an omen of divine displeasure. The storm added an element of farce. Nero had smeared the darkened body with gypsum, which was washed away by the rain and exposed the evidence of the crime. He delivered a public statement, probably written by Seneca, voicing the standard platitudes and lamenting the loss of his brother's help. This public announcement was the final word on the subject and constituted the official report of the death. No report was offered to the senate.[73]

The lurid account just provided is essentially what the ancient sources have passed down to us. Josephus' dogmatic assertion of Nero's guilt is particularly interesting. He had personal links with Vespasian's son, the future emperor Titus, who was brought up with Britannicus and had become his close friend. Titus was, in fact, present at the banquet, and he also fell ill (it was assumed later that he had consumed some of the poison). Josephus clearly reflects the version of events, whether accurate or not, that still prevailed in court circles when he published his account in the early 90s. The suspicion of murder might have been strengthened by the apparent rewarding of the tribune Pollio, who had supposedly helped in acquiring the poison. An inscription has survived recording an equestrian governor (procurator) of Sardinia with the name of Titus Julius Pollio, who may well have been Nero's henchman. The most likely time for his appointment would have been 56, the following year, when the incumbent governor Vipsanius Laenas was convicted for extortion.[74]

It is legitimate to raise the basic question – whether Britannicus was in fact murdered. He was epileptic and the possibility that he suffered a severe and fatal epileptic fit cannot be ruled out; the darkening of the body points to death by tetanoid epilepsy. No known poison except strychnine, not used in the ancient world, will turn the face dark.

The similarity of the accounts of his and Claudius' final hours, particularly in the detail of the ineffective first dose of poison, might suggest that both drew from common lore about poisonous deaths. In the *De Clementia*, published shortly afterwards, Seneca asserts that Nero is unstained by the spilling of blood, which certainly vindicates Nero's *official* version, although the exoneration suffers a blow from Seneca's deathbed pronouncement, when he lists Britannicus among Nero's murder victims. It should also be noted that so high was Nero's stock that the public generally condoned Britannicus' murder, according to Tacitus, just as the murder of Gemellus by Caligula had been considered acceptable as an example of *realpolitik* in which the state must be protected from the danger of destructive rivalries.

Modern authorities are generally sceptical about the notion that Britannicus died from foul play. The consistency of the ancient sources both in the facts and in the general details is not especially significant, given the difficulty already noted of proving or refuting a charge of murder by poisoning. Again, whether the charge was true or untrue is not the key issue. The mere *belief* that Nero was responsible would by itself create an atmosphere of tension and fear. The official public stance that Britannicus was a lamented brother was maintained for years to come. Evidence for this can be found at Amisus in Pontus, where the bases for an imperial statue group have survived. Britannicus appears among them, along with Nero and Poppaea (Nero's second wife). The group could not have been erected earlier than 63, the date of Nero's second marriage, and thus appeared at least eight years after Britannicus' death.[75]

If Britannicus was in fact murdered, Agrippina can safely be ruled out as an accessory. Only the consistently unreliable scholiast on Juvenal implies guilt on her part, *conscia matre* ('his mother being guilty'). Tacitus, hardly a friendly source, describes her as *ignara* ('unaware') and the *Octavia*, a good guide to near-contemporary public opinion, has her weeping over the body of Britannicus. Tacitus speaks of Nero distributing Britannicus' possessions after the latter's death and implies that one of the recipients was Agrippina, but that she was quite unimpressed by his generosity. According to Dio, even Seneca and Burrus were disturbed by Nero's action and from this point on lost their serious interest in public business, choosing to concentrate on their own survival. Some may well have benefited materially from the distribution of Britannicus' estate but this certainly is no proof of guilt (or even of a crime), and clearly they may not have been in a position to refuse with grace. The one person reported to have come out ahead was Locusta, who got a free pardon for all her past crimes and a country estate to show no hard feelings. Nero reputedly sent pupils to her, but her past was bound eventually to catch up with her and she would later die during Galba's purge of Nero's favourites.[76]

Whether Britannicus' death was natural or criminal, it would have concentrated Agrippina's mind and have made her even more conscious of the necessity of protecting her position. She began to cultivate friendships with the descendants of the great republican noble families. As has been stressed, there were important houses, the Junii Silani, the Aemilii Lepidi and others, who had potent memories of their distinguished past and still seem to have nursed ambitions for power. Agrippina had always seen the importance of fostering good rapport with important members of the senate. Whether her activities now constitute anything more sinister is open to question. Tacitus suggests that she had determined to build up a faction there, but it is unlikely that she could have hoped to win any sort of organized following. Nero's conduct towards the senate was still at this time marked by respect and deference; there was little more that Agrippina could offer the body as a whole. She also continued to foster her contacts in the praetorian guard, in particular with the centurions and tribunes she had been instrumental in appointing, but the notion that she was planning some sort of overt rebellion can be ruled out. Agrippina's purpose was surely limited to making herself indispensable, to prove to Nero how valuable she could be as an ally and also, should he entertain the unthinkable, to leave him in no doubt about how difficult and dangerous it would be to try to eliminate her. Even if, as Tacitus says, she drew very close to Octavia at this time, such a relationship could have been political only in the broadest sense. Octavia represented the last link with the Claudian vision that Agrippina had helped sustain. Agrippina may well have derived personal comfort from the knowledge that this link still existed. But there was no possibility that Octavia could be part of any plot to overthrow Nero.

It might be tempting to see Agrippina being steered increasingly into the position that her mother had earlier occupied, pushed out to the margin of the system instead of in her rightful place at the centre. But, unlike her mother, she still had a powerful ally in Rome in the form of the praetorians, who remained steadfastly loyal to Germanicus' memory and were in many instances her own hand-picked appointments. The wisdom of ensuring sympathetic under-officers and not merely a temporarily compliant prefect now becomes apparent. Nero understood the situation and wisely chose not to confront the guards directly. Instead he opted to follow Agrippina's lead and sought to win them over. This would account for his allotment of an extra ration of grain to them, equal to a monthly allowance, free of cost (the cost of grain was normally deducted from the praetorian's pay). He next set about manoeuvring his mother out of her close daily contact with the men. As a preliminary, he made a decision that would on the surface have seemed innocent enough. He claimed that her tumultuous daily gatherings, when her clients came to petition her, were creating a nuisance. This morning assembly of clients was an important symbolic ritual – Seneca marked his retirement from the time that his own such gatherings stopped. Because of the disturbance they caused, Agrippina was asked to move out of the palace proper to the nearby house which her grandmother Antonia had owned on the Palatine.[77]

Once Agrippina was out of the palace, it was possible to take the next, more significant, step. As wife and later mother of the princeps, she had the privilege of having her premises guarded by *excubiae* ('watches') of guards. Nero ruled that praetorians would, from now on, be used for strictly 'military' duties. To avoid any risk of confrontation, this measure was presented as part of a broader package, in which the general duties of the guard were redefined. They were no longer assigned to keep order at public gatherings, as they had in the past. In late 55 the cohort usually in attendance at the games was withdrawn. Tacitus does not link this measure with Agrippina. He claims that the withdrawal of troops from public places was intended to create an impression of increased civic liberty, while its real purpose was to prevent the soldiers from being corrupted by spending too much time at the theatre. But its real target may, in fact, have been Nero's mother. She would no longer have personal use of a praetorian detachment, and since she was no longer resident in the palace would lose contact with the men normally on guard duty there.

Nor was this all. When she left the Palatine Hill, Agrippina had been accustomed to a different form of protection, German guards. The Germans formed the personal and private bodyguard of the emperor, and were distinct from the praetorians, who were technically part of the Roman army. Noted for their strength and toughness, they had first been recruited by Augustus, mainly from among the Batavians on the lower Rhine. Their commitment and sense of purpose was well illustrated by their energy, and brutality, in suppressing the disorder at the time of Caligula's assassination. Agrippina appears to have been given a detachment of Germans after Nero's accession (in the context of mid-55 Tacitus describes their appointment as 'recent', *nuper*). These she also now lost. The removal of this personal bodyguard was not a serious assault on her power (the Germans, unlike the praetorians, had never been a significant political force), but it had important indirect repercussions. The loss marked a visible change, the first public announcement that she was no longer in high favour. In the world of political intrigue, the appearance of power and influence is almost as important as the real thing. Nero continued to visit his mother, surrounded by a throng of centurions, as if to make some sort of point, but people had got the message. He was one of her very few visitors. A few former cronies kept up their contact with her, but Tacitus observes that it was difficult to tell if they came out of affection or only to gloat.[78]

Nero had so far played a battle of nerves with his mother, seeking to edge her out of her position of influence while avoiding direct confrontation. But the dismissal of the guard brought things to a head. Tacitus provides a detailed account of the crisis that arose, although its precise character still eludes us.[79] Things were set in motion by one of the few women who continued to maintain contact, Junia Silana. She was the former wife of Gaius Silius, divorced by him to clear the field for Messalina, and described by Tacitus in stereotypically broad strokes as the equal of Agrippina in family distinction, in beauty and in immorality. The claim that she matched Agrippina in family distinction (*genus*) is puzzling. The three male sons of Marcus Junius Silanus, consul of 19, have frequently been mentioned in this narrative as belonging to a family with a strong sense of pride and clear ambitions. They had two sisters. One of them, Junia Calvina, came into prominence in 48 when she was associated with her brother Lucius in the incest scandal that led to the dissolution of his betrothal to Octavia and his suicide. The other, Junia Lepida, emerges in 65, the year of the Pisonian conspiracy, as the wife of the jurist Cassius Longinus. Despite her name, Junia Silana was not one of the daughters of the consul of AD 19, and she must have belonged to another branch of the family. She was perhaps the daughter of the suffect consul of 15, another Marcus Junius Silanus, the father-in-law of Caligula, put to death by the emperor in late 37. This would mean that at one point Junia would have been Caligula's sister-in-law. Even so, it seems an exaggeration to describe her family distinction casually as a match for Agrippina's, and Tacitus seems to have lapsed into a familiar cliché.

As victim of Messalina, Silana would have been a natural ally of Agrippina and for many years they were close friends, but a rift arose between them when Silana began to entertain hopes of marrying a young nobleman, Sextius Africanus.[80] Agrippina had clearly anticipated inheriting from her friend, a widow with no children, and made every effort to prevent the marriage. Unfortunately, she appears to have been injudicious in her public comments, and Silana heard herself described as a 'woman of no morals and getting past it'.[81] Tacitus' account must be treated with caution. He frequently reduces disputes between powerful women close to the imperial house to 'quarrels over women's things', as he does here. The clash may well conceal a serious political move against Agrippina. Silana might have harboured resentment over Agrippina's treatment of her kinsmen. In any case, she made common cause with Nero's aunt Domitia, who continued to enjoy Nero's affection. Domitia had reason to bear a grudge. Agrippina had married her ex-husband and inherited his wealth, and had been responsible for her sister Lepida's death. Two of Junia Silana's clients, Iturius and Calvisius, were set up to plant a charge against Agrippina. Their story was that she had entered into a conspiracy with Rubellius Plautus, the son of Julia, Tiberius' granddaughter. For good measure they added that the two were lovers. To get the emperor's ear they needed an entrée and worked on Atimetus (otherwise unknown) and Paris, an actor and freedmen of Domitia. Paris was a particularly valuable contact, since he enjoyed Nero's favour and regularly joined him in his entertainments. Friendship with Nero, and his professional skill, would in the end prove to be the undoing of Paris (and other artists). He was put to death in 67, apparently because the emperor was jealous of his talents.[82]

Paris chose his time carefully, late in the evening when Nero had drunk a fair quantity of wine and was particularly suggestible. The charges were so graphic that the young emperor was filled with alarm, and he not only began to suspect Agrippina and Rubellius Plautus of sedition but, according to one tradition, even decided that it was too risky to leave Burrus, Agrippina's appointee, in his command.[83] This last detail is highly significant. Paris had clearly not been able to lay any precise or specific charges against Burrus, since no punishment seems to have been planned for him, but he managed to create an impression that somehow the prefect was under Agrippina's influence.

Tacitus provides the only details of the suspicions entertained about Burrus, and in doing so allows us a rare insight into his historical methods and sources. The historian Fabius Rusticus, Tacitus tells us, reported that Nero made arrangements for command of the praetorian guard to be handed over to Caecina Tuscus. Caecina was reputedly the son of Nero's nurse, which would have created a bond between him and the emperor although he might initially have enjoyed Agrippina's favour, since he had been appointed to an official post, *iuridicus,* in Egypt in 51/52, when her influence was at its peak. Like other favourites, he would eventually fall out of favour with Nero for fairly trivial reasons; in 66 he constructed an elaborate bath for the emperor's visit to Egypt, but apparently made the mistake of using it himself. For this display of gross lèse majesté he was rightly banished. By 69 he is recorded as back in Rome and politically active. When in 55 Nero pondered handing over the praetorian command to him, it was only the intervention of Seneca, according to Fabius, that saved the post for Burrus. It is possible that Seneca persuaded Nero that removing Burrus would achieve little, since his successor as prefect would still be faced with the problem of the praetorians' attachment to the house of Germanicus. Balancing Fabius' version, however, Tacitus notes that Pliny and Cluvius say nothing of such a decision, not even raising the issue of Burrus' suspected loyalty and he observes that Fabius had a tendency to inflate the achievements of his patron Seneca. Tacitus' inclination is clearly to discount the story.[84]

Whether or not Nero actually harboured suspicions about Burrus, he took no action against him at this time. But he did believe the charge and supposedly insisted that

Agrippina be put to death summarily. Burrus, probably from a combination of loyalty and self-interest, dissuaded him. As Griffin sees it, Seneca and Burrus had no vested interest in having Agrippina removed completely. As long as she was on the scene, Nero would see in his two advisers a means of escape from her influence. A more important clue to Burrus' advice, however, is that even four years later he was still afraid to use the guard openly against her because of the great affection in which she was held by the men. Burrus might well have argued that Nero's only possible hope of winning total support from the praetorians would be to establish beyond doubt that she was, in fact, guilty of sedition. If that could be done, then perhaps they could be counted on to act against her. Accordingly, Agrippina was granted a hearing.

The following day Burrus interrogated Agrippina, in the presence of Seneca. There is a hint that Nero still did not altogether trust his prefect, since he sent a number of freedmen to sit in as witnesses to what went on. Agrippina's defence, as reported by Tacitus, came in two parts. The first consisted of an attack on her female rivals and their lackeys. Junia Silana's motives were not questioned but she was portrayed as someone totally incapable of sound judgement. Iturius and Calvisius, Agrippina suggested, had been bribed; they were destitute and needed the money. Domitia she dismissed, as not really giving a damn about her nephew. When his mother had been working for Nero's accession, Domitia had spent her time decorating the fishponds at her villa at Baiae.

Agrippina's speech so far could be seen as a preamble. She then got to the meat. She challenged anyone to come forward and accuse her of tampering with the guard or fomenting trouble in the armies in the provinces. The form of the challenge is interesting. She does not deny her influence with the troops. In fact, her statement could be interpreted as an implicit threat, one that was skilfully presented. To avoid the impression of being too provocative, she finished by pointing out that common sense put it beyond doubt that her future lay with Nero. Through him she enjoyed the protection of a son, something she could not get from Rubellius Plautus. Moreover, if Britannicus had succeeded, she probably would not even have survived. Her case was convincing enough to win her hearing with Nero. This key exchange, which seems to have marked a highly important phase in the relationship between Agrippina and her son, is given brief coverage by Tacitus, who probably had little hard information. He reports only that she did not try to defend herself or to bring up yet again all she had done for her son (she seems to have learned her lesson on that score). In fact, Tacitus provides no clue to the remarkable volte-face that followed, which suggests, if not total reconciliation between mother and son, at least the recognition by Nero that she was simply too powerful to be set aside. The result of the meeting was nothing less than astonishing. From hovering on the brink of destruction, Agrippina ended up, for a time, back in a position as powerful as the one she had occupied in the early heady days of her son's accession. Her accusers were punished. Junia Silana was exiled, destination unknown. Later, when Agrippina's power began to wane, Junia was able to make her way back to Tarentum, where she died a natural death in quiet obscurity. Calvisius and Iturius were relegated, Atimetus was condemned to death. Paris escaped only because he was a close personal friend of the emperor.

Since the charges brought against Agrippina were dismissed, the subsequent punishment of the accusers was inevitable and hardly surprising. What is much more remarkable is that she was also able to obtain positions for her friends and allies, including offices considered highly prestigious.[85] Patronage is always a useful gauge of power and influ-ence, and by that measure Agrippina would seem to have emerged from the crisis second only to Nero in status (by contrast the evidence for appointments that can be attributed to Seneca and Burrus at this time is very scant, see Appendix VIII). The highly sensi-tive supervision of the corn supply (*cura annonae*) was assigned to Faenius Rufus. This proved an excellent appointment. He performed his duties with great efficiency and honesty, to the extent that, even though initially a favourite of Agrippina's, he was sub-sequently appointed praetorian prefect (along with Tigellinus) on Burrus' death in 62. Tigellinus had little regard for his colleague and accused him of remaining attached to Agrippina's memory after her death (and of having been her lover). Faenius later became implicated in the Pisonian conspiracy and was put to death in 65.[86] An Arruntius Stella, otherwise unknown, was given responsibility for the games. Little is known of Arruntius, except that he was probably a Paduan, and the suggestion has been made that Nero's tutor Asconius Labeo, from the same place, might have had some influence in the appointment.[87]

Tiberius Balbillus was made prefect of Egypt. He was an individual who made his mark in a variety of ways. He got into the record books by sailing from the straits of Messina (between Italy and Sicily) to Alexandria in six days, but he was also a highly lit-erate man, much admired by Seneca. Among other writings, he left behind an eye-witness account of an exotic aquatic battle where dolphins, swept into the Nile delta from the sea, fought to the finish with a swarm of crocodiles. The dolphins won. Balbillus may well have held office previously in Egypt in charge of the shrines, muse-um and library in Alexandria and, possibly, in the rest of the country.[88]

Publius Anteius was designated as governor of Syria, one of Rome's most significant military commands. Griffith points out that the earlier appointment of Corbulo as legate of Cappadocia and Galatia to handle the Armenian crisis, on the recommenda-tion of Seneca and Burrus, had brought Nero's two advisers great credit. The retirement of the elderly governor of Syria, Ummidius Quadratus, provided Agrippina with an excellent opportunity to replace him with someone who might be a match for Corbulo. Anteius's antecedents are uncertain. A senator called Anteius was killed by the Germans at the time of Caligula's assassination and may well have been the brother of the new appointee. This might offer a connection with Agrippina, since the father of the Germans' victim had, like Agrippina, been exiled by Caligula. But the link is tenuous. Publius Anteius, the new governor, had been an officer of Germanicus on the German frontier and was entrusted in 16 with the task of building a fleet. He seems still to have been active in 51, by which time he is found serving as legate of Dalmatia, and his appointment there could well have been be due to Agrippina's patronage. Evidence of his loyalty to the memory of Claudius, and its continuity through his household, is pro-vided by the fact that one of Anteius' freedmen dedicated a portico to Divus Claudius at Salona in Dalmatia in 54.

Nero seems to have felt obliged to go along with the appointment of Publius Anteius but it made him uneasy, probably because of the military importance of Syria. Excuses were found to delay his departure indefinitely and Ummidius Quadratus stayed on as governor until 60, when he was in fact replaced by Corbulo. Publius, by now at least in his late 70s, died in the aftermath of the Pisonian conspiracy, allegedly because of his wealth and his suspicious obsession with horoscopes. Nero's hesitation in sending him to

Syria might have arisen in part from personal antipathy, because of his close ties to Agrippina, but his forced suicide in 66 is a hint that there may have been good grounds to distrust him.[89] Pallas had been removed from office in the course of 55, and it might have been expected that his brother Felix, procurator of Judaea, would fall with him. There are grounds for believing that Felix's recall from Judaea came in the second year of Nero's reign, following October 55. As has been recorded (p. 127), on Felix's return a delegation of Jews brought charges against him. These were dismissed, according to Josephus, because of the intervention of Pallas who, he says, was at that time held in high regard. Josephus' claim of such intervention surely reflects what the Jewish deputation must have believed was the only explanation for the failure of their case, which they no doubt considered irrefutable, even though Pallas was by then in no position to influence events. While Agrippina was unable to prevent Felix's dismissal, it may in fact have been she, rather than Pallas, who saved him from prosecution (see below).

While Agrippina benefited, albeit temporarily, from the aftermath of the Junia Silana affair, Burrus seems to have suffered, although it is not clear whether Nero was offended because he had come to Agrippina's defence or because he had exposed his inability to get rid of her.[90] In any case a curious charge was now brought by a certain Paetus, otherwise unknown, apparently a man who had made a fortune by farming uncollected debts owed to the treasury. He claimed that Burrus and the freedman Pallas had conspired to supplant Nero with Faustus Cornelius Sulla Felix, husband of Claudius' daughter Antonia. On the surface the accusation seems ridiculous (Tacitus certainly thought so) and it comes as no surprise that the charge against Burrus was dismissed on the spot, or that Pallas was subsequently exonerated (in a very garbled passage Dio credits Seneca with the dismissal of the charges). Paetus was banished from Rome. Perhaps the most interesting aspect of the proceedings is that their very existence suggests that Paetus, or his backers, felt that Burrus was somehow vulnerable, perhaps as someone who was not actually disloyal but who possessed too much integrity to do the kind of sordid job, such as the murder of the emperor's mother, that was now required of him. The trial may in reality have been an attempt to get at Pallas. As a condition of his departure from office, the freedman had secured the undertaking that there would be no examination of his books. When the present accusation failed, the account books were burned. This suggests that somehow the books were involved as evidence and that the charge of treason was a front to launch an indirect examination of Pallas' financial dealings, in order somehow to sidestep the undertaking that had previously been made to him. In that case, Paetus, who had a reputation for murky business transactions with the treasury, would have been an appropriate accuser. It is hard to see what Burrus' involvement might have been. During his time as procurator of the imperial estates he would have had financial duties, which could well have brought him into contact with Pallas, but he would have been, at best, a very small player. Equally curious is that, despite the initial charge against him, Burrus was one of the assessors who afterwards sat in judgement over Pallas. The charges against the prefect must have been rejected decisively. Since Burrus was of equestrian status, Pallas' hearing must have taken place not in the senate but in private, before the emperor. Later, praetorian prefects regularly assumed judicial duties.[91]

The failure of the charge brought by Paetus against Pallas might have enabled Agrippina to secure the modest favour on his brother Felix's behalf, suggested above, thus creating the false impression that Felix had been acquitted through Pallas' intervention. This, of course, is speculation, and even the date of Felix's recall is much disputed (it has been argued that it should be placed in about 60). Pallas remained a marked man and died in 62, poisoned, it was said, by Nero, who was eager to gain control of his enormous wealth.[92]

From late in 55 until the beginning of 59, the year of her death, there are scattered allusions to Agrippina in the archaeological record. In Rome the Arvals celebrated her birthday, 6 November, in both 57 and 58 (the November entries for the immediately earlier and subsequent years have not survived), and honoured her in their celebration of Nero's birthday in 58 (possible in 57 also, where the relevant text is missing). In Naples games were dedicated to her in 56. It is possible that she appears in other extant inscriptions outside Rome during this period, but in the absence of precise dating criteria this cannot be confirmed. Although dropped from the coins of the Roman mint, she continued to appear on local issues. Again, the vast majority cannot be dated precisely. The coinage of Alexandria, however, does carry the mint year and can be dated with accuracy; Agrippina (identified [in Greek] as Agrippina Augusta) is portrayed on that city's earliest tetradrachms from Nero's reign (56/57) and continues to appear until her death (Pl. 15).[93]

In contrast to the archaeological evidence, there is no securely datable mention in any literary source of Agrippina between 55 and 59, other than a retrospective allusion in 58 to her supposed love affair with Seneca (see below). This is a remarkable situation. Had Agrippina been totally eclipsed she might have retired into quiet oblivion, playing no role in political activities at Rome or in Nero's personal affairs. Yet this can hardly have been the case. By late 55 she was once again at the height of power. In 59 we find that she continued to be revered by the praetorian guard, and Burrus was hesitant to use them against her. She also continued to be enough of a thorn in Nero's side that he should have wanted to eliminate her. There is also a hint that Nero was anxious to play down any public notion of a rift, since in the birthday celebrations for herself and for Nero in 57 and 58 (see above) the Arvals carried out ceremonies not only to mark the occasion but also to honour Concordia. This evidence should not be pushed too hard, however, since rites for Concordia were also carried out on Nero's birthday in 60.[94]

We must conclude that during the first period of Nero's reign Agrippina's role was highly public, as during the incident of the Armenian legation, or dramatic enough to have been passed on by some source in the palace, as when she was charged with complicity with Rubellius Plautus. After 55 she seems to have assumed a much lower profile, trying to work more behind the scenes, still exercising power and influence, but doing so in a much more subtle, less easily defined way, avoiding provocation and confrontation. As a consequence, she ceases to be a dominant 'personality' except in the manner of her death and thus finds herself excluded from Tacitus' narrative. Syme notes here a familiar Tacitean technique. After introducing Sejanus, for instance, he withheld his name for several years as if to maintain suspense. Similarly Agrippina fades out of the narrative, but her presence is still felt and she returns dramatically, on the eve of her death.[95]

Suetonius alludes loosely to Agrippina's movements in the intervening years, claiming that Nero drove her from the palace and started to harass her. He bribed men to annoy her with lawsuits while she lived in Rome, and when she retired to the country agents were hired to pester her, loitering near her house and disturbing her peace with abuse and mockery.[96] The allusions are too vague to be of great use. The 'lawsuits' secured by bribery may be a confused allusion to the attacks made on her by Iturius and Calvisius (p. 175), and the harassing disturbances at her country house are probably at best a reflection of specific incidents rather than coherent policy.

The only reference to Agrippina in the literary sources between 55 and 59 appears in a curious and intriguing context in 58, already mentioned. Tacitus reports under that year actions taken against Suillius Rufus. There had been attempts to clip his wings under the revived Cincian law. This seems to have been the first stage of a continuous attack on him, which came to a climax in 58. He appears to have been careful not to infringe the new restrictions placed on advocates' fees, and he was eventually accused of extortion in Asia and of embezzlement of public funds. Suillius was a wily opponent and even this charge could not be made to stick. Eventually he was accused of the more broad crime of malicious prosecution and participation in judicial murder. Suillius realized who his real enemy was, and did not hesitate to say so publicly – Seneca. He launched into a savage denunciation of his opponent, calling him the bitter enemy of the friends of Claudius. Suillius exploited the still potent name of Germanicus, observing that while he, Suillius, had served on Germanicus' staff, Seneca had debauched his home (*illum domus eius adulterum fuisse*) and violated the beds of the imperial women (*corrumpere cubicula principum feminarum*). This incident as described by Tacitus is clearly the same as the one recorded by Dio as an attack by an unnamed individual (presumably Suillius) on Seneca. He observes that Seneca faced a number of charges in 58, including that of adultery with Agrippina. He had not been satisfied, Dio notes, with a liaison with Livilla and had not learned his lesson as a result of his banishment but had taken up with Agrippina, knowing what sort of woman she was and what sort of son she had. Dio does not make clear whether the criticisms of Seneca (whom he despises) are intended as statements of fact, or are a paraphrase of the charges made by the accuser, although the skilful ambiguity suggested by impropriety of an affair with a woman 'like Agrippina' who had a son 'like Nero' (that is, either the highest or the lowest, depending on preference) suggest that the language is Suillius'. In any case, Dio follows the reference with a litany of complaints about the historical contradictions between Seneca's personal life and his teachings, leaving no doubt that he intends the reader to take the accusations as proved. Suillius put up a good fight, but in the end he lost. Deprived of half of his estate, he was exiled to the Balearic islands.[97]

Despite the rapprochement with his mother in late 55, Nero clearly still felt uneasy about her. Their reconciliation seems to have been based on fear rather than goodwill and affection, and predictably he continued to believe that she constituted a permanent threat to his role as princeps and that while she was alive he could never feel secure about the loyalty of the guard. While it is unlikely that she had actually promoted the interests of other candidates, such as Britannicus or Rubellius Plautus, the truth is not the key factor. As Nero's reign progressed he began to fit the traditional mould of the tyrant, becoming increasingly paranoid about suspected enemies and increasingly unwilling to follow sound advice. What he believed about Agrippina is what would decide her fate, and in 59 she would fall victim to the monster that she had largely created.

8
The End

In 59 Nero decided to kill Agrippina. Why he should have reached this momentous decision, and why he should have reached it at this particular time, remains something of a mystery. Agrippina's disappearance from the narrative of the previous four years is particularly frustrating, and means that we are given no proper background to Nero's thinking. Suetonius speaks of his being driven by his mother's 'threats and violence' (*minis ... ac violentia*), but he provides no specific examples of such behaviour, and the claim may be no more than speculation. Tacitus does offer an explanation, one so unconvincing that it was probably offered out of desperation and suggests that he was as puzzled we are. He claims that the clash between Nero and his mother in 59 had origins similar to the dispute of 55, that is, Nero's infatuation with a woman. In this later affair the object of his passion was no freedwoman but a married woman of a prominent family, Poppaea Sabina.[1]

Poppaea is introduced by Tacitus in the narrative of the previous year, 58, where he describes her as a woman with every advantage in life except moral integrity. Her father Titus Ollius had fallen victim to Sejanus before he had a chance to prove himself beyond the quaestorship, and she had therefore assumed the name of her more distinguished maternal grandfather, Poppaeus Sabinus, who had achieved both the consulate and the triumphal insignia. She was a woman of striking appearance, who apparently inherited her looks from her mother, reputedly the greatest beauty of her day and driven to her death, along with Valerius Asiaticus, by Messalina. She also had a lively personality and a keen wit. Tacitus sees a similarity to Agrippina in that, although promiscuous, she was no slave to passion, and could transfer her affections wherever it was advantageous. Her first husband was Rufrius Crispinus, the praetorian prefect removed from office by Agrippina (the dismissal might have sown the initial seeds of Poppaea's emnity). There is some disagreement in the ancient sources about later events. In the *Histories* Tacitus follows a version preferred by the other sources, that while still married to Rufrius she became Nero's lover, and that Otho (the future emperor), a favourite of Nero and obviously a rising star, went through a bogus marriage with her to accommodate the emperor until he could divorce Octavia. In the later *Annals* Tacitus follows a version that Otho began an affair with Poppaea when she was married to Crispinus and eventually married her. In this variant Otho subsequently arranged an introduction between his wife and Nero, perhaps, as Tacitus suggests, playing the pander and hoping to use her to promote his own career. Nero became infatuated by her and, to ensure a clear field, arranged for Otho to be appointed governor of Lusitania, where he performed his duties with distinction, returning in 68 to Rome to become emperor himself for a short time.[2]

Book 14 of the *Annals* opens with the year 59 and in the opening sentence reintroduces

Agrippina to the narrative after a four-year absence. The context is Nero's infatuation with Poppaea and her refusal to accept the permanent condition of mistress. Agrippina's affection for Octavia was well known and Poppaea seems to have despaired of any divorce while his mother was alive. She insisted to Nero that Agrippina opposed her from the fear that if Poppaea became Nero's wife she would expose his mother's past crimes, though the logic of this argument is far from clear. While Tacitus does not claim that Poppaea actually called for Agrippina's murder and actually clouds the issue by suggesting, without further elaboration, that Nero had long been planning the crime (*diu meditatum*), he suggests that Poppaea's challenge drove him over the brink.

In fact, the removal of Agrippina from the scene would have no immediate impact on Poppaea's situation – Nero waited another three years to marry her. Her introduction at this stage seems to be little more than a literary device, utilized because Tacitus could see no plausible explanation for Nero's conduct and also incidentally serving to show that Nero, like Claudius, had fallen under the malign influence of a woman. As late as 62 Tacitus still speaks of Nero hastening to bring forward (*maturare*) the wedding with Poppaea. At this later date Poppaea schemes to have Nero rid himself of Octavia and vigorously promotes her own marriage prospects in the same year, in a situation curiously parallel to that of 59. It is possible that Tacitus recycled the events of 62 in a slightly different form to provide some motive for the murder three years earlier, although he does seem to be drawing on an earlier tradition that Nero got rid of his mother to please Poppaea, as suggested in the *Octavia*. Dio picks up the notion that Poppaea was the instigator of the murder, but her motive was not to hasten her marriage. It was far more bizarre. Poppaea had supposedly discovered that Nero had acquired another mistress. This itself might not have been a serious problem. But the newcomer was his mother's double. This made Poppaea jealous and to get rid of Agrippina she persuaded Nero that his mother was plotting against him. What Poppaea planned for the double we are not told.[3]

Once Tacitus has Nero determined on murder, he introduces a new element in the relationship between mother and son. Without specifically drawing a link to what has preceded, he cites Cluvius Rufus for the story that Agrippina was so anxious to maintain her *potentia* ('influence') that she was even willing to stoop to incest. Tacitus' earlier claim that her *potentia* had started to disappear in 55 is now forgotten. Cluvius claimed that she would dress in sexy clothes and visit her son at midday, when he was in a mellow mood after drinking. They were seen kissing and exchanging endearments (hardly remarkable behaviour between mother and son). Seneca was alarmed at the restored pre-eminence of Agrippina, but he did not intervene directly. Instead he used Acte, the freedwoman and mistress of Nero, who alerted her lover that there was widespread speculation that he was committing incest with his mother, and that Agrippina was even going about boasting of it. Her clinching argument was that the guard had become so dispirited by his behaviour that their loyalty was compromised. Fabius Rusticus agrees that Acte brought Nero's passionate reconciliation with his mother to an end, but differs from Cluvius in claiming that Nero was the instigator of the incest. Tacitus adds that Cluvius' version, attributing the impulse to Agrippina, was supported by other (unnamed) authorities. But he is reluctant to commit himself to the story and wonders if it became attached to her because she had a notorious reputation for prostituting herself for political ends. Dio reports the Cluvian version and adds that Agrippina's purpose was to wean Nero from Poppaea. He, like Tacitus, is not sure whether to believe the report. Suetonius typically accepts the story, claiming that they would commit incest in Nero's litter, and adding the sordid detail that they were given away by the stains on the emperor's clothing.[4]

As noted earlier, charges of incest are commonly made against prominent figures in antiquity. In the case of Nero and Agrippina there are particular reasons for caution, given the scepticism of Tacitus and Dio – hardly friendly witnesses. Apart from this we might note that the story of Nero's surprised reaction to the sight of his mother's body after her death (p. 190) suggests a lack of intimate familiarity with it. There is also a rational explanation for the rumours of incest. Both Dio and Suetonius report the story that Nero had a mistress with a striking resemblance to Agrippina (the one who upset Poppaea so), and Dio adds the detail that after he slept with her he would boast that he had slept with his mother. Given that the stories of incest must have originated from the palace, it is not difficult to see how Nero's flippant comments could have provoked the belief that he had enjoyed his mother.[5] What is particularly interesting is that whatever the truth of the incest charges, Nero and Agrippina were clearly in the habit of showing one another considerable affection in public, further proof that she had not been totally eclipsed by this time. Nero's affection might well have been nothing more than a show, but it is surely significant that at the very least he still felt the need to put on such a show.

Alarmed by Acte's warning, Nero began to avoid meeting Agrippina in private, and urged her to take her leisure in her gardens or to go to one of her villas at Tusculum (possibly inherited from Passienus) or to the imperial villa at Antium. Tacitus' earlier claim that Poppaea was the inspiration behind the murder-plan seems to be forgotten. He now has Nero convinced that Agrippina would be a burden to him even if she lived away from Rome, and he determined therefore to kill her. He presumably still feared the influence she had over the troops, and felt that his principate could never be secure while she was still alive.

Once he had reached the decision, Nero was faced with the dilemma of how to carry it out. He ruled out poison. Britannicus' death would have made everyone suspicious and Agrippina had in any case built up resistance by antidotes. A direct physical attack was out of the question, since no-one would be willing to take on the job, a telling reflection on the reliance Nero could place in the praetorians and of the fear that Agrippina evoked among ordinary assassins. Neither objection seems very persuasive. The method supposedly adopted by Nero was hardly one to allay suspicions, and in the end he had to rely on assassins. It seems likely that Tacitus appreciated that his account would seem implausible and he wanted to forestall the inevitable objection that a simple method of eliminating her could have been chosen.[6]

Finally someone did promise to bring off the murder. Significantly, it was not an army man but Anicetus, the prefect of the Misenum fleet. The Roman fleet since the time of Augustus had been based in two main naval stations, Ravenna on the east coast, Misenum on the west. The Misenum fleet was the more important and remained in service for four centuries. It has been calculated that there might have been over 10,000 sailors at the time of Nero, manning perhaps fifty ships in all. Certainly during the unrest of 68–9, the fleet from Misenum provided men for Legio I, and Otho withdrew over 1000 sailors from it to lead against Vitellius. There still remained enough men for Vitellius to plan to raise another legion from their ranks.[7] Apart from the two main bases, there were detachments located elsewhere. One would have been at Ostia, from which provincial officials were transported to their new duties and emperors set out for their Campanian estates.[8] There was also a detachment in Rome, perhaps from the time of Augustus, and under Commodus they were used to tend the awnings in the amphitheatre. The sailors in Rome are known to have played a political role after Caligula's assassination. They streamed into the praetorian camp, and were a key factor in deterring potential rivals from challenging Claudius.[9]

Under Claudius the governors of certain provinces, previously designated as prefects, began to hold the rank of procurator (with the exception of Egypt). The same change was applied to the commanders of the fleets at Ravenna and Misenum. This had an important consequence. Freedmen had been used as procurators of the imperial estates since the time of Augustus, and we now find the presence of imperial freedmen, without military background, as procurators in command of the fleets. Three such freedmen are known from the period 41–69.[10] Because of the close relationship that often existed between emperor and freedman, this development gave the fleets a potential role in political disputes. Nero had never had full confidence in the reliability of the praetorian guard while it was under the command of Burrus. In 59, for the first time, a prominent protective role was given to the troops of the fleet and the commander of the Misenum fleet assumes an undertaking that might have been expected to fall within the bailiwick of the praetorian commander. This was not the last occasion when this would happen. In the great Pisonian conspiracy against Nero in 65, which involved several members of the guard, it was an officer of the fleet, Volusius Proculus, who revealed the first evidence of the plot to murder Nero. Anicetus, commander in 59, had no apparent naval skills but had been Nero's tutor in his youth, and was presumably someone in whom the emperor could place total personal reliance. To help matters, Anicetus despised Agrippina – a feeling that was reciprocated.[11]

Anicetus put his engineering skills to their best use. According to Suetonius, his scheme was apparently to place a mechanical device in the panels of Agrippina's bedroom. This was designed to loosen the supports and so allow the ceiling to fall on her while she slept. We are not told where this accident was to be arranged but it was presumably to happen in one of Agrippina's own residences. This could explain why the plot was leaked and the plans scrapped. Anicetus had his second inspiration at a theatrical performance, during which a mechanical ship miraculously came apart to let out some animals, and then reassembled itself. As a result, he supposedly conceived the idea of a similar craft, not just a stage prop but a real ocean-going ship that could detach part of itself and drop the intended victim overboard. Admittedly, Nero did have a penchant for clever contrivances. His Golden House had a circular dining hall which revolved day and night. Towards the close of his reign in 68, as news of the rebellion of Vindex swept Rome, he spent most of the day showing prominent Romans some unusual hydraulic pipes and explaining their mechanics. All the same, the ingenious collapsing ship, which has brought us one of the most familiar and colourful incidents from antiquity, should be treated with scepticism. Apart from the general implausibility of such a device ever

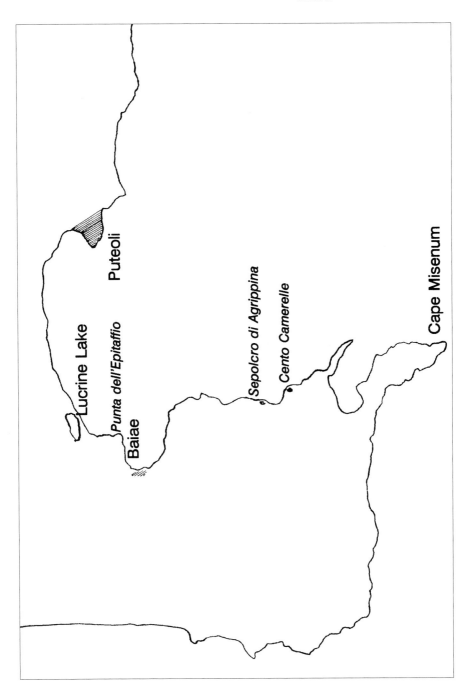

Fig. 4 Baiae and its environs

being able to work (see below), Suetonius claims that the plan was either to shipwreck Agrippina or to crush her on board in a collapsing cabin, which seems to be a confused version of the idea of a collapsing bedroom.[12]

The murder was to be carried out during the festival of Minerva, 19–23 March, which Nero usually spent at Baiae, the resort town of Rome's 'beautiful people' in the bay of Naples (Fig. 4). The emperor's visits to the Baiae area were the stuff of local legend, with pleasure booths set up on the shore for wild living. It is possible that Acte accompanied him on his trips; at any rate, she acquired property in nearby Puteoli. In particular, Nero enjoyed visiting the villa of Gaius Calpurnius Piso and in 65 would come close to being murdered there. Making a grand show of reconciliation, Nero wrote to Agrippina and invited her to join him. His mother was at Antium at the time, presumably staying at the family villa. She sailed down to the bay of Naples and came to shore to be met by Nero. He then accompanied her the short distance to her villa at Bauli (for details of the topography see Appendix X).

Agrippina's villa was almost certainly the luxury establishment once owned by the wealthy republican orator Hortensius, who built fishponds there and became so attached to one of the fish that he wept when it died. On Hortensius' death in 50 BC the villa presumably passed to his son, to be confiscated by the triumvirs after the battle of Philippi in 42 BC. Eventually it came into the possession of Antonia the Younger, possibly through her mother, Octavia. Antonia similarly had a favourite fish, which she adorned with gold rings. Word of this piscatorial marvel soon spread and curious tourists made their way to Bauli to see it.[13] In AD 55 Agrippina was obliged to move out of the imperial palace to the Palatine residence of her grandmother Antonia. It is possible that Antonia's country estates, including the villa at Bauli, were also at the same time made available to her. The surviving remains of this building, known as the Cento Camarelle, were excavated early in this century. Two separate structures have been identified on the site. The earliest seems to be the remains of a large villa. A series of galleries cut by narrow passages opens towards the sea. Above the galleries, but oriented with them, is a large cistern with four corridors linked by grand arches roofed with barrel vaulting.[14]

Since Agrippina had travelled all the way from Antium, it is likely that she stayed in the area for a few days, her visit culminating in a grand dinner Nero gave her at Baiae, rather than for the single evening that Tacitus implies. Suetonius adds the detail that the future emperor Otho was privy to Nero's plans and played host on the fatal evening.[15]

Agrippina was treated royally and occupied the seat of honour above the emperor. After a friendly and congenial meal, Nero showed considerable affection, kissing her eyes and her breasts. After midnight they went down to the shore, where several vessels were moored. One stood out above the others, as a special honour to his mother. Dio has Nero give Agrippina a close embrace, declaring as she left him, 'For you I live, through you I rule.'[16]

Tacitus' narrative continues. The sea was calm and the night starlit (ie, there was no moon). The ship was still quite close to the shore, the passengers relaxed and unconcerned. Crepereius Gallus was standing near the tiller while Agrippina's friend, Acerronia Polla, was bent over the feet of Agrippina as she reclined on a couch on the deck. Tacitus paints a charming picture of the two women discussing the happy turn of events. The scene is presumably a dramatic device to emphasize Agrippina's tragedy since, if true, it would suggest that she was naive to a degree never previously manifested throughout her life. The cheerful mood is also difficult to reconcile with the suspicions she supposedly entertained about her son right to the end. Suddenly, on a given signal, the canopy above them, which had been weighted with lead, collapsed and Crepereius was crushed to death on the spot. Agrippina and Acerronia were saved by the height of the couch balusters, which were solidly built and did not give way under the impact. That was not the only problem with the mechanism. The predicted collapse of the boat did not follow; also, not all the crew was privy to the plot, and in the confusion the plotters were impeded by those who had been kept deliberately in the dark. A farcical scene ensued. In order to capsize the vessel, the crew (or at least those in the know) rushed to one side, but they were slow to organize themselves and a counter-effort at the other side of the vessel weakened the effect. However, it did not prevent Agrippina and Acerronia from sliding somehow into the water. Acerronia made the mistake of calling out for aid, insisting that she was Agrippina, and was despatched with poles and oars. Agrippina stayed silent and, although she was wounded on the shoulder, managed to swim out to some small fishing smacks. They carried her to the Lucrine Lake (Appendix X), and from there she made her way back to her own villa. The account of Dio is slightly different. In his version the ship actually did collapse and Agrippina fell into the sea but did not drown – he attributes her survival essentially to luck rather than the bungling of the crew, which he does not mention. He adds that the sailors did try to strike her with their oars (the *Octavia* says that they succeeded) and that Acerronia was killed in the mêlée. No mention is made by Dio of the fishing boats, and Agrippina succeeds in swimming to the shore unaided, despite having consumed a considerable amount of wine. We are given no further information on casualties, or on Acerronia and Crepereius Gallus. The *Octavia* similarly makes no mention of the boats and has Agrippina carried along in the water by loyal servants.

The saga of the remarkable and ingenious shipwreck is one of the most vivid episodes of antiquity, one we would regret losing, but it raises a number of very serious questions. First of all there is the problem of the mechanism. Tacitus seems to be uncertain whether Nero decided on the collapsing bedroom or the collapsing boat, and seems somehow to merge the two. Some of the details cause concern. Crepereius Gallus is supposedly standing by the tiller but is crushed under the canopy. Agrippina and Acerronia are saved by the solid sides of the couch – but they would have had to be in decidedly uncomfortable positions for this to happen. Then there is the conduct of the crew. The notion that some knew of the plot and tried to tip the boat by standing at one side while the remainder went to the other side to keep the balance is both ludicrous and inconsistent with the remainder of Tacitus' account, since he describes chaos and confusion while such a manoeuvre would require considerable order and discipline. We also have to assume a suicidal element within the crew, willing to tip over a vessel that would be likely to dump them in the sea and roll over them. If they were prepared to carry out such an obvious manoeuvre, they clearly could have had no concern about secrecy. Why then not simply throw Agrippina overboard?[17]

One plausible explanation suggests itself. Suetonius says, that to persuade her to sail by the 'trick' boat, Nero earlier ordered one of his captains to ram her vessel as it was on its way to the Baiae area, pretending that it was an accident (the incident is not mentioned by Tacitus). If Agrippina's boat was rammed by one of the fleet triremes not some days earlier but on the final voyage (it was a moonless night, and visibility would have been limited), we would have a plausible explanation for the collapse of the canopy roof and the suicidal manoeuvre of the crew might in fact have been nothing more than a breakdown of discipline when a large number rushed to one side in an effort to escape. Such a ramming could well in fact have been accidental, but it may also have been deliberate, and if so it is highly plausible that the crew of Agrippina's vessel would have been kept completely in the dark, since to pass off her death as a convincing accident at sea would have required that some members of the crew died also. We learn afterwards that the official reports of the event were totally sanitized, which would inevitably have led to much speculation, and this speculation about the accident at sea could have merged with rumours about the scheme for the collapsing bedroom, given extra fuel by the spectacle of the collapsing ship seen in the theatre. Acerronia's death might well have been deliberate but it could also have been accidental. Tacitus does have Agrippina later ponder the event in terms which seem to suggest that there could not have been an accident, since there was no dangerous reef or sudden gale. But since these observations reflect Agrippina's inner musings on the night of her death, they presumably originate from the imagination of the author, and clearly cannot be pushed too hard for an accurate account of the events.[18]

Tacitus reports that after picking up Agrippina from the sea the boats took her to the Lucrine Lake. That body of water was renowned throughout the Roman world for the cultivation of oysters and young oysters were brought from Brundisium to feed there. The trade had been threatened by Agrippa's plans to convert the Lucrine into a naval base by connecting it with a channel to Lake Avernus and piercing the sandbar between it and the bay of Baiae. Fortunately for the oyster industry that project proved a failure, probably because of silting, and was eventually abandoned in favour of the base at Misenum. The lake was accessible by small vessels and Strabo speaks of it as providing excellent moorage. If the boats that rescued Agrippina belonged to oystermen, they would have had a plausible reason to land Agrippina here rather than at her villa at Bauli, since the shoreline would have been familiar to them and would thus have offered a safer landing on a moonless night. From there Agrippina was carried in a litter back to Bauli, naturally reluctant to risk going back by sea. It would have been a dramatic journey and she would somehow have had to skirt Nero's residence at Baiae (see Appendix X).[19]

Back in her villa, Agrippina, wrapped in warm blankets, tended to her wound and pondered on her best course of action. The scales had fallen completely from her eyes, and she now had no doubt about Nero's intentions. Her own wound and the death of Acerronia brought home to her how narrow her escape had been. She decided that the safest course would be to feign ignorance –a plan, incidentally, that could hardly have carried conviction had the crew openly and deliberately tried to tip her into the sea and deliberately hit her with poles. Accordingly she decided to play for time, and sent her freedman Agerinus with a spurious message to Nero that by a stroke of luck she had survived a serious accident. True to form, she remained the efficient businesswoman; she ordered that Acerronia's will be sought out and her goods put under seal. She no doubt assumed that she would inherit, and Tacitus notes that in this one act her motives were nothing other than what they seemed.

After his mother's departure from the banquet Nero had spent a sleepless night, waiting for the news that it was all over. At last a message arrived – she had escaped, slightly wounded. Nero was terrified (*pavore exanimis*). Agrippina could be in no doubt about what had been intended for her. Would she now rally the praetorians to her side, or charge him in the senate with the murder of her friends and the attempted murder of herself? His first concern would have been over the loyalty of the praetorian detachment stationed at Misenum. He now turned in desperation to his old advisers, Seneca and Burrus. He was able to summon them immediately, which means that they must have been in the Baiae area. Tacitus' text at this point is hopelessly corrupt, but it seems that he left open the question of whether or not they had been involved in the scheme (*incertum an et ante ignaros*).[20] Dio does claim that Seneca had pressed Nero to murder, but his account is deeply hostile towards Seneca, which should make us cautious about the claim. On the whole their involvement seems unlikely. It was not really in their interest to eliminate her. As noted earlier, it served their purpose to have Agrippina as a living thorn in Nero's flesh but, more significant, the risky, even reckless, nature of the undertaking seems to be out of character for Seneca and Burrus. Besides which, the fact that Nero seems to turn to them only as a last resort suggests that they had not been part of the plot.

Now that events had turned critical, Seneca and Burrus realized that there was no way that Nero could be dissuaded from taking the final drastic step, but they were equally reluctant to allow their own names to be tarnished. Seneca was the first to speak and skilfully deflected the problem onto his colleague. Looking towards Burrus, he asked whether the praetorians could be ordered to carry out Agrippina's execution. Burrus' response is highly significant. He assured Nero of the loyalty of the guard but emphasized that they were pledged to the imperial family as a whole, in other words their loyalty was to the emperor's kin as well as to the emperor himself. There is evidence that the *sacramentum* of the praetorians might have involved an oath to protect the whole imperial house, but Burrus' words here seem to denote general affection and loyalty rather than the legal obligations involved in a formal oath. To avoid any danger of misunderstanding, he spelled out the situation clearly to Nero – that the guard was strongly attached to the memory of Germanicus and would not take up arms against his daughter. This is powerful testimony to both the magical influence of Germanicus' name some forty years after his death, and also to the thorough preparations made by Agrippina to infiltrate the guard with her own men. Burrus was in no hurry to clean up someone else's mess. He concluded by insisting that Anicetus finish off what he had started. Thus, in the final crisis, the praetorians justified Nero's worst suspicions and failed him. Burrus does not come out of this well. He lacked the courage to object to the murder but also lacked the courage to follow the emperor's orders to carry it out.

In the meantime, Agerinus had arrived with Agrippina's message. Tradition reports that, when he was ushered into the emperor's presence, Nero threw a sword at his feet, charging that Agrippina had plotted against his life, and thus laying the foundations for the later claim that she had committed suicide to avoid a humiliating exposure.[21] By now, word of Agrippina's escape had spread; interestingly, and perhaps significantly, the first reports spoke only of an accident. Groups of people began to gather by the shore, clambering onto the boats and climbing on the sea wall; massing together, they streamed up to her villa carrying torches. Suddenly a column of troops came into view and the crowd scattered. Anicetus cordoned off the villa, then smashed down the entrance. The troops broke into the house, seizing the slaves. Finally Anicetus, along with Herculeius, a trireme captain, and a naval centurion, Obaritus, came upon Agrippina, who was attended by a single servant. In her final moments, she showed considerable dignity and loyalty to the traditions of her family. She haughtily refused to accept their announcement that they had come to execute her on the orders of the emperor. If they were intent on murder, she responded, then it could not be on the instructions of her son. Her haughty pronouncement did not help her. They came upon her as she sat on the couch and Herculeius struck her head with his club. Obaritus drew out his sword to finish her off. Her final gesture has won her a sort of immortal fame and the story deserves to be true (but may well not be); baring her stomach, she told them to strike the womb that had given birth to Nero.[22]

Tacitus notes that the authorities generally agree on how Agrippina died but that there are different versions of what happened next. Nero made his way to the villa and some sources (unnamed) claim that he inspected the corpse and expressed admiration for its beauty, while others (also unnamed) deny the story. Suetonius reports that 'trustworthy authorities' (*nec incerti auctores*) confirm the story, adding the detail that he handled the limbs, criticizing some, praising others, sipping wine as he passed judgement. Dio relates the incident without query, along with Nero's final comment that he had not realized he had such a beautiful mother. The whole episode has a theatrical quality, as if Nero were trying to act out the horrific denouement of the kind of play that was popular at that time.[23]

That very night Agrippina received the final rites. She might at one time have imagined a ceremony on the lavish scale of her father's or third husband's. Such was not to be. She was cremated on her dining couch, a ritual that would duly dispose of her body and at the same time any evidence of how she had died. Her freedman added a touch of spectacle by running himself through with his sword as the pyre was kindled, either out of devotion or through fear of the fate that awaited him. The ashes, which under happier circumstances would have been stored next to her ancestors in the mausoleum of Augustus, were given a casual burial by her servants. During Nero's reign there was never a proper burial, nor was the plot marked by any kind of enclosure. Afterwards, it is not clear when, she was given a modest tomb by the road to Misenum, near to where the villa of Julius Caesar 'looked out from the heights over the bays that lay spread beneath' (*subiectos sinus editissima prospectat*), as Tacitus lyrically expresses it. She thus, the historian observes, fulfilled the prophecy for which she had once shown such scant concern on being told that Nero would one day reign but would kill her, when she had responded, *occidat dum imperat* ('let him kill me, only let him rule!').[24]

Agrippina had played a dominant role in Nero's early life and it would have been remarkable if he could have remained indifferent to her death. According to Tacitus, he was overwhelmed by the magnitude of his own deed. He spent the remainder of the night struck almost dumb, seized by recurring bouts of panic. With dawn came some consolation. Burrus had staged a show of support from the praetorian detachment and the officers (centurions and tribunes) came to offer their congratulations on his escape from the plot. Their loyalty to Agrippina was clearly tempered by a practical realism.

Once she was off the scene self-interest took over, as it always did, and impelled them to a show of loyalty to the reigning princeps. A donation of cash no doubt encouraged their sense of duty. Contrived congratulations were organized throughout the area, with visits to temples and celebratory sacrifices in the neighbouring towns. This helped a little but Nero continued to be haunted by the thought of what he had done. He supposedly heard trumpets on the hills and sounds of lamentation from the simple grave that had been made for his mother. In fact, he could not get the picture of the grave, or the sea and the surrounding hills, out of his mind so he moved into Naples to escape the memory. It was not a total success. There are further stories told of his being pursued by his mother's ghost or by the Furies brandishing whips and flaming torches. Finally, he had expiatory rites performed at the grave to appease her restless shade.[25]

Nero's first priority had been to ensure the adherence of the praetorians. Although secondary in importance, the senate also had to be won over. To this end he despatched a letter, written by Seneca. Its elegant opening words have been preserved by Quintilian, *salvum me esse adhuc nec credo nec gaudeo* ('the fact that I am still alive, I can neither believe nor celebrate'). The remainder of the letter was designed to appeal to the senators' prejudices. He stated first that Agrippina had sought to acquire a share of power (*consortium imperii*), a charge that was probably true. The senate had been aware of her status and had responded with outward acquiescence, even sycophancy, yet, as the letter seems to suggest, had privately resented her behaviour as contrary to Roman tradition. His second charge also probably came close to the truth, that she had aspired to have the praetorians swear allegiance to her. Having won over his audience with charges that were reasonably grounded, Nero went on to make the more extravagant claim that she had been determined to secure the same oath of loyalty from the senate and the people, an assertion of third party *intent*, thus incapable of proof or disproof, but cleverly designed to appeal to deep-seated fears. Her ambitions foiled, he insisted, she had then turned against the very groups she had tried to court the soldiers, senate and people. The last two she had attacked with charges against prominent members or by the blocking of largesses; the charge about the soldiers is more difficult to understand, unless Nero was artfully reminding people of her initial purges of the praetorian officer corps. He further alleged that she had to be restrained from breaking into the sessions of the senate. Again, there was sufficient truth in this charge to make it credible, in that she had followed the proceedings behind a curtain, but there was no concrete evidence that she planned to thrust herself onto the actual proceedings. Also, he claimed, he had prevented her from taking part in negotiations with foreign nations, reminding people of the famous incident involving the Armenian ambassadors. After these specific indictments, Nero launched into a general attack on the Claudian regime, blaming Agrippina for every scandal that had occurred. From her past sins, Nero moved on to Agrippina's last night. He described the shipwreck as an accident (unfortunately we are not given particulars) and the arrival of her messenger Agerinus as an attempt on his own life.

Without going into detail, Tacitus says that the speech was received with incredulity. The supposed accident and assassination attempt were so unbelievable that the blame was directed not so much against Nero as against Seneca, that he should have put his pen to such a document.[26] But Tacitus' sour interpretation of its reception is not really borne out by the facts. The senate seemed to react with relief to the news that a woman who was feared and hated had been removed, and any temporary disgust over the conduct of Nero was forgotten. In fact, there was a scramble to be first to demonstrate gratitude. A meeting of the Arvals is recorded in Rome on the Capitol for 28 March, without indication of its purpose, and it is likely that it was summoned in response to the news that the attempt on Nero's life had been exposed, as had happened previously in October 39 under Caligula, when news of the exposure of Gaetulicus' conspiracy was received in Rome. In the senate there was a series of sycophantic measures: thanksgivings (*supplicationes*) were celebrated, occasions when gods were approached at a time of particular catastrophe (no fewer than fifty-five were decreed for Augustus). The Arvals carried out formal *supplicationes* on 5 April, to celebrate Nero's safe delivery: *pro salute Neronis Claudi Caesar[is]*. Annual games were decreed to mark the festival of Minerva, since it was then that the conspiracy had been exposed.[27] Agrippina's birthday (6 November) was classed among the *dies nefasti* (it had been celebrated annually by the Arvals up to the previous November), as had happened to her mother. Only two senators broke rank. The distinguished orator from Gaul, Julius Africanus, used irony, conveying to Nero the request from Gaul that he should bear his good fortune with courage. The renowned Thrasea Paetus registered his protest more explicitly. He listened as Nero's letter was read, then showed his contempt by walking out of the chamber. Not a single member followed his example. Dio claims, somewhat illogically, that the general populace disapproved of Nero's behaviour but made an outward show of rejoicing since they felt assured that his recent conduct had guaranteed his own destruction (if so, they would have nine years to wait).[28] Heaven's response was rather more courageous and the murder was marked by the usual crop of portents although, as Tacitus observes they could hardly have been real portents of divine intervention since Nero was able to get away with his crimes for years to come. In any case, it is duly recorded that a woman gave birth to a snake, while another was killed by a thunderbolt as she made love to her husband. The fourteen regions of Rome were all struck by lightning. One further sign of heavenly displeasure can be confirmed. Tacitus says that there was an eclipse of the sun and Dio adds the detail that it occurred during thanksgiving sacrifices held in connection with Agrippina. The event is confirmed by Pliny, who dates it to 30 April of that year and reports that it was seen in Campania shortly after midday and in Armenia three hours later. Dio adds two independent and colourful occurrences. As the elephants drew the chariot of the deified Augustus into the circus, they proceeded as far as the senators' seats then stopped and refused to go any further. Most dramatic of all, as Nero was being brought his dinner a thunderbolt fell and, like a harpy swooping down to steal its victim's food, destroyed the whole meal.[29]

Nero delayed his return to Rome, still unsure about his reception by the senate and the general public, despite assurances by his advisers that the name of Agrippina was so hated that her death had won him universal favour. They were right. The age-old resentment of powerful and ambitious women proved a strong emotion. Just to make sure, the same advisers (not named) went back to Rome ahead of him to prepare the ground. Agrippina's statues were destroyed, the traditional fate of disgraced imperial women, suffered in 32 by Sejanus' mistress Livilla and in 48 by Messalina. Her name was hacked out of inscriptions on public buildings. Neither the destruction of the statues nor of the inscriptions seems to have been carried out in a systematic fashion and, in view of the festival arranged in her honour later in the year (see below), it does not seem likely that the senate declared a formal *damnatio memoriae*.[30] On Nero's arrival senators in their festal dress, with their wives and children, streamed out to meet him and along his route bleachers were set up for spectators, as if for a triumph. Tacitus reports that Nero entered Rome like a victorious general, as a victor not over an enemy but over the servitude of the people. Like the triumphant commander, he proceeded to the Capitol to fulfil his vows. Again, Tacitus' account is confirmed by the Arval record. The rituals carried out for Nero's return to Rome (*reditu*) on 23 June were complex. On the Capitoline there were sacrifices to the Capitoline triad, Jupiter, Juno and Minerva, more at the new Temple of Augustus, and even more to Mars Ultor as well as to Nero's Genius. The reference to Mars Ultor is especially interesting. On building this temple, Augustus decreed that in it the senate would discuss matters of war and the conferment of triumphs. Holders of imperium on their departure would take their final leave from the temple and would return to it to deposit their triumphal insignia. Nero's presence there is another indication that he sought to associate the state's deliverance from Agrippina with a triumphant victory over its enemies. His conduct is reminiscent of Caligula's after the suppression of the conspiracy of Gaetulicus and Lepidus, when three daggers were deposited in the temple and an ovation (a form of lesser triumph) was held to celebrate the defeat of the conspirators.[31]

If there was any hostility felt towards Nero it was underground and scattered. Dio records a few incidents but comes far short of indicating widespread dissatisfaction. Someone hung a leather bag on one of Nero's statues, with the implication that he ought to be put into one (a common punishment of murderers was to place them in a leather bag and throw them into a river). A baby was left abandoned in the Forum with a tag fastened to it reading, 'I won't rear you, in case you murder your mother.' One of the few statues of Agrippina that had managed to survive destruction was covered with a cloak, as if it were veiled, with an inscription, 'I am disgraced and you are not ashamed.' Graffiti would be found sporadically in Rome at varying levels of wit and literary skill. One, in Greek, took the form of a reply to an implied question that asked what three famous individuals had in common: 'Nero, Orestes, Alcmeon: each one a matricide.' A particularly clever graffito, akin to the modern anagrams of prominent names found in popular satirical magazines, recorded, also in Greek: 'A novel calculation: Nero slew his own mother' (*Neron idian metera apecteine*). In Greek, numerals are represented by letters of the alphabet. The numerical value of the *Neron* is 1005, the same as *idian metera apecteine*, the suggestion being the formula, {Nero} = {matricide}. Another, in the form of an elegiac couplet, refers to Aeneas, the legendary founder of the Julian line, who distinguished himself by carrying his father Anchises to safety as Troy was being sacked by the Greeks: 'Who denies that Nero comes from the great line of Aeneas: by one his mother was carried off, by the other his father.' Nero had the good sense to play down these isolated incidents and treated anyone caught writing such lampoons with leniency. On one occasion the insult was more blunt and more public. Datus, a performer of Atellan farces (light plays in a vaudeville vein), sang in Greek: 'Farewell father, farewell mother' and as he did so imitated the gestures of drinking and swimming. Yet he suffered no greater penalty than being obliged to leave Rome.[32]

The end of any unpopular regime is invariably followed by a show of generosity from the new ruler, intended to distance him from his predecessor. A parallel phenomenon was seen now, marking in a sense the end of Agrippina's era. Two otherwise unknown senators, Valerius Capito and Licinius Gabolus, who had been banished by Agrippina (this is the first time that their original sentence is mentioned in the sources), were allowed to return. So were Junia Calvina, expelled because of the suspected incest with her brother, Lucius Silanus, and Calpurnia, forced to leave Italy supposedly because Claudius had merely praised her charms but still in exile after his death and therefore, one assumes, guilty of more than looking pretty. Lollia Paulina, Agrippina's rival for Claudius' hand, was not so lucky. Forced into exile, she had been subsequently murdered, but her ashes were brought back to Italy and a tomb was erected in her honour. Iturius and Calvisius, who had been exiled in 55 for their part in the unsuccessful attempt to bring down Agrippina, were allowed to return. Junia Silana, a key figure in the same affair, had already managed to return to Italy but died before Agrippina. It is implied that she would have enjoyed the full amnesty had she survived. Of the seven who received Nero's clemency, three are women and they are the only ones of any distinction. Of the four men, two were agents of Junia Silana; the other two are unknown.[33]

Agrippina soon ceases to be a lively political issue. Even Nero seems to have made an effort to rewrite his own history and to pretend that she was simply another revered member of the imperial family. In fact, Anicetus had recommended that after the murder he should put on the usual displays of *pietas*. Dio records a splendid festival held in Agrippina's honour occurring after her death, with events spread over several days in five or six different theatres. The festivities were certainly novel and included a performance by a tightrope-walking elephant that was hoisted to the highest gallery of the theatre and then made its way down the rope, complete with rider. It was probably Nero's own conduct that helped people to forget the abuses associated with Agrippina. Liberated from the restraint that she had always imposed, whether in person or in spirit, he gave free rein to his inclinations and his conduct was so outrageous that it eventually brought an end both to himself and the Julio-Claudian dynasty.[34]

Ironically, not all of Agrippina's foes prospered as a result of her death. Having rid himself of the incubus of his mother, Nero perhaps felt less need of the refuge that her enemies had provided him. The first victim in this group was his aunt Domitia. She had been very close to Nero and had taken care of him when his mother was exiled by Caligula. Dio places her death among the events of 59. She was elderly by this time and in her sickbed. Nero was eager to get his hands on her estates at Ravenna and Baiae, and unwilling to wait for nature to take its course. Suetonius claims that he arranged for the doctors to poison her and then suppressed her will, thus in a sense bringing to a successful conclusion his father's old squabble with her about money. The story arouses the usual scepticism.[35]

When Agrippina had returned to Rome in 47 she had been greeted with enthusiasm as the last representative of the ideals briefly promised by Germanicus and as an antidote to the evil machinations of Messalina. As a symbol Agrippina stood second to none in popularity, when the symbol was translated into actual power the public perception quickly changed. However untrustworthy Poppaea might have been generally, she is probably to be believed when in early 59 she spoke of the popular anger against Agrippina's 'arrogance and greed' (*superbiam avaritiamque*), although such anger was probably concentrated in Rome. The concern of the crowds who congregated around her villa during her last hours and the general relief on hearing that she had survived the shipwreck indicate that, like other members of the Julio-Claudian family, Agrippina was much more popular in the hinterland than in the capital. Twelve years after her triumphant return to Rome her passing seems to have been mourned by few; even the staunchly loyal praetorian guard proved true to form and became staunchly pragmatic when presented with the fait accompli of her death. The politically powerful woman would always suffer a devastating 'image' problem in ancient Rome, which could be compensated for only by consummate skill in political manipulation, by the building up of powerful alliances and by the isolation of powerful opponents. This Agrippina did brilliantly as the wife of Claudius, but tragically failed to achieve as the mother of Nero.

There seems to have been no movement to rehabilitate Agrippina after her death. She left no band of devoted followers committed to setting straight a record they considered distorted, and any revisionist tendency among historians like Cluvius Rufus would have stood little chance of flourishing while Nero was alive, or during the reign of his eventual successor, Vespasian. The only evidence of later sympathy comes from early in the second century, during the reign of Trajan. A colossal head, identified as Agrippina's, has been found in Trajan's Forum. It is doubtless from the ancestral gallery designed around the great colonnade, on the lines of the atriums of private houses (where the images of ancestors were displayed on the walls). Susan Wood has suggested that Trajan, who prided himself on his devotion to his family, was seeking to draw a distinction between himself and Nero in honouring the murdered sister, wife and mother of emperors.[36] Trajan's gesture, however, seems to have been an isolated one and history records no-one emulating him until the twentieth century. A relief of Agrippina, along with other Roman rulers associated with the city, decorates Cologne's Römischer Brunnen, a fountain built in 1915 on the foundations of a Roman tower (the fountain was restored in 1955). Finally, in 1993, the citizens of Cologne reinstated Agrippina to the place of honour she had occupied at the city's founding, when they belatedly erected a statue to her in their town hall.

Syme often argued that Agrippina, and other powerful imperial women, were weighty figures in their own day but were essentially unimportant, since they passed from the scene without any lasting impact. This is surely to under-estimate Agrippina's significance. She represents an essential stage in the evolution of the imperial system, in the attempt to give a formal definition to the political role open to a woman of ability and energy. She did not change the hardened attitudes of her contemporaries, but she did define what Romans were willing to tolerate. Her experiment may have been a failure but it was not without its long-term effects. It can surely not be a coincidence that she was the last woman to play a dominant role in Roman political life for a century and a half. Later generations of imperial wives and mothers who might otherwise have entertained aspirations to power clearly took to heart the bitter lesson that Agrippina learned when, in AD 59, she was beaten and hacked to death by her son's hired assassins.

9
Sources

I Literary Sources

Our understanding of any era depends ultimately on the extent, accuracy and bias of the source materials available. The problem of literary sources is more acute for ancient history than for other periods, since the information is especially fragmentary, confused and tainted by the preconceptions and prejudices of the authors.

Of necessity, we must in the case of Agrippina rely very heavily upon literary evidence. The general issue of the written sources for the Julio-Claudian period, their relationship to one another and their trustworthiness are all highly important matters but they can only be touched on here, to the extent that they relate to the portrait drawn of Agrippina.

The obstacles faced in antiquity by an author wishing to provide authentic and reliable information about Agrippina, or any other important figure of the period with perhaps the exception of the public career of the emperor himself, were enormous. They are well laid out by Dio, when commenting on the changes brought about by the establishment of the principate in 27 BC (loosely translated):

> The government was thus transformed then for the better and for the greater safeguard of the people, for under the republic it was quite impossible for them to be protected. But subsequent events cannot be reported like earlier ones. Previously, it is clear, issues were brought before the senate and the citizen body even if they took place far away. In consequence, everybody learned about them and many noted them down and as a result, even if the accounts of some were seriously tainted by fear or favour, partisanship or hostility, a truthful picture of the issues was to some degree manifested in others who wrote of them and also in the public records. But from this time on most things started to become secret and concealed, and though some things might happen to be published they are not trusted, as being incapable of confirmation. For there is a suspicion that everything is said and done in accordance with the wishes of the powerful and their henchmen. Consequently many things that did not happen are spread about and many things that incontestably did happen are not known and virtually everything is broadcast differently from the way it happened (Dio 53.19.1–4).

Tacitus reflects a similar problem at the beginning of the *Histories,* in his observation that with the introduction of the principate the interests of peace required that all power should be concentrated into the hands of one man. Consequently, idepen-dent writers of the stature associated with the republic were no longer found and historical truth was impaired. Tacitus adds, however, that the problem arose as much from the desire to flatter as from ignorance of matters of state. It is certainly observ-able that, as the Julio-Claudian period progresses, ever-greater emphasis is placed by Tacitus on the details of the life of the emperor at the cost of serious political analy-sis. All of this reflects the eclipse of the senate's power. As that body declined in importance, so did the political significance of its *acta*. Serious developments now result not from senatorial debate or resolutions but from the political intrigue carried out behind palace walls. And because of the absence of any public accounting it was relatively easy to falsify the record.[1] Dio testifies to how this can happen. Although he is more than happy to believe the worst of Agrippina and Nero, he admits that every-thing that they did in the palace was spread by rumour and gossip and distorted by conjecture. Any activities that could be dreamt up were spread about as the truth, and simply because a report was *feasible* it was taken as *true*.[2]

Only a tiny portion of the contemporary, or near-contemporary, historical writings on the Julio-Claudian period have survived. We are led to believe by Tacitus that this was no great loss. He contrasts the now-missing authors with those of the republic and, to a lesser degree, of the Augustan age and says that the records of Tiberius, Caligula, Claudius and Nero were falsified through cowardice while the rulers were still living, and vitiated after their deaths by the still potent feelings of hatred.

The writings of the emperors themselves, and of members of their family, were one available source of information. Little use, in fact, was made of them (Suetonius in particular refers to the imperial memoirs dismissively), and most writers generally preferred works that came from a senatorial tradition.[3] Suetonius mentions a *commen-tarius*, a brief autobiographical text of Tiberius, which he seems to have seen and which he says was composed *summatim breviterque* ('sketchily and briefly').[4] In it Tiberius says that he deposed Sejanus because of his plots against the offspring of Germanicus, an explanation that Suetonius rejects, thus providing a clue to why ancient authorities like himself place little value on imperial memoirs as a viable source. Tiberius left two other sets of writings. Suetonius refers to his *commentarii* (plural), unspecified but probably different from the brief autobiography (*commentar-ius*) even though the same Latin word is used for both, and his *acta*, probably some sort of political journal. Together they were Domitian's favourite reading.[5] They are unlikely to have contained much of interest relating specifically and directly to Agrippina the Younger but would doubtless have had a great deal to say about her mother, little of it complimentary.

There are no references to autobiographical writings by Caligula, and even if they had existed they would probably have been suppressed by his successor, Claudius, who was himself a prolific writer. Suetonius and Pliny the Elder make use of a contempo-rary history by Claudius in forty-one books, which may have covered the forty-one years from the foundation of the empire to the death of Augustus (27 BC–AD 14), thus not relevant to Agrippina.[6] Claudius also wrote an autobiography in eight volumes. Its potential value for the later career of Agrippina would have been enormous, but Suetonius dismisses it as nonsense, although he conceeded its stylistic merits. Nero seems to have consulted it during the trial of Suillius in AD 58.[7]

The most important memoirs for our present purpose are, of course, those written by Agrippina herself, unfortunately now lost. Tacitus, under the year 26, records that Agrippina the Elder sought permission from Tiberius to remarry. Apart from citing Pliny for the information about Agrippina's protection of the Rhine bridge in AD 15, this is the only place in the Tiberian books of the Annals where Tacitus reveals his source, noting that he found the information in the memoirs (*commentarii*) of her daughter, Agrippina (the younger), 'who (she was the mother of the emperor Nero) left a record for posterity of her own life and of the misfortunes of her kin' (*quae Neronis principis mater vitam suam et casus suorum posteris memoravit*). He also observes that the information has been overlooked by all other writers. Pliny the Elder records that Nero was born feet first, and gives as his source the writings of Agrippina. While he does not say what form the writings took (*scribit ... Agrippina*), their identification with the memoirs mentioned by Tacitus seems a fairly safe assumption.[8] We have no other explicit citation of the memoirs.

It is far from certain when Agrippina put together her memoirs. When Tacitus alludes to her authorship he describes her as *mater Neronis*. But does this mean that she was the mother of Nero when she wrote them? Not necessarily. The phrase could simply be a vivid way of identifying her and one that would provide a nice parallel with her mother, since both were involved in trying to promote the causes of their sons. Scholarly views of this question vary. Some have argued that she wrote the record during Claudius' reign, when planning Nero's succession, and even used it as propaganda to balance Messalina's hostility. In this case, the memoirs would have ended at the point where Agrippina became Claudius' wife.[9] Most scholars, however, have Agrippina imitating Cicero, making use of her forced absence from political activities after 55 to engage in writing.[10] Paratore relates the memoirs directly to Agrippina's falling out with Nero.[11] It will be remembered that, according to Tacitus, she threatened to publish the whole history of her unlucky house, of her marriage, of her use of poison. It could then be argued that she intended to show how much pain and suffering Nero had caused her, and thus began with his breech delivery. One difficulty is that Agrippina seems in 55 to be threatening to make known the damaging information immediately, which implies that the work was already in publishable form; it is, of course, possible that the basic memoirs had already been completed and that she intended adding only a damaging postscript to them. There is, however, a general problem that there are no acknowledged citations from the latter part of the memoirs. Moreover, as already indicated (p. 169), the whole passage of Agrippina threatening to go public is suspect and may be a rhetorical fabrication.

As noted above, concrete examples of the use made of the memoirs by later authorities are very few, nor are the events related of great political significance. The breech birth of Nero would have been a traumatic personal experience for Agrippina herself, but hardly one that would change the course of Rome's history. Syme is doubtless correct in observing that the other citation, about Agrippina the Elder's desire to remarry, is of some interest because of implications of a fresh marriage for the widow of Germanicus. But of course the marriage did not take place and one is left with the impression that Tacitus used the incident, unnoted as he proclaims by other authorities, primarily to flaunt his own scholarly thoroughness. Opinion about other possible uses of the memoirs by Tacitus ranges between extremes. Fabia has argued that Agrippina the Elder's request is the only item taken by Tacitus from that particular work, and he receives some support from Walker, who observes that the historian's manner of introducing the citation suggests that the memoirs were not normally used as a source. At the other extreme is Motzo, who believes that the memoirs consisted of several volumes, and provided a whole series of incidents and episodes for the Tiberian section of the *Annals*. The fact that Tacitus might have had a low opinion of Agrippina the Younger, Motzo argues, does not preclude his use of material which would have given him an insight into the workings of the court. Motzo includes the information in Tacitus about Agrippa Postumus, the involvement in his death of Livia and Tiberius, the story of Augustus' voyage to Planosa to see Agrippa Postumus, the story of Claudius Clemens, the false Agrippa, and also the death of Augustus, with its negative portrayal of Livia. He notes that by contrast there is no trace of any use of the memoirs in *Annals* 11–14.12 Paratore, by contrast, has argued that the reluctant admiration of Tacitus when he describes Agrippina striving to put her son on the throne originates from his use of this source. Paratore also notes that after Nero's accession, where the picture of Agrippina is much less attractive, Tacitus openly discusses the differences in the sources, perhaps because he was not relying on the memoirs at this stage.[13]

Pliny the Elder specifically cites Agrippina the Younger for the information on the breech delivery. Motzo suggests that he drew on her also for his material on the fertility of Livia and Agrippina the Elder, Agrippina the Younger's unusual teeth and Augustus' final days, when the emperor was supposedly tormented by thoughts of the intrigues of Livia and Tiberius. Motzo similarly detects uses in Suetonius. He suggests that his story of the sun's rays falling on Nero may have come from the memoirs, from the same section that provides Pliny with the information on the breech birth, and that the report of Messalina sending snakes to kill Nero originated from the same source. It is difficult to assess Dio's use of the memoirs, since much of his relevant text survives only in epitome. Motzo argues that he drew on them for two predictions – Domitius' anticipation that his son Nero would be a disaster, as nothing good would come of anything born to him and Agrippina, and the prophesy that Nero would one day kill his mother. He reasons that Dio seems to have used a source available to both Suetonius, who records the first, and to Tacitus, who records the second.[14]

There is clearly little concrete evidence for the extent and nature of the imperial memoirs. What of contemporary historians? Agrippina would have been the target of official denigration at three separate periods of her life in 39 after her banishment by Caligula, after the mid 40s when she became the target of Messalina's hostility, and in 59 when she was murdered. These attacks would have paid little attention to the truth; Dio's evidence for the way the scurrilous stories circulated about her were generally believed has already been cited. Contemporary impressions of Agrippina are thus likely to have been one-sided. Moreover, they would have tended to be fixed soon after her death. There would have been little incentive for the Flavian historians to tone down any criticism and any histories published in the reign of Vespasian would be bound to perpetuate the hostile tradition, given that Agrippina had shown such animosity towards Vespasian and done so much to impede his career.[15]

Because of the loss of much of the contemporary historical writing, we must rely heavily on later extant authorities for information on Agrippina. They, in their turn, would have drawn on material that derived ultimately from the lost contemporary sources. The extent of their debt is disputed. For long it was felt that the major ancient Roman historians were highly dependent on their sources and did not engage in original research, a notion associated in particular with the Italian scholar Fabia.[16] Syme attempted to rescue the reputation of Tacitus somewhat, arguing that he used such material as the Acta Senatus, which would have included the original texts of the imperial speeches. Occasionally we are offered glimpses of Tacitus and other authorities at work, evaluating and comparing sources, but such occasions are rare. Tacitus does promise to give the names of his authorities where they differ, but unfortunately does not on the whole honour the pledge. On one occasion, he compares Cluvius and Fabius Rusticus on the issue of Burrus' loyalty, and there is also a discussion of the sources for Nero's incest. Suetonius enters into a detailed debate on the birthplace of Caligula. Dio does at times offer differing interpretations, as in his discussion of the conduct of Verginius Rufus, but avoids actually naming his sources.[17]

The scholarship on the contemporary sources and the use made of them by the later writers on the Claudian/Neronian period is vast, and can only be touched on here.[18] It is a curious irony that the most complete contemporaneous historical work, that of Velleius Paterculus, completed in AD 30, is all but neglected by later historians, probably because of its highly flattering picture of his old commander Tiberius. Of the senatorial writers of the period, the most readily identifiable is Marcus Cluvius Rufus. He is thought to have been suffect consul under Caligula, and may have been on the Palatine Hill on the occasion of Caligula's assassination. He was the herald of Nero when that emperor performed as a singer at the Neronia in Rome and had the privilege of announcing that Nero would perform the *Niobe,* which went on until late in the afternoon; so successful did he prove at the job that he was given the same duty when Nero went on his tour of Greece in 67.[19]

Cluvius' histories, according to Syme, began with Caligula and covered the reigns of Claudius and Nero, and from the late nineteenth century he has been claimed as the major source of Tacitus' *Annals* for Claudius and Nero.[20] Townend has suggested that he was not a proper annalist but wrote a 'farrago of scandals and lampoons' to try to make up for his unfortunate association with Nero. This suggestion is now questioned. Tacitus certainly treats him with respect and Pliny the Younger saw him as a historian who was true to the events. While he may have been an honest observer of events, it is worth noting that he was able to serve in turn Nero, Galba, Otho and Vitellius, and thus succeeded in maintaining the favour of the powerful.[21]

Specific references to Cluvius' work in Tacitus all relate to the reign of Nero, while Plutarch uses him as the source for the story that for a period the usurper Otho adopted the practice of adding 'Nero' to his name.[22] He was Tacitus' source for the information that Nero did not, in fact, decide to replace Burrus in AD 55, and that Agrippina was prime instigator of the incest with her son (the latter is confirmed by *ceteri auctores*).[23] Did Tacitus use him in the Claudian books? He does seem to have used a source there that is more hostile to Claudius than the one available to Dio and Suetonius, who see some positive merit in Claudius' reforms although they do portray him as being under the sway of freedmen and wives. The only major source might have been Cluvius.[24] Syme points out that in the Neronian books Tacitus refers to him simply by his nomen 'Cluvius', the single name implying that he had been formally introduced earlier in the lost Caligulan or Claudian chapters.[25] Given his closeness to Nero in the latter part of the reign, it is not likely that he was well disposed towards Agrippina.[26]

Another named source is Fabius Rusticus, friend of Seneca the Younger, whom Tacitus, the only writer to preserve his name, describes as the most eloquent of the moderns as Livy was of the ancients. Tacitus may in fact have known Fabius personally. He, Pliny the Younger and a Fabius Rusticus, usually identified as the historian, figure in the will of a wealthy Spaniard Lucius Dasumius of Cordoba, drawn up in 108.[27] Fabius published a history in AD 83/84, but we do not know where it began or where it left off, or even its precise nature. It is thought that he might have continued a history of Seneca the Elder. It has also been suggested that what he wrote was not a history proper but in fact a monograph on the Elder's son, Seneca the Younger.[28]

Tacitus draws on Fabius Rusticus for information on the shape of Britain; otherwise all the references are to the reign of Nero.[29] He is first cited in the surviving portion of the *Annals,* where he is the source for the information that Burrus was suspected of intrigue with Agrippina and saved through the intervention of Seneca. Later he is credited with the view that Nero was the instigator of incest with his mother; Tacitus is reluctant to accept his version, preferring that of Cluvius and other authorities (Suetonius follows Fabius' version).[30] As the protegé of Seneca, Fabius is likely to have been hostile towards Agrippina.

Pliny the Elder was born in AD 23/24 and died during the eruption of Vesuvius in 79. An equestrian, he entered military service and served for several years on the Rhine. He returned to Rome probably in 57 or 58, shortly before Agrippina's death, but seems to have secured no civil position and spent the next number of years in study. During the reign of Vespasian his career prospects improved; he became a personal friend of the emperor, whose son Titus he had known during his service on the Rhine. He held a number of procuratorships and ended with the command of the fleet at Misenum. The position would prove unlucky for him, since he was at Misenum when Vesuvius erupted and he was fatally determined to inspect the event. Pliny was a prolific writer; he wrote a history of the German Wars in twenty books, a work used by Tacitus and clearly the source for the notable episode of Agrippina the Elder's defence of the bridge on the Rhine in AD 15, specifically attributed by Tacitus to Pliny. He also wrote an annalistic history in thirty-one books, perhaps covering the period between 44 and 77, by which date we know it was completed. There is much speculation that these works could have provided important information for Tacitus, Dio and Suetonius, on the grounds that Pliny's *Natural History* is often the source of information for statements found in all three authors, such as Pliny's observation that Agrippina wore a gold cloak at the Fucine Lake, echoed in both Tacitus and Dio. He is cited by Tacitus along with Cluvius to refute the tradition that Nero was convinced of Burrus' divided loyalty.[31] But there are also divergences. Unlike Dio and Tacitus, Pliny blamed Nero, not Agrippina, for the murder of Marcus Silanus in 54. Moreover, Tacitus clearly has Pliny in mind when he scorns the writers who accumulate trivial data, such as statistics on buildings. In another section Tacitus dismisses as absurd Pliny's claim that Antonia, Claudius' daughter, gave her support to the Pisonian conspirators.[32] Given Pliny's debt to Vespasian, it is unlikely that his picture of Agrippina the Younger would have been a sympathetic one. Certainly in his only surviving work, the thirty-seven books of the *Natural History*, dedicated to Vespasian's son Titus, the incidental information about Agrippina is almost uniformly hostile. Pliny was a diligent collector of facts and provides us with one of the two citations from Agrippina's memoirs, and a nice eye-witness account of Agrippina at the Fucine Lake, dressed in her finery.[33]

One contemporary writer who would have insight into the activities of the Neronian court is, of course, Nero's teacher and adviser Seneca. He is not a historian in any formal sense of the word but often drew on historical or contemporary events in his philosophical works. Seneca, for all that he was at one time close to and later estranged from Agrippina, makes no reference to her in any of his extant works. So prone was he to obsequious flattery, and so willing to denigrate earlier regimes in the hope of winning favour with the current one, that any observations that he might have made would have had in any case to be treated with some caution.

Senecan authorship is claimed for a work that does not mention Agrippina but is very important for the question of her relationship with Nero at the beginning of his reign – a piece known familiarly as the *Apocolocyntosis*, a witty extended joke in a mixture of prose and verse about the death of Claudius and his reception in the next world. The text mingles humour with serious concerns about the corruption of the Claudian court, the irregularity of judicial procedures and the large number of murders. The title alludes to a *colocynta* or pumpkin, and is thought to represent a play on the word *apotheosis*, although in the extant work Claudius becomes neither pumpkin or god. That Seneca wrote a parody on the apotheosis of Claudius is established by Dio, who also provides the name, *Apocolocyntosis*. There is broad, but by no means universal, agreement that the familiar extant work is Seneca's but caution is necessary. The manuscripts ascribe it to Seneca but the ascription may not be ancient. Nor does the title *Apocolocyntosis* appear in the manuscripts. It is generally, but again not universally, accepted that the extant text, whether Senecan or not, should be dated to 54, shortly after the death of Claudius.[34]

Apart from a massive corpus of prose works, Seneca was also a prolific writer of tragedies. One of the groups of manuscripts of his plays contains an additional work, the *Octavia*, and in those manuscripts the play is attributed to him. Both the style and the specific allusions (such as to the manner of Nero's death) have led scholars to conclude almost unanimously against Senecan authorship and most place the work during the Vespasianic period. The play relates the events of 62, when Octavia is put aside by Nero and taken off to her exile and eventual death. The *Octavia* does evoke some slight sympathy for Agrippina because of Nero's cruel treatment of her but is generally hostile, as one might expect from a work written in the reign of Vespasian. It is of some value in being fairly close in time to Agrippina's own day, and in illustrating the attitude towards her in the generation following her death.

Almost contemporary with Agrippina is Josephus, a pro-Roman Jewish nationalist born in 37/38. His *Jewish War* (*BJ*) is an account of the great Jewish uprising of 66–70; a Greek version appeared in 75–9. His *Jewish Antiquities* (*Ant*), an account of the Jews down to the time of the uprising, appeared in 93–4. Josephus does allude on occasion to Agrippina. He is useful as the only source to record her interest in affairs in Judaea, and as the only source to express some doubt about the claim that Claudius was murdered by her. Unfortunately, although he is very valuable while dealing with Jewish matters, Josephus is often muddled and confused when dealing with Roman affairs, a problem aggravated by the serious corruption of his manuscripts.

What little we know of the contemporary historians is probably of greater interest to the historiographer than to the biographer of Agrippina. In the end, for literary information on her we have to rely almost entirely on the late major authorities, Dio, Suetonius and Tacitus.

Dio was a provincial aristocrat, from Nicaea in Bithynia, who held the consulship in about 205 and in 229. His history was written in Greek and, although its extent is not certain, it seems to have ranged from the early kings to the reign of Severus Alexander (222–35). It is essentially an accumulation of information with little attempt at broad synthesis or judgement, and little true analysis. Dio's opinions seem usually to be elicited from the situation at hand and do not really combine to give an overall approach to history, nor is there any consistent political theory. He claims to have used more than one source, as in the information that several trustworthy writers claimed that Seneca incited Nero to murder his mother, but there is no source cited in the extant version of his account of Agrippina. Whether or not there may have been in his original text we cannot tell (see below); it is possible that he used a speech of Publius Suillius for information about the improper relationship between Seneca and Agrippina. Very little critical judgement is applied by Dio to the assessment of the sources and little effort is made to distinguish between the absurd and the reasonable, or to cull information patently tainted by bias. In the case of Agrippina, he usefully draws attention to the process by which unfounded gossip was attached to her name but unfortunately does not take the logical step of trying himself to eliminate unfounded and basically absurd material.[35]

Dio can be useful, especially in the absence of other annalistic sources, in that he treats his material broadly in sequence, unlike Suetonius. It might therefore be expected that he would be valuable for Agrippina's early career under her brother Caligula, for which Tacitus is missing. But there are two reservations. First, Dio's annalistic scheme is far from rigid. He will sometimes treat issues thematically, out of chronological context. Moreover, he will sometimes lump together items at the end of the year that he has omitted, as in the treatment of the marriage of Caligula and Caesonia which is of considerable importance for the motivation of Agrippina and other conspirators. On one occasion Dio places the ceremony securely before Caligula's departure for the north, since he dedicated his child, born shortly after the marriage, on the Capitol in Rome, but he also places the marriage towards the end of 39, when Caligula was already in Gaul.[36]

The second complication is that there are gaps in Dio's text and as a consequence we are sometimes obliged to rely on Byzantine summaries, or epitomes. The epitomators had a tendency to excerpt rather than to summarize, and important events can be lost entirely. The original text is missing for AD 40, a crucial phase of Agrippina's early career. Serious analysis of Dio's portrait of her later activities is hampered by the accident that his original text is missing also after AD 46, just before her return to the political stage, and does not resume (and then only in part) until well after her death. The picture of Agrippina that survives from Dio is uniformly hostile, even though he recognizes that much of what was claimed about her came from gossip and speculation. The story of Agrippina carrying the urn with Lepidus' bones is the first time that she is presented vividly centre stage in Dio, and he thus introduces her in association with adultery and immorality. She is said to have seduced Claudius before their marriage and to have had a sordid affair with Pallas. Dio is the only one of the surviving literary sources to mention Agrippina between 55 and 59, again in a context of adultery, with the claim that she was Seneca's mistress.[37] He asserts that Agrippina became a second Messalina, which illustrates how little he understands her true nature.[38] It is, in fact, only after her death that Dio recognizes her importance in the dynastic scheme, calling her the daughter of Germanicus, granddaughter of Agrippa and descendant of Augustus.[39]

Suetonius was born about AD 70, perhaps in Africa, and went on to hold a number of imperial appointments under Trajan and Hadrian. He was a highly prolific writer, the *Lives of the Caesars* being his most celebrated work, composed during his period of service to Hadrian or perhaps after dismissal from his post. He was widely read in antiquity and seems also to have been popular through the Middle Ages and Renaissance. His reputation took something of a blow very early in the century when Leo charged him with being merely a compiler who did not attempt to provide discrete portraits of individual emperors. In the early 50s Steidel argued that Suetonius did, in, fact aim to provide a coherent and congruous portrait of his subjects, his view has won wide, but not universal, acceptance.[40]

Suetonius is a biographer rather than a historian. Apart from the family backgrounds and early lives of his subjects, which introduce his biographies, he tends not to follow a chronological scheme but to group issues in a loose thematical framework. Like Dio, he shows no evidence of a broad sense of history or of great political questions. Suetonius had access to important imperial archives and there is little evidence that he fabricated material. In fact, when he chose to conduct his own research, based on such diverse material as inscriptions, imperial correspondence or public records, the results can be impressive. Unfortunately most of his material is not original and where it is not he is quite willing to give an ear to any story that has come down in the tradition, no matter how implausible it might appear. This is especially true when he has the opportunity to pass on lively anecdotes. As a source for Agrippina, Suetonius suffers another disadvantage. He did not write a biography of Agrippina specifically. Thus his information tends to be scattered and selective, and is intended essentially to illustrate anecdotes about others, namely the emperors, rather than to provide inherently interesting material about her. Suetonius' picture of Agrippina is inconsistent and probably reflects his sources or even his use of anecdote to create effect. Thus her influence over Claudius is malevolent, her personality is *ferox* and *impotens*. On the other hand, he is cautious about the mushroom story. He also stresses that it was Nero who initiated the incest with his mother, while Tacitus prefers to accept the account of Cluvius and 'other authorities', that Agrippina was the instigator.[41] There are several passages where Tacitus, Suetonius and Dio are very close in their material, as, for example, in the accounts of the events surrounding Agrippina's death. This can be attributed to the use of common sources rather than to direct borrowings. Certainly Suetonius does not seem to have used Tacitus thoroughly, although it may be that there are oblique references to him, as in his *tour de force* on Caligula's birthplace, intended to show up the inadequacies of previous treatments, or his detailed defence of Nero against the unfounded charge of plagiarism made by Tacitus.[42] There is general sentiment that Dio did not use Suetonius directly, although there are enough points of agreement to suggest very strongly that in places they used the same source.[43]

Of the three surviving main sources it is to Tacitus that we must look for anything approaching a coherent picture of Agrippina. He is the outstanding historical source for the Julio-Claudian period. His general qualities as a historian have already been eluci-dated in considerable detail by generations of scholars and will not be covered here. His famous dictum that he wrote without partisanship, *sine ira ac studio*, has been subjected to much scrutiny. There can be little question that he was biased against the imperial system, but fortunately this bias does not induce him to accept foolish rumours at face value. He can be critical of his sources and he occasionally reveals how his mind works, as in his reservations about Fabius Rusticus' account of Seneca's role in replacing Burrus because of the friendship between the two men. In considering Tacitus' portrait of Agrippina, we must recognize his hostility towards the ambitious members of the imperial family; the picture is complicated by the fact that Agrippina was a woman.

The assessment of Tacitus' attitude towards the women of the Julio-Claudian period has ranged from the extremes of Wuilleumier and Bardon – that he was a misogynist, motivated by a basic hatred of women, and thus his portrait of them is unreliable for that reason – to the view of Syme and Riposati that while the portrait of Agrippina, and of other women like her, may be devastating, it is probably a fairly accurate reflection of the truth.[44] Tacitus can surely be acquitted of misogyny, in the sense of a pathological hatred of women. He sees qualities in women, as well as faults, qualities like *constantia* and *fides*, and his women are at times capable of heroism.[45] His handling of Agrippina the Elder in particular should acquit him of misogyny in this literal sense. He can be critical of her. She is described as *paulo commotior* ('somewhat too excitable', *Ann.* 1.33.5), *atrox* ('fierce', *Ann.* 4.52.3), a characteristic inherited by her daughter (*Ann.* 12.22.1, 13.13.4) and manifested also by Poppaea (14.61.3), *accensa* ('inflamed', *Ann.* 4.52.3) and *pervicax irae* ('obstinate in anger', *Ann.* 4.53.1). But in essence Agrippina the Elder was a strong woman, fighting in a just cause, and Tacitus goes out of his way to portray her defects in a way that causes the minimum damage. He allows unattractive personalities like Sejanus or Tiberius to voice the strictures against her, such as the charge that she involved herself with the troops (*Ann.* 1.69.5) or was guilty of *contuma-cia* (*Ann.* 4.12.5), or that she committed herself to *curae viriles* ('masculine ambitions') and was *impatiens aequi* ('unable to endure not being on top') and *dominandi avida* ('hun-gry for power' *Ann.* 6.25.3). At *Ann.* 4.12.7 Tacitus refers to her *tumidos spiritus* ('swollen arrogance'), but the charge is turned around by him to criticize the viciousness of those who provoked her. He does say that Germanicus told her 'to put aside her brashness' (*exueret ferociam*, Tac. *Ann.* 2.72.1), but such criticism, while honest, is softened by the awareness that she was brash by the standards of the gentle and diplomatic Germanicus.[46]

In fact, the main problem is not Tacitus' general view of women but his assessment of a particular class of women, those who sought to participate in the political process. He reflects the attitudes of his day and of his class, attitudes that go far back into Roman history. Underlying the corruption of the Julio-Claudian period, in Tacitus' view, was the never-ending cynical manoeuvring to ensure a particular successor to the principate. The contest is dominated by women, immersed in factional feuds. Note Tiberius' reasons for refusing Sejanus' request to marry his daughter, that the marriage would serve to aggravate the already intense jealousy between the various women of the household. Another recurring detail is the ambitious woman who seeks to bring down her female rival. Apicata ruined Livilla; two concubines ruin Messalina. Domitia Lepida, who is the match for Agrippina in everything, is destroyed *muliebribus causis* ('for women's reasons'), and is driven by *infensa aemulatio* ('hostile rivalry') towards Agrippina. Junia Silana was an old friend of Agrippina, but turned against her for personal reasons.

Such women not only sought indirectly to exercise power but also attempted to place a claim on a power that belonged by right and tradition to the senate and people. Notice that Tacitus says that Agrippina had Seneca recalled to help her *ad spem dominationis* ('to further her hopes for power') and she entered an affair with Lepidus *spe dominationis*.[47] Moreover, ambitious women are invariably described as beautiful, and beautiful women are stereotypically associated with vice. Poppaea's mother was the greatest beauty of her day and had bequeathed her looks to her daughter (*Ann.* 13.45); Junia Calvina, sister of Lucius Silanus, is *sane decora* and *procax* (*Ann.* 15.59.9). Satria Gallia, wife of conspirator Piso, is beautiful but *degenerem*, and guilty of *impudicitia* (*Ann.* 15.59.9).[48]

Paratore has observed that in his portrayal of Agrippina the Younger Tacitus seems to have been torn between outright hostility and reluctant admiration. While he condemned what she represented, he admired her energy and competence. Paradoxically she alone in the dynasty was worthy of power, although for women to seek such power went against the principles of basic decency. At the point of her marriage to Claudius, her 'masculine' aspects are brought out by Tacitus. She did not behave from wantonness like Messalina but was modest in her private life and did nothing shameful unless it paved the way for her tyrannical control. Paratore says that the activities that are depicted as lust in Dio and Suetonius are shown in Tacitus to be important elements in her strategy of securing a place for her son on the throne.[49] Her attitude to money further enhances this picture, that she saw it as a means of subsidizing political ambitions.[50] During the shipwreck she is the only one who does not lose her head and panic.[51]

Bias against a particular individual is not in itself an insurmountable problem in a historical account. Once it has been identified, allowance can be made for it. Much more serious is the problem that Tacitus, like historians of all periods, is inclined to think in stereotypes. He tends not to think of women, even when as powerful as Agrippina, as individuals. Note that she is given no physical description – she is simply lumped in with Junia Silana and Lepida as three beauties. This is not a matter of misogyny but rather a form of intellectual laziness. This tendency towards stereotyping is betrayed in Tacitus' language, as has been demonstrated by L.W. Rutland. There are 30 instances of the adjective *muliebris* ('female') and its adverb *muliebriter* in his works. Ten of these are neutral usages, basically 'female' as opposed to 'male'. But two-thirds are used in contexts that make a stereotypical statement. The three instances of adverbs define activities that are supposedly feminine, lamenting (*Ag.* 29.1, cf. *Ann.* 15.38.5), grumbling loudly (*Ann.* 13.13.1), or behaving weakly (*Ann.* 13.10.3). The adjectives similarly characterize lamenting (*Ag.* 4.1) and howling (*Ann.* 16.10.5, cf *Hist.* 4.18.4) as typically feminine. Silly trifles are associated with women (*Ger.* 18.3) and a crowd is female, therefore wretched (*Ann.* 1.40.3). Frivolous motives (*Ann.* 12.64.4) are typically female and advice that is female is therefore worse (*deterius*). The most common associations convey either arrogance, irrational or foolish behaviour, or sinister scheming: hence haughtiness (*Ann.* 13.14.1), lack of self-control (*Ann.* 1.4.5, 12.57.5, cf. *Ann.* 14.32.2), passion (*Ann.* 4.39.1), fanaticism (*Ann.* 14.30.2), animosities (*Ann.* 1.33.5), jealous rivalry (*Ann.* 2.43.5, cf. *Ann.* 4.40.4, 12.12.1), seductive charms (*Hist.* 1.74.1), deceit (*Ann.* 2.71.4, 11.3.2), cronyism (*Ann.* 5.2.2) and seductive plots (*Ann.* 14.2.2). In addition, there are passages where the reference to a woman might on the surface be innocent but implicitly maintains a stereotype. For example, Agrippina seeks a special kind of poison from the notorious Locusta, and we are told that the required potion was supplied *eius mulieris ingenio* ('through the talents of that *woman*', 12.66.4), reinforcing the association between women and poison.[52] The limitations of this thinking are apparent in Tacitus' account of Agrippina: when she goes to Baiae to see Nero we are told that this shrewd and highly political woman was taken in by her son's attentions, *facili feminarum credulitate ad gaudia* ('with the lax credibility that women give to things they are happy to believe', Tac. *Ann.* 14.4.2). Now serious issues are raised by this claim. Was the relationship between Agrippina and Nero in fact cordial enough for her not to have to fear a plot? Were Nero's preparations so skilful that she was not aware of them? Was there in reality no plot at all? The danger of stereotypes is that the historian does not see the need to explore such questions – the problems are set aside in a dismissive phrase. Ironically, Tacitus himself recognizes the problem. In his discussion of the supposed incest between Nero and Agrippina (Tac. *Ann.* 14.2), he notes that the account of Cluvius (that Agrippina initiated the incest) has greater support than the version of Fabius Rusticus (that Nero was the initiator). But he tellingly goes on to observe that, while the reports of Cluvius and others might well have been based on what actually did happen, it could be that the rumours were believed simply because Agrippina's track record of sexual perversions for political ends made such a story plausible.

Thus throughout Tacitus we see a number of recurring patterns. Of course, one could argue that similar political situations will provoke similar human responses. The problem is to distinguish between occasions when the historian is honestly and conscientiously recording these responses, and when he is thinking in standard types. Thus we note the theme of the ambitious woman, already married, who attaches herself to an up-and-coming man, similarly married: the story of Livilla and Sejanus to some extent is echoed by the story of Messalina and Silius (where the prospect of marriage and involvement in political power corrupts) and, while we do not have precise details, seems to be reflected in the account of Ennia and Caligula. This standard framework may well have affected the account of the relationship of Claudius and Agrippina, creating the starting-point that it had to be the result of intrigue and plot.

The parallels between Agrippina and Livia, especially in their relationship to their sons, are striking to a degree that raises suspicions. Both sons take power through the scheming of a mother, the removal by the mother of rival claimants and the poisoning of the incumbent emperor. In each case the mother tries to rule through her son, she is rebuffed by her son, and after her death it becomes clear that, for all her faults, she did act as a check on her son. Both emperors seem moderate, but after their mothers' deaths exercise evil tendencies unrestrained.[53]

Many details in Tacitus's narrative seem to be echoes of other parts. Thus his comment at the beginning of Tiberius' reign, *primum facinus novi principatus fuit Postumi Agrippae caedes* ('the first crime of the new principate was the murder of Agrippa Postumus', *Ann.* 1.6.1) is reprised at the beginning of Nero's, *prima novo principatu mors Iunii Silani proconsulis* ('the first death in the new reign was that of the proconsul Junius Silanus', *Ann.* 13.1.1).[54] Now it may well be that each of the reigns had indeed started off with a murder organized at arm's length by an ambitious woman. But, again, the danger of stereotypical thinking is that the murder of Agrippa Postumus, the fact of which, if not the details, is beyond doubt, might precondition the historian to expect a similar event later. The reference to Tiberius as 'Nero' in the immediately preceding passage (Tac. *Ann.* 1.5.6) was no doubt intended to stress that the circumstances surrounding Tiberius' accession were as sinister as those surrounding Nero's. Note the details of the deaths of Augustus and of Claudius, and in particular the roles of Livia and Agrippina. An explicit comparison is made at *Ann.* 12.69.4, where Agrippina is said to have emulated Livia in providing the exact funeral arrangements that Augustus had enjoyed. The general context of the deaths was the same: the reigning emperor has been persuaded to adopt a stepson as his heir, and the empress mother is alarmed for the safety of the scheme for which she has so long planned and decides to put her husband out of the way. The similarity of *Ann.* 12.68.3 to 1.5.6 is striking: the emperor dies suddenly but the news of his death is kept concealed until the accession of the stepson has been made certain. The empress barricades the house in which the dead emperor lies and issues reassuring reports about his health. Livia: 'Livia blocked off the house and approaches with zealous guards, and reassuring notices were released at intervals. ...' Agrippina: 'She shut off all the approaches with guards, and frequent reports were issued that the emperor's health was improving. ...' Note also that the theme of both accounts bears a resemblance to Livy's account of Tarquinius' death by Tanaquil (Livy 1.41.5).[55]

As has been made evident in the preceding narrative, the reluctance of the sources to see women like Agrippina as distinctive personalities with their own individual qualities, and faults, is the most serious obstacle facing the biographer of women of the imperial family.

Literary citations
Octavia
21: Agrippina was cruel and fierce and murdered Claudius.

44–5: Agrippina murdered Claudius and was murdered in turn by her son.

93–6: Agrippina handed over the empire to her son and was rewarded by murder.

102: Claudius was murdered.

125–9: As a favour to Poppaea, Nero shipwrecked Agrippina then had her finished off with the sword.

141–2: Claudius' marriage to Agrippina was incestuous.

150–67: Agrippina contrived the marriage of Nero and Octavia and thus took control of the empire. There was no crime she would not commit. She eventually murdered her husband, and was in turn murdered by her son.

170–1: Agrippina was grief-stricken over the death of Britannicus.

310–76: Agrippina was shipwrecked by Nero, confessed to the murder of Claudius and responsibility for the murder of Britannicus. Nero despatched assassins who stab her in the womb.

593–617: Agrippina's reward for making her son emperor was to be shipwrecked, then murdered and her statues and inscriptions destroyed. After his death, the ghost of Claudius haunted Agrippina as his and Britannicus' murderess.

634: Agrippina was murdered by Nero.

952: Agrippina once aspired to power but was murdered by her son.

Pliny the Elder

Pliny *NH* 7, *pref.*: Agrippina is cited as a source.

Pliny *NH* 7.45: As the mother of Nero, Agrippina was a misfortune for the entire world.

Pliny *NH* 7.46: Agrippina wrote that Nero was born feet-first.

Pliny *NH* 7.71: Agrippina had a double set of canines.

Pliny *NH* 33. 63: Pliny saw Agrippina in her gold cloak at the Fucine Lake.

Pliny *NH* 35.201: Agrippina ordered the award of *ornamenta praetoria* to Pallas.

Josephus

Jos. *Ant.* 20.135: Agrippina interceded on behalf of the Jews.

Jos. *Ant.* 20.148, 151: Agrippina was rumoured to have poisoned Claudius.

Jos. *BJ.* 2.249: Claudius was persuaded by Agrippina to adopt Nero.

Juvenal

Juv. *Sat.* 5.147–8, 6.620–4: Agrippina poisoned Claudius with a mushroom. (Scholiast on:)

Juv. *Sat.* 1.155: Agrippina was the lover of Tigellinus.

Juv. *Sat.* 2.29: Claudius arranged a special law to enable him to marry Agrippina.

Juv. *Sat.* 4.81: (see Suet. *Vita Passieni*)

Juv. *Sat.* 5.109: cites Probus for statement that Agrippina recalled Seneca as Nero's tutor.

Juv. *Sat.* 6.124: Nero murdered Britannicus with his mother's connivance.

Juv. *Sat.* 6.620: Agrippina poisoned Claudius.

Juv. *Sat.* 6.628: Agrippina poisoned Britannicus.

Tacitus

Tac. *Ann.* 2.41.4: Germanicus' five children accompanied him on his triumph.

Tac. *Ann.* 3.2.4: Agrippina and the other children greeted their mother as she returned with Germanicus' ashes.

Tac. *Ann.* 4.53.3: Agrippina wrote memoirs on her family.

Tac. *Ann.* 4.75.1: Agrippina married Domitius.

Tac. *Ann.* 12.27.1: Agrippina was born in Oppidum Ubiorum.

Tac. *Ann.* 11.12.1: Messalina was hostile towards Agrippina.

Tac. *Ann.* 12.1.3, 2.3: Agrippina was Pallas' recommended choice as Claudius' wife.

Tac. *Ann.* 12.3.1–2: Agrippina charmed Claudius and planned the marriage and betrothal of Nero to Octavia.

Tac. *Ann.* 12.5.1: Agrippina and Claudius had an affair.

Tac. *Ann.* 12.6.2: Vitellius lobbied for the marriage of Claudius and Agrippina.

Tac. *Ann.* 12.7.3: The senate validated the marriage of Claudius and Agrippina.

Tac. *Ann.* 12.8.1: Silanus committed suicide on the day of the marriage.

Tac. *Ann.* 12.3.2: Agrippina ensured the betrothal of Nero and Octavia.

Tac. *Ann.* 12.8.3: Agrippina secured the return of Seneca as Nero's tutor.

Tac. *Ann.* 12.7.5–7: The state fell under an almost masculine tyranny. Money was seen as a means to power.

Tac. *Ann.* 12.22.1–4: Agrippina obtained the prosecution and death of Lollia Paulina.

Tac. *Ann.* 12.25.1: Agrippina secured the adoption of Nero with the help of her lover Pallas.

Tac. *Ann.* 12.26: Agrippina received the title of Augusta. Nero's adoption was confirmed. Britannicus was now isolated.

Tac. *Ann.* 12.27.1: Agrippina gave her name to Cologne, where she was born.

Tac. *Ann.* 12.37.5: Caratacus paid homage to Agrippina.

Tac. *Ann.* 12.41.7: On Agrippina's urging, Britannicus' tutors were removed.

Tac. *Ann.* 12.42.1: Agrippina secured the praetorian command for Burrus.

Tac. *Ann.* 12.42.3: Agrippina was granted the *carpentum*.

Tac. *Ann.* 12.42.5: Agrippina protected Vitellius from prosecution.

Tac. *Ann.* 12.56.5: Agrippina attended the draining of the Fucine Lake in a cloak of gold.

Tac. *Ann.* 12.57.4: Agrippina charged Narcissus with embezzlement.

Tac. *Ann.* 12.59.1: Agrippina destroyed Statilius Taurus.

Tac. *Ann.* 12.64.4–6, 65.1–2: Domitia Lepida was eliminated.

Tac. *Ann.* 12.65.2: Narcissus' suspicions about Agrippina's intentions grew.

Tac. *Ann.* 12.65.4: Narcissus claimed that Agrippina had an affair with Pallas.

Tac. *Ann.* 12.66–7: Agrippina poisoned Claudius.

Tac. *Ann.* 12.68: Agrippina delayed the announcement of Claudius' death to ensure the loyalty of the troops.

Tac. *Ann.* 13.1.1: Agrippina brought about the death of Marcus Silanus.

Tac. *Ann.* 13.1.4: Narcissus was forced to suicide by Agrippina.

Tac. *Ann.* 13.2.3: Seneca and Burrus had to face the *ferocia* of Agrippina. Passionate for power, she enjoyed the support of Pallas.

Tac. *Ann.* 13.2.6: Agrippina received exceptional honours.

Tac. *Ann.* 13.5.2: Agrippina opposed measures that subverted the policy of Claudius.

Tac. *Ann.* 13.5.2–3: Agrippina observed sessions of the senate and attempted to meet the Armenian ambassadors.

Tac. *Ann.* 13.6.2: There was popular concern that Nero was ruled by a woman.

Tac. *Ann.* 13.12.1: Agrippina's control over Nero began to slip.

Tac. *Ann.* 13.13.1–4: Agrippina opposed Nero's affair with Acte, first aggressively then diplomatically.

Tac. *Ann.* 13.13.5–6: Nero offered Agrippina clothes from the palace and caused offence.

Tac. *Ann.* 13.14: Pallas was removed from office, which reportedly elicited threats against Nero from Agrippina.

Tac. *Ann.* 13.15.1–2: Agrippina's threats provoked Nero to eliminate Britannicus.

Tac. *Ann.* 13.16.6: Agrippina was terrified on the death of Britannicus.

Tac. *Ann.* 13.18.3–5: Agrippina was driven to seek the support of Octavia and amassed money for the coming conflict with Nero. He deprived her of her guard and moved her to the house of Antonia.

Tac. *Ann.* 13.20–1: Junia Silana brought charges of rebellion against Agrippina, who was allowed a hearing and successfully defended herself.

Tac. *Ann.* 13.42.5: Seneca corrupted the beds of the imperial princesses.

Tac. *Ann.* 14.1.1–4: Poppaea urged the murder of Agrippina.

Tac. *Ann.* 14.2: Agrippina planned incest with her son.

Tac. *Ann.* 14.2.4: Agrippina was the lover of Lepidus and Pallas.

Tac. *Ann.* 14.3–8: Nero was determined to murder Agrippina; he contrived the device of the collapsing boat and, when that proved unsuccessful, sent agents from the fleet to murder her.

Tac. *Ann.* 14.9.1: Nero may have inspected his mother's body.

Tac. *Ann.* 14.9.2–5: Agrippina was cremated, and thus brought about the prophecy that Nero would slay her and rule.

Tac. *Ann.* 14.10: Thanks were given for Nero's deliverance from Agrippina throughout Italy, but he was haunted by her ghost.

Tac. *Ann.* 14.11: Nero charged his late mother with plotting against him.

Tac. *Ann.* 14.12.1–4: Thanksgivings and portents marked Agrippina's death.

Tac. *Ann.* 14.12.5–7: The old enemies of Agrippina returned from exile.

Tac. *Ann.* 14.13: Nero was persuaded of the unpopularity of Agrippina.

Tac. *Ann.* 14.57.1: Tigellinus accused the prefect Faenius of *amicitia* with Agrippina.

Tac. *Ann.* 15.50.4: Tigellinus accused Faenius of an affair with Agrippina.

Tac. *Ann.* 15.67.3: Subrius Flavus explained his participation in the Pisonian conspiracy as a consequence of Nero's murder of Agrippina.

Tac. *Ann.* 16.14.3: Publius Anteius' affection for Agrippina earned him the animosity of Nero.

Tac. *Ann.* 16.21.1: Thrasea Paetus was put to death, hated among other things because he walked out of the senate when charges were made against Agrippina.

Suetonius

Suet. *Cal.* 7: Agrippina and her sisters were born *triennio*.

Suet. *Cal.* 15.3: The sisters were included in oaths and consular proposals.

Suet. *Cal.* 24.1–3: Caligula committed incest openly with his sisters, gave them to his favourites and accused them of adultery.

Suet. *Cal.* 39.1: Caligula sold the property of his sisters in Gaul.

Suet. *Cal.* 59: Caligula's sisters gave him a proper burial.

Suet. *Claud.* 26.3: Claudius was ensnared by the charms of Agrippina. A special law was enacted to allow their marriage. Claudius and Agrippina attended the marriage of a centurion.

Suet. *Claud.* 29.1: Claudius was under the complete control of his wives.

Suet. *Claud.* 29.2: Claudius and Agrippina married on the first day of the year.

Suet. *Claud.* 39.2: While planning marriage with Agrippina, Claudius called her his child and ward.

Suet. *Claud.* 43: Near the end of his life Claudius regretted the marriage with Agrippina.

Suet. *Claud.* 44: Claudius was murdered by Agrippina.

Suet. *Nero* 5.2: Domitius acknowledged the son (Nero) born to Agrippina.

Suet. *Nero* 6.1: Domitius foresaw disaster from a son born of him and Agrippina.

Suet. *Nero* 6.2: Agrippina resented Caligula's suggestion that she name her son Claudius.

Suet. *Nero* 6.4: Agrippina put the snakeskin in a bracelet for Nero.

Suet. *Nero* 7.2: Nero testified against Domitia Lepida to please his mother.

Suet. *Nero* 28.2: Nero had a mistress who resembled Agrippina. Nero and his mother committed incest in his litter.

Suet. *Nero* 34.1: Agrippina offended Nero by her strict behaviour. She was deprived of her German guard and sent from the palace, and subjected to harassment.

Suet. *Nero* 34.2: Schemes to eliminate Agrippina were pondered.

Suet. *Nero* 34.3: Nero murdered his mother and viewed her corpse. He was haunted by her ghost.

Suet. *Nero* 39.3: An Atellan farce suggested that Nero tried to drown his mother.

Suet. *Nero* 52: Agrippina prevented Nero from studying philosophy.

Suet. *Galb.* 5.1: Agrippina set her cap at Galba.

Suet. *Vesp.* 4.2: Vespasian was eclipsed through the hostility of Agrippina.

Suet. *Vesp.* 9.1: Vespasian rebuilt the temple of Divus Claudius, begun by Agrippina and destroyed by Nero.

(Suet.) *Vita Passieni:* Passienus married Agrippina, Caligula perhaps implied that he had committed incest with Agrippina, Passienus was murdered by Agrippina, whom he made his heir.

Dio

Dio 58.20.1: Agrippina was the wife of Domitius.

Dio 59.3.3–4: Caligula bestowed honours on his sisters then came to hate them (except Drusilla).

Dio 59.7.4: With her sisters and Caligula, Agrippina watched races from the front seat.

Dio 59.9.2: Consuls took oaths of allegiance to Agrippina and her sisters.

Dio 59.22.6: Caligula and Lepidus had an improper relationship with Agrippina and Livilla.

Dio 59.22.8: Agrippina and Livilla were banished by Caligula, and Agrippina was made to carry Lepidus' bones.

Dio 59.23.8: The supporters of Agrippina and Livilla were put on trial and forced to resign their offices.

Dio 59.23.9: Tigellinus had an affair with Agrippina.

Dio 59.26.5: Caligula had an affair with Agrippina and her sisters.

Dio 60.4.2: Agrippina was recalled from exile by Claudius.

Dio 60.31.6: Agrippina and Claudius had a premarital affair.

Dio 60.31.8: Claudius married Agrippina with the help of freedmen and Vitellius.

Dio 60.32.1–2: Agrippina gained control over Claudius and achieved the adoption of Nero.

Dio 60.32.2: Agrippina manipulated all sectors of society.

Dio 60.32.2: Agrippina recalled Seneca as tutor.

Dio 60.32.3: Agrippina murdered Lollia Paulina.

Dio 60.32.5–6a: Agrippina removed all supporters of Britannicus and the prefect of the guard.

Dio 60.33.1: Agrippina had more power than Claudius and greeted everyone in public.

Dio 60.33.21: Agrippina received the *carpentum*.

Dio 60.33.2a: Agrippina received the title of Augusta.

Dio 60.33.2b: Agrippina secured the banishment of Calpurnia.

Dio 60.33.3a: Agrippina won over Narcissus and Pallas.

Dio 60.33.3: Agrippina wore a gold cloak at the draining of the Fucine Lake.

Dio 60.33.7: Agrippina gave audiences to ambassadors with Claudius.

Dio 60.33.9–10: Agrippina arranged for Nero to make vows for Claudius' recovery from illness, and persuaded Claudius to name Nero as successor.

Dio 60.33.12: Agrippina wanted the title of empress. She lent assistance during a fire.

Dio 60.34.1–4: On Claudius' rapprochement with Britannicus Agrippina became alarmed and murdered him.

Dio 60.34.4: Narcissus had been sent to Campania by Agrippina before Claudius' death.

Dio 60.35.2: Nero and Agrippina pretended to mourn Claudius' death.

Dio 61.2.2: Agrippina heard a prophecy that Nero would rule and kill her.

Dio 61.2.3: Domitius understood his wife's character.

Dio 61.3.2: At first Agrippina managed all matters of state. She had an affair with Pallas.

Dio 61.3.3–4: Agrippina tried to meet the Armenian embassy. Seneca and Burrus blocked her from public life.

Dio 61.4.5: Friends advised Nero to stand up both to Agrippina and to Seneca and Burrus.

Dio 61.5.4: Agrippina tried to discourage Nero's extravagance.

Dio 61.6.4: Agrippina brought about the murder of Marcus Silanus.

Dio 61.7.1–3: Nero's affair with Acte caused Agrippina distress.

Dio 61.8.4–6: Agrippina lost her guard, leading to wild rumours.

Dio 61.10.1: Seneca was charged with being Agrippina's lover.

Dio 61.11.3–4: Agrippina tried to seduce Nero, as she had seduced her uncle Claudius. Nero had a mistress who resembled her.

Dio 61.12.1–3: Nero was persuaded by Poppaea, and reportedly by Seneca, to murder his mother. Nero took his mother to Campania on the collapsible ship.

Dio 61.13: On the failure of the collapsible ship, agents from the fleet were sent to finish off Agrippina.

Dio 61.14: Nero inspected the body of his mother, and charged that she had plotted against him and claimed that she had committed suicide. Nero was haunted.

Dio 61.16.1: Nero returned to Rome after the murder of Agrippina.

Dio 61.16.2a: Agrippina's statues were destroyed.

Dio 61.16.2.2: People openly claimed that Nero had murdered his mother.

Dio 61.16.4: Sacrifices were held in honour of Agrippina.

Dio 61.17.2: A festival was established in honour of Agrippina.

Dio 62.6.3: Boudicca claimed that Rome was ruled by Messalina and Agrippina.

Sources making limited allusions

Phlegon, *Mir.* (*FGH* 2.1179, VII): A Syrian woman changed sex on Agrippina's estate at Mevania in AD 53.

Plut. *Ant.* 87.4: Agrippina bore a son to Domitius, married Claudius and was murdered by Nero.

Philostratus, *Apoll.* 5.32: Claudius was so much under the control of women that they say he was murdered by them.

Boethius, *Cons.* 2.6.4: Nero inspected Agrippina's corpse.

Orosius 7.5.9: Caligula committed incest with his sisters, exiled them and ordered their deaths.

Eutropius 7.12.3: Caligula committed incest with his sisters, exiled them and ordered them killed.

Jerome *ap Eus.* 178 (Helm) AD 40: Caligula committed incest with his sisters and ordered them exiled then killed.

Aurelius Victor *Caes.* 3.10: Caligula committed incest with his sisters.

Aurelius Victor *Caes.* 4.12–13: Agrippina married and poisoned Claudius.

Aurelius Victor *Caes.* 4.15: Through Agrippina's scheming, corrupt praetorians concealed the news of Claudius' death to ensure the succession of Nero.

Anon. *Epit. de Caes.* 3.4: Caligula committed incest with all three sisters.

Anon. *Epit. de Caes.* 3.10: Claudius married Agrippina, who poisoned him.

Anon. *Epit. de Caes.* 3.12: Through Agrippina's scheming, corrupt praetorians concealed the news of Claudius' death to ensure the accession of Nero.

II Material Sources

The material sources for Agrippina have been arranged here in three categories: sculpture, coins and inscriptions. Papyri are also of some value for occasional background information on her life and career, but have little direct relevance, in contrast to their great importance, for instance, for information on her grandmother, Antonia the Younger (see Kokkinos (1992), passim).

Sculpture

The following abbreviations are used:

F= Fittschen, K. & Zanker, P., *Katalog der römischen Porträts in den Capitolinischen Museen und den anderen kommunalen Sammlungen der Stadt Rom* III (1983, Mainz); PL.= large plates (Tafel), pl.= small plates (Beilage); P= Polaschek, K., 'Studien zu einem Frauenkopf im Landesmuseum Trier und zur weiblichen Haartracht der iulisch-claudischen Zeit', *TZ* 35 (1972), 141–210; T I= Trillmich, W., 'Ein Bildnis der Agrippina Minor von Milreu/ Portugal', *MDAI* (M) 15 (1974), 184–202; T II= Trillmich, W., 'Julia Agrippina als Schwester des Caligula und Mutter des Nero', *Hefte des Archäologischen Seminars der Universität Bern* 9 (1983), 21–38.

The sculpted heads of Roman imperial figures are rarely found in association with their inscribed bases. Their identification is therefore based primarily on their resemblance to coins, although the process can be helped by general stylistic features which provide broad clues to dating.

Identifications are often a matter of personal judgement and can be highly speculative. In the past there was a tendency to assign every superior Roman portrait to a member of the imperial family. Beginning with Ludwig Curtius, there has grown the recognition that a distinction must be drawn between private and 'imperial' portraits. The portraits of the emperors and their family would have been copied and distributed widely. This would result in a series of replicas all based on a common original type, although local craftsmen might introduce their own idiosyncracies. Important members of the family would, of course, have several types, especially if they enjoyed long lives. The methodology of much modern scholarship involves grouping extant copies in their appropriate type-categories. It has been suggested, for instance, that the small bronze of Agrippina found at Alba Fucens (see p. 130) might be an example of a 'type piece', taken out into the provinces to be copied.

The context of a sculpted piece, if known, will provide another useful clue to identity. An excellent example is the *sebasteion* (sanctuary) at Aphrodisias, discovered in 1979 to the east of the centre of the city. It was dedicated to Aphrodite and the imperial family, an appropriate pair since Venus was the mother of Aeneas, the mythical founder of the Julian line. The complex consists of a monumental gateway on the west, which led into two long porticoes on the north and south, at the east end of which stood a temple. The porticoes were three stories high, with relief panels flanked by columns in the two upper stories. The 180 panels (of which about eighty have survived) were varied in their subject matter – mythology, allegory and, important for our purposes, imperial figures of the Julio-Claudian era. This last group provides a rich store of Julio-Claudian iconography and can be surprisingly detailed. Two reliefs, probably the most striking pieces of all Agrippina's surviving sculpture, come from this source (Pls 18 & 19).

There must at one time have been numerous sculpted portraits of Agrippina through-out the empire, the great majority of which would have disappeared soon after her death. Dio 61.16.1 speaks of her statues being destroyed in Rome on Nero's return to the city in AD 59. In the near-contemporary *Octavia* 610–11, the ghost of Agrippina laments that her son ordered the destruction of her statues (and her inscriptions) throughout the empire. But it seems safe to assume that some would have escaped.

No statue base bearing Agrippina's name has been securely linked to an extant statue. The mid-nineteenth-century excavations in the Etruscan town of Caere produced an inscription of Agrippina the Younger (see below, Inscriptions, no. 8), and a full-length statue found at the same site was initially linked to the inscription (see Bernouilli (1969) II. 183, 376). The statue is now usually identified as Drusilla, for whom an inscription was also found, or as Agrippina the Elder (see Fuchs (1989), II, 76–9, Giuliano (1959), no. 32; Rose (1993), 199–200); note that de Ruyt (1972), 161 still accepts Bernoulli's attribution to Agrippina the Younger. Given the nature of the material, it is impossible to produce a secure corpus of portraits of Agrippina (or of any member of the imperi-al family), and attributions vary from scholar to scholar (see, most recently, Wood [1995]). But something approaching a consensus has emerged on the key types, based very heavily on comparisons with coin portraits.

Reliefs
Two examples from Aphrodisias (see above).

Sculpture in round
I Copenhagen/Ancona Group (Claudian)
The most influential type is represented by the Copenhagen/Ancona group. The hair is parted in the middle and lies flat for a short distance from each side of the straight part-ing, then rises in tiers of curls over the temples. The centres of the curls are normally drilled. At the back the hair is tied in a pony tail, and long corkscrew strands (usually two) fall from behind the ear. On the face the lips tend to be tightly set, with the upper one slightly protruding above the lower. The cheek bones are fairly prominent, the chin broad. The eyes are large. Most of the assigned portraits display an air of superiority and there is a slightly masculine cast to the face. The nose tends to be prominent, with a rounded tip.

1 Copenhagen, Ny Carlsberg Glyptotek 636. Fig.3
2 Ancona, Museo Nazionale delle Marche. T I pl. 39
3 Aphrodisias. Smith (1987), no. 3, pl. 8)
4 Aphrodisias. Smith (1987), no. 11, pl. 24
5 Athens. Watzinger (1901), pl. 13
6 Mantua, Galleria e Museo di Palazzo Ducale. F pls 4 a–d
7 Oxford, Ashmolean Museum. Gardner (1922), pl. 7 (identified as Livia)
8 Philippeville. T I 189, n.25. Gsell (1898) pl. 9.3
9 Philippeville. T I 189, n.25. Gsell (1898) pl. 10.1
10 Rome, Museo Nazionale (Terme). Inv. 56964. Felletti Maj (1953), pl. 110
11 Rome, Museo Nazionale (Terme). Inv. 121316. Felletti Maj (1953), pl. 111

12 Rome. Vatican, Museo Chiaramonti LIII 3 Inv 2084. F pls 3c–d, Wood (1988), fig. 12

13 Rome. Vatican, Museo Chiaramonti XIX 5 Inv. 1480. F pls 5a–d, Wood (1988), fig. 1

14 Sabratha, Museum. Caputo (1950), pl. 9

15 St. Bertrand de Comminges, Museum. Goessler BullMusImp 3 (1932), pl. 4

16 Vicenza. Museo Civico E I 254. T I pls 42,43a

17 Vienna, Kunsthistorisches Museum I 1550. F pls 5a–d

II Milan/Florence Group (Claudian)

Close to the Copenhagen/Ancona type, this group is distinguished from the others primarily by a number of small curls on the forehead.

1 Milan, Civico Museo Archeologico Inv A 1132. Fig. 1

2 Florence, Galleria degli Uffizi. Inv. 1914. 115. Poulsen (1928), pls 84

3 Chiete, Museo Nazionale di Antichità. de Ruyt (1971/72), pls 2–5

4 Cos, Archeological Museum. Guiliano (1959), 160 no. 17

5 Cuenca, Museo. Museum Guide (1979), pl. 42

6 Faro, Museu Arqueologico, T I pls 35–7

7 Madrid, Museo Arqueologico Nacional Inv. 34.433, T I pl .45

8 Olympia, Archeological Museum L147. Wood (1988), figs 8–9

9 Rome, Vatican, Candelabrum Gallery, V 23 Inv. 2762. Lippold Vat.Kat. III.2. pls 168–9

10 Rome, Vatikan, Galleria delle Statue 408 Inv. 558. F pls 3a–b

11 Tripoli, Museum, T I pl. 46

III Stuttgart Group (Neronian)

A minor variant has been identified, dated to the Neronian period, where the rows of curls start immediately at the centre parting. The features are softer, stressing the resemblances to Nero.

1 Stuttgart:Hausman, Romerbilnisse (1975) no. 8

2 Copenhagen, Ny Carlsberg Glyptotek 634

3 Naples. Mus. Naz. 5612

4 Naples. Mus. Naz. 5612

5 Petworth, Petworth House F pls 3a–b

6 Torlonia, Torlonia 528 (perhaps)

IV Naples/Parma Group (Caligulan)

This group shares certain characteristics with the Copenhagen/Ancona and Milan/Florence group, but also has links with portraits of Caligula (Polaschek 200– 10).

1. Naples Museo Nazionale 6242. Saletti (1968), 120 n.52

2. Parma, Museo Nazionale di Antichità Inv 830. Saletti (1968), pl. 3–4

V Adolphseck 22 Group (Caligulan)

This group has features of the Caligulan period, and is assigned by some to Drusilla. The features are close to the main Agrippina types, although the hair is different, with forehead curls and wavy hair laid out in concentric arcs. The identification with Agrippina is laid out in Trillmich (1983), but see Polaschek, 210–20. Trillmich thinks that the type series might have been broken with the banishment of Agrippina and Livilla in AD 39.

1 Schloss Fasanerie, Fulda, Adolphseck 22. Fig. 2

2 Cambridge, Fitzwilliam Museum, inv. GR 116 – 1937

3 Huelva, Museo MDAI(M) 22 (1981), pl.29

4 London, British Museum, Gems no. 3946. P pl.202.2, 205.7, T II 5.3–4

5 Providence, Rhode Island School of Design, Museum, acc. no. 56.097. P pl.203.5, 205.8

6 Rome, Museo Nazionale (Terme) T II pls 6.1–3

7 Toledo, Casa y Museo del Greco. inv. 146. T II pls 7.1–4

Two posthumous heads have been assigned to Agrippina. Their ascription is far from certain: (a) a colossal head from Trajan's Market (no. inv.): Fittschen (1983) 6, PL. 6, Wood (1988), 424–4, figs 15–16, Eck (1993), 88 n.196; (b) head from Cologne (Römische-Germanisches Museum, inv. 564): Wood (1988), 425; Salzmann (1990), 178; Eck (1993), 88 n.196

Cameos

1 Paris, Cabinet des Médailles. no. 277 T II pl. 2.1. Trillmich has noted the resemblance of the Adolphseck type to this familiar cameo in Paris (Megow [1986], 303, no. D.39, pl. 18.1). The profile bust (head) is accompanied by a small female figure on the left and a cornucopia on the right, in which resides a draped figure of a youth. The scene has been traditionally interpreted as Messalina with her children, Octavia and Britannicus. On close observation, however, the small female is seen to have a helmet and shield and developed breasts. She cannot be Octavia and is probably a personification, possibly Roma. The head of the youth has now been recognized as a later addition. Trillmich identifies the portrait as Agrippina the Younger's, and dates the cameo to the period after her marriage to Claudius, because of the diadem. Trillmich (1983); Sande (1985), 190; Wood (1992), 231. Megow (1986), D. 39, identifies the main figure as Drusilla; Fuchs (1990) 108 has argued for Caesonia, with her daughter Drusilla.

2 Vienna, Kunsthistorisches Museum 19 (inv. no. IX a63): Megow A81, pl.31, 32.1.2.4. Two pairs of jugate heads emerge from a cornucopia, males on the outer surface, females on the inner. First identified by Fuchs (1936) as Claudius and Agrippina the Younger on the left, Germanicus and Agrippina the Elder on the right. Wood (1988), 422; Künzl (1994). Fig. 6

3 Paris, Cabinet des Médailles no. 276. Megow A 86, pl. 27.3. Claudius as Triptolemus and Agrippina as Ceres, in a carriage drawn by snakes.

4 Paris, Cabinet des Médailles. no. 280 T II pl. 4.1

5 Paris, Cabinet des Médailles. no. 283 T II pl. 4.2; Fuchs (1990), Abb.4

6 Paris, Cabinet des Médailles no. 286; Babelon (1897), 149, no. 286 pl. 32

7 Cologne, Dom (Dreikönigenschrein IB a17) Simon (1960) 145 Anm 32 Abb 9, Weinstock (1971), pl. 39.11. A seated male at the left wears a breastplate and an aegis on his breast. In his right hand he holds a sceptre. A spike/thorn comes from his head. A female facing him holds a laurel crown in her right hand and a cornucopia in her left.

8 London, British Museum. Gems 3604. T II pl. 3.1, Fuchs (1990), abb. 3

9 Leningrad, Hermitage. inv. 335. T II. pl. 4.3

10 Leningrad, Hermitage. inv. 343 (?) T II. pl. 4.4

11 Paris, Cabinet des Médailles 276 (the Grand Camée). Kaspar (1975), 61, Jucker (1977), 211 and Megow (1987), A85 think that the Grand Camée is Claudian and that the couple on the right are Claudius and Agrippina.

III Inscriptions

For military and social history inscriptions are of crucial importance. For more narrowly political history they tend to be less significant. Inscriptions referring to the imperial family are numerous throughout the empire; *Octavia* 610–11 indicates that Agrippina's inscriptions, like her statues, were obliterated. But many survived. The honours paid to figures like Agrippina in the provinces do not in themselves provide a reliable guide to the status that they actually enjoyed in Rome, although such material might be of interest in showing the parts of the empire where they seem to be held in high regard. In Agrippina's case, it would be particularly useful if inscriptions datable to 55–9 could be identified, to indicate whether her status throughout the empire was affected by her apparent eclipse in Rome. Of indirect value is the record of the Arval priesthood. This body was made up of twelve men, in addition to the emperor. It kept a detailed account of its rituals, inscribed on stone, many of them associated with the imperial family. In the case of Agrippina, the Arval record is *directly* useful only in providing the date (though not the year) of her birthday, and, like the coins, testifying (as do other inscriptions) to the frequent use of her title *Augusta* (birthday: Smallwood 21.17; title *Augusta*: Smallwood 17.3, 21.17, 110.3, 101, 264.3–4). But the record is of considerable indirect value in recording the movements and careers of the figures who made up the brotherhood, who tend to represent the élite of the day.

The following list is meant to illustrate the range of inscriptions relating to Agrippina the Younger. It is not a complete catalogue (see also Hahn [1992], 186–207) nor does it offer the whole of the inscription (only the relevant sections of their text have been included), or a definitive reading of the part that is printed. It is assumed that where Agrippina is called Augusta an inscription is not earlier than AD 50. The Greek equivalent, Sebaste, may have been used more casually from 49.

The ascription to Agrippina the Younger cannot be guaranteed in every case, since inscriptions of Agrippina and her mother are sometimes hard to distinguish.

1   CIL 2.963

 Mora (Arrucia) in Portugal

 Known only from copies

 Hübner's reconstruction: IULIAE AGRIPPINAE [*neronis*] CAES(aris) AUG(usti) GERMAN(ici) *matri aug*(ustae) N(ostrae)

 Julia Agrippina, our Augusta, mother of (Nero) Caesar Augustus (text very uncertain)

 54–9(?)

J. de Encarnação, Conimbriga 28 (1989), 157–67 argues that the inscription refers to Agrippina the Elder

2　ILS 222 (Smallwood 100)

Rome, on Triumphal Arch over Via Lata

IULIAI AUG AGRIPPINAI GERMANICI CAISARIS F

Julia Augusta Agrippina daughter of Germanicus Caesar and wife of Claudius together with dedications to Antonia, Nero and Germanicus)

Dated: precisely to 51/52 (see Barrett [1991])

3　CIL 6.8720

Rome

AGRIPPINAE GERMANICI CAISAR F

Agrippina daughter of Germanicus Caesar

4　CIL 6.8834

Rome

AGRIPPINAE GERMANICI CAESARIS IULIAE

Agrippina daughter of Germanicus Caesar

5　CIL 6.31287

Rome

AGRIPPINA DIVI CLAUD[*i*/ GERMANIC[*i*/ CAESARIS [*f*

Agrippina wife of Divus Claudius and daughter of Germanicus Caesar

54–9

6　CIL 9. 6362

Rome

IULIA[*e agrippinae/ germ*]/MANICI CAES/*aris f*

Julia Agrippina daughter of Germanicus Caesar

Reign of Tiberius

See Torelli (1963), 255

7　CIL 10.1418

Herculaneum

iuliae germ[*anici f*/ AGRIPPINAE TI CLA[*udi*

Agrippina daughter of Germanicus and wife of Claudius

49–54

8　ILS 223

Caere

IULIAE AUGUSTAE GERMANICI CAESARIS *f*] AGRIPPINAI TI C[*laudiC*]*aisa*[*ris Augusti*

Julia Augusta Agrippina daughter of Germanicus Caesar and wife of Tiberius Claudius (Augustus)

50?–4

9　AFA (Smallwood 19.6)

Rome

AGRIPPINAE AUGUSTAE

6 November, 57

10 AFA (Smallwood 21.17, 32)

Rome

AGRIPPINAE AUG(ustae)

6 November, 15 December 58

11 Fast Ant CIL 10.6638

Rome

AGRIPP(inae) IUL(iae)

November 6

12 ILS 220

Grove of Diana at Aricia

PRO [*sa*]LUTE TI. [*CLaud*]I CAESARIS [*Aug. Germ*]ANICI ET IULIAE [*Agrippinae Aug. et T*]I CLAUDI BRITANNICI [*Caesaris et Neronis*] Claudi Caesaris

For the welfare of Tiberius Claudius Caesar and Julia (Agrippina Augusta?) and Tiberius Claudius Britannicus and Nero Claudius Caesar

After the adoption of Nero in 50, perhaps shortly after, given the prominence of Britannicus

13 Corinth AE 1927.2

p]ROCURATORI CAESARIS ET AUGUSTAE AGRIPPINAE

(To the procurator of) Caesar and Agrippina Augusta

Probably 54–9

14 Espérandieu ILG 628

Castel-Roussillon, Narbonensis

Agrippi]NA soro[RI

Agrippina (?)

Consulship of Caligula and L. Apronius, January 39

15 Espérandieu ILG 629

Castel-Roussillon, Narbonensis

Agri]PPINAE GERMAN[ICI CAESARIS FILIAE

Identical pair

Agrippina daughter of Germanicus Caesar

16 IG XII. 2.172b; ILS 8789; IGR 4.78

Mytilene (Greek)

NERONI KAI DROUSO KAI AGRIPPINA KAI DRUSILLA NEA APHRODITE TOIS KASIGENTOISI
  TO AUTOKRATOROS GAIO KAISAROS

Nero and Drusus and Agrippina and Drusilla the New Aphrodite, the siblings of Imperator Gaius Caesar

Reign of Caligula, probably after the death of Drusilla (38–41)

17 IG XII. 2.211 (CF. 213, 232); IGR 4.81

Mytilene (Greek)

TAN GYNAIKA TO SEBA [*s*] TO NEAN THEAN BOLAA[*n*]SEBATEN … IOYLIA AGRIPPEINAN

Wife of the Augustus the new Goddess Augusta Boulaia … Julia Agrippina (wife of Claudius)

Epithet of a god or goddess with a statue in the Council Chamber (Boule)

49–54

18 CIG 2960

Ephesus (Greek)

ag]RIPPEINES … [*the*]AS [*s*]YN KLAYDIA MI[…

To Claudia (daughter of Claudius) and Divine Agrippina (mother or daughter?)

19 AE 1930.85; J. Keil, 'Vorläufiger Bericht über die Ausgrabungen in Ephesos',
   Jahreshefte des österreichischen Archäologischen Instituts in Wien 26 (1930) 6–66

   Ephesus (Greek)

   [*n*]ERONI KLAYDIO KAS[*a*]RI SE[*ba*]STOI GERMANIKOI TO AYTOKRATORI [Ioulia]
   AGRIPPEINE SEBASTEI TH MATRI AYT[*oy*] KAI OCTAOYIA TH GYNAIKI TOY A Y T O K R A
   TOROS

   Dedication to Nero (as emperor), Agrippina Augusta and Octavia

   54–9

20 Ditt³ 809

   Delphi (Greek)

   SEBASTEN AGRIPPEINAN SEBASTOY NERONIS METERA

   Agrippina Augusta, mother of Nero Augustus

   54–9

21 Herzog (1922), 239 n.3; Maiuri (1925), no. 468 (cf. 475); see Robert
   (1960), 291; Price (1984), 86

   Cos (Greek)

   Pair of inscriptions on a base:

   Side A: TIBE(ri)OI KLAYDIOI KAISARI/SEBASTOI GERMANIKOI DII/ SOTERI KAI
   AGRIPEINEI/ SEBASTE(*i*)DEMETRI/KARPOPHOROI

   Side: B: SOTERI KAI AGRIPPEINIAI/ SEBASTAI DAMATRI

   Agrippina Augusta Demeter

   50–4

22 Herzog (1922), 237 n.2

   Asclepeion, Cos (Greek)

   Inscriptions written on either side of a dedication slab from a statue base:

   Side A: AGRIPPEINAN TAN GERMANIKOY KAISAROS THYGATERA, GYNAIKA
   TOY ANTHUPATOY GAIHOY SALLOYSTIOY GRISPOY PASSIENOY EKI[*tioy tan*]
   EYERGETIN TOY DAMOY

   Agrippina, daughter of Germanicus Caesar, wife of proconsul Gaius Sallustius
   Crispus

   Early 40s

   Side B: IOYLIAN SEBASTAN AGRIPPINAN TAN GYNAIKA TOY SEBASTOY TIBERIOY KLA
   DIOY KAISAROS GERMANIKOY AYTOKRATOPOS SOTEROS KAI KTISTA TAS POLIOS

   Julia Augusta Agrippina wife of Claudius (as emperor)

   50–4

   Side B was supposedly an updated version

   Hirschfeld (1905), 26 accepts the inscription as genuine, as do Vogel-Weidemann
   (1982), 327, Eck (1993), 24

23 IGR 4.208 (= CIG 3610; Smallwood 101)

   Ilium (Greek)

   TIBERIO KLAYDIO KAISARI S(ebasto) GERMANICO KAI IOYLI[a] S[*eba*]STE AGRIPPEINE
   KAI TOI[*s tekn*]OIS AYTON

   To Tiberius Claudius Caesar Augustus Germanicus and Julia Augusta Agrippina
   and their children

   50–4

24 IGR 4.560

Aezani (Greek)

[*Nerona Klay*]DION KAISARA DROYSON GERMANIKON TON HTION PHY[*s*]EI[*Th*]EAS [*agrippeines*]

Nero Claudius Caesar Drusus Germanicus, natural son of the goddess (Agrippina)

50–4

25 IG 12.5.275

Paros (Greek)

[*theas agri*] PEINES S[eb]*ASTES*

Divine Agrippina Augusta

After 49

26 IG 12.2.208; IGR 4.22 (cf. Hahn 34)

Mytilene

THEAN SEBASTAN BOLLAAN AIOLIN KARPOPHORIN

Divine Augusta, Aeolian Demeter Boulaia

49–54

27 IG 12. Suppl. 134

Mytilene

[*thean a*] *I*[o]*LIN SEBASTAN*

Divine Aeolian Augusta

49–54

28 CIG 2183

Mytilene (Greek)

Marcus Granius Carbo son of Gaius HYPOGYMNASIARCHESANTA THEAS SEBASTAS AIOLIDIS KARPPOPHORO AGRIPEINES

Divine Augusta Agrippina, Aeolian Demeter

50–9

See Robert (1960), 288

29 IGR 4.1104

Isthmus, Cos (Greek)

SEBASTEN THEAN DAMATRAN

The divine Augusta Demeter

50–

30 CIG 3858

Akmonia, Phrygia (Greek)

Iulia Severa, priestess SEBASTES EYBOSIAS

Eubosia may have been an epithet of Ceres. No certainty that the reference is to Agrippina the Younger

31 CIG 7061

Gem inscription (Greek)

A KYRIAS ARGRIPEINES

It is speculated that the A may be an abbreviation for AYGYSTES

32 Pace (1926), 419, no. 117

Adalia (Greek)

Epigraph in honour of son of Mida, winner of games held by the *hyposchesis*

TIBERIOY KLAYD[*ioy* KAI/AGREIPEIN[*es*
49–54

33 Epid IG IV2, 1, 602
Epidaurus (Greek)
AGRIPPINAN KAISAROS
49–54

34 Epid IG IV2, 1, 603
Epidaurus
[*ioylian sebasten*] AGRIPPINAN
(Julia Augusta) Agrippina (wife of Claudius)
50–4

35 AE 1980.855
Epidaurus (Greek)
[*agrippinan kaisar*]OS
49–54 (her name may have been chiselled out in 59)
33*ILS* 226
Naples
CLAUDIO CAESARI AUGUST(O) ET /////// AUGUSTAE
(Agrippina, name erased, probably in 59) Augusta
56

36 CIL 6.37591
Rome.
AGRIPPINAE AUGUSTAE
Grave memorial of freedwoman Zosime Freedwoman of Julia Agrippina Augusta
After 50

37 6. 36911
IULIAE AUG. AGRIPPINAE
Julia Augusta Agrippina
Rome? Dubious authenticity
Apparent grave memorial of slave of Trajan
Also slave of Julia Augusta Agrippina (interpretation difficult)

38 CIL 6. 20384
Rome
AGRIPPINAE AUGUSTAE
Grave memorial for freedwoman, Julia Aventina
50–

IV Coins

Coins are important tools for the historian, since they represent not only units of currency but also devices for propaganda, by means of which rulers can remind the populace of those aspects of their reign that they wish to emphasize. Agrippina was not, of course, a ruler, but coins of the period provide a vivid impression of the prominent role that she played alongside three emperors. The issues of all three reigns are unique for coins minted by the imperial authorities in the role that they give to the living sister, wife and mother of the reigning princeps, and they illustrate the progress that Agrippina made towards a form of shared rule.

Quite apart from the light they throw on constitutional and political issues, the coins provide the main evidence for the appearance of their subjects. This is important for Agrippina since there is no detailed literary description of her. 'Imperial' coins, that is, coins minted under the auspices of the central Roman authorities, although not necessarily in Rome itself, will tend to carry more individualized portraits than local coins, issued for local distribution, although there are exceptions. Of the imperial coins the most valuable for individualized portraiture is the sestertius, since its large field offers the best scope for detail. Unfortunately, in the case of Agrippina the Younger only one certain sestertius is known, that minted by Caligula depicting all three sisters on the reverse, without any scope for facial detail. One other Agrippina sestertius is known (no. 4 below) but the face, unremarkable if somewhat severe, may be modelled on that of Agrippina's mother. Certainly, the face of Agrippina the Younger on the securely identified precious metal issues is much less attractive. The Claudian denarius depicts a face with heavy rounded features, while on the Neronian issues at the beginning of his reign Agrippina has the same heavy features, rather jowly, with a large nose (nos 8–9). The likely accuracy of this portrayal (the depiction of Nero all through his reign on the gold and silver issues is certainly realistic) and the question of Agrippina's physical attractiveness or otherwise is not a trivial issue. Tacitus claims that she was a beautiful woman who used her physical charms to ensnare a defenceless Claudius, among others. The coins suggest that his claim may be unwarranted.

Imperial issues (including imperial coins of Ephesus and Caesarea in Cappadocia)

Caligula
1 RIC² 33 (sestertius). Pl. 10
37–8
Obverse: head and legend of Caligula
Reverse: Caligula's sisters, Agrippina, Drusilla and Livilla (all identified), as personifications

Claudius
Rome
2. RIC² 75 (Denarii). Pl. 16
50–4
Obverse: draped bust of Agrippina (facing right); she wears a crown of corn ears, one long tie falls down. The hair is fastened at the neck in a long plait. Two locks fall loosely down the neck.
Legend: AGRIPPINAE AUGUSTAE.
Reverse: head and legend of Nero
Kaenel (1986), 18–19, 80–1 doubts the authenticity of many examples of this issue.

3 RIC² 80–1 (aurei and denarii)

50–4

Obverse: laureate head, and legend of Claudius.

Reverse: as obverse of no. 2

4 RIC² 103 cf RIC² Caligula 55. Pl. 10

Obverse: draped bust of Agrippina (facing right) with hair in a long plait.

Legend: AGRIPPINA AUG(*usta*) GERMANICI F(*ilia*) CAESARIS AUG(*usti*) ('Agrippina Augusta, daughter of Germanicus, wife of Caesar Augustus')

Reverse: *Carpentum* drawn left by two mules. No legend

Only seven examples are known: four are in Berlin, one in Vienna, one in Sofia, one, whereabouts unknown (see *BMC* p.195; RIC² p. 129 n.103; Kaenel (1984), 141–2). They all have different reverse dies, which suggests strongly that they are genuine, but all originate from the Balkans, from Moesia-Thrace. Sutherland notes

that their style seems somewhat inferior to other imperial coinage. They might be a local series, in imitation of the Caligula memorial sesterius for Agrippina the Elder (RIC² 55), although the number of reverse dies speaks against this.

5 Kaenel (1984) 142, A8,9 (dupondius)

Obverse: draped bust of Agrippina, facing left.

Legend: AGRIPPINA AUG GERMANICI F CAESARIS AUG (Agrippina Augusta, daughter of Germanicus, wife of Caesar Augustus).

Reverse: Ceres on throne, legend CERES AUGUSTA (cf RIC² Claudius 94,110)

Only two examples are recorded, one (in very bad condition) is in the Athens National Museum; the whereabouts of the other is unknown.

Ephesus

6 RIC² 117 (silver cistophoric tetradrachms)

50/51

Obverse: Laureate head of Claudius with legend dated to 50/51.

Legend: AGRIPPINA AUGUSTA CAISARIS AUG (Agrippina Augusta wife of Caesar Augustus)

Reverse: Draped bust of Agrippina, hair in three rows of curls in front and fastened in a plait at the back.

7. RIC² 119

Undated

Obverse: jugate heads of laureate Claudius and bare-headed Agrippina.

Pl. 12

Legend: TI CLAUD CAES AUG AGRIPP AUGUSTA.

Reverse: Cult statue of Diana; legend DIANA EPHESIA.

Nero

Rome

8 RIC² 1–2 (Aurei and Denarii). Pl. 13

54

Obverse: confronting busts of Nero (facing right) and Agrippina, draped, with hair in long plait and one lock falling down her neck.

Legend: AGRIPP(*ina*) AUG(*usta*) DIVI CLAUDI NERONIS CAES(*aris*)MATER ('Agrippina

Augusta, wife of Divus Claudius, mother of Nero Caesar').

Reverse: *Corona civica* enclosing SC, and legend of Nero.

9 RIC² 6–7 (aurei and denarii). Pl. 14.

55

Obverse: jugate busts (facing right) of Nero and Agrippina (draped and bare-headed). Legend of Nero

Reverse: Quadriga and elephants, bearing two figures. Legend. EX SC and as obverse of no. 8

Caesarea in Cappadocia

10 RIC² 607 (didrachms and drachms). Pl. 17

54–?

Obverse: Nero and legend

Legend: AGRIPPINA AUGUSTA MATER AUGUSTI ('Agrippina Augusta mother of the Augustus')

Reverse: draped bust of Agrippina (facing right). The hair fastened at neck in a long plait. Two locks fall loosely down the neck.

11 RIC² 608 (didrachms)

54–?

Obverse: as no. 10

Legend: as on RIC² 607

Reverse: draped bust of Agrippina (facing right), veiled, wearing *stephane.*

12 RIC² 609 (24 – as piece)

54–?

Obverse: as no. 10

Reverse: as no. 10 but enclosed in laurel wreath. No legend of Agrippina

13 RIC2 610 (drachms)

Obverse: as no. 10

Legend: as no. 10

Reverse: draped bust of Agrippina, veiled, facing left.

14 RIC² 611 (Drachms)

Obverse and reverse: as no. 10.

15 RIC² 612 (12 – as pieces)

Obverse and Reverse: as no. 12

Local issues

The following list is based on A. Burnett, *Roman Provincial Coinage* (London, 1991) = RPC. See also Hahn (1992), no. 197

(n)= number of coins in holdings available to catalogue, if more than one

B = bust (or simple head) of Agrippina

L=legend of Agrippina

F=facing pair of heads

J=jugate pair of heads, with reigning emperor unless otherwise noted

La= legend of Agrippina, including title of Augusta

Ld= legend of Agrippina, including divine attribute

Caligula

RPC 2012 (4) (Apamea, Bithynia) B,L; RPC 2014 (2) (Apamea, Bithynia) full figure, L ; RPC 4973 (Caesarea Paneas, Judaea [coin of Herod Agrippa]) full figure, L

Claudius

RPC 1017 (4) (Cydonia, Cyrenaica and Crete) Ld; RPC 1034–6 (20) (Koinon, Cyernaica and Crete) BL; RPC 1183 (Corinth) BLa; RPC 1184 (Corinth) BL; RPC 1788 (Calchedon, Thrace) BLa; RPC 1835 (Tomi, Moesia) BL; RPC 1924 (Bosporus, Cotys I) BL; RPC 1925 (10=1924 +1925) (Bosporus, Cotys I) BLa; RPC 2100–21001 (3) (uncertain mint, Bithynia) BLa; RPC 2134 (Sinope, Bithynia) BLa; RPC 2154 (Amisus, Bithynia) BLa; RPC 2322 (Assos, Asia) FL; RPC 2380 (6) (Thyatira, Asia) BLa; RPC 2461 (12) (Mostene=Caesarea, Asia) JLd; RPC 2475 (14) (Smyrna, Asia) J; RPC 2499 (3) (Clazomenae, Asia) BL (may be Agrippina the Elder); RPC 2620 (7) (Ephesus, Asia) F; RPC 2621–4 (50) (Ephesus, Asia) J; RPC 2665 (6) (Nysa, Asia) JLa (attribution uncertain); RPC 3064–5 (13) (Cadi, Asia) BLa; RPC 3101 (6) (Aezani, Asia) BLa (identity of Agrippina not certain); RPC 3102–3 (21) (Aezani, Asia) BLa (could be Agrippina the Elder); RPC 3246 (4) (Brocchoi, Asia) BLa; RPC 3542 (4) (Claudiconium=Iconium, Galatia) BLa; RPC 4170 (5 silver) BLa; RPC 4859 (Caesarea Maritima, Syria) seated figure, La; RPC 4970 (Judaea, Jerusalem, minted by procurators) L; RPC 5188, 5190, 5192, 5194, 5196, 5199 (41) (Alexandria, Egypt) BLa

Nero

RPC 972, 973 (Crete, city unknown) BLa; RPC 1038 (7) (Koinon of Crete) F (Claudius)La; RPC 1190, 1193, 1196, 1198 (Corinth) BLa; RPC 1350 (12) (Epimel Kleonikou, Achaea) BL; RPC 1591, 1604, 1605 (5), 1606, 1606A (Thessalonica, Macedonia) BLa; RPC 1749 (Perinthus, Thrace) BLa; RPC 1929 (Bosporus, Cotys I) BLa; RPC 2052, 2054 (Nicaea, Bithynia and Pontus) JLa; RPC 2316 (14) (Ilium, Asia) FLa; RPC 2341 (Methymna, Asia) J (Agrippina and Octavia) La; RPC 2349 (2) (Mytilene) Lad; B2372 (Pergamum, Asia) (2) FLa; RPC 2386–8 (7) (Hierocaesarea, Asia) BLad; RPC 2395 (Pitane, Asia) BLa; RPC 2406 (Elaea, Asia) BLa; RPC 2434 (Cyme, Asia) BLd; RPC 2444–5 (2) (Phocaea, Asia) BLa; RPC 2457 (7) (Magnesia, Asia) standing Agrippina, as Demeter Ld; RPC 2458 (Magnesia, Asia) BLa; RPC 2478–9 (30) (Smyrna, Asia) FLa; RPC 2517 (8) (Teos, Asia) BLa; RPC 2685 (2) (Samos, Asia) FLd; RPC 2686 (7) (Samos, Asia) BLd; RPC 2722 (4) (Halicarnassus, Asia) BLa; RPC 2799 (2) (Euromus, Asia) FLa; RPC 2800 (Euromus, Asia) BLa; RPC 2823 (23) (Alabanda, Asia) BLa; RPC 2825 (3) (Orthosia, Asia) J; RPC 2862 (2) (Orthosia, Asia) J; RPC 2918 (11) (Laodicea, Asia) BLa; RPC 2977, 2979, 2981, 2983 (8) (Hieraplois, Asia) BLa; RPC 3042 (7) (Philadelphia, Asia) BLa; RPC 3107 (9) (Synaus, Asia) FLd; RPC 3136 (15) (Apamea, Asia) FLa; RPC 3151, 3152 (12) (Eumenea, Asia) BLa; RPC 3156 (8) (Sebaste, Asia) B; RPC 3172 (3) (Sebaste, Asia) BLa; RPC 3192, 3193 (7) (Iulia, Asia) BLa; RPC 3214–5 (5) (Docimeum, Asia) BLa; RPC 3218, 3221 (10) (Cotiaeum, Asia) BLa; RPC 4173, 4175 (20, silver) (Antioch,

Syria) BLa; RPC 4845 (Paneas, Syria) seated Agrippina La; RPC 4860 (3) (Caesarea Maritima, Syria) seated Agrippina La; RPC 4861 (Caesarea Maritima, Syria) BLa; RPC 5201, 5211(19), 5212 (8), 5221 (7), 5231 (6) (Alexandria, Egypt, pl. 15) BLa (dated: 56/57, 57/58, 58/59)

Appendix I
The Year of Agrippina the Younger's Birth

The day and month of Agrippina the Younger's birthday are firmly established as 6 November, from both the anniversary celebrations recorded for AD 57 and 58 by the Arval Brethren (Smallwood 19.6 and 21.15) and the entry in the AD 16 calendar record of Antium, the Fasti Antiates (EJ p.54).

The year is nowhere explicitly stated. Indications are provided by the following framework:

13: early: Germanicus leaves Rome for Germany on the termination of his consulship, held during the whole of 12 (Suet. *Cal.* 8.3; Dio 56.26.1).

14: 18 May: Agrippina the Elder is away from Rome, but not apparently in the same location as Germanicus (Suet. *Cal.* 8.4).

14: after early October: Agrippina is described as pregnant during the mutinies that followed Augustus' death on 19 August. The time is probably October, since the context follows the arrival of the senatorial commission despatched at the meeting held to consecrate Augustus, on 17 September (Tac. *Ann.* 1.14.4, 39.1, 40.2; Dio 57.5.4, 7; *EJ* 52). Agrippina is sent to Trier to deliver her child (Tac. *Ann.* 1.44.2).

17: 26 May: Drusilla and Agrippina the Younger, by inference, attend their father's triumph in Rome (Tac. *Ann.* 2.41.4, *EJ* p.49).

18: after 1 January: Tacitus records that Livilla was born on Lesbos, not long after Germanicus entered his consulship at Nicopolis, on the first day of January (Tac. *Ann.* 2.53.1–54.1).

We might add that Tac. *Ann.* 12.27.1 explicitly names Cologne (or strictly, its predecessor, Ara Ubiorum) as Agrippina the Younger's birthplace, and Suet. *Cal.* 8.4 indicates that Agrippina the Elder gave birth to two daughters in Germany. It is more than likely that the second was Drusilla, probably born at Ambitarvium, north of Coblenz, where altars were dedicated to commemorate her mother's delivery, and were seen by Pliny (Suet. *Cal.* 8.1); Suet. *Cal.* 7 however reports that two children died in infancy (*duo infantes...rapti*), and his Latin permits one of the two to have been a daughter.

Also, Suet. *Cal.* 7 tells us that, following the three surviving sons, the three surviving daughters, Agrippina, Drusilla and Livilla (in that order) were the last of Agrippina the Elder's nine children (two others died in infancy, a third in early childhood). The three daughters were born *triennio*, that is either in three successive years or in a three-year period. Suetonius is generally found to be reliable on precise biographical matters.

Suetonius lists the daughters in the order given above, and it is a reasonable assumption that this is in order of birth, as applies to the sons mentioned in the same section. This assumption is strengthened by their appearance on the famous sestertius of Caligula (Pl. 10), in which they appear in the same sequence, from left to right: Agrippina, Drusilla and Livilla. Also, Agrippina the Younger was married five years before her two sisters and is thus likely to have been the oldest.

AD 14 (November) is not *impossible* as a birth-date for Agrippina the Younger. We know that her mother was not with Germanicus in May of that year, but there is no proof that she had not already spent time in the north. She might have travelled to join Germanicus in 13, to conceive about early February. Thus the child she was carrying during the mutiny could have been Agrippina the Younger. This date is highly unlikely, however. It would have been remarkable for neither Tacitus nor Suetonius to identify the child if it was destined to become so famous. Its anonymity lends weight to the possibility that it was stillborn. Also Germanicus explicitly sent Agrippina to Trier for the delivery; it means that she would have had to return to the legionary camp (near Cologne) to give birth, without the return being noted. Moreover, a birth in 14 would mean that Suetonius' *triennio* would be meaningless. November of AD 16 can be ruled out – there would not be time for two further daughters to be born in separate births before early 18.

If Agrippina was born in November in AD 15 (the traditional date), we do face some difficulties. During the campaigns of 15 Agrippina the Elder saved the retreating Romans by defending the bridge over the Rhine. Tac. *Ann.* 1.70.2 shows explicitly that this happened after the autumn equinox. She would thus have been some seven months pregnant; in most women this would be highly visible and worth recording. But we cannot be sure that it would have been so in Agrippina's case. Also, if Agrippina the Younger was born in 15, Drusilla's birth would have to be placed in 16. Dio 59.13.8 seems to place the AD 39 celebrations for the anniversary of Drusilla's birth *early* in the year. Her birth clearly could not have fallen early in 16, nor could it have come in *early* 17, since Germanicus was on a protracted summer campaign at the required time of conception (Tac. *Ann.* 2.5.4). Nor would Agrippina's birth in November 15 and Livilla's in early 18 accommodate Suetonius' *triennio*, in the sense of three successive years.

There have been two basic attempts to reconcile these discrepancies. Mommsen, 'Die Familie des Germanicus', *GS* (1904), 4.271–90 (believing that *triennio* should mean 'in three successive years'), suggested that Tacitus placed Livilla's birth in 18 by error. Germanicus would hardly have subjected his pregnant wife to the rigours of a winter sea voyage, and he must have sent her ahead to Lesbos before the end of the sailing season in 17 for a birth later in that year. Drusilla's birthday was accordingly placed by Mommsen in late 16.

J. Humphrey, 'The Three Daughters of Agrippina Maior', *AJAH* 4 (1979), 125–43 has proposed a more radical solution. He puts particular emphasis on the testimony of Dio 59.13.8 who, as noted, places celebrations held in AD 39 for the anniversary of Drusilla's birth early in the year. The ancient sources could be reconciled if we assume that *Drusilla* is the oldest daughter, born in early 15 (thus the child carried by Agrippina in 14), followed by Agrippina the Younger, born in November 16, and Livilla in early 18 (as Tacitus states). This does leave some difficulties, however. The order of the three daughters in

Suetonius can be explained only if we assume that he was ignorant of or indifferent to their relative ages, the type of family detail that seems to have interested him. Moreover, the arrangement of the sisters on Caligula's sestertius would have to be explained by the assumption that Drusilla's mid-position suggests prominence, of which there is no hint elsewhere on the coin-type. Moreover Agrippina the Younger's earlier (by five years) and more distinguished marriage remains a difficulty. Humphrey offers some tentative evidence that there had been earlier betrothals in Germanicus' family, to Quinctilius Varus, probably the son of the notorious general, and Asinius Saloninus, but there is no way of telling which daughter(s) might have been betrothed. In any case had Agrippina not been the oldest it is difficult to see why Drusilla would not have been given to Domitius. Clearly Dio had found in his source that Caligula celebrated Drusilla's birthday in 39; unfortunately his chronology for much of that year is hopelessly muddled (witness his confused report on Caligula's marriage), and there can be no certainty that the birthday did in fact occur early in the year. We know that Caligula was still in Rome in early September in AD 39, and might have celebrated Drusilla's birthday in that month; it is possible that Drusilla was born in September in AD 16, following the birth of Agrippina in November of the previous year (Tac. *Ann.* 1.41.3 does call Agrippina the Elder a woman of impressive fecundity, [*insigni fecunditate*]). Despite these conclusions, it must be recognized that Humphrey's arguments do carry weight and have established that the question should remain open. The traditional date of Agrippina's birth, November AD 15, although accepted in this book as a convenient reference point, must be considered tentative.

Appendix II
The Husbands of Domitia and Lepida

Domitia

A marriage between Domitia and C. Passienus Crispus, later husband of Agrippina, is securely attested (Quintilian 6.1.50, 3.74; Schol. Juv. 4.81). Syme (1986), 162–3 suggests that there could have been two previous husbands. The first might have been the evil prosecutor D. Haterius Agrippa (consul AD 22) described in 17 as a relative of the imperial prince Germanicus Caesar. Haterius bestowed the cognomen *Antoninus* on his son, Q. Haterius Antoninus, the spendthrift consul of AD 53, which might imply that D. Haterius had married a daughter of Lucius Domitius and Antonia (Tac. *Ann.* 2.52.1, 6.4.2, 12.34.3). Domitia might still have been married to Haterius in 20, to judge from the consular year of Haterius' son Quintus, consul in 53.

Syme, *Papers B* 122 (1986), 163, believes that there could have been a second marriage, to one of the two Blaesi brothers. Their father was the *novus homo* Q. Junius Blaesus (suffect in AD 10), the uncle of Sejanus and the only ex-consul to be put to death in connection with the prefect's fall. They, in turn, both committed suicide in 36, anticipating the condemnation foreshadowed by Tiberius' decision to transfer to others the priesthoods marked for them. The senior of the two brothers was Q. Junius Blaesus, consul in 26, and possibly the more likely candidate. Junius Blaesus, the son of one of the two Blaesi and governor of Lugdunensis at the time of Vitellius' acclamation in 69, was attacked because he used to boast of his Junian and *Antonian* ancestors. He died shortly afterwards in Rome, possibly from poison (Tac. *Ann.* 6.40.2; *Hist.* 3.38).

Lepida

Lepida's first husband was Messala Barbatus. Syme, *Papers B* 425 (1986), 164 observes that his father died while consul in early 12 BC. Thus Barbatus had to be born no later than 12 BC, and on the basis of his family distinction could have expected a consulship by AD 23. Since he did not become consul, Syme suggests that he must have died before that date (Tac. *Ann.* 11.37.4; Suet. *Claud.* 26.2).

Lepida's second husband was Faustus Cornelius Sulla, to whom she bore a son of the same name. The marriage is confirmed by Dio 60.30.6a, who calls Faustus junior the *brother* of Messalina and thus indicates that his father was married to Messalina's mother; Faustus junior held the consulship in AD 52, which might suggest that his birth, and the terminal date for his parents' marriage, should be a little before 20. It is very possible, however, that because of his betrothal to Antonia he was given accelerated promotion of five years, as was Antonia's previous fiancé. The wedding, then, need not necessarily predate 24.

Appendix III
The Date of Nero's Birth

See Geer (1931), 58; Gallivan (1974), 300–1; Bradley (1978), 45-6; Griffin (1984), 241 n.11, 243 n.63.

The most explicit statement on the date of Nero's birth is given by Suet. *Nero* 6.1, who places it just before dawn, at Antium, nine months after the death of Tiberius, on the eighteenth day before the Kalends of January (AD 37, 15 December). The *day* is confirmed by the Arval record (Smallwood 16, 21) and the report by *SHA Verus* 1.8 that Lucius Verus was born on 15 December, the same day as Nero. The exactness of the day lends an authority also to Suetonius' year. Suetonius is supported by Tac. *Ann.* 13.6.2, who notes concerns at the end of the year of accession, 54, that the government was in the hands of a youth barely past his 17th birthday. He also receives limited support from Dio 63.29.3 who observes that Nero, who died in June 68, lived thirty years and a number of months and days; the exact figure for the months and days varies with the empitomators, but all match a birth-date of 37. It should be noted that a date of 37 generally harmonizes with the known circumstances of Nero's birth and later life.

This explicit information is apparently contradicted by other references. Suet. *Nero* 8.1 and Dio 61.3.1 report that at the time of Claudius' death in October 54 Nero was 17 years old. Both entries may go back to a source that was misled because Claudius' death happened so late in the year (13 October); otherwise a birth-date of 36 would have to be assumed. The date of 36 is supported by Suet. *Nero* 7.1, who reports that Nero died in 68 at the age of 32. Moreover, Tac. *Ann.* 12.58.1 places Nero's marriage to Octavia as the first entry for 53 and gives Nero's age as 16. This last problem might be resolved if we assume that the marriage was placed at the beginning of the year's entries for dramatic effect rather than in chronological sequence, and that it in fact occurred after mid-December. There are two problems with the birth-date of 36. It cannot be reconciled with the story of the *lustratio*, which is set under Caligula's principate. Moreover, Tac. *Ann.* 12.41.1 says that in 51 the *toga virilis* was bestowed *prematurely* on Nero. If in fact he was born in 36 he would have reached the traditional age of manhood (14) by the end of the previous year, AD 50.

Tac. *Ann.* 12.25.3 says that Nero had three years' seniority over Britannicus. This information is not of great help for absolute dating since there is uncertainty about the date of Britannicus' birth. By the usual reconstruction, it should put Nero's birth in 38 or 39, but because of the confusion over Britannicus' birth-date this calculation should not be given great weight. Suet. *Nero* 7.1 states that Nero was adopted in his eleventh year. Now the adoption is dated to 50 by Tac. *Ann.* 12.25.1, and to 25 February in the Arval record (Smallwood 21). To be in his eleventh year on 25 February 50, Nero would have had to be born in 39. Given the circumstances of the latter part of that year, this date can be confidently ruled out.

Appendix IV
The Family of Marcus Aemilius Lepidus

It is likely that Marcus Aemilius Lepidus, husband of Drusilla, was the grandson of Paullus Aemilius Lepidus, a close friend of Augustus and husband of Cornelia, daughter of Augustus' first wife Scribonia by an earlier marriage. The elder of Paullus' sons, Lucius Aemilius Paullus, was the disgraced husband of Julia the Younger. The younger, Marcus Aemilius Lepidus, consul of 6, was considered *capax imperii*, one of a handful of men who might be potential successors to Augustus (on which, see Tac. *Ann.* 1.13.2; Syme [1955], 22). Marcus maintained close connections with the imperial house. His daughter, Aemilia Lepida, married Drusus, brother of Caligula. She came to an unfortunate end, betraying her husband and then committing suicide after being charged with adultery with a slave. Most scholars believe that Drusilla's husband was the son of the consul of AD 6, and that he bore the same name as his father.

On the basis on Namatianus 1.306, J. Lipsius, *Ad Annales Liber Commentarius* (Leyden, 1585), 238 (on Tac. *Ann.* 14.22) argued, followed by Balsdon (1934), 42 and Nony (1986), 359, that Lepidus was the son of Julia Minor and Lucius Aemilius Paullus, and thus cousin of Agrippina.

See Vell. 2.114.5; Tac. *Ann.* 6.40.3; Syme, *Papers A*, 820; PIR² A371; P. von Rohden, *RE* I (1893), I 5.61–3; Meise (1962), 108; Bergener (1965), 119; Stewart (1953), 74; Hayne (1973), 501; Barrett (1990), 82.

Appendix V
Agrippina's Movements
in Late 39

The traditional reconstruction of the events of 39 has Caligula going north to Gaul and/or Germany in the company of his two sisters and Lepidus; he supposedly arranged the execution of Gaetulicus on the spot. There is no explicit ancient evidence for these assumptions.

The reconstruction offered in this chapter differs from the traditional one, essentially in assuming that Gaetulicus was executed while Caligula was still in Mevania, and that his sisters and Lepidus did not accompany him any farther than that town. The arguments for this position are laid out in Barrett (1990), 108.

They are summarized briefly as follows. Caligula was almost certainly not in Rome by the end of October, to judge from his absence from the Arval ceremonies, and seems to have been out of Rome when the condemnation of Lepidus occurred in the senate (the charges were communicated rather than delivered personally). But this tells us only where Caligula was not; it does not say where he *was*. It would have been courageous, to say the least, for him to have put himself in the lion's den by going north to Gaul or Germany while Gaetulicus was still alive. It would have been hardly less foolhardy for him to have travelled outside Italy accompanied by a group of people he suspected of conspiring against him. Lepidus was executed by a tribune, Dexter. The execution need not have been carried out in a legionary camp by a legionary tribune, since Dexter could have been a tribune in one of the praetorian units that accompanied Caligula to Mevania. When Caligula began to run short of cash in Gaul, he sold by auction the possessions of his two sisters, including their slaves and freedmen. It has generally been assumed that these goods and possessions must have accompanied the sisters, an assumption that is not warranted. Finally, Agrippina is said to have carried the urn containing Lepidus' ashes to Rome. This piece of theatre better suits the journey (already long enough) from Mevania than the almost impossibly lengthy one from Lyons or Mainz.

Appendix VI
The Date of Seneca's Tutorship

The sequence of Seneca's praetorship and appointment as tutor had been much discussed; see in particular Waltz (1909), 151; Faider (1929), 209; Giancotti (1953), 103–4; Griffin (1976), C1.

Dio 60.32.2–3 in an epitome clearly datable to 49 states that Agrippina made Nero Claudius' son-in-law (*gambron apedeixe*), and later brought about his adoption and entrusted his education to Seneca. In Tac. *Ann.* 12.8 the recall and appointment of Seneca as tutor is placed between the suicide of Silanus, which occurred on the day of the wedding of Agrippina and Claudius, and the section on the betrothal of Nero and Octavia. If we are to take this as a strict sequence of events, it means that Seneca's recall and his appointment as tutor belong to 49, before the betrothal. This sequence seems to receive some confirmation in Tac. *Ann.* 14.53.2, where Seneca says that in the eighth (*octavus*) year since Nero obtained power (that is, between October 61 and October 62) it was the fourteenth year since Seneca had been *spei tuae admotus*, which would indicate October 48 to October 49. There is, however, a problem. Tacitus says that Seneca took up the praetorship at the same time as becoming tutor. For all Agrippina's influence with her husband, it seems inconceivable that Seneca could have entered into a praetorship immediately on his return. Indeed, for Agrippina to recall a former ally and to place him immediately in charge of her son would have seemed unduly provocative, and in a sense would have made a mockery of his previous conviction. Agrippina was a patient and careful operator and would have seen the value of moving by gradual stages. It must be assumed that Seneca's recall in 49 was not linked officially to his appointment as Nero's tutor. After a few months in Rome he would have been in a position to enter the praetorship and to start the tutorship of Nero, at the beginning of 50, the following year.

Appendix VII
The Decline in Agrippina's Power

The standard view is that Agrippina's power declined in early 55, or even earlier, and that this decline was a result of her eclipse by Seneca and Burrus. This assumption raises a number of problems. There is uncertainty on the part of the literary sources over the chronology of her fall from grace. Dio 61.7.5 records that after the unfortunate diplomatic incident involving the ambassadors of Armenia, which, like Tacitus, Dio places at the end of 54, Seneca and Burrus prevented any business from being conducted by Agrippina and took authority into their own hands. But Dio also claims that in 55 they more or less gave up any serious attention to the affairs of state, following the death of Britannicus, and concentrated instead on their own protection (61.3.3–4.2). Tacitus is even more self-contradictory. In Tac. *Ann.* 13.2 the opposition of Seneca and Burrus to the slaughter of Agrippina and Pallas is mentioned even before the funeral and consecration of Claudius, and the claim is made that from the very outset the respect shown to her was a front for the benefit of the public (*propalam*). In addition, Tacitus says that the beginning of 55 saw a diminution of Agrippina's influence (Tac. *Ann.* 13.12.1). Yet in the aftermath of the Junia Silana affair, well into 55, at a time when Agrippina had supposedly been abandoned by her friends, she was powerful enough to have her opponents punished and, more significantly, to arrange the appointment of her own friends to crucial positions. Also, at the beginning of Book 14, some four years later, Agrippina's influence seems to be unimpaired. The reason given for Nero's decision to go ahead with Agrippina's murder is supposedly that Poppaea taunted him with being under his mother's thumb, *alienis iussis obnoxius*, and lacking not only *imperium* but even private *libertas*. There was popular anger, Poppaea insisted, over her conduct, and no-one refuted the claim because of a general desire to see Agrippina's *potentia* destroyed. When Nero heeded Poppaea's taunts, Agrippina resorted to incest to reassert her *potentia* (with the implication that she had surrendered it only as a result of very recent developments). It seems clear, despite Dio's assertion that Agrippina had lost power completely by the end of 54 and Tacitus' claim that it had begun to ebb by the beginning of 55, that she continued to be a powerful figure right up to the year of her death (although there is no evidence that she continued to influence appointments after 55). As late as 59 she is still able to count on the loyalty of the guard, to the extent that when Nero makes his final move against her he is obliged to use men from the fleet rather than the praetorians.

The notion that Agrippina's decline was brought about through the machinations of Seneca and Burrus poses a problem. During the Junia Silana affair Burrus also fell under suspicion as an ally of Agrippina, although by this time he was supposedly her bitter opponent. Although Burrus escaped the charge, he was immediately afterwards implicated with Agrippina's creature Pallas in an alleged attempt to remove Nero.

Tigellinus on Burrus' death made the interesting comment, that his loyalty to Nero was not divided as Burrus' had been (Tac. *Ann.* 14.57.2).

Agrippina remained an important force in political affairs right up to the end. Tacitus sees the dramatic change in the reign of Nero as occurring in 62, with the death of Burrus and the departure of Seneca from matters of state. But another important change occurs after the murder of Agrippina in 59, which suggests that she had continued to exercise an influence over events and over Nero up to this point. Tacitus concludes his account of her death and Nero's handling of its aftermath and turns abruptly and dramatically to a marked transformation in Nero, characterized by his intention to indulge his ambitions and to devote himself to chariot racing and appearances on the stage. Also, after the abortive conspiracy of 65, one of the key participants, Subrius Flavus, a tribune of the guard, justifies his conduct by stating that he had begun as a loyal follower of Nero but turned against the emperor when he went downhill following the death of his mother. Warmington (1977), 245, notes that Subrius mentions the death of Agrippina as only one of Nero's abuses that preceded the conspiracy. But it does come first in the list, with the implication that it set the other abuses in motion. Also, when Nero had finally resolved to murder his mother, he declared that *illo die sibi dari imperium* (Tac. *Ann.* 14.7.6: 'on that day power was given to him'). A similar notion is found in Dio. He sees Nero going out of control after the death of Britannicus (61.7.5), but he also sees another stage in the imperial decline after the death of Agrippina (61.11.1: 'from this point on he became generally worse – he considered that it was acceptable for him to do whatever it was in his power to do'). Indeed, unless Nero's mother still had a considerable hold over him (the rumours of incest certainly bear this out), it is difficult to understand why he should have decided to kill her at all. Tacitus clearly saw this as a problem, and was obliged, as will be shown, to provide an explanation that simply does not convince.

The nature of Nero's relationship with his mother is linked to the more general issue of the familiar *quinquennium Neronis.* There was a tradition that Rome had enjoyed a limited period of excellent government under Nero, which apparently originated in a rather obscure though frequently repeated comment of the emperor Trajan, who reputedly said that all other emperors were surpassed by five years (quinquennium) of Nero. This anecdote is related by two fourth-century historians, Aurelius Victor, *Liber de Caesaribus* 5.2, and the anonymous *Epitome de Caesaribus* 5.2, who supposedly took their material from an earlier imperial history, the so-called Kaisergeschicht (see Enmann [1884], 337 and the comments of Den Boer [1972], 22 and Syme [1978], 222). Admittedly, the only achievements they cite are public buildings and foreign policy, which in fact belong to years later than the first five and it is likely that the allusions were made loosely. That the first five years were intended as the quinquennium fits well with the sentiments expressed by Calpurnius Siculus 1.42, who talks of the second birth of the golden age and the return of the rule of law. Also, the *Apocolocyntosis,* probably written within months of the accession, opens by calling the new reign a *saeculum felicissimum.* If so, five years from Nero's accession would be October 59, only some months after Agrippina's death, suggesting very strongly that the *whole* of her Neronian period should be seen as a distinct and formative phase (the quinquennium is placed in the first five years, by, *inter alios,* Lepper [1958], Murray [1964], Griffin [1972], 423–4, [1984],

37, Levick [1982]; Syme [1971], 109 thinks that it could refer, ironically, to any five of Nero's years).

The almost total silence of the literary sources on Agrippina's activities between 55 and 59 need not cause concern. Dio has survived only in summary epitomes, and his information on the whole period tends to be scrappy and incoherent. The narrative of Tacitus is continuous but domestic political affairs in the years 56–8 receive relatively little coverage. Indeed, not only is Agrippina absent from Tacitus' account but Burrus does not appear there during the same period and Seneca makes an appearance only in an almost incidental manner, in that he is identified as the target of the attacks by Suillius Rufus (Tac. *Ann.* 13.42–3). The pattern is repeated in Dio – no mention of Burrus, and of Seneca only in the Suillius sections, where a retrospective survey of his career is provided and where Agrippina also makes her sole appearance; the information possibly originated from Suillius' speech, which explains its presence at this juncture (Dio 61.10); Dio does refer to Burrus at 61.10.6 but with reference to the charges brought against him and Pallas earlier, in 55. Seneca and Burrus return in vivid and concrete terms only at the same time as Agrippina, in the context of her murder and its aftermath. Thus no mention is made of the activities of the two men who were supposedly running Rome during the period.

Also to be noted is the fact that there is no convincing evidence of a serious rift between Agrippina and Seneca and Burrus. In Tac. *Ann.* 13.14.3, Agrippina called them offensive names in a histrionic speech where she also supposedly espoused the cause of Britannicus and declared her intention of going to the armies, but the passage is hardly believable. In 58 Suillius makes no hint of Seneca's enmity against Agrippina and in fact without any sense of irony he accuses them of having been lovers.

The Patronage of Seneca and Burrus in 54–9

There is little direct evidence that Burrus was able to secure appointments for colleagues. Duvius Avitus, who came from Burrus' home town of Vaison, was suffect consul in November and December 56, and this office had been preceded by the governorship of Aquitania. The governorship was an important position but, given the date of his consulship, can hardly have been assigned to him later than 54 and might be due ultimately to Agrippina. Duvius later went on to be legate of Lower Germany (PIR² D 210; *ILS* 979, CIL 4.3340, 12.1408; Pliny *NH* 34.47; Tac. *Ann.* 13.54.3; Syme [1958], 591; Griffin [1976], 84–5).

Seneca's family certainly prospered as a result of his ascendancy, but there does not seem to have been a dramatic shift in 55. His brother L. Junius Gallio Annaeanus did hold a consulship in 55 or 56 (*Archaeologica Classica* 10 [1958], 231–4) but he had already begun a successful career before that and was governor of Achaea earlier, in 51/52 (SEG 13.384). Seneca's father-in-law Pompeius Paulinus was actually replaced as prefect of the annona, a post he held under Claudius (referred to in *Brev. Vit.* 18–19, published between mid-48 and mid-55) by Agrippina's appointment, Faenius Rufus. Seneca's brother-in-law, the identically named son of the above Paulinus, was legate in Lower Germany in 55 (Tac. *Ann.* 13.53.2) and must have been suffect consul earlier, perhaps when his sister married Seneca after the latter's return from exile in 49. But it may have been even earlier (Eck, *ZPE* 42 [1981] suggests him as colleague of M. Junius Silanus in CIL 14.3471). The appointments are not extraordinary and do not seem to indicate any great improvement in the fortunes of the family since the time of Claudius.

Outside his family circle there is relatively little evidence of Seneca's power of patronage. Syme suggests that L. Pedanius Secundus, Praefectus Urbi in 61, when he was murdered by his own slave under murky circumstances, might have been appointed to that office in 56 through the agency of Seneca, when the incumbent L. Volusius Saturninus died. But the only link is that Pedanius was also born in Spain and the fact that he had held a suffect consulship in 43 indicates that his career had progressed well before Seneca reached Rome (PIR P146; Pliny *NH* 10.35; Tac. *Ann.* 13.30.4, 14.42.1; Syme [1958], 591). Lucilius Junior might have acquired the procuratorship of Sicily through Seneca, but the date is uncertain (PIR L286; Sen. *Ep. NQ* 4a. *pref.* 1, 21–2; Pflaum [1961], I.30,70 III, 961–2). Seneca may also have been responsible for the appointment of Annaeus Serenus, prefect of the Vigiles, who could have replaced Laelianus in that position when the latter was appointed to Armenia, apparently in 54 (Dio 61.6.6; see Griffin [1976], App. D3). He is also given the credit by Plutarch for the appointment of the future emperor Otho to the governorship of Lusitania in the late 50s (PIR S109; Plut. *Galb.* 20.1; Tac. *Ann.* 13.46.5 says that Otho was appointed in 58, confirmed by Suet. *Otho* 3.2 that he was governor ten years before 68; on this evidence

Griffin [1984], 254 n.54 rejects the tradition that Otho played host to Nero before Agrippina's murder).

In the Armenian crisis of 54 there was speculation about which general would be appointed; it was felt that the choice would provide an indication of whether Nero was being guided by advisers of integrity or by the usual court intrigues. Tacitus thus *implies* that the appointment of Domitius Corbulo should be attributed to Seneca and Burrus, but provides no detailed reasoning. Popular sentiment at the beginning of the latest phase of the crisis was that Nero was influenced by these two *and* by Agrippina. Also, Corbulo was the half-brother of the notorious Publius Suillius, the arch-foe of Seneca. In fact, Corbulo's appointment might well have been a simple case of the best man actually getting the position, as implied by Tacitus (Tac. *Ann.* 13.8.1).

Appendix IX

SC on Gold and Silver Coins of Nero

It is noteworthy that all the gold and silver issues from the imperial mint at Rome between 54 and 63/4 with the exception of one very rare issue of gold quinarii has the legend EX SC. This legend is usually limited to bronze coinage and its precise significance has been much debated. The traditional view, which goes back to Mommsen (1887), 1026–8, is that Augustus maintained the right to mint gold and silver coinage, but left bronze coinage to the senate, who would have indicated their authority by the letters SC. There is actually no clear evidence that the senate exercised such an authority. Kraft (1962) argued that the letters indicated not senatorial authority for the bronze coins but senatorial involvement in the honours depicted on them. Wallace-Haddrill (1986) claims that the main function of SC was to distinguish the official coinage in base metals from local issues. See the useful summary in Talbert (1984), 379–83.

Before Nero, SC did not appeared on the gold and silver of the empire except for very rare cases (cf. RIC I2 p.64, no.321). If Kraft's thesis is adopted, the SC of Nero's early coinage would reflect the senatorial vote of the *corona civica* (the most common reverse type), or perhaps the voting of divine honours or the triumph for Claudius; but the legend EX SC continues on precious coins after 60–1 when conventional personified figures (Roma, Virtus, Ceres) appear on the reverses (which might be explained as the result of tradition).

Sutherland (1976), 5–21, (1967), 35–8, RIC[2] 135, 149, suggests that SC on aes coins from Augustus onwards indicates the role of the senate in withdrawing supplies of aes from the aerarium for coinage, while the princeps presumably kept control over stocks of gold and silver. He argues that Nero went back to the situation which prevailed before Julius Caesar and transferred control of gold and silver back to the authority of the senate, to be taken back by the emperor in 64. There is no way of proving that such a process did take place. If it did, it would represent a striking gesture towards the senate on Nero's part. See Griffin (1984), 58–9.

Appendix X
The Final Days of Agrippina

Although the final days of Agrippina are among the best documented of any event in the ancient world, the details pose serious difficulties. The circumstances of Agrippina's death are closely associated with her villa at Bauli. The basic question still to be resolved is its location. Was it north or south of Baiae? Pliny *NH* 9.172 indicates that Bauli was in the district of Baiae: *apud Baulos in parte Baiana* and Tac. *Ann.* 14.4.4 explains that the name was given to a villa (one can safely assumed in the vicinity of Bauli) washed by *flexo mari* (literally the 'bending sea', so presumably a cove or small bay) between the promontory of Misenum and what he calls *Baianus lacus*. (i) North (suggested from the eighteenth century): see, *inter alios*, Beloch (1890), 176, 177; H. Hülsen RE 3 (1897), 154–5 (but he confusingly places it between Baiae and Misenum); Nissen (1902), 736; McDaniel (1910), 101; apart from Nissen (who argues that the villa was not near Baiae but to the east of Punta Caruso near Puteoli), most place it either just north of or on the promontory, *punta dell'epitafio*. The *punta* forms the natural boundary of the bay of Baiae some 4 kilometres (2½ miles) north-east of Misenum, quite close to the southern end of the Lucrine Lake and the Via Herculanea, the narrow strip of land separating the lake from the sea. In fourth-century writers Bauli is associated with the myth of Hercules, as the place where he penned the cattle of Geryon, the *boualia*, while building the via Herculanea (Symmachus *Epist.* 1.1; Servius on *Aen.* 7.662). Pliny *NH* 3.61 appears to confirm this location since he lists the localities of the area apparently from south to north: *Misenum, portus Baiarum, Bauli, lacus Lucrinus et Avernus*.

The association of Bauli with the via Herculanea in the fourth century is not, however, necessarily significant for its location, since the relatively distant Pompeii is also associated by Servius with the same *pompa* made by Hercules. Nor does the sequence of towns as given by Pliny necessarily preclude a southern location, since he may have mentioned Bauli after Baiae simply to indicate a subordinate status. Another problem is that Tacitus' expression *Baianus lacus* would have to mean the Lucrine Lake, even though he mentions the Lucrine by its own name (*Lucrinus lacus*) in the immediately following section. (ii) South (suggested from the sixteenth century): Maiuri (1941), 249–60, (1963), 89–91; D'Arms (1970), 181. The traditional identification of Bauli has been with the modern village of Bacoli; between the southern limits of the Bay of Baiae and Cape Misenum the sea forms a slight bay near Bacoli, to which Tacitus' *flexo mari* might refer. In this case his *Baianus lacus* would refer to the farthest recess of the bay of Baiae, between Baiae and Puteoli. Maiuri argues that the cisterns known as the *cento camerelle* on the heights of Bacoli represent the remains of Hortensius' villa, which almost certainly was the villa eventually acquired by Agrippina. D'Arms notes that Cicero (*Acad.* 2.80) states that from Hortensius' villa at Bauli one could see Puteoli, and that nothing intervened to block the sight of Pompeii. This is the case from Bacoli, while from the *punta dell'epitaphio* north of Baiae the hills of Puteoli and the ridge of Posillipo obstruct the view of any land beyond. Inscriptions mentioning an *ordo* or *collegium Baulanorum* have been found at Bacoli (CIL 10.¹ 1746–8). The southern location also has some antiquarian support; a ruined small odeon attached to a Roman villa has long been known as the *sepolcro d'Agrippina*.

Compounding the difficulty of the location of the villa at Bauli, the sequence of events leading up to the dinner is confused. Dio 61.12.3 has Nero making the journey to Campania together with his mother in the collapsing boat, with the intention of acclimatizing her to the vessel; Dio places all the subsequent action at Bauli. Suet. *Nero* 34.2 has Nero entertaining Agrippina elsewhere, and offering her the collapsing boat for her return to Bauli. Tacitus' account is the most detailed. He states that Nero spent the festival of Minerva at Baiae. On Agrippina's arrival, he meets her on the shore (it is not made clear whether at Baiae or Bauli, and Maiuri [1941], 255 has even argued that it was Misenum) and accompanies her to the villa at Bauli, where she saw a large collection of ships, one of which (the collapsing version) stood out. Tacitus says that she travelled for dinner to *Bauli* in a litter because of her suspicions about her son. This follows Nero's accompanying her to her villa and seems to create an impossible sequence of movements. One solution has been to assume a copyist's error in Tacitus' manuscripts, and to emend the text to make her destination (for dinner) Baiae rather than Bauli, by changing *gestamine sellae Baulos praevectam* ('carried to Bauli') to read *Baias praevectam* ('carried to Baiae'). The sequence would then be that he met her on the shore at Bauli and took her to the villa where she was to stay, and at some later point she went to dinner at Nero's residence at Baiae, making her way in the litter. This accords with Suetonius' comment that after the dinner Agrippina set out to return to Bauli. But, in any case, the story of Agrippina' decision to travel by litter, whether to Baiae or Bauli, because of fear that she would be murdered by her son on the evidence of an informer is totally unconvincing and presumably arose speculatively after the event. She would hardly have consented to go on board ship after the final dinner had she entertained such serious suspicions, and Tacitus' claim that Nero's charming behaviour allayed her fears (*blandimentum sublevavit metum*) does not carry conviction. The passage may be a confused reference to Agrippina's *final* journey to her villa at Bauli, presumably in a litter, *after* the shipwreck. The very dramatic nature of this particular journey would have ensured that it would stay in the popular memory, perhaps to be confused with events a few hours earlier and create an impossible sequence of movements in the unemended text of Tacitus. It is also difficult to understand why there should have been a large fleet moored off Bauli.

Tac. *Ann.* 14.5.7 says that when Agrippina had been brought to the shore after the shipwreck, she came to the Lucrine Lake, and was carried from there to her villa. This has led some to believe that she had a villa on the Lucrine, as argued by McDaniel (1910), Maiuri (1941, 1963), Bishop (1960), Koesterman (1968). The arguments are essentially that there would have been no point in her landing there if the villa was in a different location, and that a journey from the Lucrine Lake to Bauli would have required her to go past Baiae (where Nero was residing), a highly dangerous journey. Furneaux (1907), Ramsay (1909), Woodcock (1939), Bicknell (1963), D'Arms (1970) have rejected the Lucrine location and argued that the villa where she spent her last hours was the one at Bauli. She certainly was buried near the road to Misenum. The Lucrine Lake was far distant but she might have had good reason to land there. As noted earlier, the fishermen who rescued her may not have been familiar enough with the coastline near Bauli to land her in the dark. Agrippina probably realized that she did not have the sympathy of the fleet and perhaps feared the presence of ships patrolling south of Baiae. The objection that she would have been too unwell to make the long trip in a litter because of her wounds is not persuasive. Perhaps most important, Tacitus has already referred, before the shipwreck, to a villa at Bauli and a subsequent reference to a *villa*, without further modification, must surely be to the same one.

Bishop (1960), 167 has attempted to determine the precise date when the murder took place. Dio says that Agrippina sailed after midnight, and that the accident occurred fairly soon after embarkation; some time before 2 a.m. would therefore be a reasonable assumption. Dio and Tacitus both indicate that the night was moonless (despite the objections of Katzoff [1973], 77 it is difficult to understand them otherwise). The night of 26 or 27 March would be a good candidate. On that night (in 59) the moon rose at about 2.30 a.m.; it would have risen approximately 50 minutes 30 seconds earlier on each of the preceding nights. That night would suit the testimony that the Arvals met on the Capitoline on 28 March, immediately, one assumes, on receipt of the news. But perhaps not too much faith should be placed in the details of Dio's account. Suet. *Nero* 34.2 says that Nero invited his mother to celebrate the festival of Minerva with him, which would imply the period 19–23 March, possibly with the night of 23 March as the most likely date.

Abbreviations

Ancient Authors and Works

Anon. *Epit. de Caes.*	*Epitome de Caesaribus* (anonymous)
Anth. Pal.	*Anthologia Palatina*
Apoc.	*Apocolocyntosis*
Appian *BC*	Appian, *Civil War*
Ascon. *Comm.*	Asconius, *Commentarii*
Aul. Gell.	Aulus Gellius
Aur. Vict. *Caes.*	Aurelius Victor, *Caesares*
Boethius *Cons.*	Boethius, *De Consolatione Philosophiae*
Calp. Sic.	Calpurnius Siculus
Cic. *Acad.*	Cicero, *Academicae Quaestiones*
Cic. *Att.*	Cicero, *Letters to Atticus*
Cic. *Brut.*	Cicero, *Brutus*
Cic. *Cael.*	Cicero, *Pro Caelio*
Cic. *De Orat.*	Cicero, *De Oratore*
Cic. *De Rep.*	Cicero, *De Republica*
Cic. Dom.	Cicero, *De Domo Sua*
Cic. *Leg.*	Cicero, *De Legibus*
Cic. *Mil.*	Cicero, *Pro Milone*
Cic. *Phil.*	Cicero, *Philippics*
Cic. *Tusc.*	Cicero, *Tusculan Disputations*
Cic. *Verr.*	Cicero, *Verrine Orations*
C.Th.	*Codex Theodosianus*
Dem. *In Neaer.*	Demosthenes, *In Neaeram*
Dig. *De Adopt.*	Digest, *De Adoptione*
Dion. Hal.	Dionysius of Halicarnassus
Eutrop. *Brev.*	Eutropius *Breviarum*
Fast. Ant.	The Calendar of Antium
Fast. Ost.	The Calendar of Ostia
Florus *Epit.*	Florus, *Epitome*
Front. *Aq.*	Frontinus, *On the Water Supply*
Gaius *Inst.*	Gaius, *Institutes*
Hor. *Ode*	Horace, *Odes*
Jer. *ab Abr.*	St Jerome, *ab Abraham*
Jos. *Ant.*	Josephus, *Antiquities*
Jos. *Ap.*	Josephus, *Contra Apionem*

Jos. *BJ*	Josephus, *Jewish War*
Juv. *Sat.*	Juvenal, *Satires*
Livy *Per.*	Livy, *Summaries*
Lysias *In Diog.*	Lysias, *Against Diogeiton*
Macrob. *Sat.*	Macrobius, *Satires*
Martial *Spect.*	Martial, *Liber de Spectaculis*
Ovid *Ex Pont.*	Ovid, *Letter from the Pontus*
Ovid *Fast.*	Ovid, *Fasti*
Philo *Flacc.*	Philo, *Against Flaccus*
Philo *Leg.*	Philo, *Legatio*
Philost. *Apoll.*	Philostratus, *Life of Apollonius*
Phlegon *Mir.*	Phlegon, *Miracles*
Pliny *Ep.*	Pliny, *Epistles*
Pliny *NH*	Pliny, *Natural History*
Pliny *Paneg.*	Pliny, *Panegyricus*
Plut. *Ant.*	Plutarch, *Antony*
Plut. *Caes.*	Plutarch, *Caesar*
Plut. *Cat. Mai.*	Plutarch, *Cato the Elder*
Plut. *Cic.*	Plutarch, *Cicero*
Plut. *Cor.*	Plutarch, *Coriolanus*
Plut. *Gai. Gracc.*	Plutarch, *Gaius Gracchus*
Plut. *Galb.*	Plutarch, *Galba*
Plut. *Lucull.*	Plutarch, *Lucullus*
Plut. *Pomp.*	Plutarch, *Pompey*
Plut. *Quaest. Rom.*	Plutarch, *Quaestiones Romanae*
Plut. *Sull.*	Plutarch, *Sulla*
Plut. *Tib. Gracc.*	Plutarch, *Tiberius Gracchus*
Sall. *BC*	Sallust, *Civil War*
Schol. Hor. *Ode*	Scholiast, on Horace's *Odes*
Schol. Juv. *Sat.*	Scholiast, on Juvenal's *Satires*
Sen. *Ben.*	Seneca, *De Beneficiis*
Sen. *Brev.*	Seneca, *De Brevitate Vitae*
Sen. *Clem.*	Seneca, *De Celementia*
Sen. *Cons. Helv.*	Seneca, *Consolatio ad Helviam*
Sen. *Cons. Liv.*	Seenca, *Consolatio ad Liviam*
Sen. *Cons. Marc.*	Seneca, *Consolatio ad Marciam*
Sen. *Cons. Polyb.*	Seneca, *Consolatio ad Polybium*
Se. *Const.*	Seneca, *De Constantia Sapientis*
Sen. *Contr.*	Seneca, *Controversiae*
Sen. *Ep.*	Seneca, *Epistles*
Sen. *Ira*	Seneca, *De Ira*
Sen. *QN*	Seneca, *Quaestiones Naturales*
Sen. *Vit. Beat.*	Seneca, *De Vita Beata*
Serv. on Verg. *Aen.*	Servius, on Vergil's *Aeneid*
SHA	*Scriptores Historiae Augustae*

Simplicius *In cat.*	Simplicius, *On the Categories*
Stat. *Silv.*	Statius, *Silvae*
Suet. *Aug.*	Suetonius, *Augustus*
Suet. *Claud.*	Suetonius, *Claudius*
Suet. *Cal.*	Suetonius, *Caligula*
Suet. *Div. Jul.*	Suetonius, *Divus Julius* (Caesar)
Suet. *Dom.*	Suetonius, *Domitian*
Suet. *Galb.*	Suetonius, *Galba*
Suet. *Nero*	Suetonius, *Nero*
Suet. *Tib.*	Suetonius, *Tiberius*
Suet. *Tit.*	Suetonius, *Titus*
Suet. *Vesp.*	Suetonius, *Vespasian*
Suet. *Vit.*	Suetonius, *Vitellius*
Tac. *Ag.*	Tacitus, *Agricola*
Tac. *Ann.*	Tacitus, *Annals*
Tac. *Dial.*	Tacitus(?), *Dialogus*
Tac. *Germ.*	Tacitus, *Germania*
Tac. *Hist.*	Tacitus, *Histories*
Ulpian	Ulpian, *Ad Sabinam*
Ulpian *D.*	Ulpian, *Disputationes*
Val. Max.	Valerius Maximus
Varro *LL*	Varro, *Linga Latina*
Varro *RR*	Varro, *Res Rusticae*
Vell.	Velleius Paterculus
Verg. *Aen.*	Vergil, *Aeneid*
Zosim.	Zosimus

Modern Works

AA	*Archäologischer Anzeiger*
AAAH	*Acta ad Archaeologiam et Artium Historia Pertinentia*
AC	*L'Antiquité Classique*
ACD	*Acta Classica Universitatis Debreceniensis*
AE	*L'Année Epigraphique*
AFA	*Acta Fratrum Arvalium*
AHR	*American Historical Review*
AJA	*American Journal of Archaeology*
AJAH	*American Journal of Ancient History*
AJP	*American Journal of Philology*
Anc. Soc.	*Ancient Society*
ANRW	*Aufstieg und Niedergang der Römischen Welt*
ArchClass	*Archeologia Classica*
BGU	*Berliner griechische Urkunden*
BJ	*Bonner Jahrbücher*

BMC	Mattingly, H., *A Catalogue of the Roman Coins in the British Museum* (London, 1923)
BMCR	*Bullettino del Museo della Civiltà romana*
CIG	*Corpus Inscriptionum Graecarum*
CIL	*Corpus Inscriptionum Latinarum*
CJ	*Classical Journal*
C&M	*Classica et Mediaevalia*
CP	*Classical Philology*
CQ	*Classical Quarterly*
CR	*Classical Review*
CRAI	*Comptes Rendues de l'Académie des Inscriptions et Belles Lettres*
CT	*Les Cahiers de Tunisie*
CW	*The Classical World*
Degrassi	Degrassi, A., *I fasti consolari dell'impero romano dal 30 avanti Cristo al 613 dopo Cristo* (Rome, 1952)
Ditt.³	*Sylloge Inscriptionum Graecarum*, ed. W. Dittenberger, 3rd ed.
EJ	Ehrenberg, V., and Jones, A.H.M., *Documents Illustrating the Reigns of Augustus and Tiberius* (Oxford, 1952)
EMC	*Échos du Monde Classique*
FOS	Raepsaet-Charlier, M.F., *Prosopographie des femmes de l'ordre sénatorial (Ier– IIe siècles* (Louvain, 1987)
GNS	*Gazette Numismatique Suisse*
GR	*Greece and Rome*
HSCP	*Harvard Studies in Classical Philology*
IG	*Insciptiones Graecae*
IGR	*Inscriptiones Graecae ad Res Romanas pertinentes*
ILS	*Inscriptiones Latinae Selectae*
JDAI	*Jahrbuch des Deutschen Archäologischen Instituts*
JEA	*Journal of Egyptian Archaeology*
JNG	*Jahrbuch für Numismatik und Geldgeschichte*
JQR	*Jewish Quarterly Review*
JRS	*Journal of Roman Studies*
KölnJb	*Kölner Jahrbuch*
LEC	*Les Études Classiques*
MDAI(A)	*Mitteilungen des Deutschen Archäologischen Instituts (Athen. Abt.)*
MDAI (M)	*Mitteilungen des Deutschen Archäologischen Instituts (Madrid. Abt.)*
MDAI(R)	*Mitteilungen des Deutschen Archäologischen Instituts (Röm. Abt.)*
MH	*Museum Helveticum*
NC	*Numismatic Chronicle*
NS	*Notizie degli Scavi*

NZ	*Numismatische Zeitschrift*
Pap. Ryl.	*Catalogue of the Greek Papyri in the John Rylands Library at Manchester*
PBSR	*Papers of the British School at Rome*
PCPhS	*Proceedings of the Cambridge Philological Society*
PhW	*Philologische Wochenshrift*
PIR	*Prosopographia Imperii Romani*
P. Lond.	*Greek Papyri in the British Museum*
P. Mich.	*Greek Papyri in Michigan*
P. Oxy.	*Oxyrhynchus Papyri*
PP	*La Parola del Passato*
QAL	*Quaderni di Archeologia della Libia*
RA	*Revue Archéologique*
RAL	*Rendiconti dell'Accademia dei Lincei*
RBS	Bloch, H. *Roman Brick Stamps* (Cambridge, Mass., 1949–)
RCCM	*Rivista di Cultura classica e medioevale*
RE	*Paulys Real-Encyclopedie der classischen Altertumswissenschaft*
REA	*Revue des Études Anciennes*
REL	*Revue des Études Latines*
RFIC	*Rivista di Filologia e di Istruzione Classica*
RH	*Revue Historique*
RIA	*Rivista dell'Instituto Nazionale di Archeologia*
RIC	*Roman Imperial Coinage*
RIDA	*Revue Internationale des Droits de l'Antiquité*
RM	*Rheinisches Museum*
RN	*Revue Numismatique*
RPA	*Rendiconti della Pontificia Accademia di Archeologia*
RPC	Burnett, A. *et al.*, *Roman Provincial Coinage* (London, 1991)
RPh	*Revue de Philologie*
SchNR	*Schweizerische numismaytische Rundschau*
SEG	*Supplementum Epigraphicum Graecum*
Smallwood	Smallwood, M., *Documents Illustrating the Principates of Gaius, Claudius and Nero* (Cambridge, 1967)
Stud. Clas.	Studii Clasice
Stud. Rom.	Studii Romani
Syme *Papers A*	Syme, R., *Roman Papers* (Oxford, 1979–) Vols. I–III
Syme *Papers B*	Syme, R., *Roman Papers* (Oxford, 1979–) Vols. IV–V
TAM	*Tituli Asiae Minoris*
TAPA	*Transactions of the American Philological Association*
TZ	*Trierer Zeitschrift*
WS	*Wiener Studien*
WürzJbb	*Würzburger Jahrbücher für die Altertumswissenschaft*
YClS	*Yale Classical Studies*
ZPE	*Zeitschrift für Papyrologie und Epigrpahik*

Notes and References

1 Background (pp. 1–12)

1 Verg. *Aen.* 1.288, 6.789; Serv. on *Aen.* 1.267, 2.166; Livy 1.30.1–2 (emended); Dion. Hal. 3.29.7; Tac. *Ann.* 11.24.2; Suet. *Div. Jul.* 6.1; Weinstock (1971), 5

2 Syme (1986), 3, 51

3 See Allison & Cloud (1962); Syme (1958), 403; Levick (1979)

4 For general accounts, see Balsdon (1962), Pomeroy (1976), Hallett (1984), Gardner (1986), Bauman (1992)

5 Pliny's wife: Pliny *Ep.* 4.19; Cornelia: Plut. *Pomp.* 55.1; Caerellia: Cic. *Att.* 13.21.5

6 Cic. *Brut.* 211; Quintilian 1.1.6; Appian *BC* 4.4.32–4 (claiming to provide the text of her speech); Val. Max. 8.3.3

7 Juv. *Sat.* 6.434–56

8 Quintilian 1.1.6

9 Tac. *Dial.* 28

10 Cic. *Brut.* 211; Plut. *Tib. Gracc.* 1.4, *Gai. Gracc.* 4.3, 19.2; Appian, *BC* 1. 20

11 Tac. *Ag.* 4; Suet. *Nero* 52

12 *ILS* 68: Cornelia Africani filia Gracchorum (the base is still extant); Plut. *Gai. Gracc.* 19.2; cf. Val. Max. 8.3.3

13 *ILS* 8403; Suet. *Aug.* 73

14 Servius on *Aen.* 1.720

15 Sabines: Livy 1.13; Dion. Hal. 2.30: Coriolanus: Livy 2.33–5, 37–40; Dion. Hal. 6.92–4, 7.19, 21–67; Plut. *Cor.* 34–6

16 Lucretia: Livy 1.57–60; Dion. Hal. 4.64–7; Tullia: Livy 1.48.5–7; Dion. Hal.

4.28–30, 39

17 Livy 34.2–4; Plut. *Cat. Mai.* 8.2

18 Cic. *De Rep.* 1.67

19 Tac. *Ann.* 3.33

20 Livy 8.18.6; Tac. *Ann.* 2.71.4; Tacitus also speaks of the imperial house being rent by *muliebres offensiones* (*Ann.* 1.33.5, 12.64.4)

21 Livy 40.37.5

22 Popilia: Cic. *De Orat.* 2.44; Cornelia: Suet. *Div. Jul.* 6.1; Plut. *Caes.* 5.2; Julia (Caesar's aunt): Suet. *Div. Jul.* 6.1; Julia (Octavian's grandmother): Suet. *Aug.* 8.1; Quintilian 12.6.1

23 Bauman (1992), 60

24 Plut. *Cic.* 20.1

25 Valeria: Plut. *Sull.* 35.4–5; Praecia: Plut. *Lucull.* 6.2–3

26 Cic. *Verr.* 2.1.120, 136–8

27 Sall. *BC* 24.3–25; Tac. *Ann.* 12.7.6; Balsdon (1962), 47–8; Syme *Papers A* 1242–3, (1986), 198

28 Vell. 2.74.3; Plut. *Ant.* 10.3

29 Cic. *Phil.* 3.16

30 Modern scholarship has tended to follow the same lines as the ancient sources, but more recent studies exhibit a more sceptical assessment of the sources; see Babcock (1965), Pomeroy (1975), 185, 189, Hallett (1977), Dixon (1983), 109, Huzar (1986), 102; for a valuable sober re-evaluation of Fulvia's career: Delia (1991)

31 Ascon. *Comm.*25, 38

32 Cic. *Mil.* 28, 55; Val. Max. 3.5.3 (an obscure passage suggesting that Clodius was tied to her apron-strings, *adhaerens stolae*); Babcock (1965); Marshall (1985), 167 argues that Fulvia played an active political role as Clodius' wife; but note the reservations of Delia (1991), 198–9

33 Cic. *Phil.* 2.48

34 Cic. *Phil.* 3.4, 5.22, 13.18, picked up by Dio 45.13.2, 35.3; Appian *BC* 3.4

35 Dio 47.8.4

36 See Delia (1991), 205 and n.72 for a bibliography on the source material

37 Dio 47.8.2; Appian *BC* 4.29 (cf. Val. Max. 9.5.4, who makes no mention of Fulvia)

38 Appian *BC* 5.14

39 Dio 48.10.3–4; Vell. 2.74.2–3; Florus *Epit.* 2.16.2; Livy *Per.* 125; Martial *Spect.* 11.20; on the authenticity of the Octavian epigram, see Hallett (1977), 160–1

40 Appian *BC* 5.55, 59; Dio 48.28.3

2 Family (pp.13–21)

1 Daughter of Caecus: Suet. *Tib.* 2.3; Aul. Gell. 10.6.1; daughter (or sister?) of Pulcher: Cic. *Cael.* 34; Suet. *Tib.* 2.4

2 Vell. 2.75.1, 77.3

3 Vell. 2.75; Tac. *Ann.* 5.5.1–2; Suet. *Tib.* 4.2–3, 6.2; Dio 48.15.3, 54.7.2

4 Vell. 2.77.3; Tac. *Ann.* 5.1.2; Suet. *Tib.* 4.3

5 *Fasti Verulani* (*EJ* p. 46); Vell. 2.75; Tac. *Ann.* 5.1.3; Suet. *Tib.* 4.2, *Claud.* 11.3; Scribonia: *PIR* S220; Sen. *Ep.* 1.70.10; Suet. *Aug.* 62.2; for the tradition that Drusus was born three days before the marriage, see *PIR²* C857

6 Dio 49.15.5–6, 38.1; Bauman (1989), 32–4, (1992), 93–7

7 *CIL* 10.8042.41, 15.7814; Pliny *NH* 34.2.3; Dio 55.2.5–7, 56.10.1; Galba: Suet. *Cal.* 16.3, *Galb.* 5.2; Dio 59.2.3; Willrich (1911), 71; Rostovtzeff (1957), 670

8 Sen. *Cons. Marc.* 4.4; Suet. *Aug.* 69.1; Tac. *Ann.* 5.1.4; Dio 48.44; Val. Max. 6.1.1

9 Suet. *Aug.* 71.1; Dio 58.2.5; Tac. *Ann.* 1.5.3 calls her a *uxor facilis*

10 Suet. *Aug.* 84.2

11 Sen. *Clem.* 1.9; Dio 55.14–22.2

12 Tac. *Ann.* 5.1.5; Suet. *Aug.* 84.2, *Tib.* 50.3

13 Mommsen (1887), V.448

14 Béranger (1939), 183–6; Villers (1950), 236–8; Von Premerstein (1937), 267

15 Galba: Tac. *Hist.* 1.16.2; Vespasian: Suet. *Vesp.* 25 (echoed in Dio 66.12.1)

16 Suet. *Cal.* 24.1

17 Suet. *Aug.* 63.1

18 Ciaceri (1943), 295

19 *EJ* p.35; Vell. 2.93.1–2; Pliny *NH* 7.149, 19.24; Tac. *Ann.* 1.3.1; Suet. *Aug.* 66.1, 3; Suet. *Tib.* 6.4; Dio 51.21.3, 53.28.3–4, 30.1–5, 31.1–4, 33.4–5; see Syme (1939), 342, 344

20 Suet. *Aug.* 64.1; Dio 54.6.5, 8.5, 12.4, 18.1, 28; on the adoption, see Sutherland (1951), 58

21 Levick (1976), 57–60, argues that political intrigue lies behind the events

22 See Sumner (1967), 427–30 on the date

23 Livy *Per.* 142; Sen. *Cons. Liv.* 83–94, 169–86, 209–12, 465–6, *Cons. Marc.* 6.3.1, *Cons. Polyb.* 11.15.5; Pliny *NH* 7.84; Suet. *Claud.* 1.3; Dio 55.1.3–2.3; Val. Max. 5.5.3; charm and republican sentiments: Vell. 2.97.3; Tac. *Ann.* 1.33.3, 2.82.3; Suet. *Claud.* 1.4

24 Vell. 2.99.2; Tac. *Ann.* 1.53.2; Suet. *Tib.* 10.2; Dio 55.9

25 Pliny *NH* 7.45; Vell. 2.100.3; Suet. *Aug.* 64.2; Macrob. *Sat.* 2.5. Much of the information on Julia's character comes from the later author Macrobius, but is generally accepted by scholars: see Sattler (1969), 75

26 Tac. *Ann.* 6.51.3; Suet. *Tib.* 8.2–3; Macrob. *Sat.* 2.5.8; Bauman (1992), 112. For the date of the estrangement: Levick (1976), 37

27 Sen. *Ben.* 6.32.1–2, *Clem.* 1.10.3; Pliny *NH* 21.9; Tac. *Ann.* 1.53.1–4; Suet. *Aug.* 65.2, 101.3, *Tib.* 50.1; Dio 55.10.12–14, 13.1, 56.32.4. The modern scholarship on the topic is massive: for material before 1970 see Meise (1969), 3–34. Since 1970 see, *inter alios*, Levick (1972, 1975 & 1976), *Tiberius;* Ferrill (1976), Shotter (1971), 1120–1, Corbett (1974), 91–2, Lacey (1980), Syme, (1939), 427; *Papers A* 912–36, (1978), 192–8, Goold (1983), Raaflaub (1990), 428–30, Bauman (1992), 108–19

28 Vell. 2.100.4 (suicide); Tac. *Ann.* 1.10.4, 4.44.3 (execution), cf. Dio 55.10.15. Iullus'

literary pretensions: Schol. Hor. *Ode.* 4.2.25–36

29 Sempronius Gracchus: *PIR* S265; Tac. *Ann.* 1.53.6–9; Dio 55.10.15. Sempronius as poet: Ovid, *Ex Pont.* 4.16.31; Levick (1976), 41 argues against the identification of Sempronius with the tribune of 2 BC; Quinctius Crispinus Sulpicianus: *PIR* Q37; Scipio: Vell. 2.100.5; Scipio may be the son of P. Cornelius Scipio, consul 16 BC and son of Scribonia (as surmised in *PIR*² C1435); Appius Claudius: *PIR*² C760; Vell. 2.100.5; Syme, *Papers A* 926 suggests that Appius Claudius was the son or nephew of Appius Claudius Pulcher, consul of 38 BC; see T.P. Wiseman (1968), 207–9; Demosthenes: *PIR*² D47; Macrob. *Sat.* 1.11.17; Dio 55.10.16; see Sattler (1969), 517; on Ovid's possible involvement, see Thibault (1964), 55–67

30 Sen. *Ben.* 6.32.1, *Brev.* 4.5; Vell. 2.100.4; Tac. *Ann.* 3.18.1: *qui domum Augusti violasset*; 1.53.1, 3.24.2, 6.51.3 (*impudicitia*); 4.44.3 (adultery) 3.24. 3 (excessive punishment); Suet. *Aug.* 65.1; Dio 55.10.12; lists of conspirators: Sen. *Clem.* 1.9.6; Suet. *Aug.* 19.1; Sen. *Brev.* 4.5 (the 'Paulus' of Seneca's MS is clearly an error for Iullus, caused by confusion with the affair of Julia the Younger); Pliny *NH* 7. 149; Suet. *Aug.* 19.2; Tac. *Ann.* 1.10.5, 3.24.4; Dio 55.10.15; for a discussion of Pliny's evidence see Tränkle (1969), 121–3; Swan (1971), 740–1; Ferrill (1976), 344–5; Till (1977), 137; Bauman (1967), 198–245 argues that there was no political conspiracy, but that Julia and her paramours were convicted of a form of treason

31 See the comment of E. Gruen, in Raaflaub (1990), 429 n.48: 'One does not engage lightly in adulterous liaisons with a daughter of the *princeps*'

32 *EJ* p.39, 47, no. 69; Vell. 2.102.3; Suet. *Tib.* 11.4, 13.2–3; Dio 55. 10.10

33 For modern treatments, see, *inter alios*, Meise (1935), 35–48, with bibliography, Levick (1976), Syme (1978), 206–14; (1986), 117–22; Raaflaub (1990), 430–1, Bauman (1992), 119–24

34 Pliny *NH* 7.75; Tac. *Ann.* 3.24.5–7, 4.71.6–7; Suet. *Aug.* 64.1, 65.4, 72.3, 101.3; Schol. Juv. *Sat.* 6.158

35 Suet. *Aug.* 19.2; see also Norwood (1963), 153–5 and Levick (1976), 301–39; Schol. Juv. *Sat.* 6.158 (considered valid at *PIR*¹ J635)

36 Suetonius notes a conspiracy involving Lucius Paullus and a *Plautius* Rufus. If this is the *Publius* Rufus recorded by Dio as stirring up agitation in Rome in AD 6 (his name may have been Publius Plautius Rufus), we have a date of AD 6 for Paullus' conspiracy: Suet. *Aug.* 19.1; Dio 55.27.2; Paullus, according to Syme, was not executed. Lucius Paullus, a member of the Arval Brethren, is noted in their record as dying in May 14. Since an Arval cannot be deprived of his status even by exile, it is likely that banishment, rather than death, was the fate of Julia's husband: Syme (1978), 208; cf. Hohl (1937), 339–42 (dead in AD 1) and Norwood (1963) 150 (dead

in AD 6); the child: Barnes (1981), 362; Syme believes that the scholiast's information is confirmed by Suet. *Claud.* 26.1, where Suetonius observes that when Claudius was an *adulescens* (he would have been 17 in AD 8) he was forced to break off his engagement to Aemilia Lepida (daughter of Julia and Paullus) because her parents offended Augustus

3 Daughter (pp. 22–39)

1 Paratore (1952), 44

2 Tac. *Ann.* 6.25.3; Mellor (1993), 76–7

3 Syme (1958), 254

4 Tac. *Ann.* 1.33.1, 2.73.2–3; Suet. *Cal.* 3–6; Walker (1960), 232 notes the resemblances between Tacitus' depictions of Germanicus and of his own father-in-law Agricola

5 Tac. *Ann.* 1.78.2 (*male consulta*), 2.8.2 (*erratum*); Mellor (1993), 75–6; for a recent analysis of Tacitus' depiction of Germanicus, see Pelling (1993)

6 Tac. *Ann.* 1.33

7 *Fasti Vallenses* and *Fasti Pighiani*; Suet. *Cal.* 8.1; on Antium as the birthplace of Caligula, see Barrett (1990), 6–7, 255 n.10

8 Suet. *Cal.* 1.1; Dio 56.27.5

9 Suet. *Cal.* 8.4

10 *CIL* III.28 (a forgery); Sen. *Const.* 18.4; Tac. *Ann.* 1.41.3, 69.5; Suet. *Cal.* 9.1; Dio 57.5.6; Aur. Vict. *Caes.* 3.4; Anon. *Epit. de Caes.* 3.2; Eutrop. 7.12.1; Suda sv. *Kaligolas*

11 Vell. 2.132.2; Tac. *Ann.* 1.5; Suet. *Tib.* 22; Dio 56.30.1–2, 31.1. Dio and Suetonius note reports that Tiberius was responsible for concealing the truth about Augustus' death

12 Tac. *Ann.* 1.8.1–2, 14.1; Suet. *Tib.* 26.2, 50.2–3; Dio 57.2.1, 12.1.4

13 Suet. *Tib.* 50.2; Dio 57.12.2

14 Vell. 2.125; Tac. *Ann.* 1.31–49; Suet. *Tib.* 25.2; Dio 57.5–6; Schove (1984), 4–6

15 Tac. *Ann.* 1.40.3–44; Suet. *Cal.* 48.1; Dio 57.5.6. On the different versions of the

story, see Burian (1964), 25–9

16 Tac. *Ann.* 1.49.5–51.9; Dio 57.6.1

17 Syme (1958), 292–3; on the German campaigns: Timpe (1968), Syme (1978), 55, Lehmann (1991)

18 Tac. *Ann.* 1.59.3: *tradit C. Plinius, Germanorum bellorum scriptor* ...

19 Tac. *Ann.* 3.33, 4.20.3

20 Birth at Ara Ubiorum (later Cologne): Tac. *Ann.* 12.27.1 (see Tac. *Germ.* 28.4, Strabo 4.3.4 on the earlier history of Cologne); Hurley (1993), 23 argues on the basis of Suet. *Cal.* 8.3 that when Suetonius refers to Agrippina's birth *in ea regione* he makes specific reference to Ambitarvium, and that Agrippina's later claim to be born there was an unfounded boast

21 Suet. *Cal.* 8.1–4, where it is noted that Agrippina gave birth to two daughters in the region. Pliny mistakenly thought that the altars referred to Caligula; Ambitarvium: M. Ihm, *RE* 1 (1894), 1800

22 Tac. *Ann.* 2.26

23 Tac. *Ann.* 2.43.7, 3.56.5. Livilla had earlier been married to Gaius Caesar, who died in AD 4. Her marriage to Drusus is undated, but their daughter was old enough to be married in AD 20. See Eck (1993), 13 on the reasons for Germanicus' recall

24 Varro *LL* 5.54; Castagnoli (1964), 186 n.1

25 On the prestigious republican houses, see Tamm (1963), 28–45, Coarelli (1983), II.25, 31; on Marc Antony's house, Tamm (1963), 47 n.23, Kokkinos (1992), 147

26 Jos. *Ant.* 19.117; Kokkinos (1992), 149 argues that the house of Germanicus and the house of Antonia are identical

27 Tac. *Ann.* 2.41.2–4; Eck (1993), 13

28 The general stability of the area was further threatened by the uncertain future of other kingdoms of Asia Minor: Archelaus of Cappadocia (*PIR*[2] A1023) died in Rome in 17 at the latest (Tac. *Ann.* 2.42.2–6; Suet. *Tib.* 37.4; Dio 57.17.3–7); Antiochus III of Commagene (*PIR*[2] A741) and Philopator of Amanus (*PIR* P282): Tac. *Ann.* 2.42.7; Jos. *Ant.* 18.53

29 Tac. *Ann.* 3.1.5 states that on her return from the east Agrippina was accompanied by only two children (Caligula and the recently born Livilla)

30 Bauman (1992), 140

31 Tac. *Ann.* 2.55.5

32 Tac. *Ann.* 2.56.; Suet. *Cal.* 1.2; Dio 57.17.7

33 *Fast. Ant. (EJ* p. 53); Pliny *NH* 11. 187; Tac. *Ann.* 2.71–3; Suet. *Cal.* 1.2; Tac. *Ann.* 2.83.3 says that he died in the suburb of Epidaphne, a confusion with *Antioch epi Daphne*

34 Tac. *Ann.* 2.73, 83; Suet. *Cal.* 6; epigraphical evidence for the commemoration is preserved in the Tabula Hebana and Tabula Siarensis: *EJ* 94a; *ZPE* 55 (1984), 55–100; 67 (1987), 129–48; 86 (1991), 47–78; 87 (1991), 103–24; 90 (1992), 65–86

35 Tac. *Ann.* 3.17.5; on the senatorial account, see Eck, *Cahiers* (1993), 189; Rowe (1994)

36 Tac. *Ann.* 6.26.4 Dio 58.22.5

37 Tac. *Ann.* 4.8.4

38 Tac. *Ann.* 2.84.1

39 On the priesthoods of Nero and his brother Drusus, see Barrett (1990), 258 n.3

40 Tac. *Ann.* 4.2.4; Suet. *Claud.* 27.1; Dio 57.19.7; cf. Dio 58.4.3

41 Tac. *Ann.* 4.10; Dio 57.22.1–3

42 Tac. *Ann.* 4.2.1; Suet. *Tib.* 37.1; Dio 57.19.6

43 Tac. *Ann.* 4.12

44 Tac. *Ann.* 4.12.5, 17.4

45 Bauman (1992), 143; Rogers (1931) takes the extreme view in arguing for a conspiracy

46 Sen. *Ben.* 3.26.1 speaks of *accusandi frequens et paene publica rabies*; Syme (1958), 422

47 Tac. *Ann.* 3.44, 4.18–20; Bauman (1992), 146; Flaig (1993)

48 Tac. *Ann.* 4.39–40. Some have cast doubt on the supposed correspondence, and even on the incident itself

49 Tac. *Ann.* 4.52; Suet. *Tib.* 53.1; Bauman (1992), 148 suggests that the Claudia Pulchra incident comes from Agrippina's memoirs

50 Tac. *Ann.* 1.12.

51 Tac. *Ann.* 4.53; Suet. *Tib.* 53.1

52 Tac. *Ann.* 4.54; Suet. *Tib.* 53.1

53 Tac. *Ann.* 5.2.2; Suet. *Tib.* 50.3; Dio 57.12.5–6

54 Tac. *Ann.* 4.57.4; Suet. 51.1; Dio 57.12.6

55 Tac. *Ann.* 4.60.5–6

56 Sen. *Contr.* 1.3.10; Tac. *Ann.* 4.66

57 Pliny *NH* 8.145; Tac. *Ann.* 5.3.1; Suet. *Cal.* 10.1

58 Meise (1969), 240; other modern treatments include Charlesworth (1922), 260–1, V. Gardthausen, *RE* 10 (1918), 475; M. Gelzer, *RE* 10 (1918), 511; L. Petersen, *PIR²* I.217; Marsh (1931), 184–7; Rogers (1931), 160, (1935), 101, (1943), 57–9; Colin (1954), 389; Syme (1958), I.404–5; Koestermann (1963), on *Ann.* 5.3; Bauman (1992), 151

59 Sen. *Ira* 3.21.5; Tac. *Ann.* 4.67.5.; see Scott (1939), 462

60 Casa di Livia: *CIL* 15.7264; on the excavation of the house, Tamm (1963), 64 n.6; see Barrett (1990), 205, Kokkinos (1992), 148–9

61 Tac. *Ann.* 4. 68–70; Dio 58.1.1–3

62 Pliny *NH* 14.60; Tac. *Ann.* 5.1–2; Suet. *Tib.* 51.2, *Cal.* 10.1; Dio 58.2.1. On the date of the death, see Barrett (1990), 258 n.23

63 Tac. *Ann.* 5.3–4

64 Tac. *Ann.* 5.4.3

65 Philo *Flacc.* 9

66 Tac. *Ann.* 4.67.6

67 See Rogers (1931), 141–68; Boddington (1963), 1–16

68 Suet. *Tib.* 53.2

4 Sister (pp. 40–70)

1 German incursions: Tac. *Ann.* 4.72–4; Suet. *Tib.* 41. Marriage: Tac. *Ann.* 4.75; the fact that Tacitus records the marriage as the last item of 28 does not mean that it took place before 6 November, Agrippina's birthday. He often rounds off each year with scraps of information which do not fit into his narrative (despite Paratore [1952] 38, who suggests that the marriage is mentioned at the end of the year in Tacitus' narrative in order to draw attention to it). On the age at marriage, see Hopkins (1965 & 1966), Weaver (1972), 182, Shaw (1987), Treggiari (1991), 399–402

2 Tac. *Ann.* 4.75. References to the marriage: Jos. *Ant.* 20.148; Tac. *Ann.* 6.45.3, 12.64.4; Plut. *Ant.* 87.4; Suet. *Nero* 5.2, *Galb.* 5.1; Dio 58.20.1

3 *AFA* (Smallwood 16.5, 19.24, 21.25, 23.5); Sen. *Contr.* 9.4.18; Carandini (1988), 359–87; Seneca in fact refers to the building of *thermae*, hot baths which are usually public, but the context of his mother's distress indicates clearly that Domitius was involved in a private, not public, building

4 Pliny *NH* 7.71; Griffin (1984), 23 speculates that Pliny might have found the information in Agrippina's memoirs

5 Tac. *Ann.* 12.64.4, 13.19.2, 14.9.1; Dio 60.31.6, 61.14.2; Suet. *Nero* 34.4 says that when Nero examined Agrippina's body he praised some aspects, found fault with others

6 *RIC*[2] Claudius 75 (but see the comments of von Kaenel [1986], 18–19, 80–1); Nero 1–3, 6–7

7 Suet. *Claud.* 30; see Wood (1988) for the resemblances of the sculpted heads attributed to the two Agrippinas

8 Jos. *Ant.* 20.148; Vell. 2.72.3; Tac. *Ann.* 4.75; Suet. *Nero* 5.1; Juv. *Sat.* 8.224–8; Asilius Sabinus: Sen. *Contr.* 9.4.18; his actual words (in Greek) were *proton kolymban, deyteron de grammata*, alluding to the proverb found in Plato, *Laws* 689D; Eck (1993), 17

9 Mommsen (1864), 1.73; Wiseman (1971), 172; Bradley (1978), 27

10 Bradley (1978), 30; Syme, *Papers A* 815 (1986), 157

11 Brunt (1975), 619–25; Griffin (1984), 21

12 Vell. 2.72.3; Tac. *Ann.* 4.44.1–3 (Tacitus erroneously identifies his wife as the younger Antonia here, as at *Ann.* 12.64.4); Suet. *Nero* 4; Plut. *Ant.* 87.3

13 Sen. *Contr.* 9.4.18; Tac. *Ann.* 6.1.1, 45.1–3; Dio 58.20.1

14 Bradley (1978), 43; E. Groag, *RE* (1903), 5.1, 1331; *PIR*² D127; Griffin (1984), 21; Syme (1986), 155–6 bases his thesis on evidence from the frieze of the Ara Pacis. This monument was dedicated in 9 BC to commemorate Augustus' safe return from Gaul and Spain. The altar was surrounded by a walled precinct illustrating the procession on the day of its consecration 13 BC, with relief portraits of the imperial family. The boy with Domitius and Antonia is about 6 or 7, too old to be Gnaeus; see Simon (1967), 19, Pl.15

15 Suet. *Nero* 5.2

16 On Domitia: *FOS* 319; *PIR*² D171; A. Stein, *RE* 5.1 (1903), 1509–10. She is referred to only as 'Domitia', with the following exceptions: name not given but inferred by allusion to aunt and freedman Paris (Tac. *Ann.* 13.27.7); name not given but indicated by analogy with Dio (Suet. *Nero* 34.5); referred to as Nero's aunt (Suet. *Nero* 34.5 [by inference]; Tac. *Ann.* 13.19.4; Dio 61.17.1; Schol. Juv. *Sat.* 4.81; Digest 12.4.3.5, mistakenly calling her the *filia* of Nero)

17 Tac. *Ann.* 13.21.4; Dio 61.17.1

18 Suet. *Nero* 5.2; Quintilian 6.1.50

19 Dio 61.17.2; Tac. *Ann.* 13.21.6; on her Roman estates, *SHA* Pius 5.1; Aurelianus 49.1. In the same region a pipe inscribed with the name *Crispi Passieni* (*CIL* XV.7508) was found. On the possibility that the gardens of Domitia take their name from Domitia Longina Augusta (*PIR*² D181), see A. Stein *RE* (1918), Suppl. 3, 410

20 Domitia Lepida: *FOS* 326, *PIR*² D180, E. Groag, *RE* 5.1 (1903), 1511–13. She is usually called simply Lepida, except at Tac. *Ann.* 12.64.4 (Domitia Lepida); Syme (1986), 158–9, argues that the cognomen *Lepida* came from the mother's side, and suggests a first marriage to Aemilia Lepida for her grandfather Domitius Ahenobarbus, the naval commander

21 Tac. *Ann.* 12.64.5; Suet. *Nero* 5.2

22 Calabria: Tac. *Ann.* 12.65.1; Griffin (1984), 31 speculates that Nero first met Ofonius Tigellinus there; Fundi: a freedman L. Domitius Phaon, from her estate at Fundi, died 20 June 67 (*AE* 1914.219). Puteoli: two wax tabulae refer (1) to granaries on the estates (*in praedis* […]*tiacis*) of Domitia L[*iv*]ia (*AE* 1973.167), reread as *praed(i)iis B[ar]batianis* of Domitia L[*e*]pida in *AE* 1978.139, and (2) to the [*praediis*] Lepidan[*is*] in the Puteoli area (*AE* 1978 139) ; see D'Arms (1981), 76 n.17

23 See Barrett (1990), 259 n.29

24 Tac. *Ann.* 6.23.1–3, 25.2; Dio 58.3.1–6, 23.6

25 Suet. *Tib.* 54.2, *Cal.* 7; Dio 58.3.8

26 Suet. *Tib.* 54.2, 61.1; Dio 58.8.4

27 Dio 58.11.6–7

28 On Caligula's stay in Capri, see Barrett (1990), 27–41; for a recent survey of Herod Agrippa's career, see Schwartz (1990)

29 Tac. *Ann.* 5.10; Dio 58.25.1

30 Tac. *Ann.* 6.23.4–6; Suet. *Tib.* 54.2, 61.1; Dio 58.22.4, 25.4

31 Tac. *Ann.* 6.25.1; Suet. *Tib.* 53.2; Dio 58.22.4

32 Sen. *Contr.* 10.4.25; Tac. *Ann.* 6.15.1–2, 27.1; Syme, *Papers B* 177–98; Levick (1976), 208

33 On the marriage, see Barrett (1990), 61 n.63

34 Schol Juv. *Sat.* 1.155 (cf. Dio 59.23.9). On the scholia on Juvenal see Wessner (1931), xxxvi–xlv

35 Tac. *Ann.* 2.74.1, 79.1, 6.47–8, 12.52; Suet. *Nero* 5.2; Dio 58.27.2; Levick (1976), 216–7; Forsyth (1969), Bauman (1974), 130–4, (1992), 164; Vibius Marsus: *PIR* V388; Lucius Arruntius:*PIR*[2] A1130; Albucilla: *PIR*[2] A487; she was the former wife of Satrius Secundus

36 Tac. *Ann.* 6.50.6

37 Philo *Leg.* 10–13, 232, 356; Suet. *Cal.* 13

38 Jos. *Ant.* 18.236; Suet. *Cal.* 15.1; Dio 59.3.8

39 *AFA* Scheid 221.3; *AFA* (Smallwood 9.11–15)

40 Suet. *Cal.* 15.2; cf. Suet. *Tib.* 26.2; the fifth month of the year (the numeration in the Roman calendar begins with March). Quintilis, had similarly been renamed Julius, since Caesar had been born in that month, and Sextilis had been renamed Augustus, as the month of his first consulate. The choice of September for Germanicus would have provided a nice quasi-dynastic sequence following Julius and Augustus. Clearly

the arrangement was short-lived, and there is no evidence of its use in Italy. It is attested in Egypt, along with other months honouring Caligula or his family, such as Gaieos (Phamenoth) and Drusilleios (Payni), Scott (1931), 230; Rea, (1988), 10–14; Hanson, 1287–95; Balconi (1985), 84–8

41 *RIC*[2] 21–2, 25–6

42 Agrippina: Smallwood 84, 85; *RIC*[2] Gaius 55; on the coin, see Trillmich (1978), 32–5, Jucker (1980), 205–17; Suet. *Tib.* 54.2, *Cal.* 15.1, Dio 58.22.5; Nero and Drusus: *RIC*[2] Gaius 34, 42, 49; Suet. *Claud.* 9.1; Drusus: *ILS* 187 (Bergamo). Dio 59.3.5 mistakenly states that Drusus' remains were recovered (see Suet. *Cal.* 15.1)

43 *AFA* (Smallwood 3.7); Tac. *Ann.* 4.16.6; Suet. *Aug.* 44.3, *Cal.* 15.2, *Claud.* 11.2 (with Lipsius' emendation); Dio 59.3.4. Refusal to use the title in Rome during her life-time might explain the tradition that *Claudius* bestowed it on her; she is called Augusta before death on at least one non-Roman inscription, from Corinth (*CIL* 6.892; see Kokkinos [1992], 46–7). The only mints to identify her as Augusta are those of Corinth and Thessalonica (*RPC* 1176–7, 1573–5)

44 *Fast. Ost.* 14–15 (Smallwood 31); Suet. *Claud.* 9.1

45 Suet. *Div. Jul.* 80.2, *Aug.* 58.2, *Tib.* 51.1, *Cal.* 15.3; Dio 58.2.8: oaths were taken by the fortunes of Sejanus and Tiberius, and it might be implied that Sejanus was included in the oath for the emperor's safety: *euchonto hyper amphoin* (Tiberius and Sejanus)

46 Tiberius: Tac. *Ann.* 1.7.3, 34.1; Dio 57.3.2, 58.12.6, 17.2; Caligula: Philo *Leg.* 231; Jos. *Ant.* 18.124; Suet. *Cal.* 15.3; Dio 59.3.4, 9.2; Herrmann (1968), 109 on the annu-al oath. Practice in the east was clearly more casual; at the beginning of Caligula's reign the town of Assos offered congratulations to the new emperor and declared its loyalty to the emperor and his house (Smallwood 33)

47 *RIC*[2] Gaius 33; *RPC* 4977 (Herod Agrippa); 2014, cf. 2012 (Apamea); *RIC*[2] Claudius 124 (Cappadocia)

48 Jos. *Ant.* 19.204 (sister, singular); Suet. *Cal.* 24.1; Dio 59.11.1 (Drusilla) 22.6 (Agrippina and Livilla); Eutropius 7.12.3 (sisters); Aur. Vict. *Caes.* 3.10 (sisters); Anon. *Epit.de Caes.* 3.4 (sisters); Jer. *ab Abr.* 178 (Helm) (sisters); Schol. Juv. *Sat.* 4.81 (sister, singular); Orosius 7.5.9 (sisters)

49 Suet. *Cal.* 29.1 (the text reads *adiatrephia*)

50 Schol. Juv. *Sat.* 4.81, probably based on Suet. *De Oratoribus* (now lost), where Passienus Crispus is confused with Vibius Crispus

51 Tac. *Ann.* 14.2.4

52 On the dedication of the temple, see Barrett (1990), 69–70

53 Dio 59.7.4

54 On the dates and nature of the illness, see Barrett (1990), 73–4

55 *ILS* 172 (Smallwood 88); Philo *Leg.* 23–31, 62–5, 68; Suet. *Cal.* 23.3; Dio 59.8.1, 4–5, 10.8; Barrett (1990), 75–7

56 The name was Cornelia Orestina according to Dio, Livia Orestilla according to Suetonius, who is generally more reliable on such matters: Suet. *Cal.* 25.1; Dio 59.8.7; on the names, see Kajava (1984), 23–30

57 For the theory that Domitius was sterile and that Nero was not his son, see Edgeworth (1986)

58 Suet. *Aug.* 58.2; Scrinari (1975), 10–11; Blake (1959), 40; Coarelli (1982), 295–6; most of what has survived of the western section is republican in date

59 Tac. *Ann.* 14.9.5; Dio 61.2.2; cf. Suet. *Nero* 6.1; for the son of Thrasyllus, Tac. *Ann.* 6.1.6

60 Pliny *NH* 7.46

61 Suet. *Nero* 6.1; Dio 60.2.3

62 Pliny *NH* 7.45; Suet. *Nero* 6.1–2; Dio 60.33.2², 2^C, 61.2.1; Willrich (1903), 291; Balsdon (1934), 42; Edgeworth (1986), 104: Stahr (1867) 11 argues that he was given the name of Claudius Domitius Ahenobarbus. Edgeworth explains the anecdote as indicating that Domitius did not accept the child as his own

63 Machaon: Dio 59.9.3; Macro: Philo *Flacc.* 13–16, *Leg.* 32–62; Suet. *Cal.* 26.1; Dio 59.10.6. For modern theories: De Visscher (1964), 54–65; Meise (1962), 252; Dabrowski (1972), 114–72

64 Date of death: *Fast. Ost.* (Smallwood 31.30); date of consecration: *AFA* (Smallwood 5.5.15) as restored, but see Temporini (1978), 72; Geminus: *Apoc.* 1.2; Dio 59.11.4 (Dio gives the name 'Geminius'); *iustitium:* Philo *Flacc.* 56 (but see *AFA* Scheid 224–5); oaths: Suet. *Cal.* 24.2; *Drusilleios:* Boak (1927), 185–6; Scott (1931), 249–51; Rea (1988) 11, 13; P. Mich.V. 321.19 provides the last known citation (December 42)

65 Livia: Suet. *Claud.* 11.2; Dio 60.5.2; Claudia: Tac. *Ann.* 15.23.4; Poppaea: Tac. *Ann.* 16.21.2

66 Dio 59.11.1 claims that Marcus Lepidus and Caligula were homosexual lovers

67 Suet. *Cal.* 24.1; Dio 59.11.1, 22.6–7; Drusilla as successor: accepted by Mommsen (1887) II, 1135 n.5; Lepidus' statues at Aphrodisias: *SEG* 30.1251, see Reynolds (1980), 70–84

68 Pliny *NH* 9.117; Suet. *Cal.* 25.2; Dio 59.12.1

69 Tac. *Ann.* 12.2.2; Tacitus records that the argument used in favour of Lollia as a wife for Claudius was the fact that she was barren and would not present a threat to the succession; Suet. *Cal.* 25.2; Dio 59.12.1, 23.7

70 Jos. *Ant.* 19.193; Tac. *Ann.* 2.85.1–4; Pliny *NH* 7.39; Suet. *Cal.* 25.3–4, 33; Dio 59.23.7, 28.7

71 Suet. *Cal.* 23.1, 26.3; Dio 59.18.1–4, 20.1, 23.8

72 Tac. *Ann.* 6.9.5–6, *Hist.* 1.48.2–3; Plut. *Galb.* 12.1; Dio 59.18.4; see Simpson (1980), 358

73 Tac. *Ann.* 6.30.3–7; Dio 59.22.5

74 *AFA* (Smallwood 9.18–20)

75 Suet. *Cal.* 8.2, *Galb.* 6.2; Dio 59.21.4, 22.5

76 Lack of discipline: Tac. *Ann.* 6.30.3; Dio 59.22.5; cf. Suet. *Cal.* 44.1; *Galb.* 6.2–3

77 A. Stein, *RE 4* (1900), 1385; Simpson (1980), 362; Willrich (1903), 307; Linnert (1908), 81; Bergener (1965), 120; Barrett (1990), 105

78 Stewart (1953); Meise (1962), 114–15; Bergener (1965), 119; Faur (1973), 19

79 *PIR*² C 1391, 1479; Garzetti (1974), 91; Stewart (1953), 72; Bergener (1965), 121; Faur (1973), 23

80 Sen. *QN* 4A *praef.* 15, *Ep.* 31.9; see W. Kroll, *RE* 13 (1927), 1645; Pflaum (Paris 1961), III 761–2, L. Petersen, *PIR*² L388 argues that Lucilius never held an Alpine procuratorship

81 Suet. *Claud.* 9.1

82 Phlegon *Mir.* (FGH 2.1179.VII)

83 Tac. *Ann.* 14.2.4; Suet. *Cal.* 24.3, 29.2; Dio 59.22.6,8; Namatianus 1.306

84 Bergener (1965), 120

85 Linnert (1908), 81; Willrich (1903), 297; Meise (1962), 101–22; Faur (1973), 16

86 Griffin (1984), 27

87 Tac. *Ann.* 14.2.4

88 Pliny *NH* 7.39; Eck (1993), 20

89 Philo *Flacc.* 185–91

90 Willrich (1903), 308; Linnert (1908), 61–82; Meise (1962), 110–11, 119; Faur (1973), 19

91 Dio 59.23.8

92 Sen. *Ep.* 4.7; the tribune is called Dexter

93 Suet. *Cal.* 24.3; Dio 59.22.7–8; Scaevinus: Tac. *Ann.* 15.74.1; Vespasian: Suet. *Vesp.* 2.3, 4.2. Nicols (1978), 5–7 places Vespasian's praetorship in 40

94 Suet. *Cal.* 39.1

95 Dio 59.23.9 (who mentions only Agrippina); Schol. Juv. *Sat.* 1.155; Roper (1979), 347

96 Sen. *Ep.* 108.22, *Cons. Helv.* 19

97 Sen. *Contr.* 3. pr.10 calls Passienus' grandfather '*Passienus noster*'

98 Sen. *Cons Helv.* 18.6,; *Ep.* 104.2, Sen. *Vit. Beat.* 17.2; Suet. *Cal.* 53.2; Tac. *Ann.* 15.60.5, 63, 64; Dio 61.10.3, 62.25.1–2; praetorship: Griffin (1976), 46; it was bestowed after his return to Rome in 41: Tac. *Ann.* 12.8.3

99 Suet. *Cal.* 34.2, 53.2; Dio 59.18; Barrett (1990), 48–9

100 First proposed by Walz (1909), 68; see Clarke (1953), Mendell (1957), 147

101 Marchesi (1944), 11; Stewart (1953), 81 (on the connection with the Sejanians); Lana (1955), 106, 115; Griffin (1976), 53–6

102 Dio 59.22.8

103 Tac. *Ann.* 14.63.2; Tacitus refers to Livilla's expulsion by Claudius, but his silence

about Agrippina the Younger is still significant

104 Strabo 5.3.6; Columella *RE* 7.17; Dio 59.22.8; D'Arms (1970), 78. Pontia: Jacono (1926), 219–32; Ward-Perkins (1959), 154 n.4, Coarelli (1984), 381–7

105 Pliny *NH* 32.154

106 *AFA* (Smallwood 10.10); Suet. *Nero* 6.3; Bradley (1978), 48

107 Suet. *Nero* 6.3; see Geer (1931), 60–1, Bradley (1978), 48. Suetonius' entry that Domitius died before Agrippina's banishment must be a slip (he is followed by Lackeit [1918], 910)

108 Suet. *Cal.* 29.2, *Claud.* 9.1; Dio 59.22.9

5 Niece (pp. 71–94)

1 Suet. *Cal.* 60; Dio 60.1.1; Jos. *Ant.* 19.158–89

2 Suet. *Claud.* 29.1, *Vit.* 2.5

3 *Apoc.* 5.2; Suet. *Claud.* 2.1, 3.2 (with Leon [1948], 81), 4.2; Dio 60.2.1; Claudius' literary pursuits: Schmidt (1994), 119–31; Malitz (1994), 133–44

4 Momigliano (1961), 2

5 Tac. *Ann.* 12.59.1, 14.46; Dio 60.12.5

6 Jung (1972); Levick (1990), 29–39; Barrett (1990), 176–7

7 Jos. *Ant.* 19.267; Rufrius Pollio: *PIR*[1] R123; Catonius Justus: *PIR*[2] C576

8 Momigliano (1961), 44; McAlindon (1957), 281

9 *Apoc.* 14; Sen. *Clem.* 1.23.1; Suet. *Claud.* 29.1–2; Dio 60.16.1–2; McAlindon (1956), 114; Wiseman (1982), 65; Momigliano (1961), 53

10 Bauman (1992), 171

11 Tac. *Ann.* 15.35.2, 16.12.3; Koster (1994), 1–9

12 McAlindon (1956); Syme (1986), 188–99

13 Vitellius' abilities: Tac. *Ann.* 6.32.5–5, 37; Suet. *Vit.* 2.4; Dio 59.27.2–6; Dorey

(1966), 145–52: Vitellius and Caligula: Suet. *Vit.* 2.5; Dio 59.27.6; Vitellius and Antonia: Tac. *Ann.* 11.3.1; Messalina's shoe: Suet. *Vit.* 2.5; Syme (1986), 183. The inscription on his tomb read: *pietatis immobilis erga principem* ('[a man] of unswerving loyalty towards the emperor', Suet. *Vit.* 3.1)

14 Ovid *Ex. Pont.* 4.8; Pliny *NH* 7.39; Tac. *Ann.* 4.31.5–6; Syme (1949), 16–17; Cichorius (1922), 429 mistakenly took Suillius to be Vistilia's husband. Suillius Caesoninus: *PIR* S698; Tac. *Ann.* 11.36.5, 13.11.2 (he did not benefit from the amnesty granted in 55). Tac. *Ann.* 13.43.2 lists Suillius' named victims: Q. Pomponius, Julia (daughter of Drusus), Poppaea Sabina, Valerius Asiaticus, Lusius Saturninus, Cornelius Lupus; on the date of his consulship (21 or 25): Gallivan (1976), 419

15 General: Suet. *Aug.* 44.1, 74, Tac. *Ann.* 4.6.8; Augustus: Suet. *Aug.* 67.1 (Licinus and Celadus), Juv. *Sat.* 1.109 (Licinus); Tiberius: Dio 58.19 6 (Hiberus), Jos. *Ant.* 18.167 (Samaritan, perhaps 'Thallos'), Pliny *NH* 13.95 (Nomius)

16 Dio 59.26.1–2 (Protogenes); Stat. *Silv.* 3.3; Martial 6.83, 7.40 (Tiberius Claudius [his name is uncertain]); Philo *Leg.* 166–77, 181, 203, 206 (Helicon and Homilos); Sen. *Ep.* 47.9; Jos. *Ant.* 19.64–9; Pliny *NH* 33.134, 36.60; Tac. *Ann.* 11.29.1; Plut. *Galb.* 9.1; Barrett (1989), 176–7

17 Suet. *Claud.* 25.5; Scramuzza (1940), 87; Momigliano (1961), 34; McAlindon (1965), 118; Garzetti (1974), 587

18 *Apoc.* 13.3; Tac. *Ann.* 12.66.1

19 Melmoux (1977), 61: freed by Caligula, like Callistus: *ILS* 191; A. Stein, *RE* (1935), 1701; Oost (1958), 111: freed by Claudius. Schol. Juv. *Sat.* 14.329: *Narcissus ... ditissimus eunuchus*

20 Boulvert (1965), 92

21 Tac. *Ann.* 11.29.3, 37.4; Suet. *Vesp.* 4.1; Melmoux (1977), 64; McAlindon (1977), 253

22 Suet. *Claud.* 28; Dio 60.34.4

23 Tac. *Ann.* 11.29.1, 12.53.3; Duff (1928), 77; Westerman (1955), 89

24 Jos. *Ant.* 18.182; Dio 66.14.1–2. *Pap. Ryl.* II.255 (see Rostovtzeff [1957], 674 n.48) shows him as owner of an estate in Egypt during Antonia's lifetime. It is just possible, though unlikely, that it was part of his *peculium* (savings)

25 Tac. *Ann.* 12.25.1, 53.5, 65.4, 14.2.4; Dio 1.3.2, 62.14.3; Probus (in Schol. Juv. *Sat.* 1.109); on gardens, Front. *Aq.* 1.19, 20, 69; see also Pliny *NH* 33.134; Juv. *Sat.*

1.108–9; Suet. *Claud.* 28; Tac. *Ann.* 14.65.1

26 Pliny *Ep.* 7.29, 8.6; Tac. *Ann.* 12.53.5

27 Aemilia Lepida: PIR^2 A419, *FOS* 29; Suet. *Claud.* 26.1; Livia Medullina: PIR^2 L304; *FOS* 500; Suet. *Claud.* 26.1; Plautia Urganilla: PIR^1 P368; *FOS* 619; Suet. *Claud.* 26.2, 27.1; Hoffmann, *RE* 21 (1951), 54, no. 66. Levick (1990), 24–5 sees a link with the Silvanus scandal and places the divorce in the same year, 24. Ehrhardt (1978), 56 argues that the marriage to Plautia Urganilla took place some years before 20

28 Aelia Paetina: PIR^2 A305; *FOS* 18; P. von Rohden, *RE* I (1893), 539 no. 179; Jos. *Ant.* 20.150, *BJ* 2.249; Tac. *Ann.* 12.1; Suet. *Claud.* 26.2, 27.1; on the political aspects of the divorce, Levick (1990), 55; potteries: *RBS* 196–7

29 On Messalina: *PIR* V161; *FOS* 774; Syme (1958), 437, (1986), 150, 164, 178: after the death of Messalina's father, her mother remarried and produced a son Faustus, consul in 52. Faustus' consulship is unlikely to have been delayed beyond the appropriate year, which would place his birth, and hence his parents' marriage, before 20. On this principle, Messalina's birth would not be placed after 20 and Messalina would reach marriageable age some years before the wedding to Claudius (Levick [1990], 55 agrees); but estimates of the marriage date vary: Mottershead (1986), 107 (39); Syme (1958), 55 n.26 (shortly before 41); Ehrhardt (1978), 56 (mid-37). On her birth-date: Geer (1931); (AD 26); Syme (1958), 437 n.5 (earlier than 20); Ehrhardt (1978), 55 (20); Meise (1969), 152 n.122 (no later than 24). Note also that because of his betrothal to Antonia, Faustus was given accelerated promotion of five years, as was Antonia's previous fiancé. The wedding, then, need not necessarily predate 24

30 Syme (1958), 184, (1986), 182

31 Juv. *Sat.* 6.120–32; Pliny *NH* 10.172; Dio 60.18.1–2

32 Suet. *Claud.* 27.2; Tac. *Ann.* 13.15.1 states explicitly that Britannicus became 14 in 55, and thus puts his birth securely in 41. But note that in this context Tacitus wants to provide a motive for Britannicus' murder in 55 (the approach of the age of manhood). The date does receive support from a coin of Alexandria of 41 (*RPC* 5113) depicting Messalina with two small children; Suet. *Claud.* 27.2 provides impossible contradictory dates: Britannicus was born on the twentieth day of Claudius' *imperium* (ie February 41), but in his second consulship (Jan–Feb 42); Dio 60.12.5 places Britannicus' birth among the events of 42; see the discussion in Schwartz (1992), 229, n.42

33 Dio 60.12.5

34 Suet. *Claud.* 11.2; Dio 60.5.1–2; the title of Augusta, originally offered to Antonia by

Caligula, but not used by her in Rome, may have been conferred on her once again

35 Tac. *Ann.* 11.38.3; Dio 60.12.4–5, 22.2; Suet. *Claud.* 17.3; Meise (1969), 149, 151 on the significance of the *carpentum:* Tac. *Ann.* 12.42.2

36 Stahr (1967), 39; Jos. *Ant.* 19.237; Suet. *Cal.* 59.1, *Nero* 50, *Dom.* 17.3

37 Jos. *Ant.* 19.127–30, 158–9; Suet. *Cal.* 60

38 Stahr (1867), 56; Lackeit (1918), 910; Maurer (1949), on Suet. *Cal.* 7., Kornemann (1942), 226

39 Dio 60.27.4

40 Dio 60.8.5

41 Suillius' charge: Dio 61.10.1; Claudius' affairs: Suet. *Claud.* 33.2; Tac. *Ann.* 11.29.3; Dio 60.18.3; Meise (1969), 140

42 On the procedure, Bauman (1974a), under 'Manifest Guilt', (1992), 260 n.15

43 Suet. *Claud.* 29.1; *Apoc.* 10.4, 13.5

44 Tac. *Ann.* 14.63.2 (for a discussion on Pandateria as her place of exile, see p. 69); Dio 60.8.5; *Apoc.* 10.4 reports that Claudius put to death the two Julias, great-grand-daughters of Augustus, one by starvation the other by the sword. Julia wife of Rubellius died by the sword (*Octavia* 945); Fitzler *RE* 10 (1918), 938–9, no. 575 seems to confuse the two Julias; mausoleum: *ILS* 188 (Smallwood 87)

45 Dio 60.27.4. Dio's text is obscure and possibly corrupt. As it stands it seems to say that Messalina suspected Vinicius of being responsible for Livilla's death

46 Sen. *Cons. Polyb.* 13.2; Schol. Juv. *Sat.* 5.109

47 Suet. *Claud.* 17.3; Sen. *Cons. Polyb.* 13.2; Helvia: Griffin (1976), 60; *iustitia:* Sen. *Cons. Polyb.* 13.3

48 Sen. *QN* 4 praef.14

49 On Agrippina's possible intercession: Griffin (1984), 28, Kamp (1934). Messalina's role in Seneca's exile: Meise (1969), 141, Roper (1979), 347, Levick (1990), 56; on Seneca's exile: Ferrill (1966), 254, Kamp (1934), 101–8, Stewart (1953), 84f n.92; on the affair between Seneca and Livilla, Giancotti (1953), 53–62

50 Suet. *Nero* 6.3

51 Tac. *Hist.* 1.49; Suet. *Galb.* 2; Wiseman (1974), 153, (1982), 62; Menaut (1981), 268 is mistaken in asserting that Agrippina sought the hand of the *father* of the future emperor

52 Plut. *Galb.* 3.1; Suet. *Cal.* 16.3, *Galb.* 3.4, 4.1, 5.2; Dio 59.2.3

53 Dio 57.19.4; Syme (1986), 130 observes that Manius Aemilius Lepidus (*PIR²* A363) was not, as often believed, the most illustrious member of the family at that period, and that a wrong emendation of Tacitus assigned to him the achievements of his relative Marcus Aemilius Lepidus (*PIR²* A369)

54 Suet. *Galb.* 5.1, 7.1; Barrett (1990), 129

55 Schol. Juv. *Sat.* 4.81; Herzog (1922), 237 n.2 provides the text of a dubious inscription from Cos identifying Passienus as husband of Agrippina (see p. 223)

56 Sallustius: *PIR* S61; Tac. *Ann.* 1.60, 2.40, 3.30.7; Tacitus observes in Sallustius' obituary that in his final years his influence had started to wane somewhat. Passienus' grandfather (also called Passienus) was a distinguished orator. His natural father Lucius Passienus elevated the family to senatorial rank, holding the consulship in 4 BC, and went on to be proconsul of Africa and, earn the *ornamenta triumphalia* in an unspecified war, possibly the Gaetulian campaign of AD 6. An inscription from the African town of Thugga records honours paid to Lucius' son, a military tribune in the Legio XII Fulminata. Orator Passienus: (*PIR* P108); Sen. *Contr.* 3, praef. 14; *ornamenta triumphalia* Vell. 2.116.2; Thugga inscription: *ILS* 8966; Syme (1986), 162; Roman estate: *CIL* 15.7508, a pipe with the name of Crispus Passienus

57 First consulship: Degrassi 9; Vogel-Wiedemann (1982), 327; Asia: *AE* 1969.460; Vogel-Wiedemann, 326 assigns 41/42 to Passienus' proconsulship also; Syme, *Papers B* 351 argues that 41/42 should be assigned to the term of P. Lentulus Scipio

58 Sen. *Ben.* 1.15.5; Pliny *NH* 16.242; Tac. *Ann.* 6.20.1 (cf. Suet. *Cal.* 10.2); Syme (1986), 80 mistakenly has Passienus going north with Caligula

59 *CIL* 13.4565; Sen. *QN* 4A pr.6; Pliny *NH* 16.242; Quintilian 6.1.50, 3.74, 10.1.24; Dio 60.23.1; Schol. Juv. *Sat.* 4.81; Syme (1986) gives the date of the first consulship as 27 without giving his grounds; Stewart (1953), 83

60 *Anthologia Latina* nos 405, 445 (Riese)

61 See inscription no. 21; Vogel-Wiedemann (1982), 327

62 Dio 60.4.1; Pliny *NH* 16.242

63 Schol. Juv. *Sat.* 4.81; Suet. *Nero* 6.3; Martial 10.2.10; Syme (1958), 328 n.12; (1970),

82, (1986), 160 n.2.; Jerome places the death in 38, clearly impossible. R. Hanslik, *RE* 18 (1949), 2097–8, no.2 puts the death in 48 after the fall of Messalina, which would best suit the rumours that grew up afterwards. Weaver (1976), 216, with reference to *CIL* 6.10399, argues for death quite early in his second consulship; Syme (1986), 183 observes that she would be cheated of the gardens of Sallustius Crispus, since that part of the estate had previously passed into imperial possession (*ILS* 1795)

64 *CIL* 5.2848; Tac. *Ann.* 13.10.1; Parker (1946),44; Henderson (1903), 24; Hohl (1918), 350; Syme *Papers A*, 296; but see Bradley (1978), 50–1

65 Schol. Juv. *Sat.* 1.155; the MS of the scholiast actually reads Agrippina and *Fulvia*, generally emended to *Iulia* (Livilla); Roper (1979), 347

66 Tac. *Ann.* 11.29.1; Suet. *Claud.* 37.2; Dio 60.14.2–4; *PIR²* I835, 6; Levick (1990), 58; McAlindon (1956), 117–18; Stewart (1953); Dorey (1966), 147

67 Dorey (1966), 147; Bauman (1992), 170

68 Ehrhardt (1978); C. Appius Silanus' exact place in the Junian family is not clear (see Weidemann [1963], 138–45, *PIR²* I824)

69 Ehrhardt (1978), 62–5; Vinicianus: *PIR²* A701; Dio 60.15.1–2, 4; Barrett (1990), 160–1, 174–5; Q. Pomponius: *PIR* P564; Jos. *Ant.* 19.263–4, *BJ* 2.205; Tac. *Ann.* 13.43.3; Dio 59.29.5; Timpe (1960), 490–1; Barrett (1990), 176

70 Suet. *Claud.* 13.2; Tac. *Hist.* 2.75; Dio 60.15 (implies suicide); on Scribonianus' natural lineage, see Wiseman (1982), 61–2

71 Pliny *Ep.* 3.16.6–13; Martial 1.13; Dio 60.16; on the victims, Ehrhardt (1978), 64; notable among these were A. Caecina Paetus, who had been in Dalmatia and joined the rebellion, and his wife Arria, who encouraged her husband to die bravely by stabbing herself and passing the knife to Paetus, saying, 'It doesn't hurt, Paetus' (*Paete, non dolet*)

72 Rubellius Blandus was proconsul of Africa in 35/36 and is last heard of in an inscription to Diva Drusilla from Tibur dated to 38 (*ILS* 196); Picard (1963), no. 44, 71; Wolfgramm (1971), 3 believes that he died at the beginning of Claudius' reign

73 *Apoc.* 10.4, 13.5; Tac. *Ann.* 13.32.5, 43.3; Suet. *Cal.* 29.1; Dio 60.18.4; Meise (1969), 143

74 *Octavia* 944–6 (*ferro … caesa est*)

75 *Apoc.* 13.5; Tac. *Ann.* 1.29.2; Dio 60.18.3; see Pflaum (1950), 206: Rufrius Pollio (*PIR*

R123): Dio 60.23.2, Halmann (1986), 104; his name among those executed in the *Apocolocyntosis* is based on the almost certain emendation of the variants that appear in the MSS: *Roufius Pomfilius, Rusius/Rufius Pompei(i) filius*

76 Tac. *Ann.* 11.12.1

77 Suet. *Claud.* 13.2; Dio 60.27.5

78 *Apoc.* 11.2.5; Suet. *Claud.* 27.2, 29.1–2; Dio 61.29.6a, 31.8; Tac. *Hist.* 1.48.1; Plut. *Galb.* 23.1 has Crassus and Scribonianus alive under Nero; McAlindon (1957), 281, (1969), 144. Messalina's motivation: Becker (1950), 177, Bergener (1965), 160, E. Groag *RE* 3 (1899), 2801, Coursey Ruth (1916), 87, Tolde (1948), 69; Crassus' ambitions: Dorey (1966), 148 n.2, McAlindon (1956), 127, Syme (1958), 385, (1960), 19, Groag, *RE* 3 (1999), 2801; 13 (1926), 344 bases the date of 47 on the association of the trials of Pompeius and Asiaticus in Dio. H. Dessau, *PIR*[1] P 477, McAlindon (1956), 126, Pistor (1965), 110 date the death before 47 on the grounds that Tacitus, whose narrative resumes in 47, otherwise would have mentioned it. Smilda (1896), 136 on Suet. *Claud.* 27.2 gives 46 or early 47; Syme (1960), 19 n.85, gives 46, Sievers (1870), 123 n.6 between 44 and 46, Dorey (1966), 148 between 44 and 47. It is noteworthy that the *Apocolocyntosis* says that Claudius and Pompeius' father Crassus were as alike as two eggs in a basket and that Crassus was stupid enough to have been emperor, which might hint that he had exhibited imperial ambitions

79 Tac. *Ann.* 13.23.1; Suet. *Claud.* 27.2; Dio 60.30.6[a]; Ehrhardt (1978); Levick (1990), 61; Meise (1969), 145–7

80 Jos. *Ant.* 19.159; Tac. *Ann.* 11.1.1, 3.1; Dio 60.27.1–3, 29.4–6[b]. Scramuzza (1940), 93; Syme (1986), 184; the identity of motives in case of Agrippina and Statilius Taurus weakens both the cases

81 Reasons for his downfall: Bauman (1992), 176

82 Tac. *Ann.* 11.29.1

83 Tac. *Ann.* 11.11; Suet. *Nero* 6.4

84 Tac. *Ann.* 11.12.2

85 Tac. *Ann.* 12.7.5–6

86 Sources for the Messalina–Silius affair: Pliny *NH* 29.8, 20; Jos. *Ant.* 20.149; Tac. *Ann.* 11.12, 26–38; Suet. *Claud.* 26.2, 29.3; Dio 60.31.1–5; Juv. *Sat.* 6. 116–32, 10.329–45; *Octavia* 257–72, 950–1; *Apoc.* 11.1, 5, 13.4; Aur. Vict. *Caes.* 4.6–12; Anon. *Epit. de Caes.* 4.5–6; modern treatments, *inter alios*, Ranke (1883), III 1. 102–5; Duruy (1885), 627; Groag (1899), 2805; Henderson (1903), 26; Domaszewski

(1909), II. 36; Ferrero (1911), 186–92; Dessau (1924–6), II.1.165; A. Nagl *RE* 3A (1927), 69–71; Faider (1929), 178; Birt (1932); Scramuzza (1940), 90; Passerini (1941), 30; Mullens (1941/2), 62; Becker (1950), 156; R. Helm, *RE* 22 (1954), 2183; G. Herzog Hauser & B.F. Wotke RE 8A (1955), 252–4; Walter (1956); Colin (1956); Staehelin (1956), 153; McAlindon (1956), 123, (1957), 283; Oost (1958), 117–19; Syme (1958), 348, 375, 407, 539; Aalders (1961); Momigliano (1961), 76, 120; Dorey (1961), 1–10; Balsdon (1962) 103–6; Bishop (1964), 30; Kornemann (1963), II. 193; Pflaum (1963), 338; Bengston (1967), 284; Meise (1969), 158; Mottershead (1986) ad loc.; Levick (1990), 65; Bauman (1992), 176–9

87 Silius: *PIR*² I864; A. Nagl, *RE* 3A (1927), 69–71 no.4. Consul designate: Tac. *Ann.* 11.27.1; Junia Silana: *PIR*² I804, *FOS* 474; Syme (1986), 196

88 *Octavia* 257–61; it has been argued that the marriage was a fabrication of the freed-men, by Colin (1956), 25–39; Koestermann (1967), on Tac. *Ann.* 11.27

89 Suet. *Claud.* 39.1

90 There is evidence of removal of her name from a number of inscriptions: *ILS* 210, *CIL* 6.4474; *IGR* 4.1146 (Lindos), *Africa Italiana 8* (1941), 34 (Leptis); *TAM* 11.3.760 (Arneae in Lycia); on surviving statues: Wood (1992)

91 Advisers: Scramuzza (1940), 90

92 Willenbücher (1914), 7; Meise (1969), 166; Mehl (1974), 65 n.353, 74–9

6 Wife (pp. 94–142)

1 Suet. *Claud.* 26.2

2 Tac. *Ann.* 12.1.1

3 Tac. *Ann.* 12.1–2; Suet. *Claud.* 26.3; Crook (1955), 42; Levick (1990), 70

4 Narcissus may well have been Claudius' slave and have been manumitted by him; see A. Stein, *RE* 16 (1935), 1701. Caligula had a slave named Narcissus, but the name was common (cf. *ILS* 3.1,.p. 218)

5 Oost (1958), 120; Dorey (1966), 130, n.26; Ehrhardt (1978), 69; Levick (1990), 70; Stein, *RE* 16 (1935), 1701; Felix did, of course suffer from a disadvantage, that he was (half) brother of Messalina

6 Lollia: *PIR*² L328; Pliny *NH* 9.117; Suet. *Cal.* 25.2; Tac. *Ann.* 12.1.1; Dio 59.12.1; *PIR*² L312; Syme (1986), 177; Levick (1990), 71; Marcus Lollius: *PIR*² L311; Vell.

2.102.1; Lollia is described by Tacitus as *M. Lollii consularis* and some therefore assign a consulship to her father (*PIR²* 312), in addition to her grandfather; the former has been assigned a suffect consulship in AD 13 (thus registered below the line with query by Degrassi [1952], ad loc.). A consulship is considered certain, and probably in 13, by Brunt (1961), 81. Against the notion, Syme (1958), 748, (1966), 59; Syme (1986), 177 says that a consulship for the son is unlikely, in view of Lollius' disgrace in AD 2 and the enmity nourished long afterwards by Tiberius

7 Dio 61.3.2; Tac. *Ann.* 12.25.1, 65.4, 14.2.4; Oost (1958), 120

8 Suet. *Claud.* 4.1–6; Wiseman (1982)

9 *Apoc.* 10; Tac. *Ann.* 3.4.3, 13.1.2 (Marcus Silanus), 14.22 (Rubellius Plautus), 15.35.2 (Decimus Junius Torquatus Silanus); see Gagé (1934), 11–36; Kraft (1966), 100–9; Wiseman (1982), 59

10 Tac. *Ann.* 12.2.3; descent from Augustus: 63.8.2, 12.2; descent from Aeneas: Suet. *Nero* 39.2; Dio 48.52.3, 62.18.4, 63.29.3; Dio 60.2.1; Rubellius: Tac. *Ann.* 14.22.2; Kraft (1966), 113

11 *Apoc.* 9.5, 10.4; Lesuisse (1961), 277 argues the dubious proposition that Claudius could have made a claim to the name 'Caesar' through Livia, on the grounds that Augustus adopted her into the Julian family in his will (Tac. *Ann.* 1.8.2); for a different view: Griffin (1994), 310

12 Tac. *Ann.* 11.12.1, 12.2.3

13 On the motives for the marriage: Scramuzza (1940), 91; Meise (1969), 173; Coursey Ruth (1916), 51; Dessau (1924), I.167; Tolde (1948), 86–8; Villers (1950), 250; Timpe (1962), 94; Dorey (1966), 153; Koesterman on Tac. *Ann.* XII.2.3; Kraft (1966), 115; Levick (1990), 64–7; Bauman (1992), 180

14 Tac. *Ann.* 12.3.1; 5.1, Suet. *Claud.* 26.3; Dio 60.31.6; Scramuzza (1940), 92; Oost (1958), 123

15 Tac. *Ann.* 12.3.2; Dio 60.31.8 (under AD 49, but describing events preceding the marriage in that year)

16 Birth: Mommsen (1903), 126: Salii: *ILS* 9339 (the restoration of Lucius' name here is far from certain); prefect: Dio 60.5.8; betrothal: Dio 60.5.7, 31.7, Tac. *Ann.* 12.3.2, Suet. *Claud.* 24.3, 7.2, 29.1; British triumph: Tac. *Ann.* 12.3.2; Suet. *Claud.* 24.3; Dio 60.23.1, 31.7: *ILS* 957 has been restored to read *honoratus an]n XVIII [triumphalibus ornamentis.* Offices: Tac. *Ann.* 12.3.2, 4.4; Dio 60.5.8, 31.7

17 Tac. *Ann.* 12.3.2, 4.1, 9.2; Dio 61.31.8; Vitellius: Flach (1973), 267

18 Junia Calvina was married to one of Vitellius' two sons, almost certainly Lucius, rather than the future short-lived emperor Aulus Vitellius. At any rate, she is not listed among the emperor Vitellius' wives (Suet. *Vit.* 6)

19 *Apoc.* 8.2; Tac. *Ann.* 12.4; Suet. *Claud.* 29.1–2, *Vit.* 6; Dio 60.31.8 (on a possible conspiracy, McAlindon [1956], 116, Meise [1969], 173); the *Apocolocyntosis* belongs to early in Nero's reign, when Seneca might have been anxious to maintain his position with Agrippina; by the time of the *Octavia,* 149 the charge is described as false (*fictum*). On incest, see Cic. *Leg.* 2.41; Eprius Marcellus: *PIR*² 84; Tac. *Dial.* 5, *Ann.* 13.13.4, 16.22.10, *Hist.* 2.53.1, 4.6.1; Dio 66.16.3; on the completion of the lustrum Vitellius' duties would have expired; Mommsen (1887), 340.5, 413.6 suggests that Vitellius' term was renewed (on some coins of his son he is called censor ii); but he may have stayed censor for 5 years with Claudius; Smith (1963), 141–2

20 Tac. *Ann.* 12.5–7; Domaszewski (1909), 38

21 Tac. *Ann.* 14.2.4; *Octavia* 141–3

22 Tac. *Ann.* 12.9; Suet. *Nero* 28; Talbert (1984), 168

23 Livia was divorced from Tiberius Claudius Nero in order to marry Augustus; Caligula's second wife Livia Orestilla (or Cornelia Orestina) was betrothed to Gaius Calpurinius Piso just before the marriage; his second wife Lollia was married to P. Memmius Regulus before his marriage. The manuscripts of Tacitus are corrupt in this section. Vitellius' argument about Roman law and custom is ambiguous and depends on the punctuation of Tacitus' text. *Sed aliis gentibus sollemnia neque lege ulla prohibita* would mean that the custom was 'normal in other countries' and 'not prohibited by any law (in those countries)'. A more forceful interpretation would place a comma between *sollemnia* and *neque*: 'normal in other countries, and not prohibited by any law (*in Rome*)'

24 Tac. *Ann.* 12.7.1–3; Suet. *Claud.* 26.3; Dio 60.31.8; Scrammuzza (1940), 262

25 Suet. *Dom.* 22; Dio 68.2.4; Gaius *Inst.* 1.157; *C. Th.* 3.12.1; Gaius, in the *Institutes,* observed that it was permissible to marry a brother's daughter (although marriage to a sister's daughter was still forbidden) and that this principle was first established when Claudius married Agrippina. It appears to have remained in force until AD 342 when a Constitution addressed to the provinciales Foenices attacks such a relationship in very strong terms; Dio 68.2.4 claims that Nerva prohibited marriage between uncle and niece, but the reference may be to a niece on the sister's side; Weiss (1908), 340; Pigianol (1912), 153–67; Corbett (1930), 48; Godolphin (1934), 134; Scramuzza (1940), 262; Smith (1963), 139; Levick (1990), 209 n.4

26 In Athens such marriages were acceptable (Dem. *In Neaer.* 2, Lysias *In Diog.* 4) and marriage to this degree was also allowed under Jewish law. Vitellius had been legate

of Syria, where he would have had direct knowledge of Hellenistic and Jewish practices and would have been able to strengthen his arguments by firsthand experience. The possibility of influence from the Etruscans, in whom Claudius had a scholarly interest, is claimed by Piganiol (1912), 156–8

27 Tac. *Ann.* 12.7.5–7; Suet. *Claud.* 26.3; Dio 60.31.8

28 Cameo 2 (p. 218); Fuchs (1936), 232–7; Zwierlein-Diehl (1980), 36–7; Oberleitner (1985), 55; Massner (1994), 171; La Rocca (1994), 281 n.79; B. Levick has suggested in correspondence that the turreted wall on Agrippina's head might refer to Cologne, in which case the gem would be slightly later than the marriage; Künzl (1994) argues that it originally depicted Caligula and Caesonia/Drusilla, who were afterwards reworked into Claudius and Agrippina the Younger

29 *Apoc.* 8.2, 10.4, 11.2; *Octavia* 145–50; Tac. *Ann.* 12.8.1; Dio 60.81.8; the *Octavia* alludes to the defilement of Silanus' household gods, which might be taken to mean that the death took place in his house. Stahr (1967), 115 melodramatically places the death at the altar; Suetonius and the *Octavia* indicate that he was forced to commit suicide, while Dio specifically claims that Agrippina and Nero persuaded Claudius to put him to death by persuading the emperor that he was plotting against him; the *Apocolocyntosis* states explicitly in three places that Claudius murdered him

30 Tac. *Ann.* 12.8.1; Momigliano (1961), 27, 89 n.12; Wissowa (1912), 515, n.1

31 Dio 60.32.1–2

32 Pliny *NH* 35.201

33 Suet. *Vesp.* 4.1–2 (on the date of proconsulship, see *PIR²* F259); Nicols (1978), Jones (1983), Eck (1993), 48

34 Tac. *Ann.* 12.9

35 Tac. *Ann.* 12.8.3; Athens: Probus, in Schol. Juv. *Sat.* 5.109; Probus adds that he had been in exile at this point, AD 49, for three years instead of the correct eight, and his account clearly needs to be treated with caution; Suet. *Nero* 7.1; Dio 61.32.3; Griffin (1976), 62

36 Suidas I.203 [Bernardy]; Alexander Aegeus: *PIR²* A501; Simplicius *In cat.* proem p.10.13K; Chaeremon: *P.Lond.* 1912; *PIR²* C 706; Schwartz, *RE* 3 (1899), 2025–7; Jos. *Ap.* 288, 293–303; Griffin (1976), 65, 140; Levi (1949), 93

37 Opposition to philosophical education: Suet. *Nero* 52; Nero's curriculum: Morford (1968), 59–65

38 Iunius Gallio: *SEG* 19.384; *PIR*² I.757; Pompeius: post in Asia is mentioned in Sen. *Brev.* 18.3, written between mid-48 & mid-55, see Griffin (1962), 105, (1976), 84. Aulus Paullinus: Tac. *Ann.* 13.53.1–2; Eck (1981), 229 proposes him as colleague of M. Junius Silanus in *CIL* 14.3471 (see Griffin [1976], 57–9, [1984], 255, n.56)

39 Tac. *Ann.* 13.42.5; Dio 61.10.1 (in Dindorf's edition the issue is dated to 57); Giancotti (1953), 52–5

40 *PIR*² L328; Tac. *Ann.* 12.22; Dio 60.32.4

41 Tac. *Ann.* 12.22.3, 14.12.6; Dio 60.33.2b (Dio's suggestion that Calpurnia might have been put to death is contradicted by Tacitus)

42 Tac. *Ann.* 12.26.1; Dio 60.33.2a; Stahr (1867), 121; Levick (1990), 71

43 Poppaea received the title when her daughter Claudia was born at Antium, 21 Jan, 63; Tac. *Ann.* 15.23; *AFA* (Smallwood 24, 25); *ILS* 234; Griffin (1984), 103

44 Inferred from Tac. *Ann.* 13.18.5; Dio 61.33.1

45 Agrippina–Claudius official issue: *RIC*² Claudius 80–1; Agrippina–Nero official Claudian issue: *RIC*² Claudius 75 (but see the comments of Kaenel [1986], 18–19); Ephesus *RIC*² Claudius, 117, 119 (erroneously described); Tralles: *RPC* 2654. Assos: *RPC* 2322; Mostene: *RPC* 2461; Smyrna: *RPC* 2475; Nysa: (probably): *RPC* 2665; Trillmich (1978), 55–63

46 Trillmich (1974), 192–3; Wood (1988), 420. The diadem appears on the sculpted heads I.1.10 II.2 (p. 216).

47 Rose (1993), *passim.* Fittschen-Zanker (1983), 5 n.3; Saletti (1968) 26–30; Rose, ad loc, says that there are no grounds for Jucker's (1977), 206 assertion that Agrippina's head was placed on a re-cut image of Messalina, the most famous being that of Aphrodisias

48 Rose (1993), 170, n.89 believes that the same connection should be seen in the clasped right hands on the coins of Alexandria between 49 and 54; *RPC* 5176, 5183

49 Demeter association: Robert (1960), 291; Price (1984), 85–6; Smith (1987), 109; Rose (1993), 170

50 Suet. *Claud.* 17.3

51 Jos. *Ant.* 19.117

52 Domus Tiberiana: Jos. *Ant.* 19.117; Tac. *Hist.* 1.27.3; Suet. *Nero* 8; Krause (1985);

Barrett (1990), 205–7; Wiseman (1991), 18, 65; Richardson (1992), 136–7; Caligula's Capitoline residence: Suet. *Cal.* 22.4

53 *Octavia* 536; Tac. *Ann.* 12.25; Suet. *Claud.* 27.2, *Nero* 7.1; Dio 60.32.2, 33.22; Oost (1958), 129, Scramuzza (1940), 91; on the chronological problems, see Appendix III; on the adoption, see Hohl (1918), 353; Kornemann (1930), 50–7; Geer (1931), 63; Prevost (1949), 39; Koestermann (1967), on Tac. *Ann.* 12.26.1; Levick (1990), 70

54 See Bradley (1978), 54–6 for the notion that Nero was not given precedence over Britannicus

55 Tac. *Ann.* 13.16.3; Suet. *Tib.* 62.3, *Nero* 33.3, *Titus* 2; Dio 67.33.3 (Zonaras); Groag (1899), 2688; Parker (1946), 50; Esser (1958), 1; Bergener (1965), 153, 160; Koestermann (1967) on Tac. *Ann.* 13.16.3

56 Suet. *Tib.* 15.2, *Claud.* 39.2; Tac. *Ann.* 12.25; B. Levick has observed to me that Tiberius could not have adopted Germanicus after his own adoption, as he would no longer have been paterfamilias

57 Caligula was only a few years older than Gemellus; Cic. *Dom.* 13.14; Dig. De Adopt. 1.7.fr 15.2; 17.3; Ulpian, lib 26 AD Sabinum; Shulz (1951), 143–7; Augustus: Vell. 104.1 (Augustus justified his adoption of Tiberius by reasons of state); Suet. *Aug.* 65.1

58 Tac. *Ann.* 1.3.5; Ulpian D. 1.3(?), 15.2

59 Tac. *Ann.* 12.41.7

60 May (1944), 101–5; Prévost (1949), 35–41

61 *AFA* (Smallwood 21.57); Suet. *Nero* 1.2; Mommsen (1864), I. 73; Wiseman (1971), 172; Bradley (1978), 27; Nero's Name: Weaver (1965) argues that a Domitius Lemnus, described as procurator of Germanicus Caesar in *ILS* 1490, was freedman of Nero after adoption. For Germanicus as part of Nero's name during this period he cites *ILS* 222, 5025. In one dedication, probably shortly after his adoption, Nero has the praenomen Tiberius. Another hint that 'Nero' may not have been his exclusive praenomen, at least in the early part of this period, is to be found in Zonaras (Dio 61.33.2²), who says that on adoption Claudius gave him the name of Tiberius Claudius Nero Drusus Germanicus Caesar; moreover Zonaras refers to Nero as 'Nero' because that was the name that prevailed (Dio 61.33.2ᶜ). Note that Claudius used the name Germanicus before he became emperor (*CIL* 6. 4338, 4345, 4348, 4356, 4359, 4362–3)

62 *AFA* (Smallwood 14.7–9; the inscription is fragmentary but the restored order is almost certainly correct); *IGR* 4.208, 330, 560; Tac. *Ann.* 4.37.4; Frisch (1975), 193;

Rose (1993), Cat. 120

63 Tac. *Ann.* 12.26.2

64 Sen. *Ep.* 53.7–8; Suet. *Nero* 7.1; Faider (1929), 182; Fabia (1910), 263

65 Ptolemais: Pliny *NH* 5.75; Archelais: Pliny *NH* 6.8; Siculi: Pliny *NH* 3.141; Aequum: Wilkes (1969), 114; Savaria: Pliny *NH* 3.146; Camulodunum: Tac. *Ann.* 14.31.3; Frere (1987), 63

66 Tac. *Germ.* 28, *Ann.* 1.57.2, 12.27.1–2; Schmitz (1950), (1956), 31–9; Fremersdorf (1950), 31; Camulodunum: Tac. *Ann.* 14.31.3; Frere (1987), 63

67 Tac. *Hist.* 4.28, 63.2, 65.2, 5.24.1

68 Appius Claudius: Suet. *Tib.* 2.2; Lucius Antonius the brother of Marc Antony sought to have himself designated as *patronus XXXV tribuum* (Cic. *Phil.* 6.12); on municipal patrons: Mommsen (1887), 3.1202; Abbott and Johnson (1926), nos 10, 26, 44, 65, 67

69 Alpine: *CIL* 9.2142, 10.206, 3826; Spain: *CIL* 2.1525; Asia: *AE* 1909, no.41, *CIG* II.3602, 3603, 3604

70 Ilium: see 'Asia', n.69; privileges: Livy 38.39.10; Strabo 13.26, 28; Caesar: Lucan 9.950–99, Suet. *Div. Jul.* 79.3; Braund (1980), 420–5; Harmand (1957), 167–8; Augustus shared his patronage of Ilium with Marcus Agrippa, one suspects after the latter's marriage to Julia

71 *IG* IV^2 593–604

72 Canusium: *ILS* 6121 (Abbott & Johnson [1926], 136; on the attitude of reigning emperors: Eilers (1993); Demougin (1994), 22 notes that the founding of the *colonia* at Cologne is distinguished from other Claudian settlements in originating from privileged ties within the imperial house

73 Levick (1990), 72. His colleague was the loyal Ser. Cornelius Scipio Salvidienus Orfitus (*PIR*^{2} C 1444). Melmoux (1983) claims that the non-tenure of the consulship in this year by L. Vitellius (he had held one in 43 and 47) represents a loss of favour, because he was too closely connected with Agrippina

74 Tac. *Ann.* 1.3.2, consul-designate: 4 March (Smallwood 21.65–72)

75 Tac. *Ann.* 12.41.1–4

76 RIC^2 Claudius 75–9, 82–3, 124; the major priesthoods are: *pontifices, augures, quin-*

decimviri sacris faciendis, the septemviri epulones; successor on obverse: Grant (1970), 30, Griffin (1984), 29, Levick (1990), 210 n.15, Sutherland (1986), 86–7, adding that the aes sestertii once assigned to Claudius because of the obverse portraits of Britannicus (*BMC* I, Claudius 226) are now fairly securely attributed to Titus as commemorative issues to honour his old friend (*BMC* II, lxxviii and 293, no. 306; cf. Suet. *Tit.* 2)

77 Suet. *Nero* 7.2; Dio 53.28.3–4

78 Faider (1929), 185: this interpretation is based on a generally accepted emendation of Tac. *Ann.* 12.41.4, *triumphali veste* for *triumphalium veste.* The latter MS reading would mean that Nero appeared in the garb of a *triumphalis* (one who had celebrated a triumph), an arrangement which would have made him seem ridiculous. The *vestis triumphalis* would not convey this notion, since on certain occasions it was the garb of magistrates holding imperium. It doubtless reflected Nero's *imperium proconsulare*, although its appropriateness within the city walls might be questioned

79 Smallwood 100; Barrett (1991), 6–7; Rose (1993), 166; priesthood: 5 March (Smallwood 21.65–72); *sodales Augustales:* Smallwood 132b

80 Tac. *Ann.* 12.41.6–7; Suet. *Nero* 7.1; Double (1976), 178; Faider (1929), 185; Walter (1956), 45; Koestermann (1967), on Tac. *Ann.* 12.41.3; Kraft (1966), 120; Griffin (1984), 244 n.79

81 *AFA* (Smallwood 16.5, 19.22–5, 21.25, 22.5–6); Tac. *Ann.* 13.10.1; Suet. *Nero* 9; Griffin (1984), 22, 244 n. 79

82 Tac. *Ann.* 12.26.2, 41.8; Melmoux (1983), 353 argues that Britannicus' tutors might be seen to be nostalgic for absolute power, and thus in conflict with the more liberal orientation which Agrippina was preaching, more favourable to the senate and the senatorial oligarchy

83 Tac. *Ann.* 12.41.5, 8, 69.2; 14.7.4; 15.50.4; 67.3; Dio 60.32.5; Schiller (1872), I.1.342; Double (1876), 181; Groag (1899), 2689; Henderson (1903), 39; Faider (1929), 185; Parker (1946), 49; Timpe (1962), 95f; Grenzheuser (1964), 24; Bishop (1964), 32; Kraft (1966), 117; Meise (1969), 182; Melmoux (1983), 353

84 Piso: Tac. *Ann.* 2.55.4; Suetonius: Pliny, *Ep.* 3.8.1

85 Stat. *Silv.* 55.24; Juv. *Sat.* 14.195; Florus, *fragm.* p.108 (Halm); Tac. *Hist.* 3.44

86 Domaszewski (1967), 90–7; Durry (1928), 140–6; Birley (1963–4); Watson (1969), 18; Dobson-Breeze (1969); Webster (1985), 98

87 Smallwood 283; see Picard (1937), 120

88 Tac. *Ann.* 13.15.4

89 Faenius: *PIR*² F102; Tac. *Ann.* 15.50.4; Dio 62.24.1; Subrius: *PIR* S684; Tac. *Ann.* 15.67.2–3; Dio 62.24

90 Tac. *Ann.* 12.43; Suet. *Claud.* 18.2; Dio 60.33.10 (under 52–3); Eusebius-Jerome, 181 (Helm) mistakenly puts the famine in 50

91 Tac. *Ann.* 12.42.1; Dio 60.32.6ᵃ; Rufrius: *PIR*¹ R121, Geta: *PIR*² L453

92 Smallwood 259. Burrus belonged to the Voltonia tribe, who regularly came from Vaison. Tac. *Ann.* 12.42.2, 13.2.2; De la Ville de Mirmont (1910); McDermott (1949); Syme (1958), 622–3; Baldwin (1967), 430; Levick (1990), 74; Griffin (1984), 67–72

93 Tac. *Ann.* 12.42.4–5; Suet. *Vit.* 3.1; Levick (1990), 75; Melmoux (1983); 359; Lupus: *PIR*² I 766

94 Caratacus: *PIR*² C418; Tac. *Ann.* 12.37.5–6; Tacitus places the appearance of Caratacus at Rome in 50, but since it belongs to the ninth year of the war it must be dated to 51; Dio 60.33.7; *carpentum:* Tac. *Ann.* 12.42.3–4; Dio 60.33.2¹ (dated to AD 49); Koeppel (1983) argues that Claudius celebrated a second triumph in 51

95 See inscriptions nos 24 and 27 (p. 223)

96 Jos. *BJ* 2.22–3, *Ant.* 19.363–20.15, 97–9, 100–3; for the general period, Smallwood (1976), 256–70; Millar (1993), 64–5

97 Jos. *BJ* 2.223–7, *Ant.* 20.105–12

98 Jos. *BJ* 2.232–3 (one Galilean death); Jos. *Ant.* 20.118–19 (several deaths)

99 Jos. *BJ* 2.234–9, *Ant.* 20.119–24; Tac. *Ann.* 12.54

100 Tac. *Ann.* 12.54; Josephus says that Felix succeeded Cumanus. Smallwood (1976), 266 places responsibility for Felix's appointment to Samaritis on Quadratus; Momigliano (1934), 388–91 believes that Claudius himself intervened. Smallwood (1976), 266 believes that the change was made on the local initiative of Quadratus. Aberbach (1949–50) suggests that either Tacitus inherited an error in his source or there was a copyist's mistake, and that Felix was assigned *Galilee;* for a detailed recent discussion: Schwartz (1992), 223–42

101 Jos. *BJ* 2.239–44 (placing the first hearing at Caesarea), *Ant.* 20.125–33 (at Sebaste/Samaria): Jonathan's support: *Ant.* 20.162; loyalty of Ananias and his son: *BJ* 2.409, *Ant.* 20.208–10; Smallwood 182

102 Jos. *BJ* 2.245–6, *Ant.* 20.134–6

103 Jos. *BJ* 20.223, *Ant.* 20.104; Smallwood 262; on the death in 48 of Herod of Chalcis, brother of Herod Agrippa, Chalcis was placed for a short time under the legate of Syria until Agrippa II was appointed king in late 49/early 50. Agrippa II later gave up Chalcis but received an extended kingdom, Philip's old tetrarchy, with Batanea and Trachonitis and the addition of two other tetrarchies, Varus' old dominion in the Lebanon region and Lysinias' old territory of Abela

104 *Apoc.* 12.3.19–22; Suet. *Claud.* 15.2; Levick (1990), 118

105 Jos. *Ant.* 18.31, 143

106 Jos. *BJ* 2.247, *Ant.* 30.137–8; Josephus uses a fairly specific term to describe his dispatch (*ekpempei*), an inappropriate word if Felix had been in Judaea already, which suggests that he had returned to Rome for the hearing; the view of Stein (1927), 114, Sherwin-White (1939), 11 n.89 and Stockton (1961), 117 that Felix had been made an eques has no direct support in the sources. Suet. *Claud.* 28 has Felix placed in command of the troops and administration of Judaea as a libertus, as does Tac. *Hist.* 5.9.3. Two freedmen are attested as governors: Acastus, in Mauretania: *ILS* 1483; Hiberus, briefly appointed to govern Egypt: *PIR²* 168; Dio 58.19.6; Philo *Flacc.* 1; W. Ensslin, *RE Supp.* (1956), 8.540

107 *RPC* 4970

108 Jos. *Ant.* 20.141–4; Acts of the Apostles 24.24; Tac. *Ann.* 12.54.1, *Hist.* 5.9.3

109 Jos. *BJ* 2.266–70, *Ant.* 20.173–8

110 Jos. *BJ* 2.284, *Ant.* 20.182–4

111 Tac. *Ann.* 12.25.1; Dio 59.3.2; Probus: Schol. Juv. *Sat.* 1.109

112 Pliny *NH* 35.201, *Ep.* 7.29.2, 8.6.; Tac. *Ann.* 11.38.5, 12.53; Suet. *Claud.* 28; Scramuzza (1940), 133 suggests that Tacitus implies that Pallas took the money; but see Oost (1958), 131

113 Pliny *NH* 35.201, *BJ* 2.247, *Ant.* 20.137; Pliny *Ep.* 7.29; Tac. *Ann.* 11.38.5, 12.54.1; Suet. *Claud.* 28; Duff (1928), 85–6, 214–20; Oost (1958), 131–2

114 Levick (1990), 75; Flach (1973), 269; Dorey (1966), 154 implausibly suggests that Narcissus' opposition to Agrippina originated from a feud in 48

115 Dio 60.33.3[a]

116 Suet. *Tit.* 2; Dio 64.3.4; Paratore (1952), 58–9

117 *ILS* 302 (cleaning of the tunnel), *CIL* IX.3888–90; Pliny *NH* 36.124; Tac. *Ann.* 12; Suet. *Claud.* 20.1–2; Dio 60.11.5; Thornton (1983), 106; it continued to be plagued by problems. Trajan tried to improve the scheme, but it was not until the ninteenth century that the lake was finally drained

118 Pliny *NH* 33.63; Tac. *Ann.* 12.56–7; Suet. *Claud.* 32; Dio 60.33.3; Tollis (1961), 68; de Ruyt (1971/72), 165; mock naval battle: Coleman (1993), 56; ship graffito: Guarducci (1953), 199

119 Tac. *Ann.* 12.57.4–5; Dio 60.33.5; Stahr (1867), 140; fire: Dio 60.33.12 (dated ambiguously to 53–4)

120 Donatives: Tiberius: Suet. *Tib.* 76; Caligula: Dio 59.2.1; Claudius: Suet. *Claud.* 10.4; Galba: Tac. *Hist.* 1.5.2; games: Suet. *Claud.* 21; aqueducts: Pliny *NH* 36.122; Ostia: Dio 60.11.3; Fucine Lake: Suet. *Claud.* 20.2; Dio 60.11.5, 33.5

121 Tac. *Ann.* 14.6.2

122 Tac. *Ann.* 12.7.6–7; Dio 60.32.3–4

123 Cic. *Verr.* 2.3.197; Jones (1950)

124 On this issue, see in particular Millar (1963) and Brunt (1966)

125 Ulpian 43.8.2.4: *res fiscales quasi propriae et privatae principis sunt*

126 Augustus: *Res Gestae*, Appendix I; Caligula: Suet. *Cal.* 37.3; Nero: Tac. *Ann.* 13.31.2, 15.18.4

127 Tac. *Ann.* 6.2.1; Dio 53.16.1

128 Suet. *Dom.* 2.3; Vespasian: Suet. *Dom.* 2.3; for the apparent exception of Pius: *SHA* Pius 12.8 (to be treated with caution), see Brunt (1966), 78

129 Otho: Dio 64.8.3; Vitellius: Dio 65.2–4; Vespasian: Dio 66.8.4

130 Suet. *Aug.* 40.3

131 Tac. *Ann.* 3.25.1–2; Gaius II.150; Ulpian 28.7

132 Tac. *Ann.* 2.48.1

133 Tac. *Ann.* 4.20.1–2; Dio 53.23.5–7

134 Suet. *Aug.* 101.4; Tac. *Ann.* 1.11.5–7; Dio 53.30.2 cf. Suet. *Cal.* 16.2; Dio 59.9.4

135 Freedmen *a rationibus* antedate Claudius and one appears to have drawn a salary from the *aerarium* under Tiberius: *EJ* 153

136 Stat. *Silv.* 3.3.85–105

137 Tac. *Ann.* 13.14.1–2; Scrammuza (1940), 122, 271; Oost (1958), 126–7

138 Sutherland (1986), 84; cf. *RIC²* p.115, *BMC* I, xliv–xlv; Crawford (1968)

139 Tac. *Ann.* 13.13.3, 14.1–2

140 Tac. *Ann.* 13.13.5–6; *cuncta ex ea haberet* would be an unusual expression simply to convey the idea that Nero owed the principate to Agrippina

141 Tac. *Ann.* 4.15.3, 12.60; Coponius: *PIR²* C1285; Jos. *BJ* 2.117. The issue is much disputed: Stockton (1961), 116–20; Seager (1962), 377–9; Millar (1964), 180–7, (1965), 326–7; Brunt (1966), 461–89; Levick (1990), 50

142 Tac. *Ann.* 12.58; Suet. *Nero* 7.2; Stahr (1867), 142; Fabia (1911), 148; Rhodes: *Anth. Pal.* 9.178; Suet. *Claud.* 25.3; Dio 60.24.4; Ilium: Livy 38.39,10; Strabo 13.1.27; significance: Braund (1980), 420–5; Bononia: Livy 37.57.7; Vell. 1.15.2; it had been exempted from the oath taken to Octavian before the Actium campaign (Suet. *Aug.* 17.2) because of its ancestral ties with the Antonii. Nero was deploying all his ancestral connections

143 Suet. *Claud.* 4.3

144 Suet. *Claud.* 4.3: Augustus had been determined to bar Claudius from the same privilege when his brother Germanicus was consul; *Nero* 7.2 places Nero's tenure just before his marriage to Octavia, thus in 53, following Tacitus' chronology; Levick (1990), 74; Geer (1931), 65 suggests April/May 53; Schiller (1872), 82, Hohl (1918), 354 and Meise (1969), 180, place it in 52; Lehmann (1856), 348, Henderson (1903), 39 and Bradley (1976), 61, date it to 51

145 Suet. *Nero* 7.2; Dio 60.33.9–10 associates the letter to the senate with the riots over the corn shortage (which are described in the same section as Claudius' illness in 53) but it is not easy to see what the connection could be, and the date for the riots is in conflict with Tacitus' AD 51. A number of scholars have argued that the letter fits better the context of Claudius' illness, eg Stein *PIR²* 27; Groag (1899), 2813; Hohl (1918), 354; Meise (1969), 180

146 Tac. *Ann.* 12.58.1; Plut. *Ant.* 87; Suet. *Nero* 7.2; Dio 60.33.2², 11; Gaius *Inst.* 1.58; Smith (1963), 142–3. The fact that Tacitus *introduces* AD 53 with the wedding

should be seen as a dramatic device, and need not be chronologically significant; Dio and Suetonius agree in placing the ceremony later in the year

147 Plut. *Ant.* 87.2 claimed that Augustus made Marcellus, his nephew, both his son and his son-in-law, but there is no confirmation of this statement

148 Tac. *Ann.* 12.59.1; Scramuzza (1940), 97; Levick (1990), 211

149 Suet. *Claud.* 13; Dio 60.27.5; Syme (1986), 240

150 *CIL* XV.7542; Tac. *Ann.* 11.1.1; Scramuzza (1940), 98; Front. *Aq.* 2.125–8

151 Tac. *Ann.* 12.52.4, 14.46.1; Levick (1990), 211 n.24

152 *BGU* 511. Wilcken (1895), 487 read *pa[rouses Sebastes meta] ton matronon* (in the presence of [Agrippina, along with] the women); see *Corpus Papyrorum Judaicarum*, II no. 156 for a critique of Wilcken's emendation and an argument for the year 41 (see also Schwartz [1990], 96–9); Premerstein (1932), 18 first suggested that *Tarkyios* might be Tarquitius. See Griffin (1976), 82 n.4: 30 April, 53, before Tarquitius' banishment

153 Phlegon *Mir.* 7 (FGH 2.1179), see Liebeschutz (1979), 156

154 Tac. *Ann.* 12.64.4–6, 65.1–2; Suet. *Nero* 7.1; Syme (1986), 165 points out that Tacitus is mistaken in suggesting that they were close in age. Agrippina was probably born in 15 (see Appendix I), while it was about then that Lepida married Messala Barbatus. There might thus have been a dozen years' difference

155 Stahr (1867), 143; Sief (1973), 268–70

156 Ancient sources: (see Momigliano [1932], 314–7: Sen. *Apoc. 1-6;* Jos. *Ant.* 20.148, 151; *Octavia* 31: Claudius died coniugis *insidiis*, 44: *coniugis scelere*, 64: *crudeli sorte* 102: *per scelus rapto*, 164/5: *miscuit coniunx vivo/ venena saeva* (cf. Giancotti's edition of *Octavia*); Pliny *NH* 22.92; Juv. *Sat.* 5.146–8, 6.620–3 (with scholiast); Tac. *Ann.* 12.66–7; Martial *Spect.* 1.20; Suet. *Claud.* 44.2–46, *Nero* 33.1, 39.3; Dio 60.34.2–6, 35; Philost. *Apoll.* 5.32 (*hos phasi*); Aur. Vict. *Caes.* 4.13; Anon. *Epit. de Caes.* 4.10; Orosius 7.6.18; Zosim. I.6.3; only at Suet. *Nero* 33.1 is Nero indirectly linked with the murder, since he made jokes about mushrooms being the food of the god, which makes him at least privy to the deed. See Baldwin (1983), 164; the modern sources are voluminous, and include *inter alios*: Peter (1867), IIIa.292f; Double (1876), 216–21; Lehmann (1858), 375; Ranke (1883), III.1.108–10, 2. 307–10; Duruy (1885), 639–41; Smilda (1896), on SC 44.2; Henderson (1903), 44, 457; Domaszewski (1909), II.45; Fabia (1911), 153; Ferrero (1911), 210–13; Lackeit (1918), 912; Hohl (1918), 355, (1931), 389; Herzog (1922), 232–40; Dessau (1924–6), II.1.172; Kroll (1927), 197; Kornemann (1930), 56, (1942), 234, 423;

Charlesworth (1934), 696; Pack (1942), 150; Scramuzza (1940), 92; Bagnani (1946); McDermott (1949), 235; Becker (1950), 158; Babelon (1955), 140; Esser (1958), 173–5; Oost (1958), 133; Townend (1960), 109; Timpe (1962), 99; Lesuisse (1962), 45; Heuss (1964), 323; Bishop (1964), 33; Grenzheuser (1964), 24; Bengston (1967), 284; Koestermann (1967), on Tac. *Ann.* 12.66.1; Warmington (1969), 19–20; Mehl (1974), 285; Griffin (1984), 32; Levick (1990), 77; Heller (1985), 70; Grimm-Samuel (1991); Bauman (1992), 187

157 Jos. *Ant.* 19.248; Tac. *Ann.* 12.64.4; Suet. *Claud.* 43, 46; Dio 60.35.1

158 Tac. *Ann.* 12.65, 66.3; Suet. *Claud.* 43; Dio 60.34.1; Paratore (1952), 57

159 Levick (1990), 76; see Meise (1969), 185 for a summary of opinions

160 Suet. *Claud.* 44.1

161 Sen. *Apoc.* 13; Tac. *Ann.* 12.66.1; Dio 60.34.4; Sinuessa: *CIG* 5969; *CIL* 8.2583; Strabo 5.3.6; Pliny *NH* 31.8: on the thermae on the Bay of Naples, D'Arms (1970), 140–1

162 Immunity: Tac. *Ann.* 12.67.1; Dio 60.34.2; for the general belief: Livy 26.14.5

163 Tac. *Ann.* 12.66.4–5; 13.15.4; Suet. *Nero* 47.1, 3; Dio 64.3.41; Halotus: *PIR*² H11; Suet. *Galb.* 15.2

164 Suet. *Nero* 33.1; Dio 60.35.4; Domitian: Suet. *Dom.* 14.1; Serenus: Pliny *NH* 22.96; Grimm-Samuel (1991) has revived an earlier suggestion of Robert Graves, that the culprit was the *Amanita phalloides*. Unusually for a victim of mushroom poisoning, Claudius seems to have fallen ill then recovered before lapsing again, a typical reaction to this particular species. But *A. phalloides* has an initial latent period of 10–15 hours during which no symptoms appear, and it would have to be assumed that Claudius ate it in a snack before the banquet. In that case, however, since the symptoms of *A. phalloides* were so unfamiliar it is difficult to see why the tradition of the mushroom poisoning arose, without the coincidence that Claudius ate the mushroom both at an earlier snack and at the banquet. On the effect of *A. phalloides* see Ramsbottom (1960), 31–4; Litten (1975), Ruanach (1978). Graves (1960) offers an entertaining account of the earlier (1949) identification of *A. phalloides* as the murder weapon

165 Tac. *Ann.* 12.61; Pliny *NH* 29.8 reports that he and his brother between them left an estate of 30 million HS

166 Illness: *Apoc.* 6–7; Suet. *Nero* 7.2; Dio 60.33.9; death unrelated to mushrooms (whether accidental or deliberate), *inter alios*: Ferrero (1911), 450, gastro-enteritis; Pack (1943), malaria; Bagnani (1946), heart failure. Kroll thinks that the story is exploited for its dramatic purposes. Why poison an edible mushroom instead of

just using a poisonous one? The use of Locusta makes the story more vivid

167 Sen. *Apoc.* 1, 3; Tac. *Ann.* 12.68.3; Suet. *Nero* 8.1; see Pack (1943)

168 *Apoc.* 4

7 Mother (pp. 143–80)

1 Tac. *Ann.* 12.69.1: in the middle of the day; Suet. *Nero* 8.1; *Apoc. 2:* between the sixth and seventh hour. The *Apocolocyntosis,* which could not afford to offend Agrippina, treats the time as the actual hour of death, not just the announcement of death

2 Dio 61.3.2; *P. Oxy.* 1021 shows that news of the accession was known in Egypt at least thirty-five days after the event

3 Tac. *Ann.* 12.69.1–3; Suet. *Nero* 8, 61.3.1; Dio 61.3.1; Caligula would almost certainly have been acclaimed by the detachment of praetorians stationed at Misenum. The notion of a formal acclamation by the guards at the steps of the palace is strengthened by the emendation of Tacitus' *festis vocibus* to *faustis vocibus*

4 Suet. *Claud.* 9.4: 15,000HS; Jos. *Ant.* 19.247: 20,000 HS (5,000 drachmae); Dio 61.3.1

5 Tac. A*nn.* 12.69.5; Suet. *Nero* 8 (*raptim*)

6 *ILS* 244; Brunt (1977), Parsi (1963), 84–5; Barrett (1990), 56–7. For a senatus consultum to have the full force of a *lex* at this period it properly needed the consent of the popular comitia, after a legally prescribed but imperfectly understood interval. The Arval record distinguishes between the imperial proclamation on 13 October and the formal assumption of the principate, the tribunician comitia, on 4 December (Smallwood 19.15, 21.11, 20). Nero assumed his fourteenth grant of tribunician power in 67; an inscription from November of that year (*ILS* 8794) shows that he had still not assumed it by that month. See Griffin (1984), 244 n.91; Barrett (1990), 70–1

7 *Pater patriae:* Dio 60.3.2, 69.3.2; a newly discovered Arval fragment shows that Caligula adopted the title on 21 September (Scheid [1980], 225.57–8; see Barrett [1990], 70), Suet. *Nero* 8; coins show the title accepted by Nero between late 55 and late 56

8 *AFA* (Smallwood 21.10); see Bradley (1978), 64; Caligula: *AFA* (Smallwood 3.10, 8.10): *hoc die … a senatu impera[tor appelatus est*; Timpe (1962), 101

9 Augustus: Tac. *Ann.* 1.8.1–3; Suet. *Aug.* 101; Dio 56.32; Tiberius: Jos. *Ant.* 18.234 Dio 59.1.2–3

10 Tac. *Ann.* 12.69.5; Suet. *Claud.* 44.1; Dio 61.1.1–2

11 Dio 61.7.6; Mommsen (1887), 2. 1135; see also Smilda (1896), on SC 44.1; Groag (1899), 2815; Hohl (1918), 355; Josserand (1930–2), 289; Hammond (1933), 76; Koestermann (1963–8), on Tac. *Ann.* 12.69.5; Lesuisse *LEC* (1962), 47; Timpe (1962), 104; Meise (1969), 186–8; Seif (1973) 292–4; Bellen (1974), 104; Griffin (1984), 32, 96; Levick (1990), 78; Bauman (1992), 187

12 Suet. *Claud.* 46; Faider (1929), 191 suggests that neither son was given an advantage in the will but that Nero's name was written first, which seemed to imply an advantage; on which, see Josserand (1930), 290; see Béranger (1939), 171 on the distinction between bequeathing possessions and power

13 Tiberius' will: Dio 59.1.2; 68/69: Tac. *Hist.* 1.80.1; Dio 64.10.1; Barrett (1990), 52; Pius may be an exception, Brunt (1966), 78; see Bellen (1972); senatorial debate: Meise (1969), 188

14 Tac. *Ann.* 12.69.4, 13.2.6, 3–4; Suet. *Claud.* 45, *Nero* 9; Stahr (1867), 156

15 Tac. *Ann.* 1.8.7; Suet. *Aug.* 100.2–4; Dio 56.34.1–2, 42, 43.1; in the unlikely event that Suet. *Claud.* 46 is correct about Claudius' failure to designate consuls for 55, the magistrates-elect who took part in Claudius' funeral would have had to be designated by Nero

16 Tac. *Ann.* 13.3; Suet. *Nero* 9

17 Tac. *Ann.* 13.2.6 and Suet. *Claud.* 45 speak of Claudius' deification following his funeral; Tac. *Ann.* 12.69.3–5 does not distinguish separate senate meetings for the acclamation of Nero and the voting of divine honours for Claudius; at *Ann.* 13.2.6, however, Tacitus distinguishes between the vote for the public funeral (*simul*) and the consecration (*mox*) and at *Ann.* 13.3–4 indicates an important meeting of the senate immediately following the funeral; Suet. *Nero* 9 implies that divinity was granted later than the funeral; Tiberius: Dio 59.3.7; see Sage, (1983); Levick (1990), 17

18 Tac. *Ann.* 13.2.6; flamen of Claudius (*CIL* 9.1123); Vell. 2.75.3; Dio 56.46.1

19 *RIC*[2] Nero 1–7; also it was probably in this period that undated gold and silver coins were minted with an obverse of Claudius' head and the legend DIVUS CLAUDIUS AUGUSTUS, and on the reverse a chariot with triumphal decoration, pulled by horses and flanked by Victories; Suet. *Claud.* 11.2; Dio 59.13.8, 61.16.4; elephant-drawn chariots were used in association with the deified Livia and Augustus, as well as Drusilla, the sister of Caligula: Clay (1982), 26–9, 42–5 has argued that the second figure in *RIC*[2] 6–7 cannot be Augustus, since it sometimes shows breasts and the hair is arranged in a feminine manner. He argues for Fides Praetorianorum; both revers-

es are clearly inspired by two sestertii of Tiberius issued to honour the Deified Augustus, depicting the same triumphal chariot or the car drawn by elephants, the latter with the legend DIVO AUGUSTO (*RIC*² Tiberius 54, 56)

20 Knossos: *RPC* 1007, Crete: *RPC* 1037–8, Caesarea, Cappadocia: *RPC* 3631, *RPC* 3635, *RPC* 3647–8, *RPC* 3652–3, Syria: *RPC* 4122–3, Antioch: *RPC* 4174, Ptolemais: *RPC* 4749–50; Rose (1993), 174 has also suggested that a new posthumous portrait type of Claudius wearing the oak crown, the *corona civica*, was produced at the outset of Nero's reign

21 Richardson (1992), 87–8, C. Buzzetti, in Steinby (1993), 277–8; Charlesworth (1937), 57–60 claimed that the temple was dismantled to erect a distributing station for water from the Aqua Claudia (Front. *Aq.* 2.76)

22 Suet. *Vesp.* 9.1; Martial *Spect.* 2 refuted by Hartman (1906), 83–4; see Platner and Ashby (1929) 120–1; Blake (1959), 31–3; Nash (1961), 243; Ward-Perkins and Boethius (1970), 217–19 (arguing for Vespasian), Coarelli (1980), 165–6 (Claudian); *CIL* VI 10251a is the sole inscriptional reference, a grave stone of a freedman *constitutori collegi numinis dominorum quod est sub templo divi Claudi*); since the surviving wall faces on to a paved street it would hardly have been part of Nero's Golden House; marble plan: Carettoni (1955), 61–4, Tav. XVI; Rodrigez Almeida (1981), 65–9, Tav. II

23 Suet. *Nero* 9; Dio 61.3.1

24 Tac. *Ann.* 13.5.2, 14.11.2; John of Antioch (fr. 90 M v.105–5) at Dio 61.3.2; Talbert (1984), 118; Thompson (1981); meetings on Palatine, Suet. *Aug.* 29; Tac. *Ann.* 2.37.3; Dio 58.9.4; Jos. *Ant.* 19.266; Capitoline: Dio 60.1.1; Livia: Dio 57.12.3, 47.1; sons of Hortalus, Tac. *Ann.* 2.37.3

25 Tac. *Ann.* 2.37.3, 13.2.6; Livia: Tac. *Ann.* 1.14.3; Dio 56.46.2

26 *RIC*² Nero 1–3, 607–12; a precedent may be found in the innocuous children in cornucopias on a Tiberian sestertius, with the legend of Drusus (son of Tiberius) on the reverse (*RIC*² Tiberius 42). The children *may* be the twins of Drusus but they are not even identified by legends. Mattingly, *BMC* Tiberius 95 classifies the cornucopia face as the *reverse;* Sutherland (1951), 153, (1986), 84–7

27 *ILS* 225, 231, 233, 8902; *CIL* 2.4926, 4928, 4734, 4884; 3.346, 382; 7.12; 10.8014

28 See *RPC* 2221 (Pergamum), noted by Rose (1993), ad loc.

29 *Octavia* 612–13; Smith (1987), 128–9

30 Spartiaticus: *AE* 1927.2; Taylor & West (1926), 393; Eutychus: Dessau 8120; Weaver

(1972), 64; the inscription might mean that he served two Augusti in succession

31 Tac. *Ann.* 13.6.2

32 Marcus Junius Silanus: *PIR*² I 833; Pliny *NH* 7.58; Tac. *Ann.* 13.1.1–2; Dio 61.6.4–5; consulship: *ILS* 206; Dio 60.27.1; the tag of golden sheep is assigned by Dio 59.8.5 to his father Marcus, suffect 15; the ambiguous reference to greed at Dio 61.6.5 almost certainly refers to Agrippina rather than to Silanus; Dio's claim that Agrippina feared that Marcus Silanus would be preferred to Nero because of the latter's way of life is unconvincing at this period; Rogers (1955), 197–8; Baldwin (1967), 426 (inclines towards Pliny on the issue of Nero's guilt); Martin (1981), 162; Griffin (1984), 30; Syme (1986), 192; Rudich (1993), 2; Agrippa Postumus: Tac. *Ann.* 1.6.1

33 Helius: *PIR*² H55; Tac. *Ann.* 13.1.3; Suet. *Nero* 23.1; Plut. *Galb.* 17; Dio 63.12.1–3, 18.2; Celer: *PIR*² C625; Tac. *Ann.* 13.1.3, 33.2

34 Decimus Torquatus: *PIR*² I.837; Tac. *Ann.* 15.35; Lucius Torquatus: *PIR*² I.838; Tac. *Ann.* 15.52.2, 16.7.4, 8.1; Rubellius Plautus: *PIR* R85; Tac. *Ann.* 13.19.3, 14.22, 59.3; it was claimed that he stood in the same relation to Augustus as did Nero, but this was true only in the technical sense, by virtue of Augustus' adoption of Tiberius; Faustus Cornelius Sulla: *PIR*² C1464; Tac. *Ann.* 13.47, 14.57.6; Rogers (1955), 195 adds as potential rivals, Annius Pollio (*PIR2* A678) and Annius Vinicianus (*PIR*² A700), sons of Lucius Annius Vinicianus, and Meise (1969) 192 adds C. Cassius Longinus (*PIR*² C501), married to Junia Lepida, great granddaughter of Augustus. The last three can have been at best marginal candidates

35 *Apoc.* 13.4; Tac. *Ann.* 13.1; Dio 60.34.4–6; Baldwin (1967), 429; Flach (1973), 269; Melmoux (1977); Narcissus II died shortly after Nero (Dio 64.3.4)

36 *Apoc.* 4; Tac. *Ann.* 12.64.5; Suet. *Nero* 34.1; choice of friends: based on Lipsius' emendation of *inrepserat* to *inrepserant* at Tac. *Ann.* 13.12.2

37 *CIL* 6.915; Tac. *Ann.* 13.31.2–3, 51; Suet. *Nero* 10.1; Dio 61.5.3–4 (perhaps a *topes*, see Plut. *Ant.* 4.7–9); Nero reduced by 75% the amounts paid to informers against those who had violated the provisions of the Lex Papia Poppaea; he removed the 4% tax paid by the buyer on the purchase of slaves, a remission that was more apparent than real, since the tax was now paid by the vendor, who just added it to the purchase price; the inclusion of cargo-boats in the assessment of merchants' property for taxation purposes was rescinded; grants to senators: Tac. *Ann.* 13.34.1–3: (i) M. Valerius Messala Corvinus, who received half a million HS (ii) Aurelius Cotta (iii) Q. Haterius Antoninus

38 *Apoc.* 4; Tac. *Ann.* 13.6.2; Suet. *Nero* 34.1; Griffin (1984), 45

39 Tac. *Ann.* 13.2.2; Waltz (1909) saw the two as leaders of factions in the broadest sense, with Burrus as the pre-eminent equestrian and Seneca the pre-eminent senator. McDermott (1949), 249 even suggested that Burrus' name was first provided by Seneca to Agrippina (given her personal interest in the guard this does not seem likely); on Burrus' austerity: Tac. *Ann.* 13.2.2, 14.7.4, 51, 15.7; Dio 62.13.1–2: Baldwin (1967), 430; Griffin (1984), 72; Rudich (1993), 15; De la Ville de Mormont (1910) for early scepticism about Burrus' virtue

40 *ILS* 1321

41 Dio 62.20.3; Tac. *Ann.* 14.15.7 has only Burrus (and the praetorians) present at the early performances

42 Dio 61.4.1–2; Griffin (1984), 51 suggests that Dio might have been influenced by the dramatic changes that took place in his own day under the Severans

43 *CIL* IV 5514; Digest 36.1.1; Griffin (1976), 73. n.6; Bradley (1978), 107–8

44 Syme (1958), 550; for modern theories about Seneca's role see Walz (1909), 8–9, 233–4; Faider (1929); Crook (1955), 119–25

45 Tac. *Ann.* 14.52.4, 54.1, 15.62.2; Griffin (1984), 71; Rudich (1993), 10–11

46 Calp. Sic. 1.58; Sen. *Clem.* 2.1–2; Suet. *Nero* 10.2; Tac. *Ann.* 13.1.4: Griffin (1984), 47

47 Sen. *Clem.* 1.9; Tac. *Ann.* 13.11.2, 14.12.5–6; other cases of *clementia* are viewed with scepticism by Tacitus. Nero delayed the trial of Publius Celer (*PIR*² C265), charged in 58 with corruption in Asia until he died, according to Tacitus, for his services in the murder committed at the beginning of the reign (Tac. *Ann.* 13.33.1). In the same year, two former proconsuls of Africa were acquitted by Nero; in the case of one of them, Pompeius Silvanus, the motive may have been his wealth, combined with childlessness and advanced age, which might have held out the possibility of legacies. In the end Silvanus cheated such hopes by living for many more years (Tac. *Ann.* 13.52). The acquittal of Felix is attributed to the improper intervention of Pallas (Jos. *Ant.* 20.182)

48 Dio 61.4.5, 8.5, 10.6; Ferrero (1906), 449–72, (1911), 276–337 suggests that for two years Agrippina represented the old conservative Roman ideals and Seneca was opposed to them because he had ideals of his own which were strongly oriental in character; Giancotti (1953), 239 claims that Seneca began his sexual liaison for the express purpose of keeping her *ferocia* in check (a noble sacrifice!); for the love affair, Syme (1958), 308, 376

49 Tac. *Ann.* 13.2

50 Suet. *Tib.* 27; Martial *Spect.* 7.99.4

51 Tac. *Ann.* 13.4

52 Calp. Sic. 1.42, 49; Suet. *Nero* 10.1; Caligula: Dio 59.3.8; Claudius: Tac. *Ann.* 12.11.1; Suet. *Claud.* 11.2; Nero: Sen. *Clem.* 1.9.1–12, 15.3–16.1

53 Caligula's golden shield: Suet. *Cal.* 16.4

54 Tac. *Ann.* 13.5.1; Suet. *Nero* 10.2: examples of deference to senate; Tac. *Ann.* 13.11.1: discontinuance of oath to uphold his *acta;* Suet. *Nero* 15.2: no one day con-sulship; Tac. *Ann.* 13.41.5: no continuous consulship; Cal. Sic. 1.60–2 speaks of seeing the last of the funeral processions of senators in chains, and of prisons so full that only a scattered few remained to take their place in the senate house

55 Tac. *Ann.* 11.5–7, 13.5.1–2: grammatically, by the use of the singular *quod* Tacitus might seem to imply that Agrippina opposed only the second measure (relating to the quaestors and games), but *quod* applies to the general situation and the context indicates clearly that Agrippina opposed both measures; Suet. *Claud.* 12.2; Dio 54.18.2; Griffin (1984), 52; Rudich (1993), 26–7; Bauman (1992), 193 claims that since Claudius had been deified his *acta* were protected from interference and that, as priestess of his cult, Agrippina had a right to intervene on his behalf

56 Cal. Sic. 1.69–73; Tac. *Ann.* 11.1–3, 14.48.3, 62.4, 15.58.3, 16.61.2; Suet. *Nero* 15.1; Dio 60.29.4–6; Crook (1955), 106; Bleicken (1962), 96; Sherwin White (1966), 395, (1963), 13; Griffin (1984), 52

57 Tac. *Ann.* 13.43; Momigliano (1961), 104

58 Jos. *Ant.* 20.183–4; Tac. *Ann.* 13.19.4–20.1, 14.39; Dio 61.5.4; Griffin (1984), 54

59 Tac. *Ann.* 13.31.4–5, 14.17: in 57 Nero forbade provincial governors of all ranks from giving gladiatorial games and obliged provincial governors to give precedence to cases against *publicani;* procurators: Tac. *Ag.* 15.2 cf. Plut. *Galb.* 4.1; Domitian: Brunt (1966), 481, based on implications of contrast with Trajan's reign in Pliny *Paneg.* 36.4

60 Tac. *Ann.* 11.22.2–3, 13.5.1–2; Suet. *Claud.* 24.2 (quaestors already in office give the games), *Dom.* 4.1; *SHA:* Severus Alexander 43.3–4 indicates that Domitian's mea-sure was still in force in the third century; Vacca, Vita Lucani 10 asserts that in the 60s Lucan put on a show with his colleagues 'according to the prevailing custom' (*in more tunc usitato*); Talbert (1984), 58; Griffin (1984), 60

61 Tac. *Ann.* 13.5.3; Dio 61.3.3–4; Suet. *Nero* 13 deals not with this incident, but a later

Armenian deputation under Tiridates in 66

62 Dio 60.34.2–4; on the *Apocolocyntosis*, see p. 202

63 Smallwood 16, 19, 21, 22; on 11 September, 59 also Nero sacrificed a cow to the Di Penates (household gods) before Domitius' house; Tac. *Ann.* 13.10.1; Suet. *Nero* 9; Wissowa (1896), 1485; Krause (1931), 262; Scheid (1990), 413, 417

64 Pliny *Paneg.* 11.1; Suet. *Claud.* 45, *Vesp.* 9.1

65 *RIC* I² Nero 10, 613–4, 619–22; Smallwood 22.15 (*AFA*: AD 60), 149 (Luna AD 66–7), 351 (Bulgaria AD 61/62), 352 (Gaul AD 58), *ILS* 225 (Spain AD 55), 227 (Spain AD 58), 233 (Luna, Italy, AD 66/67)

66 *IGR* 1.1263.28 (September 68); *ILS* 241.53, 80; aqueducts: *CIL* 6.1257 (AD 71), 1258 (AD 80–1); oaths: *ILS* 6088 (xxv, xxvi) (Salpesa), 6089 (lix) Malaca; games: *ILS* 5285; Bradley (1978), 68; on the general question: Charlesworth (1937); Griffin (1994), 310

67 Suet. *Nero* 18; Seneca's holdings: Dio 62.2.1; on Didius: Tac. *Ann.* 12.40; *Ag.* 14; see Birley (1953), 1, 5; Webster (1878), 84; Bradley (1978), 111; Salway (1981), 107–9; Frere (1987), 68

68 Tac. *Ann.* 13.12.1; *RIC*² Nero 6–7; Ptolemy II: Morkholm (1991), 103; Claudius and Agrippina, facing: *RPC* 2322, *RPC* 2620 jugate: *RPC* 2224, *RPC* 2461, *RPC* 2475, *RPC* 2621–4, *RPC* 2665; Nero and Agrippina, facing: *RPC* 2316, *RPC* 2372, *RPC* 2478–9, *RPC* 2685, *RPC* 2799, *RPC* 3107, *RPC* 3136 jugate: *RPC* 2052, *RPC* 2054, *RPC* 2565, *RPC* 2825–6; Alexandria: Schumann (1930), 12. n.22

69 Annaeus Serenus: *PIR*² A618; Sen. *Ep.* 63.14.15; Pliny *NH* 22.96; Martial 8.81, 7.45.2; Martial lists him among Seneca's closest friends; Dialogues 2, 8, 9 of Seneca were dedicated to him. Griffin (1976), App. D3; Claudius Senecio: Tac. *Ann.* 15.50.1, 70.2

70 Tac. *Ann.* 13.12–13; Suet. *Nero* 28.1; Dio 61.7.1; Acte: *CIL* 6.11242–3, 15027, 10.7980; Suet. *Nero* 50; Caenis: Suet. *Vesp.* 3; marriage: Digest xxiii.2.44. On Agrippina's motives: McDermott (1949), 236; Fabia (1911), 158, Giancotti (1953), 252; Weaver (1972), 171, 222

71 Tac. *Ann.* 13.13.2–3

72 Tac. *Ann.* 13.2.4, 14.1–2; Dio 61.7.3; Oost (1958), 134–5; Momigliano (1961), 104

73 The murder of Britannicus: Tac. *Ann.* 13.15–17; Suet. *Nero* 33.2; Dio 61.1.2, 7.4 (at which, see John of Antioch for story of Nero's buggery); Herodian 4.5.6; Eutrop.

Brev. 7.14; Schol. Juv. *Sat.* 1.71, 6.117, 124, 8.215; Locusta: Juv. *Sat.* 1.71 (with scholium); Tac. *Ann.* 12.66.4. That the death took place early in the year is indicated by the notice by Tac. *Ann.* 13.15.1 that Britannicus would that year have assumed the *toga virilis* (normally in March): Britannicus' song: Menaut (1981), 273 argues that it echoed one or other of the fragments of Ennius' *Andromache Captiva* and *Thyestes*, preserved by Cic. *Tusc.* 3.44; Faider (1929), 194 claims that the song was ambiguous; Julius Densus: Tac. *Ann.* 13.10.3

74 Jos. *Ant.* 20.153; Pollio: *PIR²* I473; *CIL* 10.7952; Laenas: Tac. *Ann.* 13.30.1

75 Tac. *Ann.* 15.62.2; Giancotti (1953), 165; Griffin (1984), 74. Doubts about the murder are quite old: see Stahr (1867), 257, who believes that the story gained currency later when people had changed their minds about Nero's character. Titus: Suet. *Tit.* 2; Faider (1929), 196; condoning of murder: Tac. *Ann.* 13.17.2; Amisus: *SEG* 16 (1959) 748; Rose (1993), Catalogue: 98

76 Agrippina: Tac. *Ann.* 13.18.1, 3; Schol. Juv. *Sat.* 6.124; *Octavia* 170–1; Seneca and Burrus: Dio 61.7.5; Sen. *Ben.* 2.18.6–7; Faider (1929), 199; Ciaceri (1943), 292 argues for the complicity of Seneca and Burrus; Faider (1929), 195 discredits it; poisons: Dawson (1968), 256

77 Seneca: Tac. *Ann.* 14.56.6

78 Tac. *Ann.* 13.18.4–5, 19.1, 24.1; Suet. *Nero* 34.1; Dio 61.8.3–6; grain allowance: Suet. *Nero* 10.1; Brunt (1950), 53; Watson (1969), 98; some have linked this to the donative given after the Pisonian conspiracy (Tac. *Ann.* 15.72.1), see Bradley (1978), 77; German Guard: H. Bellen (1981), Speidel (1984)

79 Tac. *Ann.* 13.19–21

80 Sextius Africanus was an Arval from AD 54 at the latest and held the (suffect) consulship in 59: *PIR* S464; *AFA* (Smallwood 14.1, 34)

81 In 55 Agrippina would have been in her 40th year. Silana was almost certainly older–Agrippina later calls her an *anus* ('old woman'). If Sextius was in his appropriate year when he assumed the consulship in 59 he might have been born about 26 and thus have been at least eleven years younger than Junia

82 (L. Domitius) Paris: *PIR²* D156; at Tac. *Ann.* 13.27.7 Nero deprives Domitia of Paris. Suet. *Nero* 54 claims that Nero put him to death because he saw him as a rival, Dio 63.18.1 because he could not teach Nero to dance

83 Tac. *Ann.* 13.20; McDermott (1949), 250; Gillis (1963), 13; Baldwin (1967), 431

84 Caecina: *PIR²* C109; *Pap. Ryl.* 2.119; Tac. *Ann.* 13.20.2, *Hist.* 3.38–9; Suet. *Nero*

35.5; Dio 63.18.1, which places him in Egypt in 67, but Jos. *BJ* 2.309, 315 shows that he had left by at least June 66, by which time Tiberius Alexander had taken office; Stein (1950), 35; Pflaum (1961), I. no. 16; Sumner (1965), 138; Griffin (1976), 95, (1984), 115, 161, 187 suggests that Caecina might have become estranged from Agrippina when she secured the appointment of his subordinate Balbillus as prefect of Egypt

85 Apart from the patronage appointments listed by Tacitus, two others might have been made at this time. Agrippina is later seen to be the close friend of Acerronia Polla, who will die in the accident intended for Agrippina. Acerronia was the sister of Gnaeus Acerronius Proculus, who held a proconsulship of Achaea, some time after 44, possibly due to Agrippina's influence. Acerronia: *PIR²* A34, *FOS* 2; Tac. *Ann.* 14.5.6, Dio 61.13.3; Acerronius: *PIR²* A 34; *IG* 3.611; Bull Hell.50.442,79. He seems to be the son of rather than the same as the consul of 37 of the same name (*PIR²* A32–4: *Fasti Ostienses* [Smallwood 31.1]), who can hardly have been proconsul of Achaea which was under the administration of the legate of Moesia up to AD 44; Crepereius Gallus, who belonged to an influential provincial family from the Roman colony of Psidian Antioch, was a man of equestrian background who rose in the equestrian service to become procurator Augusti. His rise was no doubt due to Agrippina and he paid for it with his life, also dying in the famous shipwreck; Tac. *Ann.* 14.5.2; Levick (1964), Griffin (1976), 84

86 Faenius Rufus: *PIR²* F102; Tac. *Ann.* 14.51.5; 15.50.4

87 Arruntius Stella: *PIR²* A1150; a descendant (*PIR²* A1151 is cited by Martial as Paduan); Rostovtzeff (1905), 46; Hirschfeld (1905), 287–8; Griffith (1962), 105, (1976), 85; Syme *Papers A*, 296 on Labeo

88 Balbillus: *PIR²* C813; *SEG* 8.716; Smallwood 261, 391.28, 418, 439; *P. Lond.* 1912; Sen. *QN* 4a.2.13; Pliny *NH* 19. pr.3; Tac. *Ann.* 13.33.1; Suet. *Nero* 36.1 refers to an astrologer Balbillus, possibly the same man, and Dio 66.9.2 speaks of an astronomer 'Barbillus' who was given permission by Vespasian to celebrate sacred games at Ephesus; Stein (1950), 32–4; Pflaum (1961), I. no.15, 34–41; Griffin (1976), 83, 86; Bradley (1978), 219–20; Balbillus probably replaced Mettius Modestus (appointed on Nero's accession) who in turn had replaced the former praetorian prefect Lusius Geta

89 Publius Anteius: *PIR²* A731; *CIL* 3.14321.16, 14987.1; his name appears on plaques recording the rebuilding in the headquarters of the legionary fortress of Legio XI Claudia at Burnum from early 51. His name was erased after 66, and restored there after Nero's death; Tac. *Ann.;* 16.14, P.v Rhoden, *RE* (1894), 1.2349; Syme (1949), 9; Wilkes (1969), 98; Griffin (1976), 86–7; freedman: *CIL* 3.1947; brother (*PIR²* A729) and father(?) (*PIR²* A728); Jos. *Ant.* 19.125, 126; Germanican legate:*PIR²* A727; Tac. *Ann.* 2.6

90 Tac. *Ann.* 13.23; McDermott (1949), 251; Oost (1958); Gillis (1963), 15; Griffin

(1984), 75; Baldwin (1967), 432–3

91 Tac. *Ann.* 13.23; judicial duties of praetorian prefect: Durry (1928), 171–3; Dio 61.10.6 seems to place the case in 58, when Suillius made an attack on Seneca in the senate

92 Jos. *Ant.* 20.182; Tac. *Ann.* 14.65.1; Suet. *Nero* 35.5; Dio 62.14.3; Oost (1958), 137; Jerome dates the appointment of Felix's successor, Porcius Festus, to the second year of Nero's reign (October 55–October 56). The issue is much disputed: good summaries in Griffin (1976) 87, D5 (55/56); Smallwood (1976), 269 n.40 (58/59); Schwartz (1992), 223–42 (spring 56)

93 *AFA* (Smallwood 19.6, 30; 21.16, 32); *ILS* 226 (Inscription no. 34, p.224); *RPC* 5201, *RPC* 5212, *RPC* 5231, Förschner (1987), no. 93–6; some of the references to Agrippina in Suetonius are, of course, undatable

94 Birthday rites in 60: *AFA* (Smallwood 23.5); see Balsdon (1962), 122

95 Syme (1958), 308, 376

96 Suet. *Nero* 34.1

97 Tac. *Ann.* 13.42–3; Dio 61.10.1, 6

8 The End (pp. 181–95)

1 Tac. *Ann.* 13.45; Suet. *Nero* 34.2, 35.1

2 Tac. *Hist.* 1.13.8; see also Suet. *Otho* 3; Plut. *Galb.* 19; Dio 61.11.2; Tac. *Ann.* 13.45.4–46

3 *Octavia* 126–7; Tac. *Ann.* 14.59.5, 60; Dio 61.11.4, 12.1 (cf. Suet. *Nero* 28.2); Syme (1958), 376; Scott (1974), 112; Dawson (1968), 254–5, 60; Martin (1981), 171; Griffin (1984), 254, n.42; McDermott (1949), 238 seems to believe the Poppaea story

4 Tac. *Ann.* 14.2; Suet. *Nero* 28.2; Dio 61.11.3–4

5 Suet. *Nero* 28.2; Dio 61.11.4, 12.1

6 Tac. *Ann.* 14.3.1–2; Suet. *Nero* 34.2 (he claims that Nero made three unsuccessful poison attempts); Dio 61.12.2

7 Tac. *Hist.* 1.6.2, 2.12.1, 17.2, 3.55.1; Plut. *Galb.* 15.3; Starr (1960), 16–20; Kienast (1966)

8 Tac. *Hist.* 2.9.1; Juv. *Sat.* 8.167–76; Suet. *Nero* 47.1

9 Augustus: *CIL* V.938 (Aquileia); Caligula: Jos. *Ant.* 19.253; Commodus: SHA Commodus 15.6

10 Kienast (1966), 31; Starr (1960), 210–11 for a list; on prefects/procurators generally, Levick (1990), 48

11 Stahr (1867), 212; Caligula kept a fleet equipped to make a speedy escape in the event of an uprising; Suet. *Cal.* 51.3; Volusius Proculus: *PIR* V658; Tac. *Ann.* 15.51.2–8; Anicetus: *PIR²* A589; Tac. *Ann.* 14.3.5, 62.3; Kienast (1966), 56

12 Tac. *Ann.* 14.3.5–4; Suet. *Nero* 34.2; Dio 61.12.2; Nero's gadgets: Suet. *Nero* 31.2, 41.2; see Bradley (1978), 179

13 Hortensius' villa was located at Bauli by several ancient sources: Cic. *Acad.* 2.9; Varro *RR* 3.17.5; Pliny *NH* 9.172; D'Arms (1970), 68–9, 182

14 Maiuri (1963), 87; Kokkinos (1992), 153–5

15 Plut. *Galb.* 23.4.9 (implying that Seneca's intervention saved him from execution); Suet. *Nero* 34.2; *Otho* 3.1, 4.1; Dio 61.13.1; Dawson (1968) has suggested that *Otho* might well have been conspiring with Agrippina to murder Nero, and argues that this is why he was despatched to Lusitania. Otho supposedly administered Lusitania for ten years (presumably a round figure), returning to Rome in 68

16 Tac. *Ann.* 14.4; Suet. *Nero* 34.2; Dio 69.12.3–13.2; festival of Minerva: Varr. *LL* 6.14; Aul. Gell. 2.21.7; Ov. *Fast.* 3.809–14; Acte: D'Arms (1970), 94; Piso's Villa: Tac. *Ann.* 15.52.1; villa of Hortensius/Antonia: Pliny *NH* 9.172

17 See T. Barton in Elsner (1994), 62 n.57: 'an amalgamation of a variety of traditions'

18 Tac. *Ann.* 14.5–6.1; *Octavia* 125, 310–57, 955; Martial 4.63; Dio 61.2–4; on discrepancies in the story see Dawson (1968), 255

19 Strabo 5.4.6; Pliny *NH* 9.169

20 Dio 61.12.1; Fabia (1910), 268–9 says that it is impossible to believe that Seneca and Burrus were not in on the plot, since so many others were; Ciaceri (1941/2), 294 thinks they were implicated; Gillis (1963), 294 thinks that Seneca was not involved and that Burrus might have been, but held his troops back to see who would win; McDermott (1949), 230, 239, 252 argues that neither was involved; on the general problem of the sources at this point, D'Anna (1963)

21 Tac. *Ann.* 14.7.6–7; Suet. *Nero* 34.3; Dio 61.13.4; Burrus' conduct, Baldwin (1967)

22 *Octavia* 369–72; Tac. *Ann.* 14.8; Dio 61.13.5; Krappe (1940), 472 claims that the inci-

dent is inspired by Aeschylus, *Choephoroi* 896, where Clytemnaestra bares her breast and invites Orestes to strike it

23 Tac. *Ann.* 14.9.1; Suet. *Nero* 34.4; Dio 61.14.2; Boethius *Cons.* 2.6.4; on the theatrical quality: Baldwin (1979); Dawson (1968), 261; Seneca's Phaedra ends with Theseus similarly inspecting the limbs of the mangled Hippolytus

24 Tac. *Ann.* 14.9.2–5; on the narrative of the final section, Quinn (1963), 117; Dawson (1968), 259 argues that she committed suicide

25 Tac. *Ann.* 14.10; Suet. *Nero* 34.4; Dio 61.3–4

26 Tac. *Ann.* 14.11; Quintilian 8.5.18; Dio 61.14.3; formal oath: Mommsen (1887), 2.819.6; authorship of letter: Alexander (1954) suggests that Quintilian's attribution of the letter to Seneca reflects the denigration in the Flavian period of the great figures of the Julio-Claudian age; it has also been argued that the indignation was not over Seneca's morality but his incompetence. The listing of the earlier crimes would have stirred up indignation, but it would have obscured the simple fact that she was accused of trying to assassinate her son. Nero might then have written the letter himself (it is not attributed to Seneca by Dio), but in the style of his influential teacher, which could have misled people

27 *AFA* (Smallwood 22.5–12); Tac. *Ann.* 14.12.1; Stahr (1867), 235; Freyburger (1078), 1426; Talbert (1984), 388

28 Tac. *Ann.* 14.12.1–2; Dio 61.15; Agrippina's birthday: *AFA* (Smallwood 19.6, 21.16) (unfortunately no text for that date in subsequent years has survived); Agrippina the Elder: Suet. *Tib.* 53.2; Julius Africanus: *PIR*² A.120; Quintilian 8.5.15, 10.1.118, 12.10.11

29 Tac. *Ann.* 14.12.3–4; Pliny *NH* 2.180; Dio 61.16.4; Schove (1984), 11–13

30 *Octavia* 611; Tac. *Ann.* 14.13; Dio 61.16.2a; Livilla: Tac. *Ann.* 6.2.1: Messalina: Tac. *Ann.* 11.38.4; erasure of name: *ILS* 226 (inscription 31); Eck (1993), 88 n.196 argues for a formal *damnatio memoriae*

31 *AFA* (Smallwood 2225–30); Tac. *Ann.* 14.13.3. Mars Ultor: Suet. *Aug.* 29.2; Scheid (1990), 399–400; although Nero might have returned as a conquering hero to Rome he clearly did not feel comfortable back in the city. At any rate, he left again later that summer since his return is recorded in the Arval record for 11 September Smallwood 22.35; Scheid (1990), 399

32 Suet. *Nero* 39.2; Dio 61.16.22–3

33 Tac. *Ann.* 14.12.5–7; Scott (1974), 111

34 Tac. *Ann.* 14.13.3; Dio 61.17.2

35 Suet. *Nero* 34.5; Dio 61.17.1

36 Wood (1988), 424–5

9 Sources (pp. 196–239)

1 Tac. *Ann.* 1.4.–4; Dio 53.19.1–4; Flach (1973), 265–6

2 Dio 61.8.5

3 Momigliano, in Latte (1956)

4 Suet. *Tib.* 61.1 *quem de vita sua summatim breviterque composuit*

5 Suet. *Dom.* 20

6 Pliny *NH* 12.78; Suet. *Claud.* 41.2; Momigliano (1932), 317

7 Suet. *Claud.* 41.3: *composuit et de vita sua octo volumina magis inepte quam ineleganter;* Tac. *Ann.* 13.43.4; Durry, in Latte (1956)

8 Pliny *NH* 7.46; in his preface Pliny also lists Agrippina as one of sources for Book 7; Tac. *Ann.* 2.69.1, 4.53.3

9 Motzo (1927), 52; Bardon (1956), 172; Michel (1966), 124; Griffin (1984), 23, 28; Duret (1986), 3283

10 Stahr (1867), 194; Raffay (1884); Fabia (1893), 331; Syme (1958), 277; Balsdon (1962), 121; Wilkes (1972), 181; Clarke (1975), 50; Eck (1993), 22 argues that she had started to write the memoirs before her exile in 39

11 Tac. *Ann.* 13.14.4; Paratore (1952), 42

12 Fabia (1893), 332; Motzo (1927); Syme (1958), 278; Walker (1960) 139; Stahr (1867), 194 without being specific says that the memoirs would have contained attacks on Livia and Tiberius and on Messalina; Bauman (1992), 149 suggests that the confrontation over Claudia Pulchra came from the memoirs; Wood (1988), 424 assigns to them information on the conflict between Agrippina and Tiberius; Eck (1993), 52 suggests that Tac. *Ann.* 13.14.3 (Agrippina's threats against Nero) was derived from the same source

13 Paratore (1952), 41–2

14 Pliny *NH* 7.46, 57, 71, 151; Suet. *Nero* 6.1, 4; Dio 61.2.1–3; see also, Griffin (1984), 23; Clack (1975), 45–53 argues that much of the material in Juvenal's *Satires* might have come from the memoirs; Agrippina should have been an obvious target of Juvenal, but she emerges unscathed. He claims the following borrowings: the description of Messalina at the brothel (*Sat.* 6.115–132), the incest between Agrippa II and his sister (*Sat.* 6. 155-8), the beauty preparations named after Poppaea (*Sat.* 6.461–2), Caesonia's aphrodisiac for Caligula (*Sat.* 6.614-17), the description of Rome when Sejanus fell (*Sat.* 10.56–90), the castration and seduction of Sporus by Nero (*Sat.* 10.306-9), the description of the wedding between Messalina and Silius (*Sat.* 10.329–45)

15 Suet. *Vesp.* 4.2; Dio 61.8.5; Dorey (1962), 2

16 Fabia (1893); see also Momigliano (1932)

17 Tac. *Ann.* 13.20.4; Suet. *Cal.* 8; Dio 63.25

18 See *inter alia* Momigliano (1932), Syme (1958), Tresch (1965), 55–63, Questa (1967), 175–207; Martin (1981), 207–9; Griffin (1984), 235–7; Duret (1986), 3152–346; Sage (1990), 1010–16; Morford (1990), 1587–9

19 Jos. *Ant.* 19.92 (assassination of Caligula); Tac. *Hist.* 1.8.1 (Tarraconensis); Suet. *Nero* 21.2 (Neronia); Dio 63.14.3 (Greece); Barrett (1990), 168–9

20 Fabia (1893)

21 Townend (1960, 1961, 1964); Duret (1986), 3284–91; Sage (1990), 1012–13; Wardle (1992)

22 Pliny *Ep.* 9.19.5; Plut. *Otho* 3.2; In *Quaest.Rom.* 107 Plutarch cites him for the Etruscan origin of the word *histrio* ('actor')

23 Tac. *Ann.* 13.20.3, 14.2.4; Syme (1958), 179

24 Momigliano (1932), 307; Sage (1990), 1011–12

25 Syme (1958), 290

26 For differing views, see Momigliano (1932) and Townend (1960, 1961)

27 *CIL* 6.10229; Sage (1990), 1015; the Rusticus addressed by Pliny the Younger at *Ep.* 9.29 may be Fabius Rusticus, but there is no certainty; see Sherwin-White (1966), 512

28 Fabius: *PIR*² F62; Tac. *Ag.* 10.3; Sage (1990), 1015; Seneca the Elder wrote a history from the period of the civil wars, which, according to the younger Seneca came

down almost to the day of his death (*ab initio bellorum civilium, unde primum veritas retro abiit, paene usque ad mortis suae diem* [Haase Fr. 91]). We do not know precisely when his death occurred but we can place it between the death of Tiberius in 37 and the exile of the younger Seneca in 41. This is doubtless the work used by Suetonius in his account of the death of Tiberius (Suet. *Tib.* 73.2)

29 Tac. *Ag.* 10.3, *Ann.* 13.20.2, 14.2.4, 15.61.6; see Syme (1958), 179, 293; Duret (1986), 3291–4

30 Tac. *Ann.* 13.20.2, 14.2.3; Suet. *Nero* 28.2; Syme (1958), 290 suggests that because at Tac. *Ann.* 13.20.2 Tacitus refers to 'Cluvius' and 'Plinius' but the formal 'Fabius Rusticus', the last may not have been mentioned earlier. Clarke (1965), 69, however, notes that later Tac. *Ann.* 14.2.4 and 15.61.6 still cites him as 'Fabius Rusticus'. For the idea that Dio 61.7.5 is derived from Fabius, see Murray (1965), 52

31 Syme (1958), 180, 291; Townend (1961 & 1964)

32 Tac. *Ann.* 13.31.1, 15.53.4–5

33 Townend (1960, 1961, 1964) has contrasted what he considers to be the sober and careful Pliny with the frivolous and unreliable Cluvius Rufus

34 Dio 60.35.3; Münscher (1922), 50 argued that the target of the *Apocolocyntosis* was the mover of the deification, namely Agrippina, and that the work was a concealed attack on her. But Nero and the senate approved the deification. Also, nowhere is she identified as the mover of the motion. Kurfess (1924), 1308 observes that Agrippina is not mentioned in the *Apocolocyntosis*, leaving the conclusion that she approved of it. He says that its purpose was to give confirmation by silence to the official account of Claudius' death; see Kraft (1966), 98; Baldwin (1964) doubts the ascription to Seneca. For a summary, Goodyear (1982), and for recent thoughts, Hortstkotte (1985), 337–58; Nauta (1987), 69–96; Griffin (1994), 310

35 Dio 61.12.1

36 Dio 59.23.7, 28.7

37 Dio 59.22.8, 60.30.6, 61.3.2, 61.10.1

38 Dio 60.33.21

39 Dio 61.14.1

40 Leo (1901); Steidel (1951)

41 Suet. *Nero* 28.2; Baldwin (1983); 347

42 Tac. *Ann.* 14.16.1–2; Suet. *Nero* 52; see D'Anna (1963)

43 Momigliano (1932) argues that the common source was Cluvius; Townend (1960) 115–17 suggests that both Suetonius and Dio made use of information supplied by Claudius Balbillus, prefect of Egypt; see Millar (1964), 85, 87, 105

44 Wuilleumier (1949), 79–80; Bardon (1962), 283; Syme (1958), 535; Riposati (1973); the issues are clearly set out in Wallace (1991)

45 Baldwin (1972), 84

46 Walker (1960), 60; Kaplan (1979)

47 Tac. *Ann.* 4.40.3–4; 12.8.3, 64.4; 13.19.2, 4; 14.2.4; Rutland (1978), 15

48 Baldwin (1872), 86–7 has pointed out that the association of beautiful women with vice does not indicate misogyny, since handsome men have the same problem–Silius (Tac. *Ann.* 11.12.2) was handsome, as was Traulus Montanus, Messalina's one-night stand (Tac. *Hist.* 1.48)

49 Paratore (1952), 41–2 notes that the story of the snakes in Nero's bedroom is said by Suet. *Nero* 6.4 to be a plot by Messalina. In Tac. *Ann.* 11.11–6 the story is told without any reference to Messalina. This is done deliberately, since Tacitus' purpose is to enhance the role of Agrippina and to emphasize her strength in the face of her opponents

50 Tac. *Ann.* 12.7.6–7

51 Paratore (1952), 78

52 Rutland (1978), 15–16, with other examples added to the list she provides

53 Walker (1960), 70; Griffin (1984), 39

54 See Morford (1990), 1082, 1601

55 Charlesworth (1923, 1927); Martin (1955), 123; Griffin (1984), 39

Bibliography

Abbott, F.F. and Johnson, A.C., *Municipal Administration in the Roman Empire* (New York, 1926)

Abel, K., *Bauformen in Senecas Dialogen* (Heidelberg, 1967)

Aberbach, M., 'The Conflicting Accounts of Josephus and Tacitus concerning Cumanus' and Felix' Term of Office', *JQR* 40 (1949–50), 1–14

Alexander, W.H., 'The Enquête on Seneca's Treason', *CP* 47 (1952), 1–6

Alexander, W.H., 'The Communiqué to the Senate on Agrippina's Death', *CP* 49 (1954), 94–7

Alföldy, G., *Flamines Provinciae Hispaniae Citerioris* (Madrid, 1973)

Allen, W., 'The Political Atmosphere of the Reign of Tiberius', *TAPA* 72 (1941), 1–25

Allen, W., 'Imperial Table Manners in Tacitus' *Annals*', *Latomus* 21 (1962), 374–6

Allison, J.E. and Cloud, J.D., 'The Lex Julia Maiestatis', *Latomus* 21 (1962), 711–31

Allmer, A., *Revue épigraphique du midi de la France* 2 (1884–9), no. 513, 75–7, 138–9, 231–3

Arthur, M.B., '"Liberated" Women: The Classical Era', in Bridenthal (1977)

Babcock, C., 'The Early Career of Fulvia', *AJP* 86 (1965), 1–32

Babelon, E., *Catalogue des Camées Antiques et Modernes de la Bibliothèque Nationale* (1897)

Babelon, J., 'L'enfance de Néron', *RN* 17 (1955), 129–52

Babelon, J., 'Numismatique de Britannicus', *Hommages à L. Herrmann* (Coll. *Latomus* XLIV, Brussels, 1960), 124–37

Backer, E. de, *Agrippine et Néron de Tacite* (1949)

Bagnani, G., 'The Case of the Poisoned Mushrooms', *Phoenix* 1 (1946), 15–20

Balconi, C., 'Su alcuni Nomi Onorifici di Mesi nel Calendario Egiziano', *ZPE* 59 (1985), 84–8

Baldwin, B., 'Executions under Claudius: Seneca's Ludus de Morte Claudi', *Phoenix* 18 (1964), 39–48

Baldwin, B., 'Executions, Trials, and Punishments in the Reign of Nero', *PP* 22 (1967), 425–39

Baldwin, B., 'Women in Tacitus', *Prudentia* 4 (1972), 83–101

Baldwin, B., 'Nero and his Mother's Corpse', *Mnemosyne* 32 (1979), 380–1

Baldwin, B., *Suetonius* (Amsterdam, 1983)

Balsdon, J.P.V.D., *The Emperor Gaius* (Oxford, 1934)

Balsdon, J.P.V.D., *Roman Women: Their History and Habits* (London, 1962)

Balsdon, J.P.V.D., 'The principates of Tiberius and Gaius', *ANRW* II. 2 (1975), 86–94

Bang, M., 'Das gewöhnliche älter der Mädchen bei der Verlobung und Verheiratung', in L. Friedländer, *Darstellungen aus der Sittensgeschichte Roms* 4 (1922), 133–41

Bardon, H., *La littérature latine inconnue. II. L'époque impériale* (Paris, 1956)

Bardon, H., 'Points de vue sur Tacite', *RCCM* 4 (1962), 282–93

Barnes, T., 'Julia's Child', *Phoenix* 35 (1981), 362–3

Barnes, T., 'The Date of the Octavia', *MH* 39 (1982), 215–27

Barrett, A.A., 'Did Galba visit Britain?', *CQ* 33 (1983), 243–5

Barrett, A.A., *Caligula: The Corruption of Power* (London & New Haven, 1990)

Barrett, A.A., 'Claudius' British Victory Arch in Rome', *Britannia* 22 (1991), 1–19

Bartels, H., *Studien zum Frauenporträt der augusteischen Zeit* (Munich, 1962)

Barwick, K., 'Senecas Apocolocyntosis. Eine zweite Ausgabe des Verfassers', *RM* 92 (1943), 159–73

Bauman, R.A., *The Crimen Maiestatis in the Roman Republic and Augustan Principate* (Johannesburg, 1967)

Bauman, R.A., *Impietas in Principem* (Munich, 1974)

Bauman, R.A., *Lawyers in Roman Transitional Politics* (Munich, 1985)

Bauman, R.A., *Lawyers and Politics in the Early Roman Empire* (Munich, 1989)

Bauman, R.A., *Women and Politics in Ancient Rome* (London, 1992)

Becker, K., Studien zur Opposition gegen den römischen Prinzipat (Diss. Tübingen, 1950)

Bellen, H., 'Versaatlichung des Privatvermögens Römischer Kaiser', *ANRW* 2.1 (1974), 91–112

Beloch, J., *Campanien, Geschichte und Topographie des antiken Neapel und seiner Umgebung* (Breslau, 1890–2)

Benario, H.W., 'Imperium and Capaces Imperii in Tacitus', *AJP* 93 (1972), 14–26

Bengston, H., *Grundriss der römischen Geschichte mit Quellenkunde. I* (Munich, 1967)

Béranger, J., 'L'hérédité du Principat: Note sur la transmission du pouvoir impérial aux deux premiers siècles', *REL* 17 (1939), 171–87

Bergener, A., Die führende Senatorenschicht im frühen Prinzipat (14–68 n. Chr.) (Diss. Bonn, 1965)

Bernoulli, J.J., *Römische Ikonographie* (Stuttgart, 1882–94, reprinted Hildesheim, 1969)

Besnier, R., *Les Affranchis impériaux à Rome, de 41 à 54 P.C.* (Paris, 1847–8)

Best, E.E., 'Cicero, Livy and Educated Roman Women', *CJ* 65 (1970), 199–204

Bicknell, P.J., 'Agrippina's Villa at Bauli', *CR* 13 (1963), 261–2

Bird, H.W., 'L. Aelius Seianus and his Political Influence', *Latomus* 28 (1969), 61–98

Birley, E., *Roman Britain and the Roman Army* (Kendal, 1953)

Birley, E., 'Promotions and Transfers in the Roman Army II: The Centurionate', *Carnuntum Jahrbuch* (1963–4), 21–33

Birt, Th., *Frauen der Antike* (Leipzig, 1932)

Bishop, J.D., 'Dating in Tacitus by Moonless Nights', *CP* 55 (1960), 164–70

Bishop, J., *Nero: The Man and the Legend* (London, 1964)

Blake, E.M., *Roman Construction in Italy from Tiberius through the Tiberians* (Washington, 1959)

Blazquez Martínez, J., 'Cabeza de Agrippina, de Medina Sidonia', Archiva Español de Arqueologia 29 (1956), 204–6

Blazquez Martínez, J., 'Propaganda dinastica y culto imperial en las acuñaciones de Hispania', *Numisma* 23–4 (1973–4), 311–29

Bloch, G., 'Remarques à propos de la carrière d'Afranius Burrus préfet du prétoire sous Claude et sous Néron', *Annuaire de la Faculté des Lettres de Lyon* 3 (1885), 1–17

Boak, A.E., 'Men Drousilleos', *JEA* 13 (1927), 185–6

Boddington, A., 'Sejanus. Whose Conspiracy?', *AJP* 84 (1963), 1–16

Bol, R., 'Ein Bildnis der Claudia Octavia aus dem Olympischen Metroön', *JDAI* (1976), 291–307

Bonamente G., *Germanico: La persona, la personalità, il personaggio. Atti del Convegno, Macerata–Perugia, 9–11 maggio 1986* (Facoltà di Lettere e Filosofia Università Macerata, 39, Rome, 1987)

Borghesi, B., *Oeuvres Compltes* (Paris, 1862–97)

Boulvert, G., *Les esclaves et les affranchis impériaux sous le Haut–Empire romain: rôle politique et administratif* (Aix en Provence, 1965, Naples, 1970)

Boulvert, G., *Domestique et fonctionnaire sous le Haut–Empire romain: la condition de l'affranchi et de l'esclave du prince* (Paris, 1974)

Bradley, K., *Suetonius' Life of Nero: An Historical Commentary* (Brussels, 1978)

Braund, D.C., 'The Aedui, Troy and the Apocolocyntosis', *CQ* 30 (1980), 420–5

Breeze, D. and Maxfield, V. (eds.), *Service in the Roman Army* (Edinburgh, 1989)

Bridenthal, R. and Koonz C. (eds), *Becoming Visible: Women in European History* (Boston, 1977)

Brunt, P., 'Pay and Superannuation in the Roman Army', *PBSR* 18 (1950), 50–71

Brunt, P., 'The Lex Valeria Cornelia', *JRS* 51 (1961), 71–83

Brunt, P., 'The Fiscus and its Development', *JRS* (1966), 75–91

Brunt, P., 'Procuratorial Jurisdiction', *Latomus* 25 (1966), 461–89

Brunt, P., 'Two Great Roman Landowners', *Latomus* 34 (1975), 619–35

Burian, J., 'Caligula und die Militärrevolte am Rhein', Mnema V. Groh (Prague, 1964), 25–9

Cameron, A. and Kuhrt, A. (eds.), *Images of Women in Antiquity* (London, 1983)

Camporini, E., *Sculture a tutto tondo del Civico Museo Archeologico di Milano* (Milan, 1979)

Caputo, G., 'Sculture dello scavo a sud del foro di Sabratha', *QAL* 1 (1950), 7–28

Carandini, A., *Schiavi in Italia* (Rome, 1988)

Carcopino, J., *Passion et politique chez les Césars* (Paris, 1958)

Carettoni, G., *La Pianta marmorea di Roma antica: forma urbis Romae* (Rome, 1955)

Carney, T.F., 'The Changing Picture of Claudius', *AC* 3 (1960), 99–104

Castagnoli, F., 'Note sulla topographia del Palatino e del Foro Romano', *ArchClass* 16 (1964), 173–99

Charlesworth, M.P., 'The Banishment of the Elder Agrippina', *CP* 17 (1922), 260–1

Charlesworth, M.P., 'Tiberius and the Death of Augustus', *AJP* 44 (1923), 145–7

Charlesworth, M.P., 'Livia and Tanaquil', *CR* 41 (1927), 55–7

Charlesworth, M.P., 'Gaius and Claudius', *Cambridge Ancient History* (Cambridge, 1934), 652–701

Charlesworth, M., 'Flaviana', *JRS* 27 (1937), 54–62

Chastagnol, A., 'Les Femmes dans l'ordre senatorial: titulature et rang social à Rome', *RH* 103 (1979), 3–28

Christ, K., 'Tacitus und der Principat', *Historia* 27 (1978), 449–87

Christes, J., 'Elemente der Mündlichkeit in der taciteischen Erzählung der Ermorderung Agrippinas (Ann. 14.1–13)', in *Strukturen des Mündlichkeit in der römischen Literatur*, ed. G. Vogt–Spira (Tübingen, 1990)

Ciaceri, E., 'Claudio e Nerone nelle Storie di Plinio', *Processi politici e relazioni internazionali* (Rome, 1918)

Ciaceri, E., 'Nerone Matricida' *RAL* Ser.7.3 (1941/2), 289–98

Cichorius, C., *Römische Studien* (Leipzig, 1922)

Clack, J., 'To those who fell on Agrippina's Pen', *CW* 69 (1975), 45–53

Clarke, G.W., 'Seneca the Younger under Caligula', *Latomus* 24 (1965), 62–9

Clay, C.L., 'Die Münzprägung des Kaisers Nero in Rom und Lugdunum. Teil 1: Die Edelmetalprägung der Jahre 54 bis 64 n. Chr.', *NZ* 96 (1982), 7–52

Coarelli, F., *Roma* (Rome, 1980)

Coarelli, F., *Il Foro Romano* (Rome, 1983)

Coarelli, F., *Lazio* (Rome, 1984)

Coffey, M., 'Seneca, Apokolokyntosis 1922–1958', *Lustrum* 6 (1961), 239–71

Coleman, K.M., 'Launching into History: Aquatic Displays in the Early Empire', *JRS* 83 (1993), 48–74

Colin, J., 'Les vendages dionysiaques et la légende de Messalina', *LEC* 24 (1956), 23–39

Corbett, J.H., 'The Succession Policy of Augustus', *Latomus* 33 (1974), 87–97

Corbett, P.E., *The Roman Law of Marriage* (Oxford, 1930)

Corbier, M., 'Claude et les finances publiques: la création du fisc impérial', *Actes du VII Congrès intern. de l'épigr. gr. et lat. 1977* (Bucharest and Paris, 1979), 346–7

Coursey Ruth, Th. de, The Problem of Claudius: Some Aspects of a Character Study (Diss. Baltimore, 1916)

Cousin, J., 'Rhétorique et psychologie chez Tacite', *REL* 29 (1951), 228–47

Crawford, M.H., 'Plated Coins–False Coins', *NC* (1968), 55–9

Crook, J., *Concilium Principis* (Cambridge, 1955)

Dabrowski, A.M., Problems in the Tradition about the Principate of Gaius (Diss. Toronto, 1972)

D'Anna, G., 'Osservazioni sulle Fonti del Morte di Agrippina Minore', *Athenaeum* 41 (1963), 111–17

D'Arms, J.H., *Romans on the Bay of Naples* (Cambridge, Mass., 1970)

D'Arms, J.H., *Commerce and Social Standing in Ancient Rome* (Cambridge, Mass., 1981)

Dawson, A., 'Whatever Happened to Lady Agrippina?', *CJ* 64 (1968), 253–67

De la Ville de Mirmont, H., 'Afranius Burrhus', *RPh* 34 (1910), 73–100

Delia, D., 'Fulvia Reconsidered', in S. Pomeroy (ed.), *Women's History and Ancient History* (Chapel Hill, 1991), 19–217

Demougin, S., *L'Ordre Equestre sous les Julio–Claudiens* (Rome: Collection de l'École Français de Rome no. 108, 1988)

Demougin, S., 'Claude et la société de son temps', in Strocka, op. cit. (1994), 11–22

D'Ercé, F., 'La mort de Germanicus et les poisons de Caligula', *Janus* 56 (1969), 123–48

De Serviez, J.R., *The Roman Empresses* (London, 1752)

Dessau, H., *Geschichte der römischen Kaiserzeit II.* 1 (Berlin 1924–6)

Dickison, S.K., 'Claudius: Saturnalicius Princeps', *Latomus* 36 (1977), 634–47

Dixon, S., 'A Family Business: Women's Role in Patronage and Politics at Rome 80–44 BC', *C&M* 34 (1983), 91–112

Dobson, B., 'The Significance of the Centurion and Primipilaris in the Roman Army and Administration', ANRW 2:1 (Berlin, 1974), 392–434

Dobson, B. and Breeze, D.J., 'The Rome Cohorts and the Legionary Centurionate', *Ep.Stud.* 8 (1969), 100–24

Domaszewski, A. von, *Geschichte der römischen Kaiser* II (Leipzig, 1909²)

Domaszewski, A. von, *Die Rangordnung des römischen Heeres* (Cologne–Graz, 1967²)

Dorey, T.A., 'Cicero, Clodia and the *Pro Caelio*', *GR* 27 (1958), 175–80

Dorey, T.A., 'Adultery and Propaganda in the Early Roman Empire', *University of Birmingham Historical Journal* 8 (1962), 1–6

Dorey, T.A., 'Claudius und seine Ratgeber', *Altertum* 12 (1966), 144–55

Double, L., *L'Empereur Claude* (Paris, 1876)

Downey, *A History of Antioch in Syria from Seleucus to the Arab Conquest* (Princeton, 1961)

Dröpp, S., 'Claudius in Senecas Trostschrift an Polybius', in Strocka, op. cit., 295–306

Dudley, D.R., *The World of Tacitus* (London, 1968)

Duff, A.M., *Freedmen in the Early Roman Empire* (Oxford, 1928)

Duret, L., 'Dans l'ombre des plus grands. II. Poètes et prosateurs mal connus de la latinité d'argent', *ANRW* II.32.5 (1986) 3152–346

Durry, M., *Les cohortes prétoriennes* (Paris, 1928)

Durry, M., 'Le mariage des filles impubères à Rome', *REL* 47 (1970), 17–24

Duruy, V., *Geschichte des römischen Kaiserreichs* I (Leipzig, 1885)

Eck, W., 'Miscellanea Prosopographica', *ZPE* 42 (1981), 227–56

Eck, W., 'Das s.c. de Cn. Pisone patre und seine Publikation in der Baetica', *Cahiers du*

Centre Glotz 4 (1993), 189–208 (=Eck, Cahiers, 1993)

Eck, W., *Agrippina, die Stadtgründerin Kölns. Eine Frau in der frühkaiserzeitlichen Politik* (Cologne, 1993) (=Eck, 1993)

Edgeworth, R.J., 'Nero the Bastard', *Eos* 74 (1986), 103–11

Ehrhardt, C., 'Messalina and the Succession to Claudius', *Antichthon* 28 (1978), 51–77

Eilers, C., *Roman Patrons of Greek Cities in the Late Republic and Early Empire* (Oxford, 1993)

Elsner, J. and Masters, J., *Reflections of Nero* (London, 1994)

Enrile, D., *Seneca, Caio Cesare, Claudio* (Palermo, 1946)

Espérandieu, E., *Inscriptions Latines de Gaule* (Paris, 1929)

Esser, A., *Cäsar und die julisch–claudischen Kaiser im biologisch–ärztlichen Blickfeld* (Leiden, 1958)

Fabia, Ph., *Les sources de Tacite dans les Histoires et les Annales* (Paris, 1893)

Fabia, Ph., 'Sénèque et Néron', *Journal des Savants* (1910), 260–71

Fabia, Ph., 'La mère de Néron', *RPh* 35 (1911), 144–78

Faider, P., 'Sénèque et Britannicus', *MB* 33 (1929), 171–209

Fau, G., *L'Emancipation féminine dans la Rome antique* (Paris, 1978)

Felletti Maj, B.M., *Museo Nazionale Romano. I Rittratti* (Rome, 1953)

Ferrero, G., *The Women of the Caesars* (London, 1911)

Ferrill, A., 'Seneca's Exile and the ad Helviam: A Reinterpretation', *CP* 61 (1966), 253–7

Ferrill, A., 'Augustus and his Daughter: A Modern Myth', in *Studies in Latin Literature and Roman History* 2 (Coll. *Latomus* 168: Brussels 1980), 332–66

Fishwick, D., 'The Annexation of Mauretania', *Historia* 20 (1971), 467–87

Fishwick, D. and Shaw, B.D., 'Ptolemy of Mauretania and the Conspiracy of Gaetulicus', *Historia* 25 (1976), 491–4

Fittschen, K. and Zanker, P., *Katalog der römischen Porträts in den Capitolinischen Museen und den anderen kommunalen Sammlungen der Stadt Rom* (Mainz, 1983)

Flach, D., 'Seneca und Agrippina im Antiken Urteil', *Chiron* 3 (1973), 265–76

Flaig, E., 'Loyalität ist keine Gefälligkeit. Zum Majestätsprozess gegen C. Silius 24 n Chr.', *Klio* 75 (1993), 289–98

Förschner, G., *Die Münzen der Römischen Kaiser in Alexandrien* (Frankfurt, 1987)

Forsyth, P.Y., 'A Treason Case of AD. 37', *Phoenix* 23 (1969), 204–7

Fremersdorf, F., 'Neue Beiträge zur Topographie des römischen Köln', *Römisch–germanische Forschungen* 18 (Berlin, 1950)

Frere, S., *Britannia* (London, 1987³)

Freyburger, G., 'La Supplication d'action de graces sous le Haut-Empire', *ANRW* 16.2 (1978), 1418–39

Friedrich, W.-H., 'Eine Denkform bei Tacitus', *Festschrift E. Kapp* (Hamburg, 1958), 135–44

Fuchs, M., *Il teatro e il ciclo statuario giulio–claudio* (Rome, 1989)

Fuchs, M., 'Frauen um Caligula und Claudius', *AA* (1990), 107–22

Fuchs, S., 'Deutung, Sinn und Zeitstellung des Wiener Cameo mit den Fruchthornbüsten', *MDAI(R)* 51 (1936), 212–37

Gagé, J., 'Divus Augustus. L'idée dynastique chez les empereurs julio–claudiens', *RA* 55 (1934), 11–36

Gallivan, P.A., 'Some Comments on the *Fasti* for the Reign of Nero', *Historia* 23 (1974), 290–311

Gallivan, P.A., 'The *Fasti* for the Reign of Claudius', *CQ* 28 (1978), 407–26

Gardner, J.F., *Women in Roman Law and Society* (London, 1986)

Gardner, P., 'A New Portrait of Livia', *JRS* 12 (1922), 32–4

Garnsey, P., *Social Status and Legal Privilege in the Roman Empire* (Oxford, 1970)

Garzetti, A., *From Tiberius to the Antonines*, transl. J.R. Foster (London, 1974)

Geer, R.M., 'Notes on the Early Life of Nero', *TAPA* 62 (1931), 57–67

Gelzer, M., 'Iulius Caligula', *RE* 10 (1918), 381–423

Gercke, A., *Seneca–Studien. Fleckeisens Jahrbücher für Classische Philologie* Suppl. 22 (1896), 1–334

Giancotti, F., 'Il Posto della Biografia nella Problematica Senechiana: da quando e in che senso Seneca fu maestro di Nerone?', *RAL* 8 (1953), 102–18

Giancotti, F., 'Il Posto della Biografia nella Problematica Senechiana: Seneca Antagonista d'Agrippina', *RAL* 8 (1953), 238–62

Giancotti, F., 'Seneca Amante d'Agrippina?' *PP* 8 (1953), 53–62

Gillis, D., 'The Portrait of Afranius Burrus in Tacitus' *Annales*', *PP* 18 (1963), 5–22

Giuliano, A., 'Ta ritrattistica dell'Asia Minore', *RIA* 8 (1959), 146–201

Godolphin, F.R.B., 'A Note on the Marriage of Claudius and Agrippina', *CP* 29 (1934), 143–5

Goodyear, F.R.D., *The Annals of Tacitus* I (Cambridge, 1972)

Goodyear, F.R.D., 'Prose Satire: Apocolocyntosis Divi Claudii', *Cambridge History of Classical Literature* (Cambridge, 1982), II.633–4

Goold, G. P., 'The Cause of Ovid's Exile', *Illinois Classical Studies* 8 (1983), 84–107

Grant, M., 'The Pattern of Official Coinage in the Early Principate', in *Essays in Roman Coinage presented to H. Mattingly* (Oxford, 1956), 96–112

Grant, M., *Roman History from Coins* (Cambridge, 1958)

Grant, M., *Nero* (London, 1970)

Gratwick, A.S., 'Free or Not So Free? Wives and Daughters in the Late Roman Republic', in E.M. Craik (ed.), *Marriage and Property* (Aberdeen, 1984), 30–53

Graves, R., 'New Light on an Old Murder', in *Food for Centaurs* (New York, 1960)

Grenzheuser, B., Kaiser und Senat in der Zeit von Nero bis Nerva (Diss. Münster, 1964)

Griffin, M., 'De Brevitate Vitae', *JRS* 52 (1962), 104–13

Griffin, M., *Seneca, A Philosopher in Politics* (Oxford, 1976)

Griffin, M., *Nero: The End of a Dynasty* (London, 1984)

Griffin, M., 'Claudius in the Judgement of the Next Half–Century', in Strocka, op. cit., 307–16

Grimal, P., 'L' exil du roi Ptolémée et la date du De Tranquillitate animi', *REL* 50 (1972), 211–23

Grimal, P., 'Les rapports de Sénèque et de l'empereur Claude', *CRAI* (1978), 469–78

Grimal, P., 'Les allusions à la vie politique de l'empire dans les tragédies de Sénèque', *CRAI* (1979), 205–20

Grimm-Samuel, V., 'On the Mushroom that Deified the Emperor Claudius', *CQ* 41 (1991), 178–82

Groag, E., 'Claudius', *RE* 3 (1899), 2778–839

Groag, E., 'Studien zur Kaisergeschichte III. Der Sturz der Iulia', *WS* 41 (1919), 74–88

Gsell, S., *Musée de Philipeville* (Paris, 1898)

Guarducci, M., 'Alba Fucens', *NS* 7 (1953), 117–25

Hahn, U., *Die Frauen des Römischen Kaiserhauses und ihre Ehrungen im Griechischen Osten anhand Epigraphischer und Numismatischer Zeugnisse von Livia bis Sabina* (Saarbrücken, 1994)

Halfmann, D., *Itinera Principum* (Stuttgart, 1986)

Hallett, J., 'Perusinae Glandes and the Changing Image of Augustus', *AJAH* 2 (1977), 151–71

Hallett, J.P., *Fathers and Daughters in Roman Society* (Princeton, 1984)

Hammond, M., *The Augustan Principate* (Cambridge, Mass., 1933)

Hanson, A.E., 'Caligulan Month Names at Philadelphia and Related Matters', *Atti xvii cong. intern. pap.* III, 1287–95

Hardy, L.E., The Imperial Women in Tacitus' *Annales* (Diss. Indiana, 1976)

Harkness, A.G., 'Age at Marriage and at Death in the Roman Empire', *TAPA* 27 (1896), 35–72

Hartman, J.J., 'De Porticu Claudia', *Mnemosyne* 34 (1906), 83–4

Hayne, L., 'The Last of the Aemilii Lepidi', *AC* 42 (1973), 497–507

Heinrichs, A.D., *Sejan und das Schicksal Roms in den Annalen des Tacitus* (Marburg, 1976)

Heller, J., 'Notes on the meaning of cholochynte', *Illinois Class. Stud.* 10 (1985), 67–117

Henderson, B.W., *The Life and Principate of the Emperor Nero* (London, 1903)

Herington, C.J., 'Octavia Praetexta: A Survey', *CQ* 11 (1961), 18–30

Herington, C.J., 'The Younger Seneca', *Cambridge History of Classical Literature* (Cambridge, 1982), II.4.511–32

Herrmann, C., *Le role judiciare et politique des femmes sous la république romaine* (Brussels, 1964)

Herrmann, P., *Der römische Kaisereid* (Göttingen, 1968)

Herz, P., 'Die Arvalakten des Jahres 38 n. Chr. Eine Quelle zur Geschichte Kaiser Caligulas', *BJ* 181 (1981), 89–110

Herzog, R., 'Nikias und Xenophon von Kos', *Historische Zeitschrift* 125 (1922), 216–47

Heuss, A., *Römische Geschichte* (Brunswick, 1964²)

Hind, J., 'The Death of Agrippina and the Finale of the Oedipus of Seneca', *Journal of the Australasian Universities Language and Literature Association* 38 (1972), 204–11

Hirschfeld, O., *Die kaisierlichen Verwaltungsbeamten bis auf Diocletian* (Berlin, 1905)

Hoffsten, R.B., Roman Women of Rank of the Early Empire, (Diss. Philadelphia, 1939)

Hohl, E., 'Domitius', *RE* Suppl. 3 (1918), 349–94

Hohl, E., *Die römische Kaiserzeit* (Berlin, 1931)

Hohl, E., 'Zu den Testamenten des Augustus', *Klio* 30 (1937), 323–42

Hopkins, M.K., 'The Age of Roman Girls at Marriage', *Population Studies* 18 (1965), 309–27

Hopkins, M.K., 'On the Probable Age Structure of the Roman Population', *Population Studies* 20 (1966), 245–64

Horstkotte, H., 'Die politische Zielsetzung von Senecas Apocolocyntosis', *Athenaeum* 63 (1985), 337–58

Humphrey, J.W., An Historical Commentary on Cassius Dio's Roman History, Book 59 (Gaius Caligula)' (Diss. University of British Columbia, 1976)

Humphrey, J.W., 'The Three Daughters of Agrippina Maior', *AJAH* 4 (1979), 125–43

Hurley, D.W., *An Historical and Historiographical Commentary on Suetonius' Life of C. Caligula* (Atlanta, 1993)

Huzar, E.G., 'Mark Antony: Marriages vs. Careers', *CJ* 81 (1986), 97–111

Jacono, L., 'Solarium di una villa romana nell'isola di Ponza', *NS* (1926), 219–32

Jones, A.H.M., 'The Aerarium and the Fiscus', *JRS* 40 (1950), 22–9

Jones, B.W., 'Agrippina and Vespasian', *Latomus* 43 (1984), 581–3

Josserand, C., 'Le testament de Claude', *Musée Belge* 34 (1930), 285–90

Jucker, H., 'Der Grosse Pariser Kameo', *JDAI* 91 (1977), 211–50

Jucker, H., 'Zum Carpentum–Sesterz der Agrippina Major', *Forschungen und Funde: Festschrift Bernhard Neutsch* (Innsbruck, 1980), 205–17

Just, W., 'L. Annaeus Seneca', *Altertum* 12 (1966), 223–33

Kaenel, H. von, 'Britannicus, Agrippina Minor und Nero in Thrakien', *SchNR* 63 (1984), 127–66

Kaenel, H. von, *Münzprägung und Münzbildnis des Claudius* (Berlin, 1986)

Kahrstedt, V., 'Frauen auf antiken Münzen', *Klio* (1910), 291–314

Kajava, M., 'The Name of Cornelia Orestina/Orestilla', *Arctos* 18 (1984), 23–30

Kamp, H.W., 'Concerning Seneca's Exile', *CJ* 30 (1934), 101–8

Kaplan, M., 'Agrippina semper atrox: A Study in Tacitus' Characterization of Women', *Studies in Latin Literature and Roman History I* (*Collection Latomus* 164, 1979), 410–17

Kaspar, D., 'Neues zum Grand Camée de France', *GNS* 25 (1975), 61–8

Katzoff, R., 'Where was Agrippina Murdered?', *Historia* 22 (1973), 72–8

Kienast, D., *Untersuchungen zu den Kriegsflotten der römischen Kaiserzeit* (Bonn, 1966)

Köberlein, E., *Caligula und die ägyptischen Kulte* (Meisenheim, 1962)

Koeppel, G.M., 'Two Reliefs from the Arch of Claudius in Rome', *MDAI(R)* 90 (1983), 103–9

Koestermann, E., *Cornelius Tacitus. Annalen* (Heidelberg, 1963–8)

Kokkinos, N., *Antonia Augusta: Portrait of a Great Roman Lady* (London, 1992)

Königer, H., *Gestalt und Welt der Frau bei Tacitus* (Erlangen–Nurenberg, 1966)

Kornemann, E., *Doppelprinzipat und Reichsteilung im Imperium Romanum* (Leipzig–Berlin, 1930)

Kornemann, E., *Grosse Frauen des Altertums* (Leipzig, 1942)

Kornemann, E., *Römische Geschichte*, rev. H. Bengston (Stuttgart, 1963[5])

Koster, S., 'Julier und Claudier im Spiegel literarischer Texte', in Strocka, op.cit., 1–9

Kraft, K., 'S(enatus) C(onsulto)', *JNG* 12 (1962), 7–49

Kraft, K., 'Der politische Hintergrund von Senecas *Apocolocyntosis'*, *Historia* 15 (1966), 91–122

Kragelund, P., *Prophecy, Populism and Propaganda in the 'Octavia'* (Copenhagen, 1982)

Krappe, A.H., 'La Fin d'Agrippine', *REA* 42 (1940), 466–72

Krause, C. *et al.*, *Domus Tiberiana: Nuove Richerche, Studi di Restauro* (Zurich, 1985)

Krause, K., 'Hostia', *RE* Suppl. 5, 236–82

Kroll, W., 'De Claudii morte', *Raccolta di scritti in onore di Felice Ramorino* (Milan, 1927), 197–8

Künzl, S., 'Gemma Claudia?', *Römisch–Germanisches Zentralmuseum: Archäologisches Korrespondenzblatt* 24 (1994), 289–97

Kurfess, A., 'Zu Senecas Apocolocyntosis', *PhW* 44 (1924), 1308–11

Labaste, H., 'Comme Plutarque, Tacite aurait–il menti?', *Humanités (Paris), Cl. de Lettres* 7 (1930), 92–5

Lacey, W.K., '2 BC and Julia's Adultery', *Antichthon* 14 (1980), 127–42

Lackeit, C., 'Iulius (Iulia)', *RE* 10 (1918), 909–14: no.556

Laistner, M.L.W., *The Greater Roman Historians* (Berkeley, 1963)

Lana, I., *Lucio Anneo Seneca* (Turin, 1955)

La Rocca, E., 'Arcus et Arae Claudii', in Strocka, op. cit., 267–93

Latte, K. *et al.*, *Histoire et historiens dans l'antiquité* (Geneva, 1956)

Lefevre, E., 'Die Politische Bedeutung von Senecas Phaedra', *WS* 103 (1990), 109–22

Lehman, G., 'Das Ende der römischen Herrschaft über das "westelbische" Germanien: von der Varus–Katastrophe zur Abberufung des Germanicus Caesar 16/17 n. Chr.', *ZPE* 86 (1991), 79–96

Lehmann, H., *Claudius und Nero und ihre Zeit I* (Gotha, 1858)

Leipoldt, J., *Die Frau in der antiken Welt und im Urchristentum* (Leipzig, 1954)

Leo, F., *Die griechisch–römische Biographie nach ihrer literarischen Form* (Leipzig, 1901)

Leon, E.F., 'The Imbecillitas of the Emperor Claudius', *TAPA* 79 (1948), 79–86

Lesuisse, L., 'L'aspect héréditaire de la succession impériale sous les Julio-Claudiens', *LEC* 30 (1962), 32–50

Levi, M.A., *Nerone e i suoi tempi* (Milan, 1949)

Levick, B. and Jameson, S., 'C. Crepereius Gallus and his Gens', *JRS* 54 (1964), 98–106

Levick, B., 'Tiberius' retirement to Rhodes in 6 BC', *Latomus* 31 (1972), 779–813

Levick, B., 'Julians and Claudians', *G&R* 22 (1975), 29–38

Levick, B., 'The Fall of Julia the Younger', *Latomus* 35 (1976), 301–39

Levick, B., *Tiberius the Politician* (London, 1976)

Levick, B., 'Poena Legis Maiestatis', *Historia* 28 (1979), 358–79

Levick, B., 'Nero's Quinquennium', *Studies in Latin Literature and Roman History* iii (Coll. Latomus 180; Brussels, 1982) 211–25

Levick, B., '"Caesar omnia habet": Property and Politics under the Principate', *Entretiens Hardt* 33 (Geneva, 1987), 187–218

Levick, B., *Claudius* (New Haven and London, 1990)

Lewis, M.W.H., *The Official Priests of Rome under the Julio-Claudians* (Rome, 1955)

Liebeschutz, W., *Continuity and Change in Roman Religion* (Oxford, 1979)

Linderski, J., 'Julia in Regium', *ZPE* 72 (1988), 181–200

Linnert, U., Zur Geschichte Caligulas (Diss. Jena, 1908)

Litten, W., 'The Most Poisonous Mushrooms', *Scientific American* 232 (1975), 90–101

Luce, T.J. and Woodman, A.J., *Tacitus and the Tacitean Tradition* (New Jersey, 1993)

McAlindon, D., 'Senatorial Opposition to Claudius and Nero', *AJP* 77 (1956), 113–32

McAlindon, D., 'Claudius and the Senators', *AJP* 78 (1957), 279–86

McAlindon, D., 'Senatorial Advancement in the Age of Claudius', *Latomus* 16 (1957), 252–62

McCulloch, H.Y., 'Literary Augurs at the End of Annals XIII', *Phoenix* 34 (1980), 237–42

McDaniel, W.B., 'Bauli, the Scene of the Murder of Agrippina', *CQ* 4 (1910), 96–102

McDermott, W.C., 'Sextus Afranius Burrus', *Latomus* (1949), 229–54

McDermott, W.C., 'Clodia and Ameana', *Maia* 36 (1984), 3–11

McDougall, J.I., 'Tacitus and the Portrayal of the Elder Agrippina', *EMC* 25 (1981), 104–8

MacMullen, R., 'Women in Public in the Roman Empire', *Historia* 29 (1980), 208–18

MacMullen, R., 'Women's Power in the Principate', *Klio* 68 (1986), 434–43

Maiuri, A., *Nuova Silloge Epigrafica* (Florence, 1925)

Maiuri, A., 'Note di topografia campana', *RAL* Ser.7, 2 (1941), 249–60

Maiuri, A., *I Campi Flegrèi* (Rome, 1963⁴)

Malitz, J., 'Claudius (FGrHist 276)– der Princeps als Gelehrter', in Strocka, op. cit., 133–44

Marchesi, C., *Seneca* (Milan, 1944)

Marsh, F.B., 'Roman Parties in the Reign of Tiberius', *AHR* 31 (1926), 65–8

Marsh, F.B., *The Reign of Tiberius* (Oxford, 1931)

Marshall, A.J., 'Roman Women and the Provinces', *Anc.Soc.* 6 (1975), 109–27

Marshall, B.A., *A Historical Commentary on Asconius* (Columbia, Miss., 1985)

Martin, R.H., 'Tacitus and the Death of Augustus', *CQ* 5 (1955), 123–8

Martin, R.H., *Tacitus* (London, 1981)

Martin, R.H. and Woodman, A.J., *Tacitus: Annals Book IV* (Cambridge, 1989)

Massner, A.-K. 'Zum Stilwandel im Kaiserporträt claudischer Zeit', in Strocka, op. cit., 159–76

Maurer, J.A., *A commentary on C. Suetoni Tranquilli, Vita C. Caligulae Caesaris*, Chapters I–XXI (Philadelphia, 1949)

May, G., 'Notes compliméntaires sur les actes de l'Empereur Claude', *Rev. hist. droit franç. et étr.*, Ser. IV. XXII (1944), 101–14

Megow, W.R., *Kameen von Augustus bis Alexander Severus* (Rome, 1973)

Mehl, A., *Tacitus über Kaiser Claudius: Die Ereignisse am Hof.* (Munich, 1974, *Studia et Testimonia Antiqua* 16)

Meise, E., *Untersuchungen zur Geschichte der Julisch–Claudischen Dynastie* (Munich, 1969)

Mellor, R., *Tacitus* (London, 1993)

Melmoux, J., 'L'action politique de l'affranchi impérial Narcisse: un exemple de la place des affranchis dans les entourages impériaux au milieu du 1er siécle', *Stud.Clas.* 17 (1977), 61–9

Melmoux, J., 'La lutte pour le pouvoir en 51 et les difficultés imprévues d'Agrippine', *Latomus* 42 (1983), 350–61

Menaut, L., 'Une femme de tête, Agrippine', *Bulletin de Litterature Ecclesiastique* 82 (1981), 263–84

Mendell, C.W., *Tacitus: The Man and his Work* (New Haven, 1957)

Michel, A., *Tacite et le destin de l'empire* (Paris, 1966)

Millar, F.G.B., *A Study of Cassius Dio* (Oxford, 1964)

Millar, F.G.B., 'Some Evidence on the Meaning of Tacitus *Annals* XII.60', *Historia* 14 (1964), 180–7

Millar, F.G.B., *The Emperor in the Roman World* (Ithaca, 1977)

Millar, F.G.B., *The Roman Near East 31 BC–AD 337* (Cambridge, Mass., 1993)

Momigliano, A., 'La personalità di Caligola', *Annali della R. Scuola Normale Superiore di Pisa. Lettere, Storia e Filosophia NS* 1 (1932), 205–28

Momigliano, A., 'Osservazioni sulle fonte per la storia di Caligola, Claudio, Nerone', *RAL* 8 (1932), 293–336

Momigliano, A., 'Ricerche sull'organizzazione dell Giudea sotto il dominio romano 63 a.C.–70 d.C.', *Annali della R. Scuola normale superiore di Pisa* 3 (1934), 183–221

Momigliano, A., *Claudius: The Emperor and his Achievement* (Cambridge, 1961²)

Mommsen, Th., 'Die Familie des Germanicus', *Hermes* (1878), 245–65

Mommsen, Th., *Römische Forschungen* (Berlin, 1864–79)

Mommsen, Th., *Römisches Staatsrecht* (Leipzig, 1887³, reprinted Graz, 1963)

Mommsen, Th., 'Bruchstücke der Saliarischen Priesterliste', *Hermes* 38 (1903), 125–9

Mommsen, Th., *Gesammelte Schriften* (Berlin, 1904, reprinted 1965)

Monteleone, C., 'Un Procedimento stilistico in Tacito, *Annal.* 14.8–9', *RFIC* 103 (1973), 302–6

Morford, M., 'The training of three Roman emperors', *Phoenix* 22 (1968), 57–72

Morford, M., 'Tacitus' Historical Methods and the Neronian Books of the *Annals'*, *ANRW* II.32.2 (1990), 1582–627

Morkholm, O., *Early Hellenistic Coinage* (Cambridge, 1991)

Mottershead, J. (ed.), *Suetonius, Claudius* (Bristol, 1986)

Motto, A.L., *Seneca* (New York, 1973)

Motzo, B.R., 'I commentari di Agrippina madre di Nerone', *Studi de Storia e Filologia* Vol. I (Cagliari, 1927)

Mullens, H.G., 'The Women of the Caesars', *GR* 11 (1941/2), 59–67

Münzer, F., 'Clodia', *RE* 4 (1900), 105–7

Münzer, F., 'Fulvia', *RE* 7 (1900), 281–4

Münzer, F., 'Die Verhandlung über das Jus Honorum der Gallier im Jahre 48', *Festschrift zu Otto Hirschfelds sechtzigstem Geburtstage* (Berlin, 1910)

Münzer, F., 'Servilia', *RE* 2A (1923), 1817–21

Murray, O., 'The "quinquennium Neronis" and the Stoics', *Historia* 14 (1965), 51–2

Musurillo, H.A., *The Acts of the Pagan Martyrs* (Oxford, 1954)

Nash, E., *Pictorial Dictionary of Ancient Rome* (New York, 1961)

Nauta, R.R., 'Seneca's *Apocolocyntosis* as Saturnalian literature', *Mnemosyne* 40 (1987), 69–96

Nicols, J., *Vespasian and the Partes Flavianae* (Wiesbaden, 1978)

Nissen, H., *Italische Landeskunde* II (Berlin, 1902, reprinted Amsterdam, 1967)

Nony, D., *Caligula* (Paris, 1986)

Norwood, F., 'The Riddle of Ovid's *relegatio'*, *CP* 58 (1963), 150–63

Oberleitner, W., *Geschnittene Steine: Die Prunkkameen der Wiener Antikensammlung* (Vienna, Cologne & Graz, 1985)

Oost, S.I., 'The Career of M. Antonius Pallas', *AJP* 79 (1958), 113–39

Pace, B., 'Ricerche nella regione di Conia, Adalia e Scalanova', *Annuario della regia scuola archeologica di Atene e delle missioni Italiane in Oriente* 6–7 (Bergamo, 1926), 419, no. 117

Pack, R.A., 'Seneca's Evidence on the Deaths of Claudius and Narcissus', *CW* 36 (1943), 150–1

Paratore, E., 'La figura di Agrippina minore in Tacito', *Maia* 5 (1952), 32–81

Paratore, E., 'Un Evento Clamoroso nella Roma di millenovecento Anni fa', *StudRom* 7 (1959), 497–510

Paratore, E., 'Nerone (Nel XIX Centenario della Morte)', *StudRom* 17 (1969), 269–87

Paribeni, R., *Il ritratto nell'era antica* (Milan, 1876)

Parker, E.R., 'The education of heirs in the Julio–Claudian family', *AJP* 67 (1946), 29–50

Passerini, A., *Caligola e Claudio* (Rome, 1941)

Pathmanan, R., 'The Parable in Seneca's Oedipus', *Nigeria and the Classics* 10 (1967–8), 13–20

Pelham, H. F., *Essays* (Oxford, 1911)

Pelling, C., 'Tacitus and Germanicus', in Luce and Woodman (1993), 59–85

Peter, C., *Geschichte Roms* (Halle, 1867)

Pfister, K., *Der Untergang der antiken Welt* (Leipzig, 1941)

Pfister, K., *Die Frauen der Cäsaren* (Berlin, 1951)

Pflaum, H.G., *Les procurateurs équestres sous le Haut–Empire romain* (Paris, 1950)

Pflaum, H.G., *Les carrières procuratoriennes équestres sous le Haut–Empire romain* (Paris, 1961)

Picard, G.Ch., 'Rubellius Plautus patron de Mactar', *CT* 11 (1963) no. 44, 69–74

Piganiol, A., 'Observations sur une loi de l'empereur Claude', *Mélanges Cagnat* (Paris, 1912), 153–67

Pistor, H.H., Prinzeps und Patriziat in der Zeit von Augustus bis Commodus (Diss. Freiburg, 1965)

Platner, S.B. and Ashby, T., *A Topographical Dictionary of Ancient Rome* (Rome, 1929, reprinted 1965)

Polaschek, K., 'Studien zu einem Frauenkopf im Landesmuseum Trier und zur weiblichen Haartracht der iulisch–claudischen Zeit', *TZ* 35 (1972), 141–210

Pomeroy, S., *Goddesses, Whores, Wives, and Slaves: Women in Classical Antiquity* (New York, 1976)

Pomeroy, S., 'The Relationship of the Married Woman to her Blood Relatives in Rome', *AncSoc* 7 (1976), 215–27

Pommeray, L., *Etudes sur l'infamie en droit romain* (Paris, 1937)

Poulsen, F., *Porträtstudien in norditalienischen Provinzmuseen* (Copenhagen, 1928)

Premerstein, A. von, *Zu den sogenannten Alexandrinischen Märtyrerakten*, Philologus Suppl. 16 (1923), 1–76

Premerstein, A. von, *Von Werden und Wesen des Principats* (Munich, 1937)

Prévost, M.H., *Les adoptions politiques à Rome sous la république et le principat* (Paris, 1949)

Price, S., 'Gods and Emperors: The Greek Language of the Roman Imperial Cult', *JHS* 94 (1984), 79–95

Purcell, N., 'Livia and the womanhood of Rome', *PCPhS* 32 (1986), 78–105

Questa, C., *Studi sulle fonti degli Annales di Tacito* (Rome, 1960)

Quinn, K., 'Tacitus' Narrative Technique', *Latin Explorations* (New York, 1963)

Raaflaub, K.A. and Samons II, L.J., 'Opposition to Augustus', in K.A. Raaflaub and M. Toher (eds.), *Between Republic and Empire* (Berkeley, 1990)

Raditsa, L.F., 'Augustus' Legistation Concerning Marriage, Procreation, Love Affairs and Adultery', *ANRW* 2.13. 278–339

Raffay, R., *Die Memoiren der Kaiserin Agrippina* (Wien, 1884)

Ramage, E.S., 'Clodia in Cicero's Pro Caelio', in *Studies in Honour of C.R. Trahman* (1984), 201–11

Ramage, E.S., 'Strategy and Methods in Cicero's *Pro Caelio*', *Atene e Roma* 30 (1985), 1–8

Ramsbottom, J., *Mushrooms and Toadstools* (London, 1960)

Randour, M.J., *Figures de femmes romaines dans les Annales de Tacite* (Louvain, 1954)

Ranke, L., *Weltgeschichte* (Leipzig, 1883)

Rantz, B., 'Les Droits de la femme romaine tels qu'on peut les apercevoir dans le pro Caecina de Ciceron', *RIDA* 29 (1982), 56–69

Rapsaet-Charlier, M.-Th., 'Ordre sénatorial et divorce sous le Haut–Empire: un chapitre de l'histoire des mentalités', *ACD* 17–18 (1981–2), 161–73

Rapsaet-Charlier, M.-Th., 'Epouses et familles de magistrats dans les provinces romaines aux deux premiers siècles de l'empire', *Historia* 31 (1982), 64–9

Rawson, B. (ed.), *The Family in Ancient Rome: New Perspectives* (London, 1986)

Rawson, E. 'The Eastern Clientelae of Clodius and the Claudii', *Historia* 22 (1973) 219–39

Rea, J.R., 'Calendar of Gaius', *Oxyrhynchus Papyri* 55 (1988), 10–14

Reynolds, J.M., 'The Origins and Beginning of Imperial Cult at Aphrodisias', *PCPhS* 26 (1980), 70–84

Richardson, L., *A New Topographical Dictionary of Ancient Rome* (Baltimore, 1992)

Richter, G., *Engraved Gems of the Greeks, Romans and Etruscans* (London, 1968)

Riposati, B., 'Profili di donne nella storia di Tacito', *Aevum* 45 (1971), 25–45

Ritter, H.-W., 'Livia's Erhebung zur Augusta', *Chiron* 2 (1972), 313–38

Robert, L., 'Recherches Epigraphiques', *REA* 62 (1960), 285–361

Rodriguez Almeida, E., *Forma Urbis Marmorea: aggiornamento generale* (Rome, 1981)

Rogers, R.S., 'The Conspiracy of Agrippina', *TAPA* 62 (1931), 141–68

Rogers, R.S., *Criminal Trials and Criminal Legislation under Tiberius* (Middletown, 1935)

Rogers, R.S., *Studies in the Reign of Tiberius* (Baltimore, 1943)

Rogers, R.S., 'The Roman Emperors as Heirs and Legatees', *TAPA* 78 (1947), 140–58

Rogers, R.S., 'Heirs and Rivals to Nero', *TAPA* 86 (1955), 190–212

Roper, T.K., 'Nero, Seneca and Tigellinus', *Historia* 28 (1979), 346–57

Rosborough, R.R., *An Epigraphic Commentary on Suetonius's Life of Gaius Caligula* (Philadelphia, 1920)

Rose, C.B., Dynastic Art and Ideology in the Julio-Claudian Period (Unpublished m.s., 1993)

Rostovtzeff, M., *Social and Economic History of the Roman Empire* (Oxford, 1957²)

Ruanach, B. and Satzmann, E., *Mushroom Poisoning: Diagnosis and Treatment* (Florida, 1978)

Rudich, V., *Political Dissidence under Nero: The Price of Dissimulation* (London, 1993)

Rutland, L.W., Fortuna Ludens: The Relationship between Public and Private Imperial Fortune in Tacitus (Diss. Minnesota, 1975)

Rutland, L.W., 'Women as Makers of Kings in Tacitus' *Annals*', *CW* 72 (1978), 15–29

Ruyt, P. de, 'Un petit buste d'Agrippine en bronze doré provenant d'Alba Fucens', *RPA*

44 (1971/2), 151–65

Ryberg, I.S., 'Tacitus' Art of Innuendo', *TAPA* 73 (1942), 383–404

Sage, M., *Anc.Soc.* 14 (1983), 293–321

Sage, M., 'Tacitus' Historical Works: A Survey and Appraisal', *ANRW* II 33.5 (1990), 851–1030

Saletti, C., *Il ciclo statuario dell Basilica di Velleia* (Milan, 1968)

Salvatore, A., 'L'immortalité des femmes et la décadence de l'empire selon Tacite', *LEC* 22 (1954), 254–69

Salway, P., *Roman Britain* (Oxford, 1981)

Salzmann, D., *Antike Portäts im Römisch–Germanischen Museum Köln* (Cologne, 1990)

Sande, S., 'Römische Frauenporträts mit Mauerkrone', *AAAH* 5 (1985), 151–245

Sandels, F., Die Stellung der kaiserlichen Frauen aus dem Julisch-Claudischen Hause (Diss. Giessen, 1912)

Sattler, P., 'Julia und Tiberius: Beiträge zur römischen Innenpolitik zwischen den Jahren 12 vor und 2 nach Chr.', in Schmitthenner, W. (1969), 486–530

Scheid, J., *Les Frères Arvales. Recruitement et origine sociale sous les empereurs julio-claudiens* (Paris, 1975)

Scheid, J., *Romulus et ses Frères. Le Collège des Frères Arvales, Modèle du Culte Public dans la Rome des Empereurs* (Rome, 1990)

Scheider, K. Th., Zusammensetzung des römischen Senates von Tiberius bis Nero (Diss. Zurich, 1942)

Schiller, H., *Geschichte des römischen Kaiserreichs unter der Regierung des Nero* (Berlin, 1872)

Schmidt, P.L., 'Claudius als Schriftsteller', in *Strocka* (1994), 119–31

Schmitthenner W. (ed.), *Augustus* (Darmstadt, 1969)

Schmitz, H., *Stadt und Imperium: Köln in römischer Zeit* (Cologne, 1948)

Schmitz, H., 'Die Kaiserin Agrippina als Patronin der Colonia Agrippinensium', *Gymnasium* 62 (1955), 429–34

Schmitz, H., *Colonia Ara Agrippinensium* (Cologne, 1956)

Schove, D.J., *Chronology of Eclipses and Comets*, AD 1–1000 (Woodbridge, Suffolk, 1984)

Schuller, W., *Frauen in der römischen Geschichte* (Constance, 1987)

Schulz, F., *Classical Roman Law* (Oxford, 1951)

Schumann, G., Hellenistische und griechische Elemente in der Regierung Neros (Diss. Leipzig, 1930)

Schürenberg, D., Stellung und Bedeutung der Frau in der Geschichtsschreibung des Tacitus (Diss. Marburg, 1975)

Schwartz, D.R., *Agrippa I: The Last King of Judaea* (Tübingen, 1990)

Schwartz, D.R., *Studies in the Jewish Background of Christianity* (Tübingen, 1992)

Scott, K., 'Greek and Roman Honorific Months', *YClS* 2 (1931), 201–78

Scott, K., 'Notes on the Destruction of Two Roman Villas', *AJP* 60 (1939), 459–62

Scott, R.D., 'The Death of Nero's Mother (Tacitus, *Annals*, XIV, 1–13)', *Latomus* 33 (1974), 105–15

Scramuzza, V.M., *The Emperor Claudius* (Cambridge, Mass., 1940)

Scrinari, V. Santa Maria and Matini, M.L.M., *Antium* (Rome, 1975)

Seager, R., 'Tacitus *Annals* 12.60', *Historia* 11 (1962), 377–9

Seager, R., *Tiberius* (London, 1972).

Sealey, R., 'The political attachments of L. Aelius Seianus', *Phoenix* 15 (1961), 97–114

Seif, K.P., Die Claudiusbücher in den Annalen des Tacitus (Inaug. Diss., Mainz, 1973)

Setälä, P., *Private Domini in Roman Brickstamps* (Helsinki, 1977)

Shaw, B.D., 'The Age of Roman Girls at Marriage', *JRS* 77 (1987), 30–46

Sherwin-White, A.N., 'Procurator Augusti', *PBSR* 15 (1939), 11–26

Sherwin-White, A.N., *The Letters of Pliny* (Oxford, 1966)

Shotter, D.C.A., 'Tacitus, Tiberius and Germanicus', *Historia* 17 (1968), 194–214

Shotter, D.C.A., 'Julians, Claudians and the Accession of Tiberius', *Latomus* 30 (1971), 1120–21

Shotter, D.C.A., *Tacitus, Annals IV* (Warminster, 1989)

Sievers, G.R., *Studien zur Geschichte der Römischen Kaiser* (Berlin, 1870)

Simon, E., 'Zu den Flavischen Reliefs von der Cancelleria', *JDAI* 75 (1960), 134–56

Simon, E., *Ara Pacis Augustae* (Greenwich, Conn., 1967)

Simpson, C.J., 'The "Conspiracy" of AD 39', *Studies in Latin Literature and Roman History* II (Collection *Latomus* 168, 1980), 347–66

Sirks, A.J.B., 'A Favour to Rich Freedwomen (libertinae) in AD 51', *RIDA* 27 (1980), 283–94

Smallwood, E.M., *The Jews under Roman Rule* (Leiden, 1976)

Smilda, H., *C. Suetonii Tranquilli vita Divi Claudii'* (Diss. Groningen, 1896)

Smith, M.S., 'Greek Precedents for Claudius' Actions in AD 48 and Later', *CQ* 13 (1963), 139–44

Smith, R.R.R., 'The Imperial Reliefs from the Sebasteion at Aphrodisias', *JRS* 77 (1987), 88–138

Snyder, W.F., 'Nero's Birthday in Egypt and His Year of Birth', *Historia* 13 (1964), 303–6

Staehelin, F., *Kaiser Claudius* (Basle, 1956)

Stahr, A., *Römische Kaiserfrauen* (Berlin, 1865)

Stahr, A., *Agrippina die Mutter Neros* (Berlin, 1867)

Starr, C.G., *The Roman Imperial Navy* (Cambridge, 1960²)

Steidle, W., *Sueton und die antike Biographie* (Munich, 1951: Zetemata 1)

Stein, A., *Der römische Ritterstand* (Munich, 1927)

Stein, A., *Die Präfekten von Ägypten* (Bern, 1950)

Steinby, E.M. (ed.), *Lexicon Topographicum Urbis Romae* I (Rome, 1993)

Stewart, Z., 'Sejanus, Gaetulicus and Seneca', *AJP* 74 (1953), 70–85

Stockton, D., 'Tacitus *Annals* XII.60: A Note', *Historia* 10 (1961), 116–20

Strocka, V.M. (ed.), *Die Regierungszeit des Kaisers Claudius (41– 54 n.Chr.). Umbruch oder Episode?* (Mainz, 1994)

Strong, E., *La Scultura Romana* (Florence, 1923–6)

Stroux, J., 'Vier Zeugnisse zur römischen Literaturgeschichte der Kaiserzeit. II. Caligulas Urteil über den Stil Senecas', *Philologus* 86 (1931), 338–68

Stuart, M., 'How were Imperial Portraits Distributed throughout the Empire?', *AJA* 43 (1939), 601–17

Sumner, G.V., 'The Family Connections of L. Aelius Seianus', *Phoenix* 19 (1965),

134–8

Sumner, G.V., 'Germanicus and Drusus Caesar', *Latomus* 26 (1967), 413–35

Sutherland, H.C.V., *Coinage in Roman Imperial Policy, 31 BC–AD 68* (London, 1951)

Sutherland, H.C.V., *The Emperor and the Coinage* (London, 1976)

Sutherland, H.C.V., *Roman History and Coinage, 44 BC–AD 69* (Oxford, 1987)

Swan, M., review of Meise (1969), *AJP* 92 (1971), 739–41

Syme, R., *Roman Revolution* (Oxford, 1939)

Syme, R., 'Personal Names in *Annals* I–VI', *JRS* 39 (1949), 6–18

Syme, R., 'Marcus Aemilius Lepidus, Capax Imperii', *JRS* 45 (1955), 22–33

Syme, R., *Tacitus* (Oxford, 1958)

Syme, R., 'Piso Frugi and Crassus Frugi', *JRS* 50 (1960), 12–20

Syme, R., 'The Consuls of AD 13', *JRS* 56 (1966), 55–60

Syme, R., 'The Ummidii', *Historia* 17 (1968), 73–6

Syme, R., *Ten Studies in Tacitus* (Oxford, 1970)

Syme, R., *History in Ovid* (Oxford, 1978)

Syme, R., *The Augustan Aristocracy* (Oxford, 1986)

Taeger, F., *Charisma. Studien zur Geschichte des antiken Herrscherkultes* II (Stuttgart, 1960)

Talbert, R.J.A., *The Senate of Imperial Rome* (Princeton, 1984)

Tamm, B., *Auditorium and Palatium* (Stockholm, 1963)

Taubenschlag, R., 'Die materna potestas in gräko-ägyptischen Recht', *ZSS* 49 (1929), 155–28

Taylor, L.R. and West, A.B., 'The Euryclids in Latin Inscriptions from Corinth', *AJA* 30 (1926), 389–400

Temporini, H., *Die Frauen am Hofe Trajans* (Berlin, 1978)

Thibault, C.J., *The Mystery of Ovid's Exile* (Berkeley, 1964)

Thompson, D.L., 'The Meetings of the Roman Senate on the Palatine', *AJA* 85 (1981), 335–9

Thornton, M.K. and Thornton, R.L., 'Manpower Needs for the Public Works Programs of the Julio-Claudian Emperors', *Journal of Economic History* 43 (1983), 273–8

Till, R., 'Plinius über Augustus (nat.hist. 7.147–150)', *WürzJbb* 3 (1977), 127–37

Timpe, D., *Untersuchungen zur Kontinuität des frühen Prinzipats* (Wiesbaden, 1962)

Timpe, D., *Der Triumph des Germanicus. Untersuchungen zu den Feldzügen der Jahre 14–16 n. Chr. in Germanien* (Bonn, 1968)

Tolde, E., Untersuchungen zur Innenpolitik des Kaisers Claudius (Diss. Graz, 1948)

Tollis, C., *Alba Fucenses, dalle origini ai giorni nostri* (Avezzano, 1961)

Torelli, M., 'Trebula Mutuesca: iscrizioni corrette ed inedite', *RAL* 18 (1963), 230–84

Townend, G.B., 'The Sources of the Greek in Suetonius', *Hermes* 88 (1960), 98–120

Townend, G.B., 'Traces in Dio Cassius of Cluvius, Aufidius, and Pliny', *Hermes* 89 (1961), 227–48

Townend, G.B., 'Cluvius Rufus in the Histories of Tacitus', *AJP* 85 (1964), 337–77

Tränkle, H., 'Augustus bei Tacitus, Cassius Dio und dem älteren Plinius', *WS* 82 (1969), 108–30

Traub, H.W., 'Tacitus' Use of Ferocia', *TAPA* 84 (1953), 250–61

Treggiari, S., *Roman Freedmen during the Late Republic* (Oxford, 1969)

Treggiari, S., 'Jobs in the Household of Livia', *PBSR* 43 (1975), 48–77

Treggiari, S., 'Jobs for Women', *AJAH* 1 (1976), 76–104

Treggiari, S., *Roman Marriage* (Oxford, 1991)

Tresch, J., *Die Nerobücher in den Annalen des Tacitus* (Heidelberg, 1965)

Trillmich, W., 'Ein Bildnis der Agrippina Minor von Milreu/ Portugal', *MDAI* (M) 15 (1974), 184–202

Trillmich, W., *Familienpropaganda der Kaiser Caligula und Claudius. Agrippina Maior und Antonia Augusta auf Münzen* (Berlin, 1978)

Trillmich, W., 'Julia Agrippina als Schwester des Caligula und Mutter der Nero', *Hefte des Archäologischen Seminars der Universität Bern* 9 (1983), 21–38

Van Berchem, D., *Les Distributions de blé et d'argent à la plèbe romaine sous l'Empire* (Geneva, 1939)

Van Bremen, R., 'Women and Wealth', in A. Cameron and A. Kuhrt (eds.), *Images of Women in Antiquity* (London, 1983), 231–3

Verdière, R., 'A verser au dossier sexuel de Néron', *PP* 30 (1975), 5–22

Vessey, D.W.T.C., 'Thoughts on Tacitus' Portrayal of Claudius', *AJP* 92 (1971), 385–409

Villers, R., 'La dévolution du principat dans la famille d'Auguste', *REL* 28 (1950), 235–51

Visscher, F. De, 'La Politique dynastique sous le règne de Tibère', *Synteleia V. Arangio–Ruiz* (Naples, 1964), 54–65;

Vogel-Wiedemann, U., *Die Statthalter von Africa und Asia in den Jahren* 14–68 n. Chr. (Bonn, 1982)

Walker, B., *The Annals of Tacitus: A Study in the Writing of History* (Manchester, 1952)

Wallace, K.G., 'Women in Tacitus', *ANRW* II 33.5, 3556–74

Wallace-Hadrill, A., *Suetonius* (London, 1983)

Wallace-Hadrill, A., 'Image and Authority in the Coinage of Augustus', *JRS* 76 (1986), 66–87

Walter, G., *Nero* (Zurich, 1956)

Walz, R., *La vie politique de Sénèque* (Paris, 1909)

Wardle, D., 'Cluvius Rufus and Suetonius', *Hermes* 120 (1992), 466–82

Ward-Perkins, J.B., 'Excavation of a Roman Building', *PBSR* 14 (1959), 131–55

Ward-Perkins, J.B. and Boethius, A., *Etruscan and Roman Architecture* (London, 1970)

Warmington, B.H., *Nero* (London, 1969, reprinted 1981)

Warmington, B.H., review of Griffin (1976), *JRS* 67 (1977), 243–6

Watson, G.R., *The Roman Soldier* (Ithaca, 1969)

Watzinger C., 'Die Ausgrabungen an Westabhange', *MDAI(A)* 26 (1901), 305–32

Weaver, P.R.C., '*ILS.* 1489, 1490 and Domitius Lemnus', *Historia* 14 (1965), 509–12

Weaver, P.R.C., 'Freedmen Procurators in the Imperial Administration', *Historia* 14 (1965), 460–9

Weaver, P.R.C., *Familia Caesaris: A Social Study of the Emperor's Freedmen and Slaves* (Cambridge, 1972)

Weaver, P.R.C., 'Social Mobility in the Early Roman Empire: the evidence of the imperial freedmen and slaves', *Past and Present* 37 (1967), 3–20 (=*Studies in Ancient Society*, ed. M.I. Finley (London, 1974), 121–40)

Weaver, P.R.C., 'Dated Inscriptions of Imperial Freedmen and Slaves', *Ep. Stud.* 11 (1976), 215–27

Webster, G., *Boudicca* (London, 1978)

Webster, G., *The Roman Imperial Army* (London, 1985[3])

Weidemann, U., 'C. Silanus, Appia Parente Genitus', *Acta Classica* 6 (1963), 138–45

Weinstock, S., *Divus Julius* (Oxford, 1971)

Wessner, P., *Scholia in Iuvenalem Vetustiora* (1931, reprinted Stuttgart, 1967)

Wester, M., *Les personnages et le monde féminin dans les Annales de Tacite* (Paris, 1944)

Westermann, W.L., T*he Slave Systems of Greek and Roman Antiquity* (Philadelphia, 1955)

Wilcken, U., 'Alexandrinische Gesandtschaften vor Claudius', *Hermes* 30 (1895), 481–98

Wilkes, J., 'Julio-Claudian Historians', *CW* 65 (1972), 177–203

Willenbücher, H., *Der Kaiser Claudius* (Mainz, 1914)

Willrich, H., 'Caligula', *Klio* 3 (1903), 85–118; 288–317; 397–470

Willrich, H., *Livia* (Leipzig/Berlin, 1911)

Willrich, H., 'Augustus bei Tacitus', *Hermes* 62 (1927), 54–78

Wiseman, T.P., 'Pulcher Claudius', *HSCP* 74 (1970), 207–21

Wiseman, T.P., *New Men in the Roman Senate* (Oxford, 1971)

Wiseman, T.P., 'Legendary Genealogies in Late–Republican Rome', *G/R* 21 (1974), 153–64

Wiseman, T.P., 'Calpurnius Siculus and the Claudian Civil War', *JRS* 72 (1982), 57–67

Wiseman, T.P., *Death of an Emperor* (Exeter, 1991)

Wissowa, G., *Religion und Kultus der Römer* (Munich, 1912[2])

Wittrich, H., Die Taciteischen Darstellungen vom Sterben historischer Persönlichkeiten (Diss. Vienna, 1972)

Wolfgramm, F., Rubellius Plautus und seine Beurtheilung bei Tacitus und Juvenal (Diss. Rostock, 1871)

Wood, S., 'Agrippina the Elder in Julio-Claudian Art and Propaganda', *AJA* 92 (1988), 409–26

Wood, S., 'Messalina, wife of Claudius: Propaganda Successes and Failures of his Reign', *JRA* 5 (1992), 219–34

Wood, S., 'Diva Drusilla Panthea and the Sisters of Caligula', *AJA* 99 (1995), 457–82

Wuilleumier, P., *Tacite, l'homme et l'oeuvre* (Paris, 1949)

Wuilleumier, P., 'L'empoisonnement de Claude', *REL* 53 (1975), 3–4

Zappacosta, V., 'Senecae Apolokolokyntosis', *Latinitas* 17 (1969), 86–95

Zwierlein-Diel, E., 'Der Divus-Augustus-Kameo in Köln', *KölnJb* 17 (1980), 36–7

Index

Proper names are abbreviated where possible, and their alphabetical order is based on common usage; less familiar names are arranged by *nomen*. Items in the footnotes already indexed through the text are not listed separately. Unamplified citations of literary sources are not indexed.